○Cobra Mk.2 ○ Cobra Daytona Coupe ○ Cobra 4 S/C ○ Comet ○ Coppel MG TC ○ Corvette Gra Corvette SR-2 ○ Corvette SS ○ Corvette Sting Ray Racer ○ Cozzi Jaguar ○ Croslahti ○ Croslahti B ○ Crusader Formula Vee Wedge ○ Crusader Formula Vees ○ Crusader VSR ○ CRV/Piranha ○ Cunningham C-1 ○ Cunningham C-2R ○ Cunningham C-4R ○ Cunningham C-4RK ○ Cunningham C-5R ○ Cunningham C-6R ○ D and D Special ○ Dailu Mk.I ○ Dailu Mk.II ○ Dailu Mk.III ○ Dailu Mk.IV ○ Dailu Mk.V ○ Dane Formula III ○ Dane Formula Juniors ○ Darwin Special ○ David MG TD ○ Davis Special ○ Delfosse Mini-Junior ○ Devin C ○ Devin D ○ Devin Panhard ○ Devin Ryan Special ○ Devin SS ○ Devin-Crosley Super Sport ○ Devin-Roosevelt ○ DKW Formula Junior ○ Dolphin Formula Junior ○ Dolphin Formula 2 ○ Dolphin International ○ Dolphin Sports-Racers ○ Double-Ender ○ Durant Devin-Chevy ○ Durant Devin-Pontiac ○ Durlite Special ○ Durlite Too ○ Eagle Formula A (Eagle Formula 5000) ○ Eagle-Climax Formula 1 ○ Eagle-Weslake Formula 1 ○ Eave Chevy Special ○ Echidnas ○ Edgar MG TC ○ Edwards / Blume Special ○ Edwards Special ○ Edwards Special (2) ○ Eisert F-A ○ El Toro (1) ○ El Toro (2) ○ El Toro (3) ○ Eliminator ○ Elwood Porsche Special ○ Evans Saab Special ○ Excalibur Hawk ○ Excalibur J ○ Excalibur Mk.VI ○ Exner Simca Special ○ Eyerly Crosley ○ Fageol Twin-Porsche ○ Fairchild Panhard ○ Ferret ○ Fibersport-Crosley ○ Fitch Type B ○ Fitch-Whitmore Jaguar ○ Flying Banana ○ Flying Triangle ○ FoMoCo Special ○ Ford G7A ○ Ford GT Mk.I ○ Ford GT Mk.II ○ Ford GT MK.IV ○ Formcar Formula Vees ○ Formula 3 Echo ○ Forsgrini Mk.10 F5000 ○ Forsgrini Mk.10 FC ○ Forsgrini Mk.11 F5000 ○ Forsgrini Mk.12 FF ○ Forsgrini Mk.14 F5000 ○ Forsgrini Specials ○ Front-Runner Special ○ Fubar ○ Genie Mk.4 ○ Genie Mk.5 ○ Genie Mk.8 ○ Genie Mk.10 ○ Genie Mk.11 ○ Georgette ○ Georgette-the-Racer ○ Gillespie MG TD ○ Gounis Fiat-Crosley ○ Grady 1 ○ Grady 2 ○ Hagemann GMC ○ Hall-Scott Special ○ Hamill SR-2 ○ Hamill SR-3 ○ Hansen Special ○ Hansgen Jaguar ○ ○ Hawaiian Special ○

vintage american road racing cars

1950-1970

harold w. pace and mark r. brinker

MOTORBOOKS
INTERNATIONAL

Dedication

To our patient and loving wives, Shelley and Newie, who tolerate this little race car obsession of ours.

First published in 2004 by Motorbooks International, an imprint of MBI Publishing Company, Galtier Plaza, Suite 200, 380 Jackson Street, St. Paul, MN 55101-3885 USA

Motorbooks International titles are also available at discounts in bulk quantity for industrial or sales-promotional use. For details write to Special Sales Manager at Motorbooks International Wholesalers & Distributors, Galtier Plaza, Suite 200, 380 Jackson Street, St. Paul, MN 55101-3885 USA.

ISBN 0-7603-1783-6

On the front cover, top: Pedro Rodriguez in a Huffaker Genie at Riverside. **Center:** Ken Miles pilots the Porphin at Pomona. **Bottom:** Lance Reventlow's Scarabs were the best sports-racers of the 1950s. *Allen Kuhn*

On the frontis/title page: Jim Hall, in one of his glistening Chaparrals, was one of the leading lights in the Can-Am series. *Allen Kuhn*

On the back cover, top: Ken Miles works out a Cobra at Riverside in 1963. *Allen Kuhn*

Bottom: The Dailu Mk.1 had some great rides with up-and-comer John Cannon. *Mike Leicester collection*

Edited by Peter Bodensteiner & Lindsay Hitch
Designed by Rochelle Schultz

Printed in China

Contents

Acknowledgments

We are deeply indebted to hundreds of individuals who contributed information on their favorite marques and specials and helped keep us on the straight and narrow. We don't have room to list everyone here, but to them all, thanks again.

We would like to especially thank Allen Kuhn, whose splendid period photography graces this book and brings us back to the time when these monsters ruled the earth. Allen was on board with this project from its inception, and without his talent and encouragement this book would not have been possible.

We would also like to express our gratitude to Pete Lyons, Bob Harrington, Tom Cardin, Bob Tronolone, Tam McPartland, and Nick England for providing us with stunning photographs of the automotive creations from the most exciting period in American racing history. Special thanks to

Ron Kellogg for sharing the Dean Batchelor collection and Robert H. Rolofson III for allowing us to include his father's wonderful photographs.

In any project of great magnitude there is always the unsung hero. Our hero, Ron Cummings, worked selflessly to provide us with critical information and guidance throughout this ordeal. Thank you, Ron, for everything.

Below are some other individuals who were particularly helpful during our journey:

Millard Almon, Gordon Apker, Maritza Baez, Rodney Baker, Al Baurle, Charles Betz, Charles Bordin, Paul Bova, Jack Boxstrom, Newie Brinker, Peter Bryant, Ed Buck, Don Cannon, Rick Cannon, Andre Capella (Gessner), Rick Cardenis, Bill Chapin, Charles Christ, Art Evans, Mark Evans, Kip Fjeld, Bill Flemming, Jim Frostrom, Dan Gallant, Karen Gallant, William Green, Bill Hair, Keith Harmer, Barry Heuer,

Beau Hickory, Lindsay Hitch, Tinnell Hickory, Joe Huffaker Jr., Bill Janowski, Joe Kane, George Keck, Arlen Kurtis, Jim Larkin, Mike Larkin, Gene Leasure, Barry LeVan, Mike Liecester, Mike Losey, Greg Lucas, Harry Mathews, Bill Mays, John McCann, Bob McKee, Paul Meis, Raymond Milo, Gerald Mong, Deborah Narcus, Larry Narcus, Dan O'Connor, Don Orosco, Shelley Pace, Stephen Payne, Don Pereboom, Annie Plotkin, Fred Plotkin, Bill Pollack, Fred Puhn, Don Racine, James Robinson, Alva Rodriguez, Kenny Rogers, Jay Rusovich, Alex Saidel, Ray Saidel, Stuart Schaller, Andrew Schupack, Amy Shives, Christopher Shoemaker, Ellen Sohus, Chuck Tatum, Frank Townsend, Edward Valpey, Chris Wickersham, Court Whitlock, Nick Whitlow and Chuck Wood.

5

About the Authors

Harold W. Pace

Pace is an automotive journalist and historian who writes for a number of magazines in the United States and Europe. He has written two books on the history of American specialty cars and was awarded the Cugnot Award of Distinction from the Society of Automotive Historians for his contribution to *The Beaulieu Encyclopedia of the Automobile*. He is also a member of the Motor Press Guild. Pace is an active vintage racing driver and has owned and restored many classic racing cars. He lives with his wife, Shelley, in Weatherford, Texas.

Mark R. Brinker

Brinker is an avid vintage racer, and he collects American race cars of the 1950s. He is a voting member of the Writers Guild of America and has sold a number of feature screenplay works to major film studios. Brinker is also a board certified orthopedic surgeon who has written over 100 scientific articles, countless book chapters, and three textbooks in the field of medicine. He and his wife, Newie, live in Houston, Texas. This is his first automotive book.

Introduction

The world is full of books on racing cars. There are innumerable tomes devoted to Formula 1 dynasties, endurance racing legends, and specific road racing cars. But until now there has never been a book devoted exclusively to American road racing cars of all types and sizes. Sure, you can find lots of single-marque books devoted to documenting every chassis number of well-known racers like the Ford GT or famous Can-Am champs. But hundreds of cars built in America have never been mentioned in print before, and that is what you will find here.

American road racing started just after World War II and quickly blossomed into a movement. The Sports Car Club of America (SCCA) and the United States Auto Club (USAC), clubs that became fierce rivals in the 1950s and 1960s, were the principal race promoters. Race tracks popped up everywhere, at first on city streets, then at airports and U.S. Air Force bases, and finally at purpose-built circuits like Road America and Laguna Seca. America's love of road racing continues to this day.

Although most of the cars that competed in American road racing were built in Europe, an underground movement sprang up of "special builders" who constructed their racers in home garages or small-town machine shops. Some were so homely and slow that only the builders could love them. Others trounced every Ferrari in sight and are now on wish lists for wealthy collectors the world over.

In between these extremes were purpose-built race cars intended to be sold for profit by professional race car builders. Some, like Autodynamics and Zink, built hundreds of successful cars, while others expired after a single embarrassing season. They were powered by everything from two-cylinder Panhards to fire-breathing Chrysler Hemis. A few companies even built their own engines, but these were seldom successful.

We have taken a look at all the classes that were run in amateur and professional racing events, from

The Payne Special in action on the dirt.
Stephen Payne Collection

6

Typical grids included a mix of exotics and home-builts, like Lotus (No. 212) and the Twareg Special (No. 38).
Allen Kuhn

Formula Vee to Group 7 Can-Am. While we have not included street sports cars that were modified for racing by individuals or race preparation shops, we have included production-class cars that were designed solely (or principally) for racing.

This book is broken into several major sections. Chapter 2 is devoted to Racing Car Manufacturers, those companies that sold racing cars to the public or produced them for a racing team. Chapter 3 covers American Specials, one-offs built for the constructor or his driver to race. Chapter 4 is devoted to Engine Swap Specials, race cars that received a relatively simple engine exchange that did not necessitate major redesigns. Chapter 5 covers American Kit Car Manufacturers, companies that sold bodies or frames used to construct a special, and Chapter 6 covers the various purpose-built American Racing Engines. Chapter 7 describes the sometimes overwhelming myriad of Racing Classes for the various competition cars. The Appendix contains various rosters of cars arranged by Year(s) of Construction, Constructor, Body Builder, Powerplant, and Racing Class. The Bibliography will be useful to those wanting to read more on a specific manufacturer or car.

The focus of the book is the cars, although without the characters themselves, there would be no cars and no book. We pay homage to the great American race cars of the era and so doing honor those men and women who created them.

We have made every effort to document these splendid cars as accurately as possible and have interviewed as many of the actual builders as we could locate. Inevitably errors have occurred. Memories fade, car identities become jumbled together, and even period race reports sometimes contain errors. If we have missed a car or you see something wrong, don't get mad . . . please let us know. Our goal is to get each and every story straight. If you have something to contribute, we would love to hear from you. The best way to reach us is by email at zoom@vintageracecars.net.

Enjoy!
Harold and Mark

and his margin of victory was 40
in the same lap of the 1.9-mile track

Jerry Titus, Canoga Park, Calif., Firebird.
Craig Murray, San Rafael, Calif., Camaro.
Joe Chamberlain, Tigard, Ore., Camaro.
John Silva, Jr., San Lorenzo, Calif., Camaro.
Jerry Oliver, Concord, Calif., Camaro.
Wes Dawn, Venice, Calif., Mustang.

day's biggest disappointments was the
Hall's pair of Camaros to finish. Hall's

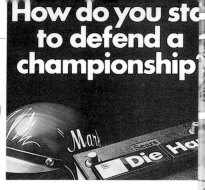

How do you sta
to defend a
championship?

WINKELMANN

GOOD DRIVING
SAVES GAS

Sports Car Club of America — Oklahoma Region SCCA

DRIVER

#7 FV

driver but for his ca
machine at their bes
The St. Louis Reg
will conduct its seco
sion National Race
Raceways Sept. 23-
ville, Mo., track and
300 drivers are expe
More important,
something that has
car buffs on cloud ni
Ford Championship
by Ford Motorsports
the SCCA, which wi
junction with the Mi
"This is the first
Ford championship
here," said John F
regional director of
probably the biggest
had here because th
Formula Ford will
Hatch (England) to r
at the International
The winner of this

Driver

ST. LOUIS
REGION

71 Fv

PRICES

All sizes A through X-6 . . . . $295.00

This includes door openings and door
jambs, separate lined doors, dash,
flanged and reinforced hood and deck
openings and flanged and reinforced hood
and deck lids. Bodies are trimmed and
crated and prices include Federal Excise
Tax. Shipping is via rail unless otherwise
specified, average freight costs $10.00 in
U.S.A.

EXTRAS

Removable Headrest for either
side (specify r or l) $25.00
Moulding for mounting plexiglass
windshield $10.00
Liner for cockpit forming two
bucket seats, driveshaft tunnel
and part of floorboard, makes installation light, strong and simple.
Molded into body when ordered . . $75.00
(Not available on bodies K, P, Q, T, V, W,
X, V-6, W-6 and X-6)

SCCA
NATIONAL
CHAMPIONSHIP
CLUB RACING

FIAT The LARGEST selling car
in EUROPE
Imported Car PARTS-SALES-SER
The Pit Stop, I

A word about our sp

For dimensions of various body sizes refer to drawing and chart. A' cowl to headrest, B' dash to center of front wheel well, D'
wheelbase limits, P' overall length, L' width at front wheel well, M' width of grille, N' width at wheel well, R' tread limits.

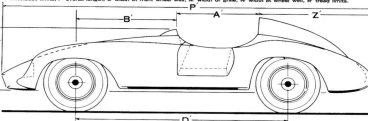

All dimensions are given in inches

Body	R'	D'	P'	A'	B'	L'	N'	M'	Z'
A	40-44	78-82	145	33	38	54	52	24	46
B	40-44	82-86	149	37	38	54	52	24	46
C	40-44	86-90	153	41	38	54	52	24	46
D	45-48	82-86	149	33	42	58	56	28	46
F	45-48	86-90	153	37	42	58	56	28	46
H	45-48	90-94	157	41	42	58	56	28	46
J	48-52	92-96	159	37	48	62	60	32	46
K	48-52	90-94	157	41	36	62	60	32	52
L	48-52	76-80	143	33	36	62	60	32	46
M	48-52	80-84	147	37	36	62	60	32	46

UNITED STATES
AUTO CLUB

NATIONAL HOT ROD
CHAMPIONSHIP
DRAG RACING
ASSOCIATION

SPORTS CAR CLUB
OF AMERICA

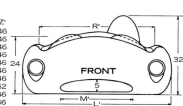

Amateur Racing 1950–1970

To appreciate the accomplishments of American racing cars, it is important to understand the competition environment. Road racing in America evolved from small prewar races put on by the Automobile Racing Club of America (ARCA) into a major spectator sport after World War II.

The most important date in the history of American road racing was February 26, 1944, when a handful of Boston-area sports car enthusiasts formed the Sports Car Club of America (SCCA). Its stated purpose was to preserve sports cars, and racing was not an initial consideration. When the war wrapped up a year later, they waited for ARCA to start putting on races again. But ARCA never revived, and the SCCA and other clubs stepped into the void and began organizing races.

The first SCCA races were held on the East Coast, where the predominately blue-blooded participants raced imported machinery, including prewar Alfas, Maseratis, and MGs. There were some notable American specials present, including Briggs Cunningham's BuMerc and the Ardent Alligator. Cameron Argetsinger was a law student at Cornell when he came upon the idea of putting on a race in the peaceful New York village of Watkins Glen. The first Watkins Glen Grand Prix was held on October 2, 1948, and was won by Frank Griswold in an Alfa Romeo coupe, with the BuMerc right behind. American iron was already holding its own!

Many SCCA members wintered in Florida and soon began looking for places to race in that area.

Early racers Cunningham, the brothers Miles, and Sam Collier lived in Florida. George Weaver and others helped steer the SCCA into race promotion.

Out West

Another important step was taken in 1947, when the California Sports Car Club (CSCC, or, more commonly, Cal Club) was born. This club was to be the hub for racing on the West Coast the way the SCCA was in the East, and the two groups would become deadly rivals. Cal Club, a Southern California group, had a more egalitarian outlook than the SCCA. Their members came from all walks of life and included former hot rodders and dirt track racers, as well as high-rolling businessmen. The SCCA established a Northern California chapter based out of San Francisco with more of an upper-crust East Coast attitude.

9

American racing took off in the 1950s, as evidenced by this grid of Ferraris, Maseratis, and specials led by Duffy Livingston's Eliminator hot rod. *Allen Kuhn*

The first track events staged by Cal Club, in December 1948, were two time trials over a hilly road. Cal Club founder John von Neumann won the first trial in an SS-100, and Tom Payne's special took the second. West Coast specials were proving as potent as their East Coast cousins!

Soon races began popping up all across the country. By 1950, events were being held at Bridgehampton on Long Island, Palm Beach Shores in Florida, and dozens of other venues. The number of entrants was climbing, and some method had to be found to classify the cars so that small 750-cc Austins were not competing directly against Grand Prix cars. A classification system was adopted that grouped cars by engine size, the way they were classified in European sports car racing. At that time most of the cars were street-driven sports models that were also used on the track, but as owners started modifying their cars it became necessary to break them into two groups—production cars and "modifieds." Once this distinction was established, few changes could be made to a street car before it was transferred to a Modified Class.

The Cars Were the Stars

Although Europe had a long lead in the manufacture of great road racing cars, there was one area of design in which Americans were way ahead—horsepower! One of the early phenomena was the feared Cadillac-Allard, an Anglo-American concoction of lightweight construction pushed along by a rodded Caddy V-8. These were the first superstars of American road racing, winning countless races in the 1950–1952 period, before others surpassed them with superior handling. One of the few cars that could run with a hot Allard was a Healey Silverstone that Briggs Cunningham's merry men had stuffed with a Cadillac engine of their own.

But even at this early stage in the evolution of American racing, a schism was forming. Many of those involved in racing wanted it to remain an amateur sport, a low-key way to enjoy driving a fine

There was much rivalry between those who preferred "proper" (European) sports cars, like this D-Type Jaguar, and mechanics who built "modifieds" with hot rod inspiration, like the Manning Mercury Special (No. 21). *Allen Kuhn*

sports car as quickly as possible. Others were ready to go pro, with spectators and prize money like that at hundreds of circle tracks across the country. Two factions formed within the SCCA and they began fighting a war that raged until the mid-1960s (and, to a certain extent, continues to this day). Initially the antipro contingent controlled the SCCA, and drivers who ran in money-paying races risked being expelled or having their SCCA competition licenses suspended. Cal Club also initially fell in with the antipro side.

Another battle was waged between those who built specials (particularly home-grown ones with hot rod overtones) and those who preferred (or sold) exotic European machinery (called "teabag-

gers" by the greasy fingernail crowd). Although this seemed like class warfare, there were rich and poor on both sides of the controversy. Various rules were implemented to bring whichever group was out of power into compliance.

Safety

Due to the high number of on-track incidents that occurred, the SCCA enforced safety requirements from the very first. Each car had to pass a technical inspection that checked the condition of the brakes, tires, wheels, and suspension. Fire extinguishers were carried even in the early 1950s, and by 1959, roll bars, safety belts, helmets, and fire-resistant suits were required.

Championships

In 1951, the SCCA devised a plan to award a national championship to the driver who had accumulated the most points in designated races over the season. The first winner was Cunningham driver John Fitch, but the concept was later expanded to include winners in each SCCA class.

American racing cars were split between home-builts like the Pickford Jaguar (left) and factory-built racers like the Kurtis 500X (right). *Allen Kuhn*

When looking over lists of SCCA champions before 1965, it would appear that the best drivers and cars were all from the East Coast as they won the lion's share of victories. However, this was because the SCCA staged most of its championship-eligible national races on that side of the country, so East Coast drivers usually ponied up the most points over the season. Cal Club had its own championship, which was naturally dominated by local drivers as well.

In 1964, *Sports Car Graphic* put on an event at Riverside Raceway in California that laid the groundwork for the current SCCA Championships. The American Road Race of Champions (ARRC) was a season-ending race for amateur drivers who qualified by finishing in the top four in class in their SCCA regions. The 1964 ARRC winners were not officially recognized by the SCCA. The next year, the ARRC received official approval, although the SCCA also continued to hand out national championships determined by the old point-total method. In 1966, the

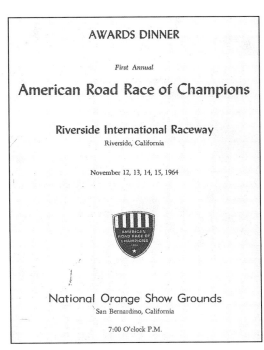

ARRC winners became the sole official SCCA national champions. (Incidentally, everyone except the SCCA record-keepers considers the 1964 ARRC winners to be the real national champs.)

The ARRC was held at Riverside in 1964, and then moved to Daytona the next year. The ARRC alternated between these two tracks until 1970 when it was moved to Road Atlanta as a permanent venue. (In the late 1990s, it moved again to Mid-Ohio.) Although Atlanta was a more central location, it resulted in the national championships always falling to cars that favored long straights and fast, sweeping turns.

The SCCA experienced continued growth through the 1960s and was able to foster a "farm system" for drivers who moved up to the professional leagues after getting experience in amateur racing. In the late 1960s, a number of manufacturers took notice of the popularity of SCCA racing and began entering factory-sponsored teams or paying contingency money to winners. Among the biggest players were British Leyland and Datsun.

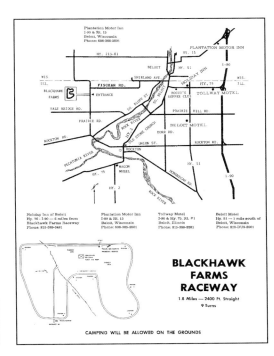

Across the country there were also small clubs like the Midwest Council of Sports Cars, which put on events at Blackhawk Farms, Virginia International Raceway, and others, and the Green Valley Racing Association, which ran the Green Valley circuit and the Austin, Texas, street races.

Formula Cars

While most early racing cars were based on two-seat sports cars (stock or modified), there was another type of racing that was slow to catch on in America. In Europe, formula cars (single-seaters with no fenders) were required for Grand Prix races, and countless amateur formulas were developed as well. Although some early Grand Prix cars made it across the pond, they usually ran in poorly supported Formula Libre (anything goes) classes. The first popular single-seater class in the United States was Formula 3 (F3), a predominately British development with cars that used motorcycle-based engines. These were relatively inexpensive, if labor-intensive,

Single-seat racing took off in popularity with the introduction of Formula Junior. *Allen Kuhn*

American factories became interested in production car racing in the 1960s, when Ford backed Carroll Shelby's Cobras. *Allen Kuhn*

little cars and as more showed up in the early 1950s, the SCCA put on events for them.

Soon, the 500-cc Club of America was formed to promote these little noisemakers, and the club blossomed into the Formula Racing Association (FRA), which put on formula car events in conjunction with Cal Club and the SCCA. The FRA was instrumental in keeping F3 alive and introducing Formula Junior in the 1960s. When the SCCA started its own formula classes in 1965, the FRA was no longer needed.

Formula Junior made a big impact in 1960 when it first arrived on U.S. shores, but it fizzled out in 1964, due to escalating costs and rapid development that resulted in new cars becoming obsolete in a matter of months. Ideally, Formula Junior was meant to provide a modern racing car (a lot like a Formula 1 car) with an affordable production-based 1,100-cc engine, but it just didn't work out. Formula Vee avoided those problems by sticking to a workable set of regulations and providing the closest racing and lowest costs of any class.

Another famous class was Formula Ford (FF), which appeared in 1968 and was approved as a national class in 1969. These single-seaters were similar in concept and appearance to the old Formula Juniors, but were equipped with a solid, dependable, and inexpensive 1,600-cc Ford street engine in a mild state of tune. The racing was close and FF proved to be an excellent training ground for future champions. Many of the top Grand Prix drivers of the 1960s and 1970s started their careers in this class.

Production Cars

In the early 1950s, SCCA production-class cars had to be close to stock. Air cleaners could not be removed, bumpers and windshields had to stay in place, and only minor service items (like spark plugs, tires, and shock absorbers) could be replaced with nonoriginal brands. This "showroom stock" concept was brought back in the mid-1970s for several popular SCCA classes. Then, as now, cheating was rampant.

As time went on, the regulations became more lenient, and manufacturers came up with long lists of "approved options" that made their cars faster. Special carburetors, cams, and suspension parts were approved for racing. Cal Club had more lenient rules than the SCCA and allowed aftermarket parts to be used as early as the late 1950s.

For all the criticism the SCCA has endured over the years from whichever side got the short end of the stick on any given issue, it had one great, glorious brainstorm that resulted in the United States having the best production sports car racing in the world. In the late 1950s, the expensive and rare Porsche Carreras were stomping everything in the 1,500-cc production-car class. There were dozens of MGAs and pushrod Porsche 356s running around the country, but they were pushovers for the four-cam Carreras and, to a lesser extent, the MGA twin cams. There was a fear that if all the drivers of cheaper, less sophisticated cars just gave up and quit, the SCCA production classes would be in danger of collapse.

In 1960, the SCCA took action. It evaluated all the approved production cars and reclassified them according to relative performance. If a 91-ci Porsche Carrera was capable of turning the same lap times as a 283-ci Corvette, then they were put in the same class. The new classifications were evaluated at the end of each season. At last, everyone had a fighting chance. As a result, there were thousands more low-cost sports cars raced in the United States than in Europe, where displacement continued to be used for classification.

One of the great amateur racing shakeups occurred in 1961, when the SCCA revoked the charter of their Los Angeles Region on trumped-up charges and adopted Cal Club as the California Sports Car Club Region of the SCCA. Thus, the two former rivals became one, with the more lenient Cal Club regulations heavily influencing the direction of future SCCA policies.

Sedans

Although sports cars were the lifeblood of SCCA racing, in the early 1960s, a number of sporty sedans needed a place to race. Some tracks, like Lime Rock and Green Valley, put on feature events specifically for these cars, but it wasn't until 1966 that the SCCA introduced sedan classes to its club racing program. Everything was raced, from Mini Coopers to Mustangs, which tied in with the new Trans-Am pro series. Sedan regulations were based on displacement, and the allowed modifications tended to be more lenient than regs for production sports cars.

Modified to Sports-Racer

When the SCCA first began splitting sports cars into two classes, most of the hotter cars were production models that had been modified for more performance. MG TDs with superchargers and cycle fenders, Jaguar XK-120s with C-Type engines, and others were put into what were called "Modified" classes. This class also included limited-edition cars (less than 500 built) and purpose-built racing cars like Ferraris and OSCAs. By the 1960s,

these classes were exclusively populated with pure racing cars, and in 1965 the term "Sports-Racer" was substituted for Modified. These cars were always classified by displacement.

Many European racing cars were modified by swapping in American engines, as with Billy Krause's Chevy-powered D-Type Jaguar, shown leading a Maserati Birdcage. *Allen Kuhn*

Professional Racing 1950–1970

The first time the rest of the world heard about American racing cars was at Le Mans in 1950, when sportsman Briggs Cunningham rolled up to the track with two Cadillac-based entries. Cunningham was a wealthy Floridian who wanted to experience racing at the highest level and convinced Cadillac to front him two Series 61 Coupe de Villes with manual transmissions. One was left mostly stock, while the other was fitted with an outrageous body resembling a giant metal cigarette pack. The two overweight, underbraked monsters rumbled through the day and night to finish a respectable tenth and 11th overall. They put the world on notice that the Americans would be back.

Back in the States, the SCCA had a serious antiprofessional bias. In the 1950s, no sponsorship

Professional sports car racing took off in the late 1950s and flowered in the 1960s with the USRRC series. Here, the Harrison Lotus 19-Ford leads a Scarab and a Genie at Laguna Seca. *Allen Kuhn*

of any kind was permitted to be displayed on the cars or in the pits, and the cars had to be entered in the name of the individual owner. Drivers were not supposed to be paid, but it was no secret that top shoes were being compensated under the table.

The no-professional rules meant many of America's star drivers moved to Europe, where they could earn a living. Phil Hill, Dan Gurney, Carroll Shelby, Masten Gregory, and others headed overseas for fame and fortune. The SCCA then added a new law allowing drivers who raced for money in Europe to race as amateurs in the United States.

Sebring

In 1950, engineer and promoter Alec Ulmann picked Sebring, Florida, as the site of America's first world-class endurance race. He desperately wanted to see sports car racing take its place beside other popular sports and believed a highly publicized endurance race was the way to do this.

The first six-hour enduro was scored by a complicated handicap system that theoretically gave any size car a chance at victory. Sure enough, a tiny Crosley Hotshot grabbed the trophy even though it finished miles behind the big Allards and such. The event was moderately successful, but was not repeated in 1951.

Although the 1950 event was sanctioned by the SCCA, by 1952 Ulmann had fallen out with the SCCA brass, and he alone put on the next Sebring race (now a 12-hour enduro sans handicapping). The SCCA reacted as it usually did to competition, threatening to kick out anyone who ran the race. They even put on a rival race the previous weekend in Vero Beach to draw away entrants. But Sebring ran anyway and was won by a Frazer-Nash.

After these two warm-ups, Sebring went big-time in 1953. Working with the American Automobile Association (AAA), Sebring was put on the Federation Internationale de l'Automobile (FIA) endurance racing championship schedule as the season opener. After a struggle with the works Aston Martin team, a Cunningham won, and American cars had won two in Florida! Sebring continued to be the premier endurance race on the American racing schedule, and American cars won it in 1964 (Chaparral), 1965–1967 (Ford), and 1969 (Ford).

Daytona

Daytona Speedway opened in 1959, and although designed primarily as an oval track, it had a usable infield road circuit that was soon put to good use. In 1962, Daytona became the site of the opening round of the FIA endurance racing championship, which was followed by Sebring to give Americans two shots at the big boys. This three-hour race was called the Daytona Continental, and Dan Gurney won the 1962 opener in a Lotus 19. By 1965, the length had changed to 2,000 kilometers and Fords were on every step of the podium with the finishing order Ford GT, Cobra, Ford GT, Cobra. The next year, the Ford GTs came back for a one-two-three victory.

RFM

In the mid-1950s, more drivers and team owners began to clamor for professional races. Popular fashion accessories at the time were bowler hats, which were nicknamed "Run for Money," or RFM hats. Several groups sprang up to put on money races, but these were usually poorly attended and run under threat of the competitors being thrown out of the SCCA, which now dominated American sports car racing.

By the early 1960s, a number of professional races paid appearance and prize money, but they were standalone events and no points were tallied. The best known was the Los Angeles Times Grand Prix at Riverside, which was turning out more than 84,000 spectators by 1963. Similar races at Laguna Seca, Pomona, Mosport, Bridgehampton, and Kent were all held in the fall and were sometimes unofficially referred to as the "Fall Pro Series."

USAC Series

In 1958, the United States Auto Club (USAC), which had been putting on oval track races for some time, announced a professional series for road racing drivers. The SCCA spit back that it would bar any driver from its events if they took part in a USAC pro race. Most drivers ignored it.

The 1958 USAC series consisted of four races and was won by congenial Californian Dan Gurney. The best-known race of the series, the Times Grand Prix at Riverside, was won by Chuck Daigh in one of Lance Reventlow's all-conquering Scarabs. The purse for the year was $24,600, a substantial sum in those days. In 1959, the USAC series expanded to 11 events and was won by Scarab-mounted Augie Pabst. The next year, popular Carroll Shelby took home the marbles, capping a successful driving career just in time to go build the Cobras. And, in 1961, acerbic Ken Miles won the series driving various Porsches. By then the Times Grand Prix was the biggest draw of

the year, with tens of thousands of spectators lining up to watch the big iron run. In 1962, Roger Penske drove his controversial Zerex Special to victory in the final USAC pro series. After 1962, the SCCA's USRRC series became the only pro series in the United States.

Nassau Races

From 1954 to 1966, the racing fraternity looked forward to one event more than any other—the Nassau Trophy Races. The tracks were terrible, the racing spotty, and the regulations prone to change at the whim of the organizers, but the parties were awesome! Nassau took place in early December, after the end of the regular racing season, and did not count toward any point championship. There were a number of races, and the competitors received free transportation, lodging, and booze all weekend. Organizer "Red" Crise put cars in whatever classes he chose and added oddball races for Formula Vees and even VW Beetles. American iron that won at Nassau included Scarabs, Chaparrals, and Corvette Grand Sports. Nassau was eventually killed by the increasingly professional nature of racing, when no one had time for parties and socializing. It was a sign of the end of an era.

USRRC

The SCCA finally got into the pro spirit in 1963, when it unveiled its own money-paying series. The United States Road Racing Championship (USRRC) series was launched to great fanfare, featuring two championships. The Manufacturers' Championship was for GT cars like Corvettes and Cobras, while the Drivers' Championship also allowed sports-racers. Sometimes the two races were separate, other times all the cars were on the track at the same time. Both race groups were broken into over- and under-2-liter classes.

The dominant GT marque was Shelby American, which was the only manufacturer to run a works team in the series. Bob Holbert won the first

Roger Penske got his shot at the big time driving this Americanized Cooper, the Zerex Special. *Allen Kuhn*

Jim Hall, in his glistening Chaparrals, was one of the leading lights in the Can-Am series. *Allen Kuhn*

driver title, using Porsche Spyders and Cobras for weapons. Shelby won the Manufacturers' Championship from 1963 to 1965, after which it withdrew from the series. After 1965, the Manufacturers' Championship was dropped. Driver titles were taken by Jim Hall (1963 and 1964) in his Chaparrals, George Follmer (1965) in a home-brew Lotus-Porsche, and Chuck Parsons (1966) who shared time in a Genie and a McLaren.

Can-Am

The Can-Am replaced the USRRC as America's premier road racing series, first run in 1966 and continuing through 1974. Unlike the USRRC, Can-Am had no under-2-liter class and allowed pretty much anything you could think of. Initially, American-built cars like the Chaparrals were in the hunt, but soon the English Lolas and McLarens took over. There were many valiant efforts from Shadow, Bryant, Ford, McKee, and others, but they did not win the series until after 1970.

International Racing

A few American teams ventured into the highly politicized world of international racing. In Formula 1, Dan Gurney carried the flag with his Eagle-Weslake, taking a popular win at Spa in 1966.

American teams did far better in endurance and GT racing. Cunningham had been the first to carry the flag to Europe. After trying Cadillacs in 1950, the Cunningham team switched to cars of its own design, frequently using Chrysler V-8s. The team's best finishes were thirds at Le Mans in 1953 and 1954, although it was always a threat.

The best-known success story was that of the Shelby American Cobras, which slithered after Ferrari in their quest for the FIA Manufacturers' Championship, finally sinking their fangs into the title in 1965.

Ford was the next to have a go at Le Mans. After stumbling in 1964 and 1965, Ford finally got it right and swept to popular wins in 1966 and 1967 (privateer Ford GTs won again the next two years). Chaparral also won in Europe, taking the Nurburgring 1,000-kilometer race in 1966 with the 2D coupe and the Brands Hatch BOAC 500 a year later with the 2F coupe.

Trans-Am

The Trans-Am was a popular series of sedan races that started in 1966 and is still hanging on today. Originally, there were two classes for over- and under-2-liters, but the small class was later dropped. American "pony cars" dominated the series, with factory entries from Chevy, Pontiac, Ford, Mercury, American Motors, Dodge, and Plymouth.

Continental F-5000

In 1967, the SCCA started the Continental F-5000 (formally known as the SCCA Grand Prix Championship), a professional series for formula cars. There were three classes, with Formula A having the same rules as Formula 1 in Europe (3-liter race engines), Formula B for 1,600-cc production-based twin cams, and Formula C for 1,100-cc race engines. The series had a low-key start with few cars and little media attention. Texan Gus Hutchison took home the trophy with a Lotus 41C Formula B car. In 1968, everything changed when the SCCA allowed 5-liter stock-block motors into Formula A. Although many American companies built Formula A cars, the only one that won a championship was Eagle, which took the title in 1968 with driver Lou Sell and again in 1969 with Tony Adamowicz. The series, renamed the Continental Championship in 1969, lasted through 1976.

Minor Series

There have also been professional series or events for primarily amateur classes, including Super Vee, Formula Ford, Formula Vee, and Formula Atlantic. Only Formula Atlantic and Super Vee lasted for long, though none were high-visibility series.

TWO

Racing Car Manufacturers

Ambro

Ambro built one complete racing car as well as a number of fiberglass bodies that were sold to special builders. Partners William Aldrich-Ames and Dewey Brohaugh assembled the first car in 1961. Both were experienced SCCA racers from the Minneapolis area. The chassis was a modified Triumph TR-3 powered by a highly modified TR-3 engine with SU carburetors. Widened Triumph steel wheels were fitted.

The fiberglass body had strong Maserati Birdcage and Lister influences; in fact, some of the body panels were molded on Don Skogmo's T-61 Maserati. Aldrich-Ames and Brohaugh shared the racer for a few years before selling it to Laurie Burford in 1963. He raced the car in Minnesota before selling it to Fred Baker, who resold the car to Burford. Burford moved to Texas around 1965 and he raced it a few times at Green Valley before selling it to Oklahoman Jerry Dewelle in 1966. Dewelle raced the car before selling it

to Ben Hineline, who converted it to Ford V-8 power and turned it into an autocross car. The Ambro has since been restored to Triumph power and is currently active in vintage racing.

(See Ambro entry in American Kit Car Manufacturers, Chapter 5.)

Anvil

Jim Hahn designed the first of a short line of Formula Vees in 1970. The prototype was based on a modified Beach FV but had a radically reworked frame and suspension. The steering box was mounted close to the middle bulkhead, with a short shaft connecting it to the steering wheel. The pitman arm projected forward toward the front end, and the steering arms were located above the driver's ankles. The car used a modified Beach body. Johnny Gable, who built a second car in 1972 for himself and named it the Anvil, fabricated the car. This car had a

different frame with the same steering system, but with a crude, wedge-shaped body. At this point, the first car was retroactively named the Anvil Mk.1, with Gable's car designated the Mk.2. Anvil later built four more FVs based on the Mk.2 design.

Apache

The Apache was one of the first American Formula Juniors. It was wider and bulkier than most other front-engined designs, partially to leave room for a variety of engines, including Simca, Peugeot, and MG. When Formula Junior was first announced, the Formula Racing Association (which was then the primary force behind formula car racing) adopted a two-tiered set of regulations that allowed older 1,300-cc MG T-series engines and Crosley overhead-cam engines as well as the 1,100-cc pushrod engines required by FIA. The regulations didn't last long, but it does explain why a few American

AMBRO

Ambro, Ltd.
1339 Third Avenue S.W.
Rochester, Minnesota

AMBRO

Year built	**1961**
Engine	**Triumph TR-3**
Gearbox	**Triumph four-speed**
Chassis	**ladder**
Front suspension	**modified Triumph**
Rear suspension	**modified Triumph**
Brakes	**Triumph disc/drum**
Body material	**fiberglass**
Wheelbase	**88 inches**
Number built	**one**

ANVIL

Johnny Gable
Dallas, Texas

ANVIL

Years built	**1970–1976**
Engine	**Volkswagen**
Gearbox	**Volkswagen four-speed**
Front suspension	**torsion bar (Volkswagen)**
Rear suspension	**swing axle (Volkswagen)**
Brakes	**drum (Volkswagen)**
Body material	**fiberglass**
Weight, approx.	**825 pounds**
Wheelbase	**81.5 inches**
Number built	**six**

APACHE

Apache Racing Cars
1414 N. Main Street
Walnut Creek, California

APACHE FORMULA JUNIOR

Year built	**1960**
Engines	**Simca, Peugeot, MG**
Gearbox	**to match engine**
Chassis	**space frame**
Front suspension	**independent, coil springs**
Rear suspension	**independent, coil springs, or swing axles**
Brakes	**drum**
Body material	**fiberglass**
Wheelbase	**83 inches**

Formula Juniors had some unusual engine choices.

The Apache was sold in kit and rolling chassis form, with a fiberglass body and double-wishbone front suspension. In back, a live axle or swing axles were options. The body was quite attractive, with a "beak" nose that presaged the later Eagle GP cars. The base price of a rolling chassis was $1,985. Few Apaches were built, and they do not show up in period race results.

Arnolt-Bristol Bolides were class winners at Sebring. *Harold Pace*

Arnolt

S. H. "Wacky" Arnolt was a Chicago-area wheeler-dealer who, in 1952, had a fortune he had made selling tiny boat motors to the government during World War II. He built that first business into many other profitable ventures, which gave him the wherewithal to enjoy his hobby—sports cars. But where others might have been content to stock their garages with Jaguars and Ferraris, Arnolt wanted to build his own road burners. He started S. H. Arnolt Inc. to import MG, Jaguar, Rolls-Royce, Aston Martin, and Bristol automobiles, and these marques served as the inspirations for his own projects.

His first venture was a street sports car based on MG TD running gear with an attractive Bertone body. The MG

Brilliant performer!

The De Luxe
ARNOLT-BRISTOL
2-Litre Sports Car

Up hills—around curves—on the straightaway—in traffic—wherever you go—the fast acceleration and superb cornering and braking qualities of this powerful American-designed sports car with British engine and chassis and Italian body will constantly amaze and delight you! A car that is safe and "forgiving" of human driving errors. Test-drive it today!

1955 VICTORIES
The Arnolt-Bristol has repeatedly demonstrated its superior performance by winning victory after victory in major 1955 racing events, including:
SEBRING, FLORIDA—1st, 2nd and 4th places in Class E Modified; 1st, 2nd and 4th places in Series Production Class 7. Winner of the Sebring Race Team Trophy Prize and the SPORTS ILLUSTRATED Trophy for Production Car Team Index of Performance. (The Arnolt-Bristol Teams was the only team to finish intact.
ELKHART LAKE, WISCONSIN—2nd, 4th and 5th places in Class E Modified.
SANTA BARBARA, CALIFORNIA—1st, 4th and 5th places in Series Production Class E.
WATKINS GLEN, NEW YORK—2nd, 3rd and 4th places in Class E Modified.

Bolide Model $4,245.00
Includes complete touring equipment
De Luxe Model 4,995.00

See the
ARNOLT-BRISTOL
NOW AT—
CHICAGO: 152 East Ohio Street
DETROIT: 15201 Kercheval
OYSTER BAY, Long Island, N. Y.: 305 Park Avenue
Berry Hill Road at South Street
ST. LOUIS: 273 DeBaliviere Ave.
ROSWELL, New Mexico: 1600 So. Main Street
LOS ANGELES: 9830 W. Pico Blvd.
SAN FRANCISCO: 1529 Van Ness Avenue
For illustrated brochure 12 RT write
S. H. ARNOLT, INC.
415 EAST ERIE STREET
CHICAGO 11, ILLINOIS

chassis were shipped to Italy, where the famed Bertone bodymen hand-formed the bodies from steel. Then they were shipped to Warsaw, Indiana, just south of Chicago, for sale. Although lovely and sporty, they were also heavy and not intended for racing. Arnolt sold 100 of them before MG switched over to the TF, and the supply of chassis ran out. He also had Bertone rebody six Aston Martin DB-2s, which he sold as Arnolt-Aston Martins.

Arnolt-Bristol Bolide

In 1953, Arnolt consummated a deal to build a new model, the Arnolt-Bristol. Based on a shortened Bristol 403 sedan chassis and engine, it was shipped from England to Italy where, once again, Bertone bodied it before forwarding it across the pond. The chassis was a solid design, based on the prewar BMW 327, which Bristol had bought the rights to after World War II. The frame rails were box section steel with independent front suspension sprung by a transverse leaf spring. In back, a live axle was sprung by torsion bars and laterally located by an upper A-bracket.

Bristol also built a sport model, the 404, which had a shorter wheelbase than the 403 (96 inches) and improved finned drum brakes. However, to save money Arnolt combined the shorter 404-length chassis with nonfinned drums from the 403. The Bristol BS1 Mark II engines put out 130 horsepower at 5,500 rpm, which at the time was adequate for a hot 2-liter engine. This engine was also based on the

BMW 327 and looked like a twin cam design. However, it had only one low-mounted cam, which drove one set of valves through pushrods. A second set of pushrods then took the action across the top of the engine to a second bank of valves, with the carburetors in the middle. The engine was theoretically obsolete by 1953 but worked very well up to 6,000 rpm and was also used in the AC Ace-Bristol, Frazer-Nash Le Mans replicas, and various Cooper racing cars.

The body was a work of art, both in style and quality. Bertone based the svelte, razor-edged shape on his BAT series of aerodynamic studies done on Alfa chassis. The bodies were made of steel with aluminum hoods and rear decks. The new model looked good from all angles. Arnolt offered the new Arnolt-Bristol in three forms: the stripped Bolide (also called the "competition" model), the DeLuxe (a convertible with a top and side curtains), and a luxurious coupe. The Bolide did not have a top, soundproofing, carpeting, a full-height windshield, or adjustable seats. The dashboard was flat and the instruments were spread out across it. DeLuxe models had a different dashboard with the gauges in front of the driver.

All three models used the same engine. Prices started at $4,245 for the Bolide and went up to $6,390 for the coupe, a bargain for a car with this level of performance and quality. The bodies were expertly hand-formed with a minimum of body putty, unlike the work of some other prominent Italian body

17

manufacturers. And it was quick, turning 0–60 in ten seconds and topping out at just over 100 miles per hour.

The first Arnolt was raced in 1954, the same year it was introduced. Fred Wacker bought a new competition model and ran it in the SCCA E-Modified class, since enough cars had not been sold for approval as a production car. Wacker tied for the class championship with a Frazer-Nash, leading many to believe the Arnolt was destined for greatness in production-class racing. But it was not to be, as it was heavier (at 2,185 pounds) than the dominating AC Aces that used the same engine. Even the Triumph TR-3 and the Morgan Plus Four (with factory-developed engine parts) were as quick.

Arnolt had his greatest successes at Sebring, where durability meant as much as speed. In 1955, Arnolt had built over 25 cars and his new toy was ready for production-class racing. A factory team was formed with Walter Inai as team manager and Juan Lopez as crew chief. Preparation was limited to a white paint job and a tune-up. Three cars were taken to Sebring for Rene Dreyfus/Bob Grier, John Panks/Ernie Erickson, and Arnolt himself teamed with Bob Goldich. Arnolt backed up the team with transporters, an army of support personnel, and plenty of spare parts. They didn't need them. The new team finished first-, second- and fourth-in-class.

The factory cars were run in midwestern and southern events and occasionally at Watkins Glen. In 1956, the three factory cars returned to Sebring, where one retired and the other two finished a disappointing second- and third-in-class behind a Ferrari 500 Mondial. The next year Arnolt was paired with Goldich, who slid off the track, overturned, and

was killed. One of the other team cars withdrew in sympathy. The remaining car finished sixth-in-class, and a demoralized Arnolt pulled out of racing for the 1958 and 1959 seasons.

But in 1960, Arnolt returned to Sebring with three new Bolides. One had a steel body, but the other two were clad in aluminum, and one sported right-hand drive. All had front-wheel disc brakes. One alloy-bodied car, driven by Max Goldman and Ralph Durbin, swept to a class victory and 14th overall, followed by another team car in fourth, and the remaining entry tenth. This was enough to win the Team Prize as well, as they were the only team to finish intact.

The factory team went on to six class wins in SCCA races in the Midwest before being disbanded. Arnolt himself had lost interest in racing. The company continued selling cars until 1963, when Arnolt passed away, by which time around 130 Arnolt-Bristols of all types had been sold. (Twelve more complete cars were destroyed in a warehouse fire.) Since Arnolt had left no one trained to take over, his hard-fought empire slowly withered away. Today Arnolt-Bristols give a good account of themselves in vintage races, where they still give battle to the AC Aces, Morgans, and Triumphs.

Ausca

Horst Kwech was an Australian mechanic who moved to the United States and worked for Knauz Continental Motors in Lake Forest, Illinois. He became a talented racing driver, and in the mid-1960s developed a line of Ausca sports-racers and formula cars that were made first at Knauz and later by his own company, Ausca Engineering. He apparently built two sports-racers, which had tubular space frames and were powered by Alfa Romeo engines. Kwech raced one and the other was wrecked in an accident. He made at least one Ford-powered Formula B car that was driven by Syd Demonsky in the Formula Continental series in 1967 with no results. Ausca also built a small number of Formula Vees. Kwech later drove Alfas and Mustangs in the Trans-Am series and built the DeKon Monzas that won the International Motor Sports Association (IMSA) Championship.

ARNOLT

S.H. Arnolt Inc.
Warsaw, Indiana

ARNOLT-BRISTOL

Years built	1954–1963
Engine	Bristol six-cylinder
Gearbox	Bristol four-speed
Chassis	ladder
Front suspension	independent
Rear suspension	live axle
Brakes	Bristol drum
Body material	steel or aluminum
Weight, approx.	2,185 pounds
Wheelbase	96 inches
Number built	130 (all models)

AUSCA

Knauz Continental Motors
Lake Forest, Illinois

Ausca Engineering
Libertyville, Illinois

AUSCA SPORTS-RACER

Year built	1964
Engine	Alfa Romeo 1600
Gearbox	Hewland Mk.5
Front suspension	independent
Rear suspension	independent
Brakes	disc
Body material	fiberglass
Number built	two

AUSCA FORMULA B

Year built	1967
Engine	Lotus twin cam
Gearbox	Hewland
Front suspension	independent
Rear suspension	independent
Brakes	disc
Body material	fiberglass
Number built	unknown

18

AUSCA FORMULA VEE

Year built . . . . **unknown**
Engine . . . . **1,200-cc Volkswagen**
Gearbox . . . . **Volkswagen**
Front suspension . . . . **trailing link**
Rear suspension . . . . . **swing axles**
Brakes . . . . **drum**
Body material . . . . **fiberglass**
Number built . . . . **unknown**

Autodynamics

Formula Vee hit the tracks in 1963 and quickly became one of the most popular classes in amateur racing. Ray Caldwell was one of the winningest drivers in this new class, and his company became one of the most successful American racing car manufacturers. Caldwell was a hot rodder in the 1950s and put his '32 Ford roadster into the "100-mile-per-hour Club." He later attended Harvard Business School and spent his weekends attending SCCA races.

Next, Caldwell signed up with the Air Force, which left him time to race a Triumph TR-3 in the Midwest. He served in Europe in the early 1960s, where he raced his Porsche Super 90 in German and Italian races and rallies. In 1962, he returned home and began work as an engineer at General Electric in Massachusetts. But his heart still belonged to racing.

Caldwell had taken note of the new Formula Vee class announced in 1962. He and two partners, Del Trott and Don MacSorely, designed a new Vee and ran an ad with a drawing of the proposed car to judge the market. It generated 1,300 replies and the first Autodynamics race car was built using advances from customers. In 1964, Caldwell drove the first car to the SCCA National Championship, thus ensuring a healthy market for his new cars. The Mk.I was a decided improvement over the Formcars, which had been the first commercially available Formula Vees.

In its first year, Autodynamics lost $9,000 (a considerable sum, since a rolling chassis cost around $1,000). The company turned a profit for the first

The Autodynamics D-1 was the first of a great marque. The capable Formula Vees won many races. *Harold Pace*

time in 1967, by which time it was selling over 60 cars a year. Its principal competitors in the early years were Formcar, Beach, and Crusader, although when the Zink came out it proved to be a more formidable adversary.

Caldwell had proven his driving ability in the Formula Vees and finished an impressive eighth overall at Daytona in 1967, driving a Ford GT40. However, he was eclipsed by a young New Englander named Sam Posey, who showed up at the Marblehead, Massachusetts, factory to learn the art of racing. As soon as he was old enough to race, Posey attached himself to the Caldwell team, where his driving ability (and financing) were appreciated.

Autodynamics Formula Vees

The D-1 was a rather sophisticated Formula Vee with a space frame chassis and a clean fiberglass body. It predated the use of Z-bars in the rear suspension, and swing axle travel was limited with steel cables. The first cars had a complicated, separate-tube exhaust system and a long, enveloping tail. The D-1A was very similar but the tail was simplified, smaller, and lighter. The D-1B was a further development of the same car, but with a bobbed tail that was not only lighter but also made it easier to get to the running gear.

A little-known version of the early FVs was the D-3, an Autodynamics FV with a Porsche 356 engine and brakes. Eight were built, and they provided a cheap entry into the very quick Formula B class.

The 1967 D-4 FV was a new design with a revamped chassis intended to take on the Zink threat. It had a Z-bar to control the rear axle travel. The D-4 "won" (and then was disqualified for illegal valve springs) at the prestigious Nassau Formula Vee race driven by Caldwell, resulting in its nickname, the "Nassau" model. Due to its more complicated design, it cost $1,195 for a rolling chassis, $200 more than the D-1B. There was also a D-4A model with a wider cockpit for heftier drivers. The last Autodynamics FV was the D-4B sold in 1969 and 1970. It was a successful design with an all-new body that is still collecting hardware in vintage races today.

In 1971, Caldwell introduced a whole new concept in Formula Vees. It was called the Caldwell D-13 and was the first customer Formula Vee to use zero-roll rear suspension in place of the Z-bars that were a standard design feature of most vees. (A few one-offs had also used zero-roll.) The D-13 was low and aerodynamically very slick, and it remained competitive well into the 1990s. Even after Autodynamics closed down, other companies picked up the design and continued to build the basic car.

Autodynamics D-4 was the last Formula Vee made before the company name changed to Caldwell. The D-4 was a very good Vee, but usually a tick of the second hand slower than the Zinks. *Harold Pace*

Autodynamics Formula Fords

When Formula Ford started up in 1969, Autodynamics was ready with a new model called the Caldwell D-9. Under the skin it was very similar to the Merlyn Mk.11 that had been so successful in England, except that Caldwell used heim joints at all suspension mounting points, whereas the Merlyn used a combination of heim joints and plastic bushings. The Caldwell body was a lovely design, with a long nose and graceful fairings back into the front suspension. The D-9 won three SCCA divisional championships that first year, and Skip Barber won the first FF National Championship over Lotus, Merlyn, and Titan FFs. In 1970, an upgraded design, the D-9B, won the Canadian and IMSA FF Championships, driven by Dave Loring.

Autodynamics Formula Super Vees

Another new class that sprang up in the 1970s was Super Vee, intended to be a step up from FF with a race-prepared 1,600-cc VW engine. Caldwell adapted the D-9 FF into the D-10 FSV, which used the VW engine as a stressed member in the chassis. According to Autodynamics' records, 17 were built (but other records say as few as eight). They were very competitive in the early days of the class.

Autodynamics Pro Series Cars

Sam Posey was busy pursuing a professional driving career, and he and Caldwell shared his Porsche 904 to win the Watkins Glen 500 in 1966. Autodynamics also ran a McLaren and various F-5000 cars for Posey. In 1966, Autodynamics built a radical new car for Posey to race in the Can-Am series. It was very light, with an aluminum monocoque chassis and a live front axle designed to help keep the ultrawide tires planted flat on the track. In back, a de Dion setup did the same. It seemed to be a retrograde step . . . and it was. Although it worked fine in theory, the straight-axle suspension was difficult for a small team to sort out and, after struggling with it during 1967 and 1968, Caldwell and Posey switched to a Lola T160. The D-7 had shown some promise in the USRRC series, finishing third at the 1968 Riverside race and qualifying second at Watkins Glen. However, in the tougher Can-Am series, it was outclassed. Two chassis were built, the first in aluminum and the second from magnesium, which saved 60 pounds. However, when the aluminum car was wrecked, the magnesium chassis was used to repair it, so only one car was completed. At different stages of its development, it was referred to as the D-7A, B, and C.

Initially, the D-7 sported an adjustable, hydraulically actuated wing that fed loads into the chassis, but it was shelved due to inadequate development time. At first, the car even used a Volkswagen steering box (shades of Formula Vee), which was replaced by a rack-and-pinion unit for the 1968

The Caldwell D-13 was the first commercially available Formula Vee to use zero-roll rear suspension. It was very successful, particularly on fast tracks. *Harold Pace*

Caldwell D-9 was the first great American Formula Ford. The basic design was borrowed from the Merlyn Mk.11, but the D-9 used heim joints in the suspension instead of the nylon bushings preferred by Merlyn. The D-9 won the first SCCA Formula Ford National Championship. *Harold Pace*

Sam Posey takes the Caldwell D-7 around Road America in the 1967 Can-Am. *Pete Lyons*

The Caldwell D-7 gets a push from driver Sam Posey (left) and builder Ray Caldwell at the Road America Can-Am in 1967. *Pete Lyons*

season. Caldwell planned two chassis for a live-axle F-5000 car using the same technology, but the cars were not completed.

Autodynamics was involved in a number of nonracing projects, including a kit car called the Hustler and the successful line of Dearborn Deserter dune buggies. The project that spelled doom for the company was getting the Dodge Trans-Am effort for 1970. Autodynamics spent a fortune tooling up for a multiyear project, only to have Dodge fold the tents after a single season. Posey and Caldwell fell out, and Caldwell tried to diversify into electric cars and other design projects, but the trail ended in 1973. Luckily, Autodynamics left a legacy of excellent racing cars that fill the grids at vintage races today.

Autodynamics published these production numbers in 1973.

Autodynamics Corp.
2 Barnard Street
Marblehead, Massachusetts

AUTODYNAMICS D-1 MK.1 FORMULA VEE
Year built **1964**
Engine . . . . **Volkswagen**
Gearbox . . . . **Volkswagen four-speed**
Front suspension . . . . **trailing link**
Rear suspension . . . . . **swing axles**
Brakes . . . . **Volkswagen drum**
Body material . . . . . . **fiberglass**
Number built **186**

AUTODYNAMICS D-1A MK.2 FORMULA VEE
Year built **1965**
Technical info . . . . . . **same as above**
Number built **194**

AUTODYNAMICS D-1B MK.3 FORMULA VEE
Year built **1965**
Technical info . . . . . . **same as above**
Number built **98**

AUTODYNAMICS D-4 MK.4 FORMULA VEE
Year built **1967**
Technical info . . . . . . **same as above**
Number built **94**

AUTODYNAMICS D-4A MK.4 FORMULA VEE (WIDE COCKPIT)
Year built **1968**
Technical info . . . . . . **same as above**
Number built **148**

AUTODYNAMICS D-4B MK.5 FORMULA VEE
Years built **1969–1970**
Technical info . . . . . . **same as above**
Number built **65**

CALDWELL D-13 FORMULA VEE
Years built **1971–1972**
Technical info . . . . . . **same as above except for zero-roll rear suspension**
Number built . . . . . . **74 (Other companies built more later.)**

AUTODYNAMICS D-3 FORMULA B
Year built **1966**
Engine . . . . **Porsche 356**
Gearbox . . . . **Volkswagen four-speed**
Front suspension . . . . **trailing link**
Rear suspension . . . . . **swing axles**
Brakes . . . . **Porsche**
Body material . . . . . . **fiberglass**
Number built . . . . . . **eight**

CALDWELL D-9 FORMULA FORD
Year built **1969**
Engine . . . . **Ford 1,600-cc**
Gearbox . . . . **Hewland four-speed**
Front suspension . . . . **independent**
Rear suspension . . . . . **independent**
Brakes . . . . **disc**
Body material . . . . . . **fiberglass**
Number built **55**

CALDWELL D-9B FORMULA FORD
Years built **1970–1971**
Engine . . . . **Ford 1,600-cc**
Gearbox . . . . **Hewland four-speed**
Front suspension . . . . **independent**
Rear suspension . . . . . **independent**
Brakes . . . . **disc**
Body material . . . . . . **fiberglass**
Number built **48**

CALDWELL D-10 FSV
Years built **1970–1971**
Engine . . . . **Volkswagen 1,600-cc**
Gearbox . . . . **Hewland four-speed**
Front suspension . . . . **independent**
Rear suspension . . . . . **independent**
Brakes . . . . **disc/drum**
Body material . . . . . . **fiberglass**
Number built **17**

CALDWELL D-7
Years built **1966–1967**
Engine . . . . **Chevrolet V-8**
Gearbox . . . . **ZF**
Front suspension . . . . **beam axle**
Rear suspension . . . . . **de Dion**
Brakes . . . . **disc**
Body material . . . . . . **fiberglass**
Number built . . . . . . **two**

AVS Shadow

Old timers who followed the Can-Am series remember the first Shadow as "the car with the tiny tires." Designed by Trevor Harris (who later penned the championship-winning Nissan GTP cars) and funded by team owner Don Nichols, the AVS Shadow Mk.1 garnered more attention during the 1970 Can-Am season than the winning teams. But the first Shadow was most emphatically *not* a winner.

The overriding goal for the radical design had been to reduce frontal area. The car had around 6 square feet less than the frontal area of a contemporary McLaren and ran the same aluminum big-block Chevy engine. The trick was to use radically smaller tires without affecting braking. Until then, most Group 7 cars had used 15-inch wheels to fit big brake rotors inside them. Shadow made a deal with Firestone to have ultrawide 10-inch front and 12-inch rear tires made up. The front wheels were wider (11 inches) than they were tall, as were the 16.75-inch-wide rears. The height to the top of the roll bar was only 24 inches!

These squat little shoes were attached to an aluminum semimonocoque tub made of multiple "torque boxes" that strengthened the structure. The suspension was unusual as well. The front A-arms were equal length and parallel, giving no camber change with body roll. This was due to the extremely limited suspension deflection expected from the stiff tires. Since there was no room up front for conventional coil-over shocks, four small die springs were used per wheel, initially damped by friction shocks (hydraulic ones were also tested). The rear A-arms were unequal length but parallel, and no radius arms were used. The rear coil springs were mounted horizontally and actuated through bellcranks.

The Hurst-Airheart disc brakes used 8-inch-diameter front rotors and cut-down calipers to fit inside the two-piece wheels. Magnesium Corvair engine cooling fans were mounted in the wheels to extract hot air. In back, Corvair fans, belt-driven off the gearbox, cooled Mustang rotors with H-A calipers. Harris initially designed the car with no wings, just a simple but functional fiberglass body. A system of air brakes that would pop out of the body was considered but outlawed by the 1970 FIA mandate against movable aerodynamic devices.

The aluminum ZL-1 Chevy put out around 620 horsepower, and Harris designed a fuel injection system based on Hillborn parts and a unique dry sump system for the low-mounted engine. A Hewland LG-600 five-speed gearbox was used. Due to the lack of room in the footbox, there were only two pedals, so the engine was shifted without a clutch. The radiators were mounted in back of the car and fed by small scoops on the rear corners.

Once on the track, everything went awry. The engine overheated, the special fuel injection system was abandoned in testing, the handling was diabolical, and a big rear wing that had to be added negated 50 percent of the frontal area savings. Driver George Follmer kept knocking the rear radiator ducts off on course markers, and eventually the radiators were stacked on top of the rear wing.

The first race appearance at Mosport almost didn't happen, due to legal problems with suppliers and a driver dispute with Andy Granatelli over Follmer's services. Finally, Follmer appeared, and the Shadow ran 25 slow laps and retired. Afterward, the SCCA outlawed the wing-mounted radiators, which were then moved to the top of the body. The rear brake cooling fan belts kept breaking, so larger air scoops were added. The horizontal rear springs were dumped in favor of multiple tiny springs like those used on the front, and they turned out to be one of the few things that worked as planned.

Just when it looked like things couldn't get worse, they did. On the way back from St. Jovite, a drunken driver hit the tow truck and trailer and totaled the Shadow Mk.1. A second car had been built and fitted with an experimental Toyota four-cam racing engine, but this engine was removed and a Chevy installed. At Mid-Ohio, the underfinanced team went through two engines in practice. Vic Elford drove it in the race but gave up after ten laps, saying the car was undrivable. It was the end of the Mk.1 (and a reported $500,000 of AVS money), but thankfully Shadow rebounded to come out on top in 1974.

The tiny AVS Shadow Mk.1 was a big disappointment for all concerned. Here, it leads a Porsche 908 at the 1970 Mid-Ohio Can-Am. *Pete Lyons*

AVS SHADOW

Advanced Vehicle Systems
Santa Ana, California

AVS SHADOW MK.1

Years built	1969–1970
Engine	Chevy V-8
Gearbox	Hewland LG-600
Front suspension	independent
Rear suspension	independent
Brakes	disc
Body material	fiberglass
Wheelbase	86 inches
Number built	two

Balchowsky

Max Balchowsky was born of Lithuanian descent in Fairmont, West Virginia, in 1924. As a kid, he showed an interest and aptitude for mechanical things. He enjoyed repairing bicycles and trucks, and at one point he considered a career as a watch-maker. Following World War II, the young Balchowsky moved to Southern California, discovered racing, and gave up on the idea of building timepieces. Instead, he decided to build cars . . . and what a glorious decision that was.

The lack of formal training in engineering or even a proper high school diploma did not dissuade Balchowsky from diving in. He taught himself the race car trade, ultimately becoming one of the best race car builders in the United States. He was that rare combination of dreamer and doer. He could think of it, and he could build it. And he didn't care if the rest of the world thought his ideas were crazy. In fact, he kind of liked being the outsider, the underdog.

In 1952, Balchowsky and his talented wife, Ina, opened Hollywood Motors at the intersection of Hollywood Boulevard and Edgemont. Ina was a skilled race car builder in her own right, and their shop quickly developed a reputation for excellence. Hollywood Motors, however, will forever be remembered as the place where the Old Yallers were born.

The identity of the person who christened the cars Old Yaller is cloudy and nearly as many versions of the story exist as spellings for the name itself (Ol Yaller, Ol' Yaller, Old Yaller, Ol Yeller, Ol' Yeller, Old Yeller, Ol Yellar, Ol' Yellar, Old Yellar). One of the most intriguing aspects of the Old Yaller story is that those who knew Max personally are absolutely convinced that they remember all of the details with great precision, although they rarely agree on all major points. It has been suggested that Balchowsky himself enjoyed the confusion surrounding his cars and intentionally dispersed various versions of each car's history throughout the years.

What is agreed is that most of the cars were painted yellow and named after Disney's beloved movie star hound, "Old Yeller." (Balchowsky did later change the spelling of his car's name, at Disney's insistence.) The name was fitting. Many of the cars were displeasing to the eye, in some cases a retinal irritant. Some have suggested that Balchowsky orchestrated the whole thing to get favorable press coverage. After all, everyone loves an ugly underdog. Balchowsky's all-American racers—built from derelict freeway signs, whitewall tires, and junkyard parts—were challenging Europe's best and most expensive. How could you help but root for the Old Yallers? Of course, Balchowsky never set the press straight. With his carefully practiced unassuming ways, he kept them convinced that his cars were overmatched

mongrels. The truth is the cars only looked crude. The Old Yallers were mechanical masterpieces—well balanced, brutally fast, and exciting to watch. On this last point, Balchowsky believed in driving the Old Yallers through the turns, sideways, foot to the floor. He designed most of the cars with rubber bushings at pivot points to promote a loose suspension. And while there was many a naysayer for this Balchowsky concept, it worked.

Balchowsky's Old Yallers were famous and frequent winners. Some of the finest drivers of the 1950s and early 1960s raced them, including Carroll Shelby, Bob Bondurant, Bill Krause, and Bob Drake. Even after the invasion of the midengined wonders from across the pond, Balchowsky's Old Yallers won eight of 13 outings in the 1963–1964, season with Ronnie Bucknum at the wheel. The cars were just that good.

Balchowsky also had a successful career prepping cars for Hollywood movies. The duties varied between preparing cars for on-screen races, crash scenes, and other stunts. In addition, Balchowsky's work included the preparation and maintenance of camera cars.

Old Yaller I

The first Old Yaller was built using the second Morgenson as the starting point. Balchowsky and investment banker Eric Hauser acquired the car from

Old Yaller I took on the fastest Ferrari in California—and won! Eric Hauser, shown here at Pomona in January 1957, was one of its regular drivers. *Allen Kuhn*

Balchowsky leads Richie Ginther's Ferrari Testa Rossa at Santa Barbara. *Allen Kuhn*

Balchowsky's racing buddy, Dick Morgensen of Phoenix, in 1956, after Margaret Prichard's tragic death while racing the car at Torrey Pines. Balchowsky worked a deal with Morgensen for Hauser to purchase the car. The homebuilt Morgensen Special (built by Morgensen and Boyd Hough in 1953 and 1954) was big, ugly, and fast, just the way Balchowsky liked his racing cars. Only one task remained—to make it faster. And that's what Balchowsky did.

Balchowsky added fire to the Morgensen Special with a '56 Buick V-8 with special pistons, six Stromberg 97 carburetors on two Crower log manifolds, and an exotic racing camshaft from Ed Winfield. With a bore of 4 3/16 inches, a stroke of 3 9/16 inches, and a compression ratio of 10.2:1, the motor produced 330 horsepower at 6,200 rpm. The gearbox was a Jaguar four-speed. Improvements were made to the steering and suspension with a hodge-podge of parts from Ford, Jaguar, Lincoln, Buick, and Morris Minor. The body was formed from aluminum sheets, Chevy truck parts, and even a Coca-Cola sign. To say that the car was displeasing to the eye would be kind. But performance was nothing short of spectacular, with 0–60 times in the low four seconds, 0–100 in nine seconds, and a top speed of 154 miles per hour. And that's what Balchowsky cared about.

Old Yaller I scored its first victory on a rainy weekend in February 1957 at the Pomona Fair Grounds, with Hauser beating the next best car in the field by some 13 seconds. In May 1957, the car scored back-to-back, Saturday/Sunday wins at Santa Barbara, again with Hauser at the helm. On Saturday, Old Yaller I beat Phil Hill (driving John Edgar's 4.9-liter Ferrari), Richie Ginther, John von Neumann, and Bill Pollack. Not too shabby for a pile of parts. On Sunday the car won again.

At the 1958 Santa Barbara Memorial Day main event, Balchowsky placed second behind Lance Reventelow in a Scarab. At the tenth Annual Santa Barbara Labor Day Races (August 1958), Balchowsky and Old Yaller I scored an impressive win in front of 20,000 fans, beating Richie Ginther's Ferrari 250 TR and Bob Oker's Aston Martin DBR-2. At the 1958 Times-Mirror U.S. Grand Prix at Riverside (a 200-mile race), the car was running near the front until its Jag transmission broke. Ironically, it was the only foreign part on the car. Balchowsky had to settle for seventh place against Chuck Daigh's Scarab, the winner. Balchowsky's disappointment was short-lived, as he beat Reventelow in a Scarab in the Sunday feature race one week later at Minden, Nevada.

Old Yaller I's final race under Balchowsky was the 1959 Examiner Grand Prix at Pomona. Balchowsky was in heavy pursuit of Bill Murphy's Buick-powered

Kurtis 500X, driven by Chuck Daigh, when the engine blew. A huge oil slick led to a terrible accident. But the car went on to win a total of 16 races, including wins at Albuquerque, Laguna Seca, Minden, Palm Springs, Paramount Ranch, Phoenix, Pomona, and Santa Barbara.

After Balchowsky had moved on to other projects, Jim Larkin fitted Old Yaller I with a small-block Chevy. After Larkin wrecked the car in a crash at Riverside, he rebuilt it and renamed it Lion Cage. The car was rebuilt with frame rails on the *outside* of the body panels, perhaps to mock the Maserati Birdcage. During its life, the car also went by some other inventive names such as the Outhauser, Dean Van Lines Special, and the Larkin-Hauser Special.

Old Yaller I was demolished at Riverside Raceway in 1961 during a Cal Club event when Eric Hauser hit the outside guardrail and cartwheeled end-over-end down the track. Hauser escaped unscathed, but the car was a tangled mess of rubble.

Old Yaller II

Max and Ina began construction of the second Old Yaller in 1959. This time they did not start with another car, as they had with Old Yaller I. Old Yaller II was pure Balchowsky from the ground up.

The chassis was formed from 13/4-inch chrome-moly tubes with a 0.058-inch wall thickness. The frame was a modified ladder configuration that

Bob Drake in Old Yaller II leads Billy Krause's D-Jag/Chevy at Riverside in 1960. *Allen Kuhn*

Old Yaller II picked up where Old Yaller I left off. Dan Gurney takes the wheel at Riverside on April 3, 1960. *Allen Kuhn*

Balchowsky termed a "distributed load frame." As Balchowsky explained in the August 1960 issue of *Sports Car Illustrated*, "My idea is a distributed load. There should be no maximum concentrated loading at any point. If there's no concentrated load, there are no failures. We figure that it will take a 110-ton impact without damage."

Torsion bars with independent A-arms handled the front suspension; the top arms were Jaguar and the bottom shortened '58 Pontiac arms. In the rear, they used a solid axle with two semielliptical leaf springs. Steering was rack-and-pinion from Morris Minor. Brakes were stock bimetallic drums from a '57–'58 Buick.

The body was a simple aluminum design built for function, not show. Jimmy Burrell built it during nights and weekends, working days at Daddy's Auto Body Shop in Burbank, California, and at night on Old Yaller II. The nose, hood, fenders, and rear deck were held on by Dzus fasteners and came off as a unit. The alloy body was designed so that it could be completely detached from the car in 10 to 20 minutes, and so that all of the mechanicals were easily accessible.

Under the hood, Balchowsky installed a monster 401-ci Buick V-8 with a bore of 4 3/16 inches and a stroke of 3.6 inches; the compression ratio was 9.5:1. Induction was from six Stromberg 97 carburetors through an Edelbrock log-type manifold. The camshaft was Winfield, with a hefty overlap of 303

degrees. The engine produced 305 horsepower at 5,400 rpm and 360 ft-lb of torque at 3,500 revs. The car accelerated from rest to 100 miles per hour in 8.6 seconds and covered the standing quarter-mile in 11.9 seconds with an exit speed of 124 miles per hour. Top speed was 151 miles per hour.

Like the first car, Old Yaller II found success at the race track. In 1960, Balchowsky piloted the car to a win at Pomona. Dan Gurney, Bob Drake, and Carroll Shelby also raced the car in 1960. Gurney was running an easy third in the Examiner Grand Prix when the engine lost a harmonic balancer, retiring the car for the day. After the race, Gurney was quoted as saying, "This is as good as the finest car I've ever driven." Shelby had two turns at the wheel. At a professional USAC race at Road America, Shelby was leading until the car suffered major mechanical

problems. The car was again unsuccessful with Shelby at the helm in the Labor Day race at Santa Barbara. Bob Drake finished second in Old Yaller II behind Bill Krause's Maserati Birdcage, beating Augie Pabst, who placed third in a Scarab in a blanket finish at the 1960 Times Grand Prix. Paul O'Shea at Las Vegas and Bob Drake at Santa Maria also scored victories in the car.

Old Yaller II continues its life in vintage racing.

Old Yaller III

Old Yaller III was initially conceived as a street machine for movie producer-cameraman Haskell Wexler. Wexler was largely responsible for getting the car finished, taking it from one shop to the next. The lineage of Old Yaller III is a bit confusing, as the car was a bit of a chameleon, changing its appearance several times during its early history.

Jack "Willie" Sutton constructed the aluminum body. Initially, the rear end was narrow, and the car rode on Borrani wire wheels. After the car was wrecked during the filming of *Viva Las Vegas*, it was rebuilt with a widened rear track and five-bolt disc wheels. The car was later fitted with another size Borrani wheel. Following a second wreck, the rear body was constructed of fiberglass and the frenched license plate became a surface-mount plate. The head faring was damaged and removed. To add further confusion, the car ran sometimes with a full

Old Yaller III was the first of a proposed line of commercially available sports-racers. It had an attractive aluminum body and was competitive against the first mid-engined cars from England. *Harold Pace*

Max Balchowsky (left) and his wife Ina work on Old Yaller III in Santa Barbara in 1963. Friend and sponsor Haskell Wexler is second from the left in the background. *Allen Kuhn*

Jerry Entin pilots Old Yaller III at Santa Barbara. *Allen Kuhn*

Ron Bucknum (in Old Yaller III) talks shop with Jerry Titus (rear) and Ken Miles (right). *Allen Kuhn*

Doretti windshield, and other times with a cutdown windscreen. The car ran with both a two-headlight and four-headlight configuration, and it ran with and without a grille.

The front end of Old Yaller III used Jaguar upper arms and Pontiac lower control arms. The car was built with a solid rear end but was converted to an independent rear suspension before it was ever finished. Brakes were Buick drum, and steering was rack-and-pinion from a right-hand-drive MGA, turned upside down. A 401-ci Buick V-8 supplied power.

The car was raced heavily and did quite well. Bob Drake won a feature race at Pomona in the early 1960s and a main event at Santa Barbara. Chuck Daigh and Ronnie Bucknum also drove the car.

Most recently, the car was owned and vintage-raced by Bruce Jacobs. In 2001, Jacobs donated the car to the Peterson Automotive Museum in Los Angeles.

Old Yaller IV

Old Yaller IV's frame was a similar, but more advanced, design compared to those of Old Yaller II and III. It was now more of a true space frame. Front suspension was sprung torsion bar and consisted of unequal arms; the upper control arms were lightened Jag, the lower were from a Pontiac. The rear suspension was via Morris torsion bars. Brakes were Jag disc in the front and Buick finned-aluminum drums with Swiss-cheesed backing plates in the rear. The gearbox was a Jaguar four-speed. The alloy body was by California Metal Shaping and was a real gem.

The car ran a Buick V-8 punched out to 430 ci fed through an Edelbrock log manifold and six single-throat Strombergs. Power output was 350 horsepower at 5,800 rpm. Balchowsky mated the Buick to a close-ratio Jag gearbox with a bell housing of his own design. Power was transferred through a fortified, 10-inch hydraulic Auburn clutch. The drive shaft was short and mated to a Studebaker Champion rear end that had a locked (solid spool) differential.

Unfortunately, Old Yaller IV is most remembered for its worst moments

rather than its best. The car was involved in a tragic accident at Pomona in 1961 when it got away from driver Bob Drake and went into the crowd. One spectator was killed and 12 others were injured. Following the accident, the car was sold to Bob Publiker. Later, Balchowsky bought the car back, removed the front bodywork and doors, and turned it into a Hollywood camera car. Sadly, the car was again badly crashed, this time during the filming of Disney's *The Love Bug*. Old Yaller IV was accidentally rolled during the filming of a mountain sequence of the movie.

Old Yaller V

When is a car with Corvette looks and Corvette power not a Corvette at all? When it's Old Yaller V, of course.

Old Yaller V began life as a Balchowsky chassis similar to that of Old Yaller IV. Corvette racer Dave MacDonald, who was looking for something lighter than a 3,000-pound stock Corvette, conceived the car. MacDonald believed that a stock Corvette had more than enough straight-line power, and he set out to build a lightened car that could out-run the modifieds.

Nat "The Glass Man" Reeder of Fiberglass Auto Body pulled the fiberglass Corvette-style body from a mold of Jim Simpson's Corvette. MacDonald, Simpson, and Jim Burrel then constructed the body with 1/16-inch glass fiber. The finished body weighed only 85 pounds.

Here's Old Yaller IV in action at Pomona in 1961. *Tam McPartland*

Dave MacDonald tries out his uncompleted Old Yaller Mk.V in Max Balchowsky's shop. *Dan and Karen Gallant collection*

Motivation for Old Yaller V came from a 327-ci Corvette engine with stock valves, pistons, rods, and crankshaft. The gearbox was a standard Corvette four-speed. The front suspension was Jag upper arms and Pontiac lowers. The torsion bars were fully adjustable. The front brakes were 11-inch Pontiac drums with aluminum fins; the rear brakes were 12-inch Buick Alfins. Initially, the car ran with a Studebaker rear end, which was later swapped for a stronger and lighter Chevy rear end with coil-over shocks to stiffen up the suspension.

The car ran with modified "reverse cone" exhaust ends with Jardine headers and wore the No. 00. The car was raced by MacDonald and was known as the Dave MacDonald/Jim Simpson Special "00" race car.

The first time out was at Cotati in 1961, where MacDonald won his class from spotty opposition. At the Pacific Grand Prix in October, MacDonald qualified poorly and spun out of the race. Unhappy with the handling, MacDonald and car owner Jim Simpson took the car to Frank Kurtis, who stiffened up the suspension to make it handle more like a Corvette. The next season, MacDonald started out strong, with a win at Riverside, but after that the car was plagued with reliability problems and was not a true contender. The MacDonald Corvette was just too late—the day of the front-engined sports-racer was over.

According to one story, the original chassis for this car sat in a field in Hawaii for several years before being cut up and scrapped. Other accounts suggest that the chassis of Old Yaller V still exists.

Old Yaller VI

This version started as a bare rolling chassis purchased by Bob Sohus. Sohus used a 383-ci Pontiac engine from the Reynolds Wrap Special and clothed the car in a hideous homemade body constructed of square and rectangular sections of fiberglass held together with pieces of duct tape. The rear section was a solid spool, rather than a proper differential, and contributed to the car's go kart

characteristics. Sohus had a falling out with Balchowsky over some money owed on the chassis. From that point on, Sohus referred to the car as *Godzilla*. At one time Walt Ward owned the car, or co-owned it with Sohus. The chassis of Old Yaller VI still exists and now wears a fiberglass body.

Old Yaller VI was fitted with this bodywork, which made even Max flinch. The car was nicknamed Godzilla. *Ellen E. Sohus collection*

Old Yaller VII

Old Yaller VII was built in 1962 and sold as a rolling chassis to Don Kirby of Rochester, New York. Kirby installed a modified Devin fiberglass body and raced it with a 327-ci fuel-injected Chevy motor in the eastern United States. Kirby crashed into a loudspeaker pole at the first turn during a USRRC race at Daytona in 1962. After this shunt, Dick Lane of Trumansburg, New York, rebodied the car in aluminum. It also was fitted with an independent rear suspension in place of the Dana live axle.

Kirby advertised the car for sale on October 27, 1962, in *Competition Press* (Vol. 9, No. 8). The car was sold to Stan

Kozlowski in 1964. He drove the car with Kirby at the Road America 500, and finished fourth in the over-2-liter class.

Kozlowski sold the car to Tim Thompson, who later sold it to Tom Palmer in 1966 or 1967. Palmer drove the car on the street and ran it at an SCCA driver's school at Watkins Glen in 1969. The car was sold again in 1980 to Dennis Manning, who stored it in his garage until it was sold to Michael Gray in 1990.

Old Yaller VIII

Old Yaller VIII was built in 1962 around a Jaguar XKE monocoque chassis that Balchowsky shortened and modified. For the front suspension, Balchowsky used Jag upper A-arms and modified '59 Pontiac lower arms. This arrangement allowed a wide range of adjustment for caster and camber. The rear suspension was another Balchowsky conglomeration. The lower arms were from an XKE, the upper arms were fabbed by Balchowsky, and the differential was from a Studebaker. Brakes were aluminum drums from a '60 Buick.

The idea for the body either came from Balchowsky or his friend Haskell Wexler, or a collaboration of the two. The center portion of the body and the tail were derived from a 1961 Jag XKE. California Metal Shaping constructed a new nose, doors, and trunk lid from aluminum. California Metal Shaping also reworked the tail section to make it look less like

Old Yaller VII had several bodies over the years. This is how it looks now. *Harry Mathews collection*

Old Yaller VIII was based on a Jaguar XKE monocoque chassis, unlike any other Balchowsky creation. *Gordon Apker collection*

a Jag and more like a one-off, installing 1958 Chevy taillights.

At some point, John Brophy purchased the car as a street machine. He installed a 327-ci Chevy V-8 and a T-10 gearbox. The car also appeared in the movie *Viva Las Vegas,* but its actual early racing record is unclear, and it may have never been raced.

In the late 1960s, Old Yaller VIII was customized for the car-show circuit. Famed customizer Dean Jeffries constructed a lovely Ferrari-like nose, and Lola T-70 wheels were fitted all around. It was a singularly great-looking car but was not raced in this guise.

In 1966, the car was sold to Richard Pekkonen, and in 1972 it was sold to Grand Strand Amusements of South Carolina. In the early 1990s, vintage racer Gordon Apker bought and restored it to original condition.

Old Yaller IX

Old Yaller IX, powered by a big FE 427-ci Ford side-oiler, won several club events, driven by Balchowsky and Ron Bucknum. Bob Drake drove it in its last race, a 1966 USRRC event at Stardust Raceway in Las Vegas. Balchowsky and Ted Peterson later converted the car to Buick power for vintage racing.

BALCHOWSKY

Hollywood Motors
Balchowsky Automotive
4905 Hollywood Boulevard
Hollywood, California

OLD YALLER I

Year built	**1957**
Engine	**5,600-cc Buick V-8 (1956)**
Gearbox	**Jaguar four-speed**
Chassis	**space frame**
Front suspension	**Ford solid axle**
Rear suspension	**live axle**
Brakes	**12-inch Lincoln with Buick front drums**
Body material	**aluminum and steel**
Weight, approx.	**2,320 pounds**
Wheelbase	**95 inches**
Length	**155 inches**
Height	**37 inches**
Cost when new	**$2,400**

OLD YALLER II

Year built	**1959**
Engine	**Buick V-8 (401 ci)**
Gearbox	**Jaguar four-speed**
Chassis	**space frame**
Front suspension	**independent**
Rear suspension	**solid axle**
Brakes	**drums**
Body material	**aluminum**
Weight, approx.	**1,870 pounds**
Wheelbase	**93.75 inches**
Length	**150 inches**
Height	**36 inches**

OLD YALLER III

Year built	**1960**
Engine	**Buick V-8 (401 ci)**
Gearbox	**Jaguar four-speed**
Chassis	**space frame**
Front suspension	**independent**
Rear suspension	**live axle, later independent**
Brakes	**drum**
Body material	**aluminum**

Old Yaller IX was the last of the famed Balchowsky line. *Harold Pace*

OLD YALLER IV

Years built **1960–1961**
Engine . . . . **Buick V-8 (430 ci)**
Gearbox . . . . **Jaguar four-speed**
Chassis . . . . **space frame**
Front suspension . . . . **independent**
Rear suspension . . . . . **live axle**
Brakes . . . . **front Jaguar disc,**
rear Buick drum
Body material . . . . **aluminum**
Weight, approx. . . . . . **1,850 pounds**
Wheelbase . . . . **91 inches**

OLD YALLER V

Year built **1961**
Engine . . . . **Chevy V-8 (327 ci)**
Gearbox **T-10**
Chassis . . . . **space frame**
Front suspension . . . . **independent**
Rear suspension . . . . . **live axle**
Brakes . . . . **drum**
Body material . . . . **fiberglass**
Weight, approx. . . . . . **1,750 pounds**
Wheelbase . . . . **92 inches**
Length . . . . **160 inches**
Height . . . . **48.2 inches**

OLD YALLER VI

Year built **1961**
Engine . . . . **Pontiac V-8 (383 ci)**
Chassis . . . . **space frame**
Front suspension . . . . **independent**
Rear suspension . . . . . **live axle**
Brakes . . . . **disc/drum**
Body material . . . . **fiberglass**

OLD YALLER VII

Year built **1962**
Engine . . . . **Chevy V-8 (327 ci)**
Gearbox **T-10**
Chassis . . . . **space frame**
Front suspension . . . . **independent**
Rear suspension . . . . . **live axle,**
later independent
Brakes . . . . **disc/drum**
Body material . . . . **fiberglass**
Price when new **$4,500**

OLD YALLER VIII

Year built **1962**
Engine . . . . **Chevy V-8 (327 ci)**
Gearbox **T-10**
Chassis . . . . **monocoque (Jaguar XKE)**
Front suspension . . . . **independent**
Rear suspension . . . . . **independent**
Brakes . . . . **drum (Buick finned**
aluminum)
Body material . . . . **center section from**
Jaguar XKE, front and
rear sections fabricated
from aluminum

OLD YALLER IX

Year built **1963**
Engine . . . . **Ford V-8 (427 ci)**
Gearbox . . . . **Ford Top Loader**
Chassis . . . . **space frame**
Front suspension . . . . **independent**
Rear suspension . . . . . **live axle**
Brakes . . . . **disc/drum**
Body material . . . . **aluminum**

Battlebirds

In the early 1950s, Ford and Chevy were engaged in a bitter fight for sales leadership, causing Ford to have some very special 'Birds built in 1957 to take on the 'Vettes at the racetracks. It was not going to be an easy job. Although the two-seat Thunderbirds easily outsold their plastic competitors, the 1956–1957 Corvettes were technologically light-years ahead of the soft, porky T-Birds. The Thunderbird was overweight, underbraked, and too softly suspended to take on a stock fuel-injected '57 Corvette on a road course. Although the Ford Y-block was more powerful than the Chevy in race tune, it was also a lot heavier, and Ford had no four-speed gearbox to match the new Borg–Warner T-10 installed in the 1957 Corvette.

The decision was made to concentrate on highly publicized events that took place at Daytona Beach. These mainly consisted of top-speed and acceleration trials, where the Ford power advantage could be put to use. Ford also wanted to try its modified 'Birds at a road race or two, including the 12-hour grind at Sebring, where durability would matter as much as outright performance.

In late 1956, Ford shipped four Thunderbirds to Pete de Paolo Engineering, which had handled other racing efforts for Ford. The cars were lightened with aluminum doors, hoods, firewalls, trunks, and other parts fabricated by Dick Troutman and Dwight Clayton. Two cars were kept relatively stock in appearance, for "stock car" classes, while the other two were more radical. The stock-appearing cars were built for straight-line and top-speed work at Daytona, but the other two cars were modified for road course use as well.

The two road racing 'Birds (nicknamed the "Battlebirds") were built by Jim Travers and Frank Coons, who would later perform miracles with Chevy engines at their Traco engine shop. They started by gutting the interior, leaving only one racing bucket and a small aluminum dashboard. The steel inner supports for the aluminum doors and hood were liberally drilled to cut weight. An aluminum tonneau cover blanketed the passenger side of the car, and finned headrests, all the rage on sports-racers in the 1950s, were fitted behind the driver's seat.

To balance the weight of the big Ford engines, they were moved rearward 6 inches and lowered in the frame 4 inches. One car got a 312-ci Y-block, while the other received a Lincoln 430-ci V-8, both estimated to be putting out over 400 horsepower. Both engines were equipped with Hillborn fuel injection for road racing and with superchargers for Daytona. Jaguar four-speed gearboxes were used, as Ford had no suitable gearbox.

29

Ford Battlebirds were Thunderbirds with major modifications. *Harold Pace*

For improved handling, Travers and Coons installed a massive front sway bar, splined like a stock car torsion bar. Stiffer coil springs were used up front, with special seven-leaf springs in back. Dual shocks were fitted at each corner to control wheel movement. Both cars received Halibrand quick-change differentials, which meant notching the gas tank. A supplementary tank was added to the trunk area.

The finned brake drums were 2 1/2 inches wide, and the rear drums were cooled by heater blowers forcing air though tubing to the drilled backing plates. The steering was modified to make it quicker and lighter, with only 1 1/2 turns lock to lock. Halibrand magnesium wheels with triple-eared knock-offs wore Firestone Super Sport tires.

The Lincoln-engined car seldom performed to expectations, except for setting the Daytona record for a standing-start measured mile at 98.065 miles per hour. In a road race at New Smyrna Beach, Florida, the Ford-powered car finished second to Carroll Shelby in a Ferrari 4.9. Unfortunately, the Automobile Manufacturers' Association (AMA) racing ban went into effect before Sebring, so the Battlebirds never got a chance to dance with the Corvettes.

Both cars were later sold to Andy Hotten, who raced them in the Midwest. The Lincoln-powered car was destroyed in an accident, but the Ford-powered Battlebird is now restored to original condition.

BATTLEBIRDS

Travers and Coons
Los Angeles, California

BATTLEBIRDS

Year built	1957
Engines	Ford 312-ci; Lincoln 430-ci
Gearbox	Jaguar four-speed
Front suspension	independent
Rear suspension	live axle
Brakes	drum
Body material	steel and aluminum
Wheelbase	102 inches
Number built	two

Beach

Beach is a respected name in both formula and sports-racing cars. Cars built by Gene Beach have won championships and competed from Nassau to Sebring, leaving hundreds of satisfied customers, who ran them with great success.

Gene Beach started racing in an MG TD in 1956. He had served in

the military during World War II and suffered a broken back in the crash of his P-47. After the war, he found work as a draftsman and then went on to become an architect in Clearwater, Florida. Beach approached racing cars as he did architecture—from a standpoint of stress calculation. After the TD came a Doretti, and then he built a special out of a modified Crosley. Beach's first complete design was a Panhard-engined car for Don Kearney. In 1959, he found a partner who would help him build serious racing cars.

The First Begras (Begra Mk.1 and 2)

Henry Grady (see Grady entry) had an automotive parts house in Miami and shared Beach's dream of building his own cars. Grady was familiar with engines, while Beach was the chassis expert, so they divided the project along those lines and set to work. Together, they bought a new Fiat 600 and cannibalized it for parts to build their first H-Modified, named the Begra (BEach-GRAdy). The two partners communicated by phone as they worked at garages 260 miles apart. Beach simplified the chassis design by stripping the Fiat chassis and bolting small steel plates to the mounting holes for the suspension pickups, then connecting the plates with a framework of electrical conduit. This was unbolted and used as a jig to weld up a light, rear-engined space frame that accepted the Fiat swing-axle suspension. To save money, he then sold the bare body back to the Fiat dealer. Beach made a very light aluminum body by hammering the panels over a tree stump. Grady bored and stroked the Fiat engine to 748 cc and fitted it with Hillman pistons and other modifications to produce a little over 40 horsepower.

The finished car weighed just over 800 pounds and was competitive right off the drawing board. Beach was a talented driver and the car scored victories in the Florida area, but Beach and Grady realized they needed more power to be nationally competitive. They sold

The Begra Mk.1 was the first of a great line of racing cars, driven here by Jerry Morgan.
Alice Bixler; Nick England collection

The Begra Mk.2 was built for Sebring and ran with a variety of engines. Hugh Kleinpeter is shown here at Nassau in 1963. *Nick England collection*

The Begra Mk.3 was the first midengined car built by Gene Beach. *Nick England collection*

the Begra Mk.1 to Jerry Morgan and began development on a Saab 750-cc engine that showed more promise than the Fiat. Unable to afford a Saab GT engine, the team upgraded a standard 750 to GT specs that produced 55 horsepower. This was adapted to the Fiat 600 transaxle in the Mk.1.

The Saab engine proved to be potent, but electrical gremlins linked to the electric tachometer dogged the car during the 1960 season. It was later uprated to an 850-cc Fiat engine and raced by Paul Kneeland.

A second car, the Begra Mk.2, was built for Bill Ward to run at Sebring in 1961. A real Saab 750GT engine was used this time, and the chassis was sturdier. The suspension and gearbox were still Fiat 600, but with Fiat 110 spindles and brakes (Fiat Multipla brakes were later installed). The body was now fiberglass and the engine was still mounted in the rear. The engine gave trouble during the race, and it retired after five hours. The Mk.2 was run once with a borrowed Abarth twin cam engine, then was upgraded to a G-Modified with a Ford 105E engine and raced by Hugh Kleinpeter.

Begra Mk.3

Beach and Grady dissolved their partnership in 1961, but Beach built four more cars that were still referred to as Begras. These Mk.3 models differed from the earlier Begras, with midmounted engines in a more sophisticated chassis that sported fabricated fully independent suspension. An Abarth twin cam-powered car was built for Team Roosevelt, a racing

team that featured Abarth-based cars. It proved to be very competitive and was raced by Beach, Bobby Richardson, and the Roosevelt team. Another was also powered by a 750-cc Abarth twin cam and raced by George Avent, who won the 1962 and 1964 SCCA Southeast Division H-Modified championships.

Beach sold two more Begras in kit form. Frank Stark bought one and powered it with a Saab 750-cc. It had Triumph Spitfire uprights and disc brakes.

The First Beach (Mk.4)

Beach set up Competition Components, with help from tuner Wayne Purdy, in 1963 and began production of the Beach Mk.4, a development of the last Begras. Beach ditched the Fiat suspension parts

and replaced them with Spitfire uprights and disc brakes, although the Fiat gearbox was retained. The nose was lowered, but otherwise it looked similar to the Mk.3. Two were built before an upgraded Mk.4B replaced it in 1964, followed by the Mk.4B/Series II and Mk.4C. A BMW 700-cc twin engine producing 65 horsepower powered the first Mk.4. It was later reengined with Deutsch-Bonnet and Sunbeam Imp engines. Mini Cooper, Datsun, and Ford four-cylinder engines powered other Mk.4/4B variations.

The most unusual version was the Mk.4B/SRV, which used the basic Mk.4 chassis with Volkswagen torsion bar/swing-axle suspension and running gear grafted on. It was intended to be a cheap sports-racer based on the VW parts that Beach used on his new love, Formula Vee. A Mk.4B/SRV was run at Sebring in 1968, where it finished too far down to be

Nick England vintage races this Beach Mk.4B.
Gordon Jolly; Nick England collection

The Beach Mk.4B/SRV was a VW-powered entry in the sports-racing classes. *Harold Pace*

Beach made winning Formula Vees. This Mk.5 is still going strong today. *Harold Pace*

The Beach Formula Vee won the lion's share of races between the Formcar and Zink dynasties. *Harold Pace*

classified. Another SRV failed to finish at Sebring the next year. Zink and Ray Heppenstall ran similar VW-based prototypes that year.

Beach Mk.8

There was one final Beach sports-racer, the lovely Mk.8 coupe. The car was intended for endurance racing, with the first model run at Sebring in 1965. It looked like a scaled-down Lola coupe and was fitted with a potent Cosworth-tuned Lotus twin cam engine. It was a hurried project and dropped out with suspension failure. Beach also advertised a street version of the Mk.8 called the Mk.8 Grand Sport, powered by a pushrod Ford Cortina GT, but none are known to have been built.

The final coupe variation was the Mk.8 1300SL, which was based on 1,300-cc Volkswagen running gear. It was intended to be a street or race car, and in 1967 one ran at Sebring, where it retired with suspension woes. Only these two Mk.8s were built.

Beach Formula Vees

When Formula Vee was introduced, Beach saw it as an opportunity to sell a lot of race cars. He introduced his first model in 1962, and it finished a promising fourth at the 1963 Nassau Formula Vee race, the premier FV race at that time. The next year, a Beach FV driven by Bruce McLaren won the event after the first two finishers were disqualified. In 1965 there was no question—Beach FVs took the first three slots at Nassau and won the SCCA runoff race at Daytona, to be crowned national champion. By 1965, Beach had sold over 150 FVs in the United States and Europe.

The FV was called the Mk.5, and there were three variations. The first cars were Mk.5As, while the 5B and 5C were made alongside each other in the mid-1960s. The Mk.5B had a square tube frame, was easy to build, and was less expensive than the more sophisticated Mk.5C.

Other Beach Formulas

When Formula Ford cranked up in the late 1960s, Beach hoped to duplicate his FV success. His Type 11 was a conventional design with a space frame, steel wheels, and an attractive body. It was a solid car but got lost in a field crowded by entries from all over the world. A second Type 11 version was intended for Formula C, which mandated the use of an 1,100-cc Ford pushrod engine, a five-speed Hewland gearbox, and mag wheels. For the big boys, a Formula B version was fitted with Lotus twin cam or Alfa engines with a five-speed Hewland and wider wheels. All three Type 11 variations had similar running gear and bodywork. Hugh Kleinpeter raced the FB versions with some success in 1968.

In 1970, Volkswagen of America decided to come up with a faster version of Formula Vee that would use larger 1,600-cc VW engines in a high state of tune. The chassis was to be similar to Formula Ford

Beach built this handsome endurance-racing coupe, the Mk.8, to run at Sebring in 1965 and 1967. *Nick England collection*

The Beach Type 11 Formula B car was offered with Alfa Romeo and Lotus engines. *Nick England collection*

The Beach SV16 was the first Formula Super Vee built. Volkswagen used it to drum up interest in the new class. *Nick England collection*

or Formula B practice, although some VW parts, like the uprights and brakes, were required. Jo Hoppen was in charge of organizing FSV for VW, and he contracted for Beach to build the first FSV prototype, which was sold to VW in 1970. The car was taken around the world to gain support of the new concept.

The Beach SV16 was a conventional design with a steel tube frame and aluminum side panels. Initially, the FSV regulations required disc brakes on the front and drums in back, although four-wheel discs were allowed by 1972. These FSVs were normally fitted with twin two-barrel Weber carbs, although at least one car had two single-barrel carburetors and a twin-nostril nose.

Beach Plan Sets

Beach also sold plan sets for all his models. These would allow buyers to build all or part of a Beach by themselves. How many were actually completed is unknown. One interesting illustration shows an FSV variation with two one-barrel carburetors and trailing-arm rear suspension like on the SV 16, but with FV-style trailing-arm front suspension.

BEACH

Competition Components, Inc.
2028 Gentry Street
Clearwater, Florida

BEGRA MK.1
Year built **1960**
Engine . . . . **Fiat 748-cc pushrod**
Gearbox . . . . **Fiat 600 four-speed**
Front suspension . . . . **modified Fiat 600**
Rear suspension . . . . . **Fiat swing axles**
Brakes . . . . **Fiat 600 drum**
Body material . . . . **aluminum**
Weight, approx. . . . . . **800 pounds**
Number built . . . . **one**

BEGRA MK.2
Year built **1961**
Engine . . . . **Saab 750-cc**
Gearbox . . . . **Fiat 600 four-speed**
Front suspension . . . . **modified Fiat 600**
Rear suspension . . . . . **Fiat swing axles**
Brakes . . . . **Fiat Multipla drum**
Body material . . . . **fiberglass**
Weight, approx. . . . . . **995 pounds**
Number built . . . . **one**

BEGRA MK.3
Year built **1962**
Engines . . . . **Abarth TC, Saab 750-cc**
Gearbox . . . . **Fiat 600 four-speed**
Front suspension . . . . **independent**
Rear suspension . . . . . **independent**
Brakes . . . . **disc/drum**
Body material . . . . **fiberglass**
Weight, approx. . . . . . **800 pounds**
Number built . . . . **four**

BEACH MK.4, 4B, 4C
Years built **1963–1968**
Engines . . . . **BMW, English Ford,**
. . . . **Honda, Imp, Mini Cooper**
Gearbox . . . . **Fiat 600 four-speed**
Front suspension . . . . **independent**
Rear suspension . . . . . **independent**
Brakes . . . . **disc**
Body material . . . . **fiberglass**
Weight, approx. . . . . . **800 pounds**
Wheelbase . . . . **88 inches**
Number built . . . . **unknown**

BEACH MK.4B/SRV
Years built **1965–1969**
Engine . . . . **Volkswagen**
Gearbox . . . . **Volkswagen**
Front suspension . . . . **trailing link**
Rear suspension . . . . . **swing axle**
Brakes . . . . **drum/drum**
Body material . . . . **fiberglass**
Weight, approx. . . . . . **800 pounds**
Wheelbase . . . . **88 inches**
Number built . . . . **unknown**

BEACH MK.8
Years built **1965–1967**
Engines . . . . **Volkswagen, Lotus TC**
Gearbox . . . . **Volkswagen four-speed,**
. . . . **Hewland five-speed**
Front suspension . . . . **independent**
Rear suspension . . . . . **independent**
Brakes . . . . **disc**
Body material . . . . **fiberglass**
Weight, approx. . . . . . **1,275 pounds**
Wheelbase . . . . **90 inches**
Number built . . . . **two**

BEACH MK.5, 5B, 5C FV
Years built **1962–1968**
Engine . . . . **Volkswagen**
Gearbox . . . . **Volkswagen four-speed**
Front suspension . . . . **torsion bar (Volkswagen)**
Rear suspension . . . . . **swing axle (Volkswagen)**
Brakes . . . . **Volkswagen drum**
Body material . . . . **fiberglass**
Weight, approx. . . . . . **825 pounds**
Wheelbase . . . . **81.5 inches**
Number built . . . . **unknown**

BEACH TYPE 11 FORMULA FORD, FC, FB
Year built **1968**
Engines . . . . **Ford 1,600-cc or**
. . . . **1,100-cc pushrod,**
. . . . **Lotus TC, Alfa 1,600-cc**
Gearbox . . . . **Hewland four-**
. . . . **or five-speed**
Front suspension . . . . **independent**
Rear suspension . . . . . **independent**
Brakes . . . . **disc**
Body material . . . . **fiberglass**
Weight, approx. . . . . . **885 pounds**
Wheelbase . . . . **88 inches**
Number built . . . . **unknown**

BEACH SV16 FORMULA SUPER VEE
Year built **1970**
Engine . . . . **Volkswagen 1,600-cc**
Gearbox . . . . **Hewland four-speed**
Front suspension . . . . **independent**
Rear suspension . . . . . **independent**
Brakes . . . . **disc**
Body material . . . . **fiberglass**
Weight, approx. . . . . . **885 pounds**
Wheelbase . . . . **88 inches**
Number built . . . . **unknown**

Begra

See Beach entry.

Bobsy

Jerry Mong built more than 100 great racing cars in his Medina, Ohio, race shops. Starting in 1958 with a midengined VW-powered special, Mong progressed to a pair of identical (hence the "Bobsy twins" nickname) cars for himself and brothers Kaye and Alan Heir. These home-built racers, the Bobsy SR1s, were attractive midengined H-Modifieds with DKW engines and aluminum frames. The use of aluminum tube frames became a Bobsy hallmark. The twin cars were run in SCCA events in 1962 with sporadic success, despite the lack of power from their stock DKW engines.

Mong had been running a tune-up shop in Medina, but decided to sell it and go into the race car business with backing from his uncle, C. W. Smith. Smith owned the C. W. Smith Engineering Company, which did government contract work and projects for GM and Ford. Mong built his third car, officially the Bobsy SR2, in his garage, but then moved to a 1,500-square-foot building to begin race car production.

The SR2

The design for the SR2 borrowed from the previous two cars and also employed an aluminum space frame with adjustable coil-over suspension. Gone were the tiny mills, replaced in the prototype by a 1,100-cc Holbay-tuned Ford 105E engine backed up with a Hewland Mk.3 transaxle. The bigger engine moved the car up to G-Modified, which had a 1,100-cc limit. This class was previously the domain of Coventry-Climax FWA-powered cars, but the pushrod Ford was beginning to take over. The Ford engine could also be quickly replaced with a 1,500-cc Ford engine for racing in the F-Modified class. At first, Mong used Triumph front uprights with Cooper wheels, but these were later replaced with parts of

his own design. Bobsy 13-inch wheels were made in 6-, 7-, and 8-inch widths.

Chuck Dietrich, who had made his enviable reputation collecting trophies in various Elvas, raced the prototype in 1963. Dietrich won the 1963 SCCA G-Modified championship in an SR2, finishing with a perfect score of nine wins. Sometimes the Bobsy crew changed engines at the track so Dietrich could win F-Modified as well!

The SR2 went into production in 1964, and some of the cars were fitted with other engines, including a 750-cc OSCA. The SR2 was designed to take engines up to 2 liters and was usually sold in kit form.

Formula Vees

The Formula Vee class was growing by leaps and bounds, so in 1965 Bobsy introduced its Vanguard Formula Vee racer. At that time, Mong also incorporated his company as Vanguard Automotive Enterprises. The Vanguard proved to be competitive, winning three SCCA divisional championships, but failed to be a contender for the national championship. In 1966, it was discontinued after more than 100 had been sold.

The Bobsy SR3 was both quick and graceful. This example packs a Porsche engine. *Harold Pace*

In 1967, Mong built a second Vee design, the Bobsy Vega. Unlike the Vanguard, the Vega had an exceptionally rigid chassis with a host of adjustable features for tuning the handling at the track. It also came standard with one of the first fuel cells fitted to an FV. A Z-bar was used in back and it hit the minimum legal weight of 825 pounds right on the head. Spax shocks were used front and rear. Mong intended to use dual-stressed aluminum side panels on the chassis with polyurethane foam squirted in

The Bobsy Vanguard Formula Vee was a good car with a simple ladder frame. *Harold Pace*

between. It was very rigid and made the car both stiff and safe, but the SCCA declared it illegal, like the early Zink. Only two were built before the car was redesigned without the stressed panels. Vegas were good but not great Formula Vees and around 20 were sold.

SR3 and SR4

The SR2 was upgraded into the similar SR3 by revising the nose and strengthening the chassis. The rounded nose of the SR2 was lengthened into a point for better air penetration. There were numerous differences between the cars, as Saab-powered H-Modifieds had thinner chassis tubes and narrower wheels than those intended for bigger engines. Some were fitted with 2-liter BMW engines, while others had wider engine bays to accommodate flat engines like the Porsche four-cam Carrera, Porsche 911, and the Corvair. Mong sold the SR3 in turnkey and kit form, and many more kits than completed cars were sold.

Like the SR2, the SR3 had a tube frame built of 6061 T-6 aluminum. The H-Modifieds had 0.083-inch wall thickness, while the bigger models had 0.125-inch walls in some of the chassis tubes. The H-Modifieds used steel, instead of aluminum, in some suspension components. Airheart disc brakes were used all the way around, two-pad units for H-Mods and four-pad for faster classes. A Mini steering rack provided quick steering, and Gabriel shocks were turned into coil-overs by clamping

Bobsy SR3s were equipped with many engines. This one now sports a Lotus twin cam. *Harold Pace*

mounts to the body of the shocks. As the cars developed, changes were made in suspension components, so there is no definitive SR3 configuration.

The SR3 was very successful. In 1965, Mong won the SCCA H-Modified championship race at Daytona in a Bobsy-Saab, besting a Bobsy-Osca in second. Two years later, John Ingleheart won the SCCA H-Sports-Racing (the new name for H-Modified) championship in a Bobsy as well.

The SR4 was a one-off prototype with a squared-off body and the last aluminum tube frame fitted to a Bobsy sports-racer. It was fitted with Lotus twin cam power. The SR5 was a production model with an aluminum monocoque that came out in 1971. Later, Mong would build more winning sports-racers, as well as Formula Fords and Formula Atlantics. The Bobsies built in the 1960s and 1970s were excellent designs and beautifully made.

The level of workmanship and fit and finish was very high on all Bobsies. Mong was aided by master machinist Louis Gilbert, who made the many precision parts needed in the suspension.

We Talk With Jerry Mong.

AUTHOR: You built your first VW-based special in 1958. Why did you decide to build your own car?

MONG: Probably money as much as anything else . . . the inability to go out and buy a Porsche or something like that to race. We built that first aluminum-bodied thing rear-engined; turned the VW engine around. I realized you could switch the ring and pinion and run the thing like a 550 Spyder. That was part of it, but basically it was just money. Racing is the kind of

The Bobsy SR4 was a one-off prototype. Number 7 (second on the grid behind an Abarth) is powered by a Lotus twin cam. *Harold Pace*

thing that takes a hold of a person and drives you; it consumes your existence, your life, and your family. There are lots of regrets involved for anyone who has been involved in racing as I was.

AUTHOR: In 1962, you built the Bobsy twins. Why did you choose to use aluminum for the frames?

MONG: At that time, lightness was the whole name of the game. There wasn't that much power available. We went with aluminum because we thought we could save some weight, and we did, but not a hell of a lot. As it turned out, we used aluminum right on through.

AUTHOR: What engines did you use in the Bobsy twins?

MONG: We used DKW engines in both of them. We reworked the transmission so we could get a quick-change rear end in them. They were semisuccessful—nothing dramatic, but unique. We learned how to work with aluminum on them.

AUTHOR: In 1964, Chuck Dietrich won his class at the ARRC in the SR2. What was it like campaigning the car with him?

MONG: It was great. You just live for the car all year long. Plus we rebuilt the car practically

**Bobsy Division
C. W. Smith Engineering Company
139 Koons Avenue
Medina, Ohio**

Vanguard Automotive Enterprises, Inc.

BOBSY SR1

Year built	**1962**
Engines	**DKW or Saab**
Front suspension	**independent**
Rear suspension	**independent**
Body material	**aluminum**
Weight, approx.	**750 pounds**
Number built	**two**

BOBSY SR2

Years built	**1963–1964**
Engines	**Ford 105E, OSCA, Saab, Datsun**
Gearbox	**Hewland Mk.3**
Front suspension	**independent**
Rear suspension	**independent**
Brakes	**disc**
Body material	**aluminum**
Weight, approx.	**750 pounds**

BOBSY SR3

Year built	**1965**
Engines	**Ford 1,100-cc and 1,500-cc, BMW 2000, Alfa 1300, Saab 850-cc, Porsche Carrera and 911, Corvair, BRM**
Gearbox	**Hewland**
Front suspension	**independent**
Rear suspension	**independent**
Brakes	**Airheart disc**
Body material	**fiberglass**
Wheelbase	**88.5 inches**
Track	**49 inches**
Weight, approx.	**750 pounds**
Number built	**estimated 50**

BOBSY SR4

Year built	**1970**
Engine	**Lotus twin cam**
Gearbox	**Hewland**
Front suspension	**independent**
Rear suspension	**independent**
Brakes	**disc**
Body material	**fiberglass**
Number built	**one**

VANGUARD FV

Year built	**1964**
Engine	**Volkswagen 1,200-cc**
Gearbox	**Volkswagen**
Front suspension	**trailing link**
Rear suspension	**swing axle**
Brakes	**drum**
Body material	**fiberglass**
Number built	**over 100**

BOBSY VEGA FV

Year built	**1967**
Engine	**Volkswagen 1,200-cc**
Gearbox	**Volkswagen**
Front suspension	**trailing link**
Rear suspension	**swing axle**
Brakes	**drum**
Body material	**fiberglass**
Number built	**estimated 20**

after every race. Chuck was a great driver, and he was used to cars that didn't handle very well. Unbeknownst to me, the SR2 didn't handle. Chuck's a real positive guy, and he was getting a free drive, and he was happy about that. He'd been over in England driving cars for Frank Nichols at Elva, and of course all the cars at that time were beastly things to drive. We didn't know about bump steer or squat. We were all dumb as a crutch, me included. But Chuck said it was a

wonderful car, and he won races in it, but he was hugely compensating for the failures of the car. When we finally started to build customer cars, people were calling up saying, "This thing handles like a piece of shit!" Of course, Chuck was compensating. But we sold cars. Structurally they were fine, but the handling was very poor. That's when I started to race the cars myself, because we had to get the things sorted out. I raced it for five or six years.

AUTHOR: You won the ARRC Championship in the SR3. How did it feel to be both the driver and the manufacturer?

MONG: It felt great. What can I say? On top of the world.

AUTHOR: Did you enjoy the driving or the building more?

MONG: The building. The driving was just a vehicle to get the thing working. I had to really know what I was selling people. You need to race a car of your own, the manufacturer does. Not to say we didn't have some fantastic customers; we did. But then again, some of your customers were pretty inept. My God, I remember one of the first cars we sold, I won't say his name, but he was at Cumberland. He had gone down on Thursday to practice, and he calls me at home Friday night around 11. He says the car's shot, the electrical system is completely out. I got up in the middle of the night, drove all the way down there, and the battery's dead. That's the kind of thing that happens. You can get a little cynical about it. Another guy was complaining about one of our C–sports-racers at Atlanta, saying it was a real stone. He was way down the list. They had posted the top speeds down the straight, and he had the fastest speed!

AUTHOR: You built two Formula Vees, the Vanguard and the Vega. Did you like the Formula Vee class?

MONG: Not really. It was a vehicle to make money. The original Vanguard Vee was a real good piece. It was a stupidly simple car with a ladder frame. It was serviceable as hell and it handled well. It had the right amount of flexibility—the torsional rigidity was zero! But people raced them and they did pretty well. The later car, the Vega, was a lot better. We didn't sell that many of those. It's a limited modification class, like NASCAR. It didn't fit with my nature. I like the modified classes, where you could do anything you like so long as the damn thing was the right displacement. Still, we must have built 120 or

150 of the first ones, maybe 20 of the last one. It sure points out how little we knew about aerodynamics. It looked aerodynamic as the dickens, but as I learned more, I realized it was a very high-drag shape. In fact, the early Vanguards, with their thick nose, would have had a lower drag ratio.

AUTHOR: Tell me about the SR3s. That was a beautiful car.

MONG: It's a real pretty car. They had low aerodynamic drag but they had a tendency to fly. Being on a shoestring, some guy would come in with some wild engine, asking if you could build a car for it. You'd say, "Hell, yes!" Some of these things were grossly overpowered. Dr. Wylie had one with a BRM V-8 in it. Wylie bought a car from us to run the BRM engine, but it was way too much for the car, so we backed up to a BMW 2-liter. Even then, the car was extraordinarily fast. That body shape was good up to about 130–140 miles per hour, then it got extremely wishy-washy. Doc made some aerodynamic dive planes for the front and got it nailed down pretty good. At one time, he had the lap record at Elkhart Lake for a little while, maybe an hour. He was a great customer.

Bocar

The outrageous Bocars built by Bob Carnes in Colorado were the wildest customer-version racing cars built in the United States in the 1950s. This does not mean they were necessarily the best, or the most successful, but they did turn heads and generate mega-ink in the enthusiast magazines of the day.

And who wouldn't be impressed by supercharged Chevies pumping out nearly 500 horsepower, or svelte aerodynamic bodies that could be purchased in kit or assembled form? The raw statistics alone made Carnes a hero to the everyday racer, who dreamed of having a sports car he could drive on the street and win with at the track. But, as usual, it didn't exactly work out that way.

Carnes started racing a Glockler Porsche Spyder in hillclimbs and road races in the Denver area in 1953. In 1954, he switched to a Jaguar XK-120 coupe and finished third at Pikes Peak (behind two other Jags) the first year that there was a sports car class. He later inserted a Cadillac engine and named it the "Jagillac." It won the Buffalo Bill Hillclimb in 1956.

But Carnes hankered for a car of his own design, something combining the power of the Jagillac with the agility of the Porsche. Although he worked for a time as an engineer, there is no record of his attaining a degree in engineering. He had been remodeling kitchens when he embarked on the Bocar project in 1957.

Bocar X-1

Carnes dove right in, building a simple frame of oval-section 4130 chrome-moly tubing (most likely pirated from a local Air Force base). Jaguar XK-120 suspension and drum brakes were fitted up front, with a Lincoln live axle in back and a Chevy 283 for motivation. The fiberglass body was formed from a plaster mold and did not resemble any other kits on the market. A low, pointed nose featured quad headlights from a 1958 Chevy, which also donated its taillights. Headrests were optional, as was a full-height windshield and a removable hard top.

Christened the X-1, the first Bocar prototype immediately took to the road . . . and the track. It had always been Carnes' intention to sell a dual-purpose machine and he was ready to start development. He ran the new car in the 1958 Pikes Peak Hillclimb, finishing a distant fifth in the sports car class. Carnes knew then he needed something more.

He soon sold X-1 to Charles Cobb, who drag raced the car quite successfully in Texas before selling it to a Chevy dealer. Next, owner Bonner Denton of Tucson, Arizona, added a GMC blower and won the AHRA Unlimited Sports Car Championships in 1964 and 1965. Denton says the interior was paneled with aluminum sheets that had aerial maps painted on the backs (probably also from the air base). Denton later built a Bocar-bodied monster for Bonneville, which ran over 200 miles per hour.

Bocar XP-4

After a few more experiments, Carnes introduced the first Bocar production car, the XP-4, in late 1958. The bodies could be purchased independently, and many specials were built on a variety of chassis. The XP-4 was available as a turnkey or in kit form. A number of changes had been made from the X-1.

The wheelbase remained at 90 inches, but the chassis now had a reasonably well-triangulated space frame made from round-section 4130 steel. The Jag front end was replaced with VW or Porsche 356 front suspension (recalling Carnes' Glockler days). The suspension was beefed up with bolts inserted into the speedometer spindles and by adding gussets to the steering arms and C-links (later standard 356 Porsche race prep). VW or Porsche steering boxes were retained. In back, an Oldsmobile live axle was

A Bocar (foreground) takes on a Porsche at Willow Springs in 1963. *Allen Kuhn*

sprung by a VW torsion bar and tube that were welded into the chassis. Four trailing links were used, along with an A-bracket similar to those used on Lotus 7s, attached on top of the differential housing. Brakes were Chevrolet drums all around; Carnes tried using Jaguar XK-150 discs on one car but did not like them.

Bocar XP-5

Few XP-4s were made before the similar XP-5 took their place. The main change was improving the brakes with Buick Alfin drums all the way around. Most XP-4 and XP-5 turnkeys (and kits) were fitted with 283-ci Chevy V-8s with four-speed T-10 transmissions. Carnes preferred the fuel-injected Corvette motor, although others were equipped with three deuces and even a Pontiac V-8. A narrowed Corvette axle with Posi-Traction supplanted the Olds rear axle.

The engines were set back a long way in the frame and offset to the right to balance the weight of the driver. The XP-5 had 44/56 weight distribution, which helped with traction on the skinny tires of the period.

On paper, it was a hot setup. Aston Martin had already used the trailing-arm front suspension on its successful DBR-series of sports-racers (as well as the street DB-

The Bocar XP-5 was a lovely car from Colorado. The XP-5s won a lot of regional races but were not up to the Scarabs. *Harold Pace*

The Bocar XP-7 (left) was the production version of the one-off XP-6 at right. *Harold Pace collection*

2), and the Jaguar D-Type had a similar rear suspension design. But Carnes did not understand the nuances of suspension development, and the cars were never developed to their true potential. One of the first XP-5s to go racing was bought by Harry Heuer, who built his Meister Brauser racing team around it. Neither Heuer nor his main driver, Augie Pabst, was enamored with the XP-5. Their early example broke regularly, and even its brightest moment, when Pabst led the first lap in it at Nassau in 1959, ended in disappointment when the fuel filter plugged up.

The Meister Brauser team opened up the nose of its XP-5 for better cooling and made the front bodywork removable for easier maintenance. Depending on who you ask, the team either ran Hillborn-injected Chevies that were shared with their Scarabs, or a single four-barrel 283. Paul O'Shea also drove this Bocar in the famous Lime Rock Formula Libre Race that Rodger Ward won in a Kurtis Midget (O'Shea soon retired). The Meister Brauser Bocar is now in a private collection.

Floridian Art Huttinger, who finished second in the first-ever televised Daytona sports car race in 1960, raced another well-known XP-5. He continued to race the car through the year without much success

before switching to a Lister. Duane Capps built a very fast XP-5 in Colorado with a 283-ci Chevy bored-and-stroked to 350 ci.

Bocar XP-6

Although his cars were not setting the world on fire, Carnes was convinced he was on the right track when he built a supercharged fire-breather called the XP-6. Stretching the chassis by 14 inches, he made enough room to bolt a Potvin chain-driven blower drive to the front of the crank and mount a GMC 4-71 blower. A Rochester fuel injection air meter was mounted on the intake side, and a metal tube carried the pressurized air back to the Corvette "doghouse" fuelie manifold and pump. It was a weird combination, but it worked very well . . . for short periods of time. With around 400 horsepower, Carnes dumped the VW front end and replaced it with something arguably worse, a live axle with trailing arms. The body was a stretched XP-5 with an extra scoop under the grille. The XP-6 was spectacular, but it was temperamental and was not a threat outside of Colorado club-level events at Continental Divide Raceway. It was a one-off and was apparently destroyed in a later shop fire.

38

Bocar XP-7

The XP-7 was an attempt to build a car similar to the XP-6 but at a lower price. The stretched frame was cursed with the VW front end again, and only a small number were sold in 1961. There was also an XP-7R race version.

One of the few XP-7s campaigned was run by Graham Shaw, who had a dismal season, breaking steering components in his Hillborn-injected Chevy-powered car (sans blower).

Bocar Stiletto

The last gasp for Bocar was the Stiletto. Intended as Carnes' ultimate weapon for the 1960 season, the original-style body was replaced with a unique design that looked like a cross between a Lotus 11 and a Bonneville streamliner. The wheels were partially shrouded and the headlights, when fitted, were in the grille opening. The first body was fitted to a DKW-powered special.

Carnes had dispensed with the "streetable" portion of the equation and made an all-out racer. The wheelbase was chopped to 101 inches, but the front-mounted blower from the XP-6 was retained. A second air metering unit was added to the inlet side of the blower, and the engine was fitted with a Racer Brown roller cam that produced a claimed 500 horsepower. Front suspension was by live axle and brakes were Corvette cerametallic racing drums. The Stiletto was a rocket in a straight line, but the Scarabs trounced it in a mock "grudge race" at

Continental Divide Raceway (recorded on film by the Meister Brauser team).

Carnes broke his Stiletto at Pikes Peak. A second Stiletto was sold to Tom Butz for driver Graham Shaw, who did everything in his power to talk Butz out of the purchase. Their car was fitted with a Hillborn-injected small-block sans blower.

In the 1960s, Bob Spooner of Missouri found a Stiletto with a blower and raced it at Midwest Division SCCA races, but with little success. One complete and one rough Stiletto are known to exist today.

An unknown number of Bocars were built, but they sold well in kit form and some 40 complete cars are on the Bocar Club register. In 1961, a fire engulfed

---

BOCAR

Bocar Manufacturing Co.
1240 Haran Street
Denver, Colorado

BOCAR XP-4 AND XP-5

Years built	**1958–1961**
Engines	**Chevrolet or Pontiac V-8**
Gearbox	**Borg-Warner T-10 four speed**
Chassis	**space frame**
Front suspension	**usually Volkswagen or Porsche 356 trailing link; one-offs with Mercedes, Jaguar, and Aston Martin**
Rear suspension	**live axle with torsion bars**
Brakes	**Chevrolet or Buick drum; one with Jaguar disc**
Body material	**fiberglass**
Weight, approx.	**1,900 pounds**
Wheelbase	**90 inches**
Length	**156 inches**
Height	**34 inches**
Number built	**fewer than 100 (plus an unknown number of kits)**
Price when new	**$6,400**

BOCAR XP-6

Year built	**1960**
Engine	**supercharged Chevrolet V-8**
Gearbox	**Borg-Warner T-10 four-speed**
Chassis	**space frame**
Front suspension	**solid axle with torsion bars**
Rear suspension	**live axle with torsion bars**
Brakes	**Buick drum**
Body material	**fiberglass**
Weight, approx.	**2,100 pounds**

Wheelbase	**104 inches**
Height	**34 inches**
Number built	**one**

BOCAR XP-7 AND XP-7R

Years built	**1960–1961**
Engine	**Chevrolet V-8 (optional supercharger)**
Gearbox	**Borg-Warner T-10 four-speed**
Chassis	**space frame**
Front suspension	**Volkswagen trailing link**
Rear suspension	**live axle with torsion bars**
Brakes	**Buick drum**
Body material	**fiberglass**
Weight, approx.	**2,200 pounds**
Wheelbase	**102 inches**
Height	**34 inches**
Number built	**unknown but few**
Price when new	**$8,700+**

BOCAR STILETTO

Year built	**1960**
Engine	**supercharged Chevrolet V-8**
Gearbox	**Borg-Warner T-10 four-speed**
Chassis	**space frame**
Front suspension	**solid axle, torsion bars**
Rear suspension	**live axle, torsion bars**
Brakes	**Chevrolet cerametallic drum**
Body material	**fiberglass**
Weight, approx.	**2,200 pounds**
Wheelbase	**101 inches**
Number built	**two or three**
Price when new	**$13,000**

The Bocar Stiletto looked like a Buck Rogers rocket ship. With a supercharged Chevy, it ran like one. *Harold Pace collection*

Carnes' factory and no more Bocars were built (although a handful were assembled from leftover parts). Frank Petersen (see Petersen Special entry, Chapter 3) raced Bocar-bodied specials, and Wendell Burgess built one on a Henry-J chassis. At least one car was built with a Mercedes coil-spring front end and brakes, and another with Aston Martin front suspension. Carnes died in 1970.

Bourgeault

Nade Bourgeault was a California race car builder who made his own line of sports-racers and formula cars. An outstanding body man, he was capable of

BOURGEAULT

Bourgeault Racing Cars
Mill Valley, California

BOURGEAULT FORMULA JUNIOR

Year built	**1959**
Engine	**Fiat pushrod four-cylinder**
Gearbox	**Fiat**
Front suspension	**independent**
Rear suspension	**independent**
Body material	**aluminum**
Number built	**one**

BOURGEAULT FORMULA B/C

Years built	**1965–1968**
Engines	**Cosworth-Ford, Alfa Romeo**
Gearbox	**Hewland**
Front suspension	**independent**
Rear suspension	**independent**
Body material	**fiberglass**
Number built	**four**

BOURGEAULT SPORTS-RACERS

Years built	**1965–1968**
Engines	**Cosworth-Ford, Alfa Romeo, BRM, Coventry-Climax**
Gearbox	**Hewland**
Front suspension	**independent**
Rear suspension	**independent**
Body material	**fiberglass**
Number built	**three**

fabricating any part in aluminum or creating an entire body from scratch. In the late 1950s, he worked with Joe Huffaker on the BMC Formula Juniors (where he did bodywork) and also rebodied a number of cars in aluminum, including the Lowe's Frazer-Nash, the Cozzi Jaguar, and the Keck Spyder. In 1959, Bourgeault started work on a Formula Junior of his own design.

Bourgeault Formula Junior

The first Bourgeault was a midengined design with a Fiat engine and an early Porsche transaxle. It would have been a superior design to front-engined Juniors, but by the time it was completed, the Lotus 18s were out and the Bourgeault was old news. This rapid pace of development eventually caused the demise of Formula Junior, and Bourgeault switched his interest to other classes.

Bourgeault Formula Cars

Bourgeault built a small number of formula cars in the mid-1960s. At least one was a Formula C car that he drove to a third-in-class at the 1966 SCCA runoffs (ARRC) at Riverside. Another was built as a Formula B with an Alfa Romeo engine. Nick Reynolds, folk music singer with the Kingston Trio, worked with Bourgeault and helped with financing. He qualified a Bourgeault FC fourth at the 1967 ARRC but failed to finish. It appears that one F-Junior and four FC/FB cars were built.

Bourgeault Sports-Racers

Bourgeault's best-known customer cars were his midengined sports-racers, also built in the mid-1960s. They were very attractive, with graceful lines and a low shovel nose. The Bourgeaults were fitted with many engines, including Cosworth-Ford, Alfa Romeo, BRM, and Coventry-Climax units. Bourgeault even made his own magnesium wheels and engine-to-gearbox adapters, which he sold separately. The sports-racers were designed for the F- or G-Modified classes, and sold for $5,800, sans engines, in 1965.

In 1966, Allan Lader won G-Sports Racing at the SCCA runoffs in a Bourgeault, besting a field loaded with Lotus 23s and Elva Mk.7s. Another Bourgeault with a 2-liter BRM Formula 1 engine was raced in B-Sports Racing, but it was destroyed in an accident. *Motor Sport International* publisher Peter Talbert ran a Cosworth-Ford-powered Mk.IV sports-racer in 1965. That same year, Bourgeault ran a sports-racer in the USRRC series, picking up a solitary point. Only three sports-racers appear to have been built.

The Bourgeaults were lovely racing cars, but the company had already folded when Nade Bourgeault died suddenly in 1974. Four cars are known to have survived, and all will hopefully return to the tracks.

This California race grid includes the Bourgeault Formula Junior (No. 104). *Tam McPartland*

Bryant

Englishman Peter Bryant moved to America in 1964 and landed right in the middle of the racing business. In 1969, he built a conventional but practical Can-Am car called the Ti22, the chemical symbol for titanium, which was used extensively in the monocoque chassis and suspension.

Ti22 Mk. 1

A big-block Chevy provided the power for the first model, driving through a Hewland LG-600 gearbox. The chassis was a full-length monocoque design without subframes. The suspension and wheels were

Peter Bryant penned the surprisingly quick Ti22. This Mk.1 is shown at Laguna Seca in 1969. *Pete Lyons*

bought from Dan Gurney, and a fiberglass body was developed that featured raised edges to force the air to stay on the body and provide downforce. The Autocoast-sponsored car ran its first outing at Laguna Seca in 1969, where it finished 13th in its shakedown race. Autocoast was a company that developed offshore powerboats and worked on car projects.

At Mount Fuji, Japan, in a nonchampionship race, driver Jackie Oliver put the Mk.1 on the pole. The next year, Oliver was hot again, qualifying third for the season opener at Mosport and finishing an astonishing second to Gurney's McLaren after a spirited dice. But at St. Jovite, Oliver got airborne at a hump and flipped, crashing down hard on the roll bar. Miraculously, Oliver walked away from the wreckage of what once had been the Ti22 Mk.1.

This improved Bryant Ti22 Mk.2 ran at Laguna Seca in 1970. *Pete Lyons*

Ti22 Mk. 2

An improved version of the Ti22 was introduced at Laguna Seca on October 18, 1970. It had a longer wheelbase and was a little lighter than the Mk.1. The chassis was stiffer and now featured a tubular titanium subframe in back to mount the engine. The wing was replaced with a tall dam across the back of the body. Bryant had rounded up a new sponsor, Norris Industries, who provided $10,000 per race. Like the other front-runners, the Ti22 Mk.2 was powered by an all-aluminum, 495-ci Reynolds Chevy engine. In the race, Oliver ran like a wild man, finishing a close second to Denny Hulme's McLaren. Oliver repeated the feat at Riverside, once again second to Hulme. The Ti22 Mk.2 was obviously the second-best car in the series at the time and more dependable than the quirky Chaparral 2J.

Unfortunately, Bryant had a falling out with his business partners and left to join Don Nichols' Shadow team for 1971. The Ti22 Mk.2 was sold to Nick Diogurdi, who had David Hobbs drive it in the 1971 Can-Am season. The car was later burned to the ground in a club race in California.

We Talk With Peter Bryant.

AUTHOR: How did the Ti22 come to be?

BRYANT: I started in April of 1969. Skip Scott had introduced me to the Titanium Corporation of America, and I asked them to supply the titanium for the car and do some of the fabrication, and they agreed. I asked Goodyear to supply tires and they agreed. I also went to Cherry rivet and asked them to supply Monel rivets, which are very expensive, and they agreed. And I went to High-Sheer Fasteners, who makes titanium fasteners, and they agreed to supply fasteners. Almost everywhere I went,

they agreed to give me pieces and parts.

AUTHOR: But no sponsorship.

BRYANT: No, but that was worth a lot of money. I designed and built the car and got it ready for the Laguna Seca Can-Am race, and the total cost of the whole thing was around $60,000.

AUTHOR: How was the 1970 season?

BRYANT: We went to the first Can-Am race with another 100 horsepower from the engine, using our own engine program. At Mosport, we led the race for 20 laps and Oliver finished second to Dan Gurney, and he and Gurney lapped the entire field twice. The car was very competitive. In the next race at St. Jovite, Oliver qualified third on the grid, went up the hill behind Dennis Hulme, lost all the downforce on the nose, and flew the car farther than the Wright Brothers did on their first flight! The chassis was destroyed. I had already started on the design of

BRYANT

Peter Bryant
California

Ti22 MK.1
Year built	**1969**
Engine	**Chevrolet V-8**
Gearbox	**Hewland five-speed**
Chassis	**monocoque**
Front suspension	**independent, coil springs**
Rear suspension	**independent, coil springs**
Brakes	**disc**
Body material	**fiberglass**
Wheelbase	**94 inches**
Number built	**one**

Ti22 MK.2
Year built	**1969**
Engine	**Chevrolet V-8**
Gearbox	**Hewland five-speed**
Chassis	**monocoque**
Front suspension	**independent, coil springs**
Rear suspension	**independent, coil springs**
Brakes	**disc**
Body material	**fiberglass**
Wheelbase	**96 inches**
Number built	**one**

the Mk.2, and after I looked at the damage on the chassis (of the Mk.1) I decided not to bother repairing it. I thought what I had here was a second-place car. I wasn't thinking straight. What I had was a first-place car with a second-place driver.

AUTHOR: I'll bet Jackie Oliver wouldn't like to hear that.

BRYANT: No, he wouldn't, but he never beat Dennis Hulme in a fair fight. I really should have tried to hire Jackie Stewart or Parnelli Jones. Jackie always raced better than he qualified, and he did a good job, but Dennis Hulme was a world champion.

AUTHOR: How did your car compare to a McLaren M8B and a Lola T-163?

BRYANT: It was better than a T-163. Then you look at the performance of the McLaren. Bruce McLaren told me personally that it [the Ti22] was a breakthrough in aerodynamics; it was the first ground-effects car. Compared to the McLaren in 1969, the McLaren still had the rounded rocker panels and rounded fenders at the front. The Ti22 had chiseled-shape front fenders and went down to a very sharp radius at the rocker panels, so the underpan was maximum flat. The body fences, which McLaren adopted in 1971, keep the air on the body. It worked very well. It was faster through Turn 9 at Riverside than the McLarens. Then McLaren was killed, which left just Denny. We went to the last two races of 1970. At Laguna Seca, we had more downforce than the McLaren and probably the same or more horsepower. Oliver finished 0.4 [second] behind Dennis Hulme; he just couldn't get past him. They lapped the entire field twice. At the last race at Riverside, Oliver was again second to Hulme, and they again lapped the field twice!

AUTHOR: You said you had your own engine program. What were you doing differently from McLaren?

BRYANT: We had a mechanic we had hired from Chaparral named Barry Crowe. One thing about the Can-Am was that it was unlimited cubic inch. We found a way to bring the engine

out to 497 cubic inches by using the crankshaft from the Keikhaefer Mercury Marine 497-inch engine in our car. We also changed the valve openings from what they were on most Can-Am cars. This required some changes to the cylinder head. The Keikhaefer crank was a billet crank that was nitrided, and it was very reliable.

AUTHOR: Tell me about your aerodynamic testing.

BRYANT: We were the first car to put a splitter on the front. Also, the height the car was run at would determine the drag. The lower it was to the ground, the more suction you got. At Riverside, we had to lift the car up slightly to get more speed down the straightaway. We were doing this before the computer. I bought a calculator from Sharp and it was $460! You open a bank account today and they'll give you one for nothing.

Chaparral

Texan oilman Jim Hall casts the tallest shadow in the history of racing technology. His Chaparral racing cars not only pioneered molded-composite chassis construction, but Hall literally wrote the book on aerodynamic downforce. He spent the early 1960s racing a variety of cars, including Lotus formula and

sports-racing cars, the first Lister-Corvette, and a potent variety of Maseratis. At one point, he alternated between his 2.9-liter T-61 Birdcage and a rocket-ship 5.7-liter 450S. Hall partnered with Carroll Shelby in a Maserati dealership in Dallas before moving to Midland, Texas, home of the booming Texas oil industry.

In 1961, he teamed with fellow oilman James "Hap" Sharp and several other Midland racers to build Rattlesnake Raceway, a 1.96-mile track with room for shops and testing facilities. About this time, he and Sharp became discouraged with buying front-line equipment from Europe. It seemed they were always getting handed down last year's model, and the parts were either outrageously expensive or impossible to get at any price. They decided the solution was to build their own cars.

Chaparral 1

As an intermediate step toward building a radical car of his own design, Hall contracted with famed West Coast race car builders Dick Troutman and Tom Barnes to build a conventional car with Hall's input. The resulting racer was a development of the Scarab sports-racers that Troutman and Barnes had worked on in the 1950s. Hall wanted to use a mid-mounted Chevy V-8, but the lack of a transaxle that would take the power caused them

Jim Hall casts a wary smile at starlet Lori Campbell at Laguna Seca in 1963. *Allen Kuhn*

to go with a front-engined design. At 1,479 pounds, the new car, named the Chaparral 1, was more than 300 pounds lighter than the previously all-conquering Scarab and had suitably upgraded suspension and brakes. Gone was the old de Dion tube, replaced with a sophisticated independent rear suspension system. Brakes were Girling AR discs, with special 6- to 8-inch-wide Halibrand wheels. The space frame was made up of 1.25-inch-diameter steel chrome-moly tubes, and the first car had an 88-inch wheelbase.

The body was built for function, not beauty, and was designed by Chuck Pelly, who had penned the lovely Scarabs. The bodies were in a continual state of development and soon sprouted various hood scoops, nose diffusers, and vents.

Up front, a 283-ci Chevy was stroked and bored out to 318 ci at Traco Engineering. However, while most racers were clamoring for more power, Hall decided to go for durability with only around 300 horsepower. Carburetion was by three Stromberg carburetors on an Edelbrock manifold, but this was soon uprated to six Strombergs. A Halibrand quick-change center section was used, usually with a spool differential but occasionally with a limited-slip unit. An aluminum-case Borg-Warner T-10 Corvette transmission completed the driveline.

Skip Hudson in a Chaparral 1 holds off Chuck Parsons in a Lotus 23B at Laguna Seca in 1963. *Allen Kuhn*

Troutman and Barnes also built four more Chaparrals. After the first car, the wheelbase was extended to 90 inches for more cockpit room. Chassis number 002 was sold to Harry Heuer, who had been running the old Scarabs under the Meister Brauser banner. His car was fitted with a much hotter engine, sporting Hillborn fuel injection. The third car built (003) was a factory team car shared with Hap Sharp. The fourth car (004) was sold to Chuck Jones for his Team Meridian, to be driven by Skip Hudson. Chassis number 005 was shipped to England for hillclimb specialist Phil Scragg.

The 1961 season had a promising start, but Hall knew he was taking on some tough competition with the new Lotus 19s driven by aces like Stirling Moss, Dan Gurney, and Jack Brabham. At the Chaparral's first race at Laguna Seca in June 1961, Hall finished second to a Maserati Birdcage, after experiencing a rocker arm failure. At the Los Angeles Times Grand Prix at Riverside, Hall and Heuer qualified well, but in the race Hall only managed a distant third. Bad luck dogged the Chaparrals the rest of the year.

The next season opened with Hall taking a fine third at the Daytona three-hour Continental, then attacking Sebring with 4-liter Chevy engines to match the FIA class regulations. The bodies were heavily modified, with raised windscreens, upholstered interiors, and extra lighting. One car, driven by Hall, Sharp, and Ronnie Hissom, finished sixth overall and first in class. At the Road America June Sprints, Hall and Heuer took a spectacular one-two finish, and in the Road America 500, Hall again clinched a victory. Although obviously outclassed by Roger Penske's new Zerex Special, Hall finished a close second at the Los Angeles Times Grand Prix at Riverside. The rest of 1962 yielded no victories.

In 1963, the Chaparrals were hanging on for dear life while Hall readied the new Chaparral 2. At Sebring, the old warriors sported tail fins and a raised rear body section to comply with new FIA regs, but both factory cars retired and were immediately sold.

The Meister Brauser racing team replaced its Scarabs with this Chaparral I. Harry Heuer won many club-level races with the car, but the day of the front-engined racer was ending. *Harold Pace*

Jim Hall raced this Chaparral 2 at Laguna Seca in 1963. *Allen Kuhn*

The Chaparral 2, driven by Jim Hall, leads A. J. Foyt in a Scarab at Laguna Seca in 1963. *Allen Kuhn*

Heuer won the June Sprints in his Chaparral, as well as an SCCA National at Meadowdale. Afterward, the Chaparral 1s slipped into obscurity. The Scragg car never amounted to much and was converted at one time into a single-seater. Today all five cars survive in some form.

The Chaparral 1 was not the runaway success the Scarab had been—by 1961 the day of the front-engined racer was over, and the Chaparral 1 was seldom a match for a good 2.5-liter Cooper Monaco or Lotus 19. However, the Chaparral 1 had fulfilled its job. It had provided Hall with an opportunity to race and develop a car while designing the dream racer he really wanted, something radically different from anything else on the track.

Chaparral 2A

Hall had been working on a new design almost from the time he started racing the first Chaparral. The Chaparral 2A was to be his baby, built at his shop at Rattlesnake Raceway. Hap Sharp became his partner on the project, so two cars were planned from the start. They settled on a monocoque structure made from fiberglass, much like the front-engined Lotus Elite. But it would be midengined like the monocoque Lotus 25 Formula 1 car. While these principals were not unique, this was the first time they had been used on a sports-racing car.

Hall collaborated with Andy Green, a composite structures engineer working in the aerospace industry. With Hall's funding, Green started his own company to develop the technology to mold the Chaparral chassis. Unlike the semimonocoque Jaguar XKE and Ford GT, the Chaparral had no

subframes to carry the suspension loads—everything was hung off the steel-reinforced fiberglass tub.

Hall spent part of 1963 running Formula 1 with BRP, but when he got back to Texas, he threw himself into the Chaparral project again. The chassis was exceptionally rigid and used suspension parts and wheels derived from proven Lotus designs. Girling AR disc brakes were used all around, with Hall's car sporting a Weber-carbureted 327-ci Chevy engine and a Colotti-Francis Type 37A Indy car transaxle. Sharp opted for an aluminum-block Buick V-8 and a Corvair or Cooper gearbox. The finished cars weighed only 1,650 pounds.

The first time out for Hall's car was at Riverside in 1963 for the Los Angeles Times Grand Prix. Hall put it on the pole and led the race until an electrical fire prompted his retirement. The rest of the season the Chaparral team chased various mechanical gremlins. During this time, Hall worked out a joint development program with General Motors that allowed him access to their aerodynamic research. This was to pay big dividends for both parties, as Chevrolet engineers became frequent guests at Rattlesnake Raceway to test their research and development projects. And the GM guys helped Chaparral develop effective chin and tail spoilers to increase downforce.

The first victory for the Chaparral 2 was in the 1964 Pensacola USRRC race, where Hall outran Roger Penske's Zerex Special. Sharp's car was converted to Chevy power with a Colotti gearbox, but for the USRRC race at Laguna Seca, Hall's car was fitted with an aluminum-block Chevy and an experimental single-speed automatic transmission

developed at GM. Penske brokered a deal to get the aluminum-block engines in exchange for rides in the Chaparral, which had proven faster than his Zerex. Hall and King Cobra driver Dave MacDonald were close in points all season until MacDonald was killed at Indianapolis. Hall, Penske, and Sharp took turns driving the automatic car, and Hall won the USRRC Championship in convincing fashion. After the USRRC season was over, Hall flipped his car at Mosport and broke his arm. Penske took over his seat and won the Governor's Trophy and the Nassau Trophy in the Bahamas, and promptly retired from racing.

Chaparral did well in 1965, expanding its theater of operations to include endurance racing and the shorter USRRC events. They did routine development work on the Chaparral 2s, including coming up with the famous spoked wheels that were later copied by several wheel manufacturers. The season started at Sebring, where the Chaparral 2 took a surprise win in the rain-soaked 12-hour enduro over the favored Ford GTs. Despite winning five races, Hall lost the 1965 USRRC Championship to George Follmer, who dominated the under-2-liter class in his Lotus-Porsche. (The overall champion was determined by class, not overall, wins.)

Chaparral 2C

Hall unveiled an all-new car at the 1965 Kent USRRC race. The 2C looked a lot like the earlier 2A, but shared almost nothing under the skin. The fiberglass chassis was replaced with an aluminum monocoque derived from a Chevrolet research vehicle, the GSIIb (since the GM research vehicle had

Jim Hall sits on the grid at Riverside for the Times Grand Prix of 1965. The car is a Chaparral 2C. *Allen Kuhn*

Hap Sharp bends the Chaparral 2C around Riverside at the 1965 Times Grand Prix. *Allen Kuhn*

Endurance racing was the forte of the Chaparral 2D coupe, shown here at Sebring in 1967. *Pete Lyons*

a "b" in its name, there would be no Chaparral 2B). The use of aluminum chopped 100 pounds off the 2A's 1,475 pounds. The 2C was 6 inches narrower than its predecessor on a 1-inch-shorter wheelbase. The 2C also pioneered the use of the "flipper" rear spoiler that could be adjusted by the driver to change the downforce. The 2C was faster than the 2A but more difficult to drive and less comfortable due to the metal transferring more heat from the engine than fiberglass had done. Hall won the 1965 Kent USRRC race on its maiden voyage. It was to be Hall's last victory as a driver.

Chaparral 2D

The Sebring win in 1965 had whetted Hap Sharp's appetite for endurance racing. Hall was not big on enduros, but Sharp was a big part of the team and the fiberglass chassis they used on the 2As were ideal for that application. Although heavier than aluminum, they were just as strong and more durable. Hall decided not to drive, so former World Champion Phil Hill and Grand Prix driver Jo Bonnier were hired to handle the driving. The first 2D built was an updated 2A with a coupe top. It was a lovely car, powered by a slightly de-tuned 420-horsepower, 327-ci, all-aluminum Chevy. At Daytona in 1967, the new car qualified second but dropped out when an upright failed. At Sebring, a second 2D (also a converted 2A) was added to the team, but internal engine problems resulted in both cars retiring early with major engine leaks. The 2A's movable rear spoiler was fixed in position on the 2D.

Everything came right at the Nurburgring in Germany, where Hill and Bonnier routed the Ferraris and Porsches to take a surprise win in their European debut. By this time, the headlights had been relocated higher in the nose and an air box and scoop were atop the roof. Unfortunately, at Le Mans they were not so lucky, and the plucky 2D dropped out with an alternator failure.

Chaparral 2E

Although a new 2E model was announced for the Can-Am series in 1966, it was actually the radically updated 2C from the previous year. A second 2E was built with a new chassis. What got everyone's attention was the enormous driver-adjustable wing mounted on pedestals atop the car. It was a radical development, the first use of a large movable wing on a big-bore road racing car. But on the Chaparrals, they really worked as designed, loading downforce directly into the wheel hubs. The radiators and oil system were moved from their traditional places in

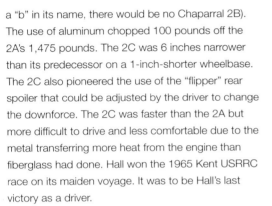

The Chaparral 2E flies around Bridgehampton in 1966. *Pete Lyons*

the nose to amidships, which allowed the nose scoops and outlet to be used solely as an aerodynamic aid for trimming the car out at high speed. The 327-ci aluminum Chevy and automatic transmission were carried over from 1965.

The Can-Am series was replacing the USRRC as the premier venue for professional sports car racing in America. Hall and Phil Hill ran the works 2Es and broke many a lap record, but the competition was intense. Hill won the Monterey Grand Prix at Laguna Seca, but elsewhere luck seemed to elude the team and Lola-mounted John Surtees won the championship. After the season, Hap Sharp wrote off one of the cars at Nassau.

Chaparral 2F

Even though it looked like a coupe version of the 2E, the 1966 2F endurance racing coupe was actually a rebody job on a 2A fiberglass chassis. It had a high wing like a 2E but used knock-off wheels for faster pit stops. Like the 2E, it used

The 2F was Chaparral's weapon for the 1967 endurance racing season. *Pete Lyons*

By 1968, the Chaparral 2G had a big-block Chevy engine. *Pete Lyons*

16-inch-diameter wheels. Under the rear deck was big news—an all-aluminum 427-ci big-block Chevy. This was basically a NASCAR engine, but cast in aluminum by Chevy for its "special friends." The engines were prepared by Chaparral engine builder Franz Weiss and produced over 500 horses, fed by four 58-millimeter Weber copies made by Chevrolet. A two-car assault was planned, teaming Hill and Mike Spence in the 2F and Bob Johnson and Bruce Jennings in the old 2D. At Daytona, both cars retired, and at Sebring, they gave the all-conquering Fords a run for their money until gremlins forced both Chaparrals out. At this point, the automatic transmission was grenading under the power of the big engines. After a string of failures, the 2F came good at the BOAC 500 at Brands Hatch in July, where Spence and Hill outran a pack of Ferraris and Lolas

The Chaparral 2H, shown at the 1969 Edmonton Can-Am, was not a success. *Pete Lyons*

to take the win. It was an upbeat end of the road for the Chaparral endurance racing cars.

Chaparral 2G

The surviving 2E was upgraded into the 2G for the 1967 Can-Am series. This entailed widening the chassis to work with wider wheels and fitting the 427-ci engine. The older chassis was not quite up to the torque of the new fuel-injected 585-horsepower monster motor. It was a depressing season, as Hall in the lone Chaparral just lacked the speed and durability of the McLarens and picked up no wins all year. At the Stardust Grand Prix at Las Vegas, disaster struck, as Hall rammed Lothar Motschenbacher's McLaren and went airborne. He flipped over in midair and landed upside down on the track. Hall was trapped inside, and once the car was rolled back over it caught fire and Hall added burn injuries to his already badly mangled legs. Although Hall survived, it was the end of his racing career.

Chaparral 2H

The 2H was an attempt at building a low-drag coupe for the 1969 Can-Am series. It looked like a big doorstop and had windows the driver could look out of on the sides. The tall strut-mounted wings that had been so much a part of Chaparral history had been banned by the FIA, so a new direction was called for. Hall hired former Formula 1 and Can-Am

champ John Surtees to take over driving chores, but the two did not get along, and the 2H was a failure. Surtees claimed he could not see out of the car, so the driving position was raised "through the roof," which fouled up the aerodynamics. The chassis returned to fiberglass construction. The suspension was new as well, with a de Dion arrangement replacing the independent system used previously. In back, a 430-ci Chevy ZL-1 was fed by a crossover fuel injection system that lowered the rear deckline.

Chaparral 2J

After the failure of the 2H, Hall rallied his forces to build the famed 2J "Sucker Car" for the 1970 Can-Am season. It used a snowmobile engine to spin fans that literally sucked the air out from under the car to radically increase traction. As usual, it was blindingly fast but fell afoul of the rule writers. Vic Elford invariably had the fastest car on the track during the season but was let down by reliability problems, usually related to the snowmobile engine. At the end of the season, the FIA banned the 2J for having "movable aerodynamic devices" (the fans). Hall pulled up stakes and shut down the racing effort. He later took up Indy car racing with a vengeance, winning the Indy 500 in 1981 with driver Johnny Rutherford.

The final Chaparral sports car was the 2J Sucker Car. Vic Elford gave it some fine rides in 1970. *Pete Lyons*

The SR-2 was a custom Corvette that looked the part of an all-out racer, but under the skin it was mostly Corvette. *Harold Pace*

Power came from a 283-ci Chevy with aluminum heads and modified Rochester fuel injection that produced 307 horsepower. A four-speed Corvette transmission was used.

Only two chassis were built, one with the lovely magnesium body and one with a crude fiberglass shell used for testing and development. Nicknamed "the mule," it would later become famous in its own right.

The SS showed up at Sebring half-ready and untested, to be driven by experienced pros John Fitch and Piero Taruffi. In practice, "the mule" and the SS both ran very well, and the two top drivers in the world, Juan Manuel Fangio and Stirling Moss, took turns around the track and pronounced the SS to be impressive indeed. However, in the race, the limited testing resulted in the SS falling out after only 23 laps with suspension, brake, and engine woes. With the lessons they learned, the SS team looked forward to running at Le Mans with a developed car, but Chevy management endorsed the 1957 AMA ban and the SS was history. Fortunately, it and "the mule" were both saved, the SS to become a museum piece and "the mule" reborn as the Sting Ray.

Corvette SR-2

Unlike the highly publicized SS, a handful of SR-2s were quietly built and raced with almost no

fanfare. The first SR-2 (Sebring Racer 2) was a lightly customized Corvette built for Harley Earl's son, Jerry, to race. He had bought a Ferrari, but his father thought it too fast and unsafe, so one of the factory Sebring production-class Corvettes was uprated with a fin in back, an extended nose, and air scoops in the side coves. It had a Corvette racing engine with 310 horsepower and the same Chrysler drum brakes run on the SS. The first time out, Dr. Dick Thompson drove it in the 1956 Road America June Sprints. Thompson found it to be heavy and unsophisticated. A second car was built with a headrest and large fin on the driver side. In top-speed runs at Daytona Beach, it hit 152.866 miles per hour and finished 16th at Sebring in 1957, driven by Pete Lovely and

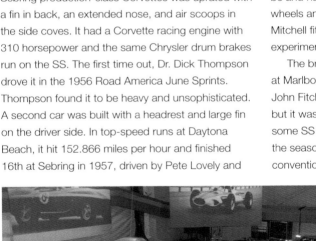

Paul O'Shea. The car was passed on to Bill Mitchell, who followed Earl as head of the GM styling department in 1958. Mitchell had the car raced on an amateur level, and Eb Rose raced it in the Southwest in SCCA events. The SR-2s were not all-out racers, too crude and heavy to take on serious sports-racers from Europe. A visually similar version with a low, center-mounted fin was built for GM President Harlow Curtice.

Corvette Sting Ray Racer

In 1959, Bill Mitchell dusted off the old SS mule and replaced the crude fiberglass body with a radical new design. Larry Shinoda, who later found fame for styling the production Sting Ray and the Mustang Boss 302, penned a razor-edged racer that foreshadowed the upcoming street car. Named the Sting Ray, it was passed off to management as a way to test public reaction to the upcoming body shape. It was much lower than the Sting Ray street car would be and had a headrest behind the driver. Halibrand wheels and side pipes added to the racer look. Mitchell fitted a 280-horsepower 283-ci, although experimental engines were later used as well.

The bright red car was driven by Dick Thompson at Marlboro Raceway in April 1959 to finish fourth. John Fitch also raced the Sting Ray at Elkhart Lake, but it was heavy at 2,154 pounds, and the troublesome SS brakes had not improved with age. Later in the season, the brake system was upgraded with a conventional power brake setup, better but still not

GM styling chief Bill Mitchell entered the Sting Ray racer for driver Dick Thompson. It was painted red at first, but later was silver. General Motors still owns this car. *Harold Pace*

51

The Corvette Grand Sport coupe was built to take on the Cobras while still looking like a production Corvette. It shared very little with the street Sting Ray. *Harold Pace*

up to the disc brakes fitted to the Listers and D-Jaguars that the Sting Ray ran against. The Sting Ray also got a new, lighter body at the end of the 1959 season.

For 1960, the Sting Ray was repainted silver and weight was reduced to 2,000 pounds. It was much quicker and better developed now, capable of keeping up with the Scarabs, Maseratis, and Porsches that dominated amateur modified racing. Although the Sting Ray wasn't the fastest car on the track, it was consistent, and Thompson won the 1960 SCCA C-Modified Championship. In 1961, the Sting Ray was cleaned up and made into a show car. Today, it is a centerpiece of Chevrolet's collection of historic Corvettes.

Corvette Grand Sport

When the street Sting Ray was introduced in 1963, it should have been big news on racetracks as well as in the showrooms. With independent rear suspension and a Z-06 racing option package, the Sting Ray was looking good. However, Carroll Shelby picked that same time to spring his Cobra pocket-rocket on the racing world. The Cobra weighed close to 600 pounds less than a Corvette and had an excellent 289-ci Ford engine with nearly as much power as the Corvette. The Cobra also had disc brakes, which the Corvette did not receive until 1965. Arkus-Duntov knew the standard Corvette could not be incrementally improved enough to beat the Cobras, so he recommended that Chevy build a special lightweight Corvette designed specifically for racing.

Arkus-Duntov found support from Chevy boss Bunkie Knudson, who could conceal the program from the GM antiracing watchdogs. The idea was to build 125 examples to qualify the Corvette Grand Sport for international GT racing, where they would have the potential to take on not only the GT-class Cobras, but hopefully also the dominant Ferrari prototypes, for overall honors.

Arkus-Duntov threw away the stock frame and replaced it with a lightweight ladder frame made from round tubes. The suspension was basically Sting Ray but beefed up and lightened wherever possible. Big Girling disc brakes were fitted all around, and a lightweight hand-laid fiberglass copy of a Corvette coupe body was added. The completed car weighed in at 1,900 pounds, about 100 pounds less than a 289 Cobra.

For power, Arkus-Duntov planned an all-aluminum small-block Chevy brought out to 377 ci, with twin-plug "hemi" heads and an experimental Rochester constant-flow fuel injection system. It produced 550 horsepower at 6,400 rpm on the test stand. But just as Cobras were starting to look like an endangered species, the myopic minions in GM upper management saved them.

In 1963, the decree came down from upstairs that the Grand Sport project was to stop immediately. The trick twin-plug engine was never installed in a Grand Sport. Five (maybe six) chassis had been made, all fitted with coupe bodywork.

Luckily, the Grand Sports were not scrapped. Two were turned over to Corvette racer Dick Doane and Gulf racing team owner Grady Davis. These were fitted with standard 360-horsepower Corvette 327 engines and raced in the tough Modified class against all-out racing cars. It was an impossible task—the Grand Sport was superior to a Cobra but dead meat for a Lotus 19 or the Zerex Special. The Doane car was seldom run, and the Davis car struggled all year to finish in the top five. One of the few Grand Sport victories was at an SCCA race at Watkins Glen, where Dick Thompson won against a lackluster field.

The Grand Sports got a new lease on life, courtesy of the season-ending Nassau Speed Week in December 1963. Shelby's Cobras had been creaming the best of the Corvettes all year long, including insults like posting a mock grave in the pits saying "Here lies the Sting Ray." Chevy honchos were steamed and looking for a way to show off what they *could* have done had upper GM management let them. Although the Grand Sports normally had no chance in the Modified classes, the Nassau organizers made their own rules and would do anything for a good race. They were persuaded to allow the Grand Sports to run against the Cobras in the GT class. Revenge was at hand.

Three Grand Sports were prepared for the race. Wider wheels were fitted, along with crude flares to cover them. Brake scoops were perched atop the

Chevrolet cut the roofs off of two Grand Sports to reduce drag for top speed at Daytona. This is the first Grand Sport built, chassis 001. *Harold Pace*

rear fenders and an oil-cooler scoop was mounted on the rear deck. Under the hood, a 485-horse-power, all-aluminum, 377-ci small-block was fed by four 58-millimeter Webers. They were entered by Texan John Mecom's team, which also featured several Chevy-powered sports-racers. This allowed Chevy to officially keep its distance, while still enjoying the exposure.

The Shelby people showed up with a full complement of Cobras, spoiling for a fight. They had no idea an ambush was waiting, and when they saw the Grand Sports they were dumbfounded. The Mecom team swept the boards, with the Grand Sports handily outgunning the Cobras all weekend.

The Grand Sports were revised at Chevrolet for the 1964 season, where they were intended to run as prototypes at Daytona and Sebring. While not competitive with true prototypes, they were expected to outrun the GT-class Cobras, which would have some good promotional value. A new vented hood was made up to fit a cross-ram manifold, and a pneumatic jacking system was installed to speed up pit stops. Two of the five coupes were converted into roadsters to provide more top speed at Daytona. However, the killjoys upstairs stepped in again and stopped the project dead in its tracks. Never before in the history of racing had a company worked so hard to fail.

The Grand Sports were sold to privateers in 1965 (with iron-block engines) and raced the rest of the season. At Sebring, Jim Hall's white coupe was shared with Roger Penske and the two of them diced with a Cobra Daytona coupe until a half shaft broke, dropping them to 18th at the flag. Delmo Johnson and Dave Morgan shared another Grand Sport, but had problems and finished 32nd. John Cannon and A. J. Foyt limped to a 23rd-place finish in a John Mecom entry.

Shelby returned to Nassau loaded for bear, with a lightweight Cobra powered by an all-aluminum 390-ci engine and driven by Ken Miles. Shelby also brought along a complement of Ford GTs to run in the prototype class. But it was for naught, as Penske drove his recently purchased Grand Sport to a win in

the Tourist Trophy, then went on to win the other two major races of the weekend in a Chaparral. Not a good time for the Ford group.

This was the last gasp for the Grand Sports, which slowly slid to the back of the grids. For 1966, the two roadsters began racing with the Penske team and George Wintersteen, and several were

converted to run big-block Chevy engines. But it was too late, and the Grand Sport was not up to handling that much power. Although five cars survive, there is a rumor that Chevrolet destroyed a sixth car at the completion of the program. The Corvette Grand Sport is a might-have-been story and would have had a happy ending, if only GM had let it.

CHEVROLET

Chevrolet Division
General Motors
Detroit, Michigan

CORVETTE SR-1

Year built	**1956**
Engines	**Chevrolet V-8 (283 or 307 ci)**
Gearboxes	**Borg-Warner three-speed or ZF four-speed**
Chassis	**ladder**
Front suspension	**independent**
Rear suspension	**live axle**
Brakes	**Chevrolet drum**
Body material	**fiberglass**
Weight, approx.	**2,700 pounds**
Wheelbase	**102 inches**
Number built	**four**

CORVETTE SS

Year built	**1956**
Engine	**Chevrolet V-8 (283 ci)**
Gearbox	**Borg-Warner T-10 four-speed**
Chassis	**space frame**
Front suspension	**independent with tubular A-arms and coil springs**
Rear suspension	**de Dion**
Brakes	**Chrysler drum**
Body material	**magnesium**
Weight, approx.	**1,848 pounds**
Wheelbase	**92 inches**
Number built	**two**

CORVETTE SR-2

Year built	**1956**
Engine	**Chevrolet V-8 (283 ci)**
Gearbox	**Borg-Warner T-10 four-speed**
Chassis	**ladder**
Front suspension	**independent**
Rear suspension	**live axle**
Brakes	**Chrysler drum**
Body material	**fiberglass**
Weight, approx.	**2,800 pounds**
Wheelbase	**102 inches**
Number built	**three**

CORVETTE STING RAY RACER

Year built	**1959**
Engine	**Chevrolet V-8 (283 ci)**
Gearbox	**Borg-Warner T-10 four-speed**
Chassis	**space frame**
Front suspension	**independent**
Rear suspension	**de Dion**
Brakes	**Chrysler drum**
Body material	**fiberglass**
Weight, approx.	**2,000 pounds**
Wheelbase	**92 inches**
Number built	**one**

CORVETTE GRAND SPORT

Year built	**1963**
Engine	**Chevrolet V-8 (377 ci)**
Gearbox	**Borg-Warner T-10 four-speed**
Chassis	**ladder**
Front suspension	**independent**
Rear suspension	**independent**
Brakes	**Girling disc**
Body material	**fiberglass**
Weight, approx.	**2,000 pounds**
Wheelbase	**98 inches**
Number built	**five or six**

Crusader

After spending World War II ousting the Japanese from various island outposts, ex-Marine Charles "Chuck" Tatum found civilian life pretty boring. But he soon discovered the joys of roadster racing, a gritty form of dirt track competition popular after the war. First as a builder and later as a stock car driver, Tatum learned his race craft. Safety was not a big concern—Tatum recalls wearing a football helmet with tape over the holes (to keep the air from whistling) and a seatbelt made out of two lengths of war surplus fabric door straps held together by a length of chain.

Later, Tatum turned to sports car racing and built the highly successful Tatum-GMC (see Tatum–GMC entry, Chapter 3). But when he took a high-paying job as sales manager for an auto dealership, one condition for employment was that he stop racing. So Tatum sold the special for $750 to finance a color television set.

Tatum Formula Junior

By 1960, Tatum had changed jobs again and no longer had to abstain from track time. He jumped on the Formula Junior bandwagon and launched into building his first formula car. He based it on a Volkswagen front axle assembly with a Goliath Tiger engine and transmission assembly in back. The Goliath was a front-driver, so the entire power unit was relocated to a midengine location. He made a body from aluminum and then cast fiberglass molds to make replacements if needed (a fortunate decision). But by 1961, when the car was completed, Formula Junior had mutated into the car-of-the-month club, and the Tatum was painfully obsolete, compared to a Lotus 18.

Crusader Formula Vees

In 1963, Tatum and his friend Jerry Demele (who raced a Lotus 7) were at a race at Grant Stadium when they saw their first Formula Vee. Colorado Formcar dealer Wendell Burgess brought the car to the event in the hopes of drumming up interest to

The Crusader VSR was an attempt to marry Formula Vee technology with a modern sports-racer chassis. *Harold Pace*

make Formula Vee an official SCCA class. After looking it over, Tatum and Demele figured they could build one themselves, and it sure looked like fun. Tatum measured the body on his F-Jr. and found, to his surprise, that it met the detailed measurements required by the first set of FV rules. Since the F-Jr. also used a VW front axle, he used the F-Jr. chassis jig and body molds to make a new car with the same chassis layout modified for the 36-horsepower VW running gear. A sturdy ladder frame was chosen for its simplicity and easy of fabrication. The first car was completed in late 1963. As there was no SCCA class yet, Tatum and Demele autocrossed the new car and stirred up interest for FV in California.

They received a warm reception, and four more Crusaders were soon built and sold. Then the California region of the SCCA threw them a curve. A powerful force of club officials was making good money selling sports cars to beginning racers, and they (correctly) saw the FV class as a potential drain on their buyer pool. So even when the SCCA national office approved FV for 1964, the California group made a new requirement—Vees would only be allowed to run in a race by themselves, and then only if they could come up with 12 cars. At the time, there were only 11 FVs in all of California. Tatum, Demele,

and an army of volunteers returned to the garage, dusted off the old Formula Junior and converted it to an FV in a matter of weeks, in time for the first race of the year. They got their race, and the rest is history.

Crusader FVs looked similar in profile to the early FVs from Formcar, Sardini, and others, but the suspension was a little different. Tatum did not believe Z-bars to be effective and did not use them on the Crusaders. Limit chains kept the swing axles from falling too far if the car got up in the air, and camber compensators were used. Tatum had soft springs made up for the back that were just strong enough to keep the car off the ground, and he used a 1-inch sway bar in front.

The Crusaders did very well, with Demele driving the ex-Junior to many wins. Tatum also drove, but usually finished behind his quick friend. The kits sold for $995, or a set of plans could be purchased that showed buyers how to build their own. Tatum recalls he built 60-something of this first series car, which helped pay for his racing habit.

In 1970, Tatum debuted a new FV with a narrower body in a wedge shape. These cars, nicknamed "Wedge" Vees, were also very quick, but only about ten were built. They also used camber compensators rather than Z-bars.

Crusader VSR

In 1968, Crusader built a short run of VW-powered sports-racers called VSRs. Tatum was a friend of Joe Vittone, who was operating the EMPI VW parts company in California. They came up with the idea of a new type of racing car that would be sold in kit form and generate parts business for EMPI as well. In order to keep setup costs down, the basic FV chassis was used, but with the driver and passenger areas bumped out on each side. The first one had a VW engine with oversize Mahle cylinders and pistons to bring displacement up to 1,788 cc. It weighed 1,100 pounds and was fitted with Porsche disc brakes and transaxle. Tatum talked to the SCCA about a prospective new class for these cars, but was rebuffed (other FV manufacturers built similar cars but the SCCA did not want to add more one-marque classes). EMPI sold VSRs in its catalog, and Tatum recalls building ten cars. Tatum later worked for Vittone as EMPI general manager.

Tatum dropped out of racing but returned when his son started racing. Once again, Crusaders are worthy competitors, and Tatum has overseen the restoration of many of his old racers.

We Talk With Chuck Tatum.

AUTHOR: Tell me about your Formula Junior.

TATUM: I heard about this new thing in Italy called Formula Junior. And my inventive mind went to work, and I thought, "I can build a Formula Junior as good as anybody." I was never lacking for confidence. To be innovative, I used a Goliath engine, a water-cooled four-cylinder that was front-wheel drive. If you put it in the rear, it was rear-wheel drive. But it took me too long to build it. I was the only guy to build an instant antique. The Goliath engine was also not up to overcoming the extra 100 pounds of weight I had in the car.

AUTHOR: So how did the Formula Vee come about?

TATUM: I went to a race at Giant Stadium. A guy named Burgess was there with a kit and a car and he let me and my buddy drive the car. Afterward, we looked at the rules, and Jerry Demele and I decided we would build a car. We got some tubing and cranked up a Formula Vee. We shortened the body by 9 1/2 inches and it worked. It was so cute, everybody loved it.

AUTHOR: Where did the name come from?

TATUM: We were filling out the race entry forms, and they wanted to know what the cars were called. I said they were Formula Vees, but they said no, they need some kind of a name. So we had six or seven guys hanging around my garage and we went through all the Indian tribes in the nation and all the reptiles known to man. Finally, one of the guys said, "You know, just getting to run these damn cars has been a real crusade." And we said, that was it, it was a Crusader. There was also a Crusader Rabbit comic strip back then and it got called the Crusader Rabbit.

AUTHOR: How did the VSR come about?

TATUM: Our idea was that if you could make a two-seater sports car that would be fun, you could sell a lot of accessories for it. We talked to the SCCA about it, but they weren't interested in adding more classes. We didn't realize anyone else was interested, although others, like Beach, built similar cars. We just ran it anyway, and most people were surprised how well the VW did against the other cars.

AUTHOR: How many did you build?

TATUM: We built ten—six the first time and four the second incarnation. I consider the car to be very successful.

CRV/Piranha

The CRV stated life as a feasibility study by Centaur Engineering, which was bought by Borg–Warner in 1965. Borg–Warner turned the project over to its Marbon Chemical division, which used the project to promote a new plastic called Cycolac (more commonly used in telephone housings). CRV stood for Cycolac Research Vehicle. The car was originally intended to take a Hillman Imp engine, but by the time the first prototypes were built, the CRVs were based on Corvair running gear. Marbon intended to get publicity by racing the CRV as well, and CRV-II, the second prototype, was built up as a sports-racer with a 170-horsepower Corvair flat-six engine and four carburetors.

CRUSADER

Crusader Cars
California

CRUSADER FORMULA VEES

Years built	1964–1969
Engine	Volkswagen
Gearbox	Volkswagen four-speed
Front suspension	trailing link
Rear suspension	swing axle
Brakes	drum (Volkswagen)
Body material	fiberglass
Number built	60-plus

CRUSADER FORMULA VEE WEDGE

Year built	1970
Engine	Volkswagen
Gearbox	Volkswagen four-speed
Front suspension	trailing link
Rear suspension	swing axle
Brakes	drum (Volkswagen)
Body material	fiberglass
Number built	ten

CRUSADER VSR

Year built	1968
Engine	Volkswagen
Gearbox	Porsche four-speed
Front suspension	trailing link
Rear suspension	swing axle
Brakes	disc (Porsche)
Body material	fiberglass
Number built	ten

Dick Carbajal's Piranha had a short but successful career in SCCA races. *Nick Whitlow collection*

The CRV used a Cycolac plastic monocoque chassis molded in three pieces and bonded together. The suspension and four-wheel Girling disc brakes attached directly to the reinforced fiberglass hull. CRV-II was raced in 1965 by Trant Jarman, who won the SCCA Central Division D-Modified Championship. In 1966, model car manufacturer AMT Corporation bought the rights to manufacture the CRV, which it renamed the Piranha. Production was moved to AMT's Arizona factory, where famed customizer Gene Winfield ran the project. Although AMT was primarily interested in selling street cars, it also advertised a Piranha kit car for $3,677. At least one was built as a racing car, although the Piranha did not reach full production before the project was shut down in 1969. Dick Carbajal raced one with factory help in 1967 and 1968, and today it is the

only known survivor from the Piranha racing project. A few street cars have also survived, as well as a Chrysler Hemi-engined dragster and a special Piranha coupe that starred in the *Man from Uncle* television series. In the 1970s, Piranha-style bodies were available from various kit car companies but were adapted to VW chassis.

Cunningham

Briggs Swift Cunningham was the first American racing car manufacturer to take the fight for sports car supremacy to Europe. Cunningham racing cars built in West Palm Beach, Florida, were a major threat at Le Mans every year they were entered, and they won Sebring as well as other American races.

Cunningham grew up rich, the son of a Cincinnati entrepreneur who made a sizeable fortune in the meat packing and banking industries. His father died when Briggs was five, and he was raised by his socialite mother, Elizabeth Kilgour Cunningham. While young, Briggs fell under the spell of an uncle, Dr. Ashton Heyl, who was a car enthusiast and drove a stately Dodge touring car crammed with an Hispano-Suiza aircraft engine. Impromptu street races in this contraption sparked Cunningham's interest in fast cars. Growing up wealthy also put him in touch with influential people in various industries who would help him out later on.

Cunningham dropped out of Yale and concentrated on spending his family money on sailboats and cars. Sailboats remained a large part of his life, peaking in 1958 when he captained the winning yacht in the America's Cup race. From his yachting friends, he learned about fancy cars, and Cunningham owned a number of fast Packards and an Alfa Romeo. The racing bug bit hard in 1939 and didn't let go for a long time.

Bu-Merc

Cunningham owned a number of racing cars in the 1930s, including a circle track car and an MG K3 Magnette, which he loaned to other drivers because he had promised his mother he would not race. He

joined the fledgling Automobile Racing Club of America to go racing as a car owner. One of the first cars he loaned out was the Bu-Merc, a hot street machine built by his friend Charles Chayne, the chief engineer at Buick. This special was based on a Buick Century chassis powered by a modified 320-ci Buick straight-eight engine. Chayne massaged the running gear for more power and road holding, and the engine was lowered and moved back in the chassis. The body was "liberated" from a wrecked Mercedes SSK that had been rebodied. The Bu-Merc had the famed Mercedes grille up front, with Buick steel wheels and the Mercedes cockpit and tail. In 1940, Cunningham loaned it to his friend Miles Collier to run in the New York World's Fair Grand Prix. Against a field of European exotica, including Alfa Romeos, Bugattis, MGs, a Maserati, an Aston Martin, and a Delage, the Bu-Merc ran as high as second before being forced out by an accident. The Grand Prix was the last American road race before World War II started.

After the war, the Bu-Merc took part in other events. After Cunningham's mother died, he began racing himself and drove the Bu-Merc to a fine second place at the first Watkins Glen Grand Prix in 1948. The race, then held on city streets, was closely fought and won by Frank Griswold in an Alfa Romeo. Cunningham's friend George Roberts drove the Bu-Merc to a third at the Glen the next year (just behind Cunningham himself in a Ferrari 166). Cunningham kept the Bu-Merc, which was later featured in his museum and then passed on to the Collier Collection.

Le Monstre

By 1949, Cunningham was hooked on racing. He met Alfred Momo, a tuning and fabricating genius who had worked for Inskip, a Rolls-Royce and MG distributor. Italian-born Momo had already lived a stellar life, first as a riding mechanic and machinist at S.C.A.T. (he rode in the winning car in the 1911 Targa Florio) and then working on aircraft, at one point climbing out on the wing to fix an engine during flight. Momo had a thriving tuning business on Long Island,

and provided guidance for the fledgling Cunningham team. Next, Cunningham met Luigi Chinetti, who had moved to America after denouncing fascism in his native Italy. Chinetti won Le Mans three times, twice in an Alfa and once in a Ferrari. His Ferrari win was in 1949, for which he was awarded two entries in the following year's race. He offered those two spots to Cunningham. All that was left was the choice of cars.

Cunningham had recently made the acquaintance of respected racing driver and tuner Fred Walters (better known as Ted Tappet), who partnered with Bill Frick in a shop called Frick-Tappet Motors. They tuned all types of cars, but their best-known product was the "Fordillac," a 1949 Ford sedan powered by a Cadillac V-8. This was a potent combination, considerably hotter than even modified flathead Fords. Frick-Tappet built a special for Cunningham to race, swapping a 331-ci Cadillac V-8 into a Healey Silverstone. This was to be a test vehicle for the upcoming Cunningham cars and was fitted with a de Dion rear end. Cunningham bought Frick-Tappet Motors and wanted to enter Fordillacs at Le Mans, but the organizers refused to allow them since they were not production cars. So Cunningham entered two 1950 Cadillacs instead.

Ed Cole, president of Cadillac, shipped Cunningham a pair of Series 61 Cadillac coupes with three-speed manual gearboxes. The Le Mans organizers (the ACO) allowed only limited performance modifications to the chassis and running gear, but allowed complete rebodies. One Cadillac was left mostly stock, while the other one (chassis number DRF 92079) got a wild, weird doorstop of a body designed by Grumman Aircraft engineer Howard Weinman. The engines were mostly stock but benefited from a special five-carburetor manifold designed by Cole himself. The huge, angular hot rod was nicknamed *Le Monstre* by the delighted French fans. It had a rough time on and off the track. First, it was wrecked while driving to the track and repaired in a two-day, nonstop marathon. In the race, Cunningham stuffed it into a sand bank and spent 30 minutes digging it out. Still, the stock Caddy finished tenth overall, with *Le Monstre* right behind (and

The Cunningham C-4R was the most successful model built by sportsman Briggs Cunningham. It won Sebring and was a strong contender at Le Mans. *Harold Pace*

ahead of a Jaguar XK-120, in Jag's first try at the event). It was the only time *Le Monstre* was run and like most of the Cunningham racers, it is currently in the Collier Collection.

Cunningham C-1

Cunningham's enthusiasm was at a high. With an excellent finish in a relatively stock Cadillac he was convinced he could do much better with a purpose-built race car. The C-1 was designed and built by the end of 1950. It had a Cadillac V-8 and three-speed gearbox mounted in a heavy tube frame. Up front, Cunningham used modified Ford suspension, with a fabricated de Dion system in back. Coil springs were used, along with Cadillac brakes (with Alfin drums) and Chrysler worm-and-sector steering. The lovely roadster body sported an oval grille with smooth, flowing lines and wire wheels. There were supposed to be four C-1 roadsters and a coupe, but Cadillac flaked out on supplying engines, so only a single roadster (Number 5101) and the coupe were built. Both ended up as street cars, although the C-1 Roadster was used as a practice car for the racing team.

Cunningham C-2R

The C-2R was essentially a C-1 powered by the then-new Chrysler 331-ci Hemi. One of Cunningham's old school chums was the son of the president of Chrysler, who subsequently sold them

engines at a heavy discount. The 180-horsepower engines were fitted with a log manifold mounting four Zenith carburetors, hotter cams, and ported heads with the compression bumped from 7.5:1 to 8.5:1. Power climbed to 270 horsepower. This was very impressive at a time when a full-race Jaguar six was only putting out 210 horsepower. Three cars were built in 1951 (Numbers 5102–5104) and promptly shipped to France to be driven by three teams—Cunningham and George Huntoon, George Rand and Fred Wacker, and Ted Walters and John Fitch. Only the latter car survived, to finish 18th after holding down second for six hours. After Le Mans, the cars were driven to International Motors in Los Angeles to be sold. (Cunningham later bought one of them back.) The C-2R was a lovely car but at 3,200 pounds was way too heavy to take on the C-Type Jags and Ferraris. It was also lacking in handling, compared to the European competition, and when driven fast put severe wear on the tires and suspension. Future Cunninghams would be much more svelte.

Cunningham C-4R and C-4RK

The next racing cars were the C-4R models (the C-3 Cunninghams were street cars). For 1952, the all-new design pared 900 pounds off the weight of the C-2R, and the suspension was in for an upgrade as well. Designed by G. Briggs Weaver, the new model sported a lighter live axle in back to replace

The Cunningham C-4RK was a coupe version of the C-4R. At Thompson Speedway in 1953, it leads a C-4R. *Ozzie Lyons*

The Cunningham C-5R finished third at Le Mans in 1953. *Pete Lyons*

the theoretically superior de Dion layout. The Hemi was now producing 325 horsepower, along with gobs of torque. It was capable of over 400 horsepower, but was detuned for endurance racing and proved to be dead reliable. The entire car was smaller, with a 100-inch wheelbase and a round-tube frame that was 6 inches narrower than the C-2R.

Two roadsters were built (Numbers 5216R and 5217R) with huge oval grilles and an aircraft oil cooler mounted on the cowl in a round housing. Festooned with scoops, bulges, and louvers, they were brutal looking machines, and the white-and-blue paint scheme made them beacons for American sports car fans. A third chassis was fitted with an evil-looking coupe body called the C-4RK (Number 5218R). The tail on the coupe was short and squared off, as per the aerodynamic theories of Professor Wunibald Kamm.

The wire wheels of the C-2R were replaced on all C-4R models with "kidney bean" Halibrand racing wheels (so named for the shape of the vents in the wheel) with knock-off hubs. Top speed was around 155 miles per hour, and a C-4R first raced at Bridgehampton in May, where Walters led but was black-flagged for a mechanical problem. At Le Mans, the coupe and one roadster retired, but Cunningham wrestled the remaining C-4R into an excellent fourth-overall finish behind two Mercedes 300SLs and a Nash-Healey. After Le Mans, the C-4Rs made the rounds at SCCA races, winning at Elkhart Lake, Albany, Allentown, and Thompson.

The C-4Rs started the 1953 season with an outright win at Sebring over the works Aston Martins.

Once again, they won at a number of SCCA events and took a third at Reims in France. At Le Mans, the C-4Rs played second fiddle to the latest Cunningham, the C-5R, which finished third. Cunningham and Bill Spear drove a C-4R to seventh place, while the C-4RK finished tenth. The final Le Mans race for the C-4R series was in 1954, when it finished a worthy third and fifth overall. Cunningham sold one C-4R and the C-4RK to Charles Moran, who kept them until 1970, when Cunningham bought them back at auction.

Cunningham C-5R

An all-new car (Number 5319R) was assembled for the 1953 Le Mans race. It was a slippery, aggressive shape that the French nicknamed The Shark. It was aerodynamically clean and featured a revised suspension design. In front, the Ford-based suspension used on previous Cunninghams was replaced

with a live axle sprung by torsion bars. The beam axle allowed huge 17-inch-diameter drum brakes to be mounted inboard of the 16-inch wheels, and a wide, gaping grille channeled air onto the brakes. The frame was similar to the C-4R and a live axle was retained in back as well.

The Chrysler Hemi was retained, but a four-speed unit borrowed from a Fiat truck replaced the three-speed gearboxes. Weight was up slightly to 2,480 pounds. Top speed was just over 160 miles per hour, and it looked like 1953 would be Cunningham's year at Le Mans. Only one C-5R was built, and it was teamed with a C-2R and the C-2RK. What Cunningham had no way of knowing was that Jaguar had a secret weapon—the new C-Types had Dunlop disc brakes that allowed them to sail past the Cunninghams under braking, even though they did not have the acceleration or top speed of the C-5R. John Fitch and Phil Walters drove steadily throughout the race but finished a distant third behind two works Jaguars. It was to be the high-water mark of the Cunningham marque. As Phil Walters wrote in *Sports Cars* and *Hot Rod*, "I don't think the Cunningham team did badly . . . three cars finished in the top ten, in perfect running order, against the best sports cars in the world." He was right. The C-5R later ran at Reims, where Fitch wrecked it in spectacular fashion. The C-5R was rebuilt on a second chassis (Number 5320R) and ran at Albany, Georgia, and March Field, California, but it proved to be too heavy for sprint races. There was also a third C-5R chassis (Number 5321R) that was never bodied.

The Offy-powered Cunningham C-6R was a victim of inadequate development. It ran in bare metal at Sebring in 1955. *Ozzie Lyons*

The C-6R was updated with a new nose and fin that resembled a Jaguar D-Type. A Jaguar engine replaced the anemic Offy. *Pete Lyons*

Cunningham C-6R

The C-6R (Number 5422) was probably the only turkey among the great cars built by Briggs Cunningham. It was intended to run at Le Mans in 1954, powered by an inverted V-12 two-stroke engine designed by Mercury Marine boss (and NASCAR team owner) Carl Keikhaefer. But the engine was never built, and Cunningham decided to power it with a Ferrari V-12. He bought a Ferrari 375 MM to "borrow" the engine, but when it became obvious the C-6R could not be completed in time, the Ferrari was run instead, alongside two C-4Rs. The Ferrari was also fitted with experimental water-cooled drum brakes, as Dunlop refused to sell them disc brakes (supposedly under pressure from Jaguar). The brakes did not work well and the Ferrari retired, but the two old C-4Rs finished third and fifth.

The C-6R was quite a bit smaller and lighter than previous Cunninghams, and a Chrysler Hemi would simply not fit. So when the Keikhaefer and Ferrari engines didn't pan out, Cunningham was left scrambling for a lightweight powerplant. He settled on a Meyer-Drake (Offenhauser) four-cylinder Indy engine destroked to 3 liters. It was changed from Hillborn fuel injection to Webers and from a magneto to a Lucas distributor. In final form, it produced 260 horsepower and was backed up with a ZF four-speed full-synchro gearbox.

The chassis was more up-to-date than the C-5R, with a lightweight tubular frame, fabricated independent front suspension, and a de Dion tube in back with coil springs. Lockheed 13-inch drum brakes were fitted, along with Halibrand alloy wheels. The new car was narrower than the C-5R and weighed only 1,900 pounds. The aluminum body was an eye-catcher, with a large oval grille and a nose much like a Ferrari 375. It was first run at Sebring in 1955, where it had no headrest (or paint) and retired with a broken flywheel. A headrest was added before Le Mans and the car was painted in the usual Cunningham bright white with blue stripe.

At Le Mans, the C-6R would only run 141 miles per hour, a good 15 miles per hour slower than the older Hemi-engined cars. The nose had been revised with a smaller grille. It retired after losing two gears in the transmission and burning a piston in the Meyer-Drake engine. The C-6R ran at Road America, where the Drake again cratered. The C-6R was not used in the 1956 season. In 1957, the Drake was dumped in favor of a 3.8-liter Jag engine and transmission, installed by Momo. At some point, the nose was also replaced with one that resembled a Jaguar D-Type. The Jag engine failed in practice at Sebring, and the car was run in some minor SCCA races without success. By then, Cunningham was racing Jaguar D-Types that were quicker and better developed than the C-6R, so the final Cunningham racer was retired. Cunningham went on to other successes with imported racing cars, but the C-6R was the end of his famous line.

CUNNINGHAM

Cunningham Car Company
West Palm Beach, Florida

BU-MERC
Year built	**1939**
Engine	**Buick Century straight-eight**
Gearbox	**Buick**
Front suspension	**independent**
Rear suspension	**live axle**
Brakes	**Buick drum**
Body material	**steel**
Weight, approx.	**2,840 pounds**
Wheelbase	**105 inches**
Number built	**one**

LE MONSTRE
Year built	**1950**
Engine	**Cadillac V-8**
Gearbox	**Cadillac three-speed**
Front suspension	**independent**
Rear suspension	**live axle**
Brakes	**Cadillac drum**
Body material	**aluminum**
Wheelbase	**122 inches**
Number built	**one**

CUNNINGHAM C-1 AND C-2R
Year built	**1951**
Engines	**Cadillac or Chrysler Hemi V-8**
Gearbox	**three-speed**
Front suspension	**independent**
Rear suspension	**de Dion**
Brakes	**drum**
Body material	**aluminum**
Weight, approx.	**3,200 pounds**
Wheelbase	**105 inches**
Number built	**one C-1 and three C-2Rs**

CUNNINGHAM C-4R AND C-4RK
Year built	**1952**
Engine	**Chrysler Hemi V-8**
Gearbox	**three-speed**
Front suspension	**independent**
Rear suspension	**live axle**
Brakes	**drum**
Body material	**aluminum**
Weight, approx.	**2,410 pounds**
Wheelbase	**100 inches**
Number built	**two C-4Rs and one C-4RK**

CUNNINGHAM C-5R
Year built	**1953**
Engines	**Cadillac or Chrysler Hemi V-8**
Gearbox	**four-speed**
Front suspension	**live axle**
Rear suspension	**live axle**
Brakes	**drum**
Body material	**aluminum**
Weight, approx.	**2,480 pounds**
Wheelbase	**100 inches**
Number built	**one**

CUNNINGHAM C-6R
Year built	**1955**
Engines	**Meyer-Drake four-cylinder, later Jaguar 3.8 six**
Gearbox	**four-speed**
Front suspension	**independent**
Rear suspension	**de Dion**
Brakes	**drum**
Body material	**aluminum**
Weight, approx.	**1,900 pounds**
Wheelbase	**100 inches**
Number built	**one**

Dane

Stuart Dane built his first road racing car in 1955, starting with a tired $100 Fiat 500 coupe as raw material for a Formula 3 car.

Dane Formula 3

Dane and friend Mark Latker welded up a space frame from 1 1/4-inch tubing and sheet steel. They also fabricated the front wishbones, which worked with the Fiat steering box. In back, a de Dion tube was located by double trailing arms and what may have been the first American use of a zero-roll stiffness suspension system, operated by bellcranks

and a single spring pirated from a folding bed. In front, a single torsion bar was fabricated from a 1/2-inch steel bar. Aircraft disc brakes were adapted to the drum brake mounting points. Johnson Motors, a Triumph dealer, built a Triumph Tiger 100 engine. The Dane won first time out at Torrey Pines in 1956 and added more wins at Pomona and San Diego. It finished 12 out of 16 races entered that year and won the Autobooks Trophy, the Formula 3 Reliability Index, and an award for the Best Home-Built Formula 3 for 1956.

Dane Formula Juniors

Dane later built two Formula Junior models in his small garage in Los Angeles. The first appeared in 1960 as a front-engined design with independent front suspension and the option of a live axle or de Dion in back. The ladder frame was basic, and the fiberglass body was simple and somewhat ungainly. Coil springs were used all around, and power came from a BMC engine and gearbox. Dane sold them in kit or completed form.

Dane later developed a midengined car based on a Fiat engine and transaxle. He was one of the founders of the 500-cc Club of America, forerunner of the Formula Racing Association (FRA), the first club to put on formula car races in the United States. In 1962, Dane teamed with "Red" LeGrand and Neil Hillier to build a formula car with a Renault engine. The team also laid out the Cheetah F3 (see LeGrand entry). Tragically, Dane was killed in an FRA race at Riverside in 1962, driving the Renault special and no more Danes were built.

Delfosse

This nice little Formula 4 machine was as American as Buenos Aires, or something like that. Curt Delfosse was a German race car builder who relocated to South America and began selling small, inexpensive formula cars in the early 1960s. They used modified NSU Prinz 780-cc engines, rear-mounted in a space frame that utilized NSU

suspension, steering, and transaxle. Delfosse's idea was for the cars to serve as a training class for young drivers who were moving up from karts. With a weight of only 550 pounds, they had a top speed of over 116 miles per hour. The Delfosse had a sleek, pointed nose and a head fairing that also enclosed the engine. Steel wheels were used all around.

Delfosse demonstrated his car for Juan Manuel Fangio and other top drivers while he was still in Argentina, but when he heard about the Formula Racing Association (FRA) Formula 4 rules, he realized his car was ideal for the class. He moved the operation to La Jolla, California, and announced he would be selling cars for $3,200. How many were sold is unknown, as Formula 4 only lasted a few years before it was rolled into Formula C.

Devin

One of the most innovative pioneers of the 1950s was Bill Devin. His career covered the gamut: racer, modifier, builder, inventor, and manufacturer. And while he was very successful at each, his accomplishments somehow did not fully reflect his considerable talents. Some suggest that funding was always a problem. Others characterize Devin as a kind-hearted cynic, stubborn and inflexible to the point that it often killed the deal. Still others think that he tried to do too many things, growing bored with

DANE

Dane Racing Cars Inc.
12969-1/2 Washington Boulevard
Los Angeles, California

DANE FORMULA 3

Year built	**1955**
Engine	**Triumph Tiger**
Gearbox	**Triumph motorcycle**
Front suspension	**independent**
Rear suspension	**de Dion**
Brakes	**disc**
Body material	**aluminum**
Number built	**one**

DANE FORMULA JUNIORS (FRONT ENGINE)

Year built	**1960**
Engine	**1,000-cc BMC**
Gearbox	**BMC four-speed**
Front suspension	**independent**
Rear suspension	**live axle or de Dion**
Brakes	**drum**
Body material	**fiberglass**

DANE FORMULA JUNIORS (MIDENGINE)

Year built	**1961**
Engine	**Fiat**
Gearbox	**Fiat four-speed**
Front suspension	**independent**
Rear suspension	**de Dion**
Brakes	**drum**
Body material	**fiberglass**

DELFOSSE

Delfosse
La Jolla, California

DELFOSSE MINI-JUNIOR

Year built	**1963**
Engine	**780-cc NSU Prinz**
Gearbox	**NSU four-speed**
Front suspension	**independent**
Rear suspension	**independent**
Brakes	**NSU drum**
Body material	**fiberglass**
Weight, approx.	**550 pounds**

Devin Panhards were potent Class H racers, particularly when powered with Devin OHC conversions or MAG blowers. *Harold Pace*

one project and jumping to another, just as the first was beginning to gel. This is not to say that Devin was not a success. He was. It's just that his creations did not take him to the heights deserved.

Devin was born in Rocky, Oklahoma, in 1915 and grew up around cars. His father owned an automobile repair garage, and young Bill quickly became a talented welder and fabricator. His first automotive creation was a single-seat amalgamation of junkyard parts powered by a washing machine engine, built for his younger brother, Gene. In the late 1930s, the Devin family moved to California, and Bill took a job with Douglas Aircraft. There he learned many skills that would become invaluable in his future automotive endeavors. In 1942, he joined the Navy as a machinist's mate and motor mechanic, furthering his skills. Back in California after a two-year stint, Devin tried unsuccessfully to open a car dealership. He wound up moving to Montour, Iowa, near the hometown of his wife, Millie, where he established a very successful Chrysler-Plymouth dealership. After selling that business, Devin made his way back to California and bought another Chrysler-Plymouth dealership. It was at that point in the story that Devin was bitten by the racing bug—in a big way.

Devin's second automotive creation was a heavily modified Crosley Hot Shot. Legend has it that he had 20 class/overall victories in 22 starts at many of the top local California venues. Energized by his Hot Shot success, Devin wanted to go bigger. Selling his dealership in Fontana, Devin teamed up with Ernie McAfee and set up an exotic car showroom in, of all things, a Quonset hut. Devin and McAfee began by selling Siatas, but the partnership ended abruptly and Devin's interest quickly flipped to Ferraris. It is often forgotten just how many great Ferraris Devin owned—the ex-Phil Hill 1952 Carrera Panamerica 2.6-liter Vignale-bodied 212 coupe, a 3-liter 250 MM Pininfarina coupe, the ex-Porfirio Rubirosa 2-liter 166, and the ex-Simon and Vincent 4.1-liter Vignale coupe. A series of forays with other exotics followed, including Porsche, OSCA, Arnolt-Bristol, and finally Deutsch-Bonnet. It was this last French jewel that steered Devin's life in a new direction.

Devin Panhard

The Devin Panhard was a car of firsts, both for Bill Devin and the world. In the 1950s, Devin became one of the best and most prolific constructors of fiberglass bodies; the Devin Panhard was his first

effort in this arena. The car was also the first ever to use a belt-driven overhead cam, a true automotive innovation for which Devin never received credit.

The Devin Panhard was born in 1954 in typical Bill Devin fashion—with inspiration and a deal. Devin sold his Ferrari 250 MM Pininfarina coupe to a man in Michigan and wound up taking a 1953 Deutsch-Bonnet Le Mans Barquette race car in partial trade. After making a deal to buy out the remaining stock of the Panhard dealership in Glendale, California, Devin pulled a mold off the stylish D.B. race car, modified it a bit, and began making fiberglass bodies for a new race car creation—the Devin Panhard. At first, he knew little about working with fiberglass, but soon he became quite proficient. (See Devin entry in American Kit Car Manufacturers, Chapter 5.)

Devin designed and manufactured his own ladder frame with an 84-inch wheelbase and a weight of 80 pounds. Each successive frame was constructed a bit differently, as Devin constantly improved on his initial design. Some frames incorporated a portion of a Panhard Junior subframe, and suspension components were taken from the same car.

Motivation for this new front-wheel drive race car came from the 750-cc two-cylinder, four-cycle, air-cooled pushrod Panhard engine (bolted to the front of the transaxle). In stock trim, this engine produced 38 horsepower. In an effort to improve performance, Devin switched from the pushrod setup to overhead camshafts. Because the Panhard engine resembled that of a motorcycle, Devin reasoned that the

Bill Devin hangs onto a trailer filled with three Devin-Panhards and Lance Reventlow's Cooper (bottom front). *Harold Pace collection*

Norton Manx camshaft setup might just do the trick. With the aid of Norton racer Don Evans, Devin fitted the stock Panhard crankcase with Manx cylinders, heads, and pistons. Horizontal twin throat Webers were fitted to each cylinder, via a custom Devin manifold.

Next came the real inspiration. Noticing an advertisement in *Business Week*, Devin contacted the Gilmer Belt Company and, with its assistance, designed a toothed rubber belt to replace the complicated Norton gear drive and run the overhead cams. This is the first known automotive application of a belt-driven overhead cam. Unfortunately, Devin never patented this innovation.

The naturally aspirated 750-cc engine placed the Devin Panhard in the H-Modified class. Initially, Devin was a relative unknown and his little racer was not considered much of a threat. This soon changed, as the cars were nearly unbeatable in their class. At 950 pounds, the cars had an outstanding power-to-weight ratio, and they became known for their superior handling.

The Devins were sold with various configurations of the 750-cc Panhard engine (pushrod, single overhead camshaft, or dual overhead camshaft). As an added treat, Devin also offered a supercharged engine using a MAG blower, which placed the car in

the 1,100-cc G-Modified class. It was not uncommon for Devin Panhard racers to decide which class to enter after checking out the competition at the event, as an engine swap was relatively easy.

A race-ready car could be purchased from Devin Enterprises for $2,850. It is not known how many Devin Panhards were produced, perhaps as few as six or as many as 12. What is known is that the cars were quick and successful. Dr. Chet Burgraff was a consistent winner in the 750-cc class and Jean-Pierre Kunstle won the 1,100-cc class at Pebble Beach in 1954 with his blown Devin Panhard. At the

same event, Jimmy Orr won the 750-cc class with his naturally aspirated Devin. In fact, Orr won the SCCA H-Modified National Championship in 1956 with his overhead cam Devin Panhard. The success was quite astounding, considering that this was Devin's first effort in race car production.

Devin SS

As a result of his abundant skill with fiberglass and his success in the $295-kit-body business, Devin received business inquiries from around the globe. American-LaFrance wanted parts for refrigerator trucks, and several engineering firms contacted Devin with various projects. There were at least two electric car company projects, a company planning to market fiberglass funeral caskets, and even an offer from a company designing a flying car. But the inquiry that forever changed Devin's life came in 1957 in the form of a letter from a couple of guys in, of all places, Belfast, Northern Ireland.

Two Irish racing enthusiasts, Malcolm MacGregor and Noel Hills, decided to build their own race car. Both were textile engineers, and both had evenings off. Noel provided the workshop facility and MacGregor designed the chassis. When Devin received the letter from the two requesting a uniquely designed fiberglass body to mount on their chassis, he saw the opportunity to build a world-class sports car, and he hopped on a plane. When Devin arrived, he inspected the prototype. The frame

Lew Spencer and Dave McDonald shared this Devin SS, named VKI. *Allen Kuhn*

62

The Devin SS was a competitive club-level car that could also be driven on the street. *Harold Pace*

was constructed of 3-inch-diameter tubes with a wishbone-and-coils independent front suspension. The rear end was de Dion—pretty racy stuff for those days. The chassis had a 90-inch wheelbase, as MacGregor favored tight, compact cars. To finish off the thing, MacGregor installed a Jag engine, a dangerous-looking gas tank, and a single seat bolted to the frame. (Devin later commented that it looked like a "farm tractor.") MacGregor took Devin and the crude prototype to an abandoned American World War II airfield in Kirkstown, 40 miles north of Belfast. The place was a cow pasture complete with, of course, cows, and . . . well . . . fresh piles of . . . you get the idea. After a few spirited "laps," Devin came in, hosed himself off, and told MacGregor, "I'll buy that, but I want a 94-inch wheelbase, set up for a Chevy V-8 engine and transmission."

While Devin was impressed with the chassis, he wanted changes, and he worked with the two Irishmen to improve it. They compromised on a 92-inch wheelbase with a front track of 52 inches and a rear track of 50 inches. The final agreement was that the rolling chassis would be built in Ireland and sent to Devin Enterprises in California, where the Devin Super Sport (SS) would be born.

In 1958, the Irish chassis began to make their way across the Atlantic. The method of construction on the "production" chassis was unusual. The basic frame was constructed of various sizes of round steel tubing (primarily 2- and 3-inch-diameter 14-gauge), which was gas welded together. In some areas, it was necessary to bend the tubes to form a corner radius. Because of limited tooling, some tubes could not be bent as required and a prebent thick-walled section was welded to much thinner-walled straight tubes, thus making a corner or radius as required. According to Devin, the Irish chassis lacked a structure at the front to support the radiator, front portion of the body, and the front bumper. A structure for the rear body support and rear bumper was also lacking. Without these pieces, the chassis could be shipped overseas in a much smaller crate, significantly reducing the shipping costs. Once received in California, Devin added the necessary front and rear supports.

Devin designed and manufactured a unique and breathtaking fiberglass body for the SS. The early bodies had a rounded tail; later bodies were modified with the headlight buckets enlarged and raised and the rear of the car flattened, with a lip to allow for a rear license plate. A 283-ci Chevrolet Corvette engine and Borg-Warner four-speed transmission were installed. When The Holley Carburetor Company emphatically dismissed Devin's request for it to manufacture a carburetor to fit the Chevy manifold, Devin designed a two-piece aluminum manifold that could accept all combinations of two- and four-barrel carburetion. It is an interesting "coincidence" that the 1963 Chevrolet Corvette came with Holleys as optional equipment.

The front suspension had double A-arms with coil-over shocks. The rear suspension of the SS was de Dion tube with four trailing links, and the rear hubs were manufactured in Ireland. Woodhead-Monroe coil-overs were used front and rear. Steering was BMC rack-and-pinion, with 2.5 turns lock-to-lock. Customers could order the car in either left- or right-hand-drive configurations. Girling disc brakes were utilized at all four corners (12-inch fronts, 11-inch rears mounted inboard). Dunlop tires (6.75x15) were mounted on Dunlop knock-off wire wheels.

One of the components designed specifically for the SS was a Devin finned-aluminum differential, although the first few cars were delivered with a 3.73:1 Salisbury unit. The cars were assembled in Devin's El Monte facility, and the SS was delivered to the customer running and completely finished, including the interior, a top, side curtains, a windshield, and instrumentation. The windshield was a particular headache for Devin, as his order at Pittsburgh Plate Glass arrived more than eight months late, with customer cars just sitting unable to be delivered. The SS instruments were Stewart-Warner with a specially manufactured Stewart-Warner/Devin oversized 200-mile-per-hour speedo and 10,000-rpm tach (both unique to the SS). The car was truly fabulous, and, boy, would it get up and go. The SS was tested in 1959 by *Sports Car Illustrated* and was clocked at an astounding 4.8 seconds for 0–60; 0–100 was accomplished in just 12.9 seconds.

Bill Devin tries out the prototype Devin D in 1958.
Harold Pace collection

In order to sell the SS, Devin named Art Evans (Evans Industries, Pasadena, California) as the sole distributor, with Evan's partner OCee Rich involved, and Pete Woods acting as the general manager. With the business end now delegated, Devin believed he could focus on his plan to build 100 Devin SSs to meet the SCCA requirements for homologation. Because of the limitations and expense associated with chassis imported from Ireland, Devin designed a similar chassis to be manufactured in his own facility to offer the SS at a more competitive price. These cars are commonly referred to as California-chassis SSs. Unfortunately, the cars were so good that they cost more to build than the selling price, even when the price was nearly doubled from $5,950 to $10,000. Devin was a self-proclaimed poor businessman, and ultimately the SS project ran out of money, but not before it scored some impressive victories at the track.

While Devin did not intend the car to be a strict racer, the car had such awesome performance that it invariably found its way to the track. Many of the known club racers of the day, including Andy Porterfield, John Brophy, Art Evans, Davy MacDonald, and Pete Woods, competed in a Devin SS. Woods won the Cal Club C-Modified Championship in a Devin SS in 1959.

Upon Devin's passing in November 2000, the SS chassis grid and all intellectual property of his estate were purchased by a group of Devin enthusiasts who are now the caretakers of Devin Sports Cars.

Devin D and Devin C

Shortly after Devin began producing the SS in 1958, he hit on the idea of making a less expensive car for those who did not have $10,000 to plunk down for an SS. The Devin D was born as a relatively inexpensive, rear-engined, Porsche- or VW-powered car that could be purchased fully finished or in component form. Devin manufactured a ladder frame with an 83-inch wheelbase and employed modified VW suspension components for the front and rear. The completed car weighed a few ticks under 1,200 pounds and would set you back $895 for the body and frame only; $1,495 for the body, frame, and all other components necessary for completion; $2,950 for a finished car with VW power; and $3,350 for a finished car with a Porsche powerplant.

When the Corvair was introduced in late 1959, Devin designed a new chassis and modified the D body for the heavier Corvair engine, running gear, and mechanicals, and created a new car, the Devin C. The C weighed in at 1,400 pounds and, like the D, was very handsome (from the firewall back, both the D and C were identical to the later version of the SS body). A complete component package to build the C was available for $2,060, and a complete car would run you $4,500. The final evolution of the Devin C was the GT coupe, which debuted at the New York Auto Show in 1964. The car was a smash hit and, in usual Devin fashion, ahead of its time with many innovations. (The tops of the doors were cut into the roof, a la the later Corvettes and the GT 40.) Only two cars were produced before the project ran out of funding.

Both the Devin C and D raced in club events. Pete Woods had a good showing in a turbocharged, Corvair-powered Devin C at the Pikes Peak Hillclimb, beaten by Ak Miller's Devin-Ford. Bill Devin estimated that over 300 Devin Cs and Ds were built.

Devin-Roosevelt

The Devin-Roosevelt was built as a one-off in 1960 for the Roosevelt-Fiat racing team owned by Franklin D. Roosevelt Jr. The car was a midengine

modified (the engine was turned around from its stock location) based on a Fiat Abarth twin cam Zagato coupe. It was built with a very light fiberglass body and a Devin-built, one-off tube frame chassis. A twin cam 747-cc Abarth engine, developing 57 horsepower, powered the car. The tranny was a four-speed Fiat 600 with a Klentz quick-change section. The suspension was modified Fiat, and the brakes were 12-inch, four-wheel Cagle discs. The finished racer weighed a petite 800 pounds.

Many Devins are currently being campaigned in vintage racing.

DEVIN

Devin Enterprises
44500 Sierra Highway
Lancaster, California

Devin Enterprises
9800 Rush Street
El Monte, California

Devin Sports Cars
35089 San Carlos Street
Yucaipa, California

DEVIN PANHARD

Year built	1954
Engine	750-cc Panhard two-cylinder; pushrod or belt-driven overhead camshaft (single or dual); optional supercharger
Gearbox	Panhard four-speed
Chassis	ladder
Front suspension	Panhard Junior (independent with transverse leaf spring)
Rear suspension	Panhard Junior (semiindependent with torsion bars)
Brakes	Panhard Junior drums
Body material	fiberglass
Weight, approx.	950 pounds
Wheelbase	84 inches
Length	150 inches
Height	39 inches
Number built	six to 12
Price when new	$2,850

DEVIN SS

Years built **1958–1959**
Engine .... **Chevy (283 ci)**
Gearbox .... **Borg-Warner four-speed**
Chassis .... **ladder**
Front suspension .... **independent with coil springs**
Rear suspension ..... **de Dion with coil springs**
Brakes .... **Girling disc**
Body material .... **fiberglass**
Weight, approx. ..... **2,170 pounds**
Wheelbase .... **92 inches**
Length .... **164 inches**
Height .... **44 inches**
Number built .... **18 Irish chassis; fewer than ten American chassis**
Price when new ..... **$5,950 (later $10,000)**

DEVIN D

Years built **1958–1965**
Engines .... **Porsche or Volkswagen**
Gearbox .... **Volkswagen four-speed**
Chassis .... **ladder**
Front suspension .... **Volkswagen trailing link**
Rear suspension ..... **swing axle**
Brakes .... **Volkswagen or Porsche drum**
Body material .... **fiberglass**
Weight, approx. ..... **1,180 pounds**
Wheelbase .... **82 inches**
Length .... **153 inches**
Height .... **46 inches**
Price when new ..... **$2,950 to 3,350, depending on engine selection**

DEVIN C

Years built **1959–1965**
Engine .... **Corvair six-cylinder**
Gearbox .... **Corvair four-speed**
Chassis .... **ladder**
Front suspension .... **Volkswagen trailing link**
Rear suspension ..... **swing axle**
Brakes .... **Volkswagen, Corvair, or disc**
Body material .... **fiberglass**
Weight, approx. ..... **1,400 pounds**
Wheelbase .... **82 inches**
Length .... **150 inches**
Height .... **44 inches**
Price when new **$4,500**

DEVIN-ROOSEVELT

Year built **1960**
Engine .... **747-cc Abarth Bialbero DOHC four-cylinder**
Gearbox .... **Fiat 600 four-speed**
Chassis .... **space frame**
Front suspension .... **independent with transverse leaf spring**
Rear suspension ..... **swing axle with coil springs**
Brakes .... **Cagle four-wheel disc**
Body material .... **fiberglass**
Weight, approx. ..... **800 pounds**
Wheelbase .... **82 inches**
Height .... **44 inches**
Number built .... **one**

Dolphin

Dolphin Engineering in El Cajon, California, built a number of successful racing cars in the brief four years of its existence. The company was started by Robert "Bud" Hull, a former commercial tuna fisherman who named the new company after one of his favorite creatures. Hull later worked in the aerospace industry and raced sports cars, starting with a Porsche Speedster and a Cooper sports-racer. He soon met John Crosthwaite, an expatriate

English designer who had worked at Cooper and Lotus. Together, they became intrigued with the Formula Junior class that sprang up in 1958. They decided to pool their resources and build some F-Jr.s of their own.

Dolphin Formula Juniors

Hull and Crosthwaite set up shop in 1960 and laid out a midengined Formula Junior with an 85-inch wheelbase. Although the original goal was to pro-

duce a competitive, affordable F-Jr., Dolphin also wanted to be able to scale up the same basic design for use in Formula 1. The slab-sided bodywork was rather bulbous and caused the car to look bigger and heavier than other midengined designs.

The lower longitudinal frame rails were 1-inch-square tubing, while the upper two were 1-inch-round. The center section was deep in order to provide increased rigidity and protection for the driver. The front suspension was typical formula car practice, with unequal-length A-arms and Armstrong adjustable coil-over shocks. NSU Prinz spindles and Fiat backing plates were used, along with Dolphin-designed rack-and-pinion steering. In back, double wishbones and coil springs provided independent suspension, with Dolphin-designed shocks and tubular radius arms. All arms were heim-jointed for full adjustability.

The engine proved to be a weak link in the concept. Although the first wave of Italian F-Jr.s from Stanguellini, Taraschi, and a host of other etceterinis used modified Fiat engines, the more muscular BMC, English Ford, and DKW mills were supplanting them by 1960. In an effort to keep the cars affordable, the engines were delivered in a low state of tune with twin 1 1/2-inch SU carbs on a fabricated Dolphin intake manifold. A Crower-Schneider cam boosted power to around 75 horsepower, and a higher-volume oil pan was baffled to increase cooling.

Fiat 600 transaxles were used with close-ratio Abarth gear sets. They were inverted so that the ring gear would rotate normally (the Fiat 600 was rear-engined, the Dolphin midengined). Five different Nardi-built final-drive ratios were available. An aluminum fuel tank was located under the driver's legs, and a front-mounted radiator was used.

Although 14-inch steel Fiat wheels were standard, Dolphin cast its own optional lightweight 8-pound magnesium wheels. They made 4x15- and 4.5x15-inch versions with cast vanes that were intended to blow air over the drum brakes.

The bodies were made of fiberglass, because they were cheaper to make than aluminum bodies,

Kurt Neumann in Dolphin Formula Junior (No. 32) trails future Can-Am star Lothar Motschenbacher in another Dolphin around Riverside in 1964. *Allen Kuhn*

even though aluminum would have been lighter. Completed cars sold for $3,895, and kit versions were available in varying degrees of completion.

The first car raced was plagued by a series of half-shaft failures, until Dolphin began heat-treating them. Dolphin's hopes were buoyed by the addition of ace wheel spinner Ken Miles to the factory team (which also included sales manager Warren Boynton and local driver John Biehl), but the bulky and oddly proportioned Dolphin was behind the curve, compared to the Lotus 18 and the "lowline" Coopers. Nine were built before a second F-Jr. model was designed.

The Dolphin International was a redesign with a much lower body, built by Troutman and Barnes. The first body was aluminum, with subsequent production bodies being fiberglass. A new, lower frame was designed, but the inverted Fiat transmission was retained. The Fiat boat anchor was dumped in favor of the English Ford 105E mill, and a reported 26 were sold. However, they were no match for the new Lotus 20.

Formula 1/Formula 2 Effort

Dolphin tried to carry out its Formula 1 plans by first building a one-off Formula 2 car with the aluminum Troutman and Barnes body from the prototype for the International. This car was fitted with a Porsche transaxle and a 1,500-cc Alfa Romeo engine. It was to be the prototype for an F1 effort with Alfa or Taylor engines, copies of which were to sell for under $7,000 each. However, it was apparently not raced and soon disappeared.

Dolphin Sports-Racers

The concept of switching from formula cars to sports-racers was more promising for Dolphin. Formula Junior had deteriorated into the "car of the month" club with generational strides taking place several times each season. Interest could not be sustained, and Hull needed something more stable to build. Meanwhile, Crosthwaite left Dolphin to design Mickey Thompson's Buick-powered, midengined Indy cars. Californian Don Maslin replaced him at the drawing board. Maslin penned the first Dolphin sports-racer, which used a widened variation on the International frame and a fiberglass body with a nose reminiscent of the "pontoon-fendered" Ferrari Testa Rossa. The chassis were available in various lengths to suit the buyer's engine choice.

The first car was powered by a 750-cc Coventry-Climax engine and ran in the H-Modified

Bud Hull's Dolphin Sports-Racers were race winners from San Diego. *Harold Pace*

class. Driver Al Cervenka of Chicago did well with the 680-pound firecracker. The second car was built for Californian Ron Cole with an 1,100-cc Climax FWA for racing in the G-Modified class. It racked up a win, two seconds, and two fourths in its first six races.

The third chassis was a giant-killer. Ordered by Porsche dealer Otto Zipper for his ace driver, Ken Miles, it sported a full-house Porsche RS-60 1,700-cc engine and transaxle. Zipper and Miles knew the venerable Porsche RS-series was at the end of its career, as it was heavier and less sophisticated than the new Climax-powered sports-racers from Cooper, Lotus, and Elva. Miles was familiar with the Dolphin operation from his time racing their F-Jr.s, so he turned to them to design a lighter package for the proven and competitive Porsche running gear.

The new car, nicknamed the Porphin in a *Sports Car Graphic* article, was an upgraded version of the smaller Dolphins. The frame was very rigid, with an estimated 3,000 ft-lb of torque per degree of deflection. This was much more rigid than the Elva-Porsches being developed by Ollie Schmidt and Carl Haas with Porsche factory assistance. It was only 30.5 inches tall and had an 89-inch wheelbase, more than 8 inches shorter than an RS-61. Triumph disc brakes with aluminum Girling calipers were used at all corners—a decided improvement over the Porsche drums. A Triumph Herald rack was used, along with Armstrong adjustable coil-over shocks all

around. The A-arms were fabricated and fitted with heim joints for full adjustability, and three thicknesses of antiroll bars were made up. Special Dolphin 15-inch wheels were made up, 5.5 inches wide in front and 6.75 inches at the back, shod with Dunlop racing tires. An RS-60 five-speed transaxle with a 4.428 final drive was fitted.

For power, the Porphin could be fitted with either a 1,600-cc or 1,700-cc four-cam Porsche Carrera engine. These proven powerhouses put out between 160 and 180 horsepower at 7,800 rpm. Carburetion was by twin 46-millimeter Weber carbs. A large oil cooler was located behind the grille, flanked by two high-powered horns for Miles to signal his fellow drivers to *move over*.

The Porphin tasted first blood at Santa Barbara in May 1963. Miles was occupied elsewhere, so famed Morgan pilot Lew Spencer took his place. In the Saturday race, the new car had brake and clutch problems, but Spencer gamely held on to a sixth-overall finish. Sunday, the car did not start.

Miles took over in June and took a close second at Riverside behind Ron Bucknum in Old Yeller III. It was a very popular race, with the 1,700-cc "David" chasing the 6-liter "Goliath." At Pamona in July, the Porphin did not finish. Soon thereafter, Miles fell out with Zipper and joined Shelby American to become a famous Cobra pilot. There was a rumor that Porsche wanted Zipper to stop running the Porphin, but it was run one last time at the American Road Race of Champions in 1964. The race was a shootout for SCCA racers to determine who was best, and Davey Jordan was chosen to drive. He practiced with a 1,600-cc engine, and a hotter 1,700-cc was installed for the race. Despite clutch trouble, Jordan finished an excellent third overall, second-in-class to an Elva Porsche. The car was then stored at Zipper's, where it remained until the 1990s when it was restored and sold to an anonymous buyer in Europe.

The most successful Dolphin racer was Dan Parkinson, who won H-Modified at the SCCA runoffs in 1964 and 1966 with his 750-cc DOHC Abarth-powered car. Dolphin is believed to have built around ten sports-racer kits and five or six complete cars, before production wound down in 1964.

Don Maslin tries out a Dolphin sports-racer at Pomona. *Allen Kuhn*

Ken Miles prepares for battle in the Porphin at Riverside in 1964. *Allen Kuhn*

DOLPHIN

Dolphin Engineering
1080 N. Johnson Street
El Cajon, California

DOLPHIN FORMULA JUNIOR

Year built	**1960**
Engine	**Fiat four-cylinder**
Gearbox	**Fiat 600 four-speed**
Chassis	**space frame**
Front suspension	**independent, coil springs**
Rear suspension	**independent, coil springs**
Brakes	**Fiat drum**
Body material	**fiberglass**
Wheelbase	**85 inches**
Number built	**nine**

DOLPHIN INTERNATIONAL

Year built	**1961**
Engine	**Ford 105E**
Gearbox	**Fiat 600 four-speed**
Chassis	**space frame**
Front suspension	**independent, coil springs**
Rear suspension	**independent, coil springs**
Brakes	**Fiat drum**
Body material	**fiberglass**
Number built	**26**

DOLPHIN SPORTS-RACERS

Years built	**1961–1964**
Engines	**Coventry-Climax, Abarth 750, others**
Gearbox	**various**

Chassis	**space frame**
Front suspension	**independent, coil springs**
Rear suspension	**independent, coil springs**
Brakes	**Fiat drum/disc**
Body material	**fiberglass**
Wheelbase	**various**
Number built	**approximately 16**

PORPHIN

Year built	**1963**
Engines	**Porsche Carrera 1,600-cc or 1,700-cc**
Gearbox	**Porsche RS-60**
Chassis	**space frame**
Front suspension	**independent, coil springs**
Rear suspension	**independent, coil springs**
Brakes	**Girling disc**
Body material	**fiberglass**
Wheelbase	**89 inches**
Number built	**one**

DOLPHIN FORMULA 2

Year built	**1960**
Engine	**1,500-cc Alfa Romeo**
Gearbox	**Porsche**
Chassis	**space frame**
Front suspension	**independent, coil springs**
Rear suspension	**independent, coil springs**
Brakes	**disc**
Body material	**aluminum**
Number built	**one**

67

Eagle

Dan Gurney was one of the most versatile drivers of the 1960s, and his Eagle racing cars left their mark on Formula 1, F-5000, and the Indianapolis 500. In 1965, Gurney assembled a team of racing wizards and called his new enterprise All-American Racers (AAR). They were based out of Santa Ana, California, and began racing cars bought from other manufacturers, including a Lotus and two Halibrand Shrikes.

However, the intent was always to build their own cars, and in 1966, they constructed the first Eagles to compete at Indy. Gurney and initial partner Carroll Shelby wanted to take a shot at Formula 1 as well, so they convinced their primary sponsor, Goodyear Tires, to fund a derivative of their Indy car to take to Europe.

Eagle Formula 1

Len Terry designed the 1966 Eagle Indy car to be the basis of a Formula 1 car as well. Terry had designed the Lotus 38 Indy winner, and the new semimonocoque Eagle was similar in many respects,

Dan Gurney (right) and master fabricator Phil Remington were the power behind the Eagle effort. *Pete Lyons*

although lighter and more rigid. The Eagles also had more cockpit room to accommodate tall team drivers Gurney and Jerry Grant, both of whom towered over Lotus driver Jimmy Clark. Unlike many Indy cars of the era, the Eagle had the same length suspension arms on both sides, so that one basic design would work for road racing as well as ovals. The Grand Prix versions had thinner aluminum skins to shave 50 pounds off the weight, and a Hewland DG300 transaxle was used. Although the Grand Prix Eagles were built in America, they were based out of AAR's European headquarters (Anglo-American Racers) in England.

The intended powerplant was a V-12 penned by ex-BRM designer Aubrey Woods and built in England by Weslake and Co., which also worked with AAR on special heads for the Ford small-block V-8. The 60-degree V-12 was a beautiful engine, but it was not ready in time for the start of the 1966 season; a 2.7-liter Coventry-Climax FPF four-cylinder was pressed into service, installed in chassis number AAR-101. The new Eagle made its debut at the Grand Prix of Belgium at Spa, where Gurney was seventh (but unclassified) at the finish. At the French Grand Prix, he finished fifth, to pick up Eagle's first two World Championship points.

At midseason, the Weslake V-12 still had not shown up; Gurney had his engine expert, John Miller, develop the aged and uncompetitive Climax for more power. The V-12 finally debuted at Monza for the Italian Grand Prix, where it was installed in chassis number AAR-102. The untested engine failed, as it did the rest of the season.

The Weslake V-12 was a combination of an advanced cylinder head design, with four valves per

The Eagle Formula 1 car, shown at Watkins Glen in 1967, was one of the best-looking F1 cars of all times. *Pete Lyons*

cylinder, and a block similar to the BRM V-12 that Weslake had also worked on. Most Weslake V-12s produced 390 to 415 horsepower. AAR was constantly developing the chassis, reducing weight by substituting magnesium and titanium for aluminum wherever possible.

The 1967 season got off to a good start at the nonchampionship Race of Champions at Brands Hatch in England. Gurney won first overall and teammate Richie Ginther was running second until brake trouble spelled his undoing. The Weslake engine was now up to 413 horsepower, making it one of the most powerful Grand Prix engines of the era. The new Eagle came right at Spa, where Gurney outlasted Jackie Stewart's BRM to notch up the first Formula 1 victory for an American car piloted by an American driver.

Unfortunately, the rest of the season was downhill, as the Weslake engine lost its reliability. The engine problems continued the next season, and AAR took over development of the V-12. The engine was a good design, but the AAR effort was underfunded by Grand Prix standards. Although a magnesium-skinned Eagle was prepared for the 1969 season, it was never raced, and AAR turned its attention to other endeavors.

Eagle Formula 5000 (Eagle Formula A)

In 1968, the Sports Car Club of America changed the regulations for the Formula A class from 3-liter racing engines to 5-liter, stock-block-and-head, production mills. A professional series, the SCCA Grand Prix Championship, followed and the class became known as F-5000 (for 5,000 cc). AAR saw this as an opportunity to sell some racing cars.

The Eagle Formula A was a development of the 1968 Indy car, designed by Tony Southgate and featuring outboard suspension and a monocoque chassis. The body was visually similar to the Indy car but was slightly slimmer due to smaller 30-gallon fuel tanks. Brakes were disc all around with 11.75-inch ventilated rotors and either Girling or Aerheart calipers. The chassis sold for $11,500, less wheels, engine, and transaxle. The power package of choice was the Hewland LG600 five-speed box and a Weber-carbureted Chevy 302-ci Z-28 engine. Eagle also offered its own cast-magnesium 15-inch wheels (11 inches wide in front and 16 inches wide in back).

In 1968, Eagle customers dominated the new series, winning all but one of the eight events. Dr. Lou Sell took the crown after winning five times. Runner-up George Wintersteen's Eagle-Chevy won at Lime Rock and Donnybrooke. The Eagles were convincingly faster than the Lola T-140 (a tube frame design) and the American-built McKee.

The next season, the series was renamed the Continental Championship, and more buyers popped up as the series grew to 13 events. The Eagle chassis was basically unchanged, except that it was offered to fit the Plymouth V-8 as well. Wings became popular, and AAR developed one that was 45 inches wide, mounted directly to the rear hub carriers. The Chevy engine built muscle, as some teams switched from carbs to Lucas-timed fuel injection, giving up to 465 horsepower in the strongest Traco-prepared engines.

Tony Adamowicz won the championship by winning twice and consistently finishing near the top in his Eagle-Chevy. Sam Posey flew his Eagle to third in the championship, followed by Eagle-mounted John Cannon in fourth and Bobby Brown in sixth.

Tony Adamowicz won the 1969 Continental Championship in this Eagle F-5000 car. *Pete Lyons*

AAR did not build any more F-5000 models and, although some Eagles were still run after 1969, they were soon eclipsed by newer designs.

Eisert

Jerry Eisert, an experienced Indy car builder, decided to try his hand at road racing machinery when F-5000 came along. He built a number of conventional Chevy-powered cars that were run in the F-5000 Championship by Jack Eiteljorg, Stew McMillan, Fred Baker, and Dennis Ott.

The first Eisert F-A was a converted Indy car, originally built for J. Frank Harrison's team. It featured inboard front suspension and was powered by a Chevy V-8. In 1968, Eisert replaced it with a new car called the ERE-Chevy, a monocoque-chassis design that was slimmer and lighter than his earlier car. The English cars generally outclassed Eiserts, but McMillan finished a credible fifth at Donnybrook in 1968.

The Eisert F-5000 car was a development of a Chevy-powered Indy car. *Barry Heuer*

EAGLE

All-American Racers
2334 S. Broadway
Santa Ana, California

EAGLE-CLIMAX FORMULA 1

Year built	**1966**
Engine	**Coventry-Climax FPF 2.7-liter**
Gearbox	**Hewland**
Front suspension	**independent**
Rear suspension	**independent**
Brakes	**disc**
Body material	**fiberglass**
Weight, approx.	**1,240 pounds**
Wheelbase	**96.5 inches**
Number built	**one**

EAGLE-WESLAKE FORMULA 1

Years built	**1966–1968**
Engine	**Weslake V-12**
Gearbox	**Hewland**
Front suspension	**independent**
Rear suspension	**independent**
Brakes	**disc**
Body material	**fiberglass**
Weight	**1,190 pounds**
Wheelbase	**96.5 inches**
Number built	**three**

EAGLE FORMULA A (EAGLE FORMULA 5000)

Years built	**1968–1969**
Engines	**Chevy or Plymouth V-8**
Gearbox	**Hewland**
Front suspension	**independent**
Rear suspension	**independent**
Brakes	**disc**
Body material	**fiberglass**
Weight, approx.	**1,470 pounds**
Wheelbase	**96.3 inches**
Number built	**14**

Excalibur

Most car enthusiasts are familiar with the huge Excalibur neoclassics that were so popular with celebrities, neocelebrities, and real estate agents in the 1970s and 1980s. Each year, they seemed to acquire more chrome, more flash, and more weight. It's hard to believe that the same designer who penned the first of these luxury touring cars also designed a successful racing car powered by, of all things, a six-cylinder Kaiser engine!

In 1952, noted American industrial designer Brooks Stevens designed a sports car that could be driven on the street, yet also compete favorably on the track. He had been working with Kaiser-Frazer for some time and felt that its Henry J sedan was the perfect starting point for a midpriced sports machine. Stevens had been an official with the SCCA and had seen the rapidly growing interest in sports car racing, which was dominated at the time by European models. He felt that the drab, boring Kaiser-Frazer was due for the injection of charisma that a hot new sports car could provide.

Excalibur J

The 1951–1954 Henry J was one of the first "compact" cars built in America. It had a 100-inch wheelbase and a choice of four- or six-cylinder Willys engines. Due to its light weight, it was surprisingly quick, but the styling was quirky and sales were slow. The reasonable size and light weight made it ideal as the basis for a sports car, and Stevens convinced Kaiser-Frazer officials to provide three chassis for him to finish out as evaluation prototypes of his design called the Excalibur J.

One car was fitted with a Willys F-head six; the other received a Henry J 161-ci L-head six. A third car also received the more powerful F-head engine. (Both engines displaced 161.1 ci.) They were modified with headers, improved ignition, and three SU carbs pirated from MG TDs. It was initially planned to power one car with a 1.9-liter Alfa Romeo engine, but none were raced with this unit. The drum brakes were fitted with angled fins that scooped cool air over their surfaces. Although stock suspension parts were used, stiffer sway bars were fitted and the geometry adjusted with input from Willys engineers.

Stevens and business associate Charles Cowdin Jr. designed the half-cycle-fendered body. It was a simple design with an enclosed back end, cycle fenders in front, a rectangular radiator opening, and an air scoop above. The body was designed to have few compound curves to make construction cheaper. Wire wheels added to the sports car flavor, as did hot rod-style lights. The only thing that gave away its pedestrian origins was a column shifter. Bumpers were fitted for street use, but could be removed for racing.

The Excalibur J ran for the first time at Janesville Airport Races in July 1952, where it finished an excellent second in class, despite suffering from development problems. The ignition system was breaking down at 4,500 rpm, although the engines were later made to rev to 6,500 rpm. In testing, the F-head version turned the quarter-mile in 15 sec-

Brooks Stevens built the excellent Excalibur J racing cars. Jim Feld and Robert Gary finished 17th at Sebring in 1954 with this car. *Ozzie Lyons*

onds and topped out at 125 miles per hour—impressive stuff at the time. At Sebring in 1953, an Excalibur J driven by Dick Irish was running well until a broken ring and pinion put them too far back to be listed as finishers.

Stevens was recognized at the 1953 International Motor Sports Show for "having created an outstanding American competition sports car in the low-priced field." Stevens estimated a production version would cost between $2,000 and $3,000. A poll at the show, where one of the Excalibur Js was on display, showed a great interest in the new car by potential customers. However, Kaiser-Frazer never took Stevens up on producing the car, and only the three prototypes were built.

Stevens continued to campaign the cars, driven by Hal Ulrich, Ralph Knudson, Bob Gary, Bob Goldich, Dick Irish, and Jim Feld. In 1952 and 1953, the Excalibur Js picked up nine first-place trophies, six second places, four thirds, and one fourth, out of 16 races. They were capable of keeping up with Jaguar XK-120s, Frazer-Nashes, and other examples of European iron.

In 1955, the fenders were fared into the body, as the cycle-fendered look became less popular. In 1957, one car was stuffed with the tired Jaguar six from an XK-140. It was duly supercharged to bump it up into the undersupported SCCA B-Modified class, where the persistent Ulrich won the National Championship. The racing effort outlived Kaiser-Frazer, which merged with Willys, then moved its passenger car operations to Argentina in 1955, leaving only the profitable Jeep production in the United States.

Excalibur Hawk

After failing to convince Kaiser-Frazer management to build a proper sports car in the 1950s, Stevens tried again with Studebaker in 1963. He felt the Avanti was pretty, but not a true sports car and certainly incapable of being raced anywhere but at Bonneville. So Stevens brewed up an unusual little coupe powered by a supercharged Studebaker R2 289-ci V-8 engine. Bob Webb built a custom space frame (using Studebaker running gear), and disc brakes were fitted up front, along with wire wheels all around.

The styling was aggressive, if not entirely harmonious. Its sleek nose and fastback coupe top still look good today, but the tailfins and side scoop arrangement could have been better integrated. Named the Excalibur Hawk, it was baptized by fire at the 1963 Road America 500, where it retired with a broken track bar bolt. It was then tested at the Indy Speedway before being raced in local SCCA races, culminating in an accident at Meadowdale. Studebaker had other paths to follow (leading to its extermination) and decided to pass on the Hawk. Too bad—it was a clever design and a better car than the lovely Avanti. The Hawk has since been restored and is active in vintage events.

Excalibur Mk.VI

The Mk.VI is one of those cars that surfaced to great fanfare, then immediately sank below the waves. Featured in *Road & Track* in 1963, the Mk.VI was designed and built by Brooks' son, David Stevens. He incorporated technology learned from racing go karts. From the outside it looked good, with a lovely fiberglass body and the injector stacks from a midmounted Lincoln V-8 poking up behind the driver. From there it got weird. There was no suspension at all in the back, where the rear axle was solid-mounted to the sheet aluminum monocoque chassis. In front, a beam axle pivoted at its center point to allow for slight road irregularities. Rack-and-pinion steering was used, along with a torque converter that gave only one forward speed,

plus reverse. The bored-out 487-ci Lincoln was modified to produce over 400 horsepower, and dry weight was listed as under 1,000 pounds. The flexing of the tall tires, 6.50x16 in front and 7.00x16 in the back, compensated for road bumps. Whether the Mk.VI was ever run is unknown.

Fibersport

Crosley Specials were the mainstay of H-Modified racing in the 1950s. And although most were one-offs built by enterprising racers, there were a few sold in kit or ready-to-race form. One of the most successful was the Fibersport, built by John C. Mays; his son, Bill Mays; and John Burmaster. Mays was a respected tuner of small, imported engines and felt there was a need for a less expensive domestic alternative to the Bandinis and Nardis of the time. Introduced in 1952, the Fibersport could be used on the street but was primarily intended for the track. The fiberglass body was contemporary in design, with slab sides and a steeply raked nose. The headlights were usually inside the oval grille, but light placement and grille shape varied.

Bodies were sold to other racers and ended up on the Siam Special and others. The street body ($750) had five layers of fiberglass and a proper trunk, two doors, molded bucket seats, and a high-quality finish with stiffening lips on all panels. The race bodies ($650) had only four layers for less weight, only one door on the passenger side, and no trunk.

Fibersport also offered two chassis, one based on a modified Crosley frame with Crosley Hotshot or Super Sport suspension at both ends. A more advanced tube frame offered similar front suspension but with a choice of leaf or coil suspension in back.

The 76-horsepower, 750-cc Crosley engine was a

Three Fibersports line up for the start at Smart Field in 1956. Note the differences in grilles and trim. *Bill Mays*

common engine choice for a racer, but street versions used bored-and-stroked versions with up to 900 cc. Mays developed and patented a "stepped" taper intake manifold that increased flow over conventional smooth-wall manifolds. A special adapter mounted the Crosley engine to a Morris Minor transmission and a Crosley rear axle.

In race tune, Fibersports were clocked at 122 miles per hour at Meadowdale, with a 0-to-60 time of 11.4 seconds and quarter-miles in the 18.2 range (very impressive for 750 cc). Turnkey racers sold for $2,450 to $2,850, depending on equipment specified.

The "works" fielded a two-car team with different grilles and headlight placement from production models, and these won many races. Bill Mays says the first car was based on a 1951 Crosley Super Sport frame, which was "dropped" and lightened with lots of holes. They also intended to make the frame more flexible, which they reasoned would make the Crosley beam axles work better over rough surfaces. The body was fiberglassed to the frame. John Mays was a half-second off the absolute lap record at Wilmott Hills and beat a Le Mans D-B at Waterloo, South Carolina. Bill Mays says the car won 32 races in 39 starts.

Bill Mays has the first car built, and he says they built three other similar cars. The last Fibersport was built for John Morse in 1962.

The Ford GT Mk.I was a classic in terms of looks and performance. With small-block Ford engines, they won Le Mans in 1968 and 1969. *Harold Pace*

FIBERSPORT	
Fibersport	
Bloomington, Illinois	
FIBERSPORT-CROSLEY	
Years built	**1952–1962**
Engine	**750-cc Crosley**
Gearbox	**Morris four-speed**
Front suspension	**live axle**
Rear suspension	**live axle**
Brakes	**drum**
Body material	**fiberglass**
Weight, approx.	**1,100 pounds**
Wheelbase	**86 inches**
Number built	**five complete cars, plus ten to 12 bodies**

Ford

The Ford GT was the result of a feud that got out of hand. In the early 1960s, Henry Ford II decided that Ford needed some more glamour to spice up its lackluster domestic lineup. Ford considered buying Rolls-Royce, but settled on the jewel in the international racing crown, Ferrari. After months of negotiation, Enzo Ferrari and Ford's representative, Don Frey, could not agree on the details, so Ford stomped away angry, vowing to beat Ferrari at his own game. The Ford GT would do just that.

Ford GT Mk.I

Although Ford press releases touted the role of Ford's newly implemented computer programs in the development of the new Ford GT racing car, all the basic design work was done in England the old-fashioned way—by trial and error. Starting with an existing Ford-powered endurance-racing car, the Lola Mk.6 GT, the newly formed Ford Advanced Vehicles (FAV) team developed the Ford GT in its Slough, England, headquarters. Powered by a 350-horsepower version of the aluminum Ford pushrod Indy engine, the GT was quick but unreliable. It was soon nicknamed the GT40 due to its low 40-inch height. In 1964, the first Ford GTs didn't exactly set the world on fire—too little time and unrealistic expectations from upper management meant the GT frequently showed up at the track untested and

inadequately developed. The Colotti gearbox was a particularly weak link, later replaced in most GT40s by a ZF five-speed unit.

The first race for the immaculate white Ford GT was at the Nurburgring in Germany, where the single car entered started second on the grid (to a Ferrari 275P) but failed to finish due to suspension failure. Then it was on to Le Mans, where the Ford brass thought it would be a walkover for their new hi-tech toy. Not quite. The three GTs entered qualified well, with Richie Ginther second to a Ferrari 330P. In the race, the Fords took off in the lead, but after four hours, one GT caught fire and soon a second succumbed to gearbox failure. The last car made it to hour 14 before its gearbox failed. The Ford team went back to the drawing board.

The next race was at Reims, France, where the entire Ford team once again retired early with engine and gearbox woes. All the stops were pulled out for a season-ending victory at Nassau, but it was not to be, as the entire team succumbed to suspension failure. The reality of endurance racing was starting to sink in at Ford headquarters, as they counted the fortune they had spent to lose every race of the season.

Ford turned the racing program over to Shelby American for the 1965 season. Shelby immediately set to work simplifying the car and making it more durable. Ford started its own race shop, Kar Kraft, in

72

Dearborn to replace FAV as the primary development team. Out went the exotic aluminum engines, replaced by the proven cast-iron Cobra 289 with four Webers. This excellent engine produced 375 horsepower and was wet-sumped for use in the GT. Other changes included replacing the original wire wheels with wider Halibrand mags, revamping all the ducting and internal aerodynamics, and painting the cars a stunning dark blue with white stripes. The brakes were also the recipients of much development, but they continued to run hot due to the considerable weight (2,200 pounds), and most changes were limited to making them easier to service and replace at the track.

Shelby American came out fighting at Daytona, taking an easy win over its own Cobra Daytona coupes and a single Ferrari 330P2. At Sebring, the Ford team was dealt a setback when the organizers invented a special class for Jim Hall's Chaparral 2A to run in. Normally, the Texas roadrunner was not legal for FIA events, and it was much lighter than the GT. Though not expected to go the distance, the lone Chaparral won going away. The second-place Ford GT won its class, but Ford was angered by the Chaparral's inclusion. The Fords faltered in the next three events at the Targa Florio, Monza, and the Nurburgring. Then it was on to Le Mans, where the Ford GT Mk.I got a big brother.

Ford GT Mk.II

Ford engine experts knew they had a secret weapon capable of pumping out lots more power than the Cobra 289, and it wouldn't even be trying hard—the NASCAR 427-ci FE engine. This powerhouse was capable of over 485 horsepower, but at 550 pounds, it was 118 pounds heavier than the 289. Ford ordered two chassis and built the first Mk.II models, with 427s sporting aluminum heads, a single 780-cfm Holley four-barrel carb, and a special Kar Kraft transaxle using production Ford top-loader gears. The big engine was detuned from NASCAR trim to last longer and run on the low-octane gasoline available at Le Mans. Initially, the Mk.II was a disaster. It was ill-handling and capable of a lot more

top speed (over 200 miles per hour) than its aerodynamic package could cope with. But Ford was determined to see the 427s run at Le Mans anyway, so two underdeveloped cars were brought along.

At Le Mans in 1965, Ford entered two Mk.IIs and three Mk.Is, along with five Cobras. Ferrari countered with 12 factory and privateer racers. When the smoke had cleared, all five Fords were among the dead, along with the works Ferraris. A privately entered Ferrari 275LM took home all the marbles, and even the previously all-conquering Cobras were beaten by a Ferrari 275GTB in the GT class. It was another downer year in the blue oval camp but, while they were running, the Mk.IIs had shown a good turn of speed, so the prospects for the next season were improved.

For 1966, Ford made some fundamental changes in its race organization. Three teams would be running GTs in all the important races, with stock car champs Holman-Moody and European sedan ace Alan Mann joining Shelby American in the hunt. (This did not go down well at Shelby American, though it had been stretched thin the previous season.) Holman-Moody did some serious development on the Mk.II program, including fabricating quick-change brake rotors that made them easier to replace at the track. Just to cover all the bases, Mann concentrated on developing two ultralightweight Mk.Is with small-block engines.

The gold Ford GT Mk.II in the lead was prepared by Holman-Moody. Two Mk.IVs follow. *Harold Pace*

The Mk.II models were assembled in the United States from chassis built by FAV in England. By now, the American teams were doing all the development. Ford went to the wind tunnel to work on the basic shape, which was subtly revised for more stability. Special dynos were rigged to run engines for up to 40 hours to simulate the grind of endurance racing. When an engine failed, it was evaluated and repaired, and the tests started again!

At Daytona in 1966, Ford GTs finished first through fifth to show they were ready for action, and then steamrolled over light Ferrari and Chaparral opposition at Sebring as well. At this point, it was obvious the Mk.II was competitive and reliable, so Alan Mann sold his GT Mk.Is and was equipped with Mk.IIs. However, Ferraris won at Monza, the Targa Florio, and Spa, and the lone Chaparral was victorious at the Nurburgring. In the face of this serious opposition, Ford pulled out all the stops for Le Mans.

Fourteen Ford entries lined up against the same number of Ferraris at Le Mans, but only two of the red cars from Maranello were factory entries. In the race, the Fords ran strong, while the Ferrari 330P3s did not. At the end, it was a question of which Ford GT would win, and they took a staged one-two-three formation to the flag. Ford capped the season by winning the FIA Manufacturers' Championship. In three years, the GT had gone from ungainly loser to unquestioned champion.

Ford GT Mk.IV

Even as the Mk.II was making good in 1966, Ford was developing a successor called the J-Car. Henry Ford was determined to defend his Le Mans win the following year, and this time he wanted it done in a car made completely in America, preferably driven by Americans. The Ford computers had been working overtime spewing out inaccurate data that was being used to build body shapes that were as unstable as they were ugly. The chassis was a radical step forward—a sandwich of aluminum sheets on each side of an aluminum honeycomb material, bonded together with an epoxy resin. This type of construction was already being used in aircraft, but this was its first use in automobiles. The chief benefit was the loss of 250 pounds, compared to a Mk.II chassis. The body was completely new, with a rear end that resembled a station wagon and a wide nose with what looked like fangs on each side. The new car proved to be a nightmare to develop. The final straw came when team stalwart Ken Miles was killed testing a J-Car built at Riverside. The bonded chassis came apart and Miles was thrown out. At this point, the J-Car was shelved for the 1966 season, but readied for 1967 when new Ferrari models were expected to surpass the Mk.II.

The Ford GT team went back to work on the J-Car, discarding theoretical solutions in favor of proven concepts. Chief engineer Phil Remington and

his crew threw away the body and made their own, based on practical experience. They ended up with a fastback tail and a more conventional (nonfanged) nose. The chassis was beefed up and attached with rivets in addition to the bonding process. Under the hood was the familiar 427-ci Ford engine, now with twin Holley four-barrels. The result was the Ford GT Mk.IV (the Mk.III was a street version of the Mk.I).

The Ford G7A was not the winner that Ford fans were hoping for in the Can-Am. *Pete Lyons*

Daytona was the first race of the 1967 season, and the results showed that Ford had been correct to anticipate a renewed Ferrari threat. The Mk.IVs were not ready, so Ford relied on the old Mk.IIs. Ferrari snatched an easy one-two-three photo finish. The danger was real.

The Mk.IV made its debut at Sebring, where it won easily after the works Ferraris didn't show and the Chaparrals broke down. The only other race run by the Mk.IV was Le Mans, where four were entered, along with three Mk.IIbs (upgraded Mk.IIs) and three GT40s in the Sports class. Against them were the

might of the Ferrari and Chaparral teams, which were much faster than the year before. But in the race, the team of Dan Gurney and A. J. Foyt took the flag in their Shelby American–entered Mk.IV, followed by two Ferrari 330P4s and the Bruce McLaren/Mark Donahue Mk.IV in fourth. When the race was over, a jubilant Gurney sprayed the crowd (including Henry Ford II) with champagne, starting a tradition that has continued to this day.

After the 1967 Le Mans win, Ford folded its tents and closed down the Ford GT program. Ferrari, Mirage, Chaparral, and Porsche traded wins the rest of the season and Ferrari emerged with the 1967 Manufacturers' Championship. But the Ford GT was not through yet. John Wyer, who had started FAV, took over a team of privately entered Ford GTs to run in 1968 and 1969. Incredibly, he won Le Mans both years, and won the Manufacturers' Championship in 1968. The old warrior had a four-year stranglehold on the most prestigious race in the world, and both the English and the Americans had much to be proud of.

Ford G7A

Ford may have conquered Le Mans, but it never got a handle on the Can-Am. In 1967, three teams were trying to turn Ford-based racers into winners, with absolutely no results. Shelby tried the lackluster

The Ford GT Mk.IV looked like no other Ford GT. One won Le Mans in 1967. *Harold Pace*

Len Terry King Cobra, Holman-Moody struggled with the Honker II, and Kar Kraft, the in-house Ford operation that had developed the Le Mans-winning Mk.IV, took its best shot with the Ford G7A.

Starting with a Ford GT Mk.IV honeycomb aluminum chassis, Kar Kraft, under the command of Don Frey and Roy Lunn, added more fuel tank capacity for 64 gallons of fuel. The conventional Mk.IV suspension was untouched, and Ford cast its own 15-inch magnesium wheels, an inch shorter than the wheels used at Le Mans.

Ford experimented with the Mk.IV's four-speed manual gearbox and a two-speed automatic transaxle. A wedge-shaped body was developed in the Ford wind tunnel, along with a two-part wing that carried the aero load directly to the wheel hubs. The driver could angle the wings via a cockpit lever. Several engines were discussed, including one called the "Calliope," which had huge intake stacks feeding two intake valves per cylinder (plus one exhaust valve per cylinder), controlled by two block-mounted camshafts. It was designed to be around 400 ci, with the possibility of being enlarged later. But it was all for naught—the endurance-racer-based G7A was too heavy to be a serious contender.

Ford spent 1967 and 1968 testing and finally threw in the towel. In 1969, the only car built was sold (along with a spare chassis) for a dollar to mechanics Charlie and Ken Agapiou. Gone were the funky wings, oddball engines, and even the gearbox. In went a Hewland five-speed and various Ford V-8s (427-, 429-, and 494-ci). A conventional wing was added as well.

The G7A was run for two years, but it was never competitive with the front-line teams. Its one brief shining moment was at the nonchampionship Mount Fuji race in Japan, where it finished second to a factory Toyota. It was later wrecked. One chassis has since been rebuilt as a Ford GT Mk.IV replica, while the other someday will be restored as the G7A.

Formcar

Formula Vee is the most popular class ever devised for amateur racing. Thousands of cars have been built, and their deceptively fast speed, for a car based on a 1,200-cc Volkswagen, has left wide grins permanently etched on the faces of racers the world over. And all those happy would-be Fangios have one man to thank—Hubert Brundage. Brundage owned the first VW distributorship to emerge after Volkswagen broke off its exclusive relationship with Max Hoffman in the late 1950s. Brundage's territory included Florida, Georgia, and South Carolina, and he established his operation in Jacksonville, Florida. His company was Brundage Motors, and this name was later shortened to its telex address, "Brumos," a name now familiar to Porsche fans the world over for its long-standing racing efforts.

Brundage was an avid racer, and he wanted a unique car that used his VW engines to compete in Formula Junior racing. In 1959, he ordered a one-off Formula Junior from the Nardi company in Italy. Brundage sent along a new VW sedan, which Nardi cannibalized for parts to build a new racer resembling a pint-sized Auto Union GP car. However, the Nardi FV was easy meat for the sophisticated (and expensive) Coopers and Loti that were dominating the class, and Brundage lost interest. At the same time, VW, which had a nonracing policy, objected to its distributor racing a car built from its components, so Brundage sold the Nardi, along with a second chassis he had ordered as a spare. Lucky us.

FORD

Ford Motor Company
Dearborn, Michigan

FORD GT MK.I

Years built **1963–1967**
Engines . . . . **Ford V-8 (256 or 289 ci)**
Gearboxes . . . . **Colotti or ZF four-speed**
Front suspension . . . . **independent**
Rear suspension . . . . . **independent**
Brakes . . . . **Girling disc**
Body material . . . . **fiberglass**
Weight, approx. . . . . . **2,200 pounds**
Wheelbase . . . . **95 inches**
Number built . . . . **approximately 105**

FORD GT MK.II

Years built **1965–1966**
Engine . . . . **Ford 427 ci**
Gearbox . . . . **Kar-Kraft four-speed**
Front suspension . . . . **independent**
Rear suspension . . . . . **independent**
Brakes . . . . **Girling disc**
Body material . . . . **fiberglass**
Weight, approx. . . . . . **2,682 pounds (wet)**
Wheelbase . . . . **95 inches**
Number built . . . . **nine**

FORD GT MK.IV

Year built **1967**
Engine . . . . **Ford 427 ci**
Gearbox . . . . **Kar-Kraft four-speed**
Front suspension . . . . **independent**
Rear suspension . . . . . **independent**
Brakes . . . . **Girling disc**
Body material . . . . **fiberglass**
Weight, approx. . . . . . **2,290 pounds (wet)**
Wheelbase . . . . **95 inches**
Number built . . . . **nine**

FORD G7A

Year built **1967**
Engine . . . . **Ford V-8s**
Gearbox . . . . **Hewland**
Front suspension . . . . **independent**
Rear suspension . . . . . **independent**
Brakes . . . . **Kelsey-Hayes disc**
Body material . . . . **fiberglass**
Number built . . . . **two**

The Formcar was the first of the Vees. Formula Vee became the most popular club racing class of all time. *Harold Pace*

The first production Formula Vee was the Formcar. It was a landmark design in club racing. *Harold Pace*

Bill Duckworth and George Smith had seen the Nardi run and were pretty impressed. They had the vision of coordinating a new racing class just for cars like it, so Brundage sold them his two Nardis for a dollar! Smith had been involved in sailboat racing for some time and had seen the success of the Star Class, which was based on a rigid set of regulations that spelled out every dimension and part that could be used. The two partners figured a similar concept would work for their new class, which they called Formula Vee.

In 1962, they approached the SCCA with a set of regulations, basically drawn up by measuring the Nardi and requiring that all Formula Vees adhere to the exact same dimensions. The SCCA took a wait-and-see attitude, so Smith and Duckworth began selling copies of their new racer, called the Formcar.

The Formcar was a simple car, with a sturdy space frame that accepted VW Type 1 (1,200-cc) running gear and suspension. It weighed 825 pounds and was fitted with stock VW steel wheels and drum brakes. The engines were tightly regulated, and stock VW transaxles were required (the sedans and vans had slightly different third gears, and either could be used). The engines were turned around and mounted in the middle of the frame, which required swapping the position of the ring gear to achieve correct direction of rotation. Coil-over shocks were used for rear springing, while one of the front torsion bars was removed and replaced with a sway bar. Although the Nardi had an aluminum body, Formcars had fiberglass panels made from molds pulled off the

Nardi originals. Most Formcars were sold in kit form for $945, and a network of dealers sprang up around the country. By 1964, the Formcars were so numerous that the SCCA accepted the new class for National events.

Rival Formula Vee manufacturers Autodynamics and Beach soon joined Formcar, which persuaded the SCCA to ease the dimensional requirements to allow some innovation in body and chassis design without diluting the basic concept. However, Formcar owners won the majority of races in 1963 and 1964, including the 1964 American Road Race of Champions and the highly publicized 1963 Nassau FV race. There had been some initial skepticism of a race car based on such humble origins, but this was soon silenced when the Formcars started lapping at the same speeds as racing Porsche 356s and Sunbeam Alpines. In short order, FV was the most popular SCCA class, and it has remained a big hit to this day.

The Formcar stayed basically the same through its life, but there were minor upgrades each year from the Mk.1 (1963), Mk.II (1964), and Mk.III (1965). After 1965, the other FV manufacturers had passed by the Formcar in terms of technology, and Formcar ceased operations. The popularity of vintage racing, beginning in the 1980s, has brought Formcars back to the tracks again. Vintage FVs are now as numerous as new FVs, and the distinctive and personable Formcars are still a winner among drivers and fans.

FORMCAR

Formcar Constructors, Inc.
1229 West Robinson Avenue
Orlando, Florida

FORMCAR FORMULA VEES
Years built	1963–1965
Engine	1,200-cc Volkswagen
Gearbox	Volkswagen
Front suspension	trailing link
Rear suspension	swing axles
Brakes	drum
Body material	fiberglass
Weight, approx.	825 pounds
Wheelbase	82 inches
Number built	unknown

Forsgrini

Brothers Lyle and Dale Forsgren started out racing karts in the 1950s, then switched to a Fiat-Abarth before building their first special in 1960. They later built a large number of specials and customer-version racing cars.

Forsgrini Specials

Their first H-Modified was built out of Renault 4CV running gear with a Crosley engine. It was midengined and wore an Almquist fiberglass body. The Forsgrens picked an Italian-ized version of their name for their new creations.

Their second car, the Forsgrini Monte Carlo, was another midengined H-Modified based on Fiat parts. This time, Dale made the body, and many other components were also made by the brothers. This car proved to be quite successful in 1961 and 1962, and in 1966 Lyle finished second at the ARRC with an upgraded version.

The Martini came next, powered by a Renault Dauphine engine. Then came the Monaco, an 1,100-cc Ford-powered car built for G-Modified. One of the best models was the Veloce, an Alfa Romeo-powered F-Modified that Lyle used to great effect against Lotus 23s in the early 1960s. In 1964, the Forsgrens built a new H-Modified and passed their old cars on to new owners.

Forsgrini Customer Cars

In 1968, Lyle quit the aircraft business to design and build race cars full time. He built the highly competitive Forsgrini Mk.10 Formula C car for Mike Campbell, who won his class at the 1968 ARRC. This car featured a hydraulically controlled, high-mounted rear wing, the first run on a winning formula car at the ARRC.

That same year, Dale finished second in D-Sports Racing at the ARRC in a Forsgrini as well. In addition to the FC cars, Forsgrini offered the Mk.12 Formula Ford, but it failed to make much of an impact.

Forsgrini F-5000

Forsgrini made a concerted effort to build an effective F-5000 car. In 1968, Lyle Forsgren came out with the Forsgrini Mk.10D, a Chevy-powered F-5000 car, to run in the professional championships. He ran it at Laguna Seca that year, finishing a promising fifth in class and 12th overall (behind four FB cars). It was to be the high point for the big Forsgrinis.

The new Forsgrini Mk.11 made its debut in 1969, driven by Harry Swanson to a 13th at the Seattle pro event. Lyle also drove one to a DNF at Riverside. For 1970, the new Mk.14 came out, but it was never in the hunt, entering three events with a best finish of 15th.

Mike Campbell took his Ford Boss 302-powered Mk.14 to Australia for the Tasman Championship in 1970, finishing in the points with a sixth at the Lady

Wigram Trophy race. Otherwise, he was a midpack runner.

Lyle Forsgren got out of the racing business in 1971, moving to Oshkosh, Wisconsin, to work for Mercury Marine. He built some fine cars and a fair number have survived to race again.

A Forsgrini sports-racer (No. 600) leads the pack. *Paul Bova collection*

Lyle Forsgren continued to build formula and sports-racing cars in the late 1960s. Here, he poses in a Formula 5000 car. *Paul Bova collection*

FORSGRINI

Forsgrini Engineering
Issaquah, Washington

FORSGRINI SPECIALS

Years built	**1960–1967**
Engines	**Fiat, Alfa, Ford, Renault, Crosley**
Gearbox	**four-speed**
Front suspension	**independent**
Rear suspension	**independent**
Number built	**six**

FORSGRINI MK.10 FC

Year built	**1968**
Engine	**Ford**
Gearbox	**Hewland**
Front suspension	**independent**
Rear suspension	**independent**
Brakes	**disc**
Body material	**fiberglass**
Number built	**two**

FORSGRINI MK.12 FF

Years built	**1968–1969**
Engine	**Ford**
Gearbox	**Hewland**
Front suspension	**independent**
Rear suspension	**independent**
Brakes	**disc**
Body material	**fiberglass**
Number built	**unknown**

FORSGRINI MK.10–MK.14 F-5000

Years built	**1968–1979**
Engines	**Ford or Chevy**
Gearbox	**Hewland**
Front suspension	**independent**
Rear suspension	**independent**
Brakes	**disc**
Body material	**fiberglass**
Number built	**unknown**

Genie

See Huffaker entry.

Grady

Henry Grady had teamed with Gene Beach to build the first three Beaches (see Beach entry), but in 1961 they went their separate ways. Grady built two more cars that resembled the original Begras. They were both midengined sports-racers with aluminum bodies. From the front, they looked a lot like the Begras, but the tails were shorter. For the first one, Grady installed a 1-liter Alfa Romeo twin cam, made by de-stroking a 1,300-cc Alfa. The car was raced in Florida, but a subsequent owner blew up the one-off engine and installed a Volkswagen. At one point, the car lost its correct identity and was sold as a Begra.

Henry Grady built this Alfa-powered Grady 1 racer after splitting with Gene Beach. *Barry LeVan collection*

The second Grady sports-racer used two Honda 305-cc motorcycle engines. *Nick England collection*

The car has recently been identified and restored to Alfa power by Barry LeVan in Pennsylvania. Grady also built a similar car that was powered by a Honda motorcycle engine, one of the first uses of these engines in SCCA racing. It was sold and promptly disappeared.

Hamill

Ed Hamill built three sports-racing cars for big-bore racing in the 1960s. The first was the SR-2, a midengined design with a steel tube frame and bonded aluminum strengthening panels, which he built in 1964. The body was an attractive shape with a low, rectangular grille. Two SR-3s followed, one raced by Hamill and one by Roy Kumnick. McKee transaxles were used, along with Ford brakes and various Oldsmobile, Repco, and Chevy V-8 engines.

Hamill ran the 1966 USRRC season, finishing an

The Hamill SR-3 (No. 99) ran at Riverside in 1965. A McKee is No. 14, while No. 55 is a Cheetah. *Allen Kuhn*

excellent fifth at Las Vegas and sixth at Riverside, powered by Oldsmobile V-8s. He ran the Can-Am series the same year, with the best result being a 12th at Riverside with a Chevy engine. Kumnick entered the 1967 Riverside Can-Am but did not start. Hamill retired at the end of the1966 season.

Howmet

Howmet was a New York manufacturer of aluminum products that decided auto racing would allow it to raise the profile (and the stock value) of the company. Since Howmet knew nothing about racing, it had Ray Heppenstall run the effort out of his shop in Philadelphia. Heppenstall was a mechanic and racing driver with vast experience with all types of road racing cars.

Howmet Falcon

Although technically a Howmet, this Falcon was a modified Ford Falcon that Heppenstall built to run at Daytona in 1967. It was a duplicate of the Falcon Monte Carlo Sprints that Ford had homologated to run in European rallies, with

fiberglass doors, hood, and trunk lid. At Daytona, it was classified as a Touring car, but the Ford factory people were not happy, as they were more interested in promoting Mustangs at that time. Heppenstall had an ongoing adversarial relationship with Ford. Heppenstall and Bill Sealey finished 12th overall and second-in-class.

The same Falcon was then modified with Triumph wheel arches, wider wheels, and a quartet of Webers, to be officially classified as a Howmet GT Sprint. Heppenstall also blanked out the rear quarter windows and installed landau bars. It next ran in the Prototype class at Sebring in 1967, driven by Heppenstall, Bob Nagel, and Sealey. Despite numerous gearbox and oil filter problems, it finished 19th overall and fourth-in-class. These respectable finishes prompted sponsor Howmet to invest in the development of the first successful American turbine-powered racing car.

Howmet Turbine

Despite his lack of formal engineering training (or perhaps because of it), Heppenstall was able to put together a race-ready turbine car in a matter of months. The FIA came up with an equivalency formula that allowed the turbine to participate as a 3-liter prototype. A used chassis was sourced from race car builder Bob McKee, and a top and gullwing doors were fabricated to go with a Porsche 906 windscreen. The chassis was typical of McKee Can-Am cars, with coil-over suspension and American

It looks like a Ford Falcon, but this was officially a Howmet Falcon. *Bob Harrington*

The Howmet Turbine, shown at Sebring in 1968, was one of the best turbine-powered racing cars of all time. *Pete Lyons*

mag wheels. McKee also built a second car and spares for the team.

A Continental turbine was obtained that was originally intended for an aborted light helicopter project. It produced 235 horsepower at 57,500 (!) raucous rpm and weighed only 130 pounds, but Heppenstall found that the engine quickly lost power as track temperatures increased. A McKee gearbox was adapted with a second set of quick-change gears in the opposite end, inverted and turned back-to-front. Although it sounds complicated, all the changes were made with a minimum of special parts or engineering work. The entire two-car project, including paying Continental for its work on the engines, was less than $160,000.

The first race for the new car was at Daytona in 1968, where Heppenstall, Dick Thompson, and Ed Lowther drove it. It qualified an impressive seventh and ran as high as sixth. Unfortunately, a butterfly valve that controlled engine speed failed, resulting in Lowther nailing the wall.

At Sebring, the car qualified third, only 1.2 seconds off the pace, but it was put out by motor mount failure after running as high as seventh. From Sebring, the team crossed the pond to the BOAC 500 six-hour race, where the throttle jammed open, sending Thompson off the track and out of the race. The Howmet also failed at the Guard's Cup Race at Oulton Park.

Back in the United States, the team ventured to the SCCA National at Huntsville, Alabama, where

Heppenstall won his class. At the Marlboro 300, Heppenstall and Dick Thompson took an easy win and also won an SCCA race at Shreveport, Louisiana.

A second car joined the team at the Watkins Glen six-hour race in July. The new car had a slightly longer wheelbase. Thompson and Heppenstall drove the new model, teamed with Hugh Dibley and Bob Tullius in the old one. They qualified ninth and 10th on the grid, with Thompson and Heppenstall finishing an excellent third overall (the first and only FIA points won by a turbine car).

The season ended at Le Mans, where the Howmets were down on top speed to the competition. One car was disqualified after losing time to a wheel bearing failure, and Thompson rolled the second car.

It was the end of the road for the Howmet Turbines in road racing, although Heppenstall had the damaged car converted into a roadster and set six turbine speed records on the access roads to Talledega Speedway. Both original Howmets survive today, joined by a third car built up from spare parts.

HSM

The HSM was an early Junior based on DKW running gear. James Reardon, Ray Heppenstall, and Harold Baumann built the car at Haverford Sport Motor in Haverford, Pennsylvania. The HSM was a midengined design with Volkswagen front suspension and a complete DKW front-drive engine and transmission package in back. The rear hubs, which had originally been on the front of a DKW, were welded up to prevent them from steering. A ladder frame was built from rectangular tubing with a 75.5-inch wheelbase. Reardon built 1,080-cc DKW engines that produced 83 horsepower. At least three cars were built.

Huffaker

Huffaker Engineering has been successful building sports-racers, production cars, Trans-Am sedans, formula cars, and Indy racers. Their engines have powered amateur and semipro drivers to hundreds of club-racing victories and dozens of SCCA National Championships. Starting with specials and front-engined Formula Juniors, Joe Huffaker left his mark on Jaguars, MGs, and many otherproduction racers.

The Marston Healey was the first road racing car built by Joe Huffaker. *Harold Pace*

Marston Healey

Joe Huffaker began his racing career building dirt track cars in California. His family moved to California when he was 18, and he was immediately interested in hot rods. After getting his degree from the College of Marin, he started building his own dirt track roadsters, which were raced by Bob Sweikert and Bob Veith. Huffaker later ran an appliance repair shop and then a Montgomery Ward service center.

Despite having no formal engineering background, Huffaker was talented, and in 1954, he was hired by foreign car salesman Mickey Marston to build a special based on a wrecked Austin Healey 100. A tube frame was built to take the Healey running gear, and a purposeful aluminum body was hand-formed to cover it. Huffaker fabricated a de Dion rear suspension system with inboard drum brakes and torsion bar springing.

Huffaker modified the Healey engine as well. Chrysler pistons were used on special rods, and the head was ported and polished. The finished car weighed in at 1,800 pounds and was completed in five months. The car was raced as a D-Modified through 1958, putting up a good showing against the Ferraris and Maseratis of the class.

Knoop Chevy

Fred Knoop was running a Healey when he approached Huffaker with the idea of building a Chevy-powered special. The 310-horsepower 283-ci

Chevy was Hillborn-injected with an Isky cam and the usual period race prep before being bolted to a Jaguar four-speed transmission. The frame was fabricated from 3-inch tubing and had a tubular front axle with a de Dion rear end made from a Halibrand quick-change center section. Brakes were disc, and the front springs were torsion bars, with coils in back. The Devin body was modified with a bigger grille and fender vents. Halibrand knock-off wheels were used, and the race-ready weight was only 1,650 pounds.

The Knoop Chevy was completed in 1957 and ran in West Coast events with minor success. Initially, it was fitted with a hood scoop and racing stripe. Knoop did better in 1958, picking up a Class C-Modified win at Vaca Valley and a class win and fifth-overall at Laguna Seca. In 1959, the car was sold to Chuck Howard, who installed a larger engine and removed the hood scoop. In 1960, Bonneville racer Bob Herda bought the car and took it to a record-breaking speed, topping 190 miles per hour on the salt. Jim Williams was the last to race the Knoop Chevy in the mid- to late-1960s. Today, the car is active in vintage racing.

Front-Engine BMC Juniors

In 1959, Huffaker went to work for Kjell Qvale at the British Motor Car Company, where he was in charge of competition activities. His first project was

a front-engined Formula Junior to take on the Stanguellinis and Elvas. The BMC Mk.1 used the Austin A-40 A-series engine. The new car was conceived in early 1959 and put into production by September. The engine was mounted at a 35-degree angle, and a four-speed BMC box was used with drum brakes all around (the drums were cast in unit with the wheels). Double A-arm suspension was used up front, with independent suspension in back as well. Huffaker constructed the space frame chassis from 16- and 18-gauge square tubing, while the body plug construction was farmed out to Nade Bourgeault. Total length was 10 feet, height was 22 inches, and at 740 pounds it was too light for the regs and had to be ballasted. Huffaker spent a reported $8,000 to develop the prototype, and production models retailed for $3,995. He sold 23 the first year, making BMC the most prolific of American F-Junior manufacturers.

To power his new racer, Huffaker developed the A-40 engine with larger valves, pop-up pistons, a hotter cam, and a single side-draft Weber carburetor. It developed 86.5 horsepower from 980-cc. Jack Dalton and Pat Flaherty were the first works drivers, and they responded by winning nine firsts and two seconds with only three DNFs in their first season. They soundly defeated the fastest Stanguellinis on the West Coast and were the quickest front-engined Juniors around.

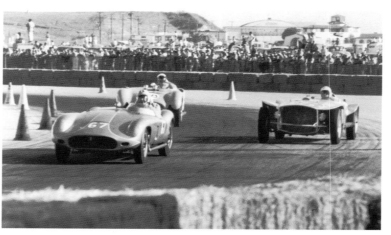

The Knoop Chevy leads the Reynolds Wrap Special at Santa Barbara. *Allen Kuhn*

The BMC Mk.1 was the quickest of the front-engined Formula Juniors. It had a short time in the sun before the mid-engined cars made it obsolete.
Harold Pace

these engines in his street-driven Morris Minor, surprising many Southern California Sprite drivers who fell within his reach. The engines retailed for $1,250 in 1962.

By early 1963, Formula Junior had turned into the "car of the month" club, with new models popping up all the time. The Lotus 22 and 27, along with the Cooper Type 3 and 4, were the dominant models, and Huffaker updated the Mk.2 to the Mk.6 with a fully fabricated front suspension derived from his new sports-racers. The wheelbase was extended from 88 to 90 inches, and the front control arms had wider pick-up points. Lockheed disc brakes were used all around, and the VW box was fitted with a Hewland five-speed gearset. The Cosworth-Ford finally surpassed the power outputs of even the Huffaker BMCs, so both engines were offered in the Mk.6. Only six were built before Formula Junior ended in 1963.

Little Genies

Huffaker saw that Formula Junior was doomed by the high cost and short life of the new models, and switched his efforts to the more stable sports-racer market. The new Genie Mk.4 was a completely new design, not a rehash of the Junior. Inboard disc brakes were fitted to the VW transaxle, and the Huffaker 1,100-cc BMC engine was competitive in the popular G-Modified class. The fiberglass body was similar in proportion to the Cooper Monaco and Lotus 19, and the suspension was softly sprung for predictable handling. The similar Mk.5 was beefed up to take Coventry-Climax FWA and Alfa Romeo engines for the midrange modified classes. Harry Banta won the 1963 SCCA West Coast Amateur Championship in G-Modified with his Genie-Climax. John Fitch drove a Genie to a win at Bridgehampton, and Art Snyder picked up a class win at the 1962 Riverside three-hour enduro. Jack Flaherty had a Mk.5 with a potent 2-liter Alfa tuned by Italian ace Virgilio Conrero.

The ultimate Mk.5 was built for EMPI, a VW parts distributor that had recently started a Corvair parts

Rear-Engine BMC Juniors

In 1960, the rear-engine revolution overshadowed the Mk.1, with the Lotus 18 and the Cooper Mk.1 F-Jr. sweeping all before them. Huffaker responded in 1961 with the BMC Mk.2. This simple design concentrated on reducing frontal area and weight. Huffaker chose a VW transaxle (fitted with close-ratio gears) with a Huffaker-designed adapter for the BMC engine. Round mild steel tubing was used to make an 85-inch wheelbase chassis with coil-over suspension at both ends. The rear suspension was similar to the front-engined car, with lower reversed wishbones, a single upper arm, and parallel trailing arms. Rear hubs were cast from magnesium, and drum brakes were retained all around. The suspension was quickly adjustable and the front lower A-arms were pressed steel BMC production parts. The Mk.2

proved to be much quicker than the Mk.1, but it was no quicker than a Lotus 18 and was inferior to the Lotus 20 and Cooper Mk.2 that came out in 1961. At $3,995 ready-to-race ($1,995 in kit form), 14 examples were sold.

To power the Mk.2, Huffaker developed a new F-Jr. engine that put out 95 horses from 1,100 cc. This was before the Sprite/Midget 1100 came out, so Huffaker took the fragile 948-cc blocks and sleeved them with high-strength liners that could be safely bored to 2.660 inches. Special racing rods, an oil pump, and a competition crankshaft were fitted, and bigger valves were installed in the head. Cam grinder Ed Winfield came up with a special grind that gave superior top-end power with passable low-end as well. A 45-millimeter DCOE Weber replaced the 40-millimeter unit used on the Mk.1. Huffaker tested

This tiny Genie was the last of the Huffaker line. *Harold Pace*

division headed by veteran SCCA racer Paul O'Shea. EMPI was developing hop-up parts for the Detroit pancake and wanted to show them off in a racer. Bill Thomas, ace Corvair engine builder, bolted together a 175-horsepower engine with four Rochester carburetors. A Porsche 356 transaxle was fitted, along with wider rear wheels. Disc brakes provided adequate stopping power, but the handling proved unpredictable until the springs were stiffened up appreciably. *Sports Car Graphic* editor Jerry Titus drove the car to fifth at the 1963 Laguna Seca USRRC race and to a handful of wins in SCCA races. In 1964, it was sold to Ed LaMantia, who ran it with some success in SCCA events. The Corvair-Genie was a one-off.

The last small-bore Genie was the Mk.11, built in 1965 as a one-off for Prudence Baxter. It was a beautiful car with an OSCA engine and distinctive bodywork. It was later owned by Bob Fox, and it won several championships before being sold to Charles Kuhn.

V-8 Genies

Attracted by the serious money and publicity that surrounded the USRRC series, Huffaker developed his first V-8-powered sports-racer, the Genie Mk.8. Although intended for the alloy 215-ci Buick-Olds-Pontiac (BOP) V-8 and the 289-ci Ford, a lighter version was designed around the Coventry-Climax FPF engine. The space frame was made from chrome-moly 4130 tubing, stiffened with an aluminum bellypan. Morris rack-and-pinion steering was used, and the front and rear subframes were bolted

to the chassis separately for ease of maintenance and repair. The suspension was similar in design to the smaller Mk.5, but spring rates were much higher to compensate for the greater weight. Dunlop magnesium calipers were fitted to the four-wheel discs. As with all his cars, Huffaker designed his own attractive spoked wheels that were also offered for sale individually. The body resembled the smaller Mk.5 and even had shrouded rear wheels. Huffaker initiated an R&D program on the BOP mill and ended up with a 239-ci mill pumping out around 300 horsepower with dual four-barrel carburetors.

To put down this power, Huffaker was forced to develop a transaxle capable of handling the torque of an American V-8. The Colotti transaxles in use at the time were inadequate and expensive, so he designed the Huffaker-BMC transaxle. This was a custom magnesium housing made in three parts to hold the differential, transmission gears, and a quick-change transfer case similar to a Halibrand QC. The 1963 Corvette close-ratio synchro gears were installed with heat-treated 4140 shafts, Getz ring-and-pinion sets, and Power-Loc limited-slip units. Although the four forward gears could not be easily swapped, the final drive ratio could be changed in minutes. This transaxle proved capable of handling up to 400 horsepower and sold for a reasonable $1,725. It was used in the factory Shelby King Cobras as well as the Genies, and Huffaker says 50 were built.

The Mk.8 was one of the more successful customer sports-racers of the pre-Lola/McLaren era. It was sold in kit and turnkey form, with at least eight complete cars built. Pedro Rodriguez, who won the 1963 Kent USRRC race over Genie-mounted Dave Ridenour, drove the factory team car. Briggs Cunningham bought an ex-works Genie-Ford for Dan Gurney to drive at Riverside (DNF). Ridenour had a Ford-powered version and captured fourth at the Pacific Grand Prix in 1963.

By 1964, the engine struggle in big-bore sports-racing was being won by the Chevy small-block, particularly as developed to produce nearly 450 horsepower by Traco Engineering. This engine was heavier and more muscular than the previous BOP and

Art Snyder in a Genie Mk.4 trails a Ferrari and a Dolphin at Pomona in 1963. *Allen Kuhn*

Jerry Titus drove the Genie Mk.5-Corvair at Willow Springs in 1963. It was quick but undependable. *Allen Kuhn*

Jim Rattenbury ran this Huffaker Genie Mk.8, powered by an Oldsmobile V-8 with a Corvair transaxle, in the Can-Am series. *Harold Pace*

The 1965 season was a good one for Genie pilots. Don Wester ran a Ford-powered example, and John Mecom bought a new chassis to be powered by a Chevy and driven by Augie Pabst. Although it was hard to catch the Chaparrals that season, Wester finished second to Jim Hall at Laguna Seca, with Genie pilots Ridenour and Paul Reinhart behind. Wester also picked up a third at Riverside, and Kent finished seventh in the USRRC championship.

One of the hottest Genies that season was the Mk.10 that belonged to actor Dan Blocker ("Hoss Cartwright" of *Bonanza* TV fame), driven by John Cannon. It was named the Vinegaroon and was first powered by a Chevy engine, then switched to a hot 300-ci, 385-horsepower Traco-Olds that weighed less than the Ford or Chevy alternatives. The chassis was extensively upgraded and the weight reduced even further. Cannon ended up second at Nassau to Hap Sharp's Chaparral.

Ford small-blocks. To put down the rapidly increasing power, wheels were getting wider to fit low-profile tires. Huffaker responded with the Genie Mk.10, an upgraded Mk.8 with open rear fenders and a stronger, all-new chassis. Bigger 12-inch disc brakes were fitted, along with stronger wheels and hub carriers. The vertical height of the frame was reduced to provide more driver room, and the bulkheads were switched from diagonally braced to scuttle-hoop construction.

Frame tubes performed double-duty, carrying the coolant from the engine to the front-mounted radiator. Spring rates were increased, and the track was increased front and rear, although the wheelbase remained at 90 inches. Huffaker recalls only building two complete cars, plus some kits and upgrading some Mk.8s to the new wheels and carriers. Rolling chassis sold for $9,500 in 1965. According to Huffaker, a single Mk.10B was built with knock-off wheels.

The next year saw Genies still in the hunt, with Cannon winning at Las Vegas, followed by Chuck Parsons in his hot Genie-Chevy. Parsons added a third at Riverside and second at Monterey to lead the USRRC scoreboard. But by midseason, the first McLarens and Lolas were up to speed, and they proved more sophisticated than the Genie. Additionally, they had Hewland gearboxes that allowed changing all the gears to suit track conditions. Parsons switched to a McLaren at midseason and won the USRRC crown, so Genie can claim at least half the victory.

83

The Genie Mk.8 was one of the first successful American midengined production racers. *Harold Pace*

The Genie Mk.10 won its share of races in the mid-1960s. *Harold Pace*

Dan Gurney and Pedro Rodriguez dice at Riverside in a pair of Genies. *Allen Kuhn*

Canadian Jim Rattenbury, who used a Corvair transaxle and BOP power, constructed another big Genie from a kit. It was run in Canada for years before being purchased by Mike Barbour and run in three Can-Ams in 1970, making it one of the few Genies to run in that series. Soon after winding down the sports-racer program, Huffaker split with Qvale and went on his own.

Formula 2

The last Huffaker formula car was a radical Formula 2 car built in 1965 with an all-fiberglass monocoque chassis. Woody Harris raced it for several seasons in England. There is no relation between this car and a similar fiberglass-chassis formula car claimed to have been built by Kellison, who built some Genie bodies. The Huffaker F2 was powered by a Lotus twin cam and was run in Europe before being brought back to the United States.

Production Race Cars

While employed at Qvale's shop, Huffaker prepared a number of BMC production cars for SCCA

racing. The most famous were a pair of Jaguar XKEs for mechanic Frank Morrill and experienced Nevada racer Merle Brennan. The Morrill roadster was built in 1962 and was the first successful XKE racer on the West Coast. It started life as a complete wreck and was rebuilt with 10-to-1 pistons, competition cams, and rejetted SU carbs. The suspension was adjusted for racing, and racing tires were fitted to the standard wire wheels. At Laguna Seca, with this very basic prep, Morrill was able to hound Dave MacDonald, at the time the hottest Corvette driver on the West Coast, until MacDonald spun and Morrill flipped the Jag, avoiding a collision.

Brennan's XKE was a special coupe prepared to do battle for the SCCA B-Production championship. It debuted in 1963 and immediately started beating Corvettes, winning 39 of 42 races entered from 1964 to 1966. This series of wins included the B-Production victory at the 1964 SCCA Runoffs at Riverside. Brennan also did well in USRRC GT events. His XKE used Winfield cams; high-compression pistons; extensive flow testing and treatment on the head, inlet manifold, and exhaust systems; triple 2-inch carbs; and lots of rpm.

Qvale bought one of the aluminum-bodied, fuel-injected XKE lightweights that were intended for FIA

endurance racing. Huffaker modified and prepared the car for the 1963 Sebring race, where Morrill and Ed Leslie drove it to seventh overall and second place in GT (behind a Ferrari GTO).

In 1966, Huffaker split with Qvale and started his own company to prepare and race British Leyland production cars. One of the first to get the Huffaker touch was Ed Leslie's Austin-Healey 3000. Huffaker's MG Midgets, MGBs, and Triumphs immediately started winning championships. He also built the unsuccessful MG Liquid Suspension Specials that

Pedro Rodriguez in a Genie Mk.8 leads Roger Penske's Zerex Special at Riverside in 1963. *Allen Kuhn*

HUFFAKER

British Motor Cars Distributors
1800 Van Ness Avenue
San Francisco, California

BMC MK.1 FORMULA JR.	
Years built	**1959–1960**
Engine	**BMC A-Series**
Gearbox	**BMC four-speed**
Chassis	**space frame**
Front suspension	**independent, coil springs**
Rear suspension	**independent, coil springs**
Brakes	**BMC drum**
Body material	**aluminum and fiberglass**
Weight, approx.	**740 pounds plus ballast**
Number built	**fewer than 50**
Price when new	**$3,995**

BMC MK.2 FORMULA JR.	
Years built	**1960–1962**
Engine	**BMC A-series**
Gearbox	**Volkswagen with CR gears**
Chassis	**space frame**
Front suspension	**independent, coil springs**
Rear suspension	**independent, coil springs**
Brakes	**BMC drum**
Body material	**fiberglass**
Wheelbase	**85 inches**
Number built	**14, plus kits**
Price when new	**$3,995 compete, $1,995 kit**

BMC MK.6 FORMULA JR.

Year built **1963**
Engines . . . . **BMC or Ford**
Gearbox . . . . **Hewland**
Chassis . . . . **space frame**
Front suspension . . . . **independent, coil springs**
Rear suspension . . . . . **independent, coil springs**
Brakes . . . . **Lockheed disc**
Body material . . . . **fiberglass**
Wheelbase . . . . **90 inches**
Number built . . . . **six**

GENIE MK.4 AND MK.5

Years built **1963–1965**
Engines . . . . **BMC, Coventry-Climax,
                           Alfa, Corvair**
Gearboxes . . . . **Volkswagen, Porsche 356**
Chassis . . . . **space frame**
Front suspension . . . . **independent, coil springs**
Rear suspension . . . . . **independent, coil springs**
Brakes . . . . **disc**
Body material . . . . **fiberglass**
Weight, approx. . . . . . **830 pounds**

GENIE MK.8 AND 10

Years built **1963–1965**
Engines . . . . **Chevy, Ford, Olds V-8,
                           Climax FPF**
Gearbox . . . . **Huffaker four-speed**
Chassis . . . . **space frame**
Front suspension . . . . **independent, coil springs**
Rear suspension . . . . . **independent, coil springs**
Brakes . . . . **Dunlop disc**
Body material . . . . **fiberglass**
Weight, approx. . . . . . **1,650 pounds**
Wheelbase . . . . **90 inches**
Length . . . . **152 inches**
Price when new . . . . . **$9,400 complete, $7,850
                           less engine.**

GENIE MK. 11

Year built **1965**
Engine . . . . **OSCA, BMC**
Gearbox . . . . **Hewland**
Chassis . . . . **space frame**
Front suspension . . . . **independent, coil springs**
Rear suspension . . . . . **independent, coil springs**
Brakes . . . . **disc**
Body material . . . . **fiberglass**
Number built . . . . **one**

ran at Indy from 1964 to 1966. In 1991, Joe Huffaker retired, while his son Joe carried on the Huffaker name. The Huffaker Company went on to win many Trans-Am and SCCA championships and is still a major force in American road racing.

Jabro

James Broadwell liked building cars. He fabricated a lovely one-off sports car in the early 1950s (named the Jabro, a contraction of his name) from scratch and raced it in the Midwest. The Jabro had a Ford six-cylinder engine and a metal body built from assorted passenger car fenders and parts.

In 1956, he decided to construct another special for the popular H-Modified class. He started by whittling a small wooden model to refine his ideas, and then bought the running gear out of a 1949 Crosley station wagon for $50. Broadwell

took time out from his job (president of Broadwell Distributing Company) to build the Jabro Jr. in seven months.

Jabro Jr.

Broadwell's choice of chassis material was unique in racing history. He welded up 1 1/4-inch TV antenna mast tubing to make a space-frame chassis. This material was chosen due to low cost, availability, and low carbon content (which simplified welding and reduced cracking). The chassis was patterned after the Jaguar C-Type and weighed only 49 pounds bare. Coil springs were chosen for their light weight, and low-pivot-point swing axles were used in front, fitted with Crosley spindles mounted to fabricated kingpins with Chevy ball-joint swivels. Tubular radius rods located the axles. A Crosley rear axle assembly was widened with spacers and extended lug bolts to give a rack of 44 inches. A Crosley torque tube was

shortened and attached to an MG TD four-speed gearbox. A torque rod was added to the rear axle assembly to take braking loads.

A stock Crosley steering box was used. The Crosley disc brakes were activated by dual master cylinders, so brake bias could be adjusted. A Crosley radiator was laid on its side and fitted with a header tank.

Broadwell built up a hot Crosley engine, based on a "Turbulator" cast-iron block. A forged crank and Stellite exhaust valves (sourced from Thermo King, the company that used modified Crosley engines as power units for its refrigerated trucks) were used. An Iskendarian T-3 cam was good for 8,500 rpm, and the head was carefully ported and polished. A single Amal motorcycle carburetor fed the juice to spark, provided by a Mallory distributor.

Broadwell made his own body from fiberglass, forming a plaster and chicken wire mold and then female molds from which to pull the actual body panels. The attractive little body looked like a D-Type Jaguar that had been left out in the sun too long, with a small headrest, fold-down doors, and hinged nose and tail sections for easy maintenance. The completed car weighed 835 pounds wet. It proved to be extremely competitive in the Midwest, taking home trophies in 18 of 20 races entered.

Jabro Mk.1 and Mk.2

In 1957, Broadwell put two versions of the Jabro on the market. The Jabro Mk.1 was visually identical to the one-off Jabro Jr., but had a slightly different (and heavier) chassis with mounting points for stock Crosley suspension at both ends. The idea was that the builder could buy a Crosley parts car and screw together an inexpensive race or street car for $500 to $750. The body sold for $295, the chassis was another $345, and an instruction book was $5. Options included racing bucket seats and aluminum valve covers for Crosley engines. Due to the number of calls he received requesting advice, Broadwell began charging a dollar per question (with a two-question minimum). He also sold complete plan sets for those wishing to duplicate his efforts on their own.

The Jabro Mk.1 was a popular customer racing car. This one uses Crosley power. *Bob Schneider; Robert Fairbanks collection*

The Jabro Mk.2 was a duplication of the Jabro Jr., with swing front axles and a lighter frame than the Mk.1. The price for the chassis went up to $595. The rear body section was subtly reshaped around the doors, and side vents were added below the hood.

Jabro Mk.3

In 1961, Broadwell designed a much more sophisticated model called the Mk.3. It had a space frame that resembled that of a Maserati Birdcage made from small diameter tubing. The new body was lower and more graceful than the earlier cars, and the mold was formed over a wood buck (easier than plaster to make smooth). It had no headrest.

The frame was built from 0.049 wall mild steel tubing in various sizes, with the 1-inch main rails being the largest diameter. Broadwell also offered a simpler space frame chassis for those who were nervous about the complexity (and cost) of the "birdcage" construction.

The front suspension was carried over from the Mk.2, but in back the torque tube was eliminated in favor of a conventional live axle. Coil-over shocks were used all around, and Crosley steering was used again. The engine was offset to the right to balance driver weight. The birdcage frame retailed for $695, with the space-frame chassis selling for $100 less. The same body fit all Mk.3 chassis and sold for

$360. Like earlier Jabros, full blueprints and plan sets were available for scratch builders.

A friend of Broadwell's converted his Mk.3 to rear-engined configuration, and an official rear-engined Mk.3 model soon followed. This version used a transaxle and independent suspension parts from a Fiat 600, with a choice of Mercury outboard or Saab engines. The midengined Mk.3 chassis sold for $695, less the Fiat parts. The Mk.3 did not sell as well as the earlier cars. The Mk.1 and Mk.2 were continued in production alongside the new model, but the Mk.3 was the last Jabro racing car.

Jabro developed its own version of the Crosley engine with eight intake and exhaust ports in a cross-flow design. The stock Crosley had only two intake ports, which Jabro welded up and reformed into four. The Jabro engine used four Dellorto carburetors, a special Kenny Harmon cam designed for the eight-port engine, and a lightweight valvetrain with Ford followers. The Jabro engine developed 65 horsepower at 9,000 rpm and cost $850 outright, or Broadwell would convert a standard Crosley engine to eight ports for $245.

JABRO

Jabro Sports Cars
1 Sunnymead
St. Louis, Missouri

JABRO MK.1

Years built	1957–1963
Engine	Crosley
Gearbox	Crosley
Front suspension	live axle
Rear suspension	torque tube
Brakes	Crosley disc or drum
Body material	fiberglass
Weight, approx.	800 pounds
Wheelbase	84 inches
Track	44 inches
Number built	unknown

Both Mk.1 and Mk.2 models sold very well and many have survived to find a new life in vintage racing events. Jabro bodies have probably found their way onto other chassis as well.

The Jabro Mk.3 was a mini "Birdcage" with Crosley power. *Harold Pace*

JABRO MK.2		JABRO MK.3	
Years built	1957–1963	Years built	1960–1963
Engine	Crosley	Engines	Crosley, Mercury, or Saab
Gearbox	MG	Gearboxes	MG or Fiat 600
Front suspension	swing axle	Front suspension	swing axle
Rear suspension	live axle	Rear suspension	live axle or independent
Brakes	Crosley disc	Brakes	Crosley disc
Body material	fiberglass	Body material	fiberglass
Weight, approx.	790 pounds	Weight, approx.	750 pounds
Wheelbase	84 inches	Wheelbase	83 inches
Track	44 inches	Track	44 inches
Number built	unknown	Number built	unknown

Jomar

Ask any racing enthusiast about the racing mecca of Manchester, New Hampshire, and you're liable to get a blank stare. But in the mid- to late-1950s, a local dealer of foreign cars at the Merrimack Street Garage turned out some of the more interesting small-bore racing cars of the day. The man was Ray Saidel, and the cars were Jomars.

The Merrimack Street Garage has been a Manchester landmark since Ray Saidel's father, Morris, first opened its doors in 1919 as a Hupmobile dealer. In the early 1930s, Oldsmobile was added to the lineup. Ray took over running the dealership when his father passed away in 1950. He decided that racing might be a good way to promote the dealership (truly a timeless racer confabulation). He started racing an HRG but, in 1954, switched to an Allard J2X Le Mans with an Olds V-8 installed at his shop. And he was really pretty darn good. In fact, in

1955, he captured the SCCA C-Modified Championship for the Northeastern region. Having been deeply bitten by the racing bug, Saidel decided to do what many were doing at the time—build all-new racing cars of his own design.

Before diving into the various Jomar creations, a few words about the chassis numbering system are in order. The Jomar Mk.I's were built on a Dellow chassis and had chassis numbers with three numbers, followed by a letter, followed by three more numbers. For all other Jomars, the chassis numbers begin with a 7, indicating that a TVR type 7 chassis was used (the 7c type was used for purpose-built race cars and the 7t type was used for road cars that were sometimes also raced). The one or two letters that follow the 7 indicate the engine fitted into the chassis; C for Coventry-Climax, FS for Ford supercharged, and C-S for Climax supercharged. The three-digit number following the letters indicates each particular car's position in either the C or FS production run. The C chassis had a smaller engine bay, with gussets on the outside of the upper frame rails. The FS chassis had gussets on the inside, creating a larger engine bay for the supercharger.

Jomar Mk.I (Dellow-Jomar)

The first two Jomars began life as a couple of English Dellow chassis. The cars' development team consisted of Louis Turner, Norman Leeds, and Saidel. The team clothed each of the two Dellow chassis in simple yet attractive aluminum panel work and installed a Ford 1,172-cc side-valve engine. The name "Jomar" was the conglomeration of the first names of Saidel's eldest daughter Joanna and eldest son Marc. These first two cars became known as the Jomar Mk.I. The first Mk.I was chassis 410M555 and carried engine number 168602; the alloy body was painted black. The second Mk.I was chassis 413B565 and carried engine number 187496; the alloy body was painted silver.

In their first season of competition, the Mk.Is were not particularly competitive, but they were durable and rarely failed to finish. The Ford powerplant was a bit underwhelming, and slippage of the archaic cable brake system was unpleasant during competition. But the cars were unique-looking and garnered a fair bit of attention.

Jomar Mk.II

Because of the Dellow's shortcomings, Saidel began looking for a replacement chassis for the next version of the Jomar race car. The answer came in the form of an advertisement by TVR in the August 1955 issue of *Autosport*. Saidel contacted TVR and learned that two chassis would soon be available— the 7t chassis would weigh 112 pounds and was

87

Number 21 is the first Dellow-based Jomar, while No. 22 is the second one. *Alex and Ray Saidel collection*

When Jomar switched to TVR chassis and Coventry-Climax engines, the cars became competitive. This Jomar Mk.II (7C104) is shown at Thompson Raceway in 1958. *Alex and Ray Saidel collection*

Another victory for Ray Saidel (left) in a supercharged Jomar Mk.II (7C-S116). Here he celebrates a 1959 E-modified win with Lou Turner. *Alex and Ray Saidel collection*

intended strictly for road-going vehicles; the 7c would be 48 pounds lighter and would be appropriate for competition sports-racers with an engine displacement of up to 2 liters. After a series of communications, Saidel placed an order with TVR of Blackpool, England, for the 7c racing chassis.

The first Mk.II chassis (chassis 7C101) was ordered on December 30, 1955, and was completed on May 4, 1956. TVR shipped the vehicle on May 13, 1956, and it was received at the Merrimack Street Garage on June 13, 1956. This was the first production racing (7c) chassis built by TVR. The chassis was ordered with magnesium drum brakes and five-lug bolt-on rims. The engine was an 1,100-cc Coventry-Climax in Stage I tune with an output of 75 horses. The car was fitted with a hand-hammered aluminum roadster body by Saidel's team and painted blue. It was first track-tested by Saidel on August 5, 1956, and subsequently had several races, and several problems. Saidel was unsatisfied with the brakes, and kingpin breakage was frequent. Saidel was concerned enough by the mechanical failures (the car experienced race-ending failure at four consecutive races) that he insisted TVR redesign the front suspension before he would take delivery of another chassis. There were so many problems with the first Mk.II that Saidel had to pull the old Mk.I out of retirement for part of the 1957 racing season.

The first Mk.II did have its good days. Saidel finished fourth at Lime Rock in April 1957 (Columbosian ran sixth in his Mk.II [7C102]), second-in-class at Marlboro in May, second-in-class at Cumberland six days later, and second-in-class again in May at an SCCA regional. Unfortunately, the car was lost at Virginia International Raceway (VIR) in August 1957, when it was crashed badly by Ray Heppenstahl.

The second Mk.II (chassis 7C102) was ordered on March 13, 1956, and was initially completed on July 21, 1956. Because of the failures with the first Mk.II, the chassis required some modification and therefore was not shipped until four months later.

Chassis 7C102, only the second TVR 7c chassis, was received at the Merrimack Street Garage on November 12, 1956. It was fitted with Alfin drum brakes. The engine was an 1,100-cc Coventry-Climax in Stage II tune. It was fitted with an alloy roadster body painted red with a white stripe. The car was sold to Bob Columbosian and raced approximately 20 times until it was wrecked at Lime Rock in July 1958.

The third Mk.II (chassis 7C104) had further chassis improvements and modifications by TVR. It was ordered on September 16, 1956, finished on February 1, 1957, and received in Manchester on March 18, 1957. The vehicle was fitted with Alfin drums, and a Stage II 1,100-cc Coventry-Climax. The alloy body was essentially a duplicate of 7C102 and was painted black. This third Mk.II became the factory team car, with Saidel as driver, and was raced at nearly 50 events between May 1957 and September 1958 to an impressive percentage of podium finishes. Class and overall wins included Thompson in June 1957, Lime Rock in July 1957, and Lime Rock again in November 1957. This factory team racer was the most fiercely campaigned of all of the Jomars.

The fourth Mk.II (chassis 7C109) was ordered on February 28, 1958, and arrived at Saidel's facility in late May. The fifth and final Mk.II (chassis 7C-S116)

Jomar sports-racers challenged the Lotus 11s in G-Modified racing. *Harold Pace*

was originally ordered on April 24, 1957, but took almost two years to complete because of problems related to the Shorrock supercharger to be delivered with the 1,500-cc Climax engine. The car arrived on February 23, 1959, so late in the year that other projects (prepping the SSR1 and the Mk.III [7C-S113] for the Daytona 1,000-kilometer road race) did not allow for the time required to build a new aluminum body for 7C-S116. The alloy body was subsequently removed from retired Mk.II 7C104 and installed onto 7C-S116. This final Mk.II was raced on numerous occasions, including a first-in-class and overall second at Thompson at a Northeastern SCCA regional on October 4, 1959.

Jomar Mk.III

During 1957 and 1958, two Jomar Mk.IIIs were built (chassis 7C103 and 7C-S113). Jomar 7C103 was ordered on March 13, 1956—the same day Saidel ordered 7C102, around which the second Mk.II was constructed. Like the Mk.IIs, chassis 7C103 was right-hand drive. The car was built with Alfin drums and an 1,100-cc Stage II Climax motor. It also had a special close-ratio gearbox. The car's completion was delayed in England, as TVR continued to work on improvements to the suspension. It arrived at Saidel Sports-Racing Cars on February 11, 1957.

Chassis 7C103 sat idle until the end of the 1957 season while Saidel was campaigning the Mk.II factory team car (7C104). For the 1958 season, Saidel decided to build a Mk.III with a new-and-improved body style. He built the first of these cars around the 7C103 chassis. The Mk.III was essentially a Mk.II with a prettier, sleeker body design and less pronounced wheel humps. In an effort to further improve performance, Turner spent countless hours working on the chassis to lighten it. The car was painted in what had now become Saidel's racing team colors—black with a white stripe with a red border, as first used on 7C104. The final touch was the addition of an egg-crate grille to the front opening of the nose. In February 1958, the car was sold to

the Foreign Motors Division of Seaman Bearing Company, and Saidel hoped that some West Coast exposure would help sales. The car was run at Riverside in March 1958; at Palm Springs a month later; later at Phoenix; and also at one of the earliest races at Laguna Seca, where it had brake trouble. By 1961, 7C103 had been painted white. Seaman's manager, Curly Brayer, who raced the car at Santa Barbara Speedway in 1961, later purchased it. Unfortunately, the car caught fire and burned to the ground. It was later rebuilt and traded to a car dealership in Las Vegas.

The second Jomar Mk.III was built around chassis 7C-S113. It was ordered on July 18, 1958, but was slow in shipping due to a delay at TVR while they awaited the supercharged Climax engine. The chassis arrived in New Hampshire in early November 1958. The car was equipped with Alfin drums and the 1,100-cc Climax, blown via a Shorrock unit. The aluminum body was painted black, Saidel's team color. This Mk.III competed in the 1959 USAC-sanctioned Daytona 1,000-kilometer road race, and was running third in the under-2-liter class when the fuel pump broke. After a 20-minute pit stop, Saidel got back in the car and managed to finish sixth overall. In the 1960s, the Climax was removed and Saidel raced the car with an aluminum Olds V-8. The car later was sold to Roger Jackson, then to Scott Woodman, and later to Harry Parkinson. In 1963, the car had a 215 Aluminum Buick. This car later became known as the Tea Kettle Special, due to an overheating problem related to the filler being lower than the engine. (This was not the same car as John McCann's Teakettle [MG TD] Special).

Like the Mk.Is and IIs that came before, the Mk.IIIs were born of the marriage of an English-built chassis and an American-built (Saidel) aluminum body. By contrast, all other Jomars, excepting the SSR1 Formula 2 Jomar Racer, were built entirely by TVR in England (they were shipped as completed cars to New Hampshire, where they were badged and sometimes modified).

Jomar Roadster

One or more similar open cockpit roadsters may have predated the Jomar Roadster, but those cars wore a TVR badge and were sold in the United Kingdom. Jomar Roadster 7C105 was ordered on April 24, 1957, just two weeks after Saidel sold the Mk.II (7C102) to Columbosian. The car was completed on August 8, 1957, at TVR and arrived in Manchester on August 14, 1957, where it received its Jomar badging. The right-hand-drive car was intended to be an all-out racer and was powered by a Coventry-Climax FWA engine. The fiberglass body was quite beautiful, but was not actually painted—red coloring was added to the fiberglass resin during its manufacture, and the car was raced that way. The roadster was sold to Nick Falcone, who campaigned the car at Thompson and Lime Rock.

This handsome sports car is the one-off Jomar Roadster. *Alex and Ray Saidel collection*

Jomar Notchback Coupe (Mk.I Road Car)

A total of four coupes (7FS101, 7C107, 7C108, 7FS102) were produced by TVR, badged Jomar by Saidel, and delivered in notchback configuration in the United States. (One additional notchback was delivered in the United Kingdom and another [7FS103] was ultimately delivered in fastback configuration.)

The notchback coupes were constructed around the heavier (and less expensive) 7t chassis and were conceived as dual-purpose cars—race on Sunday, get groceries on Monday. The notchback received a

The Jomar Notchback Coupe was a dual-purpose street and race car. *Alex and Ray Saidel collection*

fiberglass body produced in England, and all four cars were configured as right-hand drive. They were not particularly pleasing to the eye, and cockpit space was lacking. The build quality was also less than satisfying to Saidel.

The first notchback coupe (7FS101) was purchased by a disc jockey in Portland, Maine, who frequently raced it. According to Ray's youngest son, Alex Saidel, the car was later brought in with a request for installation of a heater after the disc jockey was hospitalized with hypothermia. The second notchback coupe (7C107) became the factory team notchback and was raced extensively by Saidel and Paul Manseau during the 1958 season.

After receiving the four notchback coupes (and experiencing difficulty selling them), Saidel requested that the car be restyled and improved. These improvements came in the form of the next Jomar, the fastback coupe.

Jomar Fastback Coupe (Mk. II road car)

Like its predecessor, the notchback coupe, the fastback coupes were built entirely by TVR in England, then badged and sold as Jomars by Saidel. As Saidel had requested, the body was refined with an accentuated slope to the rear end, resulting in an extended fastback roof—a much more attractive,

more interesting, if not quite beautiful, coupe. The fastback chassis remained the same basic TVR 7t. An almost identical coupe, the Grantura, was sold in Europe by TVR.

The first fastback coupe (7FS103) was ordered on October 1, 1957, and completed on March 21, 1958. This car was originally the last notchback coupe, but was changed to fastback configuration prior to delivery. The car was shipped directly to New York and arrived just in time for display at the 1958 New York Auto Show. The car was very well received and dealers placed more than 100 orders. According to Alex Saidel, "Unfortunately, TVR could not fill these orders," primarily because of financial problems. A total of only eight fastback coupes were produced (7FS103-7FS109, 7C114).

Jomar SSR1 Formula 2 Racer (Jomar Single-Seater)

By 1959, Saidel's interests had evolved to open-wheel formula racing. Racing chassis 7C111 (TVR type 7c) became the basic platform for the first of what was supposed to be a series of Formula 2 racers. However, the plan did not evolve past the first and only Jomar formula car. The car became known as the SSR1 (Saidel Sports Racing Car 1). During its construction, various tubes from the ladder frame were modified, and the torsion bars were removed from the TVR chassis. An aluminum body was constructed at Saidel's facility, designed with an elongated nose to house the front-mounted 1,220-cc Climax engine. The gearbox was MG Magnette. Saidel raced the car at Lime Rock on September 12, 1959, and was first-in-class and second overall. He finished third-in-class and fourth overall at Thompson in the unrestricted 1,500-cc class on October 4, 1959. For the 1960 season, the car received a Shorrock supercharger, and a Morris four-speed gearbox was exchanged for the MG unit. SSR1 continued to be competitive in its new blown configuration. Saidel finished second in the unrestricted class at the Thompson SCCA regional on May 22, 1960. (The Shorrock was providing 8 pounds of boost.) On September 23, he also finished third-in-class at the 1960 Watkins Glen Grand Prix.

The first Jomar Fastback Coupe (7FS103) was a handsome street car that was also raced. *Alex and Ray Saidel collection*

The Jomar SSR1 F2 was the only single-seat Jomar. *Alex and Ray Saidel collection*

Trouble in Camelot

In 1959, Saidel, frustrated with TVR's new owners, broke off their relationship, and only 23 Jomars were built between 1955 and 1959 (perhaps a 24th car in the form of a fastback coupe was delivered into the United States by TVR, but no Jomar chassis number was ever issued). Of the 23 known original cars, there were two Mk.Is, five Mk.IIs, two Mk.IIIs, one roadster, four notchback coupes, eight fastback coupes, and one Formula 2 car. Two cars were powered by Ford, nine were powered by Coventry-Climax, nine by supercharged Ford, and three by a supercharged

Climax. Of the original 23 Jomars, 13 are still accounted for, including both Mk.Is, two of five Mk.IIs (7C104 and 7C-S116), the only original Jomar Roadster, three of four notchback coupes (7FS101, 7C107, 7C108), four of eight fastback coupes (7FS103, 7FS105, 7FS109, 7C114), and the SSR1.

Today, Ray Saidel is nearly 80 years young and has officially retired from running the Merrimack Street Garage, but not from racing. When we caught up with him in August 2003, he had just returned from a weekend event at the New Hampshire

International Speedway with the VSCCA, where he and Alex, who took over running the family business in 1996, had each been racing one of the original Jomars. Not surprisingly, the Saidels are still fantastic race cars, and racers.

JOMAR

Saidel Sports-Racing Cars
Merrimack Street Garage
56 Merrimack Street
Manchester, New Hampshire

JOMAR MK.I (DELLOW-JOMAR)

Year built	**1955**
Engine	**1,172-cc Ford side-valve with Aquaplane head**
Gearbox	**three-speed, nonsynchro Ford**
Chassis	**Dellow ladder**
Front suspension	**live axle**
Rear suspension	**live axle**
Brakes	**cable**
Body material	**aluminum**
Weight, approx.	**1,500 pounds**
Wheelbase	**82.5 inches**
Length	**136 inches**
Height	**44 inches**
Number built	**two**
Chassis numbers	**410M555, 413B565**

JOMAR MK.II

Years built	**1956–1958**
Engines	**Coventry-Climax FWA or Climax supercharged**
Gearboxes	**MG Magnette four-speed or Morris four-speed**
Chassis	**space frame, TVR 7c**
Front suspension	**trailing link**
Rear suspension	**independent**
Brakes	**four-wheel Austin Healey Alfin drums, or Volkswagen magnesium drums**
Body material	**aluminum**
Weight, approx.	**1,300 pounds**
Wheelbase	**84 inches**
Length	**136 inches**
Height	**37 inches**
Number built	**five**
Price when new	**$2,895–$3,995**
Chassis numbers	**7C101, 7C102, 7C104, 7C109, 7C-S116**

JOMAR MK.III

Years built	**1957–1959**
Engines	**Coventry-Climax FWA or Climax supercharged**
Gearbox	**MG Magnette four-speed**
Chassis	**space frame, TVR 7c**
Front suspension	**trailing link**
Rear suspension	**independent**
Brakes	**four-wheel Austin Healey Alfin drums**
Body material	**aluminum**
Weight, approx.	**1,300 pounds**
Wheelbase	**84 inches**
Length	**136 inches**
Height	**37 inches**
Number built	**two**
Price when new	**$2,895–$3,995**
Chassis numbers	**7C103, 7C-S113**

JOMAR ROADSTER

Year built	**1957**
Engine	**Coventry-Climax**
Gearbox	**MG Magnette four-speed**
Chassis	**space frame, TVR 7c**
Front suspension	**trailing link**
Rear suspension	**independent**
Brakes	**four-wheel Austin Healey Alfin drums**
Body material	**fiberglass**
Weight, approx.	**1,575 pounds**
Wheelbase	**84 inches**
Length	**136 inches**
Height	**37 inches**
Number built	**one**
Price when new	**$4,095**
Chassis numbers	**7C105**

JOMAR NOTCHBACK COUPE (MK.I ROAD CAR)

Years built	**1957–1958**
Engines	**supercharged 1,172-cc Ford 100E or Coventry-Climax**
Gearboxes	**three-speed nonsynchro Ford or MG Magnette four-speed**
Chassis	**space frame, TVR 7t**
Front suspension	**trailing link**
Rear suspension	**independent**
Brakes	**four-wheel Austin Healey Alfin drums**
Body material	**fiberglass**
Weight, approx.	**1,600 pounds**
Wheelbase	**84 inches**
Length	**136 inches**
Height	**48 inches**
Number built	**four**
Price when new	**$3,495–$4,195**
Chassis numbers	**7FS101, 7C107, 7C108, 7FS102**

JOMAR

**JOMAR FASTBACK COUPE
(MK.II ROAD CAR)**

Years built	1958–1959
Engines	supercharged Ford, or Coventry-Climax
Gearbox	three-speed nonsynchro Ford, or MG Magnette four-speed
Chassis	space frame, TVR 7t
Front suspension	trailing link
Rear suspension	independent
Brakes	four-wheel Austin Healey Alfin drums
Body material	fiberglass
Weight, approx.	1,600 pounds
Wheelbase	84 inches
Length	136 inches
Height	48 inches
Number built	eight
Price when new	$3,495–$4,195
Chassis numbers	7FS103, 7FS104, 7FS105, 7FS106, 7FS107, 7FS108, 7FS109, 7C114

**JOMAR SSR1 FORMULA 2 RACER
(JOMAR SINGLE-SEATER)**

Years built	1958–1959
Engine	1,220-cc Coventry-Climax with Shorrock supercharger
Gearboxes	MG Magnette four-speed (1959) or Morris four-speed (1960)
Chassis	space frame, TVR 7c
Front suspension	trailing link
Rear suspension	independent
Brakes	four-wheel Austin Healey Alfin drums
Body material	fiberglass
Weight, approx.	1,100 pounds
Wheelbase	84 inches
Length	136 inches
Height	48 inches
Number built	one
Chassis numbers	7C111

We Talk With Ray Saidel.

AUTHOR: What made you use the Dellow chassis in the first two Jomars?

SAIDEL: I saw a Dellow chassis being advertised in a British Magazine, *Autosport*, I think it was. I ordered the chassis and we bodied it, and, of course, I didn't know what I was doing. It was so primitive. It was a trials car. It wasn't made for racing. It had mechanical brakes, no hydraulic brakes. We fooled around developing and running it.

AUTHOR: What was it like driving the Mark I?

SAIDEL: It was kind of hairy, because I didn't know any better. I mean, I started driving the Allard, which was a good thing because you couldn't make many mistakes on those old road courses, because you would go into a ditch or a tree or something. So, I think the Allard was a good training ground for me. The Mark I Jomar had a three-speed gearbox, no synchromesh, and no hydraulic brakes. I drove a race at Thompson one day. It went pretty good. I said, "Let's not touch the car." The big Labor Day race was coming up the next day. We pushed the car out on the grid for the race; they got ready and cleared the grid. I got ready to start the race, stepped on the brake pedal, and *wham*—no brakes at all. The cables had stretched out and there just weren't any brakes at all. I drove it in the race anyway. We did well, set the course record.

AUTHOR: Without brakes?

SAIDEL: No brakes. That reminds me of another race. It was a national race at the Beverly Airport, the SCCA National. They came over to me after the race and said, "Hey, you know when you go into a right-hand turn you're lifting the right rear wheel about a foot off the ground." I said, "Can't help it." It was a pretty easy car to drive. But on the other hand, I think driving something like that Allard was good training, because you can't make too many mistakes.

AUTHOR: How did the Mark II come about?

SAIDEL: We built the first two cars on the Dellow chassis and by that time, Coventry-Climax Lotuses were showing up and, of course, we didn't have a prayer against those. So then I decided to try to build something a little more competitive. I saw an ad for a chassis that the TVR people were developing. So I ordered the chassis from them. We bodied that and it was a long story. The chassis was all right, but had suspension failures. That was the early Mark II.

AUTHOR: How dangerous was the first Mark II?

SAIDEL: The only thing that was dangerous was that it was breaking kingpins. Luckily, what would happen was it would break on a real tight, slow corner. It wouldn't break on the straightaway. Turned out, it had nothing to do with the material. One torsion bar was not locked, and as the car sat on the trailer, going up and down, bouncing along, the spaces that kept the trailing arm in the right position against the housing for the torsion bar would rub against the torsion bar and it wore it away just a tiny, tiny bit, maybe the thickness of a piece of paper. It took that wear going to the racetrack and then *bang*, the thing would break, and you would have a wheel that was horizontal.

AUTHOR: Did you ever get so discouraged that you considered quitting the project?

SAIDEL: No, we never considered quitting, but we did put a hold on it a couple of times. I called England and said, "For God's sake, don't sell any of the chassis to anybody until we solve this problem." We tried all different things until we woke up to what the real cause was.

AUTHOR: What is your favorite memory of racing the Mark III?

SAIDEL: The race I enjoyed the most would be the first road race on the Daytona course. They were paving it while we were still there. That was USAC also. That was a great race.

AUTHOR: Why?

SAIDEL: Well, it was a long race. I liked the competition. I liked the USAC guys. We were practicing down there at the same time the Indy cars were practicing, because that was the only event they ever ran. They ran the oval and we ran the oval with the inner road course, so we had about a week down there practicing. We would just go out and practice maybe once. They had a lot of track time. That was the first time we ran the supercharger, and we didn't have the fuel right. We were running gasoline in it. The compression ratio we had on the supercharged car with gasoline wouldn't run good. But even then, it was still going good. I was practicing on the oval because the track wasn't finished yet. Well, it was finished for the race, but in practice we had to use the oval. You know, we could go around that oval at about 140 miles per hour with that little 1,100-cc engine with the blower. Later, we were running 50 percent methanol, 25 percent benzol, and 25 percent gasoline. But, not there. We were running gas. But even then we ran good. We finished sixth. I lost the distributor drive gear and spent 20 minutes in the pit. We had been running third before the disaster, but it was still a great event.

AUTHOR: How would you sum up the 1950s racing scene, and where do you think the Jomars fit into the picture?

SAIDEL: Actually, we were racing with the Lotus, the Elvas, and the Coopers. G-Modified was the class we mainly ran. We ran an occasionally larger engine than we might run—an E-Modified or occasionally, later, an unrestricted. But, anyway, it was mostly all G-Modified. G-Modified was a great racing class then. You know, you might have 13 G-Modified cars, all Coventry-Climax powered, usually on the grid. I think we did very well, considering we were running against

team cars for Lotus and Elva. They always had a stage higher engine, because Colin Chapman would send them the best engines. We would get gearboxes from him, too, and the same thing. One day we had a great race at Lime Rock, because we accidentally got a better set of gears from them. They gave us some closer ratios than the close ratios the others were getting. Actually, I went out for practice and thought the track was wet or something because I was going too fast. I was starting to lose it on the corners a little bit. I couldn't figure out actually what was so good. Our times were excellent. At our best, we were pretty competitive with most of the Lotuses. There was Frank Batista, who drove a factory Lotus. He had a factory-sponsored car from Lotus, and he had a higher stage engine, and we were running maximum at 7,000 rpm. He had a five-bearing cam that we didn't know about until I happened to see him with the cam cover off, and spotted that he had two more bearings on the cam. He could go higher without getting cam whip. So, we had a set made up like that locally. Then we could bring it up to about 8,000, the way he was doing.

AUTHOR: Looking back, any regrets?

SAIDEL: No, not really. You know, if I could be two people, I would have said, "Well, don't build a car, buy a good one and run in Europe, run internationally." You know, for all the effort we put into the Jomars, we could have had a real hot car that somebody else made, a factory car. But on the other hand, if I had to go back and do it over again I think I would do some things different probably. I would get more knowledge from the experts before I started, instead of having to do everything by trial and error.

AUTHOR: Which Jomar is your all-time favorite?

SAIDEL: The SSR1. That is the one I still like to race the most. You can place it exactly where you want. It's a wonderful car.

Kellison

Jim Kellison made lots of kit car bodies that were sometimes used on racing cars beginning in the late 1950s. (See Kellison entry in American Kit Car Manufacturers, Chapter 5).

Kellison J-4 Competition Coupe

In 1959, Kellison also built a racing version of his J-4 Coupe, using a tired old frame that had been hacked on for chassis development. *Motor Trend* tested it, and the handling was found to be unstable, with a worn-out Chevy V-8 that was hopelessly down on power. Andy Porterfield drove it at Santa Barbara and finished, although down the field. It was not heard from after that.

The "works" Kellison's dismal showing was the result of improper preparation, not the basic design. The Kellison kits were reasonably well thought out, if basic, kit cars. No further factory racing versions of the J-4 were built, although a number of individuals modified their own Kellisons for track use.

Kellison Formula Vee Mk.1

In 1967, kit car manufacturer Kellison announced that it was starting a new division, Grand Prix Sports and Racing, which would be developing Formula A, B, and Vee cars. However, it appears that only the FV made it into production. It was a conventional design with a very attractive semi-wedge-shaped body.

Kellison Formula 2

Kellison showed photographs of a Formula 2 body in its late-1960s catalogs, stating that the company sold Formula 1, 2, and 3 fiberglass bodies as well as a fiberglass monocoque chassis for the F2 version. This was actually a one-off all-fiberglass monocoque F-2 car built by Joe Huffaker. Kellison made the bodies for Huffaker's racing cars. Woody Harris took the fiberglass Huffaker F2 car to Europe in 1968 and entered it in a Laguna Seca pro race as a "Kellison F2." No more were sold.

Kellison Inc.
Highway 99E
Lincoln, California

Grand Prix Sports and Racing
150 McBean Park Drive
Lincoln, California

KELLISON J-4 COMPETITION COUPE

Year built	**1959**
Engine	**Chevy (265 ci)**
Gearbox	**Chevy four-speed**
Front suspension	**independent**
Rear suspension	**live axle**
Brakes	**drum**
Body material	**fiberglass**
Number built	**one**

KELLISON FORMULA VEE

Year built	**1968**
Engine	**1,200-cc Volkswagen**
Gearbox	**Volkswagen**
Front suspension	**trailing link**
Rear suspension	**swing axles**
Brakes	**drum**
Body material	**fiberglass**
Number built	**unknown**

The Kellison catalogs also show photos of a "Kellison" Formula car, but the car pictured is a Huffaker BMC Mk.II Formula Junior. It does not appear that Kellison built any complete formula cars other than the FV.

Kurtis

Frank Kurtis was one of the greatest race car constructors of all time. His career spanned four decades, and his accomplishments can only be described as legendary. Like many successful constructors of the time, Kurtis' parents were immigrants. His father, Francika Kuretich, was a talented blacksmith of Croatian descent, and he instilled the values of precision craftsmanship into Frank at an early age. In 1921, the Kuretichs moved from Utah to Southern California, the center of the sports car universe. Frank and his father found work at Don Lee

Coach and Body Works. Frank improved his skills in welding and metal shaping, building exotic coachwork for movie stars. His family name was modified to Kurtis by Lee's personnel office for ease of spelling. A few years later, Kurtis' skills benefited from his stint working under Harley Earl, the talented designer who would later make his reputation at GM.

Kurtis' first true effort on a racing car came in 1933, when he constructed a one-off radiator shell and hood for a roadster run at Jeffries Ranch, a half-mile dirt track in Burbank, California. His second effort was a body and fuel and oil tanks for the Atlas Chrome Special. He also did some work on the Stagger-Valve Fronty Ford.

In 1936, Kurtis built his first complete midget for Tommy Lee, the son of his former boss. Other projects followed, including the Jewel Box Offy midget for Charley Allen and midgets for Lou Fageol, Rex Mays, Bob Swanson, Roy Sherman, Ted Halibrand, Jack Prickett, and others. Kurtis was gifted with all things metal, and it showed.

The midget craze began to die down in 1948, and by 1950, Kurtis was only delivering a small handful. It seemed that race fans were losing interest in the little cars and moving on to bigger things—Champ cars. And, of course, Kurtis was there at the front of the pack, building some of the best Indy-type circle track cars of the day.

Total domination is the phrase that comes to mind when one recounts Kurtis' record at the Brickyard. His Offy-powered Champ cars sat on the pole at Indianapolis eight times, and won the 500 in 1950 (Johnnie Parsons), 1951 (Lee Wallard), 1953 and 1954 (Bill Vukovich), and 1955 (Bob Sweikert). His cars also ran fourth in 1947, third in 1948, and placed second in both 1949 and 1952. His cars were so good that they subjugated the entry list at Indy. Fifteen of the top 20 finishers in the 1953 Indy 500 were built by Kurtis!

While Kurtis will forever be remembered for his Offy midgets and glorious Indy cars, between 1949 and 1962, he built some fantastic road racing cars as well.

Kurtis Sports Car Beginnings

In 1949, Kurtis introduced the all-new Kurtis Sports Car (KSC). Although the car was more of a street machine, it did compete in a few select races (mostly West Coast SCCA events), marking the beginning of Kurtis' road race cars.

In an effort to generate interest in his new car, Kurtis brought an example of the KSC to Indianapolis in 1949. The car had a blown six-cylinder flathead Studebaker and was very well received. But not satisfied with the Studebaker engine, Kurtis struck a deal with Edsel Ford to buy anything he needed.

The KSC ran 130 miles per hour at a speed test at the Rosamond Dry Lake in preparation for Bonneville in August. The car was powered by a full-race Mercury engine built by Bobby Meeks (of Edelbrock Company). Driven by Wally Parks, it scored a two-way average of 142.515 miles per hour at the inaugural Bonneville Speed Week at the Utah Salt Flats.

The Kurtis Sports Car was featured on the cover of the inaugural issue of *Motor Trend* in October 1949 and garnered much attention. Kurtis offered the car in various states of completion. For $1,495, the customer received a partial kit, including basic frame, unfinished aluminum body panels and doors, windshield, linkages for brakes, and the unique hardware required to finish the car. For an additional $2,000 ($3,495), the customer received a complete kit, including an engine, tranny, and all of the accessories in ready-to-assemble form. Later, inflation drove the price up to $4,700, which made it significantly more expensive than an XK-120 Jag. As a result, the Kurtis factory produced a mere 17 kits.

Earl "Madman" Muntz purchased the rights and tooling for the KSC in early 1950s. Muntz had made his fortune selling television sets, radios, motor homes, and used cars. The KSC was renamed the Muntz Jet and underwent a number of modifications. The wheelbase was stretched, and the car became a four-seater. The flathead Ford became a Caddy and later morphed to a Lincoln. A steel body replaced the

The 500S was the most popular Kurtis production car.
Harold Pace

aluminum panels. With all of these changes, the car weighed in at nearly 4,000 pounds. In the end, the Muntz Jet outsold the KSC by more than 20 to 1, with almost 400 cars delivered. Of course, the car was no longer a sports car and Muntz lost an estimated $1,000 on each one he delivered.

Kurtis 500S

Following the sale of the KSC project to Muntz, Kurtis decided it was time to build another sports car. In 1953, he introduced the fabulous Kurtis 500S, whose chassis and suspension took heavy cues from the Kurtis 500A Fuel Injection Special. This Offy-powered rocket was leading the 1952 Indy 500 with Billy Vukovich at the wheel when the steering shaft broke, sending the car into the wall. Vukovich survived the crash, but the car was finished for the day.

The 500S frame was a ladder built from two 0.093-inch channel sections that were 7 inches deep and 1 1/2 inches wide. In order to stiffen the frame, Kurtis formed a 1 1/10-inch flange at the top and bottom of each rail; he also used tubular crossmembers at the front and rear. Kurtis was always interested in saving on weight, and he lightened the frame by drilling large holes in the rails. To extend the frame in both directions, tubular members of 1 1/2 inches were welded to the front and rear of the channel sections.

The solid chrome-moly front axle was tubular, suspended by a pair of trailing arms. Because of the trailing arm configuration, Kurtis used crossed torsion bars up front, driven by upper arms. The rear suspension was also live axle, but here the torsion bars were not crossed and were driven by lower arms. Kurtis designed the car to allow the customer some freedom of choice regarding the rear axle and the front and rear brakes. He did recommend that a single manufacturer supply all of these.

The 500S could be purchased as a completed car or in kit form, with wheelbases ranging from 88 to 100 inches. The Kurtis 500S body was an aluminum beauty with cycle fenders and an aggressive vertically oriented grille. Later in production, the car could be ordered with a fiberglass body of the same design as the alloy unit. A completed car, less engine and transmission, set the buyer back $4,986.

The first factory-completed 500S was a 100-inch wheelbase example delivered to a Hudson car dealer (Story & Ricketts, Long Beach, California) that ordered the car with a Hudson Hornet six-cylinder engine. This Kurtis-Hornet Roadster was road tested (*Road & Track*) in the October 1953 issue and received a very favorable review. Despite the somewhat anemic 160-horsepower engine, the car accelerated to 60 miles per hour in a very respectable 7.7 seconds.

Things really got cooking for Kurtis when Bill Stroppe decided to go racing in a 500S. Stroppe and Kurtis were friends, and they worked out a deal so that Stroppe could pay for the car over time. The frame was a short wheelbase version (88 inches), which Stroppe favored because of his experience racing midgets. The rear axle was Ford with a Halibrand quick-change center section, and the brakes were 11-inch Lincoln units with Frendo linings. Power was supplied by a Clay Smith–prepared 282-ci Mercury flathead V-8. Stroppe used a Ford three-speed tranny with Zephyr gears and a Ford clutch.

The Stroppe-Kurtis 500S was a winner right out of the box. Stroppe won the trophy dash, heat race,

T. W. Jones drove this Kurtis 500S with Mercury power at Torrey Pines in 1956. *Allen Kuhn*

and main event at Carrell Speedway (on dirt) in January 1953. This was followed by a DNF due to a magneto failure at the Palm Springs Road Races, where Stroppe had been in a fierce battle with Jack McAfee in a 4.1-liter Ferrari until his car broke down. Revenge came in early May at Phoenix, where Stroppe won, thoroughly trouncing McAfee by nearly a full lap. Stroppe was a winner at the Chino Airfield course in July and again at Moffett Field in August. Later in August, he was again victorious, this time at the Seattle Seafair, beating Bill Pollack's Jaguar C-Type. At the September 1953 Labor Day Races at Santa Barbara, Stroppe finished a disappointing second to Phil Hill's Ferrari 250 MM after his 500S slid into a ditch during the race. The following month, Stroppe returned to his winning ways with a victory at Reeves Field.

Stroppe's 500S was turned over to Troy Ruttman (the 1952 Indy 500 winner) to race at Riverside in November while Stroppe was in Mexico getting ready for the Carrera Panamerica. Ruttman was significantly larger than Stroppe (6 feet, 3 inches versus 5 feet, 11 inches) and did not fit the short-wheelbase car all that well. Things got so bad that the crew cut back the sheet metal on the driver's side and Ruttman raced with his left knee hanging out of the car. Ruttman was running third at Riverside until the motor jettisoned a rod. Ruttman failed to finish again in 1953 at March Field.

Stroppe returned to the wheel in 1954 and scored several more victories, including wins at Moffett Field, Santa Barbara, Sunnyvale, and Willow Springs. He also set the single-lap record (1 minute, 41 seconds) at Pebble Beach in April 1954. In the end, Stroppe was the winningest 500S driver of all time, and his was the most glorious of all 500S race cars.

An estimated 30 Kurtis 500S race cars and kits were delivered to customers between 1953 and 1955. City of Industry (California) Councilman Sam Parriott ran a blown Cadillac V-8 Kurtis 500S, mostly at Bonneville events. Indy 500 racer Manuel Ayalo bought a Chrysler-powered 500S, which passed through several owners' hands after Ayalo was tragically killed in a crash at the Brickyard. Murrell Belanger entered his Chrysler-powered 500S in the 1953 Carrera Panamerica, as did Leonard Fulkerson with his Chrysler-Hemi 500S.

Bill Murphy owned and raced two Kurtis 500S race cars. He bought the first one, powered by a V-8 DeSoto, in 1953, but didn't have too much luck with this package's reliability. He bought his second 500S, which had a Buick V-8, in 1954. This car had a unique set of clamshell fenders, which were fabricated by world-famous metal master George Barris. Murphy raced this car in 1954 and 1955 with good success. However, his greatest success was yet to come in his awesome Kurtis 500X.

Other 500S roadsters included the Cadillac-

The Bill Murphy Kurtis 500X beat its share of Ferraris in the 1950s. *Harold Pace*

Jerry Unser in Mickey Thompson's Kurtis 500X-Cadillac leads Bill Murphy in his Buick-powered 500X at Riverside in 1958. *Allen Kuhn*

powered cars of Frank McGurk, Briggs Cunningham, Ignacio Losanzo, Mickey Thompson, and Jack Ensley. Ensley won an SCCA B-Modified National Championship in his 500S in 1954. John Hammonds ran a Dodge Hemi-powered 500S, and Denny Weinberg had a Chrysler Hemi-powered 500S. Keenan Wynn ran a DeSoto-powered car out of Fresno, California, and a man named Buduron of Tucson, Arizona, ran a Mercury-powered car. Several of these cars were race winners and attest to Kurtis' skill as a designer and builder.

Kurtis 500X

The 500X was the next evolution of Kurtis' road racing cars. The ladder frames of the previous models were set aside, and Kurtis designed and built an all-new space frame of 4130 chrome-moly tubes. The tubes were of 0.083-inch wall thickness and were 1 1/2 inches in diameter. Four tubes served as the main structure and ran the length of the car in

This Chevy-powered Kurtis 500X was called the Zidar Special. *Harold Pace*

pairs. The upper tubes were bent 90 degrees to form the cockpit area. A lighter substructure built from 7/8-inch diameter chrome-moly tubing was formed to surround the driver's compartment and anchor the body via Dzus fasteners.

Suspension remained live axle with torsion bars up front crossing as an "X," and, at the rear, running parallel to the solid axle. The rear axle had a Halibrand quick-change unit, which was a major advancement over the 500S. The steering box was a Cassale unit with a short steering column.

For this all-new car, Kurtis also designed a beautiful all-alloy streamliner skin. The finished car was not only 200 pounds lighter than the 500S with a stiffer chassis, it was arguably even more beautiful.

Of all of the Kurtis road race cars, the 500X is shrouded in the most mystery regarding how many cars were actually constructed. By some accounts, as many as 12 chassis were built, but some believe six or even fewer cars were actually delivered.

The first 500X, SX-1, was built for Jack Hinkle. Hinkle had the car powered by a four-cylinder Offenhauser midget engine to compete with the smaller displacement cars of the day. The car was competitive on a regional level. This car was one of the few all-American racing cars (chassis, body, and engine) of its class.

Bill Pollack pilots Murphy's Kurtis 500X at Santa Barbara in 1957. *Allen Kuhn*

The second 500X, SX-2, was built for Albert Hoskins and Mickey Thompson. It was powered by a 389-ci supercharged Cadillac V-8 and was a real beast. Thompson claimed that the car was a 190-mile-per-hour Bonneville flyer and that it would exit the standing quarter-mile at 121 miles per hour.

The third 500X, SX-3, was built for Bill Murphy, who had previously raced two Kurtis 500Ss. Murphy had his 500X powered by a 322-ci Buick V-8, and his employee, Jack Riley, spent hours upon hours dyno testing and developing the powerplant. Bore was 4.0 inches and stroke was 3.2 inches. Early on, the car ran with Stromberg 97 carburetors; later, a 324 B-8 Hilborn fuel injection system was installed. Pistons were JE racing components, the cam was an Engle 95, and the dual ignition was a 12-volt Spalding unit. With a compression ratio of 8.2:1, the mighty Buick produced 315 horsepower at 5,500 revs. Sam Hanks was also working part-time at Murphy's car dealership and helped him dial the car in. The car ran a Jaguar four-speed transmission with a quick-change rear end that made a total of 12 ratios available.

Performance figures for Murphy's car were totally awesome, with 0-to-60 acceleration times of 4.6 seconds . . . in 1955! The car would reach 100 miles per hour from a standing start in 11.5 seconds with the standing quarter-mile taking just 13.1 seconds. While technical data does not always translate into winning weekends, this was definitely not the case with the Murphy Kurtis-Buick. In 31 starts, the car scored an incredible 18 class victories and nine overall wins at such tracks as Glendale, Palm Springs, Pomona, Riverside, Sacramento, San Diego, Santa Barbara, Santa Maria, and Torrey Pines. This was one of the winningest American race cars of the era.

The fourth 500X, SX-4, was the Chevy-powered Zidar Special, and chassis SX-5 was the one that Ak Miller modified and used in the construction of his Caballo II (see Ak Miller's Caballo II entry, Chapter 3). The sixth chassis is believed to have been used on a Mistral special, but this cannot be fully substantiated. Bob Schroeder of Texas and Joe Sexton may have run 500Xs, but sufficient information is not available. It is possible that other 500X chassis were sold. (The

500X chassis numbers include the month and year of construction and the car's place in sequence. For instance, the Murphy car's chassis number is 855 SX-3, indicating that it was built in August 1955 and that it was the third 500X built.)

Kurtis 500M

The 500M was built in 1955 as a way for Kurtis to compete with the smaller sports cars produced by Detroit and Great Britain. The "M" designation was for investor Robert McCullough, who brought capital to the project and constructed the fiberglass bodies. The 500M was built on the Kurtis 500KK kit chassis (see Kurtis entry in American Kit Car Manufacturers, Chapter 5) with live-axle suspension at both ends, Kurtis torsion bars, and a Ford rear axle.

The 500M was more a road car than a racer, with a fully trimmed interior and even a radio. At 2,700 pounds, the car was less nimble than the other models and thus less suited for the race track. The early cars were to be powered by four-cylinder Ford engines; later on, Cadillac and even Oldsmobile (Rocket 98) motors were used. Bob Schroeder raced a Buick-powered 500M in Texas and Mexico in the mid-1950s with little glory. Bob Christie of Medford, Oregon, ran a blown Nash-powered 500M in the 1954 Carrera Panamerica and did quite well until his supercharger malfunctioned.

The 500M did not fare as well as Kurtis and McCullough had hoped, and only 18 to 20 cars and kits were completed before the project died.

Final Developments

In the early 1960s, Kurtis laid out three chassis, which were essentially widened Indy Roadster units. Three cars built from these frames included Herb Stelter's 1962 Aguila (chassis 62 S-1), Sam Parriott's 1963 City of Industry Drag Car (chassis S-D-6-63), and Jack Lufkin's 1964 Bonneville Streamliner. The Lufkin car was the fastest Kurtis of all time, recording a top speed of 245 miles per hour in 1968. Kurtis also built a few other race cars in the early 1960s, including a 1962 Bonneville Ford Model A pickup truck for Buzz Lowe; a pair of dragsters for Nick Colbert and Ronnie Phelps; and a Saab-powered H-Modified, of all things, for Ed Walsh in 1962.

Kurtis Kraft
6215 South San Pedro Street
Glendale, California

1107 East Colorado Boulevard
Glendale, California

Alger Street
Glendale, California

KURTIS SPORTS CAR (KSC)

Years built	1949–1950
Engine	most powered by Ford Flathead V-8 (a few kits were fitted with other engines by the customer)
Gearbox	usually Ford but others were used
Chassis	ladder
Front suspension	Ford independent on coil springs
Rear suspension	live axle with semielliptic springs
Brakes	drum
Body material	aluminum
Wheelbase	100 inches
Number built	17
Price when new	$1,495–$4,700

KURTIS 500S

Years built	1953–1955
Engines	various V-8s (Buick, Cadillac, Chrysler, DeSoto, Dodge, Lincoln, Mercury, Chevrolet)
Gearboxes	various
Chassis	ladder
Front suspension	live axle with torsion bars
Rear suspension	live axle
Brakes	various
Body material	aluminum or fiberglass
Wheelbase	88 to 100 inches
Number built	approximately 30 (including all factory-finished cars and kits)
Price when new	$4,986 (completed car, minus engine and transmission)

KURTIS 500X

Year built	1955
Engines	various
Chassis	space frame
Front suspension	live axle
Rear suspension	live axle
Brakes	various
Body material	aluminum
Number built	six to 12 (including all factory-finished cars and kits)
Price when new	$6,000

KURTIS 500M

Year built	1955
Engines	various
Gearboxes	various
Chassis	ladder (Kurtis 500KK)
Front suspension	live axle
Rear suspension	live axle
Brakes	drum
Body material	fiberglass
Weight, approx.	2,700 pounds
Wheelbase	90 inches (most)
Number built	18 to 20 (including all factory-finished cars and kits)
Price when new	$6,200 (with the Cadillac V-8 engine)

KURTIS AGUILA

Year built	1962
Engine	Chevrolet V-8 (327 ci)
Gearbox	four-speed
Chassis	space frame
Front suspension	live axle
Rear suspension	live axle
Body material	aluminum
Weight, approx.	1,650 pounds
Number built	one
Chassis number	62 S-1

The Aguila (Spanish for eagle) was the last big Kurtis road racing car and another all-alloy beauty. Stelter paid $12,000 for the car, which was unlike any of Kurtis' prior creations. Barry Knowlton, Sylvester Fredricks, Harry Pitford, and Jim Burrell formed the body. It was constructed as a dual-purpose race car with easily removable front fenders mounted to the car via Dzus fasteners. With the fenders in place, the car ran as a modified. Without the fenders and with a single seat, it was eligible for the Formula 366 racing class which, of course, never caught on. So instead, it raced as a Formula Libre.

The Aguila pumped out gobs of horsepower from a 327-ci Chevy V-8. At only 1,650 pounds, the car could have been a world beater if it had been born just a few years earlier. But by 1962, the front-engined days were over, and the latest midengined sports racers outclassed the Aguila. After a few years of racing in the Southwest and Midwest without success, Stelter put the car away.

Of the 80 or so Kurtis sports racers and kits built between 1949 and 1962, many remain active in vintage racing.

La Boa

Al Baurle was already an experienced race car fabricator when he built his first racing cars. He worked for Bob McKee and others during his career as a fabricator and built a line of sports-racers and a Formula Ford model of his own design.

La Boa Mk.1

In 1958, Baurle built a one-off special to run in H-Modified. It was front-engined, but with lots of setback to move the weight rearward. A 750-cc Coventry-Climax engine was used, along with a BMC gearbox with Speedwell gears. The frame was a sheet steel monocoque, with tubular steel subframes front and rear. The special rear end was made for golf carts, with quick-change gears and fabricated independent suspension. The hubs were hollow, and the

La Boa sports-racers were fast and attractive. *Bob Harrington*

axles passed through them to allow less axle angularity. A narrowed and shortened Jabro body was built, and the car weighed 640 pounds. Don Moorehouse drove it and went very quickly. When it was built, this car had no name, but when the subsequent model was named the La Boa Mk.2, the first special was retroactively named the La Boa Mk.1.

La Boa Mk.2 and Mk.3

The second car Baurle built was a midengined design similar to the Lotus 23 (but introduced just prior to it in 1962). Baurle and partner John Camp set up Competition Engineering and penned a straightforward design with a steel tube space frame and fully independent suspension. To make the frame more rigid, Baurle added extra bracing in the sill areas, where most sports-racers carried their fuel tanks. Instead, the fuel tanks were located behind the driver for safety reasons. Camp named the car the La Boa after seeing boa constrictor snakes on a visit to Mexico. "He said it [the second car] was low and snaky, so we named it the La Boa," recalls Baurle. They cast their own rear hub carriers and front uprights in order to get the geometry they wanted. Various offsets, widths, and brands of wheels were tried, including American Racing, Revolution, and LeGrand.

The first Mk.2 was powered by a Saab three-cylinder engine with a Hewland transaxle. Simca 1000 rear axles were used, although they were marginal for larger engines.

The Mk.3 was a detail upgrade on the Mk.2, with a wider body to cover increasingly meaty tires. Basic kits started at $1,395 in 1968, and plan sets were available for home builders. A total of seven La Boa sports-racers were sold in kit or assembled form, plus around 50 bare bodies. The fiberglass bodies were distinctive and graceful, with Plexiglass-covered headlights. Baurle retained the headlights, even after they were no longer required; he thought they looked better that way. A variety of engines were used in the later cars, including Saab, Coventry-Climax FWA, and Lotus twin cam. La Boas won several Chicago-region championships in GSR and HSR.

LA BOA

Competition Engineering
820 E. Roosevelt Road
Wheaton, Illinois

LA BOA MK.1
Year built	1958
Engine	750-cc Coventry-Climax
Gearbox	BMC
Front suspension	independent
Rear suspension	independent
Body material	fiberglass
Weight, approx.	640 pounds
Number built	one

LA BOA MK.2 AND MK.3
Years built	1962–1968
Engines	Coventry-Climax, Saab, Lotus TC, Porsche
Gearbox	Hewland
Front suspension	independent
Rear suspension	independent
Body material	fiberglass
Weight	900 pounds
Number built	nine

R.A.C.E. FORMULA FORD
Year built	1968
Engine	Ford 1600
Gearbox	Hewland
Front suspension	independent
Rear suspension	independent
Body material	fiberglass
Number built	five

Baurle built two variations on the Mk.3 chassis for Dean Causey, who made up attractive Ferrari P-3-style bodies for them. Porsche engines powered them.

R.A.C.E. Formula Ford

After getting out of the sports-race business in 1968, Baurle became involved with building the R.A.C.E. (Royal American Competition Enterprises) Formula Fords for Hamilton Vose. At first, they planned to design a car and have it built in England, but about that time, Ron Courtney and Sam Posey were involved in a racing accident, resulting in Courtney filing legal action. Suddenly, the English race car manufacturers Vose had talked to got cold feet about building cars for litigious Americans. So instead, Baurle set up shop in Illinois and built five cars himself. They were wider than needed for a Formula Ford, leaving room for a Lotus twin cam in an anticipated Formula B version. Baurle now says this was a mistake, as a multiclass platform is seldom ideal for either class. In any case, no FBs were built, and the program quickly ran down.

Baurle later switched to building street sports cars, but he and his son Ken still provide assistance to surviving La Boas.

LeGrand

There is a special art to building a small racing car. Economies of weight and space are critical to cars with little horsepower and even less torque. One of the masters of small-displacement racing car construction was Aldin "Red" LeGrand. Armed with his training as a senior mechanical engineer in the aerospace industry, Californian LeGrand built a Renault-based special in the early 1960s. His friends Stuart Dane and Neil Hillier helped out, but Dane (see Dane entry, Chapter 2) was killed in a racing accident at Riverside Raceway. Dane had just completed laying out a new design at the time of his death, and Hillier moved away, leaving LeGrand on his own. The car was the Cheetah, and it was built to run in Formula 4.

Few racers even remember Formula 4. It was one of many racing classes that sounded promising but never caught on. In the early 1960s, the SCCA didn't have any classes for formula cars except Formula Junior. An organization called the Formula Racing Association (FRA) sprang up to promote single-seater racing in conjunction with SCCA events. The first classes they came up with were Formula Junior, Formula 3 (based on 500-cc motorcycle engines), and Formula Libre (no rules). The first Formula 3 cars came out in the 1950s and were driven by aces like Stirling Moss. There were a number of companies selling F3 cars, and at one time, the class was enormously successful (especially in England). But the cars were difficult to keep running and required constant maintenance. By the late 1950s, the F3 grids were thinning out, and soon, the class was moribund.

In the early 1960s, the FRA came up with alternate regulations to jump-start the class, renaming it Formula 4. The regs called for a 500-cc unrestricted engine, or a 750-cc engine with no more than one overhead cam. Supercharging was not allowed, but two-cycle engines were (a good thing since most were powered by motorcycle engines). The chassis regs were wide open (except for a minimum weight of 440 pounds) to encourage home builders to try their hand at creativity. It was this lack of regulations that got LeGrand's attention.

LeGrand Cheetah Mk. 1

The 1962 LeGrand Cheetah Mk.1 looked like a tiny Lotus Formula Junior and was powered by an air-cooled BMW 700 automobile engine and transaxle. The frame was made from 3/4-inch tubular steel and sported such advanced features as inboard suspension front and rear. Tiny 10- and 12-inch-diameter LeGrand-built cast-aluminum wheels were used, along with four-wheel Airheart disc brakes. LeGrand cast his own hub carriers, using Fiat bearings and hubs. The prototype had an aluminum body, but production models were fiberglass, allowing the Cheetah to tip the scales at an amazing 445 pounds. The steering was a Rube Goldbergian system that included two bellcranks, a spool, and metal cables to work the front hubs. The spool was

on the steering wheel, the cables ran from the spool to the ends of a drag link, and the drag link controlled the two bellcranks. The outer ends of the bellcranks worked the steering arms. it was weird, but it worked.

LeGrand modified the engine with dual Amal carburetors and fabricated headers. The best engines produced around 75 horsepower. Part way through the development cycle, LeGrand met Bruce Eglinton, who helped with the design and then functioned as the works driver.

The Cheetah was as fast as any Formula Junior on the West Coast. In the thinly supported FRA races, Eglinton started picking up overall victories against theoretically much faster (and more expensive) machinery. In 1964, Eglinton won the FRA season finale race, outgunning two Lotus Formula Libres with Lotus twin cam engines and a pack of Formula Juniors. Other Cheetahs finished fifth, tenth, and 13th. In May 1965, Eglinton finished fifth overall and first-in-class in a professional formula car race at

This LeGrand Cheetah Mk.2's first owner fitted it with a Warren body. The Warren bodies, built in Missouri, dressed up several LeGrands. *Barry LeVan*

A LeGrand won the first SCCA Formula B championship. *Bob Harrington*

Continental Divide Raceway in Colorado. LeGrand sold Cheetahs in several ways, including a set of plans to build your own for $25 or enough parts to build the chassis for $2,000. Reportedly, over 20 were built.

LeGrand Cheetah Mk.2

Despite the success of the Mk.1 design, Formula 4 never got off the ground. LeGrand decided to adapt the basic design to a two-seat sports-racer for the popular H-Modified class. Also called a Cheetah, the new car used the same suspension, BMW 70-horsepower engine, and transaxle as the F-4 (a Saab 750-cc three-cylinder engine could be substituted). A wider two-seat chassis was developed, but a conventional rack-and-pinion unit replaced the innovative cable steering. Weight went up to 560 pounds, so performance suffered, compared to the F-4 car. However, the new car was highly competitive in its class, at one time holding the H-Modified lap record at Willow Springs.

A strange fiberglass body was designed, with a projecting nose and bubbles over the wheels. These were also sold in kit, rolling chassis, or turnkey forms through 1965.

LeGrand Mk.3

Since Bill Thomas was also using the Cheetah name on his Chevy-powered monster, LeGrand switched to using his own name on his race cars. Also, by 1965, the SCCA had taken an interest in formula car racing and had started its own formula car classes: Formula A (1,600 cc to 3,000 cc), Formula B (1,100 cc to 1,600 cc), and Formula C (up to 1,100 cc). The majority of cars likely to contest the new class were older Formula Juniors that weighed 880 pounds, yet the minimum weight for Formula C was only 750 pounds. LeGrand saw this as an opportunity for an all-new car built right to the minimum weight. LeGrand and Eglinton cooperated on the design, benefiting from the latter's experience running a Lotus 27 F3 in Europe in 1964.

A space frame was chosen for the new car, as Eglinton's monocoque chassis Lotus had been frequently beaten by tube-frame Brabhams. The conventional space frame of the Mk.3 mounted

The LeGrand Mk.4B was an excellent small-bore sports-racer. *Harold Pace*

tubular front A-arms on the bottom and cast-magnesium upper arms. The uprights were cast-aluminum with Triumph spindles. The brakes were ultralight Airheart discs with plastic brake lines. LeGrand wheels were standard, in a variety of widths. Hewland gearboxes were used, along with a choice of Ford pushrod, Lotus twin cam, and Alfa Romeo engines. The FB versions (Mk.3B) used Hewland Mk.V boxes in place of the Mk.IV of the FC models.

The new Mk.3s immediately started wiping up the Lotus, Cooper, and Brabham opposition. Karl Knapp (president of the FRA) bought one of the first cars (a Ford pushrod-powered FC) and won four SCCA National Races in a row during the 1965 season. Eglinton won a professional FRA race at Hanford, California, driving an Alfa-powered Mk.3B, with Knapp close behind winning FC. Eglinton then won a pro race in Mexico. At the SCCA American Road Race of Champions (ARRC), the Alfa-powered

Mk.3B won the FB class, driven by Earl Jones. Not bad for the first season of an all-new design.

LeGrand Mk. 4

Following previous LeGrand practice, the Mk.4 was a sports-racing version of the Mk.3 formula car. Originally designed as a 1,100-cc racer, it was updated to take a wide variety of engines before production started and all versions were called Mk.4B. Eglinton and Don Stephan designed this car, with LeGrand providing his building skills. A variety of engines were fitted, including Maserati, Coventry-Climax, Datsun, and others. These cars were good, but not up to the lighter Lotus 23s.

An interesting one-off was the BRE Samurai, a Hino-powered coupe with a body penned by Cobra coupe designer Pete Brock. It used a LeGrand chassis stretched 1 inch to 92 inches. The engine was a 1,293-cc Hino Contessa, producing 110 horsepower, driven through a Hewland gearbox. Emil Deidt and Dick Troutman built the lovely aluminum coupe body at the famous Troutman and Barnes shop. Weight was 1,170 pounds. The Samurai was entered in the Japanese GP, but it was disqualified for insufficient ground clearance.

LeGrand Mk.5

Eglinton had run an F3 car in Europe in 1964, and in 1966 he planned a return with the one-off LeGrand Mk.5. This was an advanced formula car that could be run in F2 or F3 events. It was loosely based on the Mk.3 but reverted to conventional outboard suspension with coil-over shocks. The chassis and body were sized to fit 5-foot, 8-inch-tall Eglinton, and the Mk.5 was smaller and lighter than most European cars. Eglinton, Stephan, and LeGrand fabricated it. Eglinton installed a Cosworth MAE

engine to run as an F3 car during the 1967 season. The one-man effort was a success, with several good finishes, including a fourth at Schleitz, East Germany. The LeGrand, although running on a tiny budget, impressed the European competitors.

LeGrand Mk.6

The Mk.6 replaced the Mk.3 in 1967. This new model was a production version of the Mk.5 that Eglinton had raced in Europe. It could be run in FB or FC, depending on which engine (usually Ford, Lotus, or Alfa) was used. It ran on LeGrand 13-inch wheels.

LeGrand Mk.7

When LeGrand heard the SCCA had started a new Formula A class for American V-8-powered racers, he quickly came out with the Mk.7 model. It was a development of the Mk.6, but with the tube frame widened and strengthened. The first car used a ZF gearbox, while later cars had Hewland LG-500 transaxles. Airheart disc brakes (single spot) gripped solid 10.5-inch rotors. Both Chevy and Ford 302-ci engines could be fitted, although only one customer chose the latter. LeGrand 13-inch wheels were used—9.5 inches wide in front and 11 inches in back.

An improved Mk.7A version had wider wheels and two-spot Airheart brakes. The Mk.7 was sold ready-to-race with a 450-horsepower Chevy engine for $13,372.

Eglinton took the first Mk.7 to Las Vegas in February 1968, where he won an SCCA National. After that, it was all downhill. Eglinton was badly injured in a fiery testing accident involving the Mk.7 and missed the rest of the season. Rex Ramsey took over as works driver, but did not win any major events. Sam Posey drove Peter Bottsford's LeGrand Mk.7 with a Ford V-8 at Mosport in 1968, putting it on the pole, despite being scared to death of the car. As soon as the race started, Posey pulled into the pits and retired before he got hurt. Posey said, "That LeGrand was by far the worst F-5000 car."

LeGrand Mk.8 and Mk.9

The Mk.8 was a one-off sports-racer built from Mk.6 parts. The Mk.9 was an unfinished F3 car intended for Eglinton to take back to Europe. It was not completed after his injury in the Mk.7.

LeGrand Mk.10

Formula Ford started in England in 1967 and moved to the United States the following year. LeGrand quickly penned a new design for the Ford-based formula. The 1968 Mk.10 was based on the Mk.6, with magnesium uprights and the LeGrand cast wheels, but these were removed when the new FF rules banned them. An all-new wedge-shaped body was introduced on the production models. The wheelbase and track of the Mk.6 were increased and the chassis made more solid. The Mk.10 was a successful design and was used by the Jim Russell Racing School for driver training.

LeGrand Mk.11

For 1969, LeGrand developed a new F-5000 car to take over for the troublesome Mk.7. The Mk.11 was the last LeGrand designed by Eglinton, and was developed by LeGrand and Jim Paul. It was built to contest the USAC Pro Series races, and was a completely new design with strengthened chassis and suspension parts. Raced by Ramsey and Paul in pro events, it was uncompetitive and dogged with reliability problems. This car was also run with wings.

After 1969, LeGrand went on to build many more sports-racers and formula cars. Red LeGrand died in 1988, and the company shut down in 1991, after making hundreds of fine racing cars that proudly carried the American colors in formula and sports-racer events.

LE GRAND

LeGrand Race Cars
Lakeview Terrace and Sylmar, California

LEGRAND CHEETAH MK.1
Years built	1962–1965
Engine	BMW 700
Gearbox	BMW
Front suspension	independent
Rear suspension	independent
Brakes	Airheart disc
Body material	aluminum and fiberglass
Weight, approx.	445 pounds
Wheelbase	76 inches
Number built	20-plus

LEGRAND CHEETAH MK.2
Years built	1964–1965
Engines	BMW 700 or Saab 750
Gearboxes	BMW or Saab
Front suspension	independent
Rear suspension	independent
Brakes	Airheart disc
Body material	fiberglass
Weight, approx.	560 pounds
Number built	unknown

LEGRAND CHEETAH MK.3, 3B
Years built	1965–1966
Engines	Ford pushrod 1,100-cc, Lotus TC 1,600-cc, or Alfa Romeo TC 1,600-cc
Gearboxes	Hewland Mk.IV or V
Front suspension	independent
Rear suspension	independent
Brakes	Airheart disc
Body material	fiberglass

Weight, approx.	Formula C 760 pounds; Formula B 850 pounds
Wheelbase	86 inches (prototype was 84 inches)
Number built	approximately 30

LEGRAND MK.4
Year built	1966
Engines	Datsun, Ford, Coventry-Climax, Maserati
Gearbox	Hewland
Front suspension	independent
Rear suspension	independent
Brakes	Airheart disc
Body material	fiberglass
Wheelbase	91 inches
Number built	estimated at seven

LEGRAND MK.5 F3
Year built	1966
Engine	1,000-cc Cosworth-Ford MAE
Gearbox	Hewland
Front suspension	independent
Rear suspension	independent
Brakes	Airheart disc
Body material	fiberglass
Number built	one

LEGRAND MK.6
Year built	1967
Engines	Ford, Lotus, or Alfa Romeo
Gearbox	Hewland
Front suspension	independent
Rear suspension	independent

Brakes	Airheart disc
Body material	fiberglass
Number built	unknown

LEGRAND MK.7
Year built	1968
Engines	Ford or Chevy 5-liter V-8
Gearboxes	ZF or Hewland
Front suspension	independent
Rear suspension	independent
Brakes	Airheart disc
Body material	fiberglass
Weight, approx.	1,270 pounds
Wheelbase	90 inches
Number built	unknown

LEGRAND MK.10
Year built	1968
Engine	1,600-cc Ford
Gearbox	Hewland
Front suspension	independent
Rear suspension	independent
Brakes	disc
Body material	fiberglass
Number built	unknown

LEGRAND MK.11
Year built	1969
Engine	5-liter Chevy V-8
Gearbox	Hewland LG-600
Front suspension	independent
Rear suspension	independent
Brakes	Airheart disc
Body material	fiberglass
Number built	one

Lynx

Bill Riley became one of the top American race car designers, but he was just getting started when he and partner John Mills founded Lynx Cars Incorporated in the mid-1960s. After racing Triumph TR-2 and TR-3s, Riley built a C-Modified special he drove in the South. He then went to work for Ford in Detroit (designing the suspension for the Ford J-Car and Mk.IV race cars). He founded Lynx at the same time.

Lynx A

Riley and Mills built their first car, the Lynx A Formula Vee, in 1965. It had a space frame similar to Zink practice, and only a handful were sold. It was a good learning exercise, but Riley wanted to design a chassis that would be just as rigid but easier to build.

Lynx Mk.II and B

The next Riley FV design, the Lynx Mk.II, appeared in 1966. It was very different from most successful FVs of the time, having two 2x4 rectangular steel side rails in place of a space frame. Although technically unsophisticated, it was imminently practical, being stiff, cheap to build, resistant to damage, and easy to repair. In 1968, a new body was introduced, and the same basic car became the Lynx B. The Lynxes were mostly designed by Riley and assembled by Mills. Lynx FVs were very good race cars and one driven by James Purcell made it to the SCCA runoffs in 1967, but it failed to finish. The next year, Jim Herlinger finished ninth in a Mk.II. In 1970, Lynxes placed fourth and fifth. The Lynx B would finally taste victory in the 1971 ARRC.

Lynx C and D

The Lynx C was a one-off Formula Ford built in 1968 for driver Tony Vogele. The 1970 Lynx D Super Vee effort was star-crossed, although the cars ended up running quite well. At first, the new car was designed around the VW Type 3 engine, but before it was completed, the rules had been changed to allow the heavier Type 4 engine, as used in the Porsche 914, the 411, and the VW Van. This necessitated a

Lynx B was a landmark Formula Vee design that dominated the class in the early 1970s. *Harold Pace*

lot of redesign work, but in 1970, James Purcell won the SCCA Central Division championship and qualified for the ARRC. (He finished down the list.)

In 1971, Riley sold his part of Lynx and moved on to other things, including designing stacks of winning Indy cars and sports prototypes. In 1979, Ford bought the Lynx name and the updated FVs were renamed Caracal. The Caracal is still in production, as are parts for the Lynx FVs.

McKee

Bob McKee got into road racing after being deeply involved in stock car and Indy car racing. He built stockers for Tiny Lund and was a crew chief for Indy-great Dick Rathmann. But in 1961, McKee took on an engine swap for one of his roundy-round pals, Rodger Ward. Ward was a very capable road racing driver and had bought a Cooper Monaco, less engine. McKee swapped an aluminum Buick V-8 into the slot intended for a Climax. Although the car showed great promise, the Cooper transaxle was not up to the task, forcing McKee to design a transaxle of his own using, a Chevy T-10 gearbox coupled to a quick-change final drive unit that allowed on-the-spot gear changes. Pete Weismann assisted McKee in the development. The design was plenty stout and was used in many specials.

LYNX

Lynx Cars Incorporated
Brighton, Michigan

LYNX A

Year built	1965
Engine	Volkswagen (1,200 ci)
Gearbox	Volkswagen
Front suspension	trailing link
Rear suspension	wing axles
Brakes	drum
Body material	fiberglass
Number built	unknown

LYNX MK.II/B

Years built	1966–1979
Engine	Volkswagen (1,200 ci)
Gearbox	Volkswagen
Front suspension	trailing link
Rear suspension	swing axles
Brakes	drum
Body material	fiberglass
Number built	approximately 200

LYNX C

Year built	1968
Engine	Ford (1,600 ci)
Gearbox	Hewland
Front suspension	independent
Rear suspension	independent
Brakes	disc
Body material	fiberglass
Number built	one

LYNX D

Year built	1970
Engine	Volkswagen (1,600 ci)
Gearbox	Hewland
Front suspension	independent
Rear suspension	independent
Brakes	disc
Body material	fiberglass
Number built	four or five

Bob McKee built many successful customer racing cars. *Pete Lyons*

Chevettes

The next obvious step was the construction of a car of his own design. In 1964, he built the Chevette, a midengined special that utilized many General Motors parts from the Chevelle and Corvette (hence the name). He later wished he had trademarked the name.

The first car (Mk.I) was built for Dick Doane, an Illinois Chevy dealer and amateur racing driver who had been campaigning a Corvette Grand Sport. His Chevette used a tubular space frame influenced by McKee's experience with the Ward Monaco, but with better triangulation for increased rigidity. The main framework was round 1.5-inch-diameter seamless

Bob Montana drove this McKee Mk.V with Plymouth Hemi power at the Riverside Times Grand Prix in 1965. *Allen Kuhn*

mild steel tubing, reinforced with smaller tubing and 1.5x2 rectangular steel bulkheads. A 3/8-inch-thick magnesium plate that the steering, master cylinders, and pedals were mounted to stiffened the front bulkhead.

The front suspension was a mixture of American and European parts. The Sprite steering rack was common in sports-racers, while the front spindles and steering arms were courtesy of the Chevelle. The Girling disc brakes were 11.5 inches in diameter all around. Corvette uprights were used in back, with 'Vette trailing arms turned 90 degrees. American Racing 15-inch wheels (7 and 8.5 inches wide) mounted Firestone rubber with stock car tread patterns. A Corvette aluminum radiator was laid over up front to cool the 363-ci fuel-injected Chevy V-8 bolted to the McKee transaxle with a Z-F limited-slip unit. Doane claimed 460 horsepower from the highly modified mill.

The aluminum body was formed by McKee employee Bill Leahy from 0.050 sheet metal and was styled more to reduce frontal area than to provide downforce (typical of the time frame). It was low and rounded, with small blisters over the tires. Inside, narrowed Kellison bucket seats and an Eelco steering wheel were combined with Stewart-Warner and Sun instruments.

The first Chevette was a competent car. Doane raced it in the USRRC, and Dick Thompson also drove it. McKee followed with a series of similar cars with various engines. The very similar Mk.II was built for Jerry Hansen, who ran it in the Midwest for two years with Chevy power and won nine races in a row. The Mk.III had a Ford engine and was purchased by Cobra driver Bob Johnson. However, he never got to

drive it, because Ed Leslie crashed it in practice at Laguna Seca and it was then sold as-is to Dan Gerber.

The next two cars were bigger and had restyled bodywork with more pronounced fender lines. The Mk.IV (called the Ford LMD) was powered by a Holman-Moody 427-ci Ford V-8 and was driven in the USRRC by Mike Hall. Hall won the big-bore class at the Pensacola, Florida, USRRC race in 1964, finishing second overall to Follmer's Lotus-Porsche under-2-liter winner. Hall also finished third at Road America to be classified fifth (tied with Skip Scott) in the USRRC season totals. A very similar McKee (Mk.V) was powered by a Plymouth Hemi and raced by Bob Montana of Phoenix.

McKee Mk.VI and VII

Although the first five cars were similar in concept, McKee wanted to build customer cars that would be standardized to ease production. There were three Mk.VI models built for the 1966 season, all wearing similar fiberglass McLaren-like bodies. The Mk.VI was lighter than the Chevettes, and the chassis and suspension were more sophisticated. McKee spindles were used up front, and the rear suspension was double A-arm with aluminum hub carriers. The brakes were borrowed from the Mustang, and the steering rack was changed to Triumph. Armstrong coil-over shocks were fitted, along with Girling master cylinders.

Bud Clusserath bought the first one, powered by an Olds Toronado engine. Another went to Mak Kronn, who relied on Traco Chevy power. Former Cheetah pilot Ralph Salyer first installed an aluminum 215 Olds, then upgraded to an iron Olds 350. All used the McKee transaxle, which had been beefed up to handle more powerful engines.

Kronn was the most successful of the group, placing second at the Watkins Glen USRRC race and fourth at Las Vegas. He finished seventh in the final standings and won the prestigious Road America June Sprints. Salyer posted a big win at the 1966 SCCA runoffs, taking the C Sports Racing national championship.

This McKee Mk.VI is surrounded by celebrities. Builder Bob McKee is on the left, television star and racer Dick Smothers is in sunglasses, and the driver is Charlie Hayes. *Pete Lyons*

Gene Crowe drives the wedgy McKee Mk.VII shown in the paddock at St. Jovite in 1969. *Pete Lyons*

The Mk.VII was introduced for the 1967 season and was also built in a series of three. However, by the time the fiberglass-bodied racers hit the tracks, the stakes had been raised by McLaren and Lola, leaving the McKees to slide back down the grid. The Mk.VIIs originally had rounded bodies like the Mk.VI, but Salyer upgraded his with a wedge-shaped body. His big-block Olds-powered Cro-Sal Mk.VII starred in the movie *Winning*, driven by Paul Newman. Chevy and Olds engines powered the Mk.VIIs. Salyer joined with engine builder Gene Crower (as the Cro-Sal team), and they received some under-the-table engine development help from Oldsmobile.

Charlie Hayes switched to a Mk.VII Olds from a McLaren in 1967 and finished tenth at Elkhart Lake, three places ahead of Bob Nagel in a Mk.VII Chevy. Hayes also grabbed a seventh at Riverside and a

fourth at Las Vegas to finish ninth in the 1967 Can-Am standings. The next season, Hayes was back in the Mk.VII, finishing seventh at Elkhart Lake and sixth at Edmonton in a car now outclassed by the McLarens and Lolas. Joe Leonard finished eighth in a Mk.VII at the 1969 St. Jovite Can-Am race with a twin-turbocharged Olds V-8, the first appearance of a turbo in the Can-Am.

McKee Howmet Turbines

In 1967, McKee became involved in a radical project to run turbine-powered coupes in FIA races. The brainchild of Ray Heppenstall, the cars were sponsored by Howmet and powered by Continental helicopter engines. The chassis and bodies were essentially modified Mk.VII chassis with coupe versions of the Mk.VI bodywork. (See Howmet entry.)

Armco Cro-Sal Can-Am

McKee took one last stab at the sports-racing business in 1969, when Armco Steel offered to sponsor a radical one-off Can-Am car powered by a twin-turbocharged Oldsmobile V-8. The monocoque chassis was made from thin sheets of stainless steel. Armco selected the materials based on aerospace engineering principles, making the car very light (and challenging to build), with the idea of interesting Detroit in using stainless in place of aluminum on new models. The suspension was also made from stainless, with hollow coil springs and sway bars. Titanium was used for some items where steel was not appropriate. Another unusual feature was four-wheel drive, using a two-speed automatic transmission based on a Turbo-Hydra-matic and a Ferguson transfer case.

As if all of this wasn't trick enough, they added a twin-turbo all-aluminum Oldsmobile engine. Olds couldn't officially help due to the GM antiracing curse, but it did funnel all-aluminum big-block parts to Gene Crower, who built a piping hot 455-ci engine spinning twin TRW turbos. The fiberglass body was a development of the wedge body used on the previous Cro-Sal McKee Mk.VII. It even had a flip-up hydraulic airbrake. Although it gained McKee a lot of publicity, the new car was too complicated to be successful right off the bat, and was never fully developed. Leonard, who had earlier driven the turbo Mk.VII, practiced at the Elkhart Lake Can-Am race but did not start.

McKee F-5000 Cars

McKee built a number of Chevy-powered cars for the F-5000 series. The Mk.8 was based on a space-frame chassis, with lightweight stainless alloy frame tubes, suspension, exhaust system, bulkheads, and pivot pins made by sponsor Armco Steel. They used Kelsey-Hayes brakes, Koni shocks, a Hewland LG600 transaxle, and American Racing wheels. The Mk.8s ran in the 1968 F-5000 Championship, driven by Max Kronn (with a Shelby-prepared Ford engine) and Kurt Reinold. Reinold picked up hard-fought third places at War Bonnet and Mosport, but otherwise they were out of the hunt. Three were built.

McKee built single-seaters for F-5000 racing, like this one shown at Road America in 1969. *Pete Lyons*

Hamilton Vose ran a one-off Mk.11 in 1969. It had a monocoque chassis and was intended for both SCCA and USAC racing.

The Mk.12s were upgraded versions of the tube-frame Mk.8s, and were campaigned in 1969 by Chuck Trowbridge and Dick DeJarld. Trowbridge picked up a seventh at Continental Divide, but normally he circulated around tenth. The next season, Reinold was back in a Mk.12, picking up a seventh at Elkhart Lake. Three Mk.12s were built.

McKee moved on to build electric cars and other projects that paid much better than building racing cars.

McKee tried this ultratechie 4WD racer with a turborcharged Oldsmobile engine (the Armco Cro-Sal Can Am) in 1969.
Pete Lyons

MCKEE

McKee Engineering Corporation
411 W. Colfax Street
Palatine, Illinois

MCKEE MK.I–V

Years built	1964–1965
Engines	Ford, Chevrolet, Plymouth V-8s
Gearbox	McKee four-speed transaxle
Chassis	space frame
Front suspension	independent, coil springs
Rear suspension	independent, coil springs
Brakes	Girling disc
Body material	aluminum
Length	150 inches
Height	30 inches
Price when new	$10,500
Number built	five (one of each model)

MCKEE MK.VI AND VII

Years built	1966–1967
Engines	Chevrolet, Oldsmobile, turbo Oldsmobile V-8s
Gearbox	McKee four-speed transaxle
Chassis	space frame
Front suspension	independent, coil springs
Rear suspension	independent, coil springs
Brakes	Ford disc
Body material	fiberglass
Wheelbase	93 inches
Number built	six (three of each model)

MK.8 AND MK.12 F-5000

Years built	1968–1970
Engines	Ford and Chevy V-8 5-liter
Gearbox	Hewland LG-600
Chassis	space frame
Front suspension	independent, coil springs
Rear suspension	independent, coil springs
Brakes	disc
Body material	fiberglass
Number built	three Mk.8s, three Mk.12s

MK.11 F-5000

Year built	1969
Engine	5-liter Chevy V-8
Gearbox	Hewland LG-600
Chassis	monocoque
Front suspension	independent, coil springs
Rear suspension	independent, coil springs
Brakes	disc
Body material	fiberglass
Number built	one

ARMCO CRO-SAL CAN-AM

Year built	1969
Engine	turbocharged Oldsmobile V-8
Gearbox	two-speed automatic, four-wheel drive
Chassis	stainless steel monocoque
Front suspension	independent, coil springs
Rear suspension	independent, coil springs
Brakes	disc
Body material	fiberglass
Number built	one

We Talk With Bob McKee.

AUTHOR: What was the Howmet project like?

McKEE: Well, we only had a month or six weeks to do them in. The first one was made out of a Mk.VI that I had traded to Ralph Salyer. Doing that and a couple of other projects at the same time was bizerko.

AUTHOR: Did you have any problems packaging the turbine engine in there, or did it fit pretty well?

McKEE: The nice thing is, that engine weighed 165 pounds, and it didn't need a radiator, just an oil cooler, so that made it pretty easy. We had to design a transaxle for it, and that made it a little more difficult.

AUTHOR: Was the Howmet a variation on the cars you used to sell?

McKEE: Yeah, it was pretty much a Can-Am car, but it grew a roof.

AUTHOR: Why did you decide to build your own car in 1964?

McKEE: Well, I always wanted to build cars. I had been a stooge for A. J. Watson, and I always thought he was one of the best guys around building Indy cars. He built straightforward, simple, clean cars. After working on the Cooper, which was a simple, clean car but it had a lot of bent tubes in it, I thought we could do better than that. We had the transaxle, but I would rather build cars than transaxles and we were lucky enough to sell some of them. When Formula 5000 came out, I designed a car for that and sold three cars right off the bat. There weren't too many people making customer cars at that time, most were just one-offs.

AUTHOR: You did some of the first turbocharged engines in the Can-Am. How did that come about?

McKEE: Gene Crowe was primarily responsible for that. He worked for Ralph Salyer and was a very, very good guy . . . a good racer. He built those engines with Oldsmobile kinda looking over his shoulder and helping with parts. And he did a really good job. That engine ended up with 700 pounds of torque and 700 horsepower. It was one strong engine. We put that engine in a four-wheel drive Can-Am car we built for Armco Steel. That was technically a very interesting car and had a lot of innovations and trick materials. The B-1 bomber was made out of some of the same materials. We used a Ferguson torque-split differential that Derek Gardner designed. That was a fun car to do.

AUTHOR: I understand you ran out of sponsorship on that one.

McKEE: That's basically what happened. Oldsmobile was helping as much as they could. Armco had a budget that we certainly exceeded. They wanted to do something technically interesting to show the car manufacturers to interest them in high-strength materials, so they could lighten up cars and help them meet emissions. That's what that whole program was about. In hindsight, the four-wheel drive would really, really work in rainy weather, but the tires kept improving so fast that the McLarens and Lolas with less weight could do better all around than a four-wheel drive car. I think we were 139 pounds heavier because of the four-wheel drive. It was a fun time and lots of people were doing interesting things, and everyone was kind of helping each other out. It's hard to imagine how much fun racing was back then!

Miller

Don Miller built a series of successful H-Modified racing cars in the 1950s. He was known as the guru of all things Crosley, along with ace engine builder Nick Brajevich. Miller's cars were simple and looked crude, but they were well thought out. Each car was different, as some had envelope bodies while others had a hot rod roadster look with clamshell fenders. The roadsters weighed about 760 pounds and were powered by full-race Crosley engines. Miller sold each for around $1,500 with the proviso that he would race it first to shake it down.

Don Miller built many great H-Modifieds. No. 21 has one of the most popular body styles. *Allen Kuhn*

Miller also built at least one front-engined Crosley-powered Formula Junior for the short-lived FRA American Formula Junior regulations. It was a very attractive car that resembled a smaller Stanguellini.

MILLER

Don Miller
Inglewood, California

MILLER SPECIALS
Years built	circa 1955–1960
Engine	750-cc Crosley
Gearbox	four-speed
Chassis	ladder
Front suspension	live axle
Rear suspension	live axle
Brakes	drum
Body material	metal
Number built	eight plus

Multiplex

The Multiplex was a very early effort at an American-built production racer intended for the small-bore classes. It was built in Berwick, Pennsylvania, by the Multiplex Manufacturing Company. Multiplex had made a few cars in the early 1900s, but their first sports car was built in 1952. It was a squarish and gaudily decorated convertible with a Willys six. In 1953, the company introduced the Multiplex 186, a two-seat sports car designed for road or track by former dirt track driver "Fritz" Bingaman.

The Multiplex 186 was a decent design, with a space frame featuring a sheet steel backbone tunnel similar in concept to the later Lotus Elan. The front suspension was independent, with upper A-arms and a lower transverse leaf spring. Monroe shocks were used, and the geometry was adjusted to provide a camber curve that would keep the tires from rolling over. Perforated steel wheels mounted Goodyear 5.90x15 tires, and a Ross steering box provided a quick two turns lock-to-lock. The rear suspension consisted of a Borg-Warner live axle sprung by two parallel leaf springs. Weight distribution was 52/48, with a dry weight of 1,925 pounds. Later, the body was cleaned up from the 1952 version by replacing the tall windshield with a low windscreen.

107

Don Miller built a number of Crosley-powered specials. This car was restored by Joe Puckett, the guiding light for H-Modifieds during the early days of vintage racing, when the tiny terrors once again took to the tracks. *Harold Pace*

Multiplex wanted to build an all-American car and experimented with a Harley-Davidson twin, but reverted to an English Singer 1,500-cc engine for the car's first race at Floyd Bennett Field in New York. Works driver Henry Fanelli put in a good drive to run as high as third behind an OSCA and Jim Pauley's Bandini, before losing a wheel. Up to that point, Fanelli was leading a pack of Porsches, MG Specials, and Siata V-8s. Fanelli also drove the 186 at an AAA race at Turner Air Force Base in Georgia, but he was outrun again by the OSCAs.

Encouraged by the potential of the new car, Multiplex built two more prototypes for a planned production run. These were to have modified Willys engines with fiberglass bodies that resembled Cisitalia coupes or spyders. Apparently, the project never went beyond the three prototypes and perhaps a few bare chassis.

NTM built cars with fiberglass chassis. This Mk.2 has a Honda S-800 engine. *Paul Meis collection*

The NTM Mk.3 was a development of the Mk.2. *Paul Meis collection*

MULTIPLEX	
Multiplex Manufacturing Company	
Berwick, Pennsylvania	
MULTIPLEX 186	
Years built	**1952–1954**
Engines	**Singer or Willys**
Front suspension	**independent**
Rear suspension	**live axle**
Brakes	**drum**
Body material	**fiberglass**
Weight, approx.	**1,925 pounds**
Wheelbase	**85 inches**
Number built	**three**

NTM

A tiny sports-racer called the NTM shared something with the first Chaparral 2s—a fiberglass chassis. NTMs were built by fiberglass expert Steve Norcross and his backer, Dr. Morton Tabin, and were named after their company, Norcross-Tabin Manufacturing. Norcross made a wide variety of fiberglass products,

including displays, an economy car called the Dragonfly, and bodies for the Grand Prix Racing kart track franchise in California. With the partners' experience in automobile suspension design and composite structures, the first NTM was strong and simple.

NTM Mk.1

The first NTM was built in 1967–1968, using only standard fiberglass with polyester resins (no exotic epoxies as used in the Chaparral). It had a fiberglass monocoque with an aluminum roll bar and rear subframe. The front suspension was attached to aluminum brackets bolted to the tub. Airheart disc brakes were used at all corners, and the body was molded in colored gel coat. It had a Saab 850-cc engine driving through a Hewland Mk.VII gearbox.

The car was driven by Tabin and Ron Dennis, who failed to finish at the 1967 SCCA runoffs, the American Road Race of Champions (ARRC). In 1970, it was reengined at NTM with a Honda 750 engine, which necessitated replacing the rear of the chassis with a steel subframe and upgrading the suspension to Mk.2 specifications.

NTM Mk.2

An improved Mk.2 design was completed in 1969, with help from Jim Leach, a college professor who cast aluminum suspension uprights, hub carriers, and other parts in his backyard foundry. The Mk.2 was a major redesign, with new suspension

and a stronger tub, along with revised bodywork. Two were built, originally powered with Saab 850 engines. During the 1969 season, they were changed to Yoshimura-prepared Honda S-800 engines with Webster transaxles. Tabin immediately became competitive with the best D sports-racers

Steve Norcross sits in one of his creations, an NTM Mk.4. *Paul Meis collection*

NTM	
Norcross-Tabin Manufacturing	
Urbana, Illinois	
NTM MK.1 AND MK.2	
Years built	**1968–1969**
Engines	**850-cc Saab, 750-cc Honda**
Gearbox	**Webster five-speed**
Front suspension	**independent**
Rear suspension	**independent**
Brakes	**Airheart disc**
Body material	**fiberglass**
Wheelbase	**78 inches**
Number built	**three**

around. He finished third in the Midwest Division and second at the 1969 ARRC. In 1970, Tabin repeated his second-place performance at the ARRC.

Other models followed. The Mk.3 and Mk.4 (a B sports-racer) came out in 1972. A total of seven NTMs were built before Norcross got out of racing in 1972. An eighth car was built after the molds and spares were sold to Chuck Ulinski. A number of NTMs have survived and are currently racing in vintage events.

Old Yaller

See Balchowsky entry.

PBS

Paul and Bob Swensen (PBS) were racing fans who built Fiat-based racing engines and cars in the late 1960s. Their first product was a twin cam engine for the H-Modified class based on a Fiat 600D block. Their first engine used an eight-port pushrod "hemi" head they had made, although it didn't work. In 1964, they decided to try another angle and cast their own chain-driven twin cam cylinder heads, breathing through two 40-millimeter Weber carburetors. In final form, this 850-cc engine produced an impressive 85 horsepower at 8,500 rpm. A larger 1,000-cc engine was also added to their line, producing 110 horsepower. The engines sold for $1,600 to $1,700 depending on equipment.

PBS performed wonders with Fiat engines in its sports-racers. *Harold Pace*

PBS built two of these lovely little coupes, powered by its own line of hot Fiat engines. *PBS*

PBS	
PBS Engineering	
Garden Grove, California	
PBS MK.1 AND MK.2	
Year built	**1965**
Engine	**PBS/Fiat 850**
Gearboxes	**Fiat four-speed or Hewland five-speed**
Front suspension	**independent**
Rear suspension	**independent**
Brakes	**disc**
Body material	**fiberglass**
Weight, approx.	**740 pounds**
Number built	**two**

In late 1965, PBS built its own space-frame, midengined chassis and clothed it in a fiberglass coupe body designed by engineer Clark Adams. Airheart disc brakes were used, and the first car used a Fiat transmission (a Hewland was later substituted). Kit car builder LaDawri, who marketed the body separately as the Formula Libre, built the body. Bud Patterson and Bob Swensen drove the factory car, powered by an 850-cc engine, and ran it with some success in 1966 and 1967. A second car (Mk.2) was sold to Elliott Mendenhall, who raced it in the Southwest. Although PBS later built other racing cars, the company was not in the chassis business and preferred to sell only its engines. PBS is still in business, making Fiat performance parts and working on environmental projects.

Quantum

The success of Formula Vee inspired other groups to emulate the low-cost/tight-rules formula. In the mid-1960s, Saab was selling reasonable quantities of its three-cylinder sedans and Sonnets in the United States. They had proven to be plenty quick, though handicapped by the small displacement (850-cc) of their engines. The engines were most successful as the power unit of choice for H-Modifieds in the post-Crosley days. In 1964, Saab fanatic Henry Rudkin studied the Formula Vee rules and hatched a set of regs of his own for a Saab-based formula car class.

The class was to be called Formula S and would require Saab three-cylinder engines and transmissions with Saab-stamped suspension arms front and rear. Any chassis design could be used, along with the front spindle supports. The first (and only) company to offer Formula S racing cars was Quantum Division in Seymour, Connecticut.

Quantum Formula S

The Quantum was the brainchild of Henry "Hank" Rudkin, who had been racing since the 1950s. He designed a neat little midengined racer on a semimonocoque chassis (space frame with stressed panels). The main chassis members were two 4-inch-diameter tubes that ran from the cockpit to the front suspension. (They served double duty as fuel tanks.)

At the rear, the Quantum used Saab front hub carriers and attached the steering arms to the chassis with tie rods. In specially cast front uprights,

The Quantum Formula S was an attempt at a Saab-based series similar to Formula Vee. *Bob Harrington*

mounted steel spindles were controlled by standard Saab rack-and-pinion steering. Coil-over shocks were used all around. The fiberglass body was molded in three parts and attached with Dzus fasteners. Weight was a reasonable 830 pounds.

Although the Quantum was to be sold in kit form, Rudkin also offered tuned Saabs producing around 65 horses. The trick parts included a Saab GT crankshaft, racing pistons, and a special cylinder head and distributor. The port timing was changed, and a tricked-out Solex 40A1 carburetor was used. Rudkin would sell you an engine for $595 plus the exchange for your stock 850-cc Saab mill.

Driving the Quantum was a little tricky, as the engine had a narrow 1,500-rpm power band, and two-cycle engines have negligible engine drag for slowing down. Otherwise, it behaved much like a Formula Junior.

Saab offered to help by kitting up the parts needed to construct a Formula S, including the GT gearbox, for $1,095. Quantum sold its kits for $1,347, so a race-ready car could be assembled for around $3,300. A builder could save a few bucks by starting with a wrecked Saab GT to cannibalize.

Despite selling a number of cars, Quantum was disappointed when the SCCA refused to recognize Formula S. One driver who was impressed with the simple little car was Bill Rutan, a front-running SCCA racer. Rutan had been assembling Quantums for Saab America and racing one himself. In 1966, he finished fourth in FC at the ARRC with a Saab-

powered Quantum. The next year, he upgraded his Quantum to be more competitive with FC cars from Lotus, Brabham, and Cooper. While the original Formula S used steel Saab wheels, Rutan fitted wider mag wheels and revised the suspension. Most important, he replaced the little three-banger with a Cosworth-Ford SCA engine. At the 1967 ARRC, Rutan qualified on the pole and led the field to the finish.

We Talk With Bill Rutan.

AUTHOR: Tell me about the Quantum.

RUTAN: I got involved in the Quantum program with Saab of America; they were over in New Haven. They sold 62 kits. I raced them in 1965 and 1966. They dropped out of it in 1966, and they gave me the last Quantum I had built up for them. I had finished third in the runoffs at Riverside in it. I raced one more race the next season with the Saab engine, but I could see it was just not cutting the mustard against the SCA Cosworths that were coming to the races. I still have that Quantum, and the Tecno I won the runoffs in too. Anyway, I took that two-stroke stuff out and bought a very clapped-out SCA and rigged that all up in the car. I did quite well. I took it to Daytona and the only guy who was giving me a hard time was Bill Gobelmann, in a well-prepared Brabham GT-18. But he dropped a valve and I won.

AUTHOR: What else did you have to do to the Quantum to get it to work, other than adding the SCA Cosworth?

RUTAN: I completely reworked that dumb little car. They were tough little cars. I don't know that they cornered that quickly, but they were absolutely safe to drive. If you got in trouble with one of those things you had to do something stupid. It came with Saab wheels and brakes. I went to discs all around, newer wheels. When I had the three-cylinder engine, I bought a Colotti gearbox conversion, and boy, it didn't work. It was terrible. I ended up converting it to a Hewland.

Fred Puhn built these rapid little Quasar sports-racers before he wrote his well-known reference books on brakes and handling. *Fred Puhn*

Quasar

Fred Puhn built a series of remarkable little D sports racers (DSRs) starting in 1970. Puhn was already well known for the spun-aluminum, pie-plate wheels made by his company, Chassis Engineering, when he decided to build a car of his own design. Earlier, he had designed the Santee sports car (see Santee SS entry). The Quasar was a conventional DSR, with an aluminum monocoque center section reinforced with aluminum bulkheads and tubes. Square-tube aluminum subframes mounted the suspension front and rear. The complete frame weighed 70 pounds.

Puhn duplicated suspension geometry from a proven Brabham F3 car, adding Triumph Spitfire steering and Airheart four-wheel disc brakes. Although the rear suspension used conventional coil springs, torsion bars were used in front to allow a lower nose profile (although some customers insisted on coil springs up front). Tiny 10-inch-diameter wheels (7 inches wide) were used in front with 13-inch rims in back (9 or 10 inches wide).

For his personal car, Puhn chose a Hillman Imp engine, a SOHC design derived from the Coventry-Climax FWA. It was canted over at a 45-degree angle and race-prepared by Ian Fraser in England. It was destroked to meet the 850-cc displacement limit for DSR and put out 88 horsepower. A Hewland Mk.7 transaxle with six forward speeds was used.

It took Puhn and business partner Jim Sernink two years to build the first car. Sernink also built one, but with a 1,300-cc Ford engine. Another Quasar was also fitted with a 128-horsepower 1,300-cc Ford engine to run in CSR. *Road & Track* tested the Imp-powered car in 1970 and found it had a top speed of 124 miles per hour, ran the quarter-mile in 15.3 seconds, and did 0-to-60 in 9.4 seconds. Puhn was undefeated in class on the West Coast in 1970 and ran fourth at the SCCA runoffs at Road Atlanta.

Puhn offered Quasars with Imp power for $9,500 complete, or enough parts to build one for $3,000 (less running gear). He also sold plan sets, and several owners built their cars from scratch.

In the early 1970s, Quasar also built a 2-liter sports-racer with a Cosworth FVA engine for Chuck McCarty, but in 1973, the doors closed for good.

We Talk With Fred Puhn.

AUTHOR: You went from one extreme to the other, from the big V-8 Santee to the smallest racing class.

PUHN: At Santee, I was an employee, and we had to do what was best for the company. I couldn't build what I really wanted. The Santee was a road car you could race, like the Cobra. The Quasar was an all-out race car that you could never drive on the street. It took two years to build the first Quasar, because it was primarily

my own money. We started out building three cars. We didn't copy anything this time. I had a lot more engineering experience in the aerospace industry, so I built a monocoque aluminum car designed like an airplane. There was hardly any steel in it.

AUTHOR: I understand Jim Sernink was your partner.

PUHN: Sernink was one of the three people who bought one of the Quasars. We each paid for our own parts; I did the engineering. Sernink was my shop manager, and he worked on the styling of the body. He was more of an artist. I still have the Sunbeam Imp-powered car in my barn, waiting to be restored.

AUTHOR: How many Quasars did you build?

PUHN: I wish I knew. Memory fades, but we didn't crank out a lot of cars. Not all the cars were completed at the factory—we sold plans, we sold kits. I would guess there were probably a dozen of them out there. Every one of them was different. When I sold the business, everything went, but I recently bought a set of the plans again so I can sell plan sets to those who want a brand-new old Quasar.

AUTHOR: When did you sell the company?

PUHN: It was in 1973. We had an oil embargo and it killed the business. We were about to go bankrupt. All our supplies quadrupled in price and no one was racing anything anymore. So I sold the company.

AUTHOR: Did the new owners sell any more cars?

PUHN: No, they just went bankrupt. It lasted another year, and they sold some parts. But the wheel company survived. The Monocoque Wheel Company is in Santee, California, right across from the old Santee factory. I invented those wheels back in the 1960s.

Race Car Associates (RCA)

The RCA Formula Vee was an attractive design with an open grille that made it look more like a Formula Junior. Otherwise, it was a conventional Vee. None figured prominently at the ARRC. RCAs were sold in fair numbers and are still seen in vintage racing events.

The RCA Formula Vee was an attractive, if rare, model. *Harold Pace*

111

Reventlow Automobiles Inc.

See Scarab entry.

Sadler

Canadian Bill Sadler not only built some of the best big-bore sports-racers of the 1950s, he also successfully campaigned one of his Chevy-powered rockets in Europe a year before Lance Reventlow built his first Scarab. Sadler went on to build the predecessors of F-5000 and Can-Am cars, then disappeared from the scene as quickly as he had appeared.

Sadler's first racing special was a 1949 Hillman Minx that he repowered with a Ford V-8/60 engine. Sadler later raced an MG TD, but he really wanted to put his training as a missile technician to work on a racing car of his own design.

Sadler Mk.1

The 1954 Sadler Mk.1 was based on Jowett Jupiter running gear installed in a simple ladder frame and clothed in a crude aluminum body. Jowett suspension was used, with torsion bar springing and a live axle in back. Soon, Sadler developed a stubby fiberglass body and installed a Triumph TR-2 engine equipped with his own fuel injection system.

The Triumph showed potential, but when it threw a rod, Sadler opted for the brand-new Chevy 265-inch V-8 introduced in 1955. His family was in the auto parts business and had connections with General Motors of Canada, so a 200-horsepower two four-barrel version was delivered. Sadler adapted it to the Triumph gearbox and raced it through the 1955 season.

Sadler Mk.2

Sadler wanted to try a variety of suspension and running gear changes, so he built up a new car better suited to the powerful Chevy engine. A ladder frame was fabricated from 3.5-inch chrome-moly

tubing using the same Jowett kingpins and upper wishbones as the Mk.1. The torsion bars were replaced with leaf springs in front, which also functioned as the lower suspension arms. A 1934 ENV preselector gearbox replaced the marginal TR unit, and Austin-Healey drum brakes were fitted. In back, Sadler fabricated a low-pivot swing-axle system made from Austin-Healey parts. Later, the Chevy 265 was replaced with a 283 bored out to 300 ci. The Mk.1 fiberglass body was bolted on, and Sadler was ready to take on Europe.

Sadler decided to spend 1957 in England, then the center of the racing world, and arranged to work for John Tojiero while he raced his Mk.2 all over the island. Sadler and his wife lived in a trailer in Tojiero's back yard while he machined and designed gearboxes for racing money. It was the first good look the British had at a Chevy V-8, and at the Brighton Speed Trials, Sadler took home the trophy for fastest time of day. In addition to the trophy, Sadler won a

Bruce Kessler in the Sadler Mk.2 trails Jack Flaherty's Lister and Sam Weiss in a Porsche RSK. *Allen Kuhn*

check for £100 which he invested in a set of stylish aluminum body panels.

Upon his return to Canada, Sadler changed the Mk.2 over to Triumph disc brakes up front, installed his new body, and swapped the two quads for triple two-barrel carbs. The 1958 season was notable for fierce battles between the Scarabs and the Cunningham Listers, but Sadler's Mk.2 was able to mix it up with both forces, winning the Watkins Glen Classic over E. D. Martin's Ferrari 315S.

The Sadler Mk.2 was a race winner with its Chevy engine. *Harold Pace*

Bill Sadler himself puts the resurrected Sadler Mk.3 through its paces at the Monterey historic races. *Harold Pace*

Sadler Mk.3

Earl Nisonger was president of a large auto parts company, and he sponsored Sadler for the 1959 season. With an adequate budget for a change, a new car was designed with a proper space frame and a lower version of the Mk.2 body. Fabricated front A-arm suspension with coil-over Koni shocks replaced the Jowett parts, and in back, a low-pivot swing axle was located by trailing arms. Girling disc brakes with aluminum calipers were used all around. The engine was now a 340-horsepower 327-ci Chevy, breathing through Hillborn fuel injection and driving through a Borg-Warner T-10 four-speed gearbox. Despite being driven by Sadler and hired guns Paul O'Shea and Bruce Kessler, the Mk.3 had hard luck all through the 1959 season.

Sadler-Meyer Special

In 1959, Sadler built the Sadler-Meyer Special for John Van Meyer. It was powered by a 400-ci Buick V-8, which was a huge engine for the time. Meyer won the SCCA Unlimited Class Championship with it.

Sadler Mk.4

The Mk.4 was a simplified version of the Mk.3, designed for series production with a live rear axle in place of the swing axles. Only one was made, and it was sold to David Greenblatt and Luigi Cassiani, who used it as the concept for their Dailu 1 racing car.

Sadler Formula Junior

By the late 1950s, Formula Junior was fast becoming a battleground for racing car manufacturers striving to build the fastest cars at the highest prices. Sadler took a different approach, opting for a simple front-engined design that would be cheap to race. The company used BMC engines, gearboxes, and live axles in a conventional Elva-like body. The Sadler F-Jr. sold for $2,995 complete, and a dozen were made. Sadler said it was "the best seat in the house" to watch the races from.

Sadler Formula 3

This one-off Formula 3 car was built for a customer in Buffalo, New York. Similar to period Coopers, the Sadler had special cast-aluminum wheels and a rack-and-pinion steering unit designed by Sadler. Two Alfin drum brakes were used in front with a single one in back. A Triumph Tiger 650 engine was fitted, but the car's subsequent history is sketchy. It has survived and is currently awaiting restoration.

Sadler Sport Karts

A run of 30 single-engined Sadler Karts were built for go kart racing. These had drive from the engine to one wheel and a driveshaft to take the power to the opposite wheel as well.

Sadler Formula Libres

Sadler's first go at the Formula Libre (anything goes) class was a front-engined Sadler Formula Junior with a Chevy V-8 wedged inside. There wasn't even room for a clutch or gearbox, so the engine was connected directly to the differential. When the starter button was pushed the car would chug and lurch to life, and the engine would die if the car was going too slow. It was a deadly contraption and never raced.

Learning from this episode, Sadler built a proper F-Libre for the 1960 Watkins Glen F-Libre race. Brakes and front suspension were borrowed from the failed Libre, but a new frame with a midmounted 301-ci Chevy was made up. A clutch was added, but

This Sadler Formula Libre was called the "Formula Ferocious." *Dave Friedman; Jack Boxstrom Collection*

with no gearbox; it had only one forward speed. This car was nicknamed the Formula Ferocious and driven by Canadian Champion Peter Ryan to competitive lap times, but off-course damage caused its retirement. This car set the basic design for future F-5000 cars, with a midmounted domestic V-8 engine. It was not run again until recently when it was restored for vintage racing.

Sadler Mk.5

Sold on midengined designs, Sadler built a two-car team of Mk.5 sports-racers for the 1961 season. A sturdy space frame mounted the fabricated suspension and a handsome aluminum body. Sadler called on his gearbox-machining experience to make a two-speed transaxle out of a Halibrand quick-change rear end. Once again, hot Chevy mills provided power. The two cars ran quickly but unreliably. Sadler had a falling out with sponsor Comstock Construction and quit the team. A pity, as the Mk.5

Bill Sadler built two Mk. 5 sports-racers for the 1961 season. *Dave Friedman; Jack Boxstrom Collection*

was one of the first midengined Chevy-powered racing cars. One Mk.5 was destroyed in a fire and the other currently competes in vintage racing.

Fed up with racing at the age of 29, Sadler called it quits and became a successful electrical engineer in the aerospace industry. He later built advanced aircraft and had his own airplane company. In 1972, he built a one-off Formula Super Vee just for fun and later built a new Mk.3 from spare parts, which he runs in vintage racing. It's good to see him back!

Santee

Noted race car builder Fred Puhn (later of Quasar fame) and engineer John McCann built two prototypes for a line of sports cars to be called Santee. The company was founded in 1961 and built a prototype street sports car, plus a racing model to be called the Santee SS. The attractive fiberglass body looked a bit like the Jaguar XKE that came out the next year. The street car was intended to use the

Buick 215-ci aluminum engine, while the SS had the hotter Oldsmobile HD version, which had better cylinder heads. Santee fitted it with four Weber 45-millimeter carburetors and a hot cam, to give around 250 horsepower with a weight of 1,400 pounds. The Santee project died in 1962, after only the two prototypes and a partial street car were completed, but during 1963 and 1964 Willie West and McCann raced the SS in California SCCA races. Fred Puhn now owns all Santees.

114

SADLER

Sadler Racing Cars
St. Catharines, Ontario, Canada

SADLER MK.1
Year built	1954
Engines	Jowett Jupiter and Triumph TR-2
Gearbox	four-speed
Front suspension	independent
Rear suspension	live axle
Brakes	drum
Body material	fiberglass
Number built	one

SADLER MK.2
Year built	1955
Engine	Chevy V-8
Gearbox	ENV preselector
Front suspension	independent
Rear suspension	swing axle
Brakes	disc/drum
Body material	fiberglass and aluminum
Number built	one

SADLER MK.3
Year built	1959
Engine	Chevy V-8
Gearbox	four-speed
Front suspension	independent
Rear suspension	swing axle
Brakes	Girling disc
Body material	aluminum
Weight, approx.	1,680 pounds
Wheelbase	86 inches
Number built	one

SADLER MK.4
Year built	1959
Engine	Chevy V-8
Gearbox	four-speed
Front suspension	independent
Rear suspension	live axle
Brakes	Girling disc
Body material	aluminum
Weight, approx.	1,680 pounds
Wheelbase	86 inches
Number built	one

SADLER-MEYER SPECIAL
Year built	1959
Engine	Buick V-8
Gearbox	four-speed
Front suspension	independent
Rear suspension	live axle
Brakes	Girling disc
Body material	aluminum
Number built	one

SADLER MK.5
Year built	1961
Engine	Chevy V-8
Gearbox	two-speed
Front suspension	independent
Rear suspension	independent
Brakes	Girling disc
Body material	aluminum
Number built	two

SADLER FORMULA JUNIOR
Year built	1959
Engine	1-liter BMC
Gearbox	four-speed
Front suspension	independent
Rear suspension	live axle
Brakes	drum
Body material	fiberglass
Number built	12

SADLER FORMULA 3
Year built	1959
Engine	Triumph 650 Tiger
Gearbox	four-speed
Front suspension	independent
Rear suspension	independent
Brakes	drum
Body material	aluminum
Number built	one

SADLER FORMULA LIBRE (MIDENGINE)
Year built	1960
Engine	Chevy V-8
Gearbox	1-speed
Front suspension	independent
Rear suspension	independent
Brakes	disc
Body material	fiberglass
Number built	one

We Talk With Fred Puhn.

The Santee SS could have been a competitor against the early Cobras. John McCann drove it in the 1960s. *John McCann collection*

The secret to the Santee performance was a hot GM aluminum V-8 with four Weber carbs. *John McCann collection*

SANTEE

Santee Automobiles
Fred Puhn and John McCann
California

SANTEE SS

Year built	**1961**
Engine	**Oldsmobile V-8 (215 ci)**
Gearbox	**GM four-speed**
Front suspension	**independent**
Rear suspension	**independent**
Brakes	**Corvette drum**
Body material	**fiberglass**
Weight, approx.	**1,400 pounds**
Number built	**one**

AUTHOR: Tell me about the Santee project.

PUHN: I was working for a company called Gyrotor Incorporated. They were building helicopters. Or, rather, they wanted to build helicopters. They were building nothing. It was a start-up company, and they had gotten involved in litigation with an aerospace company that had stolen their patents. They had a factory and a staff but nothing to build. They were complaining and saying they should find something to keep the people busy and maybe make some money. Everybody in the place liked cars. My lifelong ambition since I was a kid was to build my own car, so I pushed the idea that we should build a car. I said America didn't have a good sports car. The 1961 Corvette was kind of a lemon at the time—it was only fast in a straight line. Why not build something European, like a Sprite? Everyone agreed. I took a block of wood and carved one out, kind of copying a Ferrari I liked at the time. We decided we were going to build a $2,000 sports car that looked like a Ferrari. It didn't take long to realize this wasn't going to work, particularly if there was a lot of hand-building involved. So we decided to build a high-performance sports car we could sell for more money. We found we could buy new Buick-Oldsmobile aluminum V-8s for less than the little engines we had first considered [the Fageol/Crosley engine]. Our cost was $600.

AUTHOR: Which parts did you use?

PUHN: We used that lovely aluminum engine and a Pontiac Tempest four-speed transaxle. I was the designer of the car, and I used the transaxle to get better weight distribution. Like all 21-year-old engineers, I wanted to have the ultimate in everything, so I copied from Costin's book [*Racing and Sports Car Chassis Design*] that had just come out and gave it the latest Grand Prix car suspension. Dolphin Engineering was right across the airport from Santee Automobiles. To speed things up, we used Dolphin rear suspension with magnesium uprights, just beefed up a little bit. In front, we copied the Lotus 19. We used Corvette metallic brakes because we wanted to stick with an American product. The body design was sent to an artist who made it longer, lower, and sleeker. Then we gave the drawings to a model maker, who changed it some more.

AUTHOR: It keeps changing as you go.

PUHN: Yeah, everyone had a hand in it. We made a 1/10 scale model that we used to make body bucks. Basically, it was a race car with a stock engine. It was a multitubular space frame patterned after the Mercedes 300 SLR. We built a road prototype and a race car in a year. I put together a blend of things that weren't very practical to produce, but we were idealistic car enthusiasts.

AUTHOR: How about the race car?

PUHN: The race car was paid for by one of the team members, John McCann. John was my roommate. He was a couple years older than me and had an engineering background. He had built his own race car called the Teakettle. He was quite a good driver and an engineer. I brought in Al Bond, who was an experienced mechanic and had crewed on the Jones–De Camp Crosley. The street car weighed 1,800 pounds, had 200 horsepower, and went like stink. It was really quick—probably the quickest car you could get in 1961–1962. We would go out at night and race anyone we could find. The race car was another matter; we lightened it up, sectioned the body a couple of inches, and hopped up the engine. I really wasn't an engine expert. We needed a closer-ratio gearbox, since the Tempest wasn't close enough. Corvette came up with a close-ratio transmission, so we got one of the first ones, cut the back end off, resplined it, and bolted it to the Tempest differential. We used the Corvette racing brakes. They were heavy but they stopped the car. The car weighed 1,400 pounds. I fell in love with ram tuning, so we made a manifold with four sidedraft Webers that crossed over the engine. We estimated 300 horsepower at 7,000 rpm. That car was fast. It's the fastest car I've ever ridden in, to this day.

AUTHOR: How did it perform on the track?

PUHN: Unfortunately, it takes a lot of money to develop a race car. We took it to Riverside to test it, and Carroll Shelby was there testing the prototype Cobras. McCann got in the car and hauled butt. The first lap he comes around Turn 1 at around 7,000 rpm and it sounded like a Formula 1 car. He made a couple of hot laps and came in to have it checked out, and all the Shelby crew came down and looked at it. Shelby said, "That looks real light." Our chassis was about ten years ahead of the Cobra.

AUTHOR: So what happened?

PUHN: When the money ran out we just kept on working. Four of us were sharing a room. When the food ran out we had to stop—we were starving. One of the stockholders came over and gave us a bag of groceries; then we left and went out and found jobs. It was an incredible experience.

Sardini

There were many talented self-taught mechanics who jumped on the bandwagon when Formula Vee cranked up in 1962. One of the best Vees was the Sardini, built in Manhattan, Kansas, by Don Pereboom. He had no formal engineering training, but after seeing his first Formcar, he was convinced he could build something better. "I thought, 'My God,

The Sardini was an early Formula Vee that won many races in the Midwest. *Don Pereboom*

SARDINI

Don Pereboom
Manhattan, Kansas

SARDINI

Years built	**1963–1965**
Engine	**1,200-cc Volkswagen**
Gearbox	**Volkswagen four-speed**
Front suspension	**trailing link**
Rear suspension	**swing axle**
Brakes	**drum**
Body material	**fiberglass**
Weight, approx.	**840 pounds**
Wheelbase	**83.5 inches**
Number built	**ten**

you mean to tell me people will pay money for this?'" Pereboom recalls.

Pereboom was in the Kansas State Sports Car Club, where he met Bob Hubbard, a talented driver who raced a Porsche Speedster. Pereboom became interested in racing and designed his own FV in 1963, with a comical name inspired by a Gordini he had worked on. The Sardini was pretty typical of an early FV, with an 83.5-inch wheelbase and a simple space frame, but the suspension worked very well, and the car was competitive right out of the box. Hubbard signed on as the works driver. The combination worked, with Hubbard winning the Midwest Division SCCA class championship in 1964 and 1965. The first customer car won $1,000 in an FV money race held at Aspen, Colorado. Other Sardinis ran successfully in other parts of the country.

Pereboom built ten cars, with some sold in kit form. The Sardini was a solid car with a strong regional reputation.

We Talk With Don Pereboom.

AUTHOR: Why did you pick FV to build a car for?

PEREBOOM: I bought my first new VW in the fall of 1960. I started at Kansas State that year, and I decided I wanted one of those economy cars. I made the deal and got one of the last 36-horse brand-new cars in the United States. I went to work for a VW dealer in Manhattan, Kansas, as the sales manager. Then I met Bob Hubbard, and we used to go to the races. At that time, he was racing a Porsche Speedster. Then he moved to Emporia, Kansas, as the service manager for a VW dealer. Then Hubbard bought a Formcar. I saw it run and then I took a real good look at it. With Bob's engineering background, he looked at it too. Then we put our heads together and decided there was a better way to do it. Finally I said, "If I build a car will you drive it?" He said, "Sure." I incorporated in 1963.

AUTHOR: How did you improve on the Formcar?

PEREBOOM: It was hard to get to everything on a Formcar. It was hard to work on and we improved the rear suspension by relocating the trailing arm. Of course the body had to be such-and-such dimension all the way down. You were really screwed. It was like you had a box and the body had to fit in that box. Of course, the measurements were the same as a Formcar.

AUTHOR: What did you change on the rear trailing arm?

PEREBOOM: The trailing arms, for those days, were long—way long. There's more to it than that. The axle locates at the end of the trailing arm. You have to consider what it does to the handling if that locating point is above, even with, or below the axle centerline. It alters the roll centers. I always tried to figure out why it handled so well, because everyone who drove a Sardini said how well it handled.

AUTHOR: What did you do to make it easier to work on?

PEREBOOM: All the other cars, you could spend 15 minutes taking off body panels so you could work on them. We had a lift-off body top section and in ten seconds you could have instant access to any part on the car. One time at Garnett, just for demonstration purposes, we changed an engine in ten minutes!

Lance Reventlow was the young boss at the Scarab factory. *Tom Cardin*

Scarab

There have been many great American race cars, but the best of the breed has to be the Scarab sports-racers. They were beautiful, successful, and exquisitely prepared. They soundly defeated the best Listers, Ferraris, and Maseratis in the country and looked great doing it. They were the inspiration for hundreds of specials and became the most valuable of collectible American classic racing cars. On the other hand, Scarab also built one of the slowest and least dependable Formula 1 cars of all time, one that was so bad it is only referred to in textbooks as an example of how not to go F1 racing. How the same group of people managed to hit both extremes is a great story.

The catalyst for creating the Scarabs was young Lance Reventlow. Born in 1936 as the son of Woolworth heiress Barbara Hutton and Danish Count Kurt von Haugwitz-Reventlow, he endured a childhood of massive wealth and constant publicity. His parents had a bitter divorce, followed by a custody battle that left Reventlow angry, untrusting, and bored. But by his early 30s, he found something that could hold his interest—automobiles. He made friends with another young well-to-do gearhead named Bruce Kessler, and the two of them began racing sports and formula cars in America and Europe. In 1957, they toured the great European racing car factories, in particular the Lister works in Cambridge, England. Although Reventlow had intended to buy one of their chassis to run the next year, he became convinced he and a team of Americans could build a better car back home in California.

Scarab Mk.1

The linchpin in the Reventlow plan was Warren Olsen, an experienced mechanic and race car preparation expert who had maintained Reventlow's racers. Olsen had plenty of experience with other racing efforts and knew how to get things done. He went headhunting among the best race shops in Southern California to put together Reventlow Automobiles Inc. (RAI), based out of Olsen's shop in North Hollywood, California. At Kurtis he found Dick Troutman and Tom Barnes, and from the aborted Chevrolet racing effort came driver and mechanic Chuck Daigh. Master fabricator Phil Remington, metal shaper Emil Deidt, engine mavins Jim Travers and Frank Coon (later to form Traco), and premier special builder Ken Miles all contributed to the effort.

Miles laid down the general chassis layout, but once Olsen and his crew got started, they had to improvise most of it. At a time when most big-bore machinery was based on ladder frames, the first Scarab (which Reventlow named for an Egyptian dung beetle as a joke) had a well-triangulated space frame made from 4130 chrome-moly tubing with fabricated double A-arm front suspension based on Ford spindles, coil springs, and Monroe shocks. In back, coil springs mounted a de Dion suspension system with four trailing links and a Watts Link for lateral location. The suspension system was similar to what was used by Ferrari and Lister and was superior to the live axles used on the D-Type Jaguars. A Morris Minor steering rack was one of the few non-American parts, and the brakes were Ford with custom cast-aluminum finned drums. They were the most effective racing drum brakes ever made.

The heart of the Scarab was the relatively untried Chevy small-block V-8. By 1957, it was just starting to come into its own as a performance engine, now displacing 283 ci. Daigh had some experience with the Chevy small blocks, so he built the first Scarab engines in a corner of the shop. They were soon bored out to 301 ci, then 327, and even 339 ci. Topped with Hillborn fuel injection and sparked by a

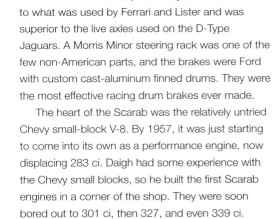

Lance Reventlow wrings out his new toy at Santa Barbara in 1958. *Allen Kuhn*

Vertex magneto, they were tuned to produce around 360 reliable horsepower. These engines were backed up by aluminum-case Borg-Warner T-10 gearboxes. A modified Halibrand quick-change center section was mounted in back, with inboard rear brakes. The lovely aluminum body was penned by art student Chuck Pelly and built by Deidt, who made a living building Indy cars. Once completed, it was painted pearl blue and pinstriped by legendary pinstripe artist Von Dutch. Halibrand wheels were chosen, and the first car built had left-hand drive.

The Mk.1 was quick from the start. The first race for the Scarab was at Phoenix in March 1958. Driver

Troutman and Barnes built both of these historic racers. A Scarab Mk.II leads a Chaparral Mk.I. *Harold Pace*

The Scarab team tried an Offenhauser engine at Santa Barbara in 1959, but it was not a success. Here, Bruce Kessler is about to be passed by John von Neumann in a Ferrari. *Allen Kuhn*

Bruce Kessler climbed into the cockpit and on his first flying lap, shattered the lap record. Unfortunately, the car was damaged before race time, but by the end of the season it was the fastest thing on wheels, winning for the first time at Santa Barbara in June. Soon thereafter, Scarab 001 had a brother.

Scarab Mk.II

Reventlow wanted to build two more cars for Kessler and Daigh to drive, while he drove 001. The next cars, 002 and 003, looked the same from the outside but had a few upgrades. Most notably, they were right-hand drive in order to be on the inside of most turns on clockwise race circuits and to provide more room for shifter assemblies in the narrow cockpit. The bottom tubes in the frame were made larger in diameter, extra tubing was added to stiffen the frame, and the rear track was slightly widened.

The Nevada Grand Prix in August 1958 was the first appearance of the Scarab two-car team. Everywhere they went the press followed, especially when Reventlow began dating (and later married) beautiful young film star Jill St. John. At Nevada, Daigh passed Reventlow in the final turn to win the race. Reventlow spun and lost his temper, but reason was restored when Daigh pointed out that if he had not taken advantage of the opportunity to pass

Augie Pabst wins at Laguna Seca in 1963 over Ken Miles in a Cobra—the last great win for a Scarab. *Allen Kuhn*

him, another car would have. By the end of the season, the team had humbled the once-mighty Cunningham-entered Lister-Jaguars twice. The Scarab had arrived.

As the FIA had imposed a 3-liter limit on its events, the Scarab engines were too large to run at Sebring and in Europe. In an effort to develop a suitable American engine, Scarab Mk.II 003 was fitted with a modified Offenhauser 220-ci Indy engine. The Offy four-banger was taller than the Chevy, so a hood scoop was fitted (a visual cue to 003, which retains the scoop to this day). But the Offy was a dud, down on power and vibrating so much it shook the car apart. It was only run once, at Santa Barbara, and then replaced with a Chevy.

The crowning race of 1958 was the Times Grand Prix at Riverside in October. Daigh had his hands full with Phil Hill in the one-off Ferrari 412MI. This fire-breather was concocted at the Ferrari factory specifically to take on the Scarab threat. Hill and Daigh were passing and repassing constantly until the Ferrari dropped back with carburetion problems. Daigh picked up a popular win in front of the home crowd.

Reventlow took an easy win at the season-ending Nassau races, and it became obvious that the Scarabs were the fastest road racing cars in the United States. It was time to move on, and the two Mk.II Scarabs were put up for sale. Reventlow kept his Mk.I and had it converted into a wild street machine.

The Mk.IIs found many more successes in the hands of later owners and were driven by Augie Pabst, Carroll Shelby, Jim Jeffords, and Harry Heuer. Jeffords drove the first car sold (002) to many victories. At one point, Jeffords was clocked at 192 miles per hour, when the front wheels actually came off the ground.

Heuer bought the second Scarab sold (003) for his Meister Brauser team and, later, bought 002 as well. Pabst won many races in the Meister Brauser Scarabs, as well as the 1960 SCCA B-Modified Championship. Heuer followed up by taking the championship the next year. Amazingly, the Scarabs were competitive right up to 1963, outrunning the agile and quick Maserati Birdcages but not the new breed of midengined cars. All three front-engined Scarab sports-racers are currently active in vintage racing events, and 002 is once again owned and raced by Augie Pabst.

Scarab Formula 1

Since his sports-racers were not legal to race in Europe, Reventlow decided to take on the Europeans in Formula 1 racing. It was a colossal failure of judgment. No one on the team had any experience in Grand Prix racing, and Reventlow insisted the car have 100 percent American content, which meant they would develop every component from scratch. Experienced firms like Ferrari and Aston Martin had languished trying to take on the midengined Coopers with front-engined cars, and the Scarab team emulated them with predictable results.

Offenhauser engineer Leo Goosen, who had a long list of great racing engines to his credit, designed an all-new four-cylinder engine. It was a laydown design, with twin plugs per cylinder and a desmodromic valvetrain that used secondary cams instead of springs to close the valves. Goosen had been against the desmo setup on development grounds, but Reventlow insisted. The engine never produced competitive power and was unreliable to boot.

The chassis was a conventional front-engined design penned by 23-year-old Marshall Whitfield, who had never designed a race car. The car looked like a small Indy car, and used a Halibrand center section attached to a special gearbox with Corvette internals. The differential was located to the left of the driver and had a single water-cooled clutch-type brake on the right halfshaft. In front, special quasi-drum brakes were fitted outboard. The all-American dictum originally meant no British disc brakes, but when the home-brewed brakes proved ineffective, Girlings were substituted.

The chassis was completed before the new engine was ready, so the old Offy that had been used in 003 was dropped in for testing. Tests showed that everything was wrong, from the brakes to the new Goodyear tires (its first effort at F1). Endless delays caused the team to miss the entire 1959 season.

The really bad news came in 1960, when the Scarab team had its Grand Prix debut at Monte Carlo. They quickly discovered they were way off the pace of even the Formula Juniors that ran in a support race. The Goosen engine was giving away over 50 horsepower to the Coventry-Climax FPF, and the brakes were abominable. Neither car qualified for the race.

At Zandervoort, Daigh qualified 15th, but when the qualifying times were questioned Reventlow threw a tantrum and withdrew the team. A third car was built as a spare chassis. At Spa, Daigh and Reventlow qualified but were way off the pace and both retired. At that point, Reventlow became discouraged and replaced himself with former Ferrari driver Richie Ginther. The next race was at Reims in France, but the Scarabs broke all their engines in practice and packed up for home.

The final Grand Prix of the season was at Riverside, so the team hoped they would have some sort of home-track advantage. They decided to only enter Daigh in one car, which they lightened as much as they could. Daigh qualified 18th out of 23 cars and finished a creditable tenth in the last race for the Scarab F1.

Chuck Daigh tries to hang on in the Scarab Formula 1 car (No. 23) at the U.S. Grand Prix at Riverside in 1960. It was an impossible job. *Allen Kuhn*

The Scarab Formula 1 car was lovely to look at, but no fun to drive. *Don Orosco collection*

At least one of the F1 cars was later reengined with a Chevy V-8, but it was never raced in that configuration.

Scarab Intercontinental

In 1961, the Formula 1 regs lowered the maximum displacement limit from 2.5 to 1.5 liters, causing English car builders to start a new series called the Intercontinental Formula (for cars up to 3 liters). The Reventlow team stuffed its old 3-liter Offy into one of the failed F1 cars and sent it and Chuck Daigh to England to contest the series. But the engine was down on power, and the chassis was still junk. Its best finish was a sixth at Goodwood, after which Daigh totaled the car at Silverstone. The car was shipped home and cut up.

Reventlow decided to build an all-new midengined car especially for the 1961 Intercontinental Formula season. It was designed by Eddie Miller (nephew of engine wizard Harry Miller) and closely followed (some say copied) Cooper Formula 1 practice. The American-only directive was shelved to allow Girling disc brakes and a Cooper-Knight transaxle. The chassis was conventional and solid, but the team was still saddled with the under-powered desmodromic engine (now fitted with dual Weber carbs). It wasn't completed in time to be run.

For 1962, the Intercontinental rules were expected to be changed to allow larger stock-block production engines. Reventlow saw this as an opportunity to make some money to keep his mother happy. She had been bankrolling the team at great expense (over $1.5 million) and was starting to have second thoughts. Reventlow's idea was to build customer versions of the car that could be sold to raise revenue. He bought a huge building and began to stockpile parts for a production run. The regulations allowed production engines to be heavily modified, so RAI launched a development program on the new Buick aluminum 215-ci V-8 fitted with four Weber carburetors. With help from Mickey Thompson (who was running the little Buick in his

Indy cars), they eventually squeezed 300 horsepower out of the lightweight V-8.

But just before the start of the 1962 season, the Intercontinental regulations were changed again, and the modifications RAI had done were disallowed. So the car was run only once, at a Formula Libre race in Australia, where Daigh took an excellent fourth overall behind three Cooper Grand Prix cars and ahead of Stirling Moss in a Lotus. The production operation was shut down and the money flow slowed to a trickle. All employees were let go except for Remington, mechanic Frank Schmidt, and designer Eddie Miller. They had one more car to build.

Scarab Midengined Sports-Racer

Although the heyday of RAI was behind him, Reventlow decided to use some of the parts they had built for the Intercontinental project as the basis for a midengined sports-racer (which never had an official name or number). Eddie Miller designed it just before he was let go. Remington built the car as a final project, before leaving to work for Carroll Shelby. The new car was a full two-seater based on the Intercontinental suspension and brakes. A Colotti T-32 gearbox was attached to the Buick, which wore a distinctive Remington-fabricated intake manifold, mounting four side-draft Webers. It was detuned to around 250 horsepower for durability and to suit the less aggressive Reventlow driving style. He ran it sporadically in 1962, dogged by reliability problems and driving with little enthusiasm. Eventually, a hotter 308-horsepower Oldsmobile version of the little aluminum V-8 was used. He wrecked it at Riverside and then ran it one last

time at Nassau in late 1962. Reventlow ran a steady race until rain started to fall, when he turned the misfiring car over to Augie Pabst, who finished in 34th place. And that was it for RAI.

The midengined car got a new lease on life in 1963 when it was sold to Texas oilman John Mecom. He sent the car to Troutman and Barnes (who by then had their own shop) to be readied for the season. Famed Indy driver A. J. Foyt drove the car at Riverside with no success, but then picked up a second at Laguna Seca.

Dick Troutman felt the car needed more power, so they stuffed a 500-horsepower Traco (Travers and Coons' new shop) Chevy V-8 and Colotti T-37 transaxle in for the season-ending Nassau races. Foyt took to the Scarab and, despite numerous off-track excursions, won the Governor's Trophy Race over Jim Hall's Chaparral 2 and Pedro Rodriguez in a Ferrari 250P. It was the first victory for the midengined Scarab, and Foyt duplicated his feat in the Nassau Trophy Race (the most prestigious race of the weekend).

Things went well the next season as well. At Daytona for the 1964 American Challenge Cup race, Foyt had an intense race with Dan Gurney in the Lotus 19B, powered by a Ford V-8. The two of them were the class of the field, swapping the lead several times a lap until Gurney's gearbox failed. Foyt came

A. J. Foyt takes the mid-engined Scarab around Laguna Seca in 1963. *Allen Kuhn*

home the winner in his last Scarab race. Augie Pabst and John Cannon also drove the car, neither with much success. But Walt Hansgen put in a great drive to win the Bridgehampton 500 over Pedro Rodriguez in a Ferrari. By this time, the Scarab had acquired a bigger bored-out Chevy and wider wheels and tires.

The final season for the Scarab was 1965, by which time it was seriously outdated. Mecom kept it as a backup, and John Cannon drove it at Riverside in May, but it retired midrace. It was retrofitted with an aluminum Olds engine, and Mecom's friend Jack Saunders won a minor SCCA race at Galveston. At midseason, Augie Pabst bought the Scarab and fitted a Chevy engine for the Times Grand Prix at Riverside, where he finished a distant tenth. At Las Vegas for the Stardust Grand Prix, he finished an amazing fifth among faster, newer equipment. Afterward, Pabst retired and has kept the last Scarab ever since as a garage mate to his front-engined Scarab 002.

The Shark Mk.1 was a popular Formula Vee in the mid-1960s. *Barry Heuer*

Shark

The Shark Formula Vees were built in Mission, Kansas, in the mid-1960s. Shark built 20 to 30 of its Mk.1 model, which was regionally competitive in the new formula. In 1969, Shark built a prototype for a new model, but the company shut down without going into further production.

The last Shark FV was a one-off. *Harold Pace*

SCARAB

Reventlow Automobiles Inc.
Los Angeles, California

SCARAB MK.I AND II
Year built	**1958**
Engine	**Chevy V-8**
Gearbox	**Borg-Warner T-10 four-speed**
Front suspension	**independent**
Rear suspension	**de Dion**
Brakes	**drum**
Body material	**aluminum**
Weight, approx.	**1,900 pounds**
Wheelbase	**92 inches**
Number built	**three**

SCARAB FORMULA 1
Years built	**1959–1960**
Engines	**Offenhauser four-cycle, Goosen four-cycle, Chevy V-8**
Gearbox	**four-speed**
Front suspension	**independent**
Rear suspension	**independent**
Brakes	**disc**
Body material	**aluminum**
Weight, approx.	**1,200 pounds**
Number built	**three**

SCARAB INTERCONTINENTAL
Year built	**1961**
Engine	**Buick V-8**
Gearbox	**Cooper-Knight**
Front suspension	**independent**
Rear suspension	**independent**
Brakes	**disc**
Body material	**aluminum**
Number built	**one**

SCARAB MIDENGINED SPORTS-RACER
Year built	**1962**
Engines	**Buick, Olds, and Chevy V-8s**
Gearbox	**Colotti T-32 and T-37**
Front suspension	**independent**
Rear suspension	**independent**
Brakes	**disc**
Body material	**aluminum**
Weight, approx.	**1,500 pounds**
Wheelbase	**91 inches**
Number built	**one**

SHARK

Shark
Mission, Kansas

SHARK MK.1
Years built	**1965–1968**
Engine	**Volkswagen**
Gearbox	**Volkswagen four-speed**
Front suspension	**trailing link**
Rear suspension	**swing axle**
Brakes	**drum**
Body material	**fiberglass**
Number built	**20 to 30**

Carroll Shelby, Dave MacDonald, and Bob Holbert jaw at Riverside in 1963. *Allen Kuhn*

Shelby American

Carroll Shelby is a legendary character in the world of racing, having succeeded on virtually every level from driver to team owner. In the late 1950s, he was one of the most successful road racing drivers in America, securing a ride in Europe for Aston Martin. The pinnacle of his career was a win at Le Mans in 1959 driving a factory Aston Martin with Roy Salvodori. But Shelby had a heart condition that forced him to retire from driving in 1961.

Shelby did not hesitate to get involved in a host of activities, including buying the western Goodyear racing tire distributorship and starting a racing school at Riverside Raceway. But what he really wanted was to build a dual-purpose sports and racing car. He tried negotiating a deal to put Chevy engines in Austin-Healeys, but it fell through. Shelby finally worked out an arrangement to install the new Ford 260-ci small-block V-8 into the British-built AC Ace-Zephyr.

Cobra Mk.1 260

The resulting Cobra turned out to be the most famous supercar of its day, and Shelby's new company, Shelby American, set to turning its new toy into a serious racing car. The immediate goal was to beat the Corvettes that dominated American amateur road racing in the early 1960s. The first Cobra chassis delivered was a street car, used as the factory show and road test car. The second chassis, CSX2002, was the first Cobra race car. Shelby American had inherited the greatest fabricator and race preparation expert in America, Phil Remington, when it bought a race shop from Lance Reventlow. Remington had been involved in the Scarab project as well as half the front-line race cars built in California. He was Shelby's ace-in-the-hole.

Remington and crew proceeded to fashion CSX2002 into a proper racing car. The AC chassis needed some serious upgrading to cope with the power and torque of a potent V-8. Contrary to rumor, the Cobra was not made from an Ace-Bristol. Bristol

discontinued production of its famous 2-liter six in 1961, forcing AC to seek a new engine source. AC settled on the English Ford Zephyr 2.6-liter six modified by tuner Ken Rudd. AC beefed up the old AC chassis for the Zephyr and changed the big, vertical Ace-Bristol nose to the low, graceful snoot later used on the Cobra. The only visual difference between an Ace-Zephyr and the first Cobras was the use of narrow flares to cover the Cobra's wider wheels. The Ace used a simple ladder frame with transverse leaf springs front and rear and fully independent suspension.

But for racing, a lot had to change on the Cobra. Initially, a near-stock 260 was installed, altered only by a Spalding Flamethrower ignition system and a crankcase breather. The windshield was replaced with a windscreen and most of the body trim was removed. The 16-inch wire wheels were fitted with Goodyear racing tires, but the clunky AC worm-and-sector steering was retained. The Cobra's first race was at Riverside Raceway in October 1962, driven by pro racer Billy Krause. Much to the surprise of the Corvettes, the crude little Cobra eased past the new Sting Rays and pulled out a 1 1/2-mile lead before dropping out with a bad hub carrier. The Corvettes won, but they knew they had a real problem on their hands.

At the season-ending Nassau races, another Cobra joined CSX2002 for a two-car effort. Both cars were painted red and ran well, but Krause failed to win, after running out of gas. For Nassau, the 260 engine in Krause's car was fitted with 12:1 pistons, a roller cam, custom headers, and a bigger oil sump. Koni shocks were used all around, as well as alloy brake calipers and many suspension upgrades. After this second promising race, the Shelby team signed up a crew of expert drivers and technicians, including Ken Miles, Dave MacDonald, and Pete Brock.

The new team tasted victory at Riverside in January 1963, with MacDonald taking first ahead of Miles. During the off season, a special manifold mounting four 48-millimeter Weber carbs was developed, as well as optional Halibrand "kidney bean" (so named for the shape of their vents) mag wheels to replace the fragile wire wheels. Shelby sold replicas of the team cars for $9,000. The last race for the 260 Cobras was at Daytona, where all three factory cars failed to finish.

Cobra Mk.2 289

By the time Sebring rolled around in 1963, the Cobras had been upgraded to 289-ci engines and rack-and-pinion steering borrowed from the MGB. Soon, street Cobras would get the same treats. The team cars were constantly being developed, and no two cars were exactly alike. A total of six Cobras entered the race, but the best finisher was 11th overall, eighth in class. But the cars were getting better, and similar Cobras won the 1963 USRRC Championship for Shelby American. The Corvettes were no longer in the hunt, but the Ferrari 250 GTO was still a threat. In 1963, two Cobras were entered at Le Mans, one by AC and one for privateer Ed Hugus. Both had aluminum hardtops (for more speed down the long Mulsanne straight) and Shelby-prepared 289 engines. The AC-entered Cobra finished seventh overall and third in the GT class, behind the Ferraris.

A visually different series of Cobra racing cars was built for the 1964 season. These came to be called "FIA roadsters" since they were intended to

Ken Miles works out a Cobra at Riverside in 1963. *Allen Kuhn*

Bob Holbert, Dave MacDonald, and Ken Miles fling their Cobras around Laguna Seca in 1963. *Allen Kuhn*

compete in Europe for the FIA Manufacturers' Championship. They had wider rear fenders to cover 7.5-inch-wide Halibrand pin-drive spoked mags in back, 6.5-inch-wide in front. All had Weber carbs, alloy Girling brake calipers, and extensively developed suspension and drivetrain components. The FIA roadsters partnered with the Daytona coupes to contest the events on the FIA calendar. The Cobras started out slow, suffering from problems at the Targa Florio, Spa, and the Nurburgring. Bob Bondurant won the Freiburg Hillclimb in a roadster, and roadsters won the season-ending Bridgehampton Double 500. The Daytona coupes won at Le Mans and at the Tourist Trophy, but it was not enough to take the 1964 FIA championship.

There were two other versions of the 289 Cobra racing cars. The USRRC roadsters were similar to FIA roadsters but had different dashboards and mechanical rear-end coolers. Versions of the USRRC roadsters that ran in SCCA production car races were required to use cast-iron brake calipers and an electrical rear-end cooler, and they had no oil cooler scoop under the nose. Shelby American once again swept the USRRC series, as well as the 1964 SCCA "amateur" A-Production Championship. The only big loss for the Cobras was at Nassau, where the Corvette Grand Sport (see Chevrolet entry) showed its mettle.

When Shelby first went after the Ferraris in Europe, he did it with the FIA Cobra roadsters. *Harold Pace*

Ken Miles built the one-off Cobra "fliptop" to take on the Corvette Grand Sports at Nassau. Power came from an aluminum 390-ci Ford. *Harold Pace*

Cobra jockeys wait on the grid at the Los Angeles Times Grand Prix in 1963. Bob Bondurant is closest, then Dan Gurney and Lew Spencer. *Allen Kuhn*

Ken Miles built a special lightweight version of the 289 Cobra race car to run at Nassau in 1964. Anxious to avenge their defeat at the hands of the Corvette Grand Sports the year before, Shelby had Miles fabricate an ultralight (1,800 pounds) roadster with an ungainly thin aluminum body and an all-alloy 390-ci experimental stock car engine. It was nick-named the "fliptop" because the nose and tail tilted up for maintenance. It only ran once in factory hands, when Miles led the GS Corvettes at Nassau until the roadster gave up the ghost.

There were no upgrades to the roadsters for the 1965 season, when FIA races were primarily con-tested by the Daytona coupes. Shelby did not enter the USRRC Championship, having its hands full developing the Ford GT. In 1967 SCCA events, the 289 Cobras were reclassified to B Production. (The 427 Cobra was accepted for A-Production.) However, at this time the SCCA made the smaller Cobras run true production equipment, like a single Holley four-barrel, skinny wheels and flares, and no oil cooler scoops.

Cobra Daytona Coupe

The Cobra roadster was a blisteringly fast car—on a short track. It accelerated, handled, and braked with the best Ferraris, but on a long straight it lacked the top speed to be competitive. The basic Cobra shape was an aerodynamic barn door, with the cockpit opening and driver catching too much wind

compared to the sleek Ferrari GTO and lightweight Jaguar XKEs. Shelby took advantage of a loophole in the regulations to build coupe versions of the 289 Cobras, which were nicknamed the Daytona coupes after the first race in which they competed.

Pete Brock, who had been a stylist at General Motors, designed the aerodynamic bodywork. He did it by eye, without the aid of a wind tunnel or massive calculations, and it worked the first time. Ken Miles strengthened the Cobra chassis to make it the most stable of the Cobras. The first car was bodied in aluminum in California, but Carrozzeria Grand Sport bodied the remaining five in Italy. In 1964, the coupes showed that they had the speed to take on the previously all-conquering Ferraris. A coupe won the GT class at Sebring, and then Dan Gurney and Bob Bondurant captured the jewel in the crown with a fourth overall and first in class at Le Mans. It was close at the end of the season, but with some political machinations, Ferrari managed to hang on to the GT championship by a small margin. (Ferrari pressured the organizers to cancel a race at Monza, Italy, that the Cobras would probably have won.)

The story was different in 1965, when the Shelby American team swept the championship. This was in no small part due to the FIA's reluctance to accept the Ferrari 250LM as a GT car (there were not enough built), leading Ferrari to boycott the series. Shelby ended up running against privateer Ferrari teams with obsolete equipment. The Daytona

coupes won six events and took eight seconds and three thirds. The only black eye was at Le Mans, where the Cobras faltered and a red-hot Ferrari 275 GTB ringer won the class.

In addition to the Daytona coupes, two coupes were built on Cobra chassis in England, one by AC and one by the Willment team. Shelby began con-struction of a 427-powered Daytona "super coupe," but it was not completed in time. It had a radical long-tailed body made by Radford Coachbuilders in England. It was finished in the early 1980s and has been run in vintage events.

Cobra 427 Competition

Although the 289 Cobra had dominated American racing in 1963 and 1964, Shelby knew he had to keep improving or the competition would catch up. The rumor (which turned out to be true) was that Chevy would drop the 396-ci V-8 into the Sting Ray in 1965, and Ferrari was trying to homolo-gate its technically advanced midengined 250LM as a GT car. In 1964, a 427 was shoehorned into a leaf-spring 289 roadster chassis and run at Sebring with Ken Miles and John Morton as drivers. It was an ill-handling pig, leading Shelby to decide a new chassis was a must.

A team at Shelby American designed the new Cobra, supposedly with help from Ford's computer geeks. However, it was later acknowledged that the computer info was so impractical most of it was discarded. The frame was similar to previous Cobra practice, but the leaf springs were replaced by coil-over shock units all round. The new chassis was 5 inches wider, but the body looked a lot like an FIA Cobra with a larger front grille. Actually, the first 427 Cobra race car, CSX3002, had a 289 FIA body that was hand-widened, as the new body panels were not completed in time. It became the works develop-ment car and was raced by Ken Miles, Phil Hill, and Bob Bondurant without success. It was the only 427 Cobra raced by the Shelby American factory team.

The Cobra Daytona coupes finally won the FIA Manufacturer's Championship in 1965. *Harold Pace*

Shelby replaced the 289 Cobra with the 427 and continued his winning ways. *Harold Pace*

Dr. Dick Thompson operates the Essex Wire 427 Cobra at Riverside in 1965. *Allen Kuhn*

In order to satisfy the FIA GT-class requirement that 100 examples be built, the first 100 Cobras were to be racing versions. Production started in 1964, but only 51 cars were completed when the FIA inspectors arrived, so the 427 Cobra would not be allowed to run in 1965 events (the same thing happened to the Ferrari 250LM that year). Shelby told AC to switch to building street models. By 1965, the FIA dropped the required number to 50, so the 427 Cobra was in. Meanwhile, Shelby had been busy racing the Ford GTs, and decided it would be politically expedient to not race 427 Cobras themselves, lest they prove a threat to the Ford GTs.

Only about a dozen of the 51 competition cars had been sold to racing teams by July 1965. They were homologated for SCCA racing, where they proved to be faster than the 289 Cobras and were also slotted into A-Production. The 37 unsold racing cars were fitted with street-version 425-horsepower engines and sold as 427 S/C (street/competition) cars. Racing cars differed from street Cobras in having oil coolers, roll bars, flared fenders, hood scoops, 42-gallon fuel tanks, and cut-outs for side pipes. Private teams successfully raced the 427 Cobras in SCCA events, where they won the A-Production Championship from 1965 to 1968, and again in 1973.

GT-350R

Shelby American introduced the GT-350 version of the Mustang in 1965. To publicize the hot street machine, racing versions (GT-350R) were built for sale to private teams. The first two prototypes were built in 1964 from notchbacks and were later sold as sedan racers. They did not carry Shelby American chassis plates. All the GT-350R race cars were fastbacks, although Shelby built a run of notchbacks (again without Shelby plates) for sale as Trans-Am cars. Those cars are not officially called GT-350s, since the number of cars that had to be sold to qualify as a sedan was much higher than the number of GT-350s that Shelby could sell, so they were homologated as Fords. The SCCA only recognized notchbacks as sedans and fastbacks as GT-350 B-Production cars. To run with the Corvettes, the Mustang was put on a diet that included ditching the

rear seat, making it a two-seater. Unlike the normal Mustang, the GT-350R had a fiberglass lower front apron with a cutout for an oil cooler, Plexiglass side and back windows, and radically modified suspension. All the sound deadening and insulation was left out, and the engine was modified to put out at least 350 horsepower using a Holley 715-cfm carburetor on a high-rise manifold.

The front A-arms were lowered 1 inch, and a 1-inch front sway bar was fitted. The engine compartment was stiffened, and torque arms were used in the rear. Koni shocks and faster steering completed the picture. A fiberglass hood was fitted, along with 7-inch-wide American Racing wheels. The interior was gutted and only a single racing seat remained, along with a bare racing dash with five or six gauges and a hefty roll bar.

Ken Miles developed the GT-350R, and one car was retained to run as a factory entry in SCCA events. In 1965, Jerry Titus drove it to the National Championship in B-Production against the 327 Sting Rays and the XKEs. It appears that 37 GT-350R models were made, possibly more. In 1966, Walt Hane won the B-Production Championship in his GT-350, while Fred VanBeuren took the honors in 1967. After that, the factory withdrew support and the Corvettes took over again.

King Cobra

Although the Cobras were the hottest things going in GT racing, by 1963 the handwriting was on the wall for front-engined sports-racers. The Scarabs, Listers, and Ferraris were being pushed to

The Shelby GT-350R was a Mustang that could take on a Corvette. *Harold Pace*

Dave MacDonald at Riverside hangs on to his slightly battered King Cobra. *Allen Kuhn*

the back of the grids by the new generation of midengined lightweights from Cooper and Lotus. Even with small 2.5- and 2.7-liter Coventry-Climax FPF engines, these cars could easily upstage a massive, bellowing V-8 sitting in the nose of a heavier and less sophisticated American special. Carroll Shelby, along with many others, came to the conclusion that the hot setup would be a healthy V-8 in the middle of a featherweight English chassis. With that in mind, Shelby American placed an order with Cooper Cars in England for two Cooper Monaco sports-racing cars, set up for Ford V-8 engines.

The Monaco and the Lotus 19 were the most successful of the new breed, and the Monaco had the advantage of being stronger (if a little heavier) than the 19. The Monacos had space frames with coil-over-shock suspension all around, aluminum bodies, and five-speed Colotti T-37 transaxles. When the chassis arrived, the Shelby team tore them down to the bare frames and rewelded all the frame and suspension parts (quality control at Cooper was frequently a hit-or-miss affair). The brakes were Dunlop discs and the wheels were skinny at 5 inches wide in front and 6.5 inches in back. The engine chosen was basically the same 289 used in the Cobra race cars, pumping out 370 horsepower with four Weber carbs. With a dry weight of around 1,300 pounds, it was quick.

The King Cobra was a Shelby American project and received no funding from Ford. Four were built to contest the professional races held at Kent (Washington) and Laguna Seca and Riverside Raceways in California. These races were held at the end of the normal racing season. The first outing for the King Cobra was at Kent in 1963, where Bob Holbert and Dave MacDonald both retired with overheating after breaking the track lap record. Bigger radiators were added for the Los Angeles Times Grand Prix at Riverside, where the competition included Jim Hall in his flying Chaparral, Dan Gurney in a Genie, and Roger Penske in his Zerex Special. Hall retired, and MacDonald blitzed the field to take an

easy win for the King Cobra in only its second race.

The last pro race of the season was the Pacific Grand Prix at Laguna Seca. Holbert and MacDonald fought it out with Hall and A. J. Foyt (driving the Scarab-Olds), with MacDonald taking the win over Foyt. After that, it was off to Nassau for the Trophy Races, which would have been a lot of fun, had the Shelby team not been ambushed by the Bow-Tie Brigade. Suffice it to say, the King Cobras, along with the Cobras, cratered while the Corvettes and the Scarabs got their revenge.

The 1964 season was not so successful, mostly due to the time expended on running the new Cobra Daytona coupes in Europe. Plus, the competition was getting better, with the sophisticated Chaparrals hitting their stride. However, Shelby wanted to win the 1964 USRRC series championship using a combination of Cobras and King Cobras, and he was counting on MacDonald and Holbert to bring the title home. The King Cobras were mildly uprated, and other transaxles were tried to replace the marginal Colottis, including a four-speed BMC transaxle built by Joe Huffaker. The first race of the season was at Kent, which also marked the appearance of a customer King Cobra built for brewery heir Craig Lang. It was driven by Holbert, who wiped it out in practice, escaping with painful, but not serious, injuries. MacDonald stepped into Holbert's team car and won the race for Shelby American. It seemed 1964 might be a repeat of the previous year, but it was not to be.

From Kent, MacDonald headed for Indianapolis, where he was to drive Mickey Thompson's midengined racer. On the second lap, he was involved in a two-car crash that took his life and

that of Eddie Sachs. On hearing the news, Holbert announced his retirement. Suddenly, Shelby had lost its two King Cobra stars. Shelby ran the Cobra roadsters in the other USRRC events but Jim Hall won the championship. The next event for the King Cobras was the Times Grand Prix, where four factory King Cobras and a new Lang Cooper showed up.

The Lang Cooper (an all-new car, as the wrecked one was too far damaged to repair) was a King Cobra with a lovely and distinctive body designed by Pete Brock. Ed Leslie normally drove it, and although it didn't win anything, it did put in some good performances. Lang continued to run it through the 1964 season, and was then sold to the Essex Wire team for Skip Scott to drive in 1965.

Bob Bondurant, Richie Ginther, Ronnie Bucknum, and Indy star Parnelli Jones were to drive the factory cars. Jones took to road racing like a fish to water and won the race pulling away from Penske (driving a Chaparral), Jim Clark in a Lotus 30, Leslie in the Lang Cooper, and Bondurant.

The Chaparrals struck at Monterey, with Penske (subbing for an injured Hall) winning both heats over Dan Gurney in his one-off, Ford-powered Lotus 19B. Bondurant kept up appearances with a third. It was the last race for the King Cobras under the Shelby banner, although the Lang Cooper ran in

The Shelby Group 7 was too little, too late to be a winner. *Harold Pace*

1965 with Charlie Hayes. In late 1965, Shelby sold the team cars.

King Cobra Group 7

Shelby American built a special car (also called the Terry T-10) to race in the 1967 Can-Am series. Although called a King Cobra, it was an all-new design by former Eagle and Lotus designer Len Terry. Power came from a 289-inch Gurney-Weslake Ford with fuel injection, although Terry intended for it to have a Ford Indy engine. The chassis was an aluminum monocoque with a single transversely mounted coil spring at each end. These spring units were attached to the opposing suspension members, and roll was controlled by small sway bars. It was similar in concept to the zero-roll rear suspension systems used on modern Formula Vees. While this worked great on Vees, it was a disaster on the King Cobra. After testing, a conventional suspension system was installed.

At Riverside, Jerry Titus qualified 13th in a stellar field, but the car only made three laps before the fuel pump packed up. The only other time it ran was at Las Vegas, where Titus crashed in practice after the suspension collapsed. The running gear was transferred to a second chassis and sold (a third unused chassis was built as well). Mike Kosloski ran it in SCCA events in 1968 and 1969. The Can-Am series became too competitive to run on a part-time basis and the King Cobra Group 7 was quickly dropped. A Chevy-powered T-10 ran in the 1970 Riverside Can-Am race, driven by Skeeter McKitterick. In 1968, Shelby ran a Ford-powered Lola in the USRRC series and a McLaren in Can-Am, with few results.

The King Cobra Group 7 was the last road racing car built by Shelby American, though the company went on to run Mustangs in the Trans-Am and Toyota 2000s in SCCA racing before closing its doors in 1969. The company was revived in the 1990s after Carroll Shelby received a heart transplant.

Shelby American
1042 Princeton Drive
Venice, California

COBRA MK.1 (RACE CARS)

Years built **1962–1963**
Engine . . . . **Ford V-8 (260 ci)**
Gearbox . . . . **Borg-Warner T-10 four-speed**
Chassis . . . . **ladder**
Front suspension . . . . **independent**
Rear suspension . . . . . **independent**
Brakes . . . . **Girling disc**
Body material . . . . **aluminum**
Weight, approx. . . . . . **2,100 pounds**
Wheelbase . . . . **90 inches**
Number built . . . . **five for road racing**

COBRA MK.2 (RACE CARS)

Years built **1963–1964**
Engine . . . . **Ford V-8 (289 ci)**
Gearbox . . . . **Borg-Warner T-10 four-speed**
Chassis . . . . **ladder**
Front suspension . . . . **independent**
Rear suspension . . . . . **independent**
Brakes . . . . **Girling disc**
Body material . . . . **aluminum**
Weight, approx. . . . . . **2,100 pounds**
Wheelbase . . . . **90 inches**
Number built . . . . **40 for road racing**

COBRA DAYTONA COUPE

Years built **1964–1965**
Engine . . . . **Ford V-8 (289 ci)**
Gearbox . . . . **Borg-Warner T-10 four-speed**
Chassis . . . . **ladder**
Front suspension . . . . **independent**
Rear suspension . . . . . **independent**
Brakes . . . . **Girling disc**
Body material . . . . **aluminum**
Weight, approx. . . . . . **2,515 pounds (wet)**
Wheelbase . . . . **90 inches**
Number built . . . . **six**

COBRA 427 COMPETITION AND S/C

Years built **1964–1965**
Engine . . . . **Ford V-8 (427 ci)**
Gearbox . . . . **Ford four-speed**
Chassis . . . . **ladder**
Front suspension . . . . **independent**

Rear suspension . . . . **independent**
Brakes . . . . **Girling disc**
Body material . . . . **aluminum**
Weight, approx. . . . . . **2,300 pounds**
Wheelbase . . . . **90 inches**
Number built **56**

GT-350R

Year built **1965**
Engine . . . . **Ford V-8 (289 ci)**
Gearbox . . . . **Borg-Warner T-10 four-speed**
Chassis . . . . **welded platform with side rails**
Front suspension . . . . **independent**
Rear suspension . . . . . **live axle**
Brakes . . . . **disc/drum**
Body material . . . . **steel and fiberglass**
Weight, approx. . . . . . **2,550 pounds**
Wheelbase . . . . **108 inches**
Number built **37**

KING COBRA

Years built **1963–1964**
Engine . . . . **Ford V-8 (289 ci)**
Gearbox . . . . **Colotti or BMC transaxle**
Chassis . . . . **space frame**
Front suspension . . . . **independent**
Rear suspension . . . . . **independent**
Brakes . . . . **Girling disc**
Body material . . . . **aluminum**
Weight, approx. . . . . . **1,300 pounds**
Wheelbase . . . . **91 inches**
Number built . . . . **six**

KING COBRA GROUP 7

Year built **1967**
Engine . . . . **Gurney-Weslake Ford V-8 (289 ci)**
Gearbox . . . . **ZF five-speed transaxle**
Chassis . . . . **aluminum monocoque**
Front suspension . . . . **independent**
Rear suspension . . . . . **independent**
Body material . . . . **aluminum**
Weight, approx. . . . . . **1,435 pounds**
Wheelbase . . . . **95 inches**
Number built . . . . **three**

127

Spectre

The early days of Formula A racing saw a number of small companies build racers for the new class. One was the Spectre HR-1, driven by well-known ace Ron Grable in the 1968 season. Grable was an engineer with Raytheon Corporation who later drove for the American Motors Javelin team in the Trans-Am Series. Ken Holden, owner of Spectre Race Cars, designed and built the Spectre HR-1. It was an unusual car for the time, featuring rear-mounted radiators and an odd fan-shaped rear wing. Initially it had side radiators, but they proved inefficient and were relocated beneath the rear wing. The Spectre had adjustable rising-rate suspension all around. Although the Spectre was outclassed in professional events, Grable won the SCCA Formula A class at the ARRC in 1968. In 1969, Tony Settember drove the HR-1, but failed to finish in the Laguna Seca pro race.

SPECTRE	
Spectre Race Cars Limited	
Bellmont, California	
SPECTRE HR-1 FA	
Year built	**1968**
Engine	**5-liter Chevy V-8**
Gearbox	**ZF**
Front suspension	**independent**
Rear suspension	**independent**
Brakes	**disc**
Body material	**fiberglass**
Number built	**unknown**

Templeton

Harvey Templeton was over 50 when he bought his first Zink Formula Vee in the late 1960s. He was a quick driver and soon gained the respect of his competitors. But Templeton found his lasting fame in three odd, but highly successful, cars of his own design.

Templeton Ringwraith

In 1967, Templeton decided to try his hand at race car construction and built a radical FV he called the Ringwraith, after the ghostly horsemen in the *Lord of the Rings* trilogy. The resulting car would not win any beauty contests but did feature a technical advancement unseen on previous Formula Vees—zero-roll rear suspension (meaning zero resistance to roll for improved handling). This system eliminated vertically mounted shocks and replaced them with two nonfunctional horizontally mounted shocks, which did not provide any resistance to rear roll (the rules required two rear shocks and springs). He also dispensed with the Z-bar that had been used for suspension control and fabricated a linkage to connect both sides of the suspension at a pivot point above the gearbox. His first try had some rough edges, and the car was reluctant to settle down after exiting corners due to its lack of damping. In 1969, Templeton sold the Ringwraith to his friend Jeff Carlin, who fitted small shock absorbers and transformed the Ringwraith into a formidable contender.

Templeton Shadowfax

The suspension system used on the Ringwraith was not completely satisfactory, so Templeton built a second car in 1969 for the 1970 season and, naturally, named it the Shadowfax (another *Lord of the Rings* figure). The car was very short in height, with the driver almost completely reclined. In his quest for low frontal area, Templeton basically built the car around himself.

When the slab-sided nose lifted on long straights, he made a boatlike "keel" that fit on the bottom of the nose to split the air as if it were water. Like most of the shade-tree engineering done on the Shadowfax, it worked great. He revised the zero-roll suspension with a lower pivot point for the suspension to rotate around, which solved the handling problem, and the car was fast right out of the box.

Harvey Templeton's first Formula Vee was the radical Ringwraith. Note holes in the front bodywork to accommodate the driver's knees! *Marvin Scruggs; Nick England collection*

Templeton beat the Caldwell D-13 in adapting zero-roll technology by a year. Templeton won an incredible number of races in the car, and even sat on the pole at the SCCA runoffs twice, but did not win the national championship.

When Templeton turned 65 (around 1975), he sold the Shadowfax and built a Formula Ford with a lever that the driver could pull to lean the tires over into a turn. Once again, it looked funny but it worked. Templeton lived to be 94, passing away in 2003. He left racing fans with three classic race cars, which thankfully have all survived. The Monoposto Group, which puts on the most exclusive vintage formula car races, only allows one car with zero-roll rear suspension—Harvey Templeton's Shadowfax.

Harvey Templeton's weird and wonderful Shadowfax was the King of the Vees. *Harold Pace*

Vulcan

In the early days of the F-5000 series, a number of American companies built cars for the new formula. One such company was Vulcan, which built at least two Chevy-powered cars, run in 1968 by Steve Durst and George Garrett. They were very effective on a national level, picking up wins in the SCCA Northeast Division. In 1968, Durst qualified for the ARRC but failed to finish.

Vulcans also ran in the SCCA F-5000 Championship. In 1968, Durst ran a Vulcan-Chevy and finished fifth at Elkhart Lake, but slipped to midpack elsewhere. The next season, Durst returned, but his best finishes were an eighth at Mosport and a ninth at Thompson.

In 1970, Durst moved up to a McLaren, and Bill Seeley drove a Vulcan-Chevy at Elkhart Lake but

Steve Durst raced this Vulcan F-5000 race car.
Nick England

finished well back. Tom Wood had a Plymouth-powered Vulcan, but it was never in the hunt. Wood returned in 1971 for a solitary run in a Vulcan-Chevy at Elkhart Lake, but failed to finish.

Yenko

The Yenko Stinger was to the Corvair what the GT-350 was to the Mustang—an example of what could be done when really talented racers got their hands on a basically sound design. Don Yenko, a Chevy dealer in Canonsburg, Pennsylvania, was famous for racing Corvettes in SCCA events. By the mid-1960s, he had tired of getting his plastic Chevy outrun by Shelby-prepared Cobras and GT-350s, so he looked for a GM product that could be made competitive. He chose the Corvair.

Like the Mustang, the 1965 Corvair was basically a good design in need of some fine tuning. The 1965 model was much improved over previous Nader Baiters, with independent rear suspension and a svelte body to replace the previous two-box styling. The SCCA would not homologate the Corvair for production sports car racing because it had a back seat, technically making it a sedan. The same fate had befallen the Mustang, so Yenko could draw upon what Shelby had done to transform a pony into a GT-350.

Yenko built a prototype of his dream Corvair racer, which he intended to call the Yenko Bonanza.

Starting with a 1965 Corvair Corsa, he and industrial designer John Salathe (who later built his own midengined sports car) cut up four pizza boxes to mock up fiberglass add-on landau extensions (which visually widened the rear top pillars) and a rear deck with a spoiler. The back seat was removed and replaced with a plywood panel covered with carpeting. The suspension was improved and, after a satisfactory shakedown by Stirling Moss, the concept (now renamed the Stinger) was developed enough to begin production.

The goal for the project was to get the new car approved for SCCA production car racing, which required that 100 cars be completed before the start of the 1966 season. Yenko invested over $350,000 buying 100 identical white Corsas and having them express delivered to Yenko Chevrolet for transformation. Chevy was only too happy to sell 100 more Corvairs, but contributed nothing to the project beyond that point. The Yenko team completed all 100 Stingers between their delivery date of December 8, 1965, and the January 1, 1966, deadline. Although Stingers could be driven on the street if desired, the main goal was to build a racing car, and a substantial number of owners raced their Stingers.

The Stinger was a product of Yenko's racing experience, combined with a careful selection of options from the Chevy catalog. In addition to the fiberglass body panels, Stage 1 Stingers had factory heavy-duty suspension and a quick-ratio steering box with fabricated arms to give only three turns lock-to-lock (much faster than standard). An exclusive dual master cylinder setup was used to adjust the brakes front-to-rear. A close-ratio four-speed transaxle was included, along with a 3.89 rear axle ratio not shared with other Corvairs. Chevy provided more effective drum brakes, fitted with metallic linings. Inside the all-black interiors were a Yenko roll bar, headrests for the bucket seats, and racing seat belts to meet SCCA safety requirements. All 100 of the first Stingers were white with blue stripes; the race versions sported blue hoods.

The Yenko Stinger looked like a Corvair, but it outran the Triumphs and Jaguars. *Harold Pace*

The stock Corvair Corsa came with a 140-horsepower engine fed by four Rochester carburetors. The Stage 1 Stinger also had a high-capacity cast-aluminum Crager oil pan, rejetted carbs, a Tuftride crank, quick-bleed cam lifters, and a low-restriction exhaust system that helped it produce 160 horsepower. Stage 1 Stingers retailed for $3,272 in 1966.

The Stage 2 engine had a hotter cam kit, a smaller cooling fan, notched pistons, blueprinted internal parts, a deep sump oil pan pickup, 10:1 compression heads, modified carburetors (to prevent flooding in corners), and a lightened flywheel. This version made 175 horsepower.

For ultimate performance, the Stage 3 kit included a race-prepared engine with ported heads, a hotter cam, a revised oiling and cooling system, and comprehensively reworked carburetors to produce a whopping 220 horsepower. Yenko offered hotter Stage 4 and Stage 5 engines, but these were not SCCA-legal.

Due to the hand-built nature of the Stingers, there were many variations, and some did not have the Landau panels in the top, or even the fiberglass rear

decks. Street versions weighed 2,225 pounds, but racing Stage 3 Stingers were stripped down to 2,120 pounds. The SCCA required all Stingers to have their special Yenko chassis numbers, and regular Corvairs could not legally be converted to Stinger specification.

The Stinger was classified in the D-Production class, where it had a tough time with the Triumph TR-4 A, Jaguar XK-series, and Lotus Super 7 opposition. Yenko ran a two-car team in 1966, driven by Yenko and former SCCA National Champion Donna Mae Mimms (who painted her Yenko in her favorite shade of pink). Jerry Thompson took over one of the factory cars and won the 1966 Central Division SCCA Championship, while Stinger-mounted Dick Thompson took Northeast Division honors and Jim Spencer captured the Central Division. At the season-ending SCCA runoffs (the ARRC), Jerry Thompson took a respectable fifth-in-class.

In 1967, Yenko ordered some more Corvairs to convert and offered other color choices (even a one-off convertible). The four-carb Corsa engine was officially dropped, but Yenko special-ordered them for his cars. At the 1967 ARRC SCCA runoffs held at Daytona, Jerry Thompson took the D-Production win

over a strong field of Triumphs and Jaguars.

After that, Chevy scaled back the Corvair, and a handful of Stingers trickled out as late as 1969. Yenko affiliate dealers in other parts of the country assembled some of them. Stingers continued to be competitive in SCCA racing through the 1970s, finishing in the top four from 1973 to 1975. They were less successful in endurance racing; in 1966, they failed to finish at Sebring and limped home 27th at the Daytona 24-hour race. Today, Stingers are still potent and highly prized vintage racers, and proof that the Corvair could have been a great car.

YENKO

Yenko Chevrolet
Canonsburg, Pennsylvania

YENKO STINGER

Years built	**1966–1969**
Engine	**Corvair flat six**
Gearbox	**Corvair four-speed CR**
Chassis	**welded platform**
Front suspension	**independent**
Rear suspension	**independent**
Brakes	**drum**
Body material	**steel and fiberglass**
Weight, approx.	**2,120 pounds**
Wheelbase	**108 inches**
Number built	**121**

Zeitler

John Zeitler was one of the most successful American formula car builders of the 1960s, with a long list of wins to his name. His first race car was an MG TD he ran in 1952, followed by a Jaguar XK 120 and an MGA. But by 1959, the young engineer decided to build his own Formula Junior.

Zeter Mk.1 Formula Junior

Starting with a very rough and well-used Cooper Formula Junior rolling chassis, Zeitler adapted a

DKW engine and gearbox to produce the Zeter Mk.1. Although the frame proved to be decidedly flexible, Zeitler learned to make allowances and began winning races. Unfortunately, in 1960, he totaled it in a hillclimb.

Zeter Mk.2 Formula Junior

The Mk.2 became Zeitler's first production model. Four chassis were built for this midengined Formula Junior design, which once again used DKW engines but with Porsche transaxles. Borgward brakes and 13-inch wheels were used. The customer cars were sold in 1960 for $2,800 each.

Zeitler Formula Vee

When Formula Junior was winding down in 1963, Zeitler bought an Autodynamics Formula Vee kit and went racing. In 1965, he came out with a Vee of his own design. He welded up the prototype chassis and then had a jig made to go into production at his shop in Connecticut. Starting with an Autodynamics body, he cut and patched up a body of his own that could be molded in fiberglass. He sold the Zeitler FV in kit form for $1,900, and built more than 40 of them between 1965 and 1971. The Zeitlers were very competitive, and Steve Burtis finished third at the 1968 ARRC in one. They won many divisional and regional championships.

Zeitler Formula Super Vee

In 1969 and 1970, Zeitler was instrumental in helping Volkswagen of America's Jo Hoppen write the rules for the new Super Vee class. Zeitler built some of the first cars for the class, with three ready in 1970. Zeitler himself won the first SCCA FSV race, a two-car promotional event against Harry Ingle in a Zink. The first SCCA National Championship for the new class was held in 1970, and Tom Davey won it in a Zeitler. He repeated that feat the next year, edging out John Zeitler, who drove to a well-deserved second place after an accident. After that, Zeitler became a team engineer and crew chief for other racing teams, and imported Modus and Lola racing cars from England.

Zink

Ed Zink started racing around 1950, but not at road racing circuits. His school of hard knocks was on the dirt ovals in Tennessee and North Carolina, where he learned to design, build, and drive hot rod roadsters. He always liked to do things his own way, running a Chevy six instead of the usual Ford flatheads. Zink's real fame was not to be made on hard-packed clay, but rather on the smooth asphalt of American road racing circuits.

Zink Petit

By the early 1960s, Zink was interested in road racing, building his first sports-racer, the Zink Petit, in 1962. It was a tiny, basic H-Modified with a DKW engine clothed in a Jabro Mk.3 body. DKW supplied the full-race, factory-built engine directly to Zink. One or two more Petits were built and driven by Tommy Van Hoosier, Bill Greer, and Tom Watts. Greer proved to be very quick in the car, resulting in his capture of the 1963 SCCA National Championship for H-Modified.

Zink Z-4

The Z-4 was a vastly more sophisticated sports-racer introduced in 1964 (the model number was based on the year the car came out). It was a midengined design for small modified classes. Three were built—two with DKW power and one with a Coventry-Climax FWA. But Zink didn't spend much more time on the sports-racers, moving his efforts to the new FV class in 1965.

ZEITLER

Zeitler Racing Design
Stamford, Connecticut

ZETER MK.1 FORMULA JUNIOR

Year built	**1959**
Engine	**DKW**
Gearbox	**DKW four-speed**
Front suspension	**independent**
Rear suspension	**independent**
Brakes	**drum**
Body material	**fiberglass**
Number built	**one**

ZETER MK.2 FORMULA JUNIOR

Year built	**1960**
Engine	**DKW**
Gearbox	**Porsche four-speed**
Front suspension	**independent**
Rear suspension	**independent**
Brakes	drum
Body material	**fiberglass**
Number built	**four**

ZEITLER FORMULA VEE

Years built	**1965–1971**
Engine	**1,200-cc Volkswagen**
Gearbox	**Volkswagen four-speed**
Front suspension	**trailing link**
Rear suspension	**swing axle**
Brakes	**drum (Volkswagen)**
Body material	**fiberglass**
Number built	**40-plus**

ZEITLER FORMULA SUPER VEE

Years built	**1969–1971**
Engine	**Volkswagen**
Gearbox	**Hewland four-speed**
Front suspension	**independent**
Rear suspension	**independent**
Brakes	**disc/drum**
Body material	**fiberglass**
Number built	**seven**

The Zink Z-5 was the dominant Formula Vee from 1967 to 1970; hundreds were sold. *Harold Pace*

Zink Z-5

Zink's first FV was introduced in 1965 and immediately started mopping up the opposition. It had an original chassis concept, wrapping a simple space frame with stressed steel panels to make a semi-monocoque chassis. It sold like crazy. The Z-5 proved superior to the best efforts from Autodynamics, Beach, and Formcar, allowing Zink drivers to win the FV class in SCCA racing in 1966 and 1967. In 1967, Zinks finished first through fifth, and enough competitors complained that the SCCA outlawed the stressed-skin metalwork. Zink designed an upgrade kit to convert older Zinks to a strong space frame without the metal panels, and the later Z-5s came standard with the extra tubing. The change didn't hurt anything—Zinks continued to win the SCCA championship through 1970. Hundreds were sold well into the 1970s.

Zink Z-8

In 1968, Zink took another shot at sports-racing cars with the Z-8. At the time, there was a move among FV fans to develop a sports-racing class based on VW Type 3 running gear. This new class was to be called VSR (Vee Sports Racing), and Crusader, Beach, and other FV manufacturers built prototype models. The Z-8 ran a mildly modified fuel-injected VW Type 3 engine, gearbox, and suspension. The prototype ran at Sebring in 1968, but driver Bill Scott retired early with clutch problems. VSR never caught on, and only one car and a spare

chassis were built. The spare was later finished out with a Corvair engine.

Zink Z-9

When the new Super Vee rules were announced, Zink decided to give it a try. The Z-9 came out in 1969, and once again used a stressed aluminum skin over a space frame made from round and square mild steel tubing. Rack-and-pinion steering was used. At the time, Super Vees were required to use VW disc brakes in front and drums in back. Fully adjustable suspension was used at both ends, along with a Hewland transaxle. Zink also built his own engines, mounting Weber 38-millimeter carburetors on cast Zink manifolds. But few Z-9s were built.

Zink was one of the most successful racing car manufacturers of the 1960s, and continued to build championship-winning cars well into the 1980s. Ed Zink passed away in 2003, but his cars are still winning races in SCCA and vintage events.

This Zink Z-8 ran at Daytona but retired early. Hugh Heishman; *Bill Fleming collection*

ZINK

**Zink Cars
Middlebrook Pike
Knoxville, Tennessee**

ZINK PETIT
Years built	1962–1963
Engine	DKW
Gearbox	DKW four-speed
Body material	fiberglass
Number built	two or three

ZINK Z-4
Year built	1964
Engines	DKW or Coventry-Climax
Gearbox	four-speed
Front suspension	independent
Rear suspension	independent
Brakes	disc
Body material	fiberglass
Number built	three

ZINK Z-5
Years built	1965–1970
Engine	1,200-cc Volkswagen
Gearbox	Volkswagen four-speed
Front suspension	trailing link
Rear suspension	swing axles
Brakes	drum (Volkswagen)
Body material	fiberglass
Number built	unknown

ZINK Z-8
Year built	1968
Engine	Volkswagen Type 3
Gearbox	Volkswagen four-speed
Front suspension	trailing link
Rear suspension	swing axles
Brakes	Volkswagen disc/drum
Body material	fiberglass
Number built	two

ZINK Z-9
Year built	1969
Engine	Volkswagen
Gearbox	Hewland four-speed
Front suspension	independent
Rear suspension	independent
Brakes	disc/drum
Body material	fiberglass
Number built	fewer than ten

American Specials

THREE

Aardvark

Californians John Porter and Dean Banks built the Aardvark in 1952. Porter built the little H-Modified as a trainer car, hoping to gain racing experience before stepping into a larger bore machine.

They built the car on a modified Panhard Dyna chassis. Porter and Dean stiffened the frame by adding small diameter tubes, and they lowered it significantly. The lower stance necessitated the fabrication of custom exhaust headers, which Banks designed to allow the exhaust pipes to course alongside the car.

The body was assembled from a combination of aluminum and fiberglass sections. The nose section was an unattractive narrow snout, constructed as a two-piece unit. The front portion of the nose was designed for quick removal to facilitate examination and work during pit stops. The hood contained a large unsculpted air scoop, and the cycle fenders were not all that flattering. While the overall con-

The Aardvark was a well-known Class H special with a Panhard engine. *Harold Pace*

AARDVARK	
Constructors	John Porter and Dean Banks
Location built	California
Year built	1952
Engine	750-cc Panhard two-cylinder
Gearbox	Panhard four-speed
Chassis	Panhard Dyna
Front suspension	independent
Rear suspension	torsion bar
Brakes	drum
Body material	aluminum and fiberglass
Weight, approx.	1,000 pounds

struction of the car was to a high standard, to say that it was interesting to look at would be kind. The precise impetus for Porter dubbing the car with its unusual name remains a matter of speculation.

Porter powered the Aardvark with a 750-cc, two-cylinder, four-cycle, air-cooled pushrod Panhard engine. In race trim, the motor produced 42 horsepower, which was plenty good for the diminutive "anteater." The car was competitive in H-Modified, and Porter learned to drive foot-to-the-floor all the way around the track.

When he had learned all that he could from the Aardvark, Porter put it up for sale and bought a Porsche 550 Spyder. Stew Haggart purchased the Aardvark when he found he could not resist Porter's fabulous advertisement: "Aardvark Panhard. Get into racing in the most reasonable class. This car has worn down many faster opponents with its dependability. Two engines, two transmissions, two chassis, 13 wheels and tires. Two new pistons and rings, Amal carburetor, my blessings, $2,000. REMEMBER: A LITTLE AARDVARK NEVER HURT ANYONE."

The car continues to race in vintage events and is highly competitive. It is a gemstone of American automotive racing history and remains a real crowd pleaser.

A.J.B.

See Butterball Special entry.

Ak Miller's Caballo de Hierro

Following their DNF in the 1952 Carrera Panamericana in a stock Oldsmobile, Ak Miller and co-driver Doug Harrison began to make plans for an all-new car for the 1953 event. Miller owned a shop that built and worked on hot rods in Whittier, California, so it was only natural that he should design and build a hot rod for the upcoming race. The car was dubbed Caballo de Hierro ("horse of iron"), a fitting name for a mechanical donkey designed to race for nearly 2,000 miles across the treacherous Mexican terrain.

The Caballo de Hierro rocketed across the Mexican desert in 1953. *Dean Batchelor*

133

Miller started with the frame from a '50 Ford and shortened it to create a 100-inch wheelbase. The frame was also narrowed to fit the body from a 1927 Model T roadster. The front suspension was an independent Ford unit with Houdaille shocks and custom coil springs fit with Air-Lift cushions, inflated with 8 pounds of pressure. In the rear, the '50 Ford axle was retained but the stock semiellipitics were replaced by a transverse leaf spring; as in the front, the rear shock absorbers were Houdaille units. Brakes began as 13-inch Chrysler units that were procured from a junkyard. The brakes were heavily modified to fit the Ford hubs, the backing plates were Swiss-cheesed, and air scoops were added for cooling. Steering was by way of a '40 Ford assembly.

The motor was a '51 Oldsmobile V-8 with '52 Olds cylinder heads, producing 250 horsepower. Induction was via four Stromberg 97 carburetors on a Nicson manifold, and Miller designed the special twin-ignition system. The gearbox was a '37 Cadillac floor shifter three-speed, and the clutch was from a '53 Oldsmobile.

The finished car was definitely a hot rod with a low aggressive stance. The bullet-shaped nose had a menacing, toothy grin with a beady-eyed headlamp on each side. The car ran on stamped Ford steel wheels. The spare tire was mounted atop the rear deck lid, and sponsors, lettered onto the T-bucket body, read like a history of the American hot rod industry. All gassed up and ready to go, the car cut the wind like an anvil.

The car competed at the Carrera in 1953 and 1954 and finished the race both times. In 1953, the car finished eighth-in-class and 14th overall, covering 1,912 miles in 22 hours, seven minutes, and 36 seconds, with an average speed of 86.5 miles per hour. In 1954, the car finished an impressive fifth-in-class and 7th overall, covering the distance in 20 hours, 21 minutes, and nine seconds, with an average speed of 94.1 miles per hour.

Ak Miller's Caballo II

Ak Miller and Doug Harrison followed up on their success with the Caballo de Hierro by building an all-new car, the Caballo II. The initial plan was to take the car to the Carrera Panamericana, but the event was canceled after the 1954 race because of deaths among drivers and spectators.

Ak Miller ran the Caballo II in the Mille Miglia in 1957.
Robert Rolofson Jr.; Robert H. Rolofson III collection

Undaunted, the two men proceeded with construction of the car, confident that if they built it, a race would come.

The Caballo II began with the purchase of a 500X space frame from Frank Kurtis (chassis SX-5). Miller admired the fine craftsmanship of Kurtis' frame, made of 1 1/2-inch (0.083-inch wall thickness) 4130 steel tubing, but felt that he could improve its stiffness. He and Harrison went to work, adding tubes and replacing some smaller tubes with larger ones. The lower frame rails were doubled, and gussets were welded in at all bends. The result was a highly modified 500X frame with vastly enhanced rigidity. The front suspension was live axle with torsion bars. The rear suspension was by torsion bars; the rear axle was from Lincoln with a Thornton limited-slip differential. Twelve-inch drums from Lincoln, with Chrysler inner components and a Micro-lock double master cylinder, provided stopping power. The gearbox was a Moss four-speed from a Jaguar Mk.VII, and steering was by a Ross cam and lever.

The sexy all-aluminum body was penned and built by Jack Sutton of Hollywood, California. The roadster body was distinctive, with a low-slung nose designed to produce front-end downforce at high speeds. Perhaps the most unique features of the body were the dual head-fairings, each of which housed a structural roll bar. Sutton constructed a light framework and attached the alloy body to it. The body was then secured in place by welding the framework to the Caballo II's frame. Miller added Lincoln 15-inch stock wheels at all four corners.

The Caballo II's power came from a 6,420-cc (392 ci) Chrysler Hemi V-8 with a bore of 4.0 inches and a stroke of 3.9 inches. With Jahns pistons, a Howard Camshaft, Hilborn fuel injection, and a compression ratio of 10:1, the beast produced a ground-pounding 400 horsepower at 5,400 rpm. At a mere 2,100 pounds, this translated to an astounding 5.25 pounds per horsepower, a dramatic advance over the Caballo de Hierro, which had a quotient of 12.4.

With the Mexican Carrera road race on hold, Miller and Harrison had a new idea—why not take Caballo II to Italy for the 1957 Mille Miglia? Since neither man could think of a reason to dissuade them, they headed to Europe for the 24th running of the great race. Miller and Harrison stirred up interest in their upcoming journey and received press coverage and support from the National Hot Rod Association (NHRA). As it turned out, the U.S. military stationed in Europe included lots of NHRA members, so they made advanced arrangements to assemble a crew of interested servicemen for the race. Unfortunately, the fairy tale came to an abrupt end 300 miles into the race, when the Caballo II broke down with a cracked brake drum. The 1957 race turned out to be not only Miller's last effort in long-distance open-road racing, but the end of the greatest of all such races, the Mille Miglia.

When Miller returned to the United States, he took the Caballo II to Bonneville in August 1957. He went through the traps at an impressive 176 miles per hour. The car was entered in 1958 at the first Los Angeles Times Grand Prix at Riverside.

Unfortunately, the car was crashed during a practice session and Bobby Unser was unable to race it as planned.

Ak Miller's Devin Specials

Ak Miller was already a legendary hot rodder when he got involved in road racing. His Caballo de Hierro had worried the European teams at the Carrera Panamericana and the Caballo II was the first all-American entry at the famed Mille Miglia in Italy. But Miller also built a number of sports cars to run the Pikes Peak Hillclimb and in road racing events. Most of these cars had Devin fiberglass bodies.

Ak Miller's Devin-Chevy

The first Miller road racer was built for the 1958 season, spurred on by an offer of sponsorship from *Hot Rod*. The technical editor, Ray Brock, was interested in the new sports car class, which had been won the previous years by Jaguars. Miller set to work building a low-tech, high-performance blend of hot rod and sports car.

Miller fabricated a steel tube frame with 1956 Chevy coil-spring front suspension and a Ford rear axle (with a Halibrand quick-change) sprung by torsion bars. A Devin kit car body gave it a decidedly exotic look. The 1957 Chevy 283 was bored and stroked to 340 ci and featured Hillborn fuel injection, Hedman headers, and a special cam ground just for Miller. A Corvette four-speed gearbox was used.

At Pikes Peak, the car, now christened the Hot Rod Magazine Special, was fast, but the 1,800-pound weight combined with Miller's lack of dirt driving experience produced handling problems in practice. The HRM crew bolted a truck flywheel in back and filled up the gas tank to put more weight on the rear, and things got a little better. In the final timed runs, Miller eked out a narrow victory over Dan Morgan's

Victress special. It was the first in a long string of victories for Miller at the Peak. The Devin-Chevy even became a movie star, when it squared off against the Caballo II in a B-movie titled *Road Racers*.

AK MILLER'S DEVIN SPECIALS

AK MILLER'S DEVIN-CHEVY

Constructor	**Ak Miller**
Location built	**Whittier and Pico Rivera, California**
Body by	**Devin Enterprises**
Year built	**1958**
Engine	**Chevy V-8 (340 ci)**
Gearbox	**Corvette four-speed**
Front suspension	**independent**
Rear suspension	**live axle**
Brakes	**drum**
Body material	**fiberglass**

AK MILLER'S DEVIN-OLDS

Constructor	**Ak Miller**
Location built	**Whittier and Pico Rivera, California**
Body by	**Devin Enterprises**
Year built	**1959**
Engine	**Oldsmobile V-8 (420 ci)**
Gearbox	**Corvette four-speed**
Front suspension	**independent**
Rear suspension	**live axle**
Brakes	**drum**
Body material	**fiberglass**

AK MILLER'S DEVIN-FORD

Constructor	**Ak Miller**
Location built	**Whittier and Pico Rivera, California**
Body by	**Devin Enterprises**
Year built	**1962**
Engines	**Ford V-8 (289, 406, and 427 ci)**
Gearbox	**Ford four-speed**
Front suspension	**independent**
Rear suspension	**live axle**
Body material	**fiberglass**

Ak Miller's Devin Specials were more at home in hillclimbs than on a racetrack, as here at Santa Barbara in 1959. *Allen Kuhn*

Ak Miller's Devin-Olds

Miller went to Pikes Peak the following year with an all-new but visually similar car. It had a new name as well, the Miller-Hanson Special, to recognize Miller's partner, George Hanson, who had helped pony up the $1,800 it cost to build the car. A ladder frame was once again welded up from oil field drill pipe (3-inch chrome-moly purchased surplus for ten cents a foot). The front suspension was '53 Chevy, the same suspension the Corvette carried until 1962. The brakes were pirated from a '52 Lincoln, and the steering box was off a '37 Ford.

For the 1959 run, Miller wanted more power, so he chose a 1959 Oldsmobile block and an offset-ground crank to bring it up to 420 ci. Miller had his own cam ground, and he fitted 9.5:1 pistons for reliability. Four Rochester carburetors were mounted on a Weiand Drag Star manifold, and big valves were installed. A Corvette four-speed backed up the big mill. The car weighed 2,100 pounds, but the beast had stump-pulling acceleration.

Miller's car blew a head gasket and suffered from overheating but still pulled out the win. He took home a check for $1,500, making his Devin-Olds a very good investment indeed.

The next year, there were weather troubles at the Peak and Miller finished fourth. But in 1961, there were no mistakes and Miller took the win over Billy

Krause's Chevy-powered D-Jaguar, the Petersen Special, and an assortment of cars including a Maserati Birdcage. Miller also ran the Devin-Olds at several California tracks, including Pomona, Stockton, and Stead Air Force Base with no great success.

Ak Miller's Devin-Ford

The next Ak Miller special, built in 1962, wore the newer style Devin body also used on the Devin SS sports car. For motive power, Ford convinced Miller to use a dead-stock 406 FE engine. It worked, and Miller notched up another Pikes Peak victory. Miller and the car were featured in Ford ads in 1962. Miller road-raced the Devin-Ford at Laguna Seca and other California tracks. The next year, the special was powered by a Ford 427 and took yet another Pikes Peak victory.

But 1964 was not as successful. Miller opted for a 289-ci Ford, and the car was known as the Cobra Kit Special (for a hop-up package Ford sold to fit on 289 engines). That year, Bobby Unser won the sports car class in a Lotus 23.

In 1965, Miller won with the red Devin Cobra Kit Special. Miller also entered a "Cobra," that was actually an elderly AC Ace he had repowered with a Ford 289. The nose was mildly revised to look more like the smaller Cobra nose. Miller also raced this car at Bonneville.

The 427-powered Devin was back in 1966 (now painted yellow), and Miller won his last sports car class victory. This car was later clocked at 189 miles per hour at Bonneville. After 1966, the Pikes Peak Sports Car Class was eliminated, and Miller went on to drive other types of cars at Pikes Peak, Bonneville, and in off-road racing.

Albi Devin Special

John Albi of Arcadia, California, began building his special in the summer of 1960. The chassis was a simple tube frame built by a friend of Bill Devin's. Drag racer Larry Cooke assisted Albi in the finishing weld-work for the frame brackets on the pedal

assembly and other components. The front end utilized a Mercury solid axle with stock transverse leaf springs. Brakes were Mercury at all four corners.

The body was a fiberglass skin from Devin, and Albi mounted it to the frame by himself. The roller was then taken to Bob Sorrell who fabricated and installed an aluminum floor and firewall. Circle-track man Don Borth made the fuel tank.

Power for the special was derived from a small-block Chevy, which Albi rescued from a junkyard. He built the motor to 4,980 cc so that he could run the car as a C-Modified. The camshaft was ground by Kenny Harmon, the pistons were forged units, and a lightened flywheel was installed.

The Albi Devin Special participated in a drivers' training session at Riverside in June 1961. After solving some overheating problems, the car ran an SCCA Novice Race at Pomona in July 1961. Albi was leading the pack when a steering problem forced him to retire early. That September, the car finished well at Santa Barbara during the Saturday race but failed to finish on Sunday with a broken rear trailing link.

The race car was later sold to a sports car enthusiast, who drove it on California's streets and highways. Albi went on to race a BMW sedan in SCCA events.

The Albi Devin Special used a Devin body and a Chevy engine. *Ron Cummings*

Altemus Auto-Banker

James Altemus built the Altemus Auto-Banker, also sometimes referred to as the Altemus Stabilizer Special, in 1950. Altemus was born in Wynnewood, Pennsylvania, in 1901, and it soon became obvious to all that he was a true genius. His early education was at the prestigious Lawrenceville School in New Jersey and St. George's School in Rhode Island. He later attended MIT.

During World War II, Altemus served as a lieutenant in the U.S. Navy. During that time, he contributed to the development of the side-launching

ALTEMUS AUTO-BANKER

Constructor	James Dobson Altemus
Year built	1950
Engine	Studebaker V-8
Chassis	Jaguar SS1 ladder
Front suspension	independent
Rear suspension	live axle with auto banking
Brakes	drum
Body material	aluminum

electric torpedo and the government's efforts with magnetic mines.

Following the war, Altemus' inventive mind continued to work, and he was issued several patents. Some of his more interesting works included vertical airplane take-off equipment, an infrared device for de-icing airplane wings, and the Altemus Peanut Harvester, which dug, shook, husked, and bagged peanuts in a single machine.

But to racing aficionados, Altemus will forever be remembered as the inventor of the outrageous Auto-Banker, a race car designed with a feature that enabled the rear wheels to lean (automatically bank) into turns. The chassis of Altemus' car included a hydraulic cylinder apparatus capable of producing 500 pounds per square inch of pressure. During high speed corners, the system tipped the rear wheels 12 degrees from vertical (in the appropriate direction) to reduce tire scrub and stabilize or brace the car against centrifugal moments.

Altemus built the car on a Jaguar SS1 chassis and powered it with a Studebaker V-8 motor. The body resembled an Indy two-seater, with a small central grille and cycle fenders. The July 1951 issue of *Motor Trend* included photographs and diagrams of the car and described the workings of the specialized apparatus.

The car was raced at East Coast road circuits in the early 1950s, including Watkins Glen. Unfortunately, on the racetrack, the system proved no advantage, and Altemus moved on to other projects.

Ambulance

See Morlang Porsche entry.

Andreé Special

Built over two years at a cost of nearly $2,000 and some 2,500 hours, the Andreé Special was Chuck Nerpal's labor of love. The car was constructed on a space frame of 1-inch tubing. Front suspension

The Altemus Auto Banker races across the stone bridge at Watkins Glen. *William Green Motor Racing Library*

was by Volkswagen trailing arms with a single torsion bar and Andrex shock absorbers. Rear suspension was by swing axles with coil and oil suspension. Brakes up front were Alfin drums with Volkswagen shoes; rear brakes were disc Goodyear-Hawleys. Steering was through a Fiat unit mated to a bell crank.

Claude Hampson of Reseda, California, built the Andreé Special's body of 0.051-gauge aluminum. The open-wheeled Grand Prix-style shell incorporated a head fairing that blended gracefully into the tail section.

ANDREÉ SPECIAL

Constructor	Chuck Nerpal
Location built	California
Body by	Claude Hampson
Engine	500-cc single-cylinder (BSA Gold Star)
Gearbox	four-speed (Burman)
Chassis	space frame
Front suspension	trailing arms
Rear suspension	swing axle
Brakes	fronts drum; rears disc
Body material	aluminum
Weight, approx.	532 pounds
Wheelbase	81 inches
Length	120 inches
Height	37.5 inches
Cost when new	just under $2,000

The Andreé Special was one of the few American Formula 3 cars. *Robert Rolofson Jr.; Robert H. Rolofson III collection*

For power, Nerpal chose the BSA Gold Star 500-cc single-cylinder four-stroker, with a compression ratio of 9.5:1; carburetion was via a 1.5-inch Amal RN Grand Prix unit. The car was built to compete in Formula 3 racing, but Nerpal designed the engine compartment with sufficient room to accept a Porsche 1,500-cc engine, in the event he decided to go Formula 2 racing. The transmission was a Burman four-speed in a magnesium case. The fuel tank was mounted in front of the cockpit between the frame rails.

Nerpal's idea was to use the lightest components available and not overengineer the car in terms of strength. The completed car weighed a waiflike 532 pounds but suffered from some early mechanical problems. Because there were early problems with severe vibrations from the diminutive four-stroke motor, Nerpal mounted the single cylinder on Lord mounts. The car was clocked at 79 miles per hour for the standing quarter-mile.

Nerpal decided to take his car to the Bonneville Salt Flats to see just how fast he could go on a half-liter. Since he was the editor of *Motor Trend* at the time, he was in an excellent position to make such boyish dreams come true. The car was converted from road racing trim to a streamliner. An all-new alloy tail section and steel canopy were fabricated and fit on the car. Dean Moon provided aluminum wheel discs with tires from Pirelli. In this new streamliner configuration, the car was known as the Motor Trend Special. Nerpal's best run at Bonneville was 99.11 miles per hour, only 0.89 miles per hour short of his dream.

Apache

Although they were built during the same general time period, this Apache has no connection to the American Formula Juniors built by Apache Racing Cars of Walnut Creek, California (see Apache entry, Chapter 2). This one-off race car began life as a Lister-Corvette and was heavily modified and rebodied on its way to becoming a special.

Bud Gates of Indianapolis was looking for a way to make his Lister-Corvette more competitive in the early 1960s. By then, the Listers were no longer running at the front. So he turned to Ron Kaplan, who was well known for his race car magic on Indy cars.

Kaplan removed the independent front and de Dion rear suspensions in favor of Kurtis-style solid axles at both ends with a Halibrand quick-change differential. This was likely done to make the car stronger and easier to adjust. The Lister body was likewise set aside, and Bob Webb constructed a sleek alloy skin. The engine was a Chevy fuel-injected V-8.

Gates raced the car in the Midwest during the 1962 and 1963 seasons. The car ran well, and Gates won at more than one SCCA regional event. The Apache was sold in 1963 to Jack Ensley, who raced it in 1964. The car is believed to have survived in storage, but its exact whereabouts remain obscure.

APACHE

Constructor	**Ron Kaplan**
Location built	**Indianapolis, Indiana**
Body by	**Bob Webb**
Years Built	**1961–1962**
Engine	**Chevy V-8**
Gearbox	**four-speed**
Chassis	**ladder**
Front Suspension	**live axle**
Rear Suspension	**live axle**
Brakes	**disc**
Body Material	**aluminum**

Arciero Special

The Arciero Special was built from a hodge-podge of parts from some of the greatest-ever 1950s road racing cars. The car belonged to Frank Arciero, a well-known racing enthusiast and friend to up-and-coming drivers. Several racers destined for stardom, including Bob Drake, Skip Hudson, Dan Gurney, and Bob Bondurant, took a turn at the wheel in one or more of Arciero's big-bore machines, including the fabulous Arciero Special. Bondurant was running fourth in the car at the 1960 Examiner Herald-Express Grand Prix at Riverside when a wrist-pin broke with six laps to go.

The car's chassis was formed from an amalgamation of several cars, starting with the frame of a Ferrari 375 MM (Chassis Number 0362 AM) that was crashed at Sebring in 1955. The frame was a multitube space design. The front suspension was from an early Ferrari with cross-leaf springs and a rubber block arrangement, with A-arms and Gabriel adjustable shock absorbers. The rear suspension had coils springs with internal Air Lift bags to allow for adjustment of weight and chassis height, longitudinal torque rods, and A-arms from a Jaguar D-type. The gearbox was a Ferrari four-speed and the steering was a worm-and-roller Ferrari unit. The brakes were Ferrari Alfins, 16x2 1/2-inch up front and 13x2 1/2-inch at the rear.

The body was a right-hand-drive Mistral fiberglass shell, sold by Sports Car Engineering Company for $345. A lot of postdelivery work was done on the shell, including narrowing it 6 inches, shortening it 8 inches, and incorporating an aluminum scoop into the hood. The car's interior was custom fabricated with a central instrument pod.

The 4,200-cc DOHC Maserati V-8s (Arciero had two of them) were donated from one of Arciero's former Indy 500 cars. The motors were reworked to run on gasoline, and they breathed through four 45-

millimeter Weber carburetors (bore was 94 millimeters, stroke was 75 millimeters). Each engine produced a reported 407 ponies at 6,800 rpm and rocketed the Arciero Special to a top speed of 180 miles per hour.

Ardent Alligator

The Ardent Alligator is a particularly intriguing car, because its story reveals much about the history of early road racing in the United States. But, the car's story began in England. It was born in 1929 as a small-displacement Riley Brooklands two-seat racer, owned and raced by Freddy Dixon, a well-known constructor of the time. In 1934, Miles Collier and his brother, Sam, bought the Riley and had it shipped to the United States. Their plan was to race the car under the sanction of the Automobile Racing Club of America (ARCA), the club they themselves founded for the purpose of going road racing.

The car was stored until 1939, at which time the Collier brothers decided it was time to go racing. The diminutive 1,100-cc, 55-horsepower engine was removed, and a 3,900-cc Mercury flathead V-8 motor was installed. This was an easier job than one would suspect, as the Riley was not nearly as small a car as its 1.1-liter motor might suggest. So

139

Dan Gurney exercises the Arciero Special at Riverside. *Allen Kuhn*

The Ardent Alligator was a prewar special that continued its career after the war ended. *Harold Pace*

in went the 175-horsepower Mercury engine, along with a Ford gearbox, rear axle, and brakes—the birth of an American special. The car was dubbed the Ardent Alligator, likely because of its green color and its American home in the Florida Everglades.

World War II put the Colliers' racing plans for their special on hold. The car was again put into storage, this time for another ten years.

Twenty years after its original completion as a Riley in 1929, the reworked special made its United States debut at an SCCA race at Bridgehampton in June 1949. The car was driven by Miles Collier but dropped out of the race with overheating problems. Undaunted by the setback, Collier readied the car for the upcoming feature race at Watkins Glen. This proved to be the greatest moment in the Ardent Alligator's history and one of the most astounding come-from-behind wins in the history of motor racing.

MILES COLLIER WINS AT WATKINS GLEN
USING ISKENDERIAN RACING CAM

ED ISKENDERIAN   5000 W. Jefferson   Los Angeles 16, Calif.

In that second year of the Watkins Glen Grand Prix, the race was to be run on the same 6.6-mile road course as the previous year with one exception—instead of eight laps, the race distance was nearly doubled to 15 laps. The race was run without a single practice session, and the starting grid was arranged by a random draw. Miles Collier and the Ardent Alligator were gridded 12th in a field of more than 40. When the flag dropped, George Roberts in the Bu-Merc stormed into the lead, with Briggs Cunningham in second in a 2-liter Ferrari 166 Spyder Corsa. Meanwhile, Collier went backward at the start and fell to 17th place.

At the end of the first lap, the Ardent Alligator was in 14th place and was a full minute behind the leader. Collier settled into the race during the second lap and made numerous passes, moving up to fourth place. In the third lap, Collier moved into third place, but he was still 52 seconds behind the leader. With each lap, Collier became a little quicker and inched toward Cunningham and Roberts. On lap 13, Collier set the single-lap record for the course at five minutes, 39 seconds. The following lap, he chopped an amazing 14.5 seconds off the previous lap, now circling the course in just five minutes, 24.5 seconds. But the best was yet to come.

The Ardent Alligator continued its charge and passed the Bu-Merc, going up the hill toward White House Corner. Now running second with Cunningham's Ferrari in sight, Collier pushed even harder than before. He caught Cunningham near

Milliken's Corner and was in the lead by the time he hit the front straightaway. As he crossed the finish line ahead of Cunningham (second), Roberts (third), Tommy Cole (fourth in a '49 H.R.G.), and John Fitch (fifth in a '48 MG TC), the timekeeper was at a total loss—Collier had run the last lap in a mind-boggling five minutes, 12.5 seconds!

While the Ardent Alligator story did not end here, the rest of the tale does not measure up to that fall day in 1949 at the Glen. The Collier brothers continued to campaign the car with some success, and Sam set a course record at the Mt. Equinox Hillclimb in Vermont in 1950. The car was sold later to Cameron Argetsinger. It was raced and changed hands several times. Owners included Brete Hannaway, George Rabe, J. D. Englehart, Bill O'Donnell, Don Lefferts, and Peter McManus. The car continues to be raced in vintage events.

Austin Chevy Special

Little is known about this home-built special, constructed by East Coast racer Addison Austin. The car was raced at Watkins Glen in 1954, powered by a six-cylinder Chevy engine, but failed to finish.

AUSTIN CHEVY SPECIAL

Constructor	**Addison Austin**
Year built	**early 1950s**
Engine	**Chevrolet six-cylinder**

Baird-Jag Special

Jack Baird and Jay Joyce of Albuquerque, New Mexico, converted a wrecked Jaguar XK-140MC roadster into a successful C-Modified racer. They built it with the intention of running in the Carrera Panamericana, but did not complete it before the race was canceled. They lightened the frame and

Constructor	Jack Baird
Location built	Albuquerque, New Mexico
Year built	1956
Engine	3.4-liter Jaguar
Gearbox	four-speed
Chassis	ladder
Front suspension	independent
Rear suspension	live axle
Brakes	drum
Body material	aluminum

lowered the engine and gearbox in the frame. Baird made the aluminum body himself with crude but functional lines, somewhat reminiscent of a Cooper-Jaguar. The suspension was beefed up, and the engine was modified with more compression, an Isky XM-3 cam kit, ported head, and Hillborn fuel injection. The Baird-Jag was estimated to have 260 horsepower. Baird drove the car in Southwestern SCCA events and, in 1956, won his class on several occasions, outrun for overall honors only by Ferrari Monzas. The car also took Top Eliminator at Albuquerque drag races.

Baldwin Mercury Special

Following the success of his first special, the Payne Special, Willis Baldwin set out to build a second car. This car came to be known as the Baldwin Mercury Special.

The car's chassis came from a '46 Ford that Baldwin shortened some 14 inches to produce a wheelbase of 100 inches. As he had done in the Payne Special, the stock crossmember was removed and a tubular crossmember was installed. In an effort to improve the car's weight distribution, Baldwin set

the engine back 22.5 inches, 7 inches more than in the Payne Special. The suspension, front and rear, was stock Ford, with the front leaf spring positioned ahead of the front axle and the rear leaf spring positioned behind the rear axle.

The transmission was a '46 three-speed Ford unit with a remote linkage (to a 3.78:1 Ford rear axle) that Baldwin custom-fabricated. The clutch was a Mercury unit, and Baldwin removed the centrifugal weights from the pressure plate to facilitate rapid shifting at high revs. The steering unit was likewise from a '46 Ford, but was fabricated with a 9-inch pitman arm to be more responsive for the quicker turns required for road racing.

Baldwin selected a Mercury V-8 engine for power. He began with a 59A cylinder block and bored it out to 3.312 inches and stroked the crankshaft to 4.125 inches; this increased displacement to 284.4 ci. Other performance modifications included installing aluminum cylinder heads and an aluminum intake manifold, regrinding the camshaft, fabricating exhaust headers, and installing a Baldwin-designed dual-point ignition setup.

The body for the Baldwin Special was constructed from found bits and pieces. Donor parts transplanted from sections of Chrysler fenders,

Constructor	Willis Baldwin
Location built	Santa Barbara, California
Year built	1949
Engine	Mercury (59A) V-8 (284.4 ci)
Gearbox	three-speed Ford
Chassis	modified '46 Ford
Front suspension	live axle
Rear suspension	live axle
Brakes	drum
Body material	conglomeration of junk
Wheelbase	100 inches

The Baldwin Mercury Special was built by Willis Baldwin and powered by a Mercury V-8. *Harold Pace*

141

The Baldwin Mark II won at Willow Springs with Bill Pollack at the wheel. *Bill Pollack collection*

headlamps, and metallic parts from a radiator shell were added to sheets of aluminum. As a final touch of class, a front grille was formed from the remains of a refrigerator shell.

Baldwin Mark II

Willis Baldwin, the builder of the earlier Payne Special and Baldwin Mercury Special, constructed the Baldwin Mark II in 1955. The car wore cycle fenders and was powered by a flathead Ford.

The Mark II had a distinctive front end with a square opening without a grille and two hood scoops. The unique hood scoop arrangement allowed for the use of two radiators, which Baldwin believed would cut down on the car's frontal area and improve performance. The second radiator was set behind and above the first and necessitated the second hood scoop.

BALDWIN MARK II	
Constructor	Willis Baldwin
Location built	Santa Barbara, California
Year built	1955
Engine	flathead Ford V-8
Gearbox	Ford three-speed
Chassis	ladder

The car was competitive and won a feature race at Willow Springs with Bill Pollack at the wheel.

Barlow Simcas

Roger Barlow and Louis Van Dyke were business partners at International Motors, a foreign car agency in Los Angeles, California. With American road racing heating up in Southern California in the early 1950s, it was only natural that two men with the automotive resources and manpower of Barlow and Van Dyke should decide to design their own race car and have it built. In fact, in the end, it was not one Simca Special that rolled out of their shop, but three.

The first Simca Special was built at International Motors in 1951, constructed by service manager Bill Pringle and mechanic Joe Thrall. It began as a ladder frame from a stock Simca Huit. The center section of the frame was widened in order to position the driver lower in the cockpit. Front and rear suspension were from Simca with the independent front receiving lightened coil springs and some of the leaves of the semielliptics of the live-axle rear removed. The brakes were Simca units with cast-aluminum shoes and finned-aluminum drums. Although these were essentially left stock, they provided exceptional stopping power for the diminutive race car and contributed heavily to Barlow's racing success in the car.

The lovely left-hand-drive, torpedo-shaped alloy body was built by Emil Diedt after a design by Barlow and Murray Nichols. The nose had no headlights, and the grille struts were oriented horizontally. The spare tire was positioned in a recess formed in the bodywork of the rear deck and was then secured in place by a knock-off spinner that also functioned as a fuel filler cap. The cycle-fendered masterpiece was finished in French racing blue, and it rode on Borrani center-lock knock-off wire wheels.

Power was provided to the rear wheels by a 1,200-cc Simca inline four-cylinder motor with

a reground camshaft, stronger valve springs, and a lightened flywheel. The engine ran with a compression ratio of 9.25:1 and induction via dual Zenith Torino carburetors. Twin SU fuel pumps kept the petrol flowing. The team mounted the engine 6 inches to the rear of stock to improve weight distribution and handling. The radiator was positioned in front of, and lower than, the stock location. The gearbox was a Simca four-speed.

The Barlow Simca was a smashing success at its first-ever race, at Pebble Beach during the last weekend in May 1951. The car was an impressive winner in the under-1,500-cc class for modifieds and placed fifth overall. This first victory was followed by many more class wins in 1951, including Reno and Palm Springs in October and Torrey

The first Barlow Simca bested the MGs until Ken Miles came along. *Harold Pace*

The Louis Van Dyke International Motors Simca Special was part of the Barlow Simca team. *Tom Cardin*

142

BARLOW SIMCA

BARLOW SIMCA NUMBER 1

Constructors	Roger Barlow, Louis Van Dyke, Bill Pringle, Joe Thrall
Location built	Los Angeles, California
Body by	Emil Diedt (design by Roger Barlow and Murray Nichols)
Year built	1951
Engine	1,200-cc Simca four-cylinder
Gearbox	Simca four-speed
Chassis	modified Simca Huit ladder
Front suspension	independent
Rear suspension	live axle
Brakes	drum
Body material	aluminum
Weight, approx.	1,112 pounds

BARLOW SIMCA NUMBER 2

Constructors	Roger Barlow, Louis Van Dyke, Bill Pringle, Joe Thrall
Location built	Los Angeles, California
Body by	Emil Diedt (design by Murray Nichols)
Year built	1952
Engine	1,200-cc Simca four-cylinder
Gearbox	Simca four-speed
Chassis	modified Simca Huit ladder
Front suspension	independent
Rear suspension	live axle
Brakes	drum
Body material	aluminum

LOUIS VAN DYKE INTERNATIONAL MOTORS SIMCA SPECIAL

Constructors	Roger Barlow, Louis Van Dyke, Bill Pringle, Joe Thrall
Location built	Los Angeles, California
Year built	1952
Engine	1,200-cc Simca four-cylinder
Gearbox	Simca four-speed
Chassis	space frame
Front suspension	independent
Rear suspension	live axle
Brakes	drum
Body material	aluminum

Pines in December. The car was so phenomenal that it was written up in *Road & Track* twice during the 1951 racing season (July and October). Pringle raced the first Simca Special after Barlow had a second one built to race for the 1952 season. With Pringle now behind the wheel, the first car was often referred to as the "ex-Barlow Simca Special." Later, Harvey Simon purchased the car and converted it to an MG-powered special (Harvey Simon's MG Special). Later still, Simon radically changed the car's look and ran it as a Formula Junior (Harvey Simon's MG Formula Junior) powered by a motor built by Bud Hand.

Diedt also constructed the second Simca Special at International Motors with a Simca frame and running gear, and an alloy body from a design by Nichols. This car was a bit smaller but retained the torpedo shape, French racing blue color scheme, cycle fenders, and rear-mounted spare tire. The second car differed from the first in that it was right-hand drive, the body incorporated headlights, and the grille was more of an egg-crate design. Once the second car was completed, Barlow began to race it.

Barlow captured the Pebble Beach Trophy in April 1952, winning the 48-lap race for cars under 1,500-cc in front of a crowd of 60,000 fans. The field included Alfred Coppel's MG TC, Bill Pringle's "ex-Barlow Simca Special," Tracy Bird's MG TD Special, Charles Dancey's modified MG TC, and Bill Devin's Crosley Hotshot.

A month later, Barlow was victorious at Golden Gate Park in San Francisco. There, he won the Mayor's Trophy Race in front of a crowd of 90,000, beating Pringle and Coppel, plus Bill David in his MG TD Special and Bob Gillespie in his MG TD Special.

The third Simca Special was built for Van Dyke in the middle of the 1952 race season and was known as the Louis Van Dyke International Motors Simca Special. Unlike the previous two cars, this car was constructed on a tubular space frame (not a modified Simca ladder). Again, the running gear

was Simca and the body was an aluminum torpedo with cycle fenders, a rear spare tire, and blue paint. This car was right-hand drive, without headlights, and had a small egg-crate grille with a smaller frontal area than the previous two cars. It was the lowest and lightest of the three and had the most highly developed engine. However, it was not successful at the track, as the earlier two cars had been. It lacked two important features of the first and second cars—mechanical reliability and Barlow's driving skills.

Barneson-Hagemann Chrysler

John Barneson had talked at length with Jack Hagemann about building a road racing special, but the project never seemed to get the green flag. That was until Barneson crashed his Allard at Pebble Beach in 1955—then everything changed.

Barneson gave Hagemann the go-ahead in August 1955, and things really got hopping. Hagemann designed and constructed a ladder frame of steel tubing. Front suspension was live axle with torsion bars and radius rods. The rear

BARNESON-HAGEMANN CHRYSLER

Constructors	Jack Hagemann, George Naruo (engine),
Location built	California
Body by	Jack Hagemann
Year built	1955
Engine	Chrysler Hemi V-8 (375 ci)
Gearbox	Jaguar four-speed
Chassis	ladder
Front suspension	live axle
Rear suspension	live axle
Brakes	disc
Body material	aluminum
Weight, approx.	2,180 pounds
Wheelbase	95 inches

suspension was live axle with a Halibrand unit, sprung by torsion bars and radius rods. Brakes were discs all around; the front had four spots per wheel and the rears had two spots per wheel. A Jaguar four-speed gearbox was mated to the Halibrand rear axle via a 25-inch-long driveshaft.

Hagemann built an alloy body with a large oval grille opening and a hood scoop. The car was painted white with a blue stripe, and there was something Cunninghamesque in the car's appearance. The car was finished off with a lovely interior, a short windscreen, and Halibrand Indy-style magnesium wheels.

While Hagemann was toiling away, George Naruo was hired to build an engine. Naruo began with a 375-ci Chrysler Hemi 300 motor. The cylinders were overbored 0.060 inches, and the heads were ported to improve performance. Stock valves were used with heavy-duty valve springs from Oldsmobile. A hot camshaft with 270 degrees

duration was obtained from Chet Herbert's shop. Induction was by four two-barrel Stromberg 97 carburetors. Power output was in the neighborhood of 360 to 370 horses, with red line at 6,500 revs.

The Barneson-Hagemann Chrysler was competitive in its class and scored numerous podium finishes. The car was a winner in May 1956 at Santa Rosa Airport. In July of that year, the car also finished second at Buchanan Field and third at Santa Maria.

This beautiful car is a piece of American racing history and today continues to compete in vintage racing events.

Batchelor/Frostrom Silver Bomb Special

See Silver Bomb entry.

Batmobile

See Masterson Batmobile entry.

Beast

The Beast began life as a stock '52 Crosley Hotshot and, over the next decade, was morphed by various owners into successive versions of a small-displacement road racer. The most impressive thing about the Beast was its "iron man" ability. The car finished approximately 90 percent of the time, while logging some 8,000 racing and practice miles.

In 1952, Chuck Sassel, a skilled Southern California metal shaper, bought a stock Crosley Hotshot with the idea of turning it into a race car. Sassel modified the body, making it longer, lower, and sleeker. He sent the engine to Nick Braje, one of the best Crosley engine builders of the day. Braje overbored and hopped up the engine with his dual-carb intake manifold, finned-aluminum oil pan, and finned-aluminum side plates and cam cover.

Before the Beast was completed, Sassel sold the car to Jim Stabuck of Norwalk, California. Stabuck bought the car cheap, with the idea of quickly reselling it for a profit. After having some engine tuning work done by Cecil Holloway of Long Beach, California, Sassel sold the Beast to Bob Hollbrook for $500.

Hollbrook brought the car to his home in Westwood Hills, California, and finished it off with a windshield, hood, and seat belt. Hollbrook finished second-in-class in his first race, at Torrey Pines in November 1954. Hollbrook's second-place finish was particularly impressive considering his minimal racing experience. He also overcame the challenges of 27 starters in his class and running in the under-1,500-cc G class (not the 750-cc H class) because of engine overbore.

Following two disappointing finishes in G class in early 1955, Hollbrook switched to a stock 748-cc

The Barneson-Hagemann Chrysler was both competitive and beautiful. *Allen Kuhn*

144

BEAST

Constructors	Chuck Sassel with Braje engine (1952); Jim Starbuck with engine tuning by Cecil Holloway; Bob Hollbrook with body modification help from Cecil Holloway
Location built	California
Year built	1952
Engine	Crosley
Gearbox	initially, stock Crosley three-speed; switched for an Austin A-40 unit in 1956
Chassis	initially, stock Crosley Hotshot; switched for a tubular space frame in 1956
Front suspension	live axle
Rear suspension	live axle
Brakes	initially, stock Hotshot; switched for spot discs in 1957
Body material	initially, modified Crosley Hotshot; switched to aluminum in 1956; switched to fiberglass in 1957

The Beast was one of the better Crosley specials. *Allen Kuhn*

Crosley powerplant with 9:1 compression, a billet crank, Isky T3 cam, and twin Carter WO carburetors. The switch proved to be an excellent decision, and the Beast began to rack up podium finishes, occasionally winning, but more often running behind Eyerly's Crosley and the Aardvark.

Hollbrook continued to develop the car and made several changes for the 1956 season. The Hotshot frame was discarded, and a lighter, stiffer space frame was constructed of 1 1/4-inch-square tubing. A new alloy body was fabricated, and the Crosley gearbox was exchanged for an Austin A-40

unit. The car continued to do well, and the trophies continued to pile up.

For the 1957 season, Hollbrook, with the help of Holloway, constructed a fiberglass body that was 70 pounds lighter than the alloy skin. He also traded the stock Hotshot brakes for spot disc units. With these improvements, Hollbrook was able to keep pace with the other improving cars of the class and consistently placed well. He eventually sold the car to a student at Whittier High School. The student later sold the car to Donn Hale Munson, who raced it for several years.

Beavis Offenhausers

George Beavis was an Aussie with a passion for Offenhauser power. In the early part of 1941, Beavis moved to Los Angeles and raced an Offy midget. After much success, including the 1950 Pacific Coast Midget Championship, Beavis turned his attention to road racing.

Beavis was a skilled mechanic and machinist, which came in handy when he decided to build his own car to go road racing. Over the years, Beavis made substantial

changes to his car. It is not known exactly how much of each prior car was retained to build the next. It is a matter of semantics as to whether Beavis built only one car that evolved over time, or whether three distinct Beavis Offenhausers were actually built.

The first version of the Beavis Offenhauser was built in 1952 on a tube frame designed and built by Beavis. The car's running gear, excepting the engine, was principally MG, including the body off of an MG TD. The engine was a 1,700-cc midget Offenhauser unit altered to run on gasoline (rather than alcohol). The car finished 12th in the over-1,500-cc class at Torrey Pines in December 1952. The following month, the car scored a win in the under-2-liter class and placed sixth overall at Carrell Speedway.

The second version of the car was built on a space frame of 1.25-inch tubing. The front suspension was MG as were the gearbox and steering unit. The rear suspension was via torsion bar from Morris Minor. A quick-change differential was mated to the MG rear axle. The brakes were DeSoto drums and backing plates, and the hubs were MG. Jack Sutton of Autocraft in Los Angeles constructed the alloy body, a cycle fender design with the spare tire mounted in full view on the rear deck.

The Beavis Offenhauser used a variety of Offy midget engines. This is the Sutton-bodied second version. *Dean Batchelor*

Beavis thought that his special would be more competitive in the under-1,500-cc class, and he began to modify the Offy engine. His goal was to decrease engine displacement from 102 to 91 ci. The block and connecting rods were sectioned, and the camshafts were redesigned (with assistance from Meyer-Drake Engineering) with a first-ever chain-drive system for Offenhauser cams. Induction was via Weber carburetors.

The second car was more successful than the first, and more is known about its California road racing history. The car ran at Chino in July 1953 but did not finish. The car failed to finish again in November 1953 at March Field. The car finished ninth-in-class at Bakersfield in March of the following year. Two months later, the car ran at Willow Springs and scored its first class victory. In July 1954, the car scored another class win at Torrey Pines, followed by a fifth-in-class at March Field in November. In 1955, the car finished first at Willow Springs in February, second-in-class at Bakersfield in May, and second-in-class at Hansen Dam in June.

The third and final version of the Beavis Offenhauser was brought to life in 1957, with many parts again taken from the previous car. The front suspension was completely rebuilt from a hybrid of Fiat and OSCA components. The front brakes were redesigned with Alfin drums, and the rears got Fiat drums. Steering was rack and pinion, with 1.75 turns lock-to-lock. Sutton again formed the body, this time as a single-seater, much like an Indy roadster. The cycle fenders and exposed tires were gone, and the car was built with a distinctive (if not huge) head fairing/roll bar/stabilizing fin. Again, the powerplant was Offenhauser, but now the engine was laid over to the right, with the driver offset right and the driveshaft offset left. The engine had a bore of 2 15/16 inches, a stroke of 3 5/16 inches, and it developed 118 horsepower at 6,800 rpm, with a compression ratio of 10.4:1. Top speed was 136 miles per hour, and the car reached 91 miles per hour for the standing quarter-mile.

BEAVIS OFFENHAUSER

BEAVIS OFFENHAUSER—FIRST VERSION

Constructor	**George Beavis**
Location built	**Los Angeles, California**
Year built	**1952**
Engine	**1,700-cc (102 ci) Offenhauser four-cylinder**
Gearbox	**MG four-speed**
Chassis	**tube**
Front suspension	**MG independent**
Rear suspension	**MG live axle**
Brakes	**MG drum**
Body material	**MG TD**

BEAVIS OFFENHAUSER—SECOND VERSION

Constructor	**George Beavis**
Location built	**Los Angeles, California**
Body by	**Jack Sutton**
Year built	**1953**
Engine	**1,486-cc (91 ci) Offenhauser four-cylinder**
Gearbox	**MG four-speed**
Chassis	**space frame**
Front suspension	**MG independent**
Rear suspension	**torsion bar (Morris Minor) live axle**
Brakes	**drum (DeSoto)**
Body material	**aluminum**

BEAVIS OFFENHAUSER—THIRD VERSION

Constructor	**George Beavis**
Location built	**Los Angeles, California**
Body by	**Jack Sutton**
Year built	**1957**
Engine	**1,486-cc (91 ci) Offenhauser four-cylinder**
Gearbox	**MG TC four-speed**
Chassis	**space frame**
Front suspension	**Fiat/OSCA hybrid independent**
Rear suspension	**live axle**
Brakes	**drum (Alfin front, Fiat rear)**
Body material	**aluminum**
Weight, approx.	**1,100 pounds**
Wheelbase	**86 inches**
Length	**110 inches**
Height	**29 inches**
Cost when new	**$6,500**

Regrettably, the new configuration did not prove successful at the track, and the car either ran poorly or did not run at all. Beavis continued to try to develop the car and at one point even tried to run the Offy engine with an S.C.O.T. blower. The car was sold in 1961, following another DNF at Riverside. The fate of the car remained unclear until it resurfaced in the late 1980s. At that point, David Kopf of Tujunga, California, planned to restore the car for vintage racing.

Bellesiles Special

After Jacques Bellesiles bought the Manning Mercury Special (see Manning Mercury Special entry), the car was referred to as the Bellesiles Special.

Blume Special

See Edwards/Blume Special entry.

Brand X (Christ)

Joe Christ built this special to run in races and hillclimbs in the late 1960s. The chassis was a copy of an Elva Mk.6 fitted with Saab suspension and brakes. A Begra body was fitted, along with a Saab 750-cc engine and transaxle. The name was a

BRAND X (CHRIST)

Constructor	**Joe Christ**
Location built	**Pennsylvania**
Year built	**1967**
Engines	**Saab 750GT**
Gearbox	**Saab four-speed**
Chassis	**space frame**
Front suspension	**independent**
Rear suspension	**independent**
Brakes	**drum**
Body material	**fiberglass**

humorous reference to 1960s-era commercials comparing their products to an unnamed "Brand X." Joe's son, Chuck, is currently running the Brand X in vintage events.

Brand X (Davis)

Homer Rader owned a Lotus dealership in Dallas, Texas, in the 1960s and raced a number of cars, including a Lotus 30 and a 23. In 1965, he teamed with friend Dan Davis to build their own cars (to be called Brand X) for the under-2-liter division of the USRRC series. The idea was to start with a modified Lotus 23 chassis, then add a 2-liter version of the Coventry-Climax V-8 Formula 1 engine. Davis wanted to build his own fiberglass monocoque in place of the Lotus space frame, but Rader vetoed the idea on practical grounds. Rader ordered five bare Lotus 23 frames and an equal number of Climax V-8s, but after they arrived, the SCCA announced it would no longer pay prize money for the under-2-liter class. Rader pulled the plug after one chassis (modified from the Lotus chassis) had been competed, and sold the Climax engines.

Victory Lane magazine publisher Dan Davis wrestles with the Brand X. *Dan Davis collection*

Davis took the remaining car and installed a Lotus twin cam. He raced it at Mid-America Raceway in 1965, when Brand X caught fire and nearly burned to the ground because the corner stations didn't have fire bottles. Fortunately, fellow racers came running from the pits and tossed their bottles over the fence. Davis still has Brand X in storage.

Brundage Duesenberg-Ford

This special was constructed using components from the two-man Duesenberg race car driven to a second-place finish by Fred Frame in the 1931 Indy 500. The impetus for the deconstruction and reconstruction of the car was the dismal next-to-last-place finish by owner and driver Ira J. Brundage at the Watkins Glen Junior Prix in October 1948, when it was powered by a Ford flathead V-8.

Following the event, Brundage and buddy Karl Sundman harvested the frame, alloy body, springs, radiator, and various other Duesie components from the car and got down to work. The special received Ford front and rear axles with parallel springs at both ends. The brakes were hydraulic drums at all four corners, but the car ran in the 1950s with disc brakes. The gearbox was a Ford three-speed with Lincoln Zephyr gears.

The Brundage Duesenberg-Ford was successful in the early 1950s. *Dean Batchelor*

A 280-ci Mercury V-8 with 8.75:1 Edelbrock heads and a Winfield racing camshaft powered the special. Twin Stromberg 97 carburetors were mated to a Grancor intake manifold. In an effort to prevent engine overheating, Brundage decreased the size of the water pump's impellers, a trick that seemed to work very well.

The Brundage Duesenberg-Ford was completed in 1949 and soon had its greatest day in the sun (. . . make that the rain). At the 1950 Round the House road race at Palm Beach Shores, an island on the Florida coast, driver George Huntoon let it rip. In a difficult race in a torrid rainstorm, the car immediately leapt into the lead and was never challenged, beating

147

BRAND X (DAVIS)	
Constructors	**Homer Rader and Dan Davis**
Location built	**Dallas, Texas**
Year built	**1965**
Engine	**Coventry-Climax/ Lotus TC**
Gearbox	**Hewland five-speed**
Chassis	**space frame**
Front suspension	**independent, coil springs**
Rear suspension	**independent, coil springs**
Brakes	**disc**
Body material	**fiberglass**
Weight, approx.	**750 pounds**

BRUNDAGE DUESENBERG-FORD	
Constructors	**Ira J. Brundage and Karl Sundman**
Location built	**Florida**
Year built	**1949**
Engine	**Mercury V-8 (280 ci)**
Gearbox	**Ford three-speed**
Chassis	**Duesenberg ladder**
Front suspension	**live axle**
Rear suspension	**live axle**
Brakes	**hydraulic drum; later disc**
Body material	**from the Duesenberg Indy car**
Weight, approx.	**1,900 pounds**

a field of superstars. First-through-tenth finishing order was Brundage, followed by Briggs Cunningham's Cadillac-Healey, George Rand's Ferrari, Leslie Johnson's Jaguar XK-120, Phil Walter's Healey Silverstone, Miles Collier's Ardent Alligator, Tom Cole's Cad-Allard, Sam Collier's Jaguar, Steve Lansing's MG, and John Fitch's MG.

Journalists were so impressed with the win that the car was featured on the cover of *Road & Track* in February 1950. Brundage's son, Hubert, continued the family racing tradition by starting Brundage Motors, which later evolved into the famed Brumos Porsche dealership. He was also pivotal in starting the Formula Vee racing class (see Formcar entry, Chapter 2).

Brundage VW Special

Hubert Brundage was a pivotal character in American automobile racing. His father, Ira, had raced the Brundage Duesenberg-Ford (see Brundage Duesenberg-Ford entry) just after World War II, and Hubert followed in his footsteps. Brundage ran the family's chain of hardware stores and soon became interested in cars. In 1951, he picked up an early Volkswagen Beetle and was surprised that a car so slow could be fun to drive. The pre-1950 Beetle had a 1,130-cc engine with only 30 horsepower, sloppy

BRUNDAGE VW SPECIAL	
Constructor	**Brundage Motors**
Location built	**Miami Springs, Florida**
Year built	**1952**
Engine	**1,200-cc Volkswagen**
Gearbox	**Volkswagen four-speed**
Front suspension	**trailing link**
Rear suspension	**swing axles**
Brakes	**drum (Volkswagen)**
Body material	**aluminum**
Number built	**one**

mechanical brakes, and a nonsynchronized gearbox. Despite these drawbacks, Brundage wanted to enter it in the 1952 Sebring race, and he set about making a new body for it from aluminum. This slab-sided creation would not win any styling contests, looking more like a bumper car than a racing machine. However, Brundage and his brother, Jack, finished 11th overall and fifth-in-class in the 12-hour enduro.

In 1953, Brundage basically reinvented his special by replacing the VW platform with a tubular chassis, switching to hydraulic brakes, and adding a Shorrock supercharger. It was much faster, but the blower made the overstressed VW engine marginally reliable.

Brundage went on to lay the groundwork for Formula Vee (see Formcar) and start Brundage Motors, which morphed into Brumos Porsche, home of many famous Porsche racing cars. Although Brundage was killed in 1964 while riding his motorcycle, his legacy lives on to this day.

Bud Hand Special

Bud Hand of Santa Monica, California, built one of the more delightful specials of the day. It took Hand a full three years to complete the car (1953–1956), but the final result was well worth the wait. The car was not only superb from a mechanical perspective, but its hand-rubbed orange alloy body was so spectacular that it won honors as a show car at local events in Southern California.

Hand's jewel box was built on a space frame constructed from 1.5-inch-diameter mild steel tubing of 0.054-inch wall thickness. The frame was gas-welded to form a rigid unit with a wheelbase of 90 inches (front track was 54 inches, rear track was 49 inches). Additional hoops were placed at the firewall (providing a mounting point for the transmission and support for the cowling) and just behind the driver, where thicker walled tubing (0.083 inches) was used to add rigidity to the frame and to function as a roll hoop.

Alan Kerns takes the Bud Hand Special (No. 26) around Santa Barbara in 1959. *Allen Kuhn*

The front suspension of the Bud Hand Special was independent, with unequal A-arms and transverse leaf springs cut down from a '36 Ford unit. The rear suspension was live axle from an MG with trailing upper radius arms and lower quarter-elliptic springs. Brakes were cross-drilled Alfin drums front and rear. The front brakes were MG TF, cooled via funnel-shaped air scoops. The rear brakes were MG TC, and Hand designed a system to cool these by forcing air through the frame tubes, which he left open. The tranny was a four-speed MG, and the steering mechanism was from a Morris Minor with modified MG steering arms.

Hand selected the 1,466-cc MG factory-option Stage 4 Competition engine with dual SU carburetors

BUD HAND SPECIAL	
Constructor	**Bud Hand**
Location built	**Santa Monica, California**
Years built	**1953–1956**
Engine	**1,466-cc modified MG Competition**
Gearbox	**four-speed (MG)**
Chassis	**space frame**
Front suspension	**independent**
Rear suspension	**live axle**
Brakes	**Alfin drum (MG TF front, MG TC rear)**
Body material	**aluminum**
Weight, approx.	**1,175 pounds**
Wheelbase	**90 inches**

as his powerplant. As received from the factory, the engine produced 82 horsepower at 6,500 rpm. Hand reworked and tuned the motor, fabricated headers, and increased power output by 10 percent.

The body was a cycle-fendered masterpiece, constructed in seven sections from sheets of 16-gauge aluminum. Dzus fasteners were used to secure the body and to allow rapid access to all sections of the race car. The belly pan was divided into two full sections and provided access to the car's underside. To finish off the car, Hand used beautiful wire wheels and added a handmade steering wheel.

By 1956, the competition had advanced, and the Bud Hand Special was a bit late to the dance, overmatched by the latest racers from Cooper, Lotus, and Porsche. Still, the car was quick, reliable, fun to drive, and absolutely stunning.

Burgraff Devin Panhard

This Panhard-based special, with a $295 Devin body, was run with great success out of Southern California by Dr. Chet Burgraff.

Burnett Specials

The cars of Stan Burnett of Seattle, Washington, were well-built sports-racers that lagged just a bit behind the factory-built cars.

Burnett Mk.1-Chevy

This Burnett Mk.1 was built in 1959. Burnett built a tube frame and fit on an attractive fiberglass Devin body. A 327-ci Chevy V-8 was installed in the right-hand-drive racer. For some added pizzazz, Burnett painted the car a rather loud shade of orange.

Burnett drove his car to victory in the first heat of the Pepsi Pro race at Westwood in 1962. He was also running third in a field of superstars at Pacific

Raceway during the 1962 Northwest Grand Prix when he suffered a mechanical failure.

The car was later sold to Gary Gove, who raced it at a USRRC race at Kent. Later still, the car was totaled in a racing accident.

Burnett Mk.2

The Mk.2, Burnett's first midengined design, wore a Huffaker Genie body with a Chevy V-8. Burnett made his own transaxle out of a Corvette transmission and a Halibrand quick-change unit

BURNETT SPECIALS

BURNETT MK.1

Constructor	Stan Burnett
Body by	Devin Enterprises
Location built	Seattle, Washington
Year built	1959
Engine	Chevy V-8 (327 ci)
Gearbox	Borg-Warner T-10 four-speed
Front suspension	independent
Body material	fiberglass

BURNETT MK.2

Constructor	Stan Burnett
Year built	1964
Engine	Chevy small-block V-8
Gearbox	Burnett
Front suspension	independent
Rear suspension	independent
Brakes	disc
Body material	fiberglass

BURNETT MK.3 AND 4

Constructor	Stan Burnett
Years built	1968–1970
Engine	Chevy big-block V-8
Gearbox	Burnett
Front suspension	independent
Rear suspension	independent
Brakes	disc
Body material	fiberglass

The Burnett Mk.3 (No. 0) was a home-built Can-Am car. This photo was taken at Riverside in 1968. *Pete Lyons*

The improved Burnett Mk.4 (No. 22) ran Riverside in 1968. *Pete Lyons*

(similar in concept to the McKee and BMC transaxles). Two were built—one for Burnett and one for Don Jensen. They were raced in SCCA events in the mid-to-late 1960s.

Burnett Mk.3 and Mk.4

The Burnett Mk.3 was a one-off update of Burnett's Mk.2, but with a big-block Chevy engine and revised suspension to take bigger wheels and tires. The body was also all-new, with modern angular lines. The car was wrecked at the 1969 Elkhart Lake Can-Am race, injuring Burnett. Burnett then built a Mk.4 version with a rear-mounted radiator and a 427 Chevy engine. It ran at the 1970 Donnybrook Can-Am, but retired. Burnett was killed testing the car in 1970.

Butterball Special

The Butterball Special started life in Great Britain as an experimental four-wheel-drive vehicle of inventor Archie J. Butterworth. Butterworth started with the chassis from a four-wheel-drive Jeep and a 3,700-cc air-cooled Steyr V-8 engine. The engine was bored to 4,500-cc and Butterworth set compression at 14:1. Equipped with a special camshaft, two Amal carbs, and running on alcohol, the motor produced a very respectable 250 horsepower. Butterworth raced the car in England in sprints, hillclimbs, and road races between 1948 and 1951. In 1949 and again in 1951, Butterworth ran the fastest time of the day at the Brighton Speed Trials. Later in 1951 at the Shelsley Walsh Hillclimb, Butterworth crashed the car badly. After the crash, Butterworth sold the car to the American Four-Wheel-Drive Company, which imported it to the United States.

William "Bill" Milliken became the driver of the Butterball Special on this side of the pond. The car was raced principally on the East Coast in hillclimbs and road races. The car's four-wheel-drive nature made it a natural for hillclimbs, but its road race record was mediocre at best. During a practice session at the 1952 Seneca Cup race at Watkins Glen, Milliken hit a light pole after spinning the car in a high-speed turn. As a result, the Butterball Special was unable to compete at that year's race. Ironically, the same turn had already been named after Milliken (Milliken's Corner) following his dramatic accident in 1950 when he rolled a Bugatti on the sixth lap while trying to overtake Erwin Goldschmidt in an Allard J2 for the lead.

The car was again entered at the Glen in 1953, but failed to start. At the 1955 Seneca Cup race, the car finally made it to the starting line but did not finish. Nevertheless, a couple of moments of glory for the Butterball were still ahead. The first came at the Giant's Despair Hillclimb, where the car posted the third best time of the day and ran second in the unrestricted class. Another came the following year

(1956), when the car finally finished the Seneca Cup race, running third-in-class and 15th overall.

The Butterball is not remembered for stunning beauty, nor impressive racing wins, nor famous personalities associated with it. But the Butterball was unique—a one-of-a-kind, four-wheel-drive Jeep race car. It took form from the ideas of a single man, an innovator who dared to challenge conventional wisdom. And that's what racing used to be about, and it's why we love to recall race cars like the Butterball Special.

BUTTERBALL SPECIAL	
Constructor	**Archie J. Butterworth**
Location built	**England**
Year built	**1948**
Engine	**3,700-cc air-cooled Steyr V-8**
Chassis	**Jeep four-wheel-drive**

Caballo de Hierro

See Ak Miller's Caballo de Hierro entry.

Caballo II

See Ak Miller's Caballo II entry.

Campbell Special

The Campbell Special was just another midengined, Chevy-powered sports-racer. But one thing made it special—it was the *first* one built in America. In fact, the only other midmounted Bowtie at the time was the Sadler Mk.5, constructed just across the border in Canada. The Campbell was an amalgamation of parts and design ideas that happened to come together in spectacular fashion.

Owner Bill Campbell was a famed powerboat builder who wanted to build a race car around an

1,100-cc JAP engine. Wayne Ewing, who had worked on Indy cars for A. J. Watson, constructed a tube frame from 4130 chrome-moly steel. Unequal-length A-arm front suspension was matched to a swing-axle rear end. Coil-over shocks were used all around with Morris Minor steering. The fiberglass body was purposeful, if not altogether graceful.

By 1961, the car was sorted out, but the JAP engine was obsolete in the small-bore classes, so a swap to a Chevy 283 was arranged. It's a tribute to the original construction that the same frame was capable of digesting that much more power. The engine was left largely stock, with triple Stromberg carbs sitting on a Weiand manifold sparked by a Joe Hunt magneto. To fit into the existing frame, the engine was canted down 5 degrees at the nose. An early Corvette aluminum radiator handled the cooling chores.

Since no available transaxle would take that much power and torque, a Chevy three-speed gearbox was bolted directly to a Halibrand quick-change rear end. This setup was long but effective. The previous swing axles were replaced with a de Dion system using a Watts link for lateral location and a four-link setup for front-to-back action. Brakes were 11-inch Halibrand discs all around.

Up front, the A-arms were replaced with stronger ones mounting Corvair spindles and uprights. Halibrand 15-inch magnesium wheels were used all around with Goodyear Blue Streak tires. Carrying only 1,375 pounds with a near-stock Corvette engine, the Campbell Special was easy to drive and did not need more gears to keep the engine in the power band. And the weight distribution was an impressive 50/50, with a short 88-inch wheelbase. The entire car was beautifully fabricated and very well thought out.

Actors Dan Blocker and Pernell Roberts, TV cowboys on the popular *Bonanza* series, sponsored the car. (Blocker later sponsored many racing cars.) The first time out was at Santa Barbara in 1961,

Jim Parkinson drove the Campbell Special at Del Mar in April 1963. *Allen Kuhn*

Jim Parkinson in the Campbell Special takes on Jerry Grant's Lotus 19 at Laguna Seca in 1963. *Allen Kuhn*

when stuntman Bob Harris drove the Campbell Special. It ran at the front until it retired. Once dialed in, the Campbell was a rocket, capable of running with most of the big modifieds on the West Coast. At the Times Grand Prix, Harris finished 13th of 33 cars.

The big Chevy's best race was at Riverside in March 1962, when Harris matched the Campbell against thundering Dave MacDonald driving a Corvette-bodied Old Yaller. By that time, the Campbell had been upgraded to a 327-ci fuel-injected Chevy engine, and the car was a lot faster in a straight line. But when the rear brakes acted up in Saturday practice, they were simply unhooked, leaving Harris with only the front brakes. He finished second to MacDonald in the Saturday race, ahead of a Lotus 19 and a field of Italian exotica and Porsche Spyders. The brakes were fixed in time for the main race on Sunday, and Harris smoked MacDonald at the start to take off in the lead. The Campbell was handling much better than MacDonald's pseudo-'Vette, and soon the two of them pulled clear of the rest of the field. They passed each other back and forth, dicing for the lead until Harris was forced to retire because of overheating. This was disappointing, but at least Harris and the Campbell had shown their mettle against a recognized star.

Harris wrecked the car at Santa Barbara, but it was repaired and driven at Del Mar in 1963 by Jim Parkinson, who broke the lap record on the way to a win in the feature. That year, the car won twice and finished third-in-class at the USRRC race at Laguna Seca.

The Campbell Special is thought to have survived and, we hope, will be restored.

CAMPBELL SPECIAL

Year built	**1961**
Engine	**Chevy V-8**
Gearbox	**Chevy three-speed**
Front suspension	**independent**
Rear suspension	**de Dion**
Brakes	**disc**
Body material	**fiberglass**
Weight, approx.	**1,375 pounds**
Wheelbase	**88 inches**

Cannon Specials

Ted Cannon owned Cannon Engineering, a machine shop in North Hollywood, California, and was knowledgeable, resourceful, and inventive.

This combination of skills enabled him to whip up race cars from thin air and on a shoestring budget. He wasn't just able to do it once—he built three unique and fabulous race cars that bore his name. The Cannon Mk.I was his first road racing effort.

Cannon Mk.I

Cannon built the Mk.I, sometimes referred to as the Cannonball or the Vacuum Sweeper, in 1950. The Mk.I was built from odds and ends already on hand at Cannon's shop. The frame was taken from a '30 Dodge. The channel rails were boxed to improve rigidity, and the wheelbase was shortened to 100 inches. The front suspension was an independent Dodge unit. Cannon removed the Dodge rear axle and replaced it with a Ford axle with transverse leaf springs. Brakes were Dodge up front and Ford at the rear, and Cannon fabricated a bias bar that he could adjust while driving to modulate the front and rear brake pressure. The three-speed gearbox was scavenged from a Lincoln Zephyr corpse, as were several body panels. As a finishing touch, Cannon used spare tire covers to construct the car's cycle fenders.

Power for the Mk.I was supplied by a Mercury flathead V-8. Cannon ground his own camshafts and machined the stock Merc heads. Induction was initially via a single Stromberg carburetor but was later exchanged for a hotter triple Stromberg setup.

The car competed at road racing events and hillclimbs in the early 1950s, most often driven by Cannon's friend Jim Seely. Seely was no stranger to being in a hurry behind the wheel, as he was a firefighter. The car ran at the first Pebble Beach road race in November 1950. Seely finished third behind two Jaguars: Phil Hill's XK-120, and Don Parkinson's XK-120. The car also raced at the Sanberg Hillclimb in 1950. For the hillclimb, Cannon fitted dual rear tires, with the outermost tires running totally outside the cycle fenders. The car was campaigned in 1951 as well, including a race at Torrey Pines.

The Cannon Mk.I races around Torrey Pines in 1951. *Rick Cannon and Dave Seely collection*

The Cannon Mk.II never raced in SCCA, due to regulation changes. *Rick Cannon and Dave Seely collection*

Cannon Mk.II and Mk.III

The Cannon Mk.II was a rear-engined race car powered by a flat six-cylinder aircraft engine. The car competed in a single hillclimb with little success. Because of changes in the SCCA rules, the car was dismantled after the event and little else is known about it.

The Cannon Mk.III never made it past the chalk-line-on-the-floor stage.

Cannon-Offenhauser Mk.IV

In 1953, Cannon built the fourth and final car in his series of specials. Like the cars that came before, the Mk.IV was built from parts that Cannon was able to accumulate. The car began as chalk markings on the cement floor of Cannon's shop. The space frame was built from steel tubing of 1.75- and 2.0-inch diameter. The space frame was built very tall as a safety feature so that the driver was surrounded in a cage just below shoulder height.

The front axle was live with transverse leaf springs and radius rods. A similar setup was used at the rear with a Ford axle, transverse leaf springs, and a Halibrand quick-change center unit. Brakes were Goodyear spots from a Ryan Fireball fighter plane with three spot disc calipers per wheel and

six brake pads per wheel. The front brakes were actuated by a pedal, the rear brakes by a hand lever. The brake pads wore quickly, and overall braking ability was far from perfect. The clutch and flywheel were from Ford as was the three-speed gearbox with Zephyr gears.

Los Angeles-based California Metal Shaping built the alloy body. The unusual-looking coupe had the driver set far back, with a short tail section. The high roofline was meant to accommodate even the tallest of drivers. The gullwing doors were used to comply with the rules, which stated that doors had to measure at least 11 by 17 inches. Because of the height of the space frame, conventional doors were not possible. The car had a long hood, simple wheels, a front bumper, and working headlights and turn signals. It was registered for street use, and Cannon used it as a daily driver. He believed that the more regularly he drove the car, the better he would do with it on the racetrack. According to Cannon's son, Don, it was the best daily driver his father ever owned. Cannon did not tow the Mk.IV to the races, but rather drove it there and back. Equipped with a trailer hitch at the rear, the car actually towed a small trailer with Cannon's tools and equipment.

While the coachwork was interesting, the powerplant was truly exotic. From Cannon's first notion of the car, he had planned to shoehorn a mammoth Offenhauser engine under the hood. The only problem was money. At the time, a brand-new 270-ci Offy engine ran $7,500—far more than Cannon had to spend. So he began to assemble Offy bits from all over the United States, and over a two-year period was able to cobble together a complete engine from Offenhauser scraps. The crankshaft had been tested by Magnaflux and rejected by its first buyer, sent back to the manufacturer because of a significant crack. Cannon knew that the damaged area on the crank was seldom an area of failure, so he bought it for next to nothing and used it.

Cannon converted the engine from alcohol to gasoline and used special pistons that lowered compression from 12:1 to 9.5:1. He used a pair of Stromberg E-E dual-throat downdraft carburetors instead of the more conventional Offy setup of Hillborn constant-flow fuel injection. For ignition, he installed a modified Ford double-breaker V-8 distributor. Cannon installed the engine laid over on its side in order to lower the car's center of gravity. He canted the Offy down on the left, 5 degrees from horizontal. The engine was also offset 4.5 inches to the right to counterbalance the weight of the driver and improve handling. This was one of the first ever 270 Offy-powered road race cars, and the first to use a flywheel and a starter.

The car was a rocket, but somewhat unreliable. Despite problems, the car finished seventh in the C-Modified national points standing in 1955, bested by five Ferraris and a Jaguar C-Type.

This car is often simply referred to as the Cannon Special. Because Ted Cannon designed four race cars, this has led to some persistent confusion regarding the various cars' histories. To add further to the confusion, when this car was written about in period, it was incorrectly referred to as the Cannon Mk.III.

This Cannon Special is the Mk.IV. It was originally powered by an Offenhauser Indy engine, but was later changed to a V-8. *Harold Pace*

Capella

The Capella was Andre Capella's third and final road race special. He built it in 1965, about the same time he went to work for Carroll Shelby. His goal was to win an amateur championship.

The Capella was Chevy-powered and was clothed in vibrant pink graphics. *Andre Capella collection*

We Talk With Andre Capella.

AUTHOR: How did the Capella come to be?

CAPELLA: When I went to work [for Carroll Shelby], I only worked on two cars for a while—the Daytona coupes, which weren't very fancy, and the GT40s. And when I worked on the GT40s, I could see that the rear-engine was gonna be the thing of the future, so I decided to build a rear-engined car. Because we did a lot of experimenting with the GT40, I knew exactly how the suspension had to be. I built everything on the new car, the A-frames, the frame. But I kinda copied the same ideas as the GT40, and using a Cobra-type frame of 4-inch tubes. The brakes were the big aluminum calipers off the Cobra. I made the body myself. I used a Cooper front end from Shelby and made a front section copying that and borrowed the Lotus 23 mold that Dan Gurney had and made the back section out of that.

AUTHOR: Tell me about the engine.

153

CAPELLA: Chevrolet gave me the first 427s ever run in a road race car. They gave me two motors. Beach City Chevrolet was helping me and they arranged for me to get the motors.

AUTHOR: But you were working for Shelby?

CAPELLA: Right. Shelby was gonna give me a 427 Ford but I told him I wanted to win races. The Fords had a lot of trouble—bearing problems, the motors weren't dependable. They were blowing up all the time. That's why Ford spent millions to be Le Mans winner and sent so many cars. Anyway, the Chevy had a lot of power, about 610 horsepower. I ran it with Webers.

AUTHOR: Was it a winner?

CAPELLA: I won ten out of 14 races in the first year. I was amateur champion in '67 or '68, I can't remember, in the Cal Sports Car Club. I ran at some USRRC events but didn't do too well. But, I never got beat by a home-built special.

CAPELLA	
Constructor	Andre Capella (Gessner)
Location built	Seal Beach, California
Body by	Cooper front, Lotus 23 rear
Years built	1965–1966
Engine	Chevrolet (427 ci)
Gearbox	T-10 four-speed
Chassis	space frame
Front suspension	independent
Rear suspension	independent
Brakes	disc
Body material	fiberglass
Weight, approx.	2,200 pounds
Cost when new	$4,000

Checkerboard Special

See Mangham-Davis Special entry.

Cheetah

Any vintage race car aficionado worth his salt remembers the outrageous Cheetahs of Bill Thomas. Perhaps only those who have had a particular affection for the cars of LeGrand know much about their Cheetah racing cars. But how many can recall the very first American race car to bare the Cheetah name?

The first Cheetah race car was built by John "Stutz" Plaisted of Massachusetts in 1954 (the other two Cheetah race cars were built in the early 1960s and share no lineage with this first car or with each other). Plaisted's car was built on a '52 Ford chassis. Front suspension was independent with Air Lift bags inside the coil springs. The rear suspension was live axle with quarter-elliptic springs. Motivation was provided by a 331-ci V-8 Cadillac engine with a single carburetor. At some point, the package was upgraded to four two-barrel carburetors on a manifold from Edelbrock. The gearbox was a three-speed from LaSalle with a

Stutz Plaisted's Cheetah (No. 54) is a V-8-powered modified that is still racing today. *Ozzie Lyons*

quick-change rear end from Franklin, and the steering box was borrowed from a Thunderbird.

The car was raced on the East Coast from 1954 through 1963, winning numerous hillclimbs and scoring top-five finishes in many road races. The car could run with most of the European iron of the day, including the Ferraris, Allards, Jag 120s, and 300SLs from Mercedes. Plaisted's son, Stutz, and Bob Holbert also raced the Cheetah. The car was still competitive when Stutz stopped racing it in 1963 in favor of a Lotus 22.

CHEETAH	
Constructor	John "Stutz" Plaisted
Location built	Massachusetts
Year built	1954
Engine	V-8 Cadillac (331 ci)
Gearbox	LaSalle three-speed
Chassis	1952 Ford ladder
Front suspension	independent
Rear suspension	live axle
Brakes	drum
Body material	steel and aluminum

Chukkar Mark II

C. W. "Chuck" Cornett and George R. Harm, both of Fresno, California, built the Chukkar Mark II. They were successful businessmen who had founded the KARM racing stable. Together they owned nearly 40 sports cars prior to conceiving the Chukkar Mark II, and Cornett had a world of experience racing many types of cars in a variety of racing classes. Cornett is perhaps best remembered for being one of the first drag racers to break the 100-mile-per-hour barrier while spinning backward through the traps.

Three other men had a hand in the construction of the Chukkar Mark II. Jim Larkin built the chassis, Bob Sorrell formed the body, and Phil Landresse, a senior high school student in Fresno, designed and constructed the aluminum-paneled interior. Larkin built a ladder frame from exhaust tubing of 3 3/4-inch diameter and 0.065 wall thickness. The front suspension was a tubular solid axle with transverse leaf springs and twin radius rods. The rear suspension was live-axle, also with transverse leaf springs and radius rods, and had a Ford Banjo housing with a Halibrand quick-change unit. The gearbox was a four-speed unit from Jaguar, and the clutch was from a '55 Austin-Healey. Brakes were finned-aluminum drums from Buick; the shocks were fully adjustable. The steering unit was from a '40 Ford that was converted to right-hand drive.

The fiberglass body was a wild and beautiful Sorrell design. Sorrell and Larkin performed the fiberglass work. The rear section was permanently mounted to the chassis via bulkheads and outriggers. The front half of the body was removable by Dzus fasteners. Phil Landresse fabricated the aluminum panels, floor boards, and underskin.

The engine for the Chukkar Mark II began as a 401-ci Buick Wildcat from a station wagon. The engine, gearbox, driveline, and rear end were

installed offset 6 inches to the left. A Cook adapter was used to mate the Buick powerplant to the Jag gearbox. Corbett hired International Red to make special cylinder sleeves, resulting in an overbore of 0.185 inches and a whopping displacement of 437 ci. Forged pistons were provided by ForgedTrue and Iskenderian provided a specially ground roller tappet cam. A special racing oil pan was also used. Induction was by six Stromberg carburetors sitting on a Crowder log manifold. In this configuration, the engine produced a mighty 410 horsepower at 6,500 rpm and launched the car from 0-to-60 in 4.1 seconds, 0-to-100 in 9.5 seconds, and an estimated top speed somewhere north of 200 miles per hour.

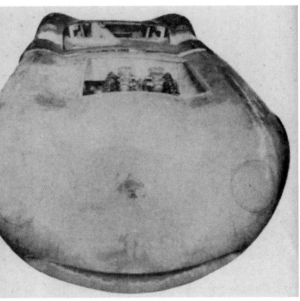

Bob Sorrell designed the body for the Chukkar Mark II. *Robert Rolofson Jr.; Robert H. Rolofson III collection*

CHUKKAR MARK II

Constructors	C. W. "Chuck "Cornett and George R. Harm; chassis by Jim Larkin
Location built	Fresno, California
Body by	Sorrell Engineering (Bob Sorrell and Jim Larkin)
Year built	late 1950s
Engine	7,123-cc Buick
Gearbox	Jaguar four-speed
Chassis	ladder
Front suspension	live axle
Rear suspension	live axle
Brakes	drum
Body material	fiberglass
Weight, approx.	1,750 pounds
Wheelbase	89 inches
Height	34 inches

Civit Jr.

Performance Engineering in Detroit built this front-engined Formula Junior. Partners John Camden, Bill Bradley, John Woodhouse, and Harry Constant assembled a clean design, using Triumph Herald power and running gear mounted on a space frame.

CIVIT JR.

Year built	1960
Engines	Triumph Herald four-cylinder
Gearbox	Triumph four-speed
Front suspension	independent
Rear suspension	swing axle
Brakes	drum
Body material	fiberglass

Cleary Special

Notre Dame engineering student Michael Cleary built the Cleary Special in 1956. Cleary built the car on a chassis donated from a Fiat Topolino, and for power he installed a Crosley CIBA four-banger. The gearbox was also harvested from the Topolino. The beautiful body was a $295 fiberglass shell from Bill Devin, finished in bright yellow paint. Midget-style magnesium wheels completed the package.

Cleary placed third at the Johnson Park Hillclimb in Grand Rapids, Michigan, in 1956. He campaigned the car in 1956 and 1957, mostly in the upper Midwest. In 1958, he tried an engine swap with a Mercury outboard, but that didn't work out very well. So he returned the car to Crosley

CLEARY SPECIAL

Constructor	Michael Cleary
Body by	Devin Enterprises
Year built	1956
Engine	Crosley CIBA four-cylinder
Gearbox	Fiat Topolino four-speed
Chassis	Fiat Topolino ladder
Front suspension	Fiat Topolino independent
Rear suspension	Fiat Topolino live axle
Brakes	drum
Body material	fiberglass

power and raced it in that configuration until 1964 when he parked it for good . . . or so he thought.

Cleary, with the help of his son, Jamie, resurrected the Cleary Special in the early 1990s and fully restored and race-prepared it. Cleary is now approaching his 70th birthday and is actively racing the Cleary Special in vintage events.

Coffield Specials

Paul Coffield was an SCCA racer in the Midwest who built a total of six small-displacement specials between 1960 and 1972. Early on, he used the Crosley four-cylinder for power, but later on he switched to Saab. His most successful car was the 750-cc Honda Special that he campaigned in 1970. Coffield was from the same mold and region as Martin Tanner, who built the fabulous specials that bore his name, and they and their cars were known and respected.

Comet

The Comet began its life in 1951 when Paul Clovis of Northbrook, Illinois, began building a racer using an MG TD frame he bought from Wacky Arnolt. At the time, it was a bare frame without a body. Clovis installed a modified Mercury flathead with dual carbs, built up from a 59A Ford block. The tranny and rear end were also Ford.

The project was later sold to Bob Ballinger of Highland Park, Illinois, who clothed the car in a lovely Glasspar fiberglass body, which required substantial shortening (8 inches) to fit the TD frame.

Ballinger named the car the Comet and raced it between 1952 and 1953. In 1952, the car competed at the Chicago Hillclimb and was victorious at the inaugural Janesville Airport races. In early 1953, the Comet raced at MacDill Air Force Base in Tampa, but retired early with a blown engine.

The destroyed Merc flathead was exchanged for a Ford flathead, and the Comet was bought by

The Comet had a Glasspar body and went through a variety of engines. *Glen Glendenning; Deborah and Larry Narcus collection*

Glenn Glendenning, who raced the car in hillclimbs, SCCA events, and fairgrounds races through 1959, making various modifications along the way. The modifications included exchanging the MG front end with a Ford unit, installing Alfin drum brakes, and exchanging the detonation-prone flathead Ford for a 283 Chevy V-8 with three Stromberg carbs. One of the unique features of the car was the installation of red, green, and yellow lights to signal the pits, presumably when the flathead let go.

The high-water mark in the Comet's career occurred in 1957, when the car was codriven by

COMET	
Constructor	**Paul Clovis**
Location built	**Northbrook, Illinois**
Body by	**Glasspar Company**
Year built	**1951**
Engine	**Mercury flathead**
Gearbox	**Ford**
Chassis	**MG TD**
Front suspension	**independent**
Rear suspension	**live axle**
Brakes	**drum**
Body material	**fiberglass**

Augie Pabst in the Milwaukee 500. The car was retired in 1960 and laid to rest in a barn in Lake Geneva, Wisconsin. It surfaced at an auction in 1976 in Minnesota and changed hands several times until it was purchased and restored by Larry and Debby Narcus in 1989–1990.

Coppel MG TC

The Coppell MG TC was one of the more successful early 1950s MG-powered specials. It was relatively light compared to many of the other MG modifieds (the stock TC was lighter than the stock TD, 1,764 pounds to 1,932 pounds) and its owner, author Alfred (Al) Coppel of San Francisco, was a very capable driver.

The tale began in 1951, as most did. Coppel owned a street MG TC and decided to take it racing. The MG body was tossed, and the engine was moved toward the rear to improve weight distribution and handling. No other major modifications were made to the chassis. The 19-inch factory wheels were discarded and the car was fitted with 16-inch Borrani wire wheels. This change provided two advantages: The car's center of gravity was markedly lowered, which vastly improved its handling characteristics, and it allowed for the use of wider tires to augment the car's grip.

Coppel enlisted Bill Harper to help with the TC engine. The valves were enlarged, the valve springs were stiffened, the camshaft was reground, and the crankshaft was race-prepped. The car was raced with stock pistons and no other major modifications were made to the block. The gearbox was a stock MG production unit without modification.

With heavy input from Coppel, Bob Allinger crafted all of the alloy body panels, designed for easy on and off, using Dzus fasteners. Allinger was a genius with aluminum, and it showed. In fact, the body was so perfect that Coppel ran it in bare aluminum with red trim accents.

In order to shed weight, Coppel fitted the car with two small 9-pound batteries in place of the stock MG 50-pounder. This one modification lightened the car by 32 pounds, a weight reduction of 2.4 percent. The finished car tipped the scales at 1,320 pounds.

The Coppel MG TC began its racing career at Watkins Glen in September 1951. Coppel finished a dismal 25th in a field of 32, completing only four of 11 laps. At its second race, at Reno in October, Coppel's special performed better, but it still wasn't looking all that promising. Things changed quickly at the Fourth Annual Palm Springs Road Race in March 1952. In the 33-lap race, Coppel scored an impressive win in the under-1,500-cc class, beating the second-place ex-Barlow Simca Special driven by Bill Pringle and the third-place 1,400-cc Siata GS owned by John Edgar and driven by Bill Pollack.

Coppel finished second in April 1952 at Pebble Beach to Roger Barlow, who was magnificent in his second Simca Special, winning the Pebble Beach Trophy for cars under 1,500 cc in front of a crowd of 60,000. A disappointing fifth followed at Golden Gate Park in May, when Barlow and Pringle in their Simca Specials, as well as Bill David and Bob Gillespie in MG TD Specials, beat Coppel. Another poor showing at Torrey Pines followed.

But perhaps the best was yet to come. Coppel regained his composure for the Stockton Road Races in August and readied himself for stiff competition. In front of throngs of screaming fans, he captured the Children's Hospital Trophy, beating all comers under 1,500 cc, including Ken Miles in the R-2, Barlow, and Pringle. This was a glorious day for Coppel and his fabulous MG TC special.

Cozzi Jaguar

In the mid-1950s, Dan Cozzi of San Francisco, California, decided to go racing. So he bought a crashed Jaguar XK-120M coupe and hired Bill Nielsen to help him design and build a special that would exploit the mechanicals from the vagrant Jag. A ladder frame was constructed from tubes with a wheelbase of 96 inches. The front and rear suspensions were transplanted from the Jaguar coupe.

For the body, Cozzi definitely did it right. He hired master metal man Jack Hagemann to build the all-aluminum skin after Nielsen's design. The car was very attractive with a lightly wedged front end, covered headlights, wire wheels, a small driver's windscreen, a driver's headrest (on the left), and a lovely rounded tail. The body was fastened to the frame via steel flanges. This made taking the body on and off a longer process than Dzus fasteners would have, but the mounting technique did produce an ultra smooth, seamless, streamlined body that was very much to Cozzi's liking. The body did not even have a driver's side door.

The engine, a mildly tuned XK-120 powerplant, was also from the wrecked Jaguar. The gearbox and brakes were Jaguar.

COZZI JAGUAR	
Constructors	**Dan Cozzi and Bill Nielsen**
Location built	**California**
Body by	**Jack Hagemann**
Engine	**Jaguar XK-120M**
Gearbox	**XK-120 four-speed**
Chassis	**ladder**
Front suspension	**Jaguar XK-120 M independent**
Rear suspension	**Jaguar XK-120 M live axle**
Brakes	**Jaguar drum**
Body material	**aluminum**
Weight, approx.	**2,520 pounds**
Wheelbase	**96 inches**

Croslahti

Starting with a 1949 Crosley street machine, Abbott Lahti of Wolfeboro, New Hampshire, decided to build himself a car to go racing. He combined the donor car's name and his surname and came up with, well . . . Croslahti.

Croslahti

The frame and mechanicals for the Croslahti (sometimes referred to as the Croslahti A) were all essentially Crosley. The engine was an early copper-brazed (COBRA) Crosley unit. The most unique part of the car was the bodywork . . . because there wasn't any. Lahti used aluminum and wood strapping to support the cowling. Other than that, the car ran naked.

COPPEL MG TC	
Constructors	**Alfred Coppel, Bill Harper (engine)**
Body by	**Bob Allinger (after a design by Al Coppel)**
Year built	**1951**
Engine	**MG TC four-cylinder**
Gearbox	**MG TC four-speed**
Chassis	**MG TC ladder**
Front suspension	**MG TC live axle**
Rear suspension	**MG TC live axle**
Brakes	**MG TC drum**
Body material	**aluminum**
Weight, approx.	**1,320 pounds**

At the track, the Croslahti was no slouch. The car ran second to Bill Spear's 2-liter Ferrari at an early SCCA event in Dover, New Hampshire. After this car retired, Lahti built a second homespun race car—the Croslahti B.

Croslahti B

This second car ran the updated Crosley cast-iron block (CIBA) and was a better performer than the first car. In 1951, Lahti recorded the fastest SCCA lap at Thompson in Connecticut driving the Croslahti B.

Lahti eventually sold the car to Jim Hoe, who later sold it to Hank Rudin, who put a fiberglass body on it and supercharged the engine.

CROSLAHTI

CROSLAHTI A

Constructor	Abbott Lahti
Location built	Wolfeboro, New Hampshire
Year built	1951
Engine	Crosley COBRA four-cylinder
Gearbox	Crosley
Chassis	Crosley
Front suspension	Crosley
Rear suspension	Crosley
Brakes	Crosley
Body material	none

CROSLAHTI B

Year built	1951
Engine	Crosley

Dailu Specials

Canadians David Greenblatt and Luigi Cassiani built the first Dailu Special in 1961. It was heavily influenced by the Sadler Mk.IV and had a tubular chassis with fully independent suspension and a Chevy V-8 for power. The attractive aluminum body built by Mike Saggers had a menacing stance, with two small air inlets and a low, protruding nose. It was raced by

The Dailu Mk.I had some great rides with up-and-comer John Cannon. *Mike Leicester collection*

The Dailu Mk.II was a great-looking car with a Chevy V-8 engine. *Mike Leicester collection*

The Dailu Mk.III was similar to earlier Dailus. *Mike Leicester collection*

rising star John Cannon, who frequently outran supposedly more modern cars. In 1962, Cannon took first overall at Mosport and won a race at Riverside as well. Unfortunately, the Dailu Mk.I was burned to the ground at Nassau in 1963.

The Dailu Mk.II was built in 1962 and was similar to the earlier car, but with a Jaguar XKE rear suspension. It had a fiberglass body and was raced by Don Horner and Gordy Dewar. With a short wheelbase and over 400 horsepower, it was a twitchy car to race. The Mk.II has survived and is currently raced by Mike Leicester.

The 1963 Mk.III, similar to the Mk.II, was given a more angular body. By that time, the era of the front-engined racer was coming to a close, and the Mk.III did not have the impact the first Dailu had. Peter Lerche raced it in the 1963 Canadian Grand Prix. The Mk.IV coupe came out in 1963 and was raced in the 1963 Players 200 and at Nassau. It reportedly later had its top removed and was used by an American racing school in the 1960s. The final Dailu, the 1965 Mk.V, had a Sadler-style chassis that was similar to the previous Dailus, but

The weird top looked out of place on the Dailu Mk.IV.
Mike Leicester collection

It looks like a Corvette, but check out those wire wheels!
The Dailu Mk.V was a strange combination.
Mike Leicester collection

it was fitted with a body resembling a Corvette Sting Ray roadster with wire wheels. There was also a Dailu Mk.VI, but it was a modified Lotus 19 and not a special.

D and D Special

Little is known about the D and D Special's racing history. It is believed to have been named after Arthur Dury and Frank Dominanni, who raced the car into the early 1950s. The chassis was from a '46 Ford, and the motor was a Ford V-8.

Darwin Special

The Darwin was a special-bodied one-off road racer with a flathead Ford powerplant in a 1926 Chevy frame. The car was originally built in 1937 with a Cadillac V-16 for dry lake racing. It was road raced from 1948 to 1951.

David MG TD

The David MG special was built in Jack Hagemann's shop in Castro Valley, California, in 1951. The car's owner, Bill David, was from nearby San Francisco and was involved in the television broadcasting industry.

Hagemann and David started the project with a stock MG TD. The body was immediately removed and discarded. Next, the MG motor was lowered 3 inches and set back 6 inches to improve balance and handling. The chassis was essentially left stock, other than relocating the motor mounts. In order to add some oomph to the package, the TD's engine displacement was increased to 1,498 cc. The crankshaft was race-prepared, and compression was raised to 9.6:1.

Hagemann formed the stylish alloy body, with David providing ideas and input along the way. Cycle fenders were used up front, but the rear fenders were faired into the tail section. The long sculpted nose terminated in a grille with vertical

members, and a short left-sided head fairing was incorporated into the body. When the metal work was complete, the car was painted a lovely shade of metallic blue. With the contrast of Borrani-Rudge wire wheel knock-offs and nerf bars at both ends, the David MG TD was stunningly beautiful. The car was raced in 1951 at Buchanan Field and Reno. It also finished 12th overall at the second Pebble Beach Road Races in 1951.

The David MG TD had a handsome Hagemann body.
Dean Batchelor

The Davis Special was good at both road racing and hillclimbs. *Dean Batchelor*

Davis Special

Bob Davis grew up in Boone, North Carolina, with the childhood dream of being a race car driver. When he returned home following duty as an aircraft mechanic in the U.S. Navy during World War II, he started work on making that dream come true. Because of the financial realities of the time, Davis was not in a position to buy an all-out European racer. So he did what so many other would-be racers did—he went into his garage and whipped up a special, all in just 2,200 hours.

The Davis Special began with the purchase of a '41 Ford chassis for $35. Davis shortened the chassis to obtain a wheelbase of 100 inches. The chassis was strengthened by adding crossmember tubes and was further modified by removing the

crossmember to permit installation of the engine of Davis' choosing. The leaf springs and brakes were also heavily modified.

The body of the Davis Special was constructed from a conglomeration of junked body scraps and metal sheets. The nose was fabricated from a section of the cab of a '47 Chevy truck. The rear section was formed from the front fenders of a '47 Plymouth. The front fenders and hood were formed from metal sheets. The delightful grille was fabbed from rods of steel and finished off with a "D" (for Davis) insignia offset to the left. The finished car was quite nice, particularly considering Davis' budget and source of parts.

Davis powered his special using an overbored Ford flathead V-8, borrowed from a '47 truck. The race-prepared motor featured three Stromberg 48 carburetors, an Isky camshaft, a crankshaft from a '51 Mercury, and a lightened flywheel. Davis set the engine back 22 inches from its stock location in the chassis in an effort to improve the car's weight distribution. The gearbox was a Ford three-speed with Zephyr gears.

Sometimes a race car is better than the sum of its parts, and such was the case of the Davis Special, a frequent top-three-finishing hillclimber in North Carolina in the 1950s. With Davis behind the wheel, the car won the Fourth Annual Hillclimb at Pilot Mountain in November 1955. In June 1956, the Davis Special was victorious at a climb at Grandfather Mountain, with hot shoe Ed Welch driving. Welch also drove the car to victory six months later at a Chimney Rock hillclimb.

In the spring of 1957, Phil Styles of Burnside, North Carolina, purchased the car and continued its winning ways. Styles won three races in a row at Chimney Rock in 1957 and 1958 and was awarded the Baugh Memorial Trophy for his accomplishment. He also won three in a row (1957–1959) at the Grandfather Mountain annual hillclimb. The last win at Grandfather Mountain came after an engine and gearbox swap following a crash at Chimney Rock at

DAVIS SPECIAL	
Constructor	Bob Davis
Location built	Boone, North Carolina
Years built	1951–1953
Engine	Ford flathead V-8
Gearbox	Ford three-speed
Chassis	1941 Ford ladder
Front suspension	modified '41 Ford truck live axle
Rear suspension	modified '41 Ford truck live axle
Brakes	modified '41 Ford truck drum
Body material	hodgepodge

the end of the 1958 season. Although the car's performance was greatly enhanced by the 283-ci Chevy V-8 and the Jag four-speed, the competition caught up, and the Davis Special was no longer invincible. Styles continued to hillclimb and road race the car until he sold it in 1965. Jimmy Dobbs rediscovered the car in 1992 in a junkyard not far from Waynesville, North Carolina.

Devin-Crosley Super Sport

Bill Devin made quite a splash in the specialty car and racing world in the 1950s, but his first road racing car was a modified Crosley Hotshot. Devin bought the car in stock form and entered it at Buchanan Field in August 1951, taking a win first time out in the novice race. Devin soon set to changing the car around, starting with a lower nose and an oval grille that resembled period Ferraris. He also restyled the rear fenders and lightened the car extensively. He then fabricated an improved exhaust system and a home-built manifold to accept a Weber carburetor. A racing cam was added, and Devin set about winning his class in 20 races. When Devin moved up to Ferraris, he sold the car to Dr. J. H. Thompson, who raced it in California until it was wrecked. Devin maintained the remains were used to build the Little Digger H-Modified, although it has not been verified.

Devin Ryan Special

The Devin Ryan Special was built in 1957 on a rectangular tube ladder frame with two 2-inch by 4-inch main members that ran the length of the car.

The Devin Ryan Special combined Jaguar suspension with Chevy power. *Harold Pace*

Smaller 1-inch-square tubes were welded to the main structure to support the body and floor.

Front suspension was from a '57 Jag Mk.I with unequal A-arms with coil-over shocks and splined hubs. Front brakes were cross-drilled discs with Jag (Mk.9) calipers. The rear suspension was also Mk.I Jag.

The fiberglass body was a 98-inch-wheelbase Devin design with a hinged (externally mounted) hood and trunk. The powerplant was a Chevy 283 V-8.

Little is known of the car's early race history. According to Mike Leicester (who bought the car in 1988), it was built on the East Coast by Peter Ryan and reportedly raced in 1958 and 1959 at Harewood Acres Raceway in Ontario. In 1962, the car was put away for winter storage in Alcove, Quebec, where it stayed until 1988. Leicester took five years to restore the car, which is currently very active in vintage racing.

DKW Formula Junior

This front-wheel-drive Formula Junior was designed and built by DKW guru Erick Sobriery. The body was an aluminum shell formed from 0.051-inch sheet material with lines reminiscent of those of the much larger Indy cars. The motor was tilted almost

The DKW Formula Junior was a front-wheel-drive Formula Junior. *Robert Rolofson Jr.; Robert H. Rolofson III collection*

90 degrees, to allow the car to be built with a very low hood line. A special aluminum manifold was fabricated for the car's Amal TT carburetors. The Formula Junior was equipped with a Dixco electronic tach with revs readable to 10,000 rpm. The cockpit was well designed and comfortable, with the gearshift lever located on the driver's left.

The Double-Ender looked the same coming and going. *Robert Rolofson Jr.; Robert H. Rolofson III collection*

Double-Ender

So is the engine up front or in back? And which end is the front end, anyway? Did you say that thing has three cylinders? And parts from Sweden and Germany? Indeed, this was a car of intrigue.

Ingvar Lindqvist of Southern California built the Double-Ender in 1958. Lindqvist was a Saab dealer, who was racing a Saab GT in production class. One day while he was racing, Lindqvist hit on the idea of building a lightweight racer of his own design to race with the modifieds. Since Saab parts were readily available to him, the powerplant decision was easy.

Lindqvist constructed a fiberglass body using a single mold. The result was a car with nearly identical-looking front and rear ends. The engine was placed at the rear, and the driver was located to the left and slightly in front of center. The roadster had a somewhat unconventional, streamlined appearance. That is not to say that the car was unattractive—far from it. It was a pretty little thing, and it was different.

The space frame was built from chrome-moly steel tubing. Volkswagen suspension was used up front. The rear suspension was independent and was a modified Volkswagen assembly with coil-spring shocks, trailing arms, and stabilizer bars from Porsche. Lindqvist used a Porsche transmission, Porsche brakes at all four corners, and a Volkswagen steering box.

The little two-stroke, three-cylinder 748-cc Saab engine sounded like Jimmy Durante clearing his throat, and it smoked like Jackie Gleason, but it produced an impressive 57 horsepower at 4,800 rpm—13.2 pounds per horse, very respectable for 1958 technology. The motor was run with a compression of 9:1, and it breathed through a Solex carburetion system.

The car proved to be very competitive, and Lindqvist generally finished among the leaders in class. The car also proved to be significant, as it led the way for others in the small-displacement class to put the engine where it belonged.

DOUBLE-ENDER	
Constructor	Ingvar Lindqvist
Location built	Southern California
Year built	1958
Engine	748-cc Saab GT
Gearbox	Porsche four-speed
Chassis	space frame
Front suspension	Volkswagen trailing link
Rear suspension	Volkswagen swing axle
Brakes	Porsche drum
Body material	fiberglass
Weight, approx.	750 pounds
Wheelbase	82 inches
Length	90 inches
Height	30 inches

Durant Devin Specials

Dick Durant of Florissant, Missouri, raced everything from tiny D-sports racers to Lola Can-Am cars, but in the 1960s, he burned up tracks in the Midwest in a potent pair of V-8 specials. Durant was an airplane engineer and a disciplined designer who put much thought into his race car before setting about to build it. He was also a heck of a race car driver.

Durant ran a Devin-bodied special with a Pontiac engine and took a class win at the 1964 SCCA Lake Garnett National.

In 1965, Durant was back with either a new car or an upgraded version of the old one. This special had a space frame of Durant's design. Prior to its construction, Durant mocked up various models of the frame's structure using match sticks and a strain gauge. Once he settled on a design, the frame was fabricated from metal tubing.

For power, Durant selected a 327 Chevy V-8 with a Corvette fuel-injection system. It was getting late in the game for front-engined racers, but

Dick Durant ran well in this Chevy-powered road racer.
John Lee

162

Durant knew that a midengined car was not within his budget. So he put the motor up front and figured that he would do the best he could.

To finish the car, Durant heavily modified a Devin fiberglass shell. It had a wide grille, slab sides, and two chin spoilers. This wasn't the prettiest Devin-bodied car to ever see a racetrack; in fact, it may have been one of the ugliest. But that wasn't the point. Durant was about one thing, and that one thing was going fast.

As it turned out, Durant did go fast. So much so that he captured the 1964 Midwest SCCA C-Modified class title and qualified for the 1965 American Road Race of Champions in Daytona Beach, Florida. Although on paper Durant should have been thoroughly outclassed by the more modern midengined invaders, incredibly, the old front-engined car qualified on the front row of the grid. Even more amazing, at the start of the race, he took off in the lead ahead of several McLarens and other more modern designs. He was actually leading and looking like a winner when an injector

drive cable broke on the next-to-last lap, leaving Durant stranded. This was to be the last time that a sports-racer with an engine up front led at a major road racing event until the advent of the Panoz.

Durant continued to race the special, but later switched to small-displacement sports-racers and then a Lola T-163 in the Can-Am series.

Dürlite Special and Dürlite Too

The Dürlite Special and Dürlite Too were designed and built by Bob Webb of Indianapolis. Webb served as an aeronautical machinist during World War II and was a skilled mechanic and fabricator.

Webb's first car, the Dürlite Special, was built between 1956 and 1958. The special was built on a tube frame of Webb's design with suspension components from Porsche. He then whipped up one of the most gorgeous polished aluminum bodies to ever clothe a sports-racer. The package was finished with a pushrod four-cylinder from Stuttgart. The car was raced in this configuration at Stout Field in Indianapolis and Lawrenceville, Illinois, in 1957.

For the 1958 season, SCCA Porsche racer Jim Ray became the driver of the Dürlite Special, and the car received a Porsche Carrera four-cam pow-erplant. At only 780 pounds, the car had tremendous potential. Sadly, this was never to be as the Dürlite Special's story came to a sudden end at Road America in June 1958, when the car was balled up in a tumbling crash.

A year later, Webb was hired by Bob Staples of Indianapolis to construct a second car modeled after the Dürlite Special. This second car, the Dürlite Too, was very similar to the first and had an equally lovely alloy body. The car was campaigned by noted Porsche racer Chuck Richert with a Porsche 550 four-cam engine. As with Webb's first car, the Dürlite Too did not live up to its potential.

DURANT DEVIN SPECIALS

DURANT DEVIN-PONTIAC
Constructor	**Dick Durant**
Location built	**Florissant and Hazelwood, Missouri**
Body by	**Devin Enterprises**
Year built	**early 1960s**

DURANT DEVIN-CHEVY
Constructor	**Dick Durant**
Location built	**Florissant, Missouri**
Body by	**Devin Enterprises**
Year built	**1965**
Engine	**Chevrolet V-8 (327 ci)**
Gearbox	**four-speed**
Chassis	**space frame**
Front suspension	**independent**
Brakes	**disc**
Body material	**fiberglass**

DÜRLITE SPECIAL & DÜRLITE TOO

DÜRLITE SPECIAL
Constructor	**Bob Webb**
Location built	**Indianapolis, Indiana**
Years built	**1956–1958**
Engines	**Porsche four-cylinder pushrod, four-cylinder Porsche Carrera four-cam**
Gearbox	**four-speed**
Chassis	**space frame**
Front suspension	**trailing link**
Brakes	**drum**
Body material	**aluminum**

DÜRLITE TOO
Constructor	**Bob Webb**
Location built	**Indianapolis, Indiana**
Year built	**1959**
Engine	**four-cylinder Porsche 550 four-cam**
Gearbox	**four-speed**
Chassis	**space frame**
Brakes	**drum**
Body material	**aluminum**

Eave Chevy Special

Larry Eave was no stranger to car construction when he built his Chevy-powered special in 1956. Eave had worked on Bonneville cars and built an Oldsmobile-powered sports car before setting out with friends Orville Withey and Chuck Rich to design and construct a road racer. The frame was a steel box made from 4-inch-diameter tubing. Suspension was by live axles at both ends, with a transverse leaf spring in front and torsion bars in back. A Halibrand quick-change was used, along with Dayton wire wheels and 1955 Chevy steering. Drum brakes were mounted all around, and GMC truck spindles were machined to fit.

The 265-ci Chevy V-8 was treated to JE pistons, an Isky Revmaster cam, a lightened flywheel, and an Edelbrock triple-carb manifold. Spalding ignition threw the spark. An Auburn clutch connected the Chevy to a Ford side-shift three-speed gearbox.

A Jones Meteor R-100 body was attached to the chassis with square-tube framework, and Ford Anglia seats were installed. The Eave Special weighed 2,000 pounds and ran the quarter-mile in 13 seconds.

EAVE CHEVY SPECIAL

Constructor	**Larry Eave**
Location built	**Portland, Oregon**
Year built	**1957**
Engine	**Chevy V-8**
Gearbox	**Ford three-speed**
Chassis	**space frame**
Front suspension	**live axle**
Rear suspension	**live axle**
Brakes	**drum**
Body material	**fiberglass**
Weight, approx.	**2,000 pounds**

Echidnas

Three remarkable specials were built in Hibbing, Minnesota, in the late 1950s by a team of enthusiasts who substituted practicality and dependability for technology and cash. The Echidnas were always a force to be reckoned with in the North, where they had a long streak of wins to their credit.

The team that built the Echidnas consisted of Ed Grierson, John Staver, and Bill Larson. All three had raced Corvettes and Jaguars before deciding to build a team of big modifieds. They ignored the high-tech stuff considered necessary for a hot modified, like disc brakes, space frames, or de Dion rear suspension. Starting with '55–'57 Chevy sedan frames, the team shortened them 20 inches to a 93-inch wheelbase. The frames were also cut in half and narrowed 6 inches at the front and 8 3/4 inches in back. The crossmember behind the engine was eliminated, and a new K-member fabricated to hold

The Echidnas were always fast, and their simple design made them easy to service. *Raymond Milo collection*

the transmission mount. Another crossmember was added behind the driver to mount a tripod-style roll bar and strengthening tubes. The frame proved to be sturdy and light.

Front suspension was a modified Chevy sedan with steel upper wishbones and Chevy Corvette cerametallic finned drum brakes. The Echidna team later designed and cast its own finned drums. In back, a Chevy rear axle was sprung by shortened leaf springs. Staver got the first car that was completed, running it in 1958 with this axle setup. However, axle windup was a problem so Larson and Grierson fitted their cars with single radius rods for axle control. Staver's car was updated with a Watts Link fabricated from Chevy steering arms and knuckles, and the update worked.

Staver's car was originally fitted with stock Chevy steel wheels, but was converted to Dayton wires simply because they looked better. The other two cars were raced on steel Chevy wheels. Although all three cars originally had Chevy steering boxes, Staver's car was converted to rack-and-pinion steering with a Morris Minor rack.

All three Echidnas had Devin fiberglass bodies painted in the same shade of light blue. The long

snout prompted Grierson's wife, Marilyn, a crossword puzzle fan, to suggest they name the car after a long-nosed anteater.

All used Chevy 283-ci engines, but Staver's car was bored and stroked to 339 ci so it could run in B-Modified (the smaller engines ran in C-Modified). Grierson, who did most of the mechanical work on the cars, opted for Rochester fuel injection, which most special builders swore would not work. Racer Brown roller cams were used, and the heads were ported and polished to produce around 340 horsepower for the bigger engine. The Echidna engines were capable of keeping up with the Scarabs in a straight line, yet all the engines were run over 900

Ed Grierson drove his Echidna to a win at the Evaleth, Virginia, airport in 1959. John Staver is pinning the hood. *Raymond Milo collection*

racing miles in a season without failure or being taken apart—impressive stuff.

In their first three seasons of racing, out of 35 starts the Echidnas won 25 first-in-class victories (eight of which were overall wins as well). The only modifieds that could outrun them were the Scarabs (now in Meister Brauser trim), George Constantine's Aston Martin, and the Cunningham Lister-Jags—not bad company for three home-built specials made from scrap Chevy frames at an average cost of around $7,500 each. Today, the Echidnas still terrorize the big-bucks cars in vintage racing. Some traditions should never change.

ECHIDNAS

Constructors	Ed Grierson, John Staver, and Bill Larson
Location built	Hibbing, Minnesota
Body by	Devin Enterprises
Years built	1958–1959
Engine	Chevy V-8
Gearbox	Borg-Warner T-10 four-speed
Front suspension	independent
Rear suspension	live axle
Brakes	Chevy cerametallic drum
Body material	fiberglass
Weight, approx.	1,925 pounds
Wheelbase	93 inches
Number built	three

Edgar MG TC

John Edgar's MG TC began life as a 1947 MG TC. Over the next few years the car was gradually modified and upgraded in an effort to constantly improve its performance as an all-out racer.

To start, Edgar equipped the car with an Arnott supercharger in the early part of 1948. As others would later emulate (such as Alfred Coppel on his MG TC), Edgar cut the wheel height from 19 to 16

inches and widened the rims. After destroying a supercharged engine with a compression ratio that was foolishly high (12:1), Edgar wisely decided that he needed some help. He took the car to Ernie McAfee's shop and put him in charge of the project.

McAfee understood blown motors and immediately reduced the MG's compression ratio. Upgrades were made to the crankshaft, rod assembly, cylinder head studs, rod bolts, camshaft, valves, and valve springs. The Arnott blower was set aside and an Italmeccanica Roots-style unit was installed. It was no accident that this choice coincided with Edgar being named the Western United States distributor of this product. (Later the Italmeccanica Company was restructured as Societa Compressori Torino, and the blower became known as an S.C.O.T. supercharger.) With a compression ratio of 6:1 and 12 psi of boost, the MG TC motor produced a very respectable 148 horsepower at 6,500 rpm.

McAfee left the TC chassis essentially stock. It was one of the few areas of the car that remained undisturbed throughout the various stages of the project. McAfee fabricated new finned brake drums from solid pieces of aluminum (those were the days!) and reconfigured Bendix aircraft units to mate with the MG hubs.

After McAfee prepared the car, it was taken to the Santa Ana European Road Race in June 1950. With

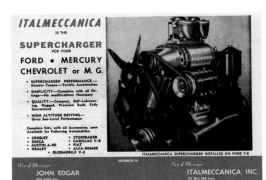

Bill Pollack at the controls, the supercharged Edgar MG TC finished a close second in the under-3,000-cc class just behind Sterling Edwards' Ford V-8 60 Special (the first Edwards Special; see Edwards Specials entry). This was followed by a class win in July at the El Segundo drag races.

EDGAR MG TC

Constructors	John Edgar and Ernie McAfee
Location built	Southern California
Body by	initially run with a stock MG TC body; later rebodied by Emil Diedt
Years built	continuously upgraded from 1947 to 1951
Engine	MG TC
Gearbox	MG TC four-speed
Chassis	MG TC ladder
Front suspension	live axle
Rear suspension	live axle
Brakes	drum
Body material	initially stock MG TC, later aluminum streamliner

The Edgar MG TC was one of the best-known specials of the 1950s. *Dean Batchelor*

More improvements followed. McAfee wanted to decrease the air temperature in the blower to make the system run cooler. Since no intercooler was readily available, he produced one by heavily modifying an aircraft oil cooler. He also installed a larger radiator. Now running cooler, the car took second at the Sandberg Hillclimb in September 1950.

The following April (1951), the car was raced at the Second Annual Palm Springs Road Race. Because Pollack was taking the bar exam and unavailable to drive, Edgar enlisted the services of driver Jack McAfee (no relation to Ernie McAfee). The car was gridded 17th, and McAfee slowly worked his way through the field. At the end, he came home a very respectable fifth overall and second-in-class.

The car's most startling transformation was first displayed at the Third Annual Palm Springs Road Race in October 1951. Other than running under the same racing number, 88, the car's appearance was radically different. Ernie McAfee had discarded the old TC body, replacing it with a magnificent streamliner skin constructed by Emil Diedt. Unfortunately, the visual punch of the rebodied special was greater than its on-track performance, as the car dropped out of the race with a piston failure. The Edgar MG TC was destroyed during the filming of the movie *On the Beach*.

Edwards/Blume Special

Forrest Edwards of San Jose, California, built the Edwards/Blume Special (also known as the Edwards

The Edwards/Blume Special started life with Morris Minor power, but later switched to Crosley. *Harold Pace*

Morris Minor Special) in 1953. Edwards did not set out to build a special, but some garage tinkering and his fondness for superchargers eventually led him in that direction. Edwards had a stock Morris convertible street machine that he decided to supercharge. The supercharger idea was probably fed by his previous favorable experience racing a blown MG TC. In any event, Edwards was so taken by the improved performance of the blown Morris engine that he decided to build an all-out racer.

The project began with the purchase of a wrecked '51 Morris sedan. Edwards scavenged the mechanicals and set them off to the side. Next, an all-new frame was constructed of 4130 chrome-moly tubing. The front suspension was taken from the Morris with little or no alteration. Edwards reengineered the rear suspension with Morris torsion bars and Ford shocks.

Edwards designed and built the all-aluminum body. Although he was not a trained metal-crafter, the alloy body was quite lovely and was one of the best-looking home-builts of the day. The body had a single door on the driver's (left) side, a beautiful oval egg-crate grille, and a sporty windscreen.

The Morris engine displaced 919 cc and produced 27 horsepower from the factory. Edwards improved the car's performance by installing modified Ford V-8 60 valves and a Harmon & Collins full racing camshaft. In addition, a lightened flywheel was used and the basic Lucas ignition system was upgraded by a Lucas sport coil. The engine

EDWARDS/BLUME SPECIAL

Constructor	**Forrest Edwards**
Location built	**San Jose, California**
Year built	**1953**
Engines	**919-cc Morris with Wade supercharger, Crosley four-cylinder**
Gearbox	**four-speed**
Chassis	**ladder**
Front suspension	**independent**
Rear suspension	**live axle**
Brakes	**drum**
Body material	**aluminum**

breathed through a single Stromberg 81 carburetor, and a belt-driven, Roots-style Wade blower was installed. At 14 psi of boost and with compression lowered to 5.3:1, the Morris engine's horsepower was greatly increased over a stock unit.

The car was completed in approximately 1,000 man-hours and made its racing debut at Pebble Beach in 1954. In a star-studded field, the car finished a very respectable seventh. The car was campaigned at several of the best West Coast tracks and always made a respectable showing for itself.

Sometime in the mid-1950s, Edwards sold the car to Tip Blume, a long-time racer and owner of San Jose British Motors. Blume removed the Morris engine in favor of a Crosley four-banger and raced the car on the West Coast in 1955 and 1956. With the new owner and powerplant, the car became known as the Blume Special. The car was not raced again until David Brodsky restored it in 1985.

Edwards Specials

Sterling Edwards was a prominent business and social leader in San Francisco in the late 1940s and early 1950s, as well as a sports car aficionado. On an overseas trip, he got a close look at the finest cars being produced in Europe and became inspired to build a high-quality American sports car. Edwards' idea was to build a vehicle that could be driven around town during the week and raced on the weekend—a true dual-purpose sports car. In the end, Edwards built a series of cars, making changes and modifications along the way. Period documentation suggests that only the first and second Edwards Specials were raced.

The first Edwards Special began when Edwards hired Norman Timbs to start on design plans for his new sports car. He then hired Emil Diedt, Lujie Lesovsky, and Phil Remington to handle construction and fabrication.

The frame for Edwards' first car was a sturdy ladder built from two 4-inch longitudinal tubes. Smaller tubes were used as crossmembers. The front suspension was independent with coil springs and A-arms. The rear suspension was by way of trailing arms and transverse torsion bars. The brakes were a set of spot discs from a Beechcraft Bonanza that Ted Halibrand modified for road racing. The gearbox was a Ford column-shift three-speed with Zephyr (Lincoln) gears. The steering unit was also Ford.

The gorgeous coupe body was hand-formed from aluminum, principally by Diedt and Lesovsky from a wooden buck constructed by William Zimmerman. Dale Runyon designed and installed the lovely leather coachwork. The flowing body lines paid homage to the cars of Cisitalia, and the car looked equally at home on public roads and on the racetrack. In keeping with the dual-purpose concept of the car, the hardtop and windshield were designed to be fully detachable. For racing, the roof and windshield were removed, with a metal tonneau cover converting the four-seater to a sleek roadster race car.

The second Edwards Special was built on a Henry J chassis. The body was a fiberglass shell from a modified mold from Edwards' first racer, and the motor was a Chrysler V-8. The car first appeared at the 1952 races at Pebble Beach but did not enjoy the same success as the first car. Over the next few years, Edwards' interest changed to European race cars, and his friends raced the car. The car was not very competitive.

The first and second Edwards Specials were followed by a series of fiberglass-bodied touring cars built in Edwards' wire cable factory in San Francisco. These road cars were well built but failed to catch on, and Edwards moved on to other things.

The first Edwards Special had a custom chassis and a Ford V-8 60 engine. *Robert Rolofson Jr.; Robert H. Rolofson III collection*

The second Edwards Special was built on a Henry J chassis and powered by a Chrysler V-8. *Robert Rolofson Jr.; Robert H. Rolofson III collection*

EDWARDS SPECIALS

EDWARDS SPECIAL

Constructors	Norman Timbs, Emil Diedt, Lujie Lesovsky, and Phil Remington
Location built	Los Angeles, California
Body by	Emil Diedt, Lujie Lesovsky, and William Zimmerman
Interior	Dale Runyon
Years built	1948–1950
Engine	153-cc Ford V-8 60
Gearbox	Ford column shift three-speed
Chassis	ladder
Front suspension	independent
Rear suspension	live axle
Brakes	disc
Body material	aluminum
Weight, approx.	2,000 pounds
Wheelbase	100 inches
Height	56 inches (with the hardtop on)

EDWARDS SPECIAL (2)

Constructor	Sterling Edwards
Location built	Los Angeles, California
Year built	1952
Engine	Chrysler V-8
Chassis	ladder (Henry J)
Front suspension	independent
Rear suspension	live axle
Body material	fiberglass

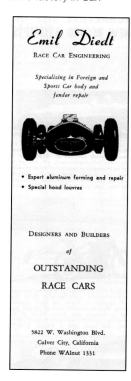
167

Eliminator

Jay Chamberlain eventually became America's pipeline to Lotus sports and racing cars, but right after World War II he was still a hot rodder with a circle track roadster in the garage. He built the roadster from Essex frame rails and a 1925 Ford Model T body before installing a lovely steel track roadster nose formed by Emil Deidt. He raced it around Southern California before selling it to Duffy Livingston, who had a muffler shop in Pasadena with Roy Desbrow. Plumber Paul Parker also had a stake in it. In 1953, they set to bringing the old racer up-to-date for sports car racing.

Livingston boxed the old Essex rails and installed hydraulic drum brakes with aircraft internals. A bored-and-stroked Mercury flathead was installed, along with a Cadillac three-speed gearbox. The car was driven by Parker and Livingston and ran as a C-Modified with fenders or a Formula Libre without. In 1956, Livingston swapped in a 265-ci Chevy V-8 opened up to 302 ci. It was treated to an Isky cam, three Stromberg carbs on an Edelbrock manifold, and a Spalding

ELIMINATOR	
Constructor	**Duffy Livingston**
Location built	**Pasadena, California**
Body by	**Ford T**
Year built	**1953**
Engines	**Mercury flathead V-8; Chevrolet V-8**
Gearbox	**four-speed**
Chassis	**ladder**
Front suspension	**live axle**
Rear suspension	**live axle**
Brakes	**drum**
Body material	**steel**
Weight, approx.	**1,920 pounds**
Wheelbase	**96.0 inches**
Length	**122.0 inches**
Cost when new	**$2,500**

Flamethrower ignition. With these improvements, the Eliminator came alive, placing near the top in races all over California. It was later upgraded with a Corvette four-speed transmission.

The old rod's best race was at the 1959 Los Angeles Examiner Grand Prix at Pomona, where it ran midpack in a star-studded field of Ferraris, Maseratis, and Porsches.

Livingston also owned the Go-Kart Manufacturing Company, which popularized the kart racing craze.

The Eliminator has survived and was restored at So-Cal Speedshop.

Duffy Livingston, in the Eliminator, climbs all over John von Neumann's Ferrari at Pomona in 1958. *Allen Kuhn*

Duffy Livingston racing the Eliminator at Paramount Ranch in 1957. Note the custom racewear. *Allen Kuhn*

El Toro

Jack Baker was a Minnesota steel fabricator who decided to go racing in 1954. Over an eight-year period he built a series of cars known as El Toro and Goldenrod.

The first El Toro was built in 1954 with the help of Ed Grierson, who later became known for his work on the Echidna project. The car was built on an MG frame. The front suspension was from a Henry J and the rear suspension was a live axle from Ford. A Cadillac V-8 supplied the power, and gear change was accomplished by way of a Ford three-speed. The lovely body was a fiberglass shell produced by Allied, from a mold pulled off a Cisitalia Coupe. Baker raced the car in regional events in the mid-1950s, though the car's suspension and brakes were suboptimal. He also took the car to the inaugural Road America 500 in 1955. By 1957, El Toro's roof section had been cut away and the car was competing in roadster form. Baker's final race in this car was a hillclimb at Rib Mountain in Wisconsin. Halfway up the mountain, Baker went off course in order to avoid a family picnicking. The car and Baker crashed hard; Baker survived but the first El Toro did not.

The second El Toro was built on the frame of Bill Peters' crashed Jaguar XK-120. The frame was shortened, lowered, and lightened. Again, Baker used a Caddy V-8 for motivation, but the car now raced with a T-10 four-speed gearbox. The body was a Mistral fiberglass roadster from Sports Car Engineering. Baker campaigned the car in 1958 without any major incident, although the car did have a tendency to lose its Dayton wire wheels during races. One of the Echidna's mechanics borrowed the car for a novice race at Met Stadium in Minneapolis in 1959 and crashed the car.

The third El Toro was built in 1959 from the crashed remains of the second car. The frame was okay, but the Mistral body was a broken mess and was exchanged for a Byers SR 90 shell. The Cadillac engine was set aside and a Pontiac V-8

EL TORO (1)

Constructors .... **Jack Baker and**
Ed Grierson
Location built .... **Minnesota**
Body by .... **Allied Fiber-Glass**
Year built **1954**
Engine .... **Cadillac V-8**
Gearbox .... **Ford three-speed**
Chassis .... **MG ladder**
Front suspension .... **Henry J independent**
Rear suspension ..... **live axle**
Brakes .... **drum**
Body material .... **fiberglass**

EL TORO (2)

Constructor .... **Jack Baker**
Location built .... **Minnesota**
Body by .... **Sports Car Engineering**
Years built **1957–1958**
Engine .... **Cadillac V-8**
Gearbox .... **four-speed Chevrolet T-10**
Chassis .... **modified Jag XK-120**
ladder
Front suspension .... **independent**
Rear suspension ..... **live axle**
Brakes .... **drum**

EL TORO (3)/ GOLDENROD

Constructor .... **Jack Baker**
Location built .... **Minnesota**
Body by .... **Byers**
Year built **1959**
Engine .... **Pontiac V-8**
Chassis .... **modified Jag XK-120,**
from the second El Toro
Front suspension .... **independent**
Rear suspension ..... **live axle**
Brakes .... **drum**
Body material .... **fiberglass**

installed. The engine had an Isky cam and was bored and stroked to 422 ci. Induction was via six carburetors. The power output was stupendous, but braking and handling remained a problem. Just before the start of the 1961 season, the car was sold to Charlie Cox.

Goldenrod

Cox replaced the trouble-prone Daytons with 15-inch Buick disc wheels. He had the car repainted in metallic gold and renamed it the Goldenrod Special. It was raced at numerous SCCA events, including those at Elkhart Lake. The Goldenrod even raced at the Land O' Lakes ice race in St. Paul, Minnesota, in January. For the 1962 race season, Cox and Bob Von Edeskudy lowered the engine 3 inches and moved it 6 inches toward the rear. This failed to improve the handling as much as was hoped, and the Goldenrod was sold. Today, the whereabouts of the Goldenrod remain unknown.

Elwood Porsche Special

This Devin-bodied VW was powered by a Porsche engine and driven by a young Jo Hoppen, who went on to run Volkswagen's racing operations in the United States. The Elwood ran in Florida in the late 1950s.

ELWOOD PORSCHE SPECIAL

Location built .... **Florida**
Body by .... **Devin Enterprises**
Year built **1957**
Engine .... **Porsche**
Gearbox .... **four-speed**
Chassis .... **Volkswagen floorpan**
Front suspension .... **trailing link**
Rear suspension ..... **swing axles**
Brakes .... **drum**
Body material .... **fiberglass**

Evans Saab Special

Tom Evans built this Saab-powered special in the mid-to-late 1960s. The chassis was a one-off space frame,

and the engine was mounted up front. Evans formed the alloy body by hand, and it was a somewhat crude-looking H-Modified.

EVANS SAAB SPECIAL

Constructor .... **Tom Evans**
Year built .... **mid-to-late 1960s**
Engine .... **Saab GT**
Gearbox .... **BMC**
Chassis .... **space frame**
Front suspension .... **NSU**
Rear suspension ..... **live axle**
Brakes .... **disc**
Body material .... **aluminum**

Exner Simca Special

Virgil Exner Jr. had automotive passion running through his veins. His father was a world-renowned automotive stylist responsible for such gems as the Chrysler 300-series cars, the 1947 Studebaker, and the Ghia Dart show cars. It was little wonder that the young Exner began to dream up his own designs at an early age.

The Exner Simca Special competed in a hillclimb without a body. *Beau Hickory*

169

During his early teens, Exner spent time at the shop of Paul Farago. There he collected parts from Simcas and Fiats. He began to make drawings and worked countless hours modifying a Fiat chassis for a new car. Exner took one of the 1,200-cc Simca engines he had collected and mounted it as low and far back as possible in the Fiat chassis. With the addition of Dayton wire wheels, the car became a roller.

Exner spent his early years as a fine arts student at Notre Dame, studying design in Vienna and Paris, and eventually returning to Notre Dame. During that time Exner had created a quarter-scale fiberglass model of a car that was so lovely, so outrageous, that it landed him Notre Dame's *Emil Jacques Gold Medal of Fine Arts.*

By 1957 Exner had made great progress on the car. He even raced the bodyless runner at a local hillclimb and finished second to a BMW 328. Using the award-winning model as a starting point, Exner made a full-scale clay model of his special. Next, he cast a mold of epoxy resin and had the whole project shipped back to the Dual Ghia factory in Detroit, where a full-scale body was produced. It was a radical bubble-top canopy design, with enormous rear fins and an exposed exhaust pipe. It was striking and, in its own way, quite lovely. The car appeared at numerous shows, including the 1959 Paris Salon and the 1960 Oakland Roadster Show, where it won an award. It was also seen in a feature article in the April 1959 issue of *Road & Track.* At

1,650 pounds, the car was not exactly a rocket with the 1,200-cc Simca engine, but it was long on pizzazz, which is precisely what Exner was after.

Eyerly Crosley

Harry Eyerly was a hydroplane racer from Oregon who decided to go road racing in the early 1950s. Since he had a world of experience racing 45-ci hydroplanes, the H-Modified class was a natural fit. His plan was to build a car that was simple, light, and dependable, and that's exactly what he did.

Eyerly began with the mechanicals from a Crosley Hotshot. He built a ladder frame of heavy-walled mild steel tubing. Additional hoops of 1/2- and 3/4-inch tubing supported the body.

Front suspension was semielliptic leaf springs and rear suspension was by quarter-elliptic springs, in each case mated to a stock Crosley solid axle. The rear hubs were special steel units that Eyerly replaced after every third race. The brakes were Crosley discs; the steering box was also Crosley. The transmission was a Jowett Jupiter Meadows four-speed unit that required an unusual shift linkage; the clutch was a solid disc. The wheels were stock 12-inch Crosley steel discs.

Eyerly designed the body and constructed it of lightweight aluminum. Because he had no prior experience as a metal-shaper, Eyerly kept the lines

Harry Eyerly sits in the Eyerly Crosley.
Edward Buck collection

neat and simple, without compound curves or complex designs. The body was secured to the frame using self-tapping sheet metal screws. The right-hand-drive cockpit was simple and without frills. The 6-gallon fuel tank, 2 1/2-gallon reserve tank, and lightweight 6-volt battery were mounted in the trunk.

The engine was a 736-cc Crosley CIBA marine unit with a steel crankshaft, one of the original hydroplane units that had been raced on water at 10,000 rpm. For road racing, Eyerly detuned the motor to produce peak output at 7,000 rpm with a compression ratio of 9.5:1. The pistons had a butterfly-shaped crown and were designed for high compression. The rods were lightened by removing material at the big end, and an Isky cam was used. Induction was by two MC-2 SU carburetors.

Eyerly understood the value of a light and nimble race car and liberally drilled all of his special's nonstressed components. The finished car weighed only 760 pounds for an impressive 1 cc of engine displacement per pound. The plan worked like a charm and, despite a top speed of only 95 miles per hour, the car was nearly unbeatable in its class.

Eyerly drove the car the way an H-Mod ought to be driven, flat out the whole way around. He thought nothing of drifting around a high-speed corner, foot to the floor, on two wheels, and he would often buzz past the big-iron boys who had to throw out the anchor. At a 2 1/2-hour enduro at Stead Air Force Base in October 1953, Eyerly won the index of performance and finished 15th overall. In April 1954, Eyerly finished first-in-class at Pebble Beach. Four months later, he won his class again at the Seattle Seafare race. For the next two years, Eyerly ruled the class on the West Coast.

The car is currently competing in vintage races.

Fageol Twin-Porsche

Lou Fageol was a man who epitomized the racing scene of the 1950s. He had an outlandish idea for a racing car, and he actually got it built. Two engines in one race car? Why not?

Fageol was no stranger to speed. He was a very successful unlimited-class hydroplane pilot and a Gold Cup winner. He was a racer, an innovator, and a manufacturer, all rolled into one. His first experience with a dual-engine race car was the Fageol Twin Special, powered by two Offy engines, which qualified on the front row at the 1946 Indy 500. This was followed in 1952 by a twin-engined 356 Porsche.

The Twin-Porsche was Fageol's third effort with dual engines. The car was built in the factory of Fageol's Twin Coach Bus Company in Ohio in 1953 and was constructed on a box channel frame with Porsche suspension. The engines were stock 1,500-cc Porsche four-cylinders with carburetion by two downdraft Solex units to each. The body was constructed from airplane drop tanks from Fletcher Aviation, and the finished coupe (with a fighter-pilotlike hinged roof canopy) was reminiscent of Buck Rogers' spacecraft.

While one engine drove the rear wheels in typical Porsche preparation, Fageol designed an arrangement for the second engine to drive the front wheels via CV

The Fageol Twin-Porsche had one 356 engine in back, and another in front! *Tom Cardin*

joints connected to modified outer Porsche housings. The shift, clutch, and accelerator were each connected to both powerplants to ensure that everything worked as one package. A particularly clever Fageol innovation was the design of a single pedal to simplify and speed up heel-toe downshifting. The pedal was designed as a swing mechanism. To apply the brake, Fageol would depress the pedal; to accelerate, he would simply roll his foot.

In an effort to increase power output, Fageol experimented with several different supercharger configurations until he hit on the idea that stuck—driving the blower units with chain saw engines. In this configuration, the car became a quad-engined racer. The Porsche powerplants were brought to life via a conventional push-button starter, and the blower units were started with pull-cords activated from the driver's compartment.

Fageol was not simply clever, he was a very capable driver as well. The Twin-Porsche competed in its first event in October 1953 at the Sowega Air Force Base Races at Albany, Georgia. The car finished second-in-class in both a prelim and the feature race. During the 1954 and 1955 seasons, the car competed at events coast to coast. In May 1954, the car was leading at Cumberland until it had a mechanical problem. Later that month, the car finished third behind two over-4-liter Ferraris at Atterbury Air Force Base in Columbus, Ohio. The car was first run with the blower setup in June 1954 at Westover Air Force Base (Chicopee,

Massachusetts) where it failed to finish. The following month, the car finished third overall at the Giants Despair Hillclimb in Pennsylvania. In September, the car finished tenth at Watkins Glen and, in November, it failed to finish at March Air Force Base in Riverside, California.

The car's final outing was at the Pebble Beach races in April 1955. In an ironic twist of fate, the car was destroyed in an episode of twin crashes. Exiting a high-speed turn, the car lost traction and flipped end-over-end in a spectacular cartwheel, coming to rest on its roof. The second part of the crash occurred when another competitor lost control of his car and crashed into the motionless Twin-Porsche. Fortunately, Fageol escaped with only minor injury.

FAGEOL TWIN-PORSCHE	
Constructor	Lou Fageol
Location built	Ohio
Year built	1953
Engines	Twin Porsche 1,500-cc four-cylinder engines
Gearbox	Porsche
Chassis	ladder
Front suspension	cross-mounted torsion bar (Porsche)
Rear suspension	cross-mounted torsion bar (Porsche)
Brakes	drum
Body material	metal
Weight, approx.	1,600 pounds
Wheelbase	90 inches
Height	51 inches

Fairchild Panhard

One of the most successful H-Modifieds of the 1950s was the front-wheel-drive Fairchild Panhard. Perry Peron designed and built the chassis and raced the car early in its career. But the car's greatest achievements came at the hands of Dr. Bill Mollé who

The Fairchild Panhard was one of the most successful front-wheel-drive H-Modifieds. *Allen Kuhn*

campaigned the car in the late 1950s on the West Coast. Mollé won the California Sports Car Club Pacific Coast H-Mod Championship in 1958 and again in 1959 and became known as the Flying Dentist. He also finished second in the SCCA regional standings in 1958 and captured second-in-class in 1959 in *MotoRacing*'s Pacific Coast Championship.

The Fairchild Panhard's chassis was a multitube space frame with lightweight stressed aluminum inner panels that provided uncommon strength. The front suspension was independent with dual transverse springs. Rear suspension was by swing axle, a flexible center-mount, and six transverse torsion bars. Drum brakes were used at all four corners, as were adjustable Houdaille shocks. Steering was rack and pinion. Murray Nichols designed the original fiberglass body, although a body from Jim Byers later replaced it. The car was painted a shade of pea green, accented by a stripe of cream.

The most unique innovation on the car came from Jerry Fairchild, for whom the car was rightfully named. Fairchild designed the first-ever successful fuel injection system for a two-cylinder four-stroke engine. The combination of Mollé's heavy right foot and the extraordinary performance from the diminutive engine was often unbeatable. (The car weighed a mere 984 pounds with a weight distribution of 60 percent front, 40 percent rear.) The engine ran with a compression ratio of 9.5:1 and developed 67 horsepower at 6,500 rpm. The car's top speed was 118 miles per hour, and it reached 84 miles per hour in

the quarter-mile, both of which were quite good for a car of its class back in the day.

Today, the car continues to campaign in vintage racing.

FAIRCHILD PANHARD	
Constructors	Perry Peron (chassis), Jerry Fairchild (fuel injection system)
Bodies by	Murray Nichols and Jim Byers
Year built	1955
Engine	745-cc Panhard, two-cylinder four-stroke, air cooled, fuel injected
Gearbox	four-speed
Chassis	space frame
Front suspension	independent with two transverse springs
Rear suspension	swing axles
Brakes	drums front (aluminum) and rear (steel)
Body material	Fiberglass
Weight, approx.	984 pounds (weight distribution 60 percent front, 40 percent rear)
Wheelbase	84 inches
Length	112 inches
Height	32 inches

FCA (Future Craftsmen of America) Mk.I

See Papier Mache Special entry.

Ferret

The Ferret was a small-displacement sports-racer built by Peter Dawson and Chris Kennedy of Detroit in 1959–1960. They started with a space frame

The tiny Ferret was powered by an outboard boat motor. *Edward Valpey collection*

fabricated from 3/4-inch and 1/2-inch boxed tubing. Front suspension was independent with equal-length A-arms and utilized rod ends at all mounting points. The rear suspension was trailing link with a low-pivot swing axle specially designed by Kennedy to produce camber gain in roll. The brakes were Airheart discs.

The car was powered by a 1,050-cc McCulloch three-cylinder outboard motor that produced 75

FERRET	
Constructors	Peter Dawson and Chris Kennedy
Location built	Detroit, Michigan
Years Built	1959–1960
Engine	1,050-cc McCulloch three-cylinder outboard
Gearbox	Harley-Davidson Knucklehead sequential four-speed
Chassis	space frame
Front suspension	independent
Rear suspension	swing axle
Brakes	disc (Airheart)
Body material	magnesium and aluminum
Weight, approx.	575 pounds
Wheelbase	71.375 inches
Length	120.5 inches
Height	27 inches
Cost when new	$4,000

horsepower. The gearbox was a Harley-Davidson Knucklehead sequential four-speed.

Dawson and Kennedy were committed to saving weight wherever possible. To this end, the main portions of the body, including the nose, side-pods, bulkhead, and tail, were constructed from thin-gauge magnesium sheet. Even the wheels were specially cast magnesium units. Only the fenders were formed from aluminum. The plan worked, as the Ferret weighed in at 575 pounds. Dawson and Kennedy finished their special in 1,300 hours at a cost of $4,000.

Dawson actively raced the Ferret for three seasons. Dawson estimates that he ran a dozen races each year, including starts at Elkhart Lake; Blackhawk Farms; and Palatine, Illinois, just to name a few.

Fitch Type B

In 1949, John Fitch built his Type B, called the Fitch Bitch by some in period. The frame for the car came from a 1,100-cc Fiat. Up front, the suspension was independent with coil-in-oil springs. At the rear, the suspension was live axle with semielliptic springs. Hydraulic brakes with finned aluminum

drums provided stopping power at all four corners. Gear-change was accomplished by way of a Fiat four-speed transmission. The car was cloaked in a much-modified Crosley Hotshot body.

Fitch chose a 2,262-cc Ford V-8 60 to motivate the "bitch." With stock bore and stroke, aluminum heads, and a racing intake manifold, the motor produced 105 horsepower at 5,300 revs. While this was certainly not ground-pounding power, it was enough to propel the car to a second-in-class and an eighth overall in a field of superstars, after a pit stop cost him the win at the International Sports Car Grand Prix of Watkins Glen in September 1950.

Fitch-Whitmore Jaguar

The Fitch-Whitmore Jaguar was a well-known special and an early 1950s collaboration of John Fitch and Coby Whitmore. Whitmore was a well-respected illustrator, whose work was often seen in national magazines. Fitch was soon to become an icon of the international racing scene, winning an SCCA National Championship in 1951. In 1953, he

won at Sebring and finished third at Le Mans, and in 1955, he and co-driver Stirling Moss dominated their class at the Mille Miglia and took home the Tourist Trophy. Fitch and Whitmore were no strangers. Together they had raced a stock XK-120 Jaguar at the first race at Sebring in December 1950. Seeking a hotter ride for the following season, the two men teamed up in 1951 to build a race car of their own design—the Fitch-Whitmore Jaguar.

The project began with a brand-new Jaguar XK-120. The stock body was removed and chassis modifications commenced. The stock Jag springs were lightened and the shocks were reconfigured. The stock brakes were discarded and new Alfin drums were installed.

Andy Salada shaped an all-new alloy roadster body, based on drawings provided by Fitch and Whitmore. The cycle-fendered special was not only extremely attractive, but it had shed a full 800 pounds during its transformation.

The engine development program was kept simple and only involved products sold by Jaguar. The principal upgrade was to a dual-exhaust system that boosted power output from 160 to 180 horsepower. Unlike many similar specials of the day, such as the

FITCH TYPE B	
Constructor	John Fitch
Location built	Connecticut
Year built	1949
Engine	2,262-cc Ford V-8 60
Gearbox	Fiat four-speed
Chassis	Fiat ladder
Front suspension	independent
Rear suspension	live axle
Brakes	drum
Body material	steel
Weight, approx.	1,520 pounds
Wheelbase	95 inches
Cost when new	$2,850

John Fitch built the potent Fitch-Whitmore Jaguar in the early 1950s. *Bob Harrington*

FITCH-WHITMORE JAGUAR

Constructors	John Fitch and Coby Whitmore
Location built	Connecticut
Body by	Andy Salada
Year built	1951
Engine	Jaguar XK-120
Gearbox	Jaguar four-speed
Chassis	Jaguar XK-120 ladder
Front suspension	Jaguar XK-120 independent
Rear suspension	Jaguar XK-120 live axle
Brakes	drum
Body material	aluminum
Weight, approx.	2,160 pounds

Parkinson Jaguar, the engine was not relocated within the chassis.

Fitch raced the car in the beginning. His best finish in the special was third at a race at Bridgehampton in 1952. Following this, Whitmore took over the driving duty and Fitch went on to fame racing other cars.

Flying Banana

This car was built by Kenneth Hill in the late 1940s and named after its bananalike shape. It ran on a Lincoln chassis, powered by a 239-ci V-8 Mercury. This was a quirky-looking machine with open wheels, huge side pipes, tandem seating, and no windscreen. It ran at Watkins Glen up through 1950 without distinction, sometimes appearing as the Merlin (a combination of the first three letters of the engine and the chassis).

FLYING BANANA

Constructor	Kenneth Hill
Year built	late 1940s
Engine	Mercury V-8 (239 ci)
Chassis	Lincoln ladder

Flying Triangle

The Flying Triangle was a Panhard-based special that never took itself too seriously. The car's stance was short and dumpy, its lines were an acquired taste, it ran on only two cylinders, and it had a goofy smiley face painted up front around the grille opening. This was certainly not a package that engendered fear and loathing in the paddock. But make no mistake about it—the little triangle could fly. It was a terrific competitor, and its self-effacing makeup only served to heighten awareness when time and time again it came home a winner.

Manuel Betes and Dick Seifried constructed the Flying Triangle on a space frame of 1 1/4-inch-diameter 4130 tubing of 0.064-inch wall thickness. Front suspension was stock Panhard with one of the leaf springs removed. The rear suspension was also Panhard, with torsion bars and a trailing Y-yoke. Brakes were Lockheed drums, 10-inch units up front and 9-inch units at the rear. The gearbox was a Panhard four-speed with a rudder-type shifter mounted top dead center in the dashboard. The rack-and-pinion steering unit was on the left.

The all-alloy body was constructed from 5250 aluminum sheets of 0.050-inch thickness. Betes did all of the body sculpting by hand. The finished product had a distinctive look with a small head fairing and a tall hood scoop for clearance of the supercharger.

The engine was a highly developed Panhard two-cylinder. Displacement could be modulated

Manuel Betes bends the Flying Triangle around Santa Barbara in 1956. *Allen Kuhn*

FLYING TRIANGLE

Constructors	Manuel Betes and Dick Seifried
Year built	mid-1950s
Engine	Panhard two-cylinder
Gearbox	Panhard four-speed
Chassis	space frame
Front suspension	independent
Rear suspension	live axle
Brakes	drum
Body material	aluminum
Weight, approx.	825 pounds
Wheelbase	80 inches
Length	138 inches
Height	31 inches
Cost when new	$1,500

from 745-cc to 850-cc by changing sleeves, pistons, rings, and pins. Induction was by way of dual Solex carburetors. Bates and Seifried experimented with a Constantini supercharger for some time before getting the blown engine package fully sorted. Much of the $1,500 they spent on the car was in engine development. Once dialed in, the blown 745-cc engine produced an impressive 50 horsepower at 4,800 rpm.

FoMoCo Special

Jim Saunders of Houston, Texas, put a lot of miles on his special in 1956 and 1957. It was a cycle-fendered roadster with a Ford flathead V-8, later replaced with a bored-out 340-ci Ford Thunderbird engine. The FoMoCo Special was a primitive-looking beast, with a crude homemade exhaust system that exited from the side of the hood and ran down the sides like an old Indy car. But it worked very well, with Saunders winning B-Modified at most events he entered in the Southwest and even taking a few overall wins against serious European opposition. Saunders won first overall in a ten-lap race at

The FoMoCo Special Mk.II ran at Green Valley Raceway in Texas. *Millard Almon*

Mansfield, Louisiana, in 1956, outrunning a pack of Ferraris, Maseratis, and a 2-liter OSCA. After 1957, Saunders retired, and the special disappeared for a while, but then came back as the FoMoCo Special II with a more streamlined body. It was raced into the early 1960s.

FOMOCO SPECIAL

Constructor	Jim Saunders
Location built	Houston, Texas
Year built	1956
Engine	Ford V-8
Gearbox	Ford
Front suspension	live axle
Rear suspension	live axle

Formula 3 Echo

Although Formula 3 racing never quite caught on in the United States to the same extent as Europe, some Americans couldn't resist the urge to build one of the little 500-cc screamers. One such individual was Mike Siakooles, who spent over 18 months and more than $1,500, with coowner Tom Bailey, piecing a car together.

The Echo rode on a space frame constructed of tubing of 0.035-inch wall thickness. The crossmembers and roll bar were from a heavier stock of 0.049 inch. The front suspension was a heavily modified Fiat. The rear suspension consisted of a low-pivot swing

FORMULA 3 ECHO

Constructor	Mike Siakooles
Body by	California Metal Shaping
Engine	500-cc SOHC Norton single cylinder
Gearbox	Burman
Chassis	space frame
Front suspension	independent
Rear suspension	live axle
Brakes	Crosley disc
Body material	aluminum and fiberglass
Weight, approx.	620 pounds
Wheelbase	87 inches
Length	152 inches
Height	42 inches

axle with tubular shock absorbers and coils. The brakes were Crosley discs, with four up front and two at the rear. The steering unit was from a Fiat 500. The gearbox was a Burman from an Aerial Square Four.

The Echo's streamlined body was produced by the California Metal Shaping Company. The sides, tail, and belly pan were fabricated from aluminum. The nose was constructed from fiberglass and had deep cutouts on the sides to enable wheel angulation to produce a sharp turning radius.

The powerplant was a 500-cc single overhead cam Norton single cylinder. The car ran with a compression of 15:1 and carburetion was by Amal. The engine produced a very respectable 50 horsepower at 6,200 rpm and pushed the Echo to a top speed of 80 miles per hour.

Front-Runner Special

After he built the Twareg, Andre Capella was determined to build a front-wheel-drive racer. He did, and called it the Front-Runner Special.

The car was built on a space frame with independent front and rear suspension. Capella used

Andre Capella built the Front-Runner Special to showcase front-wheel-drive technology. *Andre Capella collection*

Citroen axles, hub carriers, and wheels. Brakes were disc front and rear. It was powered by a 327-ci Chevy with six two-barrel carburetors that Capella took off of the Twareg Special. At the rear was a Halibrand quick-change unit. Power was transferred through a T-10 four-speed.

FRONT-RUNNER SPECIAL

Constructor	Andre Capella (Gessner)
Location built	Seal Beach, California
Year built	1964
Engine	Chevy V-8 (327 ci)
Gearbox	T-10 four-speed
Chassis	space frame
Front suspension	independent
Rear suspension	independent
Brakes	disc
Body material	fiberglass and aluminum
Weight, approx.	2,000 pounds
Wheelbase	95 inches
Length	150 inches
Height	30 inches
Price when new	$1,000

We Talk With Andre Capella.

AUTHOR: How did the whole front-wheel-drive thing come about?

CAPELLA: I got reading about front-wheel drive and started looking at it, and I said, "A front-wheel-drive car has to be a hell of a cornering car," and I was right. No one had ever built a front-wheel-drive, independent-suspension, high-horsepower car. I did a lot of engineering on the car. It cornered unbelievably, better than any car running at the time. I built my own positraction and transaxle to help with traction. It [the car] was written up in *Hot Rod Parts Illustrated* in November 1964. Some of the engineers from General Motors came by to look at it too.

AUTHOR: Did you use a Sorrell body like your first car, the Twareg?

CAPELLA: No, it was a body I built myself. I really didn't have a choice. It was such an oddball car that there was just no body that would fit it. I painted it orange.

AUTHOR: Were there any problems?

CAPELLA: Front-end lift. By the time you got going 140, 150 miles an hour, the front end was coming up high on you. I got black flagged at the first race in the car. The reason they black flagged me was that the back wheel came off the ground a foot. They thought there was something wrong with the car. I said, "It's a front-wheel drive, you morons!"

AUTHOR: You wound up getting a sponsor.

CAPELLA: Yes, Beach City Chevrolet started giving me a little bit of help. I never won a race in the car but I did come within two seconds of the Pomona track record. I was always up there. I didn't have enough power, but it cornered so well that I was just beating people in the turns all over the place. It was just amazing how bad I beat them in the corners, but they all beat me in the straightaways. You could just give it full throttle all the way around the corner. And that's what I did. It was an amazing car—I just needed more power. I knew I could be amateur champion if I had a good car. So that's when I built the Capella.

Fubar

One can only imagine what Dave Dunbar was thinking about when he built and named his special the Fubar.

The Fubar (right) ran at Santa Barbara in 1958. *Allen Kuhn*

The car was painted refrigerator white, which turned out to be an appropriate choice considering this appliance's racing abilities. It was a consistent back-marker . . . oh well, someone had to be.

Fury Special

The Troutman-Barnes Special was renamed the Fury Special by Jimmy Pfluger of Honolulu, Hawaii, when he purchased it from Dick Troutman and Tom Barnes in November 1957. Chuck Daigh raced the car in July 1959 at the first USAC-sanctioned professional road races at Riverside. Powered by a Scarab-Chevy V-8, the car led for the first 15 laps, but ultimately finished sixth.

Georgette-the-Racer

Henry Manney III was one of the most respected (and popular) journalists of the 1950s and 1960s. He was a salesman at Jim Barlow's International Motors who then morphed into a journalist. He wrote for *Car and Driver* and a number of English magazines, but found fame as the editor-at-large for *Road & Track*. He wrote about everything from nudist beaches to Formula 1, always with wit and a touch of sarcasm. He also owned a number of famous cars, including a Ferrari 250 GTO. In the early 1950s, he built a

Crosley special named Georgette-the-Racer, which he ran without great distinction. The body was later recycled on Chet Lancaster's Georgette (see Georgette entry).

Georgette

An article entitled "'Georgette the Crosley" appeared in the February 1953 issue of *Auto*. The article was about a lovely small-displacement home-built constructed by Chet Lancaster of Hermosa Beach, California. While Lancaster had considerable experience working with his hands, the Georgette was his first attempt at building a race car. The project commenced some time in the latter part of 1950 or early 1951 and took two years and thousands of hours to complete.

Lancaster initially began the project by reworking a prewar Crosley frame. That was eventually abandoned, and he constructed an all-new frame from 0.049-inch steel tubing of 3-inch diameter. For simplicity and budget, Lancaster used an array of stock Crosley parts, including the engine, front and rear axles, gearbox, driveshaft, torque tube, hubs, and wheels. Brakes were Goodyear-Hawley single-spot discs.

The engine was a 750-cc Crosley unit with a stock bore and stroke. Initially, Lancaster's information was derived from a Crosley repair manual. Later, he received help from noted experts Frank Pankratz, Nick Brajevich, and Lujie Lesovsky. To improve lower end rigidity, a Braje cast-aluminum pan was installed. Induction was improved with the use of a Carter carburetor on a Braje log manifold.

Lancaster's original plan was to design and build his own body. Due to time constraints, he purchased the old fiberglass body from Henry Manney's Georgette-the-Racer (see Georgette-the-Racer entry). Within two weeks, Lancaster had totally reworked the body into a sleek little gem, ready to hit the track.

Gillespie MG TD

Another MG Special of the early 1950s was owned and raced by Bob Gillespie, a salesperson at Kjell Qvale's San Francisco-based British Motor Car Company. Gillespie had seen Bill David's gorgeous MG TD Special race, and he hired Jack Hagemann to build a similar car.

The Gillespie MG TD used a Jack Hagemann body.
Dean Batchelor

The car was built in 1952 and was a real jewel. As was the plan from the outset, Gillespie's special shared much in common with David's car. But unlike David's car, Gillespie's lacked a head fairing and grillework.

The car was raced primarily on the West Coast and was never a winner, but it was a beautiful example of an American special, and it provided its owner with hours of road racing joy.

GILLESPIE MG TD	
Constructor	Jack Hagemann
Location built	Castro Valley, California
Body by	Jack Hagemann
Year built	1952
Engine	MG TD four-cylinder
Gearbox	MG TD four-speed
Chassis	MG TD ladder
Front suspension	MG TD independent
Rear suspension	MG TD live axle
Brakes	MG TD drum
Body material	aluminum

Glasspar Comet

See Comet entry.

Godzilla

See Balchowsky Old Yaller VI entry, Chapter 2.

Goldenrod

See El Toro entry.

Gounis Fiat-Crosley

This Crosley special was built and raced by Charles Gounis of television's *Willie the Wolf* fame. Gounis built the car on a ladder frame and clothed it in a lovely body with a head fairing. Motivation came

Charles Gounis built the Gounis Fiat Crosley (No. 1), driven here by John Brophy. *Allen Kuhn*

from a 743-cc Crosley four-cylinder engine with a compression ratio of 9.5:1, which developed 50 horsepower at 7,000 rpm. Bore was 2.520 inches and stroke was 2.250 inches. Carburetion was via two SUs, and the four-speed gearbox was from a Fiat. Top speed was 110 miles per hour. The car accelerated from 0-to-60 miles per hour in ten seconds, 0-to-100 miles per hour in 20 seconds, and ran the standing quarter-mile in 13 seconds (with a terminal speed of 75 miles per hour).

Gounis enjoyed arriving at each race with a new, and sometimes wild, paint scheme. He ultimately became quite competitive in the car with several podium finishes in the H-Modified class.

177

GOUNIS FIAT-CROSLEY	
Constructor	Charles Gounis
Year built	early 1950s
Engine	743-cc Crosley four-cylinder OHC
Gearbox	four-speed Fiat
Chassis	ladder
Front suspension	transverse leaf springs with A-arms
Rear suspension	coil springs and trailing links
Brakes	Crosley discs
Weight, approx.	760 pounds
Wheelbase	80 inches
Length	144 inches
Height	40 inches
Cost when new	$2,000

The Hagemann GMC had a lovely Jack Hagemann aluminum body wrapped around a GMC six, but a Jaguar engine recently replaced the GMC. *Harold Pace*

Hagemann GMC

The Hagemann GMC, occasionally referred to as the Sulprizio-Hagemann GMC, was built in 1955. Babe Sulprizio of Hayward, California, was a coowner of United Engineering & Machine, and he had a hankering for a Jaguar C-Type. The only rub was he couldn't afford it. So he did what many did back in the day—he built his own car fashioned after his dream car.

Sulprizio built a ladder frame from steel tubing. The front suspension was borrowed from a Mk.VII Jaguar and modified. It was no coincidence that the final

HAGEMANN GMC

Constructors	Babe Sulprizio, Jack Hagemann
Location built	Hayward, California
Body by	Jack Hagemann
Year built	1955
Engine	GMC six-cylinder (302 ci)
Gearbox	Moss four-speed
Chassis	ladder
Front suspension	independent
Rear suspension	live axle
Brakes	disc
Body material	aluminum

setup was dimensionally nearly identical to the C-Type. The rear axle was also harvested from a Mk.VII, and trailing arms connected torsion bars to the underside of the axle housing. Brakes were discs of aircraft origin. The steering unit was Morris Minor rack-and-pinion, and the steering column was Jaguar.

Sulprizio installed a 302-ci GMC six-cylinder and a Moss four-speed. The roller was then taken to Jack Hagemann's shop for construction of an alloy body. Sulprizio had an idea of what he wanted, and he furnished Hagemann with sketches of what he envisioned. The great metalworker was up to the task, and he produced an outstanding rendition of Sulprizio's dream. The car was painted bright red and was a real head turner.

The car was both road raced and driven on the street. Currently, the car is competing in vintage races, powered by a Jaguar engine.

Hall-Scott Special

Chalmers "Chal" Hall and Don Scott built the Hall-Scott Special. Hall had previously built and raced the very successful Little Digger, a lightweight Crosley-powered special. Scott owned Scott Technical Instrument Company in Phoenix, Arizona, which, at the time, was one of the highest quality machine shops in the United States.

The car was a true one-off, as Scott's company machined nearly every part on it. While this was no small task, it was made possible by the capabilities

HALL-SCOTT SPECIAL

Constructors	Chalmers "Chal" Hall and Don Scott
Year built	early 1950s
Engine	635-cc Lloyd
Gearbox	Lloyd four-speed
Chassis	ladder
Front suspension	independent
Rear suspension	swing axles
Brakes	disc
Body material	aluminum
Weight, approx.	550 pounds
Wheelbase	74 inches
Length	106 inches
Height	28 inches

of Scott's company, a military supplier of specialty parts for missiles.

The frame was a tubular ladder of the team's own design. Front suspension was independent with unequal A-arms and spring shocks. The rear suspension was by swing axles and spring shocks and was located by trailing arms. The brakes were disc front and rear. Up front, the discs were located at the wheels; in the rear, a single disc ran off the pinion shaft. Steering was a Scott rack-and-pinion unit; lock to lock was accomplished with only 7/8 of a turn. The transmission was a Lloyd all-synchro four-speed unit.

The body was simple and tidy and was constructed from lightweight aluminum panels. Because of the car's diminutive status, tipping the scales at only 550 pounds, Hall and Scott put a lot of thought and effort into weight distribution. The motor was mounted at the rear and was offset to the right in order to counterbalance the weight of the driver on the car's left. The fuel tank and spare tire were put up front, with the latter also offset to the right.

The Hall-Scott Special was one of the few racing cars to use a Lloyd engine. *Robert Rolofson Jr.; Robert H. Rolofson III collection*

ally even engineers. But how many specials of the era were actually designed and built by a rocket scientist?

Harry King was an aerospace engineer working in Southern California in the 1950s and 1960s. An expert in advanced materials, he headed the materials research group for Aerojet General. He was working on some new ideas when he hit on the notion of building a sports-racer from some of the newest materials as a way of showcasing their potential. This was a natural marriage of two of his greatest passions—materials science and race cars. Since the car was intended to be light, agile, fast, and beautiful, King decided to name it the Hummingbird.

King began the project with vim and vigor in 1959. He formed the company King Research under which the Hummingbird prototype would be designed and built. (Very likely he was the sole working employee.) King estimated that he could complete the project in six to nine months. Eight years and $20,000 later, he finished the car in 1966, having logged a tick over 7,000 hours of work. Along the way, the project took on a life of its own, with King acquiring new skills for each task at hand, including welding, fabricating, and machining at all hours of the night, every night! But in the end, it was worth the struggle. The finished car was glorious—light, powerful, innovative, and even beautiful.

The first of the car's many innovations involved a remarkable monocoque platform constructed of space-age materials. A 1 1/2-inch honeycomb core of Douglas Aircomb (Kraft paper honeycomb impregnated with phenolic resin) was sandwiched between layers of woven fiberglass cloth. The cloth was soaked in curing epoxy to augment toughness, and poured urethane foam was used to reinforce all important honeycomb joints. The finished monocoque was extremely lightweight and rigid. Its undersurface (belly pan) was designed to be perfectly smooth in an effort to improve the car's overall aerodynamic qualities. King laminated two aluminum tubes into the platform to provide for

Advanced for its day, the Hummingbird featured a fiberglass chassis and a supercharger. *Joe Kane collection*

mounting points for the engine, and various other driveline mechanicals. Each of these components, including the driveshaft and suspension, was mounted above the platform. Voids were created in the platform through which the oil pan and transmission case could hang.

King's next innovations regarded the Hummingbird's suspension. The front suspension used heavily modified Volkswagen torsion bar components with coil-over shocks. King fabricated a spiral-wound 1-inch-diameter fiberglass axle that he felt would allow some flexibility over bumps but would keep the wheels vertical. The rear suspension used a swing-axle design with torsion bars, transverse upper springs formed of fiberglass, lower A-arms, and adjustable coil-over shocks. The rear center section had a custom-built Halibrand unit that incorporated both quick-change gears and a limited-slip differential. King waited ten months for it to be delivered.

The brakes were disc at all four corners. King fabricated the front calipers from magnesium castings. The rear twin-piston Halibrand brakes were inboard and built from aluminum. King went so far as to fabricate his own brake rotors built from a steel outer surface and an aluminum core. The aluminum cores were milled with special cooling channels.

The Hummingbird's body was of a similar construction to that of the frame. The fiberglass

cloth surrounded a thinner (1/2-inch) honeycomb core of Douglas Aircomb. One exception was the construction of the car's fenders. King built these from simple fiberglass cloth rather than the more involved honeycomb core sandwich, because he didn't believe that honeycombed fenders would add much to the car's overall stiffness. Beneath the fenders, the wheelwell liners were made of epoxy-impregnated corrugated cardboard.

Like the frame, the body was incredibly strong and resilient. King was convinced that he could have jumped up and down on the surface of the body without it breaking, although there is no evidence that he ever actually attempted it. The finished body was bolted to the perimeter of the frame, further stiffening the chassis platform. Dual fuel tanks were built into the body on either side of the driver's compartment. The tanks were linked to one another and were designed to automatically equalize the fuel levels in each.

In addition to being expertly engineered and constructed, the body was an aesthetic masterpiece finished in a striking shade of blue-green (a Kaiser color, according to King). Every aspect worked in unison to make the car look great from any angle. The nose was long and distinctive and hinged forward to allow unfettered access to the engine bay. The large oval grille opening and covered headlights were appropriately sporty. The car had a smooth streamlined appearance accentuated by the sculpted left-side driver's headrest (with a roll hoop), a large body matching passenger-compartment tonneau cover, and the absence of both the driver and passenger side doors.

Other features of the coachwork included recessed taillights, side pipes, magnesium racing wheels, hood bulges for clearance of the supercharger and quad carb setup, and a rear deck lid that hinged forward to allow access to the battery and rear suspension. The windshield was from a 1955 to 1957 Thunderbird, which was cut down and modified. When King made his pass at Bonneville in 1966, he ran it with a wraparound driver-only windscreen. The twin bucket seats were positioned very low in the cockpit to aid in King's goal of a low center of gravity. Interior gauges included fuel level and pressure. As a final detail, King installed a fire extinguisher painted the same color as the body.

The engine was a 283-ci Chevy Corvette equipped with a Latham Axial Flow supercharger. King estimated that power output was in the neighborhood of 600 horsepower, although the engine was never dynoed. Induction was by way of four Carter YH single-barrel carburetors on a special intake manifold. One of the more innovative aspects of the powertrain was the gear-driven variable valve timing, designed to allow the driver to actually alter the valve timing from the cockpit during a race. The gearbox was a 1959 Corvette four-speed unit.

King took the Hummingbird to the Bonneville Time Trials in 1966 and made one unofficial pass at approximately 160 miles per hour. Apparently he backed out of it during the run and decided not to try for the 210-mile-per-hour class record. King later recalled, "I thought to myself, 'What the heck am I doing here?'" Ironically, the Hummingbird likely would have broken the speed record. King's 160-mile-per-hour pass was in third gear, 3,000 revs to the left of redline.

Following the Bonneville trip, King returned home and parked the Hummingbird in his garage. He never road raced the car as he had planned, nor

did he ever run another time trial. In fact, when he sold the car to Joseph Kane in September 2001, the odometer showed an amazing 13.1 miles, redefining the meaning of low-mileage classic. This car was one of the greatest "would have, should haves" of the era.

HUMMINGBIRD	
Constructor	Harry Alden King
Location built	Covina, California
Years built	1959–1966
Engine	supercharged Corvette V-8 (283 ci)
Gearbox	Corvette four-speed
Chassis	monocoque
Rear suspension	swing axle
Brakes	disc
Body material	experimental fiberglass composite
Weight, approx.	2,000 pounds
Wheelbase	90 inches
Length	148 inches
Height	37 inches
Cost when new	$20,000

Hussein I

Texan John Mecom made quite an impression on auto racing in the mid-1960s and just as quickly disappeared from view after his team won the Indy 500 in 1968. The 24-year-old son of a Texas oilman had burst on the scene when his team, reinforced by the unofficial Chevrolet racing operation, steamrolled the Shelby Cobras at the 1963 Nassau Trophy Races. Mecom went on a buying spree, picking up Roger Penske's Zerex Special, the rear-engined Scarab, several Corvette Grand Sports, 250LM and 250 GTO Ferraris, a Genie, a Lola Mk.6 coupe, a Lotus 19, and a Cooper Monaco. He had the Scarab, Lotus, and the Monaco reengined with Chevy V-8s, and several others already had Detroit muscle under their decks.

A. J. Foyt boots the Hussein I around the track. *Harold Pace collection*

But Mecom had enlisted famed roundy-rounder A. J. Foyt to drive for him and wanted a suitably spectacular weapon for West Coast pro races. Mecom obtained a new Cooper Monaco chassis, and mechanics Max Kelley and Gordon Chance went to work beefing it up for more muscle. Larger diameter brake rotors (12.25-inch in front and 11.5-inch in back) were added, along with stiffer springs, beefed up hubs, and American Racing five-spoke mag wheels with triple-eared knock-offs. In back, a massive 426-ci Chrysler Hemi stock car engine was bolted to a Colotti T-37 transaxle. Master body builder Jack Lane formed a brutal one-off aluminum shell. The resulting road rocket was named after King Hussein of Jordan, a diehard car freak who was allowing Mecom and his father to look for oil in his kingdom. (They never found a drop.)

Mecom was promised an aluminum-block engine from Chrysler, but it was not to be, and the overweight cast-iron lump was hung in back. Initially, the Hemi breathed through a single Holley four-barrel carb, but later eight two-barrel Webers were tried.

The first time out for the new car was at the Riverside Grand Prix for Sports Cars in 1964. Foyt strapped the Hussein on and took off after leader Parnelli Jones. After holding on to second for a while, the Hussein fell victim to fuel starvation problems and retired.

At Nassau in 1964, Mecom was confident Foyt and the Hussein could do the trick, but troubles plagued the team. In the Governor's Trophy preliminary race, Foyt ran as high as second but fell back again with fuel starvation problems. The Nassau Trophy Race was the feature event, but pouring rain made handling a 500-horsepower, tail-heavy monster an impossible job. Foyt worked his way up to second behind Pedro Rodriguez, but spun attempting to pass and finished back in 18th. The Hussein only ran once more, at an SCCA race at Galveston in 1965.

The Hussein has survived, but is in storage and is unlikely to reappear anytime soon.

The Ingalls Special was a blend of hot rod and sports car themes. *Harold Pace*

HUSSEIN I	
Constructor	Mecom Racing Team
Location built	Houston, Texas
Body by	Jack Lane
Year built	1963
Engine	Chrysler Hemi (426 ci)
Gearbox	Colotti T-37
Front suspension	independent
Rear suspension	independent
Brakes	disc
Body material	aluminum
Weight, approx.	1,820 pounds

Ingalls Special

Ed Ingalls of Lafayette, California, built this hot rod special. Ingalls wanted to go road racing but didn't have the finances or connections to run a foreign job. What he did have was a pair of skilled hands and an innovative mind.

He started with the frame rails from a DeSoto Airflow and swapped out the front and rear cross-members for Ford. The front axle was from a Ford Model A and the rear axle was also early Ford. The brakes were Ford hydraulic assemblies. The steering box was from a '36 Dodge Gemmer.

The body started as a 1931 Ford Roadster, and Ingalls added cycle fenders to the front and bobbed rear fenders from a '31 Ford. Later, he designed

and hand-formed more streamlined aluminum rear fenders. For wheels he chose the Ford wide-bolt-pattern type. Ingalls hand formed the hood, side panels, and radiator. He also hand fabricated the instrument panel and installed Stewart Warner gauges and dual windscreens. A large lap belt kept the driver from sliding around on the bench seat.

Power came from a 1941 260-ci Chrysler Spitfire flathead six-cylinder with upped compression and three Stromberg carburetors. Power was applied through a massive accelerator pedal and

INGALLS SPECIAL	
Constructor	Ed Ingalls
Location built	Lafayette, California
Year built	1949
Engines	Chrysler Spitfire flathead six-cylinder (260 ci); later, Ford flathead V-8
Gearbox	Ford three-speed
Chassis	ladder
Front suspension	live axle
Rear suspension	live axle
Brakes	drum
Body material	steel; later aluminum rear fenders were added
Wheelbase	98 inches
Length	141 inches
Height	34 inches

was transmitted through a Ford three-speed stick shift. The Ingalls Special was later reengined with a Ford flathead V-8.

This was one of the more interesting of the early American specials and was built by a true enthusiast and craftsman.

Irons FC

Charlie Irons had been racing a Renault R-8 sedan in the Southwest when he decided to build a Formula C car. He built a simple frame resembling Formula Vee practice but used Renault running gear. The resulting car was dependable but not very quick, though Irons did well in Texas Region SCCA events, finishing second in national points one year.

IRONS FC	
Constructor	Charlie Irons
Location built	Texas
Year built	circa 1968
Engine	Renault 1100
Gearbox	Renault four-speed
Front suspension	independent
Rear suspension	swing axle
Brakes	drum
Body material	fiberglass

185

Jack Baker El Toro and Goldenrod

See El Toro entry.

Jack Baker's Black Jack Special

After Baker was finished with the El Toro specials, he began working on an all-new car built around a frame from a totaled Jaguar XK-140MC. He built a lightweight fiberglass body by taking a splash off the front end of a D-Type Jaguar and the rear end of a Maserati. Other panels were hand formed as needed.

Initially, he ran the car with the Jaguar power-plant, but in 1964 swapped it out for a Ford Cobra engine. Even with the new engine, the car remained uncompetitive, and by the mid-1960s Baker lost interest and moved on to other race car projects.

JACK BAKER'S BLACK JACK SPECIAL	
Constructor	Jack Baker
Location built	Minnesota
Year built	1961
Engines	Jaguar; later Ford Cobra
Gearbox	Jaguar four-speed
Chassis	Jaguar XK-140MC ladder
Front suspension	Jaguar XK-140MC independent
Rear suspension	Jaguar XK-140MC live axle
Brakes	disc
Body material	fiberglass

James Special

Don James was a racing enthusiast on a budget who decided to build his own car. The resulting

The James Special was built on a tight budget.
Dean Batchelor

modified was based on a ladder frame made from 2-inch chrome-moly tubing welded up by friend Don Lewis. Semielliptic springs were used all around, with a Dodge tubular front axle and a 1932 Ford Model A rear axle. Ford drum brakes with drilled and scooped backing plates provided stopping power.

A 1949 Ford flathead V-8 engine was built up, using a Mercury crankshaft with a 4-inch stroke and a 3 3/8 bore that gave 286 ci. This put the James Special into Class C Modified. A Winfield Super 1-A cam, Mallory ignition, and a Sharp manifold wearing triple Stromberg 97s provided extra boost. James smoothed the ports with a hand grinder but did not enlarge them. A 1938 Ford gearbox with a remote shifter drove through a lightened flywheel and a beefed-up clutch.

James, an industrial arts major in school, made his own distinctive body from fiberglass using a male mold. James built the plug over a wooden frame covered with pottery plaster. The ultralight seats were made from metal tubing laced with nylon straps. To save money, James made his own mufflers from aluminum Thermos jugs filled with fiberglass, and fabricated an oil cooler from a used refrigerator cooling unit. By scrounging and adapting, he came up with a dashboard and all the instruments in it for only $2.

With a weight of 1,850 pounds and a top speed of around 125 miles per hour, the James was quick but not a world beater. But at a total cost of only $850, it was a terrific bargain!

JAMES SPECIAL	
Constructor	Don James
Location built	San Jose, California
Year built	1954
Engine	Ford V-8
Chassis	ladder
Front suspension	straight axle
Rear suspension	live axle
Brakes	drum
Body material	fiberglass
Cost when new	$850

Jaybird Mark X

Another beautiful and unusual racer of the period was Joe Jordan and Jim Troy's Jaybird Mark X. The car had stunning looks and always got plenty of attention when it showed up for a race. It was built at a cost of $2,500 and took approximately 18 months to finish.

The car was designed as a center-seat stream-liner, and was built on a space frame. Front and rear

A Triumph motorcycle engine powered the Jaybird Mark X. *Robert Rolofson Jr.; Robert H. Rolofson III collection*

suspension was independent by A-arms with coil-spring shock absorbers. Brakes were disc front and rear; the front used spot discs at the wheels and the rear brakes were located on the sprocket. Steering was rack and pinion.

Hollywood Plastics of Glendale, California, constructed the extraordinary fiberglass body. It was sleek with a wraparound windscreen and a monoposto-style head fairing, reminiscent of a fighter plane cockpit.

A Triumph TR 110 motorcycle engine with a displacement of 650 cc (40 ci) supplied power. Induction was via Amal carburetion. With 9.5:1

compression, the pocket rocket produced 50 horsepower at 7,000 rpm. The Jaybird reached the quarter-mile mark in 17 seconds with a terminal speed of 80 miles per hour. The car's top speed was 110 miles per hour.

While the car is certainly remembered for its awesome appearance, it is most often recalled for its first outing. Jordan lost a wheel on the long, fast, back stretch at Palm Springs. A dramatic slide was followed by an even more spectacular flip, with the car landing sunny-side down. Both Jordan and the car escaped the graveyard and lived to see another race.

Jocko Formula Junior

"Jocko" Maggiacomo, a prolific stock car builder and driver, built an attractive front-engined Formula Junior. It looked like a cross between a circle-track

JAYBIRD MARK X	
Constructors	Joe Jordan and Jim Troy
Location built	California
Body by	Hollywood Plastics
Engine	650-cc Triumph TR 110 motorcycle
Gearbox	Triumph-Berman
Chassis	space frame
Front suspension	independent
Rear suspension	independent
Brakes	disc
Body material	fiberglass
Weight, approx.	550 pounds
Wheelbase	80 inches
Length	120 inches
Height	26 inches
Cost when new	$2,500

JOCKO FORMULA JUNIOR	
Constructor	Jocko Maggiacomo
Location built	Rhinebeck, New York
Year built	1959
Engine	Fiat 1,100 cc
Gearbox	Fiat four-speed
Chassis	ladder
Front suspension	independent
Rear suspension	live axle
Brakes	Fiat drums

Midget and a Stanguellini, with torsion-bar springing and a Fiat engine and running gear. The 1,100-cc engine was fed by dual-side draft Webers, and a four-speed Fiat gearbox was used. Fiat front suspension was used, but the lower wishbones were cut and welded to Morris Minor arms so the Morris torsion bars would work. In back, a Fiat live axle was

The Jocko was a graceful Formula Junior that ran against the Stanguellinis. *Christopher Shoemaker collection*

sprung by Midget-style torsion bars; the suspension was fully adjustable. A Fiat rack-and-pinion steering unit was used. A simple ladder frame was made from 2 1/4-inch tubes, and Borrani wire wheels gave the Jocko a polished, sophisticated look. As per Midget practice, the suspension members were chrome plated. Owner Jim Haynes, who finished ninth at the 1960 Sebring Formula Junior race, drove the Jocko. The Jocko was later Sam Posey's first racing car and has been competing in vintage racing events with its current owner, Chris Shoemaker.

Maggiacomo later built a Kellison-bodied sports-racer with a Chevy V-8 engine.

John Bull Special

Charles A. Bull was a Jaguar and MG dealer in El Paso, Texas, in the early 1950s when he and his friend James Cassidy designed an MG-powered special. Starting with a 1949 Fiat 500 station wagon chassis, they added Nash brakes, Borrani 15-inch wire wheels, and a handsome aluminum body. The Fiat featured independent front suspension with a transverse leaf spring, while semielliptic springs held up a live axle in back. The car had minimal overhang at both ends, giving it a "bulldog" look, in keeping with its name. A 1952 MG 1,250-cc T-Series engine was uprated to TD Mk.II specs and attached to an MG TC transmission.

JOHN BULL SPECIAL	
Constructors	Herman Kluge, Charles A. Bull, and James Cassidy
Year built	1952
Engine	1,250-cc MG
Gearbox	MG TC four-speed
Front suspension	independent
Rear suspension	live axle
Brakes	drum
Body material	aluminum
Wheelbase	78.75 inches
Number built	unknown

Inside, a black walnut dash housed a Sun tachometer and standard gauges. Employee Herman Kluge, a former circle-track midget builder, built the special. The John Bull Special won the first two races it entered, beating MGs and a Porsche Super at the Ruidoso Rally Road Races and at the Iraan, Texas, hillclimb. Bull intended to replace the 1,250-cc engine with a 1,500-cc engine and sell replicas to other racers, but it's unknown how many, if any, were made.

Johnson Jaguar Special

Sherwood Johnson raced a Jaguar-based special on the East Coast in the early 1950s. It had an agricultural look with a cycle-fendered cigar-shaped body with two small front grilles. Johnson raced the car in hillclimbs and road races.

John Von Neumann's MG TD Competition Super Sport

See Von Neumann MG Special entry.

Jones-De Camp Crosley

One of the most beautiful of all 1950s West Coast H-Modifieds was the Jones-De Camp Crosley. It was built by a team of four, each with an area of particular expertise. Harry Jones and Lyn De Camp of the Rich and Jones Body Shop in Glendale, California, owned the car. Jim Troy designed the space frame, and Charles Gardner of Mustang Cycle built the hopped-up Crosley engine.

Jones had been actively racing a 750-cc Moretti coupe (formerly Ernie McAfee's car) but grew weary of the repeat episodes of downtime waiting for engine parts to arrive from Italy. Thus motivated, he decided to switch to an American powerplant and assembled a team to help him build a race car. The car took approximately 18 months to design and build.

The special began as a space frame constructed of 1 1/8-inch seamless steel tubes. Smaller diameter diagonal and vertical members were added to increase strength and stiffness. Front suspension was independent by unequal A-arms, Lotus coil springs, and hydraulic shocks. The rear end was derived from a Crosley Hotshot with coils and tubular shocks. Brakes were disc units from a Hotshot. The gearbox was MG, the clutch was Morris Minor, and the flywheel was Crosley. Steering was rack and pinion from a Morris. The gas tank was aluminum and was from a Panhard.

The engine was a Crosley four-cylinder over-bored to 748.36 cc. The cam was a billet unit by Winfield. The little four-banger breathed through a dual-barrel Weber carburetor that fed to a custom Gardner manifold through enlarged intake valves.

A Devin body graced the Jones-De Camp Crosley.
Dean Batchelor

Exhaust was through oversized valves to specially designed Gardner headers.

The fiberglass body was a right-hand-drive Devin design and was a delight to behold. Two important modifications to the body were made. The first involved forming a hood scoop to clear the Weber carburetor; the second involved adding material at the wheel arches to follow the contour of the small (12-inch) wheels. The inner panels were designed to save weight and were made from thin sheets of aluminum. The interior was nicely finished with black upholstery. The well-designed dash contained a tach (8,000 rpm) and gauges for oil pressure and water and oil temperature. The body was finished in white with gold trim and numbers; a racing stripe ran the length of the car.

JONES-DE CAMP CROSLEY

Constructors	Harry Jones, Lyn De Camp, Jim Troy, Charles Gardner
Location built	Glendale, California
Body by	Devin Enterprises
Year built	early 1950s
Engine	748-cc Crosley four-cylinder
Gearbox	MG four-speed
Chassis	space frame
Front suspension	independent
Rear suspension	Crosley Hotshot live axle
Brakes	disc
Body material	fiberglass
Weight, approx.	880 pounds
Wheelbase	82 inches
Cost when new	$1,200

Jones Racing Team Special

After selling their lovely Devin-bodied Jones-De Camp Crosley, sans engine, Harry and Vi Jones still wanted to go racing. So they built a new special that mated the engine from the Jones-De Camp Crosley with the body and chassis of a Lotus 11. The car was an instant winner and in 1959 scored 16 victories and ran second an additional seven times. The car won the Sports Car Club of America Pacific Coast Championship for H-Modifieds and was third-in-class nationally. It also won *MotoRacing's* Pacific Coast Championship in the H-Modified class. For the 1960 season, the Crosley engine was swapped for a 750-cc Fiat-Abarth twin cam.

JONES RACING TEAM SPECIAL

Constructors	Harry Jones, Charles Gardner (engine)
Location built	Glendale, California
Year built	1959
Engines	748.36-cc Crosley four-cylinder; 750-cc Fiat-Abarth twin cam
Gearboxes	Austin A-30, four-speeds
Chassis	Lotus 11
Body	Lotus 11
Weight, approx.	890 pounds

Kangaroo-Fiat

Fred Plotkin built this Fiat-powered sports-racer in the mid-1960s. The car was constructed on a one-off monocoque chassis with the front suspension and

KANGAROO-FIAT

Constructor	Fred Plotkin
Year built	mid-1960s
Engine	850-cc Fiat four-cylinder
Gearbox	Fiat four-speed
Chassis	monocoque
Front suspension	independent
Rear suspension	independent
Brakes	drum
Body material	fiberglass

The Kangaroo-Fiat was competitive for a long time.
Fred Plotkin collection

drum brakes from an NSU Prinz. A highly developed Fiat 850-cc engine with elevated compression and dual SU carburetors provided the power, which was transmitted through a Fiat four-speed gearbox. The body was a fiberglass creation painted in a loud shade of yellow. The car was light, nimble, and responsive and was a real contender in its class.

Keck Spyder

Nade Bourgeault built the Keck Spyder for George Keck from the remains of a Porsche 550 RS Spyder. But this was not just "any old, washed up" Porsche race car. It was Chassis Number 0104, the 1956 factory entrant at the 24 Hours of Le Mans. At Le Mans, the car raced to a Group Sports 1500 victory with Richard von Frankenberg and Wolfgang von Trips sharing the driving. Perhaps equally impressive was the overall fifth-place finish.

Following the car's legendary finish at Le Mans, Ken Miles raced it for a season. J. P. Kunstle took a turn at the wheel, and later Pete Lovely raced it. Keck eventually purchased the car with plans to refurbish it for racing. When he realized that the project was not getting finished, Keck hauled the Porsche to Nade Bourgeault's Sports Car Center in Sausalito, California.

Over the next ten months, Bourgeault spent 600 hours redesigning the car. The car was shortened and lowered 4 inches. The body shell was fabricated of light alloy into two major sections. The top section was built as four panels, and the bottom section was a one-piece unit that was riveted directly to the frame. The nose and tail segments were designed to be completely removable, allowing unfettered access to all of the major mechanical components. The finished, restyled car was breathtaking—perhaps even more beautiful than the RS Porsche from which it came.

The Keck Spyder sits in the pits at Laguna Seca in 1958. *George Keck collection*

The Keck Spyder looked as good from the back as it did from the front. This photo was taken at Laguna Seca in 1958. *George Keck collection*

KECK SPYDER

Constructor	**Nade Bourgeault**
Location built	**Sausalito, California**
Year built	**1958**
Engine	**Porsche Carrera**
Gearbox	**Porsche five-speed**
Chassis	**space frame**
Front suspension	**trailing link**
Rear suspension	**swing axle**
Brakes	**drum**
Body material	**aluminum**
Chassis number	**0104**

Keil Porsche

The Keil Porsche is one of the oddest one-off specials ever built. Lots of sports-racers had movable wings, but how many had movable bodies? Ike Eichelbarger and Bob Buck built the Keil, starting with an Elva Mk.7 powered by a Porsche 904 four-cam engine. By 1969, the Elva was no longer the hot setup and car owner Eichelbarger looked to designer Buck for help.

"Keil" is German for "wedge," and the body certainly looked like a big doorstop. However, when the car was on the track the body did some amazing things. The body was hinged just behind the front wheels and when a switch was activated, the body would raise upward to increase the angle of attack from seven degrees to 20 degrees. After completing the turn, the body would be returned to

KEIL PORSCHE

Constructors	**Ike Eichelbarger and Bob Buck**
Location built	**Raleigh, Virginia**
Year built	**1969**
Engine	**Porsche 904**
Gearbox	**five-speed**
Chassis	**space frame**
Front suspension	**independent, coil springs**
Rear suspension	**independent, coil springs**
Brakes	**disc**
Body material	**fiberglass**

The Keil Porsche had a body that tilted up to provide downforce. *Ed Cabaniss; Nick England collection*

190

its normal position. The Keil was completed in 1969 and tested at Virginia International Raceway prior to being raced there in SCCA events. Eichelbarger reported the new body added 2 miles per hour to his lap averages.

Knoop Chevy

See Huffaker entry, Chapter 2.

Le Biplace Torpedo

Ah, the early 1950s, a time when almost anything was possible. Close your eyes and imagine this. You and a friend are at a major racing event, not racing, just watching. You think it looks pretty cool out there, so you decide that you're going to build your own race car. Pretty crazy, right? But wait. You also decide that you're going to take the car to Europe and race it at Le Mans. You can open your eyes. This isn't a dream. It really happened!

Phil Stiles and George Schrafft were on hand at the first Sebring race in 1951 and witnessed a nearly stock Crosley win the Index of Performance. After the race, the two men were dreaming of going to Le Mans when Stile's wife proclaimed, "Why don't you let Crosley build you a car?" This preposterous idea set the wheels in motion for one of the most outrageous adventures in motor racing history.

The next day, Stiles wrote two carefully worded letters. The first was to Powell Crosley Jr. informing him that his company had been invited to field a car at Le Mans. The second was to the l'Automobile Club de l'Ouest, requesting an entry form. Somehow Stiles was able to set the hook at both ends and the two men were off and scheming. Now all they needed was a race car.

Crosley took some convincing, but eventually Stiles and Schrafft wore him down. He gave them a Hotshot chassis and a machined steel crankshaft. He also allowed his chief engineer, Paul Klotsch, to help with the project. Orders went out in all directions—Bell Auto Parts, Iskenderian, Braje, and Harmon & Collins. A call also went out to renowned Indy car designer Floyd "Pop" Dreyer to build a one-off aluminum body. Dreyer answered the call with a lovely torpedo-shaped envelope reminiscent of some of the prewar Grand Prix racers. The finished car was dyno tested to 42 horsepower, but the dyno was only equipped to read to 6,000 revs. Even at this modest measure, the car had a superb horsepower-to-displacement ratio for a car of its time. This was also precisely what was needed to achieve Stiles and Schraffts' goal—to win the Le Mans Index of Performance.

So off they went to France for the 1951 24-hour race. The car barely passed through tech inspection on the first try. The inspectors loved the car's triple-chromed intake manifold, but there were some problems. The car needed stronger headlights to run at night, and the larger generator that had been ordered for the car from Crosley had not arrived. So a generator and lights from Marchal were installed instead. In addition, the team had goofed on the size of the fuel tank and had to install a larger one on the fly with the help of the Cunningham crew.

With all seeming well, Schrafft hit the pavement running hard for the Le Mans start. He was going well, averaging 73 miles per hour and running in tenth place for the Index. Then the trouble began.

Le Biplace Torpedo was a Crosley-powered Le Mans racer. *Edward Buck collection*

The Marchal generator began to discharge. After a driver change, Stiles was racing hard when the generator seized up, ending the dream.

LE BIPLACE TORPEDO

Constructors	Phil Stiles and George Schrafft
Location built	Indiana
Body by	Floyd "Pop" Dreyer
Year built	1951
Engine	Crosley four-cylinder
Gearbox	three-speed
Chassis	Crosley Hotshot
Front suspension	live axle
Rear suspension	live axle
Brakes	Crosley
Body material	aluminum

Leson Simca

Seymour "Chick" Leson owned and raced this Simca-based special in the early 1950s. Leson had taken notice of Barlow's success racing his Simca Specials and had ideas of getting into the mix. So he bought a Simca Huit cabriolet and started thinking about going fast. The project started to take shape when Leson brought the Simca street machine to Jack Hagemann in hopes that he would make him a race car. Hagemann agreed to do the job in exchange for the Simca's carcass, once all the race car's essential components had been removed.

Hagemann built a chrome-moly space frame with large lower tubes and smaller upper tubes. The independent front suspension used custom-fabbed upper arms and stock Simca lower arms. The rear axle was Simca. Rack-and-pinion steering was borrowed from an MG TC. The engine was a stock 1,200-cc Simca four-banger with dual carburetion. The body was a typical Hagemann alloy masterpiece with a long, graceful nose, cycle-fenders, and wire wheels.

The car was a runner, but it did not achieve the success of Barlow's cars. Perhaps Leson was too late to the dance, or perhaps he couldn't match Barlow's Simca-driving skills. Whatever the case, this very good race car was capable of an occasional second- and third-place finish, but it was not up to the task of beating the very best under-1,500-cc iron of the day.

LESON SIMCA

Constructor	Jack Hagemann
Location built	California
Body by	Jack Hagemann
Year built	early 1950s
Engine	1,200-cc Simca four-cylinder
Chassis	space frame
Front suspension	independent
Rear suspension	live axle
Brakes	drum
Body material	aluminum

Lindqvist Saab Double-Ender

See Double-Ender entry.

Lipe Pooper

The Pooper marque is a contraction of the two parts to the equation—Porsche and Cooper. Gordon "Tippy" Lipe built such a machine in 1954 from a Cooper Formula 3 car, powered by a Porsche pushrod engine. Initially, he ran the combination in the Unrestricted class.

Around 1955, Lipe changed his Pooper into a sports-racer. He left the driver in the center and made an aluminum envelope body. In this form, the Lipe Pooper was much lighter and quicker than a Porsche Spyder, and Lipe was very successful with this car in the 1955 season. Ken Miles and Pete Lovely raced other Poopers.

LIPE POOPER

Constructor	Gordon Lipe
Location built	Marion, Massachusetts
Year built	1954
Engine	1,500-cc Porsche
Gearbox	Porsche four-speed
Front suspension	independent
Rear suspension	independent
Body material	aluminum

The Little Digger was a race winner. *Dean Batchelor*

Little Digger

The Little Digger was the brainchild of Chalmers "Chal" Hall, who wanted to conquer the H-Modified class. Hall built the car at a cost of $3,500 over the course of a full year and continued to develop the car for an additional three years.

Hall constructed a ladder frame of 1 1/4-inch 4130 chrome-moly tubing of 0.030 wall thickness. According to Bill Devin, the car was built from the wreckage of his Devin Crosley Special (a heavily modified Crosley Hotshot), but Hall never acknowledged this. The front and rear suspension had semielliptical springs and Columbus shock absorbers. Hall chose Goodyear-Hawley spot disc brakes for both front and rear. The gearbox was a highly modified MG TC four-speed unit, and the clutch pressure plate was Morris. The steering mechanism was Crosley.

The Little Digger's engine was an extensively developed Crosley with a bore and stroke of 2 1/2 inches. Carburetion was by way of a 39DC03 dual-throat side-draft Weber unit on a custom intake manifold. Other engine improvements included a hard-chromed steel crankshaft, a one-off Clay Smith cam, special lightweight tappets, a Braje valve cover, and porting, lightening, relieving, and polishing throughout. The engine produced 55 horsepower at 8,500 rpm.

The finished car was petite, but the interior was surprisingly spacious, no doubt to accommodate Hall's nondwarf physique. The body was eye pleasing and crafted of lightweight aluminum. The finished car weighed in at only 760 pounds, which helped it move along. Terminal speed in the quarter-mile was 84.6 miles per hour, and the car's top speed was 114 miles per hour.

In 1958, Hall and the Little Digger captured the H-Modified Pacific Coast Championship with ten class wins in 12 starts. Hall went on to build the Hall-Scott Special with Don Scott.

LITTLE DIGGER

Constructor	**Chalmers ("Chal") Hall**
Location built	**Phoenix, Arizona**
Year built	**mid-1950s**
Engine	**Aerojet-Crosley**
Gearbox	**modified MG TC four-speed**
Chassis	**ladder**
Front suspension	**live axle**
Rear suspension	**live axle**
Brakes	**disc**
Body material	**aluminum**
Weight, approx.	**760 pounds**
Wheelbase	**84 inches**
Length	**121 inches**
Height	**33 inches**
Cost when new	**$3,500**

Lil Stinker

See Wright Specials entry.

Long's Renault Special

Al Long was an experienced midget racer and talented fabricator who worked for Meyer-Drake of Offenhauser engine fame. Sometime in the mid-1950s, he caught the road racing bug and decided to build a race car.

He started with a rear-engined Renault sedan and used many of its parts in the construction of his car. A steel tube frame was fabricated and Renault crossmembers and front suspension components were mated to it. Long shaped the body by hand from a combination of aluminum and steel. The finished body was a lovely cigar that raced very close to the track. The driver sat on the left side in front of a short head faring.

For power, Long used the donor car's 750-cc engine and developed it just a bit. The powerplant was installed in the middle, and the ring gear in the Renault twin axle was reversed. The fuel tank was located at the front on the opposite side of the driver.

LONG'S RENAULT SPECIAL

Constructor	**Al Long**
Location built	**Los Angeles, California**
Year built	**1956**
Engine	**750-cc Renault**
Gearbox	**Renault three-speed**
Chassis	**ladder**
Front suspension	**independent**
Rear suspension	**independent**
Brakes	**drum**
Body material	**aluminum and steel**
Weight, approx.	**826 pounds**
Wheelbase	**85 inches**

193

The car was no world beater at the racetrack, but it was certainly eye catching and innovative, which, after all, was part of what the whole American specials movement was about.

Lo-Test Special

The Lo-Test Special, built by Scott Beckett in 1959–1960 while he attended the University of Minnesota, was morphed into existence from an Allard J2X that Beckett purchased from Don Skogmo for $1,250. After running the Allard at some regional SCCA events, Beckett decided that the car was in need of some serious improvements.

To improve the car's overall handling, he shortened the chassis in the cowl region a full 6 inches. The stock steering unit was removed, and a Morris Minor rack-and-pinion assembly was installed.

Next, Beckett turned his attention to the engine compartment. The Hemi powerplant was removed and a Balchowsky-prepped 402-ci Buick V-8 monster with six carburetors was installed. A Chevy T-10 four-speed gearbox completed the driveline.

To improve cooling of the brakes and engine, Beckett enlarged the grille opening.

In 1959, following a series of mechanical failures related to the de Dion rear end, Beckett installed a Jag solid rear axle with trailing links. He also upgraded to cast finned drums that he purchased from the Echidna builders just down the way. The front suspension became a swing-axle setup with trailing arms.

Following all of the modifications, the Lo-Test Special did have its share of shining moments. In September 1959, the car ran third at Meadowdale, bested only by the greatest American race cars of the day—the Scarabs, driven by Augie Pabst and Harry Heuer. In addition to some local wins in the Midwest, Beckett and codriver Dewey Brohaugh were class winners in B-Modified at the 1961 Road America 500.

Pete Lovely humiliated the Porsche Spyders in the Lovely Pooper. *Tom Cardin*

The Lo-Test Special (No. 91) was barely recognizable as a much-modified Allard. *Raymond Milo collection*

LO-TEST SPECIAL	
Constructor	Scott Beckett
Location built	Minnesota
Years built	1959–1960
Engine	Buick V-8 (402 ci)
Gearbox	Chevy T-10 four-speed
Chassis	ladder
Front suspension	swing axle
Rear suspension	live axle
Brakes	drum
Body material	aluminum

Lovely Pooper

Pete Lovely was a Volkswagen and Porsche dealer in Seattle, Washington, who built one of the most successful Porsche-powered specials on the West Coast. In 1954, he was offered a Cooper Mk.8R record car that had been built to set speed and endurance records at the banked French Montlhery track. John Cooper himself drove the car in a Formula 3 race at Avus, where he easily outdistanced the field. The car

was then powered by a variety of Norton motorcycle engines, depending on which records they were chasing. In 1954, it was shipped to the United States, along with an earlier record car, for Cooper importer John Fox. Fox sold the Mk.8R, less engine, to Lovely, who was also a Cooper dealer.

Being a Porsche dealer meant Lovely had access to any Porsche engine he cared for. He had previously built a VW-based special and was ready for something faster. He opted for a near-stock 84-horsepower 1,500-cc 356 Super engine attached to a Volkswagen transaxle. With a total weight of 920 pounds, the new car would be plenty fast. The more powerful four-cam Carrera engine was considered but rejected for being too heavy for the Cooper's spindly frame, and it would have upset the weight distribution.

The body was striking, with very low lines and the driver laid back to the point of being almost completely enclosed in the car (to lower wind resistance in record runs). The driver sat in the center of the car, with a tiny offset second seat that only small children and SCCA regulators could love. The suspension was standard Cooper practice, single upper transverse springs at both ends with lower wishbones. The resulting special was nicknamed the "Pooper," a name that was subsequently applied to other Porsche-powered Coopers.

The revised car ran for the first time at Santa Barbara in May 1955, when it came up against the most fearsome under-1,500-cc special in the country—Ken Miles' R-2 Flying Shingle (see Miles Specials entry). The Shingle had been beating up on every Porsche and OSCAs on the West Coast and was not expecting a fight from the little Pooper. To everyone's surprise, Lovely actually led Miles for part of the race before dropping back with mechanical woes.

The Pooper picked up the pace at Torrey Pines, capturing a class win there and at Seafair. At Sacramento, Lovely, Miles, and Johnny von Neumann (in a Porsche Spyder) had a tremendous contest with von Neumann passing on the straights and the two featherweights squeezing past in the corners. At the flag, it was Lovely over Miles.

Perhaps the Pooper's greatest victory came at Glendale, California, in late 1955, when Lovely squared off against von Neumann and ace Porsche pusher Jack McAfee in 550 Spyders. When the flag dropped, 550-mounted Bill Thomas took an early lead before spinning out. That handed the lead to von Neumann, closely shadowed by Lovely and McAfee. On Lap 16, Lovely barged past into the lead. Then disaster struck—Lovely traded paint with a Renault special and had to pit to have his fender pulled away from the tire. That put him half a lap down to a flying von Neumann and McAfee. Sure enough, Lovely cut the lead down lap after lap, passing first McAfee, and then going after von Neumann to edge past and take the win.

Lovely started the 1956 season with a second to Miles, who had now joined von Neumann's stable driving a 550 Spyder. At Pebble Beach, the throttle linkage came apart while Lovely was leading, but he finished fourth by driving with one hand while he reached over the back of the car and worked the

throttle linkage by hand. The last win for the Pooper was at Sacramento, after which Lovely was rewarded with a ride in one of Tony Parravano's 1,500-cc Maseratis.

In all, the Pooper racked up five class wins and the 1955 SCCA F-Modified class championship. In 1956, *Road & Track* road tested the little car and found it to have a top speed of around 100 miles per hour, running a 15.1-second quarter-mile and turning 0-to-60 in seven seconds. It was pretty impressive stuff for such a comparatively inexpensive car.

Lovely went on to run his own Lotus in Formula 1. The Pooper is still active, now in vintage racing, where it once again can hold its own with some pretty impressive company.

LOVELY POOPER

Constructor	**Pete Lovely**
Location built	**Seattle, Washington**
Year built	**1955**
Engine	**Porsche 1500S**
Gearbox	**Volkswagen four-speed**
Front suspension	**independent**
Rear suspension	**independent**
Brakes	**drum**
Body material	**aluminum**
Weight, approx.	**920 pounds**
Wheelbase	**87 inches**

Lovely VW-Porsche Special

Pete Lovely will always be famous for his Porsche-powered Cooper that bested Ken Miles and his famous Flying Shingle (see Miles Specials entry). But in 1954, before Lovely built the Pooper, he and a group of friends built a Volkswagen-based special. Starting with VW suspension, brakes, and transaxle, Lovely and crew built a steel tube

Before he raced his Pooper, Pete Lovely built the Lovely VW-Porsche Special. *Dean Batchelor*

frame at Seattle Sports Car, a VW and Porsche dealer that agreed to contribute parts and fund the effort. Lovely was working there as a salesman and mechanic.

Lovely had built and raced roadsters on oval tracks, but switched to a series of sports cars, including a Jaguar XK-120, a Giuar, and a Porsche 356. He knew enough to want a midmounted engine, so the VW transaxle was turned around and the ring gear reversed (as later done on Formula Vees). The frame was made from 2 1/2-inch steel tubing, and a VW torsion bar assembly was attached in front. The special was so light that Lovely removed the center mounting block in the upper tube and let the springs function as a sway bar.

A dead stock Porsche 1500S engine was removed from a street car and installed in the middle of the chassis. With 80 horsepower it would be dead reliable and still powerful enough to make the 1,050-pound car a screamer. Zeke Zigler and Del Fanning, who ran a local body shop, devised a basic, functional body. Every nonstructural part was drilled to reduce weight, including the steel VW wheels.

The completed special weighed about 150 pounds less than a Porsche 550 Spyder and 300 pounds less than the customer-version 550A. Even giving up power to the four-cam engine in the 550, the little special had a competitive power-to-weight ratio and immediately began to win races.

The first time out was at Bakersfield, where Lovely bested Johnny von Neumann's Porsche 550. The rest of the season it continued to do well. Lovely left Seattle Sports Car to start his own VW dealership, but the special stayed and was later driven by Dr. D. Villardi. Its fate is not known. Next, Lovely built the Lovely Pooper (see Lovely Pooper entry).

LOVELY VW-PORSCHE SPECIAL

Constructor	**Seattle Sports Car**
Location built	**Seattle, Washington**
Body by	**Zeke Ziegler and Del Fanning**
Year built	**1954**
Engine	**Porsche 1500S**
Gearbox	**Volkswagen four-speed**
Chassis	**ladder**
Front suspension	**independent**
Rear suspension	**swing axle**
Brakes	**drum**
Body material	**aluminum**
Weight, approx.	**1,050 pounds**

Lowe's Frazer-Nash

Jim Lowe enjoyed racing his lovely cycle-fendered Frazer-Nash, but decided that something more aerodynamic might be interesting. So he commissioned Nade Bourgeault to construct an all-new, curvaceous alloy body at a cost of $2,500. The result was an eye-catching roadster with a wide grille opening, a sculpted hood scoop, a low windscreen, and a beautiful padded headrest.

Lowe's Frazer-Nash ran at Santa Barbara in 1956. *Allen Kuhn*

The car raced on a ladder frame. Front suspension was by an unequal wishbone with torsion bar springing. The rear suspension was de Dion with torsion bars. Brakes were Alfin drums front and rear, and the steering was rack and pinion.

A 1,978-cc Bristol B54 Mk.I fed by three Solex carburetors powered Lowe's race car. With 10:1 compression, the engine produced 143 horsepower at 5,750 rpm and launched the car from 0-to-60 in 6.2 seconds; top speed was 135 miles per hour.

Lowe was a very capable driver, and his special proved to be quite competitive. In 1956, Lowe captured the Class E Sports Car Club of America Championship. Unfortunately, the car was destroyed in an accident at Paramount Ranch in December 1957.

LOWE'S FRAZER-NASH

Constructor	**Jim Lowe**
Location built	**California**
Body by	**Nade Bourgeault**
Engine	**1,978-cc Bristol B54 Mk.I**
Gearbox	**four-speed**
Chassis	**ladder**
Front suspension	**unequal wishbone with torsion bar springing**
Rear suspension	**de Dion with torsion bars**
Brakes	**Alfin drums**
Body material	**aluminum**
Weight, approx.	**1,625 pounds**
Wheelbase	**100 inches**

Lucas-Whitehead Climax

Harry Lucas and Don Whitehead built this Canadian special in Toronto between 1956 and 1958. Lucas was a design engineer and a veteran pilot of World War II. Whitehead was a Ford automotive technician. The two men formed an excellent team and made meticulous plans prior to beginning the project. Every component was machined to exacting specifications from a set of blueprints.

The two men were Coventry-Climax enthusiasts, and they selected the old fire pump engine for their special. Their goal was to improve upon the ideas of the other Climax-powered cars of the day (i.e., Cooper, Lola, and Lotus) and build a more durable, yet lightweight race car. The car was built on a space frame and the body was a delightful fiberglass shell.

The whole plan worked to perfection, and the Lucas-Whitehead Climax was competitive in its class in Canada. The car's best outing was a class win in a 500-mile race at Harewood, Ontario, in May 1959 at a Canadian Racing Drivers Association event, in front of 10,000 fans. The car finished third overall behind a Jaguar XK-SS and a Maserati 300S. The class win got the car much media attention and even landed it in a Sunoco advertisement.

LUCAS-WHITEHEAD CLIMAX	
Constructors	Harry Lucas and Don Whitehead
Location built	Toronto, Canada
Years built	1956–1958
Engine	1,100-cc Coventry-Climax
Gearbox	four-speed
Chassis	spare time
Body material	fiberglass

The Mabee Drilling Special set the sports car record at Bonneville. *Jim Robinson collection*

Mabee Drilling Special

Guy and Joe Mabee were Texas oilmen who wanted to build a sports car for Carroll Shelby to race. Unfortunately, by the time the car was completed in the early 1950s Shelby had other fish to fry on the racetracks of the world. Although primarily intended for the salt flats, the Mabee Special was also designed for road racing.

It was a conventional design, with a chrome-moly steel tube ladder frame mounting Kurtis-style live axles front and rear with torsion-bar springing. A Halibrand center section provided quick-change capability; a nitro-burning Chrysler Hemi was the muscle. Ray Brown built the powerhouse, boring it out to 353 ci and installing Hillborn fuel injection, a magneto, and a Chet Herbert roller cam. A Ford three-speed gearbox was initially fitted, along with Lincoln drum brakes and 16-inch steel Ford wheels. Much of the chassis design came from plan sets sold by Chuck Manning (see Manning entry in American Kit Car Manufacturers, Chapter 5). A commercially available Victress fiberglass kit car body was used.

First time out for the new car was at the 1953 Bonneville meet, where Joe turned a sensational 203.105-mile-per-hour run, earning the special the title of World's Fastest Sports Car. The car received nationwide attention and was featured in many racing magazines.

The next year the Bonneville regs forbade nitro so the speeds were lower. The Mabees decided to also go road racing. The suspension was upgraded with the latest Kurtis parts, and the drum brakes were replaced with the notoriously unreliable Halibrand discs. Halibrand alloy wheels replaced the Ford items. The Ford three-speed gearbox was discarded in favor of a rare ZF four-speed box. A new 389-ci Hemi pumped out around 350 horses and prodigious torque on its new gasoline diet, and triple two-barrel carburetors replaced the injectors for road racing. Back on the salt flats, Joe ran 187.66 miles per hour.

Meanwhile, Shelby was ready to go to Europe and the Mabee Special was not looking like a world-beater yet, so Guy Mabee financed Shelby's

197

The Mabee Drilling Special was restored to road race form with Halibrand wheels. *Mike Downey; Jim Robinson collection*

early career in Europe driving Aston Martins. Joe raced the special in the Southwest, frequently running at the front in SCCA events. In 1955, the Mabees decided the time was past for their dream car and sold it to Tommy Deal, who raced it in Texas as well. Later, the car was fitted with a supercharger and raced as the Chrysler Special.

In the late 1950s, the old warrior was rebodied in aluminum by panel-beater Herman Kluge. It now sported twin headlights and a big grille on a simple body that vaguely resembled a Kurtis 500X. The Hemi was replaced with a fuel-injected Buick V-8, and the revamped racer was entered in the 1960 Pikes Peak Hillclimb, only to be denied its run by bad weather. It ended its racing days in Mexico, retiring in the mid-1960s. The Mabee Drilling Special has since returned to the United States and is restored to its 1954 road racing configuration.

MABEE DRILLING SPECIAL

Constructors	**Guy and Joe Mabee**
Location built	**Midland, Texas**
Year built	**1953**
Engines	**Chrysler Hemi, Buick V-8**
Gearbox	**four-speed**
Chassis	**ladder frame**
Front suspension	**live axle, torsion bars**
Rear suspension	**live axle, torsion bars**
Brakes	**drum, disc**
Body material	**fiberglass, aluminum**

MacDonald Corvette

See Balchowsky Old Yaller V entry, Chapter 2.

Mangham-Davis Special

The Mangham-Davis Special was a very successful Chevy-powered modified raced in Texas and the

MANGHAM-DAVIS SPECIAL

Constructors	**Stormy Mangham and Frank Davis**
Location built	**Smithfield, Texas**
Body by	**Devin Enterprises**
Year built	**1958**
Engine	**Chevy V-8**
Gearbox	**Chevy three-speed**
Front suspension	**live axle**
Rear suspension	**live axle**
Brakes	**drum**
Body material	**fiberglass**
Weight, approx.	**1,800 pounds**

Southwest during the late 1950s. It was nicknamed the Checkerboard Special for the red-and-white checkered flag painted on the tail. Owner Stormy Mangham said it looked like a Purina feed sack.

Mangham was a pilot who decided he could build a better racing car than those he had seen at local SCCA races. He teamed with Frank Davis, a talented mechanic and driver, who built the car at Mangham's private airport in Smithfield, Texas, outside Fort Worth.

The chassis was similar to circle track practice, with a lightweight tube frame carrying live axles at both ends. A narrowed Devin fiberglass body was fitted over it, with steel wheels all around. The engine was a 283 Chevy stroked out to 301 ci, with four Stromberg carburetors modified to produce 325 horsepower. A three-speed Chevy transmission was used, since the Chevy had plenty of torque to pull out of tight corners. The Mangham-Davis Special weighed only 1,800 pounds, which was less than most C-Modified machinery. The cost was also less. At $4,500 it was a fraction of the going price for a Ferrari or Maserati race car.

The car began racing in 1958 and soon picked up a string of wins. More remarkably, Davis never spun out and only left the course once, and then as a safety precaution. At Mansfield, Louisiana, Davis outran a field that included Ferrari Testa Rossas,

Maserati 250 and 300S sports-racers, and a Jaguar XK-SS. Davis won again at the Oklahoma Petit Prix held at the Oklahoma Fair Grounds. By the end of the season, Davis had won eight of 12 races entered, beating Maserati-mounted Carroll Shelby three for three. The Mangham-Davis Special has since disappeared, awaiting, we hope, discovery in the back of some garage.

Manning Mercury Special

Of all the early race car homebuilders, stress engineer Chuck Manning of Douglas Aircraft was one of the most capable. Unlike many constructors of the day, Manning approached his project from a scientific standpoint, applying the engineering principles that he used every day of his working career. What Manning set out to build was a race car that was powerful, light, nimble, and cheap, and he was a winner on each account.

Manning built a frame of 2.75-inch mild steel with two stacked parallel tubes that ran longitudinally on each side. The 1939 Ford parts bin provided axles, hydraulic brake assemblies, drum brakes, wheels, lever-action hydraulic shock absorbers, and transverse leaf springs (which were

The most successful of the Ford flathead-powered specials was the Manning Mercury Special, here driven by Chuck Manning. *Dean Batchelor*

modified by removing every other leaf). The steering wheel and steering column were also Ford. The body was an alloy roadster with cycle-fenders and an egg-crate grille.

A 259-ci 59A Mercury V-8 with a Weiland intake manifold, aluminum cylinder heads, and a camshaft from Iskenderian provided power. Manning used a Ford three-speed with Zephyr gears and fabricated a remote linkage to put the shift lever exactly where he wanted it.

The Manning Special was a real runner at just 1,700 pounds. It was an outright winner at Palm Springs in March 1952, beating the Cunningham C-2Rs and a gaggle of Allards. Manning published an article about his car and chassis in the October 1951 issue of *Road & Track* and offered chassis plans for $2 (see Manning entry in American Kit Car Manufacturers, Chapter 5).

The Manta Ray had a distinctive body with a recessed grille. *Robert Rolofson Jr.; Robert H. Rolofson III collection*

MANNING MERCURY SPECIAL

Constructor	Charles "Chuck" Manning
Location built	California
Year built	1951
Engine	59A Mercury V-8 (259 ci)
Gearbox	three-speed Ford
Chassis	ladder
Front suspension	live axle
Rear suspension	live axle
Brakes	drum
Body material	aluminum
Weight, approx.	1,700 pounds
Wheelbase	100 inches

Manta Ray

Bob Snow built this Crosley-powered special as a way to go racing on a nickel. In actuality, the car cost Snow about 20,000 nickels ($1,000) and took approximately 400 hours to complete.

The race car was built on a ladder frame from 3-inch tubes. Suspension front and rear was

English Ford without modification. Likewise, the brakes were stock English Ford.

The body was constructed of aluminum and fiberglass in right-hand-drive configuration. The car's name came from the very prominent manta raylike "feelers" that protruded some 12 inches forward of the air intake, headlights, and grille. The bodywork was designed for easy on-and-off for maintenance and repair work. Other unique features included a functional and properly triangulated roll hoop with a skid bar and a particularly well-engineered side pipe system with secure frame fasteners.

The car ran a Crosley four-banger SOHC with a displacement of 748 cc; compression was 10.5:1. Induction was via dual Amal carburetors and the transmission was from a Morris Minor.

MANTA RAY

Constructor	Bob Snow
Year built	early 1950s
Engine	748-cc SOHC Crosley
Gearbox	Morris Minor
Chassis	ladder
Front suspension	English Ford live axle
Rear suspension	English Ford live axle
Brakes	drum
Body material	aluminum and fiberglass
Weight, approx.	835 pounds
Wheelbase	79.5 inches
Length	136 inches
Height	27 inches
Cost when new	$1,000

Mar-Chris Special

The Mar-Chris Special was a lovely racer powered by an interesting variation on the famed Crosley engine. The little Crosley was the scourge of H-Modified in the early 1950s due to its light weight and ability to rev effortlessly. Bob Montgomery and West Coast midget racer and machinist Whitey Thueson decided two Crosleys would be just the ticket for the F-Modified (1,500-cc) class. They achieved this by machining a crankcase from steel and attaching two '51 Crosley cast-iron blocks to make a tiny 45 degree V-8. A billet crank was lubed by a dry-sump system fed by Franklin aircraft oil pumps. Four Amal carburetors fed the beast, which was fired by a '29 Studebaker President distributor.

An Indian motorcycle multidisc clutch and three-speed gearbox were used in conjunction with a Pat Warren two-speed rear end, which gave a total of six forward speeds.

A simple chrome-moly ladder frame was chosen, reinforced with body stringers. Suspension was fabricated from Torsilastic engine mounts

199

Bill Cantrell drove the Offenhauser-powered Solitary Wasp (formerly the Mar-Chris Special). *Allen Kuhn*

Constructors	Whitey Thueson and Bob Montgomery
Body by	Bob Pankratz, Harry Lewis
Year built	1954
Engines	Crosley-based V-8; later Offenhauser four-cylinder
Gearbox	Indian Chief three-speed and two-speed rear end
Chassis	ladder
Front suspension	live axle
Rear suspension	de Dion
Brakes	disc (Bendix aircraft)
Body material	aluminum
Weight, approx.	1,200 pounds
Wheelbase	85 inches

attached to custom-machined torsion arms to form a rubber springing system. A live axle lived up front with English Ford hubs and spindles, while in back Thueson fabricated a de Dion system. Stopping power was guaranteed by large Bendix aircraft disc brakes, and the steering system was a midget dirt track type.

The body was started by Bob Pankratz in 1953 and finished by Harry Lewis later that year. It was formed from 14-gauge aluminum and attached to the frame by Dzus fasteners. Total weight was 1,200 pounds. The beautifully fabricated special started the 1954 season with great hopes, running a promising third at Willow Springs, but the more technically advanced Porsche 550s took over the class, and that was it for the Crosley V-8. As the rules evolved, so did the car. The body initially was built without fenders, but cycle-fenders were added early on. Later, the car was run with full fenders. Like the body, the powertrain also evolved with the times. After the car was no longer competitive with the Crosley motor, it was run with an Offenhauser. Billy Cantrell raced the car with Offy power at the Los Angeles Times Grand Prix at Riverside in October 1959.

Martin Tanner Specials

See Tanner Specials entry.

Masterson Batmobile

This lovely Corvette-powered special was owned and raced by John "Bat" Masterson, who was a heck of a driver. The car was built on a box-tube frame fabricated by Merle Brennan of Reno, Nevada. Front suspension was live axle from an early Ford with double wishbones and Houdaille shock absorbers. Rear suspension was with Packard torsion bars, upper and lower torque arms, and Houdaille shock absorbers. Stopping power was provided by 1948 Mercury drum brakes with Lasco linings.

The body was a lovely Victress fiberglass roadster shell, a unit previously manufactured by Byers as the CR-90, until the rights and molds were sold to Victress in 1960. The Batmobile was painted in a deep, dark shade of blue lacquer and

Constructors	John "Bat" Masterson (Masterson Motors)
Location built	California
Body by	Victress Manufactoring
Year built	mid-1950s
Engine	5,200-cc Chevy Corvette V-8
Gearbox	Corvette four-speed
Chassis	ladder
Front suspension	live axle
Rear suspension	live axle
Brakes	drum
Body material	fiberglass
Weight, approx.	2,000 pounds
Wheelbase	94 inches
Length	155 inches
Height	40 inches
Cost when new	$6,000

was a real eye-catcher. A central white stripe ran the length of the hood, over the top of Masterson's helmet, and down the tail. A semicircular roll hoop was centered left-to-right, as was a short head

The Masterson Batmobile used a Victress body (the former Byers CR-90) and a Chevy V-8 engine. *Robert Rolofson Jr.; Robert H. Rolofson III collection*

fairing. The interior was neat and tidy with a row of gauges located to the right of the steering wheel. The clutch pedal was conventionally located, but the brake and gas pedals were located to the far, far right.

Masterson used a 5,200-cc Corvette V-8 to propel the Batmobile. Speed equipment included J7E pistons, valves from McQuirk, a Racer Brown cam, and Headman headers. With 9.5:1 compression and Edelbrock carburetion (six-pot 97s) the motor produced 350 horses at 6,500 revs. Acceleration was impressive with 0-to-60 times in the 5-second range, 0-to-100 in 9.5 seconds, and the quarter-mile in 11 seconds (with an exit speed of 120 miles per hour). Top speed of Masterson's Batmobile was 145 miles per hour with 4.11 gears.

Meyer Special

John Meyer built an early 1950s special that started with a two-place sprint car. He powered the car with a V-8 Cadillac and drove it to and from the track on public roads. The passenger's seat served as his "trailer" and a place to carry his toolbox.

MEYER SPECIAL	
Constructor	John Meyer
Year built	early 1950s
Engine	Cadillac V-8

Mickey Mouse and Mighty Mouse Specials

These two Porsche-powered specials were built in Florida in the late 1950s. Constructed at Al Sager Volkswagen in Jacksonville, the two cars wore distinctive mouse graphics. The Mickey Mouse was a simple car based on a VW floorpan with a Porsche Super engine. The Mighty Mouse was more sophisticated, with a tube frame, a midengined Porsche pushrod engine, and a highly modified Devin body.

MICKEY MOUSE AND MIGHTY MOUSE SPECIALS	
MICKEY MOUSE SPECIAL	
Constructors	Pete Laffe, Jim Harcum, Karl Hloch
Location built	Jacksonville, Florida
Body by	Devin Enterprises
Year built	1958
Engine	Porsche 1600 Super
Gearbox	four-speed
Chassis	Volkswagen floorpan
Front suspension	trailing link
Rear suspension	swing axles
Brakes	drum
Body material	fiberglass
MIGHTY MOUSE SPECIAL	
Constructors	Pete Laffe, Jim Harcum, Karl Hloch
Location built	Jacksonville, Florida
Body by	Devin Enterprises
Year built	1958
Engine	Porsche
Gearbox	four-speed
Chassis	space frame
Front suspension	trailing link
Rear suspension	swing axles
Brakes	drum
Body material	fiberglass

Miles Specials

Ken Miles was one of the pivotal characters in American racing history. His impact on the history of road racing cannot be measured, because he was a part of so many legendary teams and races. He surely deserves his sterling reputation as a driver and fabricator par excellence. But before he first strapped on a svelte Porsche Spyder or an asphalt-munching Cobra, Miles was famous for building the most successful specials to hit the West Coast, leaving tire marks on the backs of every OSCA and Porsche that dared get in his way. He only built three complete cars, but they have become legends, works of art that just happened to collect checkered flags wherever they went.

R-1

The first Miles masterpiece was built in 1953. Miles was working as service manager for Gough Industries, a California MG distributor. He was racing MG TDs for Gough, but the dated TDs were also-rans against the modern Porsches that were starting to show up. Miles had built a few specials (including a very hot Mercury V-8-powered Frazer-Nash) in his native England before moving to California in 1951. He realized if he wanted something faster than a TD he would have to build it himself.

Gough offered him use of any MG or Morris parts they had in stock, but little in the way of cash. Miles and his friend Laurence Melvold welded up a simple ladder frame from 3.5x.062-inch mild steel tubing. (Miles preferred mild steel to chrome-moly

Ken Miles flies through the woods in his famous R-1.
Tom Cardin

201

as it was cheaper, easier to weld, and less prone to cracking.) The front suspension was based on MG Series Y sedans. The lightweight spindles were adapted to MG TC front hubs, and then modified to work with a fabricated double A-arm suspension. The Y series drum brakes were modified to take two-wheel cylinders and lightweight Alfin aluminum racing drums intended for the TC. Morris Minor rack-and-pinion steering was used.

Miles fabricated the front A-arms from 1x.062-inch steel tubing and settled on 8-inch-long upper arms and 12-inch lowers. Miles carefully laid out the front suspension to give zero bump steer, showing a degree of sophistication not fully appreciated by many frontline racing car manufacturers. Tube shocks and torsion bars were used for springing, and weight was an impressive 1,225 pounds.

Morris Oxford leaf springs were cut in half, and trailing links were used above the MG TC rear axle to control torque. Axles ratios were limited, so a friend in England made a 4.5:1 final drive ratio.

The MG factory blessed the project by providing an experimental racing engine built to go in the EX-179 MG record car. This was essentially an MG TD Mk.II block recored to a 72-millimeter bore size, giving 1,466 cc. (This would later form the basis for the XPEG engine used in the MG TF 1500.) Compression ratio was up to 10.5:1 (later increased to 11.6:1), and to prevent gasket failure, the special head had no water passages cast in its face. An external pipe connected up the cooling system. Twin 1 3/4-inch SU carbs were used, and the resulting powerhouse belted out 83 horsepower at 6,300 rpm. A stock MG TD gearbox proved to be adequate (but just) for handling the power.

To reduce costs and simplify construction, the sheet aluminum body was bent without compound curves except for the nose cone. As Miles described the process, they would attach the body on one side of the car, bend it over the top, then drill and mount it on the other side before they let go. Originally, a piece of wire mesh cut from the

Gough parts department cage was mounted as a grille in the nose. Soon, a more professional grille was made from a Morris Minor unit. The cycle fenders were carefully mounted to make sure they didn't fall off. Miles estimated the cost at $1,000 for the complete car, not including labor.

The first time out for the newly completed and untested car was at Pebble Beach in 1953, where the lovely little special splashed through the rain and soundly defeated a field of expensive OSCAs and Porsches. Beginner's luck? Hardly. The amazing R-1 won all but two races over the next year, humbling the fastest Continental iron and even embarrassing the big-bore Ferraris and Jags on occasion. The R-1's history stopped at the same track where it started, at Pebble Beach in 1954, when the flywheel bolts fractured, allowing the flywheel to come loose. This sudden failure caused the engine to overrev and throw a rod. It was time for Miles to move on to his next weapon.

R-2 (Flying Shingle)

Some SCCA officials disliked cycle fenders. Whether it was because they resembled *hot rods*, or because they weren't used on the high-dollar Italian iron preferred by the bucks-up crowd, change was in the wind. Miles and Melvold started in on a new car with an envelope body. MG parts were used again, and Miles now had some cash and a lathe in exchange for the R-1. The new car used the same front suspension as the R-1 but with a sophisticated space frame that would save weight and provide more rigidity. The frame was made from 250 feet of 1-inch steel tubing. The driving position was lowered by 3 1/2 inches to reduce frontal area.

In back, torsion bars replaced the quarter-elliptics, and a more reliable Morris Minor rear axle (with a wider choice of ratios) replaced the MG TC unit used on R-1. Miles formed 1/8-inch-thick welding wire into supports for ace panel beaters Dick Troutman and Jack Sutton to mount the handsome aluminum body panels (rolled by

The R-2 Flying Shingle was Ken Miles' second special. It was also a winner. *Harold Pace*

Autocraft). The main goals were to reduce frontal area over the R-1 and also, for promotional purposes, to have a stronger family resemblance to the standard MG TF. The new body had a vague resemblance to the MG line and was flat on top with a cut-down MG grille in front. It was quickly nicknamed the Flying Shingle.

Once again, MG provided an experimental racing engine, this time from the 1954 MG

Ken Miles drives the R-2 Flying Shingle at Torrey Pines in 1956. *Allen Kuhn*

Bonneville campaign. It was similar in performance to the previous engine, but Miles tilted it down in the front to reduce frontal area and devised a baffling system to control the oil in the pan during cornering. To fit the carburetors under the hood, the stock MG intake manifold was installed upside down so that the carburetors angled up into the port, which necessitated flipping the float bowls upside down. With a lot of asbestos to keep the heat from the headers away from the float bowls, the odd-looking setup worked. A stronger, more reliable gearbox from an MG TC replaced the MG TD gearbox used in R-1.

The first race for the R-2 was at Willow Springs in early 1955, where it retired. It then went on to win at

Palm Springs, Pebble Beach, Santa Barbara, and Torrey Pines. Porsche 550 Spyders were getting faster, and Pete Lovely's Pooper (a term now used for any Porsche-powered Cooper) beat Miles at Sacramento, but the R-2 had reinforced the image of Miles as the Number One force to be reckoned with in small-bore racing. He was so good that his old nemesis, Porsche dealer Johnny von Neumann, hired Miles to be his service manager and to drive his collection of Porsche Spyders. The R-2 was sold and later raced by Phil Washburn with a Chevy V-4 engine (see Shingle Corvettie entry). Like the R-1, it has been restored and is active in vintage events today.

R-3 (Pooper)

Miles spent 1956 winning races in von Neumann's Porsche 550 Spyder. When the much-improved 550A Spyder came out, von Neumann had trouble getting one, and he and Miles plotted to build another special. Miles remembered Lovely's effective Pooper that had defeated the R-2 the previous season. Lovely's car was a low-budget marriage of a tiny Cooper Bonneville racer with a modified Porsche 356 pushrod engine.

With a generous budget from von Neumann, Miles went first-class all the way. A new Cooper Bobtail (so named for its short Kamm-style tail) rolling chassis was acquired with a modified nose,

Ken Miles pilots the R-3 Pooper (Porsche-Cooper). *Allen Kuhn*

sans air inlet. These tiny Coopers were intended for 1,100-cc Coventry-Climax FWA four-cylinder engines and featured state-of-the-art handling for 1956. A new Porsche 1,500-cc four-cam Carrera engine (as used in the Spyders) and transaxle were added to the mix.

Putting the two together was a lot harder than it looked. There was very little room in the engine compartment for the flat engine, and six engine mounts were added to distribute the drivetrain loads into the fragile chassis. The Spyder distributors were replaced with street Carrera units that took up less room. The 550 transaxle was modified to accept Morris Minor driveshaft flanges so that it would mate up with the Cooper rear suspension.

Dick Troutman subtly reworked the body with a more graceful tail than the truncated Cooper, adding blisters on the rear deck to cover the carburetors.

MILES SPECIALS

R-1
Constructor	**Ken Miles**
Location built	**Los Angeles, California**
Year built	**1953**
Engine	**1,466-cc MG XPEG**
Gearbox	**MGTD four-speed**
Front suspension	**independent**
Rear suspension	**live axle**
Brakes	**drum**
Body material	**aluminum**
Weight, approx.	**1,225 pounds**
Wheelbase	**90 inches**
Cost when new	**$1000**

R-2 (FLYING SHINGLE)
Constructor	**Ken Miles**
Location built	**Los Angeles, California**
Year built	**1954**
Engine	**1,466-cc MG XPEG**
Gearbox	**MGTC four-speed**
Front suspension	**independent**
Rear suspension	**live axle**
Brakes	**drum**
Body material	**aluminum**
Wheelbase	**90 inches**

R-3 (POOPER)
Constructor	**Ken Miles**
Location built	**Los Angeles, California**
Year built	**1956**
Engine	**1,500-cc Porsche Type 547**
Gearbox	**Porsche four-speed**
Front suspension	**independent**
Rear suspension	**independent**
Brakes	**drum**
Body material	**aluminum**
Weight, approx.	**940 pounds**

The resulting contraption weighed in at 940 pounds and developed around 114 horsepower. It was all Miles needed to even the score with the 550A Spyders.

Miles finished second at Pomona in late 1956, and then got hauling at Paramount Ranch, winning not only the under-1,500-cc race, but the big-bore modified event as well. At the season-ending Nassau races, Miles finished an amazing fourth overall behind a trio of Maseratis and Ferraris. He started the 1957 season with a win at Pomona, but Porsche was beginning to take a dim view of what the Miles/von Neumann equipment was doing to its latest Spyders. Suddenly, the pipeline was cleared, and von Neumann received a 550A, along with orders to sell the Pooper. It was subsequently campaigned by Stan Sugarman and Chuck Howard, and is still on the tracks in vintage events today.

Three Miles American specials were built, all became race winners, and all survived to race again in historic races—a perfect score. Some consider the Fliptop Cobra run at Nassau to be another Miles special (see Shelby American entry, Chapter 2). In any case, Miles, along with Jim Hall and Lance Reventlow, must be considered royalty among special builders.

Miller-Sparks Crosley

Don Miller built the Miller-Sparks Crosley as a training car for owner/newcomer Jack Sparks to hone his racing skills. The car took three months to finish and was built at a cost of $1,360.

The frame was a ladder built from 10–20 steel tubes. Suspension was Fiat front and rear with transverse leaf springs. The brakes were stock 8-inch Fiat drums at all four corners. Steering was a Fiat worm-and-gear unit. The gearbox was also Fiat and was a close-ratio four-speed.

The body was built by Miller and was a curvaceous left-hand-drive treasure with a small windscreen and a head fairing. The beautifully sculpted round tail contained a single left-sided taillight.

The engine for the car was a stock 750-cc SOHC Crosley four-cylinder with Carter carburetion. The car ran a compression of 7:1 and developed 26 horsepower at 5,500 rpm. Starting from rest, the car would accelerate to 60 miles per hour in 14 seconds and reached top seed (98 miles per hour) in 40 seconds.

The Miller-Sparks Crosley won a novice H-Modified race at Palm Springs and ran fifth-in-class at a race at Willow Springs. The car was never particularly well known or famous but is a lovely example of a Crosley-powered H-Mod racer of the day.

MILLER-SPARKS CROSLEY	
Constructor	**Don Miller**
Year built	**early 1950s**
Engine	**750-cc Crosley**
Gearbox	**Fiat four-speed**
Chassis	**ladder**
Front suspension	**Fiat independent**
Rear suspension	**Fiat live axle**
Brakes	**drum**
Body material	**aluminum**
Weight, approx.	**730 pounds**
Wheelbase	**80 inches**
Length	**97 inches**
Cost when new	**$1,360**

Mirage

A number of cars built for the Can-Am series never made much of an impact. Most were underfunded or built by well-meaning amateurs, out of their league in the big time. The Mirage was different. It was expertly designed by experienced professionals and funded to a generous degree by an understanding patron. It was even driven by top wheel spinners, but it was a flop of the first degree anyway.

The Nethercutt Mirage was built too late to be competitive.
Pete Lyons

Jack Nethercutt was a good amateur racing driver who had been racing a Lotus 19 when he decided to build his own car in 1965. It wasn't for him to drive, but to run against the best in professional events. Nethercutt was in the cosmetics business and had the money to bankroll the effort. He hired Ted Depew, an aerospace engineer who had been working with Nethercutt's racing effort for several years, to design the car. Depew penned a sophisticated aluminum monocoque chassis mounting a 375-horsepower Traco-tuned aluminum Oldsmobile V-8 with four downdraft 48-millimeter Webers. The chassis was very rigid and total weight came to an amazing 1,280 pounds. The wheels were even fabricated from aluminum sheet to save weight and to provide more room for bigger brakes. The powerful little engine was backed up with a Colotti T-37 transaxle.

The fiberglass body was a thing of beauty. Legendary race car stylist Pete Brock was brought in to perfect an aerodynamic package that reduced frontal area and cut through the air with the greatest of ease. Although they didn't know it yet, that was the *last* thing they should have tried to do.

The Mirage had a better power-to-weight ratio than the McLarens, Chaparrals, and Lolas that dominated big-bore sports car racing at the time, along with less frontal area, which translated into high top speed. (The Mirage was clocked at over 170 miles per hour.) But when it came out in 1966, the aerodynamic war was over and the wings had won. Cars with lots of power could afford to push around wings, spoilers, and high-downforce bodies that cut top speed but added to cornering speed. Ironically, the Mirage could keep up with the big Chevys and Fords on the straights, but not in the corners.

Grand Prix star Richie Ginther failed to qualify the Mirage at the Riverside Can-Am race in 1966, by which time a small spoiler had been added above the engine. Scooter Patrick drove it at the Las Vegas Can-Am at the end of the season, but it did not finish. In 1967, Patrick returned with the car, now Chevy-powered, to run without success at Bridgehampton and Riverside.

That was it for the Mirage . . . almost. In 1968, Nethercutt sold the Mirage name for $7,500 to Gulf Oil for use on its Ford GT-based Mirage racing cars.

MIRAGE

Constructor	Jack Nethercutt
Location built	Las Vegas, Nevada
Year built	1965
Engine	Oldsmobile V-8 (280 ci)
Gearbox	Colotti T-37
Chassis	monocoque
Front suspension	independent
Rear suspension	independent
Brakes	disc
Body material	fiberglass
Weight, approx.	1,280 pounds

Mollé Panhard

See Fairchild Panhard entry.

Monsterati

It's the classic love story: Boy meets car and falls in love, boy loses car and is heartbroken, boy is reunited with car and the two live happily ever after. Oh, how we love these stories. Like Cary Grant and Ingrid Bergman in An Affair to Remember, or Gregory

Bill Janowski built the Monsterati from a plan set by Chuck Manning. Today, Janowski still races the beloved beast, which is capable of sinking its fangs into all manner of imported iron. *Harold Pace*

Peck and Audrey Hepburn in Roman Holiday . . . or Bill Janowski and his beloved Monsterati?

Who could possibly tell this story better than Janowski himself?

"Back in 1952, I had a real desire to go sports car racing, but I was in my freshman year of engineering school at SMU, and finances made it all but impossible. I might have been able to dredge up some money for a used MG or something, but small production car racing never really appealed to me. About this time, a

car called the Manning Special was featured in *Road & Track*. It was a car that utilized a Mercury flathead and Ford running gear, and it was running relatively successfully on the West Coast. This tweaked me and, with the limited time and budget that one has in school, seemed like a project that I could work on and finance on an ongoing manner. Consequently, in December 1953, I bought a 1939 Ford chassis, sans body, and began my race car program, which I worked on for the next several years, as time permitted with the dedicated help of Bob Guest."

Janowski developed the car by Z-ing the frame and moving the engine back. The front solid-axle radius rods were modified to allow the front axle to function as an anti-roll bar. Janowski continues, "We did other fine hot-rodding things like incorporating Zephyr gears in the three-speed transmission, using a tractor pitman arm to speed up the steering, and shrouding all of this in a not-too-aerodynamic fiberglass and aluminum body shell." Janowski estimates that he spent approximately $900 to build the car, which was licensed for street use in July 1956 and first raced in 1957. According to Janowski, "It was an

MONSTERATI

Constructor	**Bill Janowski (with help from Bob Guest)**
Years built	**1953–1956**
Engines	**Mercury flathead Ford, later Chevy V-8**
Gearboxes	**three-speed Ford, later Chevrolet four-speed**
Chassis	**modified 1939 Ford**
Front suspension	**modified 1939 Ford wishbone**
Rear suspension	**solid axle, 1939 Ford changed to dual trailing arms**
Brakes	**drum (1939 Ford)**
Body material	**aluminum and fiberglass**
Weight, approx.	**2,170 pounds**
Wheelbase	**100 inches**
Length	**132 inches**
Height	**38 inches**
Cost when new	**$900**
Chassis number	**T57626**

'all-purpose' car. I called it the 'Janowski Special,' as was in vogue at the time.

"Things were pretty loose in SCCA racing in those days, so I qualified for a national license after one 'petite' race. Our first major race was in June 1957 at the abandoned Eagle Mountain Air Force Base near Fort Worth. It rained so hard that all the boat races in the area were canceled; the sports cars ran on regardless. All the big names were there with their Ferraris, Maseratis, Mercedes, etc. In the first race it was raining so hard and the car spray was so bad that I went through the first turn without ever seeing it. Carroll Shelby and Paul O'Shea came together in that first turn and wiped out both their cars. I ran as high as sixth overall in the preliminary race and the feature but each time, due to my inexperience, spun out and could not get the very wet engine restarted. Had I played it a little cooler, I might have placed well in a national race and my

whole future could have changed. As you know, 'ifs' don't count in this game."

Following the race, Janowski got back in the Monsterati and drove it to Nebraska, where the car raced in some local hillclimbs. He recalls, "The car was great for acceleration but somewhat short on handling and brakes. A race at Mansfield, Louisiana, left me back in the pack. It became obvious that we needed more horsepower than the old flathead would provide. The small-block Chevy was becoming quite popular, so we installed one with three two-barrel carburetors and a Corvette four-speed transmission and went to Midland, Texas, for a race. Would you believe it took us all weekend to find out that we didn't have a vent hole in the gas cap? Back at Mansfield in the feature race, I out-accelerated everybody to the first turn, including some mighty big Ferraris. That surprised me so much that I didn't make the first turn. Ended up first-in-class and fourth overall in the feature. The car was becoming very popular, as much as anything because the fans liked to root for an underdog trying to compete against the big, expensive 'furrin' equipment.'"

Janowski then took the car to Eagle Mountain. As he had experienced in the past, the crankshaft pulley kept coming off. Janowski now finds it a bit amusing. "This was before everybody learned that you had to tap that crankshaft and bolt the pulley on." Following Eagle Mountain, the special was brought to Austin, Texas, for a hillclimb. Janowski put in one of his famous all-night thrashes to prepare the car for the next day of racing. "While waiting to run, I stretched out to catch a few winks. Upon awakening and getting ready to go up the hill, I found that someone had taken a piece of masking tape, stuck it on the car, and written 'Monsterati .001' on it. To this day, I don't know who did it, but the car was renamed at that point." Janowski then set the fastest time up the hill.

The next outing for the Monsterati was at an airport course in Hondo, Texas. Unfortunately, the car suffered a mechanical failure in the rear drivetrain.

Janowski recalls, "Jim Hall was racing a Latham supercharged Chevrolet-powered Lister. He set the fastest time but used up all his supercharged drive belts in the process. We offered to loan him our three two-barrel carburetor manifold so he could run. We put it on, modified the throttle linkage accordingly, and he went out and won the feature race. At least a little part of the car did well.

"I retired the car in frustration after Hondo, one of several times it was retired in frustration. We revitalized the Monsterati in 1960 as the Mark III, with a small-block Chevy bored and stroked to 352 cubic inches. It was the largest Chevrolet engine being run in the Southwest at the time. We took two second-place finishes in C-Modified and third overall at Mansfield. I'll always remember that race due to the large number of spectators who came over to see the car when the pits were opened. At Longview, Texas, we set a second fastest time behind Jim Hall in his Birdcage Maserati, but a transmission synchronizer failed. We now had so much torque that I was having to run illegal slicks from Inglewood Recapping just to get the power to the ground. We would go through tech on legal racing tires and then replace them with the recaps for the races. Everyone knew I ran recaps but did not protest since they knew I couldn't afford to race if I was forced to run on new racing tires."

What followed was perhaps the zenith of the Monsterati's career. "At Louisiana Hilltop Raceway, a hilly road course, we set constantly improving overall lap records for the first three races. Unfortunately, the car continued to be plagued by little mechanical problems. While leading the feature, the Chevrolet gearshift lever broke at a retaining pin (later modified by the factory) and we had to settle for second place. In another race, we had a flat tire, and in the third race, we blew our big engine.

"The big engine reminds me of a story. It occurred to me that we had lots of acceleration but lacked the handling and brakes of say, a Lister. Why not put the engine in a Lister and really go? One day I went to the old lumberyard in Dallas that Jim Hall and Carroll Shelby were using as their base of operations and suggested to Jim that he let me run his old Lister with my big engine and he could step on up to bigger and better things. After discussing this a bit, Jim said, 'Let me think about it.' He's still thinking about it, I guess.

"In Oklahoma City, we raced on a road course at the state fairgrounds where we won the preliminary big modified event and finished second overall to Ronnie Hissom's Lister in the feature. In both races, the linings literally came off the old '39 Ford shoes. At Hondo, Texas, I took second overall behind the XK-SS Jaguar that I had driven. At this point, I retired the car. During the entire time we raced, the only support we ever received was wholesale prices on Chevrolet parts and one set of racing tires from an admirer. I sold the car in 1962 and it was raced locally, but I lost track of it. I continued to race with a well-used Lotus 18 Formula Junior in Texas and then in the Midwest. When the Lotus blew its engine at Mid-Ohio in 1965, I dropped out of racing except for a little off-road racing in Baja in the late 1960s."

Then Janowski attended a vintage car race at Laguna Seca in 1981. He was so enthused that he began searching for his old car. According to Janowski, "I could trace it through the first two owners, but that's where the trail went cold. In 1983, Paul Lamb, a friend from Dallas who had helped me with the car during the early years, called and said he had located the car in Balch Springs, Texas. On my next trip to Texas, I went by to see it. Although the basic body panels were intact, it had been through numerous engines and had been thoroughly brutalized. After a year of negotiations, I bought the chassis and had it shipped to Reno, where I began a frame-up restoration."

The car is now completely restored and is a frequent competitor in vintage racing events, again driven by Janowski.

We Talk (More) With Bill Janowski.

AUTHOR: What is your favorite memory of the Monsterati?

JANOWSKI: We held the track record for the first three races at Hilltop Raceway in Bossier City, Louisiana.

AUTHOR: What was it like to find your car after all of those years?

JANOWSKI: Both exciting and depressing.

AUTHOR: Depressing?

JANOWSKI: The car was in terrible condition, basically, brutalized to say the least. It had been used as a road car and modified with many different engines. I had heard a rumor that the car was also used as a dragster. Someone had used a cutting torch on the aluminum, which, of course, you don't do. When I found it, it had been registered as a Thunderbird.

AUTHOR: Do you think that you could ever sell the Monsterati again?

JANOWSKI: Never. My wife, yes. My dog, maybe. But the Monsterati, never.

AUTHOR: Is it OK if we print that?

JANOWSKI: Absolutely.

Morgan Special

The Morgan Special was named after its creator, George Morgan of Webster, New York, and is in no way related to the Morgan motorcars of Great Britain. The car was constructed using many of the mechanical components from a 1950 Crosley. During the project, Morgan received help from his son, Gary, and fellow racing enthusiast Ed Bassage.

Construction began with a tube frame fabricated from 2 3/8-inch cold-rolled, welded seam tubing of 0.060-inch wall thickness. The frame was designed to mimic the Crosley's overall dimensions and allow for the use of stock Crosley suspension without

significant modification. The center portion of the frame was lower than the front and rear, which were "kicked up." Morgan reinforced the stock Crosley front axle and added an additional caliper to the Crosley disc brake unit. This enhanced the car's overall braking characteristics, particularly when the racetrack was wet. Morgan built the car as a right-hand-drive racer using an off-the-shelf steering assembly turned upside down, with a steering column that was shortened 20 inches.

The alloy body was designed around five basic principles: (1) accept Crosley headlights, (2) accept '54 Chevrolet taillights, (3) produce a low frontal area, (4) be constructed without welding, and (5) possess no compound curves. Despite this purely functional approach, the finished car was delightful indeed.

For power, Morgan began with a stock Crosley four-banger. The steel crankshaft was stroked, and a race cam was installed. Induction was accomplished with dual Webers, and the compression ratio was 10:1. The transmission was a '51 Morris Minor unit.

MORGAN SPECIAL

Constructors	**George Morgan, Gary Morgan, Ed Bassage**
Year built	**early 1950s**
Engine	**Crosley four-cylinder**
Gearbox	**1951 Morris Minor**
Chassis	**space frame**
Front suspension	**live axle**
Rear suspension	**live axle**
Brakes	**modified Crosley discs**
Body material	**aluminum**

Morgensen Specials

Dick Morgensen was a Phoenix-based Porsche-Volkswagen dealer with a passion for racing. During

Dick Morgensen built the third Morgensen Special with a Chevy engine and a Devin body. *Robert Rolofson Jr.; Robert H. Rolofson III collection*

the 1950s, he built a total of three cars known as Morgensen Specials.

The first Morgensen Special was built in 1951–1952 and was successful on the West Coast. The car was powered by a Cadillac engine and wore a Glasspar fiberglass body.

Morgensen and Boyd Hugh built the second Morgensen Special in a barn in 1953. The car was built on a welded-up space frame from 2-inch chrome-moly tubing, and the chassis was assembled from bits and pieces found around Morgensen's ranch. The car had a '38 Ford front end, a '49 Ford rear end, and a Plymouth six-cylinder engine. Steering was borrowed from a 1940 Ford pickup. The car won a race in New Mexico with Morgensen driving, competed at the final event at March Field, and finished third at Torrey Pines in 1954. Max Balchowsky and investment banker Eric Hauser bought the car in 1956, following Margaret Prichard's fatal accident racing the car at Torrey Pines. The car later became Old Yaller I (see Balchowsky Old Yaller I entry, Chapter 2).

The third Morgensen Special was built on a chrome-moly tubular ladder frame with a live front axle, torsion bar suspension, and finned Buick drum brakes. The engine was Chevy Corvette fed through six carburetors, and the body was a Devin fiberglass shell. The car was built in less than 30 days at a cost of roughly $2,000.

MORGENSEN SPECIALS

MORGENSEN SPECIAL (1)

Constructor	**Dick Morgensen**
Location built	**Phoenix, Arizona**
Body by	**Glasspar Company**
Years built	**1951–1952**
Engine	**Cadillac V-8**
Gearbox	**three-speed**
Chassis	**ladder**
Body material	**fiberglass (Glasspar)**

MORGENSEN SPECIAL (2)

Constructors	**Dick Morgensen and Boyd Hugh**
Location built	**Phoenix, Arizona**
Year built	**1953**
Engine	**Plymouth six-cylinder**
Gearbox	**three-speed**
Chassis	**space frame**
Front suspension	**live axle (1938 Ford)**
Rear suspension	**live axle (1949 Ford)**

MORGENSEN SPECIAL (3)

Constructor	**Dick Morgensen**
Location built	**Phoenix, Arizona**
Body by	**Devin Enterprises**
Year built	**late 1950s**
Engine	**Chevy Corvette**
Gearbox	**four-speed**
Chassis	**ladder**
Front suspension	**live axle**
Rear suspension	**live axle**
Brakes	**drum**
Body material	**fiberglass**
Cost when new	**$2,000**

Morlang Porsche

Wow, this was a cool car—wild body styling, powerplant from Stuttgart, Jack Sutton body, gullwing doors . . . and all from the humble beginnings of a pile of Porsche coupe scraps.

The Morlang Porsche was the brainchild of West Coast racing enthusiasts Bill Morlang and

Odd styling caused the Morlang Porsche to be nicknamed the Ambulance. *Robert Rolofson Jr.; Robert H. Rolofson III collection*

Bert Taylor. Both men worked together over a three-year stint to bring the car, which was actually owned by Taylor, to life. The men built the car on a ladder frame of 2-inch mild tubing. Most of the chassis components were stock Porsche. Front suspension was by Porsche trailing arms; rear suspension was by leading arms.

Morlang designed the alloy body, and Jack Sutton shaped the panels. Morlang also performed the final fitting and assembly of the body panels.

MORLANG PORSCHE

Constructors	**Bill Morlang and Bert Taylor**
Location built	**California**
Body by	**Jack Sutton**
Year built	**mid-1950s**
Engine	**1,498-cc Porsche Super four-cylinder**
Gearbox	**four-speed**
Chassis	**ladder**
Front suspension	**trailing link**
Rear suspension	**swing axles**
Brakes	**drum**
Body material	**aluminum**
Weight, approx.	**900 pounds**
Wheelbase	**80 inches**
Length	**122 inches**
Cost when new	**$1,200**

Each panel was attached to the frame using Dzus fasteners so that the entire body could be removed in three minutes for service and repairs. The assembled coupe was outrageous-looking, with a short, swoopy front end; surface-mounted headlights; a wide, short windshield, which also functioned as a roll bar; gullwing doors; and distinctive tail fins. The interior was tidy and functional with a stock Porsche steering wheel and instruments.

For power, Morlang and Taylor selected a stock 1,498-cc Porsche Super four-cylinder engine. The team positioned the motor in front of the transmission and achieved a nearly perfect 50/50 weight distribution.

The total cost to build the car was $1,200—not a lot for such a crowd pleaser. The car was so striking that it was nicknamed the Ambulance.

MPX Crosley

The MPX Crosley was designed and built by Walter Manske in his garage in Manhattan Beach, California, in 1958. Manske utilized his engineering talents as, literally, a rocket scientist to create an inexpensive, durable, lightweight race car with a low center of gravity. The finished car tipped the scales at a mere 722 pounds and measured just 24 inches in height.

The frame for the MPX was formed from small-diameter mild steel tubes. The front suspension came from a Fiat Topolino, and the rear was from Crosley. The flywheel was lightened, the clutch was Morris Minor, and the gearbox was from a Fiat Topolino.

The all-alloy body was constructed of thin-gauge material to conserve weight. Manske hand formed the MPX's body in his garage using home-spun tools made from stuffed socks and sandbags. The attractive body was kept in raw aluminum without any sealant or paint. Regular maintenance was needed to keep the shell looking good, which Manske accomplished with a Brillo pad.

In order to make the thing go, Manske installed a 750-cc Crosley CIBA engine. The engine was mounted

MPX CROSLEY	
Constructor	Walter Manske
Location built	Manhattan Beach, California
Year built	1958
Engine	750-cc Crosley CIBA
Gearbox	Fiat Topolino
Chassis	space frame
Front suspension	Fiat Topolino independent
Rear suspension	Crosley live axle
Brakes	drum (11-inch Crosley front, 9-inch Fiat rear)
Body material	aluminum
Weight, approx.	722 pounds
Height	24 inches

in a laid-over position to keep the car's overall height to a minimum. The engine ran with twin SU carbs, an Isky cam, and a compression of 11:1.

After racing the car for one season with little success, Manske sold it to Joe Puckett. Shortly afterward, Manske and Puckett devised a plan to go racing together—Puckett would drive, and Manske would wrench. From that point on, the car was known as the MPX, the Manske-Puckett-Experimental.

Despite the introduction of the rear-engined Saab specials into the ranks of H-Modified, the MPX Crosley remained surprisingly competitive. With the capable Puckett at the helm, the MPX ran second-in-class at Pomona, Tucson, and Las Vegas (twice). The car also finished third-in-class at Pomona and Palm Springs.

In 1962, the car was sold to two students from Cal State who ultimately butchered it while trying to "improve" it. Today, the ultimate fate of the MPX Crosley remains obscure.

Nethercutt Mirage

See Mirage entry.

Nichols Panhard

Murray Nichols' first Panhard-based special (he built a total of four) was not his most successful car, but it was an iron horse, competing from early 1956 to late 1965 with owner/driver Stan Bucklein at the helm.

The front-wheel-drive beauty was built on a Panhard Junior chassis, powered by an air-cooled two-cylinder, four-stroke Panhard engine. While the car's best race finish in period was a second-in-class at San Diego, the absence of a trip to the winner's circle never dissuaded Bucklein, who raced the car for more than ten seasons.

NICHOLS PANHARD	
Constructor	Murray Nichols
Year built	1954
Engine	Panhard two-cylinder, four-stroke, air cooled
Gearbox	Panhard four-speed
Chassis	Panhard Junior
Brakes	drum
Body material	fiberglass

209

Jack Wilder ran the Nichols Panhard (No. 33) at Paramount Ranch in 1957. *Allen Kuhn*

Nickey Nouse

The Nickey Nouse was Scarab chassis 002 renamed by the Stephani brothers, Jack and Ed, after they bought the car as a means of promoting their hugely successful Nickey Chevrolet dealership in the Chicago area. The car was purchased from RAI (Reventlow Automobiles Inc.) for the sum of $17,500 with Jim Jeffords named as the driver. In order to fit the non-petite Jeffords into the car, Lujie Lesovsky cut the chassis and moved the seat back 1 1/2 inches. Dean Jeffries was commissioned to repaint 002 in a purple scheme. The car also received a Nickey Nouse logo to publicize the dealership's racing effort. (See Scarab entry, Chapter 2.)

The Nickey Nouse was a purple Scarab raced by Jim Jeffords. *Tom Cardin*

Odenborg Specials

Dan Odenborg and his friend Scott Hamilton built a pair of well-known and race-winning sports-racers in the mid-1960s.

Odenborg Mercury H-Modified

The first Odenborg special was built in 1963 as a midengined design for H-Modified. Odenborg and Hamilton were college students working for a painting contractor in McMinnville, Oregon, when they started on their design. A well-triangulated space frame featured independent suspension all around and BMW brakes (two in front and one in

back). A modified 747-cc Mercury outboard engine was mounted in the middle and used a chain drive to spin the rear axles. The fiberglass body was made over plugs formed by Odenborg and Hamilton. Odenborg drove the H-Modified to many wins in 1963 before selling it to finance their next project.

Sceptre

The next year, a new racer emerged from Odenborg and Hamilton's garage, this time aided by Ron Courtney. The Sceptre was a bigger version of their H-Modified, but with a six-cylinder 1,492-cc Mercury outboard engine that ran in F-Modified. Once again, a light steel space frame was used, but this time with a Fiat 600 transaxle with Abarth gears. Airheart disc

brakes were fitted all around. The engine required a lot of development to get it to cool correctly. An all-new and very attractive fiberglass body was built, and LeGrand wheels were fitted. The Sceptre was clocked at 141 miles per hour—really quick for a small modified. Unfortunately, the Sceptre had engine trouble and never attained the record the earlier car had, but it was a beautiful car and fortunately has survived in the hands of Dan's son, Ben Odenborg.

Dan Odenborg's Sceptre had a Mercury outboard engine for power. *Ben Odenborg collection*

Orgeron Talbot-Lago

The Orgeron Talbot-Lago began its life as a 1949 Talbot-Lago T26C Formula 1 factory team race car. None other than Juan Manuel Fangio drove the car to victory in the 1950 Chilean Grand Prix. In addition to winning the race, Fangio broke the single lap and overall race records and was clocked at 181 miles per hour on the main straightaway.

In the late 1950s, the car was owned and raced by Ice Follies skater Terry Hall. Hall had been racing the car in Formula Libre but wanted to convert it to race as a C-Modified. Hall hired master bodybuilder Jack Sutton to create a magnificent center-seat aluminum skin. Sometime later, Roger Bloxham modified the body. The body and chassis were ultimately sent to Bob Ray Wood of Hollywood, California, for assembly and race preparation.

The frame was a heavy box channel with front suspension by transverse leaf springs, A-arms, and Houdaille shocks. The rear suspension was by semielliptic springs with friction and Monroe tubular shock absorbers. Brakes were 15x2 1/2-inch aluminum drums at all four corners. Power was transmitted to the rear axle through a Wilson preselector transmission. Steering was by way of a ZF worm-and-crown unit. The motor was a 4,487-cc Talbot overhead valve straight six-cylinder with 10.5:1 compression. With three 2-inch SU carburetors, the engine produced between 250 and 300 horsepower.

Hall, who had a large unpaid bill at Wood's shop, only raced the new car once, in Phoenix, in 1958. Wood invoked a mechanic's lien and sold the car to three road racing enthusiasts, who became equal partners in the car: Fred Orgeron was in the auto parts business, Phil Carter was a hotel bellman, and Jack Eubank was an industrial engineer. From that point forward, the car was known as the Orgeron Talbot-Lago.

With the hood off, the Orgeron Talbot-Lago reveals its Grand Prix car origins. *Bob Tronolone*

Carter and Eubank raced the car in a number of events with little success. The car was heavy and could not match the performance of the latest racers from Italy. The high points in the Orgeron Talbot-Lago's racing career were a third-in-class at an event at Riverside and a fourth-in-class at a Los Angeles Examiner Herald-Express–sponsored race.

The three owners could not reach an agreement regarding how to proceed after Carter spun a bearing in the Talbot engine while racing at Pomona. After the car sat idle for a while, Eubank bought out his two partners and took possession of the car. In the early 1960s, Eubank showed the car at the Vista del Mar Concourse d'Elegance. Lindley Locke took notice of the engineless car and was able to make a deal to buy it. In the late 1970s, Locke traded the car to Peter Giddings of Walnut Creek, California, who returned the car to its Grand

Driver Phil Carter wheels the Orgeron Talbot-Lago around Santa Barbara in 1959. *Bob Tronolone*

Prix configuration. Butch Gilbert of Westley, California, later became the owner of the body of the Orgeron Talbot-Lago.

211

ORGERON TALBOT-LAGO

Constructor	**Bob Ray Wood**
Location built	**Hollywood, California**
Body by	**Jack Sutton; later modified by Roger Bloxham**
Year built	**late 1950s**
Engine	**4,487-cc Talbot overhead valve straight six-cylinder**
Gearbox	**Wilson preselector**
Chassis	**space frame**
Front suspension	**independent**
Rear suspension	**independent**
Brakes	**drum**
Body material	**aluminum**

Outhauser

See Balchowsky Old Yaller I entry, Chapter 2.

PAM
Project Group 7

Sooner, rather than later, most Lotus 30s ended up wrecked. The flexible chassis and limited adjustments doomed the much-anticipated machine to also-ran status almost immediately, as California VW/Porsche dealer John "Bat" Masterson found out the first time he raced one in 1964. Two years later, he hauled the wreckage to PAM Foreign Cars in Manhattan Beach, California, to have it made into something usable. The man behind PAM was Hans Adams, an experienced race car builder with the successful Platypus-Porsche special to his credit.

The only usable parts from the Lotus were the Shelby-prepared 289 Ford, the ZF transaxle, the Lotus bell housing, and the fuel filler. The front suspension A-arms were transformed into the pedals. (They were the only decent parts of the Lotus.)

A neat space frame was drawn up using 1-inch 4130 chrome-moly tubing, which Adams welded up on the floor of his shop. He made his own suspension using Corvette spindles, fabricating sheet steel hub carriers for the rear. Airheart disc brakes were used with Corvette rotors in front.

The Shelby 289 put out 398 horsepower at 6,500 rpm, breathing through four Weber carburetors. American Racing wheels were used, 8-inch-wide in front and 10-inch in back. With a weight of around 1,500 pounds, it should have been a solid midpack car.

The fiberglass body was one of the most beautiful shapes put on a Can-Am car. It was designed and built by Skeet Kerr, a designer who had worked with Carroll Shelby. An adjustable wing was built into the roll bar area and a low, pointed nose stuck out in front.

The first race for the PAM was at Laguna Seca, where Corvette wizard Dick Guldstrand ran it at the back. He tried it again at Laguna Seca, where it went airborne and suffered a spectacular crash. Fortunately, Guldstrand recovered to race again, but the PAM did not. However, kit car manufacturer Kellison later offered the bodies for sale.

PAM PROJECT GROUP 7	
Constructor	PAM Foreign Cars
Location built	Manhattan Beach, California
Body by	Skeet Kerr
Year built	1965
Engine	Ford V-8
Gearbox	ZF five-speed
Front suspension	independent
Rear suspension	independent
Brakes	disc
Body material	fiberglass

PAM Special

The PAM (Patrick-Adams-Mitchell) Special was the car that launched Scooter Patrick's professional racing career in the early 1960s. It was light, nimble, responsive, and was motivated by a Porsche powerplant. Patrick was looming large in the under-2-liter class at the Riverside Grand Prix in October 1961 but failed to finish. Less than a month later, he brought the PAM Special home a winner at Del Mar.

Papier Mache and PMY Specials

Walt Martin was a high school shop instructor and a racing enthusiast from Cumberland, Maryland. Sometime in the late 1950s he was struck with an idea for a project for his students—his class, which was a chapter of the Future Craftsmen of America, would build an H-Modified special to go road racing.

Martin and his students began by constructing a frame from 1-inch tubing. The supporting members were drilled to reduce weight, and the finished frame weighed just 35 pounds. Martin reasoned that American racing surfaces were relatively smooth, and he did not believe that independent suspension would improve the performance of his

The PAM Project Group 7 was built from parts from a wrecked Lotus 30. Dick Guldstrand is driving here. *Bob Tronolone*

Young craftsmen surround the Papier Mache Special. The driver is Walt Martin. *Edward Buck collection*

The PMY-2 (No. 217) sits on the grid ahead of PMY-3 (No. 713). *Edward Buck collection*

PMY-3 (No. 88) was similar to PMY-2 but had no headlights. *Edward Buck collection*

special. Therefore, a simple live axle suspension was fitted front and rear. Martin was able to achieve his desired goal of 4 inches of wheel travel through the use of 18-inch quarter-elliptic springs and an adjustable retaining arm.

Two clapped-out 1951 Crosley station wagons were harvested for various other mechanical parts. Brakes were stock Crosley drums, drilled to aid with cooling and reduce the car's overall weight (by 8 pounds). The transmission and differential were also stock Crosley units.

The engine was a ported '51 Crosley four-cylinder Supersport. The cylinders were bored 0.030 inch, resulting in a displacement of 740 cc. The camshaft was from a '47 Crosley. Engine compression was 10:1. The exhaust was custom-fabricated (from a dozen pieces of 6-inch tubing) as was the intake manifold, which was fitted with two Tillotson carburetors.

Martin's class placed an order for a fiberglass body shell with one of the manufacturers of the day and readied the car for its first outing at the Cumberland Nationals. Weeks passed, the race grew closer, but much to everyone's dismay, no body shell arrived. Because the rules required a race car to have a body, things started looking pretty bleak—until one of the Future Craftsmen of America came up with the inspiration that is now legendary: "Let's build our own body, out of papier-mâché!"

Martin's class created a body form using chicken wire stringers soldered to the tube frame.

Six rolls of paper towels were procured from the boy's bathroom and fashioned into 3-inch strips. The strips were dabbed with waterproof glue and encrusted onto the chicken wire to form a papier-mâché shell. A total of 14 layers of strips were applied, ten to the exterior and four to the interior. The doors were fabricated from aluminum sheets and were made to swing open. The hood was from a '51 Crosley. The papier-mâché body was finished off in white with a rubberized paint product and then hand waxed.

The Papier Mache Special did make that race at Cumberland and was doing quite well, with Ross Wees driving, until it suffered a mechanical failure

two-thirds into the race. The car had a podium finish in class at the Giant's Despair Hillclimb and had a second DNF at Berwick, Pennsylvania, while leading in class. Little else is known for certain about the car's racing history, except for the episode at a race in Akron, Ohio, when the skies suddenly opened up and down it came—rain. A buzz circulated through the crowd. Would the little car melt away? No worry. The rubberized paint and wax did the trick. No damage whatsoever.

The tech school then got huffy about students building racing cars, so Martin and his son, Phillip, built two more cars that were similar in layout to the Papier Mache Special. They were not built by

213

PAPIER MACHE AND PMY SPECIALS

PAPIER MACHE SPECIAL

Constructors	**Walt Martin and his high school shop class**
Location built	**Cumberland, Maryland**
Years built	**1958–1959**
Engine	**740-cc Crosley four-cylinder**
Gearbox	**Crosley three-speed**
Chassis	**ladder**
Front suspension	**live axle**
Rear suspension	**live axle**
Brakes	**drum**
Body material	**papier-mâché**
Weight, approx.	**somewhere between 710 and 900 pounds**
Wheelbase	**78 inches**
Cost when new	**$325**

PMY-2 AND 3

Constructors	**Walt and Phillip Martin**
Location built	**Cumberland, Maryland**
Years built	**1960–1961**
Engine	**740-cc Crosley four-cylinder**
Gearbox	**Crosley three-speed**
Chassis	**ladder**
Front suspension	**live axle**
Rear suspension	**live axle**
Brakes	**drum**
Body material	**fiberglass**
Weight, approx.	**somewhere between 710 and 900 pounds**
Wheelbase	**78 inches**

students and were named by Martin the PMY-2 and PMY-3. (Note: others called them the PMY-1 and PMY-2, as if the Papier Mache Special was not part of the series, but Martin always considered the first car to be PMY-1.) For these two Crosley-powered cars, the Martins made a body plug from papier-mâché, then used it to make molds for fiberglass body panels. PMY-2 ran briefly with a papier-mâché nose and tail until the fiberglass ones were ready. Although the Papier Mache Special was right-hand drive, the next two cars switched to left-hand drive. The PMY-2 had square instrument panel inserts, while the last car had two round instrument recesses. PMY-2 also had headlight buckets, which the other two cars did not. The suspension was revised from car to car, but all were based on Crosley parts with leaf springs. Both PMY specials survive, but the Papier Mache Special has disappeared.

Parkinson Jaguar

The Parkinson Jaguar story begins as so many of the era did—with a racing accident and a crashed production car.

Don Parkinson was a professional architect in Los Angeles in the early 1950s. He was a sports car nut and was just getting his feet wet in road racing with some early success. He had finished second to his brother-in-law, Phil Hill, piloting a Jag XK-120 at Pebble Beach in November 1950. He returned to Pebble in May 1951 determined to take a stroll to the winner's circle this time around. Of course, things didn't go that way. Parkinson was pushing too hard and rolled the car during a high-speed turn. He walked away from the wreckage, but the car did not fare nearly as well.

The car was dragged back to Los Angeles and, with the assistance of Joe Thrall (who was a mechanic at International Motors in Hollywood, California), the twisted XK-120 body was removed. At this point in the story, Parkinson thought to transform what remained into a special.

As for a new body to clothe the car, Robert Cumberford penned a cycle-fendered, cigar-shaped design and Marvin Faw did the actual aluminum work. The finished body was sporty and visually appealing.

Thrall performed much of the drivetrain modification with Parkinson's assistance. The flywheel

PARKINSON JAGUAR	
Constructors	**Don Parkinson and Joe Thrall,**
Body by	**Marvin Faw (from a design by Robert Cumberford)**
Location built	**Los Angeles, California**
Year built	**1951**
Engine	**Jaguar XK-120**
Gearbox	**Jaguar four-speed**
Chassis	**Jaguar ladder frame**
Front suspension	**Jaguar independent**
Rear suspension	**Jaguar live axle**
Brakes	**Jaguar XK-120 drum**
Body material	**aluminum**

was lightened and a factory racing camshaft was added. The engine was repositioned 2 inches lower, 3/4 inches to the right, and 10 1/2 inches back in the chassis.

Parkinson raced his Jag-powered special several times at the close of the 1951 season. The highlight was a win at the third Palm Springs Road Race in October in the main event, the Palm Springs Cup. Parkinson beat some pretty fair talent that day, with Bill Stroppe finishing second in an MG TC powered by a Ford V-8 60 motor and Hill finishing third in a modified Jaguar XK-120.

In 1952 and 1953, Parkinson campaigned the car heavily and scored numerous podium finishes at multiple venues, including Palm Springs, Pebble Beach, Torrey Pines, and Golden Gate Park, just to name a few. At the sixth Palms Springs Road Race in 1954, the car was driven by Chuck Daigh and finished second behind Sterling Edward's Ferrari MM.

The Parkinson Jaguar reemerged in the 1970s when Faw began restoring it. By 1983, the car was owned by Bradley Buffum and had been fully restored. This wonderful car remains active in vintage racing events.

The Parkinson Jaguar was a sturdy old race car that had more lives than a stray cat. *Harold Pace*

214

Payne Special

Phil Payne and his wife, Vicky, emigrated from England to Los Angeles following World War II. Part of the trip was by sea, and the remainder was a cross-country jaunt in the couple's Brooklands Riley. When they arrived in Los Angeles, Payne took a job with International Motors, a dealership specializing in exotic automobiles. At some point, Payne took a liking to American hot rods and bought the car that later became known as the Payne Special from Willis Baldwin, the car's constructor. Baldwin is considered by many to be the father of American road racing specials. The Payne car was Baldwin's first special and therefore may represent the first-ever American car of its kind. Baldwin later went on to construct the Baldwin Mercury Special and the Baldwin Mark II.

The chassis of the Payne Special was from a 1932 Ford. The stock X-member was removed and a tubular crossmember was installed. The wheelbase was shortened to 103 inches. Front and rear suspension was via live axle with split radius rods connected to the frame rails at the "nonaxle" ends. Ford transverse leaf springs were used front and rear as were hydraulic brakes (Ford 1940–1948). The transmission was a three-speed Ford unit with a remote linkage (to a 3.78:1 Ford rear axle) that Baldwin custom-fabricated for the car. The clutch was a 10-inch Mercury unit, and Baldwin installed a lightened flywheel to improve performance.

Here's the Payne Special in action on the dirt.
Stephen Payne collection

Motivation for the car came from a 268.4-ci Mercury V-8 that Baldwin installed 15 inches to the rear of its typical location. The engine included a pair of Evans cylinder heads (9:1), an Evans triple carburetor manifold, and an Isky racing camshaft.

The body was constructed of aluminum and steel and took heavy cues from hot rods of the day. The instrument panel was set into an aluminum housing and was derived from a 1930s Auburn. Steering was accomplished via a monstrously large banjo-style steering wheel. The finished car had an attractive and purposeful appearance.

The Payne Special weighed a tick over 2,100 pounds and had plenty of get-up-and-go. Payne was a very competitive driver and posted many fastest times of the day. In addition to enjoying the victories, Payne took particular pleasure in letting everyone know that he was driving a "mere" hot rod. In 1948, Payne won a times trial at the Tommy Lee Ranch near Lake Hughes, California. The following year, Payne

finished third behind a Talbot-Lago (John von Neumann) and the Beetle Special (G. Thatcher Darwin) in the Tujunga Canyon (California) Hillclimb.

Today, Phil and Vicky's son, Steve, owns the car and lives in England.

PAYNE SPECIAL	
Constructor	**Willis Baldwin**
Location built	**Santa Barbara, California**
Year built	**1948**
Engine	**4.4-liter (268.4 ci) Mercury V-8**
Gearbox	**three-speed Ford**
Chassis	**modified 1932 Ford**
Front suspension	**live axle**
Rear suspension	**live axle**
Brakes	**drum**
Body material	**aluminum and steel**
Weight, approx.	**2,100 pounds**
Wheelbase	**103 inches**

PBX Crosley Special

It was a nation of two Crosley specials. In the West, Harry Eyerly's potent box-shaped bomb ruled the H-Modified class (see Eyerly Crosley entry). But in the East, Candy Poole's curvaceous PBX Crosley Special gave fits to its competition, sometimes even to those in much higher classes.

The PBX was born in 1952, distilled from the partnership of Crosley Hotshot racer Chandler "Candy" Poole (the "P") and engineer Bob Bentzinger (the "B"). The "X" denoted that the car was experimental. Poole was a gifted driver but was convinced that the Crosley engine (with its overhead camshaft and single-unit block-and-cylinder head construction) had vastly more potential than the Hotshot chassis and mechanicals. So he decided to build his own car, and with

The Payne Special was one of the best-built combinations of hot rod and sports car themes.
Harold Pace

Candy Poole's PBX Crosley Special was one of the best and most beautiful small modifieds. *Bob Harrington*

the assistance of Bentzinger, the two began the process on Thanksgiving Day.

The car was built upon a modified '49 Fiat 500 station wagon (Model B). Poole worked out a deal to sell off all of the Fiat's mechanicals for the same $200 he paid for the station wagon, so that his net investment in the frame came to precisely what it was worth. The frame was stripped, received new structural members, was drilled extensively, and was totally reworked. The PBX's wheelbase of 82.5 inches was derived in a most scientific fashion—add the wheelbases of the Hotshot and the Fiat donor car together and divide by two.

The front suspension remained Fiat with transverse springs and wishbones. The rear suspension was Crosley, with coil springs and a torque tube driveshaft. The transmission was a four-speed MG TC. The clutch was a Borg and Beck single dry-plate unit with a diameter of 7 1/4 inches. The drum brakes were drilled and finned for enhanced cooling. The steering was a Fiat worm-and-sector unit.

The coachwork of the PBX was splendid. Sven Johnson of the Aerform Company (New Haven, Connecticut) constructed the body after a scaled balsa wood model that Poole had designed. In order to comply with the regulations of the day, a small door that resembled a wing, hinged at the bottom, was added to the passenger (right) side. The nose and grille opening was thin and graceful,

ran the entire width of the car, and contained one headlight at each end. The fuel tank was located behind the seats and a spare tire sat atop it. The dash was constructed of beautifully finished wood, and the seats were comfortable and attractive. For instrumentation, the team used Stewart-Warner gauges and a Sun tach. The car was finished off with a Nardi steering wheel and a beautiful set of Borrani wire wheels.

The engine was a 0.040 overbored Crosley four-cylinder with the updated cast-iron block (CIBA), rather than the earlier copper-brazed (COBRA) engines formed from welded sheet steel. With the overbore, engine displacement grew to 748 cc (45 ci). Cylinder bore was 2.54 inches, and stroke was 2.25 inches. Compression was 10.5:1. Initially, stock pistons were used but were later discarded in favor of cast-aluminum units with full skirts, flat tops, and Grant rings. Poole and Bentzinger experimented with a variety of carburetion systems, including a Tillotson unit, a Carter 870-S package, twin Morris Minor SUs, and two downdraft Webers. After much experimentation, the team finally settled on twin Amal carburetors.

Poole and Bentzinger spent most of their engine development time working and reworking the Crosley camshaft. Starting from a stock engine, a Harmon & Collins cam with duration of 260 degrees and a lift of 0.400 inches was tried. This resulted in useful revs up

to 7,500. But Poole wanted more. So he tried even hotter cam grinds from Harmon & Collins and Weber but was dissatisfied. Finally, Poole worked out his own grind contour that mimicked the Harmon & Collins design in terms of opening and closing points, but reduced lift to 0.350 inches and changed the full open characteristics. This pushed the revs to 8,000 and improved power output to 55 horses.

The completed car was a real eye grabber and could get up and go. Acceleration from 0 to 60 miles per hour took just 8.5 seconds—pretty impressive for a 750-cc unit. The estimated top speed was 118 miles per hour. But what was most impressive was the PBX's reliability and winning record. In 35 starts, the car only failed to finish on three occasions. And in the 32 races that saw Poole's car still running at the end, the car scored an astounding 26 class wins.

Poole sold the car to Dolph Vilardi in 1956. A year later, he bought the car back and raced it a bit more, ultimately replacing the Crosley powerplant with a Bandini-Crosley DOHC motor. The car was sold to J. D. Iglehart in 1970 and was run in vintage events with a 750-cc Coventry-Climax engine.

PBX CROSLEY SPECIAL

Constructors	Chandler "Candy" Poole and Bob Bentzinger
Location built	Connecticut
Body by	Sven Johnson of the Aerform Company
Years built	1952–1953
Engine	748-cc Crosley (CIBA) four-cylinder
Gearbox	MG TC four-speed
Chassis	ladder
Front suspension	Fiat independent
Rear suspension	Crosley live axle
Brakes	drum
Body material	aluminum
Weight, approx.	1,000 pounds
Wheelbase	82.5 inches
Length	138 inches
Height	33 inches

216

Pete Lovely Pooper

See Lovely Pooper entry.

Peterson Special

The Pikes Peak Hillclimb was always a major event for Colorado racing enthusiasts. The sports car class was popular with both drivers and spectators in the 1950s and 1960s. One of the most successful car and driver combinations was the Peterson Special and its builder, Frank Peterson. He was a friend of Bob Carnes, who built the Bocars, so Peterson bought a Bocar body for his new special. Peterson shortened a Jaguar XK-120 chassis to 90 inches and installed a 283-ci Chevy with triple carbs. He ran the car at Pikes Peak in 1959 and 1960 and at local tracks like Continental Divide, Lowrie Field, and Buckley Field.

For 1961, Peterson reworked the car, lengthening the chassis to 96 inches, and he talked Carnes into letting him lay up his own body in the Bocar molds. It was much smoother (and heavier) than the standard Bocar body. A Halibrand quick-change unit was installed in back along with rear Buick drum brakes to go with the Jag drums in front. Rochester fuel injection was added to a hotter 283-ci Chevy engine.

The Peterson Special was a combination of Jaguar and Chevrolet parts with a Bocar body on top. *Harold Pace*

In 1961, Peterson finished third at Pikes Peak, a fine finish at the time. He installed a 327-ci Chevy for the next year and moved up to second place behind Ak Miller's Devin-Ford. The Peterson Special was upgraded with Corvette independent rear suspension and disc brakes and competed through the 1965 season. It has recently been run in vintage events in Colorado.

PETERSON SPECIAL

Constructor	Frank Peterson
Location built	Colorado
Body by	Bocar Manufacturing
Year built	1958
Engine	Chevy V-8
Gearbox	four-speed
Chassis	ladder
Front suspension	independent
Rear suspension	live axle
Brakes	drum
Body material	fiberglass

Peyote Special and Peyote Mk.II

William (Bill) Aldrich-Ames of Minneapolis, Minnesota, bought a crashed '57 Triumph TR-3, fixed it up, and went racing. He was a fixture at the local SCCA events and was not one to be satisfied with "also-ran" status. So when it became apparent that his Triumph was never going to be competitive in E-Production, he decided to turn the car into a special and run it as a modified.

Off came the body and many of the car parts. Ames removed the X-member from the TR-3 frame to allow him to relocate the engine in a lower and more posterior (10 inches toward the rear) position. He also constructed a roll bar and reworked the steering assembly and mounting points for the gas, brake, and clutch pedals. The engine and driveline components from the Triumph were retained.

Next came the body. A replacement was needed for the discarded Triumph skin, but Ames' bankroll for the project was limited. So he did what so many homebuilders of the day did—he went to the junkyard. There he found scrap sheets of aluminum and a supply of discarded hoops of electrical conduit. Ames created the artless body-form by welding the conduit hoops to the frame and then wrapping that with alloy sheets. A description of the fabrication process might lead one to conclude that the finished body was unattractive—in actuality, it was just plain awful looking.

In response to the frequent cries of, "Oh my God, shield your eyes," during the car's earliest outings, Ames decided to rebody the car. Back to the scrap yard he went, and again a shell was formed from conduit and alloy sheet metal. The car was now far more attractive and was renamed the Peyote Mk.II. Ames raced the car up through 1962 and then sold it.

The Peyote Special was based on Triumph parts with a distinctive body. *Harold Pace*

PEYOTE SPECIAL AND PEYOTE MK.II

Constructor	Bill Ames
Location built	Minneapolis, Minnesota
Year built	1959
Engine	Triumph TR-3
Gearbox	Triumph four-speed
Chassis	modified TR-3 ladder
Front suspension	TR-3 independent
Rear suspension	TR-3 live axle
Brakes	disc/drum
Body material	aluminum

Ames later entered into a joint business venture with Dewey Brohaugh, an avid racer who had scored a class win at the 1961 Road America 500, codriving the Lo-Test Special. The two men combined their last names and formed Ambro (see Ambro under Racing Car Manufacturers and American Kit Car Manufacturers).

Phil Payne Ford Special

See Payne Special entry.

Philson-Falcon

The Philson-Falcon was an East Coast special built in the late 1950s. The car's constructor was Norbert Philson, a highly skilled machinist by trade and a USAC tech inspector. Philson had previously constructed several midget racers, but in 1957, he became interested in building a sports-racer. His

The Philson-Falcon was probably the only racing car with a Ford Falcon six. *Charles Bordin collection*

idea was to create a car that was extremely safe with superb handling characteristics, and that's exactly what he did. Over a three-year period (1957–1959), Philson saw his dream grow from an idea, to blueprints, to a roller, and ultimately to a completed race car.

Philson constructed an all-tubular ladder frame that was welded into one rigid structure. The body was a beauty of all-aluminum construction. The engine used was a six-cylinder Ford Falcon (a preproduction example). With the help of his friend Robert Shirley, who had a top brass connection at Ford, Philson took delivery of the new engine in the form of a pallet of parts from Ford Motor Company. In order to reduce hood height, Philson installed the engine at a 30-degree angle (laid over on its side). The slant engine configuration necessitated special modification of the oil pan and pickup. Induction was via three SU carburetors.

Front suspension was TR-3 with Girling disc brakes. The rear suspension was MGA with drum brakes. Steering was a modified Morris rack-and-pinion.

According to the car's current owner, Charles Bordin, the car was road raced on the East Coast in the late 1950s and early 1960s. Today, the car remains active, participating in vintage race events.

PHILSON-FALCON

Constructor	Norbert Philson
Location built	Springfield, Pennsylvania
Years built	1957–1959
Engine	Ford Falcon six-cylinder
Gearbox	four-speed
Chassis	ladder
Front suspension	TR-3
Rear suspension	MGA
Brakes	front-Girling disc; rear-drums
Body material	aluminum
Weight, approx.	1,500 pounds
Wheelbase	88 inches
Length	139 inches
Height	29 inches

Phoenix Saab

This small-displacement special was built in 1960 and was powered by a three-cylinder, two-cycle Saab engine. The car had front-wheel drive and was owned and raced by famed and beloved H-Modified guru and cartoonist Joe Puckett.

The Phoenix Saab, shown here behind a Tanner, was raced by Joe Puckett. *Gene Leasure collection*

Pickford Jaguar

The Pickford Jaguar was one of the first-ever Jaguar-based American specials. Bill Pickford of Coronado, California, built the car in 1953. Pickford started with a space frame that he built from chrome-moly tubing. The front and rear suspension were from an XK-120 Jag, as were the brakes. The clutch was Jag, as was the four-speed gearbox.

The delightful alloy body was built by Joe Thrall and featured a beautifully sculpted nose with an egg-crate grille, clamshell fenders, and a wonderfully bulbous rear end. A spare tire was mounted on the right, between the front and rear fenders, helping to counterbalance the weight of the driver. The cockpit was simple and purposeful.

The engine was a stock Jaguar 3,443-cc six-cylinder. Pickford used three dual-throat Weber side-draft carburetors and set compression at 9.5:1. In this configuration, the engine developed 230 ponies at 5,750 rpm. The car would accelerate from 0 to 60 in 5.5 seconds; top speed was 141 miles per hour.

Pickford raced the car with reasonably good success. He won an over-1,500-cc feature race at

Torrey Pines in July 1954. He also had podium finishes at Santa Barbara (third) in September and Torrey Pines (second) in December 1954. The car was sold to Fred Woodward, who raced it with varying degrees of success in 1955 and 1956. Don Hulette then purchased the car for $3,200, cheap considering Pickford's initial cost of $8,000, not to mention time. Hulette won a race at Torrey Pines and another at Santa Barbara. He later removed the Jag powerplant and installed a Chevy V-8. In this configuration, he ran second at Santa Barbara in 1959 and won a race at the Pomona Fairgrounds in July 1961.

Don Hulette repowered the old Pickford Jaguar with a Chevy V-8. *Allen Kuhn*

Pink Elephants

Jim Chaffee of Mount Baldy, California, built a total of five Pink Elephants (I, II, III, IV, and V) in the late 1950s and early 1960s. These were essentially Devin Specials, built on various chassis using Devin $295 bodies. All of the cars were painted pink and wore distinctive Pink Elephant graphics.

Pink Elephant I was built in 1957 on an MG TD Mark II chassis. An MG TD four-cylinder motor provided power. It was raced for many years under a variety of names, including Devin MG. The car passed through several owners, including Chaffee, Jack Reasnor, and Frank Blachley.

Pink Elephant II was built on a platform constructed from Miller frame rails in 1958, with a Chevy V-8 motor providing the power. Period photographs indicate that the car rode on 1920s-style circle-track wire wheels.

Pink Elephant III was built in 1959. This third car was constructed using Healey parts, including the frame, floorpan, steering, wire wheels, radiator, firewall structure, and pedals. Front suspension was also Healey and was by independent A-arms; the rear suspension was live axle. Brakes were disc up front and drum at the rear. A custom dash panel was fabricated, and Stewart Warner gauges (tachometer, fuel, oil pressure, and water temperature) were installed. Aluminum was used to form the transmission tunnel, and panels were also constructed to separate the driver's compartment from the trunk area. A custom-made fuel tank was positioned in the trunk area.

Jim Chaffee slides Pink Elephant I around Paramount Ranch in 1956. *Allen Kuhn*

The fiberglass body for Pink Elephant III began life as a Devin J style. A head fairing was added, and originally it housed a roll bar. Later, a more conventional roll bar was added. The hood was modified to incorporate a scoop for improved air inlet to the carburetors. The front section of the body was fashioned to tilt forward to allow easy access to the engine compartment; the hood was also made removable for minor engine service. A one-off plexiglass windscreen was fitted to the cowl.

Motivation for the third Elephant came from a modified 283 Chevrolet with a Corvette four-speed transmission. The engine was offset to the right and set back for better weight distribution. Induction was via a three two-barrel intake manifold with Rochester carburetors. Headers and side pipes were used for exhaust.

Chaffee raced Pink Elephant III from 1959 to 1968 and constructed a small, enclosed trailer that also carried the Pink Elephant graphics. Over the years, the car underwent some typical modifications. Rear fender flares were added to allow the use of wider tires, and the chassis was modified to accept a '63 Corvette independent rear end.

Pink Elephant III finished 13th overall at the Stardust USRRC Championship in 1966, competing against some real modern monsters, including the winning Genie of Dan Blocker, driven by John Cannon.

Pink Elephant III was retired in 1967 and remained in its custom trailer until 1984, when Floyd

PICKFORD JAGUAR

Constructor	Bill Pickford
Location built	Coronado, California
Body by	Joe Thrall
Year built	1953
Engine	3,443-cc Jaguar six-cylinder
Gearbox	Jaguar four-speed
Chassis	space frame
Front suspension	independent with torsion bars
Rear suspension	live axle with torsion bars
Brakes	Jaguar drum
Body material	aluminum
Weight, approx.	1,920 pounds
Wheelbase	95 inches
Height	36 inches
Cost when new	$8,000

Fred Woodward in the Pickford Jaguar leads a young Dan Gurney in a Porsche. *Allen Kuhn*

PINK ELEPHANT I

Constructor	Jim Chaffee
Location built	Ontario, California
Body by	Devin Enterprises
Year built	1957
Engine	MG TD four-cylinder
Gearbox	MG TD four-speed
Chassis	MG TD Mark II
Front suspension	independent
Rear suspension	live axle
Brakes	drum
Body material	fiberglass

PINK ELEPHANT II

Constructor	Jim Chaffee
Location built	Mount Baldy, California
Body by	Devin Enterprises
Year built	1958
Engine	Chevy V-8
Gearbox	T-10 four-speed
Chassis	ladder
Front suspension	independent
Rear suspension	live axle
Brakes	drum
Body material	fiberglass

PINK ELEPHANT III

Constructor	Jim Chaffee
Location built	Mount Baldy, California
Body by	Devin Enterprises
Year built	1959
Engine	Chevy V-8
Gearbox	T-10 four-speed
Chassis	Austin-Healey ladder
Front suspension	independent
Rear suspension	live axle
Brakes	front disc; rear drum
Body material	fiberglass
Weight, approx.	2,028 pounds
Wheelbase	91 inches
Length	158 inches
Height	40 inches

PINK ELEPHANTS IV AND V

Constructor	Jim Chaffee
Location built	Mount Baldy, California
Body by	Devin Enterprises
Years built	late 1950s
Engines	Austin-Healey and Triumph
Chassis	Austin-Healey and Triumph

Garrett of Montclair, California, tracked down Chaffee and purchased the car and the trailer. The car lived in Garrett's shop for the next 19 years, virtually untouched, until purchased by Devin enthusiast Chris Wickersham of Pasadena, California, in 2003.

Chaffee built two additional race cars—Pink Elephants IV and V. Little is known about these two cars. It is believed that one rode on a Healey chassis with a Healey powerplant, with the other based on a Triumph.

Plass Mistral

Bob Plass, an engineer and former circle track midget racer, built the Plass Mistral. Plass was a keen observer of all things mechanical, and he borrowed several ideas from the successful specials of Ken Miles.

Plass started with a ladder frame constructed of 3 1/2-inch seamless tubing with a wall thickness of 0.065 inch. The front suspension was designed around MG components. The rear suspension was modeled after Miles' R-2 (Flying Shingle), with transverse torsion bars (Morris Minor) and 50-50 Gabriel shock absorbers. Plass used an MG TD rack-and-pinion steering unit.

The body was a Microplas Mistral fiberglass shell from Surrey, England. Modifications performed by Plass included making provisions for lights, a hood, a door, and the radiator. As a finishing touch, the car was fitted with MG wire wheels.

The motor was a special 1,496-cc MG unit—one of five imported to the United States by Miles for his record runs at Bonneville. The engine had 10.9:1 compression and breathed through dual SU carbs. Special racing rods and pistons, a hot cam, oversized valves with heavy-duty valve springs, and specially balanced rocker arms completed the engine package. Acceleration from 0 to 60 was accomplished in eight seconds, and the car topped out at 106 miles per hour.

PLASS MISTRAL

Constructor	Bob Plass
Body by	Microplas
Year built	mid-1950s
Engine	1,496-cc MG Bonneville
Gearbox	MG TD four-speed
Chassis	ladder
Front suspension	MG independent
Rear suspension	live axle
Brakes	drum
Body material	fiberglass
Weight, approx.	1,155 pounds
Wheelbase	90 inches
Length	124 inches
Height	28 inches
Price when new	$3,500

Platypus-Porsche

Hans Adams built this Porsche-powered race car in the 1960s. Adams also built the PAM Group 7.

Hans Adams built this Platypus-Porsche. *Allen Kuhn*

Pooper

This term was used for Porsche-powered Cooper specials. See Lipe Pooper, Lovely Pooper, and Miles R-3 (Pooper) entries.

Porter SLS

Chuck Porter had a body shop in Hollywood, California, and wanted to build his own racing car. He got his chance when he happened upon a seriously wrecked Mercedes 300SL coupe. It had been overturned and burned on the way to be delivered to its first owner. The delivery driver (who escaped alive) was reportedly exceeding 100 miles per hour, which would explain the serous damage the car suffered. The height, from the ground to the top of the gullwing doors, was about 3 feet. The wreckage sat in a junkyard for six months before Porter found it. It was his for $500.

Porter stripped the body off and spent some time straightening the bent frame. He then designed a lovely body that resembled his dream car, the Mercedes 300SLR, which had run so successfully in Europe. Porter kept the basic shape, raising the nose to allow for a stock radiator, and moved the headlights from the fenders to the grille. Porter had Jack Sutton build the body from 0.064 aluminum sheets and then named his creation the SLS (for SL-Scrap).

Chuck Porter in the Porter SLS leads a C-Type Jaguar at Santa Barbara in 1956. *Allen Kuhn*

Unfortunately, the fire had melted the aluminum brake drums and the fuel injection pump, and the engine was in need of an overhaul after sitting in the junkyard with a damaged valve cover. While it was apart, Porter installed a Mercedes factory performance cam to provide around 240 horsepower. Otherwise, the running gear was left largely stock.

Porter had raced midgets, but the SLS was his first road racing car. His first race was at Pomona in 1956, where he finished third-in-class. At Santa Maria, Porter won a novice race, and then he claimed his class in the main event. At San Diego, the SLS was second to a Ferrari Monza in a preliminary race, which it beat for a class win in the feature.

Porter later installed a McCulloch supercharger on the Mercedes engine. The blower produced 5 pounds of boost, and a hole had to be cut in the hood to get it to fit. Porter estimated that the blower increased power by 30 percent, but in the long run it still wasn't enough to suit him.

In 1957, Porter was running at Pomona when a '57 Corvette passed him and pulled away. Porter removed the Mercedes engine and looked around for something more muscular. He settled on a Buick V-8, as modified by the Old Yallermeister himself, Max Balchowsky. Starting with a '57 Buick block, Balchowsky bored and stroked it, then added an Isky cam and Hillborn fuel injection.

Since the Buick was a lot heavier than the Mercedes engine, Porter moved it back 10 inches in the frame, and Balchowsky fabricated adapters to mate the Buick to the Mercedes gearbox. Headers were made, and the exhaust now exited out the side vents.

The swap added 120 pounds to the weight, but the SLS was now capable of 13.9-second quarter-mile times and was seven seconds faster around Willow Springs than it had been. Porter ran the SLS in 1957, but without any notable success. In 1958, the Buick was replaced with a small-block Chevy.

After that, the obsolescent SLS was driven by a number of drivers, including Indy star Johnny Parsons, who wrecked it at the 1958 Times Grand Prix. In 1959, it failed to finish race after race, then won an event at Riverside, driven by Billy Krause. Krause continued to do well with the car through

Chuck Porter built this lovely Mercedes-based special and named it the SLS for SL-Scrap. *Harold Pace*

1961, winning several events. Ken Miles also drove the car. The SLS is restored and now in a private collection in Europe.

PORTER SLS

Constructor	Chuck Porter
Location built	Hollywood, California
Body by	Jack Sutton
Year built	1956
Engines	Mercedes 300SL, Buick V-8, Chevy V-8
Gearbox	four-speed
Chassis	space frame
Front suspension	independent, coil springs
Rear suspension	swing axle
Brakes	drum
Body material	aluminum
Weight, approx.	2,500 pounds

Powell Formula Junior

When Formula Junior was introduced in 1959, an army of would-be Colin Chapmans ran out and grabbed production car running gear to hammer into racing cars. One such pioneer was Dr. Lyle Powell, who had previously built two H-Modifieds. For running gear, he chose a DKW engine coupled to a VW transaxle with Fiat 1100 spindles, modified A-arms, and MG TD rack-and-pinion steering. The

space frame was made from small-diameter steel tubing covered with an attractive aluminum body (formed by Powell) that resembled a 1950s Formula 1 car. Swing axles were used in back, located by arms and trailing radius links.

The engine was placed in the middle, with a VW transaxle machined to take Porsche 356 gears. The DKW engine was purchased in a junkyard and bored out to 980 cc. The combustion chambers were reshaped and compression rose to 11:1. Powell also fabricated his own intake manifold for three Amal carburetors. Powell invested $2,000 and nine months of hard work into his Junior, and it repaid the favor by winning races in the early days of F-Jr. racing. But the pace of change was rapid, and it wasn't long before the Powell was outdated.

POWELL FORMULA JUNIOR

Constructor	Lyle Powell
Location built	Walnut Creek, California
Year built	1960
Engine	DKW
Gearbox	Volkswagen four-speed
Chassis	space frame
Front suspension	independent, coil springs
Rear suspension	swing axle
Brakes	drum
Body material	aluminum
Weight, approx.	975 pounds
Cost when new.	$2000

The Powell Formula Junior (No. 197) was an early mid-engined design. *Tam McPartland*

Priest Volvo

Eric Priest, Reg Wilson, and Ron Pearson built the Priest Volvo at a cost of roughly $4,000. The car was built upon a tubular frame with coil springs at all four corners. The brakes were hydraulic and were self-centering and self-adjusting. Steering was worm-and-sector. The gearbox was a five-speed and gave the car a real advantage in class, both in acceleration and engine braking.

The Victress-bodied Priest Volvo (No. 271), shown at Pomona in 1959, leads two other specials. *Allen Kuhn*

A 1,587-cc Volvo four-cylinder provided motivation, fed by a 1 1/2-inch SU carburetor. With 8.9:1 compression, the Swedish powerplant produced a healthy 85 horsepower at 5,500 rpm. The body was from Victress and was finished off with a beautiful paint job, an elegant grille, and a proud nose emblem that announced the car's underpinnings to the world: "VOLVO."

The Priest Volvo did enjoy some success at the racetrack. At a race at Pomona, the car finished third in E-Modified. It also finished second-in-class at a race at Paramount Ranch. The car recorded the fastest time of the day for novice drivers at the Pomona Time Trials.

Pupilidy VW

The Pupilidy VW, a fiberglass-bodied Volkswagen-powered special was run in the early 1950s on a highly modified Volkswagen chassis. It was competitive in class but unreliable. It was fitted at some point with a Porsche 1,100-cc engine and sold to Charles Rutan around 1955, to become the Rutan Porsche (see Rutan Specials entry).

Purina Feed Sack Special

See Mangham-Davis Special entry.

Rattenbury Crosley Special

This innovative Crosley-powered special was the third Crosley special to come from the mind and hands of Canadian builder James Rattenbury. Rattenbury was a real thinker, and his rationale for this car's design was well documented in an article that he authored in the April 1957 issue of *Road & Track*. Simply stated, his goal was to build a race car that was vastly superior to his previous two Crosley racers. During the journey, problems were solved with sound but unorthodox solutions. These solutions not only made the car better, but also made it somewhat of a fascination.

Rattenbury started with a space frame that he constructed from two different materials. The upper tubes were 18-gauge chrome-moly of 1 1/4-inch diameter; the lower tubes were 16-gauge mild steel of 1 1/2-inch diameter. As was often done in the day, the frame was engineered on a concrete floor using a pencil, and the tubes were cut to fit this full-scale drawing.

The car was built with independent suspension at both ends. Up front, the suspension was constructed with both long and short wishbone arms in a somewhat innovative arrangement. By augmenting the downward slope of the upper wishbones, Rattenbury was able to keep the wheels vertical during body roll and was able to use soft springs to enhance overall grip. The front brakes were outboard drums. The rear suspension looked like a live axle but was actually independent with a swing axle working through U-joints hidden from view by the inboard drum brakes and a Watts-style linkage. Steering was rack-and-pinion and was specially fabricated to allow a central seating/wheel position.

Rattenbury selected a Harley-Davidson gearbox because he believed the more conventional MG unit was too heavy for the application. In addition, the Harley box was more durable, had close ratios, and had a seven-plate clutch. The builder's gearbox choice led to an interesting problem in mating it with the Crosley four-banger. Rattenbury solved this by mounting the engine at the rear, just in front of the gearbox. Primary drive and final drive were by chains to the gearbox and a sprocket on the rear axle.

The four-cylinder Crosley engine was run with a stock bore and stroke and a compression ratio of 7.75:1. To this he added a Marshall Roots-style supercharger. The engine was mounted transversely at the rear, just forward of the gearbox. With 12 pounds of boost, the powerplant produced 50 ponies at 5,000 revs; with an additional pound of boost it intermittently produced 10 more horsepower at 7,000 revs.

The body was constructed from 16-gauge Alcoa utility aluminum sheet. D. Belson of New Westminster, British Columbia, performed most of this work. The front and rear sections were constructed to hinge open for easy access to all mechanical components. The most striking portion of the center-seater's body was the massive tail fin that also served as a headrest and roll bar. This was more quirky-looking than attractive. But that was not what its creator cared about. According to Rattenbury's article, "The completed car may not be handsome, but it abounds in interesting technical details."

It is believed that this car was later reengined with a Porsche powerplant and became known as the Rattenbury-Porsche Special. This was indeed an interesting car from a most inventive and interesting man.

Rattler and Finch F3

The Texas-built Rattlers and the Finch F3 from the West Coast had something in common, but just how much is not certain. The first Rattler came out of Mark Bratton's shop in Corpus Christi, Texas, and was powered by a converted Mercury outboard engine. It had separate exhaust pipes, and these combined with the two-cycle engine to deafen everyone in the vicinity, leading to its name. The Rattler had a graceful and very professional metalflake blue fiberglass body that was inspired by the Corvair Astro I show car. It was very competitive. Bratton built a second Rattler with a Honda S800 engine that he took to the ARRC in 1969, finishing a fine fifth in DSR. In 1971, a Rattler was second in DSR, driven by Joseph McClughan of Houston.

The Finch F3 was another DSR built by noted automotive author Richard Finch, who, literally, wrote the book on welding topics and Corvair maintenance. It had the same body as the first Rattler and also used spun aluminum wheels on the rear (the Rattler used them all around). However, the roll bars were different and the Finch was left-hand drive, while the first Rattler was right-hand drive. Finch built his chassis himself, so it is probable that the two cars only shared a body design.

RATTLER/FINCH F3	
Constructors	Mark Bratton and Richard Finch
Location built	Corpus Christi, Texas
Year built	1968
Engines	Mercury outboard/ Honda S800
Chassis	space frame
Front suspension	independent, coil springs
Rear suspension	independent, coil springs
Body material	fiberglass
Number built	fewer than five

R. B. Snow Crosley

This R. B. Snow Crosley was previously known as the Manta Ray. The car became known as the R. B. Snow Crosley (or the Snow Crosley) later in its life, following the addition of a new nosepiece. As the Manta Ray, the car's front end had "feelers" that projected forward a full 12 inches in front of the air intake. The reworked front end of the R. B. Snow Crosley had a more graceful, rounded appearance.

In its R. B. Snow form, the car ran with slightly higher compression (11:1 versus 10.5:1) and the Amal carbs were replaced by Stromberg 81 units.

(See Manta Ray entry.)

The R. B. Snow Crosley was previously known as the Manta Ray. *Robert Rolofson Jr.; Robert H. Rolofson III collection*

Reynolds Wrap Special

Max Balchowsky did not build this car, although its visual offensiveness rivaled Old Yaller I. The two men who built the Reynolds Wrap Special both had connections to two of Balchowsky's most hideous-looking machines. Jim Larkin was an avid period racer and the second owner of Old Yaller I, which he later renamed the Outhauser. Bob Sohus was the original buyer of Old Yaller VI, which was powered by a Pontiac mill that he removed from the Reynolds Wrap Special. It goes without saying that

The Reynolds Wrap Special had distinctive bodywork not easily mistaken for any other special. Driver Bob Sohus trails the field here. *Allen Kuhn*

Sohus and Larkin were men of good humor and never took themselves too seriously. They loved to race and loved their race cars, no matter what they looked like.

The Reynolds Wrap Special was constructed on a sturdy ladder frame made from 2 3/4-inch tubing of 0.049 wall thickness. The body was constructed from ultrathin alloy. The front and rear suspension was made of modified live-axle units from a 1940 Ford. The brakes were Ford with aluminum bonds, and the steering was also Ford. A massive radiator up front maximized cooling while being protected by a "tubular bumper." The open port at the tail housed the spare tire, which also functioned as a rear bumper.

For power, Sohus and Larkin selected a 4,700-cc (296 ci) Ford flathead ('48 Mercury) with three Stromberg carburetors. Bore was 3 3/8 inches, and stroke was 4 1/8 inches. With 9.5:1 compression, the engine developed 200 horsepower at 4,800 rpm.

The project was completed in two years at a cost of $1,800 and was well worth the time and cash. With an impressive ratio of 9.2 pounds per horsepower, the car ran the quarter-mile in 13.4 seconds (with a terminal speed of 102 miles per hour) and had a top speed of 125 miles per hour.

The Reynolds Wrap Special competed often and was run at Pomona, Paramount, and Santa Barbara, to name a few. The car had numerous top-ten overall finishes and several trips to the podium in class, including a win in class at Pomona. After sorting out the car's handling, Sohus and Larkin removed the flathead Ford in favor of the more powerful 383-ci Pontiac V-8.

REYNOLDS WRAP SPECIAL

Constructors	Bob Sohus and Jim Larkin
Year built	mid-1950s
Engines	4,700-cc (296 ci) Ford flathead ('48 Mercury); Pontiac V-8 (383 ci)
Gearbox	Ford three-speed (with Zephyr gears)
Chassis	ladder
Front suspension	live axle
Rear suspension	live axle
Brakes	Ford with aluminum bonds
Body material	aluminum
Weight, approx.	1,840 pounds
Wheelbase	100 inches
Length	140 inches
Height	38 inches
Cost when new	$1,800

Rutan Specials

Bill and Charles Rutan left their marks on road racing, but had even more impact on that most Northeastern of motor sports—hillclimbing. In 1952, the two brothers each bought new 26-horsepower Volkswagen Beetles and set to making them go faster. On Sundays, they would take their steeds to Thompson Speedway, where they could stage impromptu races. While Bill hopped up his engine by conventional methods, Charles relied on a supercharger.

Bathtub

Along the way, Bill sold his VW, but Charles bought a nasty '47 VW body and bolted it onto his '52 pan and running gear. At some point, he sawed off the top and removed the fenders, earning his raw-edged racer the nickname the Bathtub.

Originally it was supercharged, but Charles kept burning pistons, so he switched to an Okrasa kit with improved heads and carburetors. He was the terror of the Mount Washington Hillclimb, amassing a number of class wins in the early 1950s. In mid-1955, Bill bought the car from Charles.

Would you believe this decapitated VW took a minute off Carroll Shelby's best time (in a Ferrari F1 car) up Mount Washington? Bill Rutan did the trick in his Bathtub!
Mount Washington Auto Road collection

Rutan Porsche Special

About that time, Charles bought an ungainly VW special from Emil Pupilidy. It was based on a shortened VW Beetle platform with a fiberglass body that looked as if it had been poured over the chassis rather than molded. In back was a Porsche 1,100-cc engine with pistons and jugs leftover from one of the 1,100-cc Porsche Le Mans entries. Charles ran it in G-Modified for a while before selling it to Bill in 1957. Bill picked up a wrecked and burned Porsche 356

Carrera GS convertible and cannibalized it for parts. The four-cam 1,500-cc Carrera engine and drum brakes went onto the special, called the Rutan Porsche. Some improvements were made in the body, including the addition of a headrest. "It was absolutely evil," says Bill today. He was running on Michelin X radials and they would hold on tight, then suddenly let go with no warning.

In 1958, the little special got its big break. USAC fired up a road racing series for professional drivers. There were only four races on the schedule, and three of them were within easy towing range for Bill, so he signed up. At Lime Rock, he amazed the crowd by finishing fifth overall and third-in-class behind a Ferrari Testa Rossa and a Porsche RS Spyder. The next race was at Marlboro, and things got even better. He flew to fourth overall, second-in-class to another RS Spyder. Watkins Glen was the third round, and he picked up sixth overall, third-in-class at the checker. He would have had a shot at the championship if he made the tow to Riverside for the final race, but funds were short, so he passed.

After the season, Bill pulled out the Carrera engine and Porsche brakes and sold the car with a pushrod Porsche engine to a friend. According to Rutan, it was later destroyed.

The Bathtub Rides Again

But the engine lived on. Bill popped the hot Carrera into the Bathtub and it was once again the terror of the hills. In 1961, he streaked to fastest

225

time of day at Mount Washington, slashing over a minute off a record set in 1956 by Carroll Shelby in a Ferrari Formula 1 car. At that time, the road was gravel, and since Rutan still held the record when the road was later paved, his "gravel road" record still stands today.

Bill Rutan went on to bigger things. He won FC at the ARRC in 1967 (see Quantum entry, Chapter 2) and again in 1969 in a Tecno. Along the way, he drove many fast cars, and today he and Charles are still active in amateur-level racing. The Bathtub (with its hot Carrera powerplant) is still active on the hills, in the hands of the same drivers who took it to glory so long ago. Some stories do have happy endings.

RUTAN SPECIALS

BATHTUB
Constructors	**Bill and Charles Rutan**
Location built	**Moodus, Connecticut**
Year built	**1952**
Engines	**Volkswagen 1100, Porsche Carrera**
Gearbox	**four-speed**
Chassis	**platform**
Front suspension	**trailing link, torsion bar**
Rear suspension	**swing axles**
Brakes	**drum**
Body material	**steel**

RUTAN PORSCHE SPECIAL
Constructors	**Bill and Charles Rutan**
Location built	**Moodus, Connecticut**
Year built	**1958**
Engine	**Porsche Carrera**
Gearbox	**four-speed**
Chassis	**platform**
Front suspension	**trailing link, torsion bar**
Rear suspension	**swing axles**
Brakes	**Porsche drum**
Body material	**fiberglass**
Weight, approx.	**1,000 pounds**

We Talk With Bill Rutan.

AUTHOR: Tell me about the USAC car.

RUTAN: The Pupilidy Special is the one I had at those USAC races. It was built by a man in Long Island named Emil Pupilidy. I changed the brakes, went to larger brakes, but it was still absolutely evil. It had a short wheelbase, and all I had for tires were Michelin Xs. With a rear-engined concept, they were a little bit treacherous. They would stick, but when they let go they did so right away. It went right away on me a couple of times! Anyway, I was the highest aggregate finisher after the first three races, but I didn't go to Riverside because it was too far away and there was not enough money to even think about.

AUTHOR: What happened to it after you owned it?

RUTAN: I sold the car to a friend of mine, Bill Davis. We put a 1,600-cc rocker arm Porsche in it. We had a terrible time keeping rod bearings in it, I don't know why. We ran it in a couple of six-hour enduros they ran at Marlboro, Maryland. I loved those. We never did very well because we always ended up with rod bearings out of it, but it kept running anyway. You wouldn't believe the noise it made! We used Oilzum Crystal, a contemporary of Castrol R. It was thicker than hell. And although the bearings would burn up, it was still getting lubrication. We had fun with it.

AUTHOR: Tell me about the Bathtub.

RUTAN: It went pretty well for 61 cubic inches. In the middle of 1955, I bought the car and took the engine apart and put a Porsche 1,500-cc crank in it. I ended up with 1,280 cc or thereabouts. I ran it at Mount Washington and I did some hillclimbs in Pennsylvania, too. I did all right. When I got done with the USAC racing, I pulled the Carrera engine out [of the Rutan Porsche] and put it in the Bathtub. I

started taking it down to some hillclimbs in Pennsylvania and damned if I didn't start setting fastest times! It was a weird-looking creation, but it really went.

Sanitary Special

The Sanitary Special was built and raced by Ray Ingalls of Northern California. According to at least one source, the car was named for its neat and tidy construction. Ingalls used lightweight tubes to construct a lovely space frame. The front suspension and steering unit were from a Fiat Topolino. The rear suspension and gearbox were Volkswagen.

The body's center section was constructed of lightweight aluminum. The attractive nose and tail sections were fabbed of fiberglass by Lyle Powell and Malc Allen. The car was left-hand drive and had a small hood scoop and nose opening, the latter of which contained two recessed headlights. The fuel tank was mounted above the Volkswagen transmission and was an aircraft drum design.

A Crosley 750-cc single overhead cam engine that was overbored 0.030 inch provided power. Ingalls used Solex carburetors and set the compression ratio at 10:1. The engine produced 50 horsepower at 7,500 rpm and propelled the Sanitary Special to a top speed of 100 miles per

Ray Ingalls built the Sanitary Special (No. 199) from Fiat and Crosley parts. *Robert Rolofson Jr.; Robert H. Rolofson III collection*

hour. The use of the four-speed Volkswagen gearbox necessitated the fabrication of a special bearing to mate it to the front-mounted Crosley engine. The modification worked well—so well that Ingalls won the H-Modified class in the Northern California Region of the SCCA.

Satcher Special

D. G. Satcher built his California special in the late 1940s or early 1950s. Satcher built the car on a frame from a Miller sprint car and used a hodgepodge of parts from various cars. Power was supplied by a '37 flathead Ford V-8 with dual carburetors.

A Miller sprint car was the basis for the Satcher Special. *Dean Batchelor*

Schaghticoke Special

One car that was constructed very close to the Manning plan sets (see Manning in American Kit Car Manufacturers, Chapter 5) was the Schaghticoke Special, built by Wally Chapman in 1955. He bought the Manning plan set and built the car in the upstairs back bedroom of his grandmother's farmhouse in upstate New York. It was equipped with a Mercury flathead, a three-speed Ford gearbox, and Lincoln drum brakes. In 1955, John Streets arrived in the United States from England and bought the car from Chapman. He moved to Canada and raced the car there and in New York during the late 1950s. He sold the car in 1959, and it was soon wrecked. In 1991, Streets had the car replicated using the remains of the original car.

Chuck Manning sold a number of plan sets to prospective special builders. The Schaghticoke Special was one of them. *Harold Pace*

Schrafft-Fitch Crosley

George Schrafft (of Le Biplace Torpedo and 1951 Le Mans fame) and 1950s racing superstar John Fitch built this beautiful alloy-bodied Crosley special. The car was built in 1951 after Schrafft returned from Le Mans. Fitch designed the body, which was mated to a Crosley chassis. Although the car was quite attractive, it proved better as a street machine than as a racer.

Scorpion

The Scorpion was designed and built by the famous team of Dick Troutman and Tom Barnes in 1963. As the story goes, Troutman and Barnes were hired by J. C. Agajanian to build an Offenhauser-powered midengined Indy car to be entered in the 1964 Indy 500 with Parnelli Jones driving. As the ambitious constructors began to design Agajanian's car, they

227

SCORPION

Constructors	Dick Troutman and Tom Barnes
Location built	California
Year built	1963
Engine	Chevy V-8
Gearbox	Colotti T-37
Chassis	space frame
Front suspension	independent
Rear suspension	independent
Brakes	disc
Body material	aluminum

hit on the idea of doubling their output for the effort, so they simultaneously built a sports-racer with the same dimensions and suspension as the Indy car. This sports-racer became the Scorpion.

The special was constructed on a tube frame with a midship Chevy V-8 thumper built by Traco. Induction was by way of cross-flow Webers with power transferred through a Colotti T-37 transaxle. Brakes were disc all around, with the rears being inboard units. The body was a lovely alloy design reminiscent of the first Chaparral, also built by Troutman and Barnes. The Scorpion even rode on Chaparral "wobble wheels."

J. R. Fulp of South Carolina purchased the car in 1963. The two builders and Fulp settled on the car's name. The Scorpion was raced by Fulp during the 1964 and 1965 seasons and made a fair but not memorable showing. Later, John Lewis of Deland, Florida, bought the car from Fulp and began racing it with more success. In 1966, Lewis won the points championship for the Southeast Region of the SCCA.

The Scorpion was eventually put up and stored in a warehouse. Sadly, the building and car burned to the ground in a fire in the late 1960s.

Seifried Crosley

The Seifried Crosley was a frequent West Coast competitor in the H-Modified class. The Seifried father-

Don Miller takes the Seifried Crosley (No. 72) for a spin at Bakersfield in 1956. *Allen Kuhn*

and-son team, both named Richard, built the car. Seifried Sr. was a master craftsman and metal worker. In addition to building the body for the Seifried Crosley, he built the body for the lovely Seifried Special, also known as the Seifried Ford V-8 (see Seifried Special entry). The Seifried Crosley was an exceptional example of an early Crosley special—the build quality was outstanding, the design was lovely, and the car was competitive in its class.

SEIFRIED CROSLEY

Constructors	Richard Seifried Sr. and Richard Seifried Jr.
Location built	California
Year built	early 1950s
Engine	Crosley four-cylinder
Gearbox	three-speed
Chassis	ladder
Front suspension	live axle
Rear suspension	live axle

Seifried Special (Seifried Ford V-8)

In 1950, Richard Seifried Jr. decided to build a track roadster and commenced on its construction with great enthusiasm. At some point in the early stages

of the car's construction, Seifried had a change of heart and determined that what he really wanted to do was go road racing. So he tore down what he had started, tossed the frame to the side, and started over.

The Seifried Special (or Seifried Ford V-8) was built on a ladder frame of steel tubing. Seifried designed the frame with live-axle suspension with transverse leaf springs at the front and rear. Ford springs and Houdaille hydraulic shocks were used at all four corners. Brakes were Ford hydraulic units, and steering was from a 1924 Franklin, selected for its 8:1 ratio. The gearbox was a Ford three-speed with a column shifter. First and second gears were derived from a Lincoln Zephyr, a standard practice of road racers of the day. Drive went through a Hudson rear axle; a Cooke quick-change was located to the rear of the differential.

The beautiful alloy body was built by his father, Richard Seifried Sr., a master craftsman and sheet metal expert who had honed his craft while working on the famed Auto Unions prior to World War II. The sleek design had an elegant round grille, exposed head lamps, and cycle fenders at all four corners. The car was painted a stunning Chariot Red in a 12-coat lacquer finish. The car was so nice that it was featured on the September 1952 cover of *Mechanix Illustrated*.

To move the delightful creation, Seifried Jr. installed a 296-ci Mercury V-8 with Offenhauser heads. Induction was by way of three Stromberg 97 carburetors, and a Potvin ignition and cam were used. With a compression ratio of 10:1, the engine produced 190 horsepower at 5,200 rpm. The car ran 14.88 in the standing quarter-mile with a terminal velocity of 104 miles per hour. The car's top speed was 140 miles per hour.

At the racetrack, the car had its share of success. The Seifried Special won the El Segundo Sports Car Drags in June 1951. Seifried won again in August at the Carrell Speedway Road Races and finished fifth in October at Palm Springs.

The Seifried Special was a well-built car that got a lot of press in its day. *Dean Batchelor*

SEIFRIED SPECIAL

Constructors	Richard Seifried Jr. and Richard Seifried Sr.
Location built	California
Year built	1950
Engine	Mercury V-8
Gearbox	Ford three-speed
Chassis	ladder
Front suspension	live axle
Rear suspension	live axle
Brakes	drum
Body material	aluminum
Weight, approx.	2,030 pounds
Wheelbase	103 inches
Height	36 inches
Cost when new	$2,600

SHE Special

Jack Ensley was an Indy car driver in the late 1950s when he decided to build a Chevy-powered special to go after the road racing crowd. A space frame was constructed by J. Silnas and H. Hudler (whose initials, combined with Ensley's, formed the name SHE) and fitted with solid axles at both ends. Kurtis-style torsion bars provided springing, and four-wheel disc brakes, knock-off hubs, and Dunlop perforated wheels were borrowed from a D-Type Jaguar. The body was built from 16-gauge aluminum and had a Scarab look to it.

A McGurk-prepared 341-ci Chevy wore Hillborn fuel injection, a Winfield cam, Spalding ignition, and an aluminum flywheel. The engine was also offset to the right 1 1/2 inches. Although it was a neat and professionally built special, the era of live axles was over and SHE never featured prominently in the results.

SHE SPECIAL

Constructor	Jack Ensley, J. Silnas, and H. Hudler
Location built	Indianapolis, Indiana
Year built	1959
Engine	Chevy V-8
Gearbox	Corvette four-speed
Front suspension	live axle
Rear suspension	live axle
Brakes	disc
Body material	aluminum
Weight, approx.	1,860 pounds
Wheelbase	87 inches

Shingle Corvettie

After Ken Miles had moved on to other projects, his fabulous R-2 (see Flying Shingle entry) was sold and raced at local events in Northern California. Later on, the car was again sold, beginning the story of the Shingle Corvettie.

The new owner of the Flying Shingle was Phil Washburn, an auto mechanic from Oakland, California. Washburn removed the R-2's MG burner and began to dream up ideas for a new under-2-liter powerplant. When he couldn't find what he was looking for, he set out on a plan that could hardly be classified as an obvious choice. With help from Bob Eelsing and Guy Singleton, Washburn built a Chevy V-4 by cutting a V-8 in half.

In order to accomplish this trick, the team welded the open side of the transected '55 Chevy block with steel plate. Vulcan Grinding was called on to design a new crankshaft, but Washburn performed the actual

SHINGLE CORVETTIE

Constructors	Phil Washburn, Bob Eelsing, and Guy Singleton
Location built	Oakland, California
Year built	late 1950s
Engine	1960-cc Chevy V-4 (from a V-8 cut in half)
Gearbox	Corvette four-speed
Weight, approx.	1,330 pounds

fabrication. Numerous additional engine modifications were carried out to make the chopped motor perform. A custom exhaust manifold was fabricated for Stromberg 97 carburetors. The finished V-4 had a displacement of 1,960 cc and produced 121 horsepower. At just 1,330 pounds, the car exited the standing quarter-mile at just under 100 miles per hour.

Shiva

J. D. Snyder built this G-Modified sports-racer in the late 1950s from the remains of a Lotus 11. However, Snyder built his own midengined chassis to house the Coventry-Climax FWA engine and Volkswagen transaxle. The Lotus Wobbly Web wheels were also used.

The Shiva was a midengined sports-racer built from Lotus 11 parts. *Barry Heuer collection*

The Siam was an engineering student project that made it to the track. *Harold Pace*

Siam Special

The Siam Special was built in 1954 at Purdue University as a class project for engineering students. They chose to build their race car for the popular H-Modified class, where they thought the competition would be easier. For power, they went with the usual Crosley 750, backed up by a Standard (later Triumph) four-speed transmission. The team made its own simple ladder frame based on 4-inch round tubes. In front, Crosley front suspension was widened with spacers for a wider track, and in back, a Fiat Topolino axle and drum brakes were sprung with coil springs. Crosley drums provided stopping power up front.

A Fibersport fiberglass body was used, somewhat modified with a homemade grille and a small aluminum hood that could be raised for maintenance. Aluminum aircraft seats saved weight inside, and the Siam sported right-hand drive. The grille was later removed and a set of headlights located inside the grille opening. The colorful name came from the car's nose emblem, which was pried off a Siam refrigerator the builders had found in a trash dump.

The Crosley engine was modified over the time it was raced, finally receiving a billet crank, Divco truck dual-point distributor, a one-off Weber cam, and dual Solex 32 PBIC carburetors. The compres-

sion was raised by removing the steel plate between the block and crankcase, and the pistons were stock Crosley. Bruce Townsend, who also built the Townsend Special (see Townsend Specials entry), built the engine. The exhaust pipe ran through the side of the body and connected to a piece of flex pipe that bent down the side of the car. The car was originally painted blue, but was later refinished in dark green.

The Siam was bought and first run by Frank Isaacson, one of the students involved in the manufacture. Bill Mays, whose father built the Fibersport body, recalls the first time the Siam crew came to the races. "At the first race, the guys from Purdue were talking about how the 'H' cars didn't have any real engineers designing the cars, so

Purdue was going to show everybody how to really design and build race cars. The first race, they ran dead last in a field of about 20 'H' cars. They went back to the drawing boards!" The Siam improved to be an occasional winner and was later run out of legendary H-Modified guru Sandy MacArthur's shop. After Isaacson sold the car in the late 1950s, it went through many hands and was raced through 1964. The Siam was parked that year and has survived in unmodified form.

Sidewinder

Emmet Draddy in Fort Worth, Texas, built a regionally successful A Sports-Racer called the Sidewinder. The first version had a midmounted transverse Buick aluminum V-8 (reportedly with chain drive) combined with a simple body shell and go kart-style suspension. It was light, quick, and deadly.

It was rebuilt with real suspension following a crash. A final incarnation appeared around 1970, when the Sidewinder was switched to a conventional longitudinal engine mounting and a homemade two-speed transaxle. Draddy was tied in with the various aerospace companies in the Texas area (such as Bell Helicopter) and could have components fabricated to a high standard. Sporting a sleek, modern, wedge-shaped body, a high-mounted wing, and a full-house

The Sidewinder started life with a transverse engine and simple white bodywork. *Harold Pace*

Later, the Sidewinder acquired a more angular body, a longitudinal engine mounting, and a big wing. *Harold Pace*

Rover V-8 with four Webers, it was a potent weapon in SCCA national races. Driven by Walt Mays and sponsored by Texas Leisure Chair, it frequently outran McLarens and Lolas at tracks such as Green Valley in Texas and Ponca City, Oklahoma.

SIDEWINDER

Constructors	**Emmet Draddy (International Motorsport Enterprises)**
Location built	**Fort Worth, Texas**
Year built	**late 1960s**
Engine	**Buick/Rover V-8**
Gearbox	**two-speed**
Front suspension	**independent**
Rear suspension	**independent**
Brakes	**disc**
Body material	**fiberglass**

Silver Bomb

Dean Batchelor and Captain Jim Frostrom were each very active in racing and building cars from the late 1940s to the mid-1960s. Batchelor had many successful Dry Lakes cars and Frostrom was an avid tech inspector and aircraft mechanic. They were both members of the Valley Drifters car club. In the mid-1950s, the two got together and began to dream of an all-new car . . . the Silver Bomb.

The Batchelor/Frostrom Silver Bomb had an attractive Mistral body. *Keith Harmer collection*

The Silver Bomb was constructed in a 300-foot-long chicken coop-turned-garage in Sun Valley, California, adjacent to the runway at Lockheed. The original plan was that the car would be built as a street rod/sports car special based on Batchelor's Jag XK-120. When an offer too good to pass on was received on the Jag, a new chassis was made with the same basic dimensions of an XK-120. Ford was the hot setup for rods of the day, and '34 Ford C-rails were formed into box rails on each side. Suspension was live axle front and rear. Brakes were Nash drums, and instruments were Ford.

A Microplas fiberglass nose and rear section formed a portion of the bodywork. Dean's good friend Neil Emory of Valley Customs fabricated the remainder (center section, cockpit, cowl, firewall) of aluminum. Emory, a top-notch aluminum man, also built the body for a Batchelor Bonneville car. The original powerplant was a 283 Chevy with three two-barrels on an Offy manifold with a Duntov cam. A Ford three-speed was installed with a custom-made remote shifter located 10 inches behind the transmission in order to avoid using a side shifter. The three-speed was quickly changed out for a Chevy four-speed for its obvious advantages.

The Silver Bomb competed in the Lockheed Sportscar Club drag races and other local events. At one point, the car won a Lockheed 24-hour rally. It also competed in SCCA rallies and minor events. The car underwent some development, and the front end was changed to Jag XK-140/150 as soon as it became available.

Eventually, Frostrom bought out Batchelor's half of the car and relocated to Atlanta. In 1963, the car was converted to an all-out racer when Frostrom installed a Chevy 327 engine, Corvette independent rear suspension, and larger rims and tires. The car competed through the 1965 race season. Later, Frostrom sold the car and lost track of it. It eventually resurfaced and changed hands a few times. The car is now owned and vintage raced by Keith Harmer of New York.

232

We Talk With Jim Frostrom.

AUTHOR: What is your most vivid memory of building the car with Batchelor?

FROSTROM: Halfway through the construction, I moved from Burbank to Sunland. There was a single-story garage apartment/guesthouse around back that was not attached to the rest of the house. The garage wasn't big enough for all the work we had to do. So we took out the wall and finished the car in the bedroom of the guesthouse.

AUTHOR: And your fondest memory of racing the car?

FROSTROM: I finished second in West Virginia in '61, or '62, or '64, beaten by a pure Ferrari racing car. That wasn't too bad.

Simca Specials

See Barlow Simcas entry.

Simon LaDawri-Packard

David Simon, an architect from Youngstown, Ohio, built this one-off special with the help of David Dangerfield. A space frame was constructed from 2-inch tubing (0.065-inch wall thickness), with master welder Dangerfield doing most of the work.

Most of the other components, other than the LaDawri Conquest fiberglass body, were harvested from mechanical corpses found at local junkyards. Front suspension was by Ford transverse leaf springs with equal A-arms and Monroe piston shock absorbers. The rear suspension was a Studebaker live axle with the transverse leaf springs from a '34 Ford and Monroe shocks. Brakes were aluminum drums from Buick with backing plates from Packard. A modified steering unit from Pontiac was utilized on this left-hand-drive special. The 20-gallon fuel tank, borrowed from an airplane, was located in the rear.

Simon powered his car using a 6,511-cc Packard V-8 from a '56 model. With 11:1 compression and two Carter four-barrel carburetors, the mighty block produced 380 ponies at 5,500 rpm. The gearbox was a three-speed unit from a '54 Packard.

Singer Special

The Singer Special was the brainchild of Kelly Buchanan, who bought a totaled '52 Singer and built it up as a race car. Buchanan constructed a space frame from metal tubing with the help of Bob Arnt. The front suspension and rear axle were salvaged from the Singer, as were the brakes and the disc wheels. A specially designed torque reactor arm was used in the rear with Morris Minor torsion bars. The rack-and-pinion steering unit was from a Morris Minor mated to a 1940 Buick steering column.

The body was one of the first totally epoxy constructions of its kind. Singer hired North American Aviation to do the work, and Dick Seifried and Dick Snider were largely responsible for the project. The finished roadster was quite attractive and reminiscent of a Jaguar C-Type.

To motivate the 1,200-pound missile, Buchanan did a lot of work on the 1,500-cc Singer motor. A Harmon & Collins racing camshaft was used, and many of the internals were balanced and reworked by Edelbrock. In an effort to lower the car, the motor was laid over on its side 45 degrees; a dry-sump oiling system was therefore installed.

The car was completed in 1,500 man-hours, at a cost of $900, and was very fast. It scored an impressive five consecutive top-qualifying times at five different events. Unfortunately, the Singer Special turned out to be more of a qualifier than a racer and was plagued by spins, DNFs, and crashes.

Snow Crosley

See Manta Ray entry.

Sohus-Larkin Special

See Reynolds Wrap Special entry.

Solitary Wasp

This car was also known as the Mar-Chris Special (see Mar-Chris Special entry).

The rebodied Solitary Wasp dices with Ken Miles' Porsche at Riverside. *Allen Kuhn*

Sorrell-Larkin Special

Bob Sorrell was one of the real talents of the 1950s and 1960s, and his fabulous creations were seen across many arenas, including road racing, land

The Sorrell-Larkin Special had a short life.
Tam McPartland

speed record attempts, and drag racing. He was a gifted fabricator and a genius with aluminum and fiberglass bodywork. Wadded-up race cars did not scare Sorrell, so it was no surprise when he bought the twisted wreckage of a Lister-Chevrolet that the Fike Plumbing Racing Team of Phoenix, Arizona, had been campaigning. (Al Dean of Dean Van Lines previously owned the car.) After winning the consolation race in the Lister, driver Don Hulette found himself in the field of the 1960 Los Angeles Times Grand Prix. Unfortunately, the glory of the win was short-lived, as Hulette flipped the car end-over-end in turn two and set it on fire, just for good measure. Sorrel wound up with the car and became determined to make it a winner.

Sorrell had a shop in Westchester, California, and brought the balled-up mess back to work on it. He straightened and modified the frame, changed out the brakes, and installed a monster Chevy V-8 built by Jim Larkin. The car received a Sorrell fiberglass body that was laid up by Jim's younger brother, Mike. It was finished off in a unique red, white, and blue paint scheme, with the colors applied as three stripes running the length of the car.

The racer, now running as the Sorrell-Larkin Special, first appeared at a Cal Club race at Riverside Raceway in 1961 with Eric Hauser at the helm. Hauser found the car's handling and braking diabolical and had a poor showing. Sorrell thought a

different driver might make a difference and had Jack Breskovitch give it a try. Breskovitch wasn't a fan of the car either, and he didn't like its manners. So Sorrell got another driver, who turned out to be the car's last driver. Bob Johnson was given the duty at a race at Riverside in March 1962, and it didn't take long for things to heat up. During the first practice session, Johnson put the car over the fence at turn one. Just as in Hulette's incident, the car burst into flames. Unfortunately, the magnesium wheels caught fire, and this time it could not be extinguished. The car was so badly burned that it was buried where it had come to rest near turn one. In an ironic twist, the Sorrell-Larkin Special's final resting place was not far from the spot where Hauser had ended Old Yaller I's career, one year earlier.

SORRELL-LARKIN SPECIAL

Constructors	Bob Sorrell, Jim Larkin
Location built	Westchester, California
Body by	Bob Sorrell, Mike Larkin
Years built	1960–1961
Engine	Chevrolet V-8
Gearbox	four-speed
Chassis	Lister ladder
Front suspension	independent
Rear suspension	de Dion
Brakes	disc
Body material	fiberglass

Sorrell-Manning Special

Bob Sorrell designed and built this road racing special in the early 1950s. The frame was a chrome-moly ladder from Chuck Manning and was set up for an American V-8 powerplant. Sorrell designed and hand laid an outrageous fiberglass streamliner body and fitted the car with Borrani wire wheels. This car was continuously owned by Sorrell, and was in storage until the time of his passing. The car was found in a storage container in California in 2002.

The Sorrell-Manning Special had a chassis from Chuck Manning and an outrageous streamliner fiberglass body from Bob Sorrell. *Mark Brinker collection*

SORRELL-MANNING SPECIAL	
Constructors	Bob Sorrell, Chuck Manning
Location built	Westchester, California
Body by	Bob Sorrell
Year built	early 1950s
Chassis	ladder
Brakes	drum
Body material	fiberglass
Wheelbase	101 inches
Length	173 inches
Height	38 inches

SPAD

Don Bolen built a nifty H-Modified in 1964 with the idea of promoting the sale of its fiberglass body to other special builders. Bolen's SPAD bodies weighed 48 pounds and were molded in four parts: nose, tail, and two center sections. The chassis was conventional, with a space frame mounting fabricated A-arm suspension and coil-over shocks. A Fiat 600 transaxle was bolted to a Fiat 600 engine, although Bolen planned to change to Renault Dauphine power.

SPAD	
Constructor	Don Bolen
Location built	Portland, Oregon
Year built	1964
Engine	Fiat 600/Renault
Gearbox	four-speed
Chassis	space frame
Front suspension	independent, coil springs
Rear suspension	independent, coil springs
Brakes	Fiat drum
Body material	fiberglass
Weight, approx.	800 pounds

Starkweather Crosley

Ralph Starkweather was the quintessential low-budget specials builder. By his own account (in a hilarious article in the March 1960 issue of *Sports Car Graphic),* the car was the result of a deal he struck with his wife and a traffic accident. He agreed to quit racing in Class C and D and to limit his activity to the low-budget Class-H cars. The traffic accident provided him with an insurance check that provided a new racing "bankroll." With cash to spend, Starkweather found a man with a storage room full of small-bore equipment. He handed over the insurance check. Feeling like an H-Modified fat cat, he trailered the stuff home and filled the family garage with Crosley engines, a chrome-moly space frame, and the like.

Starkweather thoroughly reworked the space frame until all that remained original were the basic 1 3/4-inch backbone tubes. At the front, a plan was executed to allow for the mounting of a solid axle and stock Crosley elliptic springs. Because Starkweather planned to build the racer as a right-hand driver, several modifications were performed on the steering mechanisms and assemblies. At the rear, the members were designed to accept inverted Crosley elliptic springs.

Starkweather selected the Crosley engine because it was cheap . . . and he got four in the insurance deal. He built a special hoist from 2x4s, because he was unable to lift the 150-pound four-banger by himself (and was unable to obtain assistance from his wife or comrades). As he wrote, "Incidentally, one of the problems confronting the special builder is 'aloneness,' for the attrition rate of able-bodied helpers is quite high. Friends, avid sports car enthusiasts though they may be, some-how are not driven for long by the same burning ambition as the builder's to see the bomb blaze away from the start-finish line." The hoist did the trick and he lowered the engine and tranny into position. Starkweather then finished the frame with additional supporting structures and a roll hoop and went inside for a rest.

"I emerged from the garage long enough to reestablish an acquaintance with my wife, whose name I fortunately recalled, and with my children, who by this time had grown several inches. They all seemed to be quite happy and well adjusted, so I beat a hasty retreat back into the shop to start work on the body."

Starkweather built a male mold for his all-new body from plyscore formers, expanded metal lath, and Hydrocal molding plaster. He built the mold directly on the car's space frame. Next, he built a female mold and used it to pull the final body shell, which was cut into sections and then reassembled on the car. The finished body was a real eye-catcher, somewhere between a Lotus 11 and a Bonneville streamliner.

After $1,100 and 1,000 man-hours, the car's first outing at the Riverside Grand Prix was less than auspicious. Pulling out of the pits for the first practice session, the water pump failed and the engine internals melted. Undaunted, Starkweather returned to his garage and went back to work.

Sterling Edwards Special

See Edwards Special entry.

Stiles/Shrafft Crosley

See Le Biplace Torpedo entry.

Stovebolt Special

Few racing cars, if any, had so many legendary personalities work on them as the HWM-Chevy known as the Stovebolt Special. The car started life in 1949 at Hersham and Walton Motors (HWM) in England, where it was fitted with a 1,960-cc Alta four-cylinder engine. As one of three cars designed to contest the 1950 Formula 2 series, the Stovebolt Special featured fully independent suspension via transverse leaf springs and a simple but strong ladder frame. Enter the first legend—the team of cars was prepared by Alf Francis, one of the best-known mechanics and team managers in English racing history. Despite being underfinanced and down on power to the Italian opposition, mechanic/fabricator/tuner/team manager Francis made sure the cars were always neatly turned out and prepared to the limit. One was driven by a youngster all would come to know in short order—Stirling Moss. Moss first made his name at the Bari Grand Prix, where an underdog HWM driven by the unknown kid finished third to two supercharged Alfa Romeo Alfettas and ahead of all the factory Maseratis and Ferraris. Moss was the second legend associated with this car.

After setting Moss off on his legendary career, the Stovebolt Special was sold to a Swiss driver, then to 20th Century Fox for a movie called *The Racers*. (In England, it was called *Such Men Are Dangerous*). At the start of the movie, the HWM (painted red and identified as an early "Burano") was driven by fiery Italian upstart Gino Borgesa, played with an American accent by Kirk Douglas. The HWM came to a fiery end early in the film when Borgesa swerved to avoid a dog that had run into the road. The film showed the car bounding over a curb and crashing into a wall before catching fire.

That scene broke Tom Carstens' heart. Carstens was the Tacoma, Washington, business executive who owned the most successful Cadillac-Allard J2X on the West Coast. He loved big, brutal racing cars with muscular V-8s, but by 1955, the day of the Allard had passed. When he saw the HWM, it was love at first sight. Here was a no-nonsense racer with independent suspension, rack-and-pinion steering, and a low, lean, cycle-fendered body. Carstens contacted 20th Century Fox to see about buying the wreckage and was relieved to find the car was unhurt; the crash scene had been done with models. However, the movie company would only sell the HWM as a package with two late-model Ferraris and two Maseratis also featured in the film. Carstens accepted, and immediately unloaded the Italian iron and set to work on the HWM.

To power his creation, Carstens chose the spanking new 1955 Chevy 265-ci V-8. Although hot rodders and stock car aces were already snatching them up, only a few Corvettes had ventured onto a road racetrack with Chevy Chief Engineer Ed Cole's rip-roaring V-8. Carstens was impressed with its potential. It was much lighter than any other domestic OHV V-8 and no heavier than the flathead Ford. But in 1955, there weren't many people who knew how to modify one for racing.

The crew that Carstens rounded up for the project reads like a who's who of American racing royalty. First stop was at Vic Edelbrock's shop, where Carstens' Cadillac engines had been built. Engine wizard Bobby Meeks was turned loose on the project. The block was bored out 1/8 inch and

The Stovebolt Special was the happy marriage of an English Formula 2 car and a Chevy V-8. *Harold Pace*

The Stovebolt Special was the first Chevy-powered special to take on the Italian exotica. *Harold Pace*

the crank welded up and offset-ground to increase the stroke, bringing displacement to just under 5 liters. Special JE pistons were made up, and the heads were milled 0.060 inches to give 10.5:1 compression. The heads were ported and cleaned up. Edelbrock also ground a one-off cam that made

power up to 7,000 rpm. An Edelbrock intake manifold mounted three Holley carburetors with linkage fabricated by Carstens' crew. Spaulding dual-point, twin-coil ignition replaced the stock Chevy distributor. An adapter was fabricated to attach the Chevy to a four-speed, close-ratio Jaguar D-Type gearbox.

Eddie Kuzma, the Los Angeles fabricator already famous as an Indy car builder, took on the job of installing the engine into the tight confines of the old F2. Kuzma fabricated engine mounts, moved back the firewall, and fabricated a new tail with a headrest from aluminum. After Kuzma was finished with his part, the car was shipped across town to Ted Halibrand's shop. (Legend number six so far, and that's not counting Kirk Douglas).

Halibrand cast a special housing for his quick-change rear end unit that would allow it to be bolted to the frame and made side plates to hold the U-joints that attached to the half shafts. Halibrand also replaced the stock drum brakes with his own disc brakes (a mixed blessing). Any other legends we haven't mentioned? How about Dick Troutman and Tom Barnes, who fabricated a tubular steel clamp to hold the rear end in place? After that, Carstens and his volunteer pit crew finished the detailing and got it ready to race.

So with all this talent and experience, the Stovebolt Special was a screaming winner, right? The first time out at Pebble Beach in 1956 found driver Bill Pollack blasting past every Ferrari on the straights but sliding luridly around the turns after the differential locked up and stopped differentiating. The Stovebolt was a nifty car, but a few years too late. By 1956, the Ferraris, Maseratis, and D-Type Jaguars had advanced to another level and the Stovebolt was never in the hunt. It faded into the obscurity of club racing during the early 1960s. It was restored by John Masterson in the 1980s and has been involved in vintage events ever since. In 2004, it even appeared at the Pebble Beach concours, a testament to its fine looks and splendid pedigree.

STOVEBOLT SPECIAL

Constructor	**Tom Carstens**
Location built	**Tacoma, Washington**
Year built	**1956**
Engine	**Chevy V-8**
Gearbox	**Jaguar four-speed**
Chassis	**ladder**
Front suspension	**independent**
Rear suspension	**independent**
Brakes	**disc**
Body material	**aluminum**

Sulprizio-Hagemann GMC

See Hagemann GMC entry.

Summers Ford Roadster

See Vogel/Balchowsky Special entry.

Super Sport Special

Although Joe Goss and Jerry Richards originally built the Super Sport Special to take MG power, it is best known as the temporary home of the Taylor Super Sport engine (see Taylor Super Sport engine entry, Chapter 6). The car had a simple space frame with a Kurtis-style solid axle in front and swing axles in back sprung by torsion bars. A Halibrand rear end and Lincoln 12-inch drum brakes were used.

Goss, Richards, and John Adykes made an aluminum body that featured simple lines with a clumsy nose, protruding headlights, and a low-slung grille. After two years of racing, it was sold to Hank Tubman, who installed the prototype Super Sport SOHC engine in 1958. It was not a success.

The Super Sport Special still had an MG engine when this photo was taken. *Dean Batchelor*

Ted Roberts soon bought the car and completely reworked the body with a graceful nose featuring covered headlights. He rebuilt the Taylor engine with Hillborn fuel injection and bolted it to a Corvette four-speed gearbox. In testing, the Super Sport Special was clocked at 162 miles per hour, but the engine was plagued with development gremlins, and a Corvette V-8 was later installed. The car has survived, but the Taylor engine has disappeared.

SUPER SPORT SPECIAL

Constructors	Joe Gross and Jerry Richards
Year built	circa 1956
Engines	MG, Taylor, Chevy
Gearbox	Borg-Warner T-10 four-speed
Front suspension	live axle
Rear suspension	swing axle
Brakes	Lincoln drum
Body material	aluminum
Weight, approx.	1,160 pounds
Wheelbase	94 inches
Number built	1

Swiss Cheese Special

Jack Anderson of Barnyard Autoworks, Fresno, California, built the Swiss Cheese Special in 1953 from a wrecked right-hand-drive 1950 MG TD. Anderson widened the front crossmember 9 inches and lowered it 6 inches. The engine was mounted 10 inches back and was lowered 4 inches. The original bodywork was discarded, and the car-to-be was lightened substantially by drilling a multitude of holes in the frame rails and running gear, creating a Swiss cheese appearance. To complete the package, Anderson and his brother fabricated a lovely one-off aluminum body and installed a custom grille.

Anderson raced the car through 1958, competing at many of the premier venues of the day, including Pebble Beach, Palm Springs, Golden Gate Park, Stockton, and Santa Barbara. Anderson kept the car in as-raced condition (including its original engine) in a barn until 1994, when it was sold to Kenny Rogers, who restored it for vintage racing.

The Swiss Cheese Special never won a race, nor was it ever driven by anyone famous, but it continues to be raced in its original state more than 50 years after its birth.

SWISS CHEESE SPECIAL

Constructor	Jack Anderson
Location built	Fresno, California
Year built	1953
Engine	MG
Gearbox	four-speed
Chassis	ladder
Front suspension	independent
Rear suspension	live axle
Body material	aluminum

The Swiss Cheese Special was lightened to within an ounce of its life. *Kenny Rogers collection*

Tanner Specials

Martin Tanner wore many hats: artist, athlete, businessman, painter, bridge champion, boat builder, advertising executive, sculptor, and, of course, race car designer and driver. Although he was unquestionably eccentric, he was well liked and equally respected. In the summer of 1954, Tanner decided to go racing. His earliest rides were in an MG and an Austin-Healey, but as with all other aspects of his life, Tanner decided to do things a little differently. He decided to build his own race cars.

Tanner T-1

His first effort was the Tanner T-1, also sometimes referred to as the Martin-T. The car was a jewel box, no doubt the result of Tanner's countless hours spent planning every aspect of its construction. From simple drawings he moved to more detailed plans and then to a full-scale mock-up built from cardboard. The planning phase took a full six months, but it was well worth the effort. Once under way, the actual construction time was only about 30 weeks.

Tanner built the T-1 frame from aluminum tubing. To keep weight down, he drilled extensively in all nonstressed areas. All formed surfaces were constructed of aluminum; the firewall and floorboards were constructed from magnesium. The front suspension was a leaf spring from Fiat with two wishbones. The rear suspension was composed of a system of parallel leading arms with a Panhard rod for lateral location. Brakes at both ends were Alfin drums from a Fiat 1100; 10-inch units were used up front with 8-inch units at the rear. The steering mechanism was from a Fiat 500.

The left-hand-drive car had a very pretty aluminum-skinned body, which Tanner formed by hand. The car had a short windscreen, full-width roll bar, wire wheels, and a lovely grille, which was also a Tanner design. The headlights were from an Indian motorcycle with 12-volt bulbs from a 1942 fire truck.

To move the 720-pound T-1, Tanner selected what many H-Moders of the day were using—the mighty little Crosley four-banger. Not content with a stock CIBA unit, Tanner installed a stroked forged-steel crankshaft. He also used a racing camshaft, a Braje crankcase and sump, and magnesium connecting rods. Induction was by twin Amal carburetors with compression set at 10.25:1. The car produced 45 horsepower at 7,000 revs.

After a few initial outings in 1957, Tanner decided that the car needed more oomph. The Crosley motor was set aside, and a 750-cc Saab powerplant was installed, which turned out to be a very good decision. Tanner and the T-1 captured the 1958 National Championship in the H-Modified class.

Tanner T-2 through T-7

The Saab-powered T-2 and T-3 followed the T-1. The T-3 was a real runner and beat a gaggle of OSCAs at Cumberland in 1960. The T-3 was rebodied as the T-4 after a racing incident at Meadowdale. Tanner raced this new car through the 1962 season, scoring several class wins.

The T-5 was Tanner's first fiberglass-bodied car and was essentially a plastic version of the T-4. A mold was made of the T-4 that served as a source for future Tanner fiberglass bodies. Tanner used an Austin-Healey gearbox in the T-5 and fabricated his own gear-sets. He also designed special magnesium racing wheels for the car. Weber carburetors were now used, and the Saab's compression was upped.

When the frame of the T-5 started to fatigue, Tanner purchased a frame made of steel tubing and built the T-6. Later, he built his final car, the midengined Tanner T-7.

Tanner was forced to retire from racing in the latter part of the 1960s because of problems with his eyesight. By that time, he was on to a new and exciting career designing and selling kayaks. Unfortunately, he passed away suddenly of a heart attack in 1969. While his time here was all too short, his fabulously constructed specials from Saginaw serve as a reminder of what this period of American racing history was all about.

Martin Tanner's first racer was the T-1; it won an SCCA National Championship in 1958. *Gene Leasure collection*

The Tanner T-3 was very quick and could take on an OSCA in an even fight. *Gene Leasure collection*

The Tanner T-2 (No. 53) was an improved design that switched from Crosley to Saab power. *Gene Leasure collection*

The Tanner T-4 was a rebodied T-3. *Gene Leasure collection*

The Tanner T-6 was the last front-engined Tanner racing car. *Gene Leasure collection*

Tanner switched to a fiberglass body for the T-5. *Gene Leasure collection*

TANNER SPECIALS

TANNER T-1

Constructor	**Martin Tanner**
Location built	**Saginaw, Michigan**
Years built	**1956–1957**
Engines	**Crosley CIBA four-cylinder; later 750-cc Saab three-cylinder**
Gearbox	**four-speed**
Chassis	**space frame**
Front suspension	**independent**
Rear suspension	**live axle**
Brakes	**drum**
Body material	**aluminum**
Weight, approx.	**720 pounds**

TANNER T-2

Constructor	**Martin Tanner**
Location built	**Saginaw, Michigan**
Year built	**1959**
Engine	**Saab three-cylinder**
Body material	**aluminum**

TANNER T-3 AND T-4

Constructor	**Martin Tanner**
Location built	**Saginaw, Michigan**
Year built	**1960**
Engine	**Saab three-cylinder**
Body material	**aluminum**

TANNER T-5 AND T-6

Constructor	**Martin Tanner**
Location built	**Saginaw, Michigan**
Year built	**1962**
Engine	**Saab**
Body material	**fiberglass**

Tatum-GMC

In 1952, Chuck Tatum attended a sports car race in his hometown of Stockton, California. That evening in the watering hole of a local hotel, Tatum and three friends (Phil Hill, Sam Weiss, and Doug Trotter) were discussing the relative merits of the cars they saw racing earlier in the day. The group concluded that most of the front-runners were cars imported from Europe. At one point in the discussion, Tatum stated he could build a car out of American parts that would beat all of the foreign stuff. He considered the Allard, one of the fastest cars at the races, to be nothing but a big American hot rod in English disguise. The next day, Tatum shared some of his ideas with Trotter regarding how to build a winning all-American road race car. Tatum was young and energetic and had several years of experience with both building and driving stock cars, sprint cars, and track roadsters. His ideas for a road racer incorporated features from these types of cars.

Over the winter of 1952–1953, Tatum began constructing the car in a shop behind his house. He assembled a light but very rigid frame using thin wall (0.049 inch) seamless tubing of 2-inch diameter. Front suspension was taken from a '32 Ford, and the spindles were '39 Ford. The rear suspension was initially from a '41 Ford pickup truck with leaf springs. Later during construction, Tatum designed a coil spring suspension system with bars to locate the position of the rear axle. Steering was '40 Ford with a custom-made, extra long pitman arm to improve steering.

Tatum considered several options for the engine before choosing the six-cylinder 270-ci GMC truck engine. The GMC unit was very strong and when bored out resulted in 302 ci. The GMC engine was 25 pounds lighter and more reliable than the popular V-8 flathead Ford and 200 to 300 pounds lighter than powerplants from Cadillac and Chrysler. At the time, the GMC engine was being used in sprint

Two classics take to the track. The Parkinson Jaguar and the Tatum-GMC look as if they stepped out of a time machine. *Harold Pace*

cars, and some speed equipment was available. Tatum used a modified truck cylinder head and installed a Mallory distributor for the ignition. He designed a special intake manifold to mount three side-draft Carter carburetors from a '53 Corvette. The transmission was a Lincoln Zephyr, and the brakes were Kinmont discs. Both the transmission and brakes proved to be less than satisfactory and were later changed.

The finished chassis was taken to Jack Hagemann of San Leandro, California, for the

The Tatum-GMC used a GMC engine instead of the more common flathead Ford. *Harold Pace*

construction of an alloy body, to be formed after a design by Arden Farey, a friend of Tatum. Hagemann was accustomed to doing his own design work and didn't care much for the shape of Farey's design, but agreed to take the job anyway. When the body was complete, Hagemann modified his usual badging from "Designed by & Built by Jack Hagemann" to read "Built by Jack Hagemann." The original body had cycle fenders, but they had a propensity for falling off and being run over during race outings. After several unsuccessful attempts to fix the problem with various arrangements of brackets, the car was returned to Hagemann for the construction and installation of more conventional fenders.

Construction was completed in the spring of 1953 and the car was entered in its first race at Golden Gate Park in San Francisco. At that time, the Sports Car Club of America was a strictly amateur organization and didn't allow professional drivers to compete. Tatum had been racing sprint cars professionally and didn't qualify as an amateur, so he asked his friend Chuck Manning to pilot the Tatum in its first race. The car was an immediate success with Manning driving the car to a first-place finish. The car went on to another three wins during the 1953 season at Madera, Stockton, and Santa Barbara. After sitting out a full year, by SCCA rules, Chuck Tatum was able to return to amateur SCCA racing in the Tatum-GMC.

With his car's success in 1953, Tatum was able to secure sponsorship for an engine from Wayne Engineering, manufacturers of speed equipment for six-cylinder Chevrolet and GMC engines. For the 1954 season, Wayne sent Tatum a new GMC engine fitted with the famous Wayne 12 Port cross-flow cylinder head. The ignition system was still Mallory, but the carbs were changed to three Zenith two-barrels from a GMC fire truck. The new engine produced considerably more horsepower than the engine raced in 1953. Tatum also took his special to the Bonneville Salt Flats in 1954, where he drove the car to a top speed of 157 miles per hour. At the conclusion of the 1954 season, the engine was sent back to Wayne for an overhaul. During the 1955 season, the Wayne engine was stolen while the car was being worked on in a Palo Alto garage. The engine was never recovered, and Tatum finished the season with a borrowed flathead Ford.

Sometimes a race car takes on an identity of its own, beyond the measure of its racing success. The Tatum-GMC was just such a car, and it always seemed to attract much attention. *Hot Rod* chose the Tatum special as its feature car for the October 1953 issue. While this publication typically featured hot rods, drag cars, and dry lakes racers, the Tatum was recognized as unique—a hot rod that just happened to race in sports car events.

At the Santa Barbara Road Races in 1953, several Hollywood people were in attendance, looking for unique cars to appear in an upcoming movie. They tried to strike a deal to rent Tatum's car, but he would only agree if he did the driving himself. Tatum was made a member of the Screen Actors' Guild and drove his car in the motion picture *Johnny Dark*, starring Tony Curtis and Piper

Laurie. In 1954, Tatum entered his car in the National Roadster Show at Oakland, California. It was awarded the title of Best Sports Car.

The Tatum special also appeared in the September 1954 issue of *Motorlife,* where it was characterized as a "3-Way Sports Car" (race car, show car, movie car). The car was even used to promote professional wrestling matches.

During the three glorious years that Tatum raced the car, he competed successfully at most of the major raceways on the West Coast, including Pebble Beach, Palm Springs, Torrey Pines, Willow Springs, March Field, Buchanan Field, Golden Gate Park, Madera, Stockton, and Santa Barbara. At one of the races, an English woman commented, "I say, is this that beastly car with a lorry engine in it?" From that point on, Tatum's pit crew referred to the car as the Beast.

In 1956, Tatum went to work for a Stockton car dealer as manager of sports car operations. His boss was easy to work for but had one hard and fast rule—his managers could not compete in car

TATUM-GMC

Constructor	**Chuck Tatum**
Location built	**Stockton, California**
Body by	**Jack Hagemann**
Years built	**1952–1953**
Engine	**GMC six-cylinder (302 ci)**
Gearboxes	**Lincoln three-speed, later Jaguar**
Chassis	**ladder**
Front suspension	**1932 Ford**
Rear suspension	**1941 Ford pickup truck**
Brakes	**Kinmont discs; later Tatum finned drums**
Body material	**aluminum**
Weight, approx.	**2,159 pounds**
Wheelbase	**102 inches**
Length	**164 inches**
Height	**43 inches**

racing. Tatum sold the car, and over the next few years, various owners installed several different engines. According to Tatum, "Some of the owners didn't treat the car with much respect." As time passed, Tatum lost track of the car and assumed it had been scrapped. In 1983, acting on a tip from a friend of his son, he tracked down the remains of the Tatum-GMC in a small junkyard just a few miles from Tatum's home in Stockton. The major portions of the original body, frame, suspension, and dash were all there. The engine and transmission were gone, as were many of the smaller pieces. Tatum and his son restored the car to run in vintage races with a GMC engine and production truck cylinder head. In 1996, Chris Wickersham of Pasadena, California, purchased the car and returned it to its most glorious configuration with the Wayne head.

We Talk With Chuck Tatum.

AUTHOR: How did you get into racing?

TATUM: After I got out of the Marine Corps in 1945, they cranked up racing again. I had been to midget races before the war. After the war they got midget racing going and I would watch from the stands and I could envision myself behind the wheel of a racing car. I was looking for adventure after having been at Iwo Jima and places like that.

AUTHOR: How did you get involved in sports car racing?

TATUM: I guess in 1951 or so, I heard about the first Pebble Beach road race, and I thought, how great would it be to drive on a real race course? Some of my hardtop (stock car) racing friends had bought MG TDs, and my wife and I bought one and joined the sports car club, and we went to the races. I got interested in sports cars. I knew I had a great interest in designing and building racing cars. I drew up some sketches. I had heard of the Allard, and I knew it used Ford parts to some extent. And then I saw some of them race. They were winning races with Cadillac and Chrysler engines in them. And I thought, why don't I build a car with a GMC six-cylinder engine and I'll make a tubular Ford frame and use Ford front suspension and put it on coil springs and have an aluminum body made for it? And I did.

AUTHOR: Did you choose the GMC because of the weight?

TATUM: Yes. I had a magnesium flywheel and a magnesium bell housing on it. Everything else was lightened. Once you got it lightened, it didn't weight but about 20 pounds more than a Chevy (six-cylinder). I believe the GMC may have weighed just a little more than a Ford (flathead). They could be bored out to 305 cubic inches, the class limit. And they had the ability to deliver pure, undiluted torque when you needed it coming out of a turn. Everyone laughed when they heard I was going to use the GMC, but they were winning races all over California in roadsters and sprint cars. I had an engine that had nearly a horsepower per cubic inch.

AUTHOR: Tell me about racing it.

TATUM: To make a long story short, we raced it for the first time at Golden Gate Park, and Chuck Manning drove it. He was a pretty fast race car driver. He had a license then and I didn't, so he drove it.

AUTHOR: How did it do?

TATUM: Not very well; it kept running over its own fenders. It had motorcycle fenders and they kept falling off. I had Jack Hagemann redesign it with gullwing fenders on it for Stockton. I drove it at Stockton. I could tell it went; it couldn't have weighed over 1,900 pounds. I was out practicing, and I came up on an Allard, and I dove past him going into a turn and then went off and left him. A little while later, an SCCA official showed up and said, "You know, you're new at this, but you could learn a lot working with Dr. Skiffington in the Allard. He's an experienced driver and you

could learn something by following him." I said, "I wouldn't mind following him at all, if he'd just speed it up a little bit."

AUTHOR: How did the race go?

TATUM: They drew for numbers for the race on Sunday. Around 33 cars, and I got last. In front were six Allards. I thought, "Well, you thought you could beat the Allards. . . ." Fortunately, I won the race, going away. This opened peoples' eyes. Then I rented it to the people putting out the movie *Johnny Dark*.

AUTHOR: Did you drive it in the movie?

TATUM: Yes, I did. I wouldn't rent it to them unless I drove it. I couldn't believe I had the opportunity to associate with Tony Curtis and Piper Laurie and Janet Leigh. It took about a month to do my part. We filmed it up in Reno, Carson City, and Lake Tahoe. It was the time of my life . . . and I was getting paid! By the time that gig, as they say in Hollywood, was over, I guess I made over $6,000. That was a lot of money to me.

T-Bug

See Beast entry.

Tea Kettle (Jomar) Special

This was a Jomar Mk.III (see Jomar entry, Chapter 2) rebodied with a fiberglass body. It was named for its tendency to overheat.

Teakettle (MG TD) Special

This Teakettle Special was built by John McCann while he was an engineering student at the University of Colorado and was named for its

John McCann built the Teakettle (MG TD) Special with a Mistral body. *John McCann collection*

tendency to overheat. McCann built the car on an MG TD chassis and modified the front spindles so that they would accept Triumph TR-3 disc brakes. The rear axle was from an Austin-Healey 100-6, and the coil springs were Volvo. The beautiful fiberglass body was a Mistral design.

Motivation for the car came from a 283-ci Chevy V-8 with three Stromberg 97 carburetors on a Weiand manifold. Later, McCann upped the oomph by installing a fuel-injected 327-ci Chevy V-8. The gearbox was a T-10 four-speed.

The Teakettle was raced in SCCA events from 1961 through 1963, including Pomona, Tucson, Riverside, and Del Mar. Its finest hour was a third in C-Modified at Riverside.

The car was somewhat of a celebrity, having appeared in a print advertisement for Valvoline. The car was seen in the photo used in the ad; the start of a race at Riverside in March 1962; and in MGM's 1966 Elvis Presley movie, *Spinout*.

By 1963, McCann was a senior at San Diego State University. He entered into a business deal with Fred Puhn at Santee Automobiles and sold his Teakettle Special for $1,500. The money from the sale was used to help pay for McCann's next race car, the Santee SS (see Santee SS entry, Chapter 2).

Tholen Crosley

Dale Tholen built the Tholen Crosley over a period of four years at a cost of $1,100. The car was constructed on a square tube ladder frame of Tholen's design. Front suspension was a modified Crosley axle with coil springs, adjustable Gabriel shocks, and trailing and Watts linkage. Rear suspension was by live quarter-elliptic springs, Gabriel shocks, and Watts linkage. Brakes were Bendix 9-inch drums at all four corners.

The engine was a SOHC 750-cc Crosley with a bore of 2 1/2 inches and a stroke of 2 1/4 inches; the compression ratio was 9.5:1. The pistons were from Turner, the camshaft was a K&H Sport unit, the flywheel was a 5-pound aluminum design, and induction was by a progressive Stromberg 81 carburetion system. Tholen fabricated custom headers and a custom manifold. The car also had a special oil pan and sump to prevent oil pressure loss. Tholen selected a Fiat four-speed, and a significant effort was required to modify the Crosley bell housing and U-joint to mate with the Italian unit.

The Tholen-designed fiberglass body was delightful. It was made from a female mold, cast from a plaster and plywood buck made in Tholen's garage. The completed body had 12 sections that were easily

The Tholen Crosley was featured on the cover of *Road & Track* magazine. *Dean Batchelor*

installed and removed. The car was finished off in a delicious two-tone cream and black paint scheme with an attractive grille and windscreen.

The car ran well and was competitive. In his first eight races in the car, Tholen finished second once, third on four occasions, and fourth twice.

Thundermug

The Thundermug was Dale Tholen's second road racing car. It was named after the slang term used for the portable lavatories (typically a porcelain bowl) in use during the winter months prior to the advent of indoor plumbing.

Apparently, the sound of the car's unique engine was reminiscent of a large man relieving himself into a porcelain "thundermug."

Tholen built a lightweight chassis from steel tubing. He constructed the stylish one-off fiberglass body using a mold carved from Styrofoam blocks; the finished body weighed in at just 24 pounds. The most unique feature of the car was the powerplant. Tholen mated three Maico 250-cc single-cylinder, two-stroke air-cooled units by way of an ingenious ten-piece crankcase. Webco made the specially manufactured cylinder heads, and the rods were from BMW.

This lovely racer continues to actively participate in vintage racing.

Tomcat

The Tomcat was a 1960s-era midengined special raced in the southwestern United States. Roger Hill, an engineer at Bell Helicopter in Texas, built the Tomcat. It was powered by a 302-ci Chevy V-8 engine and was run with a Corvair four-speed transaxle. It had a fiberglass body styled by Cecil Haga. The delightful grille emblem depicted the rear view of a tomcat with a pair of immense testicles hanging down for all the world to see. Gary Valant later raced the car.

TOMCAT	
Constructor	Roger Hill
Location built	Fort Worth, Texas
Body by	Cecil Haga
Years built	1963–1964
Engine	Chevy V-8
Gearbox	Corvair four-speed
Chassis	space frame
Front suspension	independent
Rear suspension	independent
Body material	fiberglass

244

The Tomcat was an early Chevy-powered, mid-engined racer from Texas. *Millard Almon*

Townsend Specials

Frank Townsend and a group of his friends built a series of spectacular specials in their Tucson, Arizona, shop. Townsend had a background in hot rodding and frequently ran his cars at drag strips and on road courses, and he held records both places. The Townsends were among the best built and engineered specials of their era.

Townsend Typhoon (Townsend Mk.1)

While still in high school, Townsend built a fiberglass sports car body for his 1949 Plymouth chassis powered by an Oldsmobile engine. The car was attractive and soon led to another car for drag and road racing. It had the same running gear as the first car but featured an abbreviated tail and three carburetors sticking through the hood. Townsend and his brother, Robert, together with friends Pete and Jack Voedodsky, built three Typhoons for street and track use. Two more bodies were sold to customers.

The Townsend Typhoon (Mk.1) was an attractive sports-racer from Arizona. *Owen Gibson collection*

Townsend Mk.2

In 1957, the same team (plus Butch McDaniel and Larry Randell) built an improved Typhoon for SCCA racing. It had a fuel-injected Pontiac engine and a different grille. The chassis was all-new, with Kurtis-style live axles at both ends. Before it was completed, the front axle was switched to a 1955

Chevy IFS system. The team had access to surplus aircraft parts, and built the chassis out of tubing from scaffolds used to overhaul bomber engines. The belts, gauges, switch-gear, and seat were also aircraft parts. The brakes were Buick Alfin drums, and an Oldsmobile rear axle was used. The car was painted a brilliant purple and was soon nicknamed the Purple People Eater, as were all purple race cars after the song became popular. Pete Voedodsky regularly drove the car.

Townsend Mk.3

Townsend and Pete Voedodsky realized that they needed an all-new design to remain competitive in the 1960s. In 1962, they unveiled their new design, a beautifully constructed special called the Townsend Mk.3. The new car was influenced by the Maserati Birdcage and was made from 250 feet of 1-inch or smaller diameter 4130 chrome-moly steel tubing. The front suspension featured fabricated A-arms and coil-over shocks with Pontiac spindles and an MGA steering rack. Corvette cerametallic brake backing plates were mated to 1961 Pontiac Grand Prix finned drums and hubs. Special 15-inch rims with eight small "ears" were machined to bolt to the Pontiac hubs. The chassis was paneled in aluminum, and the rear axle was a narrowed Chevy unit.

Power was from a mildly modified 1961 Pontiac V-8. It was stroked from 371 to 389 inches, and the

The Townsend Mk.3 had a sophisticated space frame chassis with a Devin body. *Owen Gibson collection*

heads were ported and polished. Hillborn constant-flow fuel injection was used, and a Mallory magneto was driven off the front of the engine. What was not generally known at the time was that Townsend had acquired two all-aluminum Pontiac engines that had been made for an aborted NASCAR program. Each had plenty of muscle to propel the car at outrageous speeds. Originally, it was fitted with a Borg Warner T-10 transmission, but this was upgraded to a Muncie M22 when it became available. The car was fitted with a Devin fiberglass body while the team developed a body of its own. The Mk.3 ran the quarter-mile in 12.1 seconds and was shaken down at Santa Barbara in 1962 by Don Hulette.

Townsend Mk.4

In 1963, the new body was ready and the old Mk.3 became the Mk.4. It was a beauty, strongly resembling a Maserati Birdcage. The car was in a constant state of development, receiving first front disc brakes from a TR-3, then rear discs as well. When disc brakes were installed, the Pontiac hubs and wheels were replaced with American Racing five-spoke mags. The Mk.4 was raced through the early 1960s, driven by Hulette at the 1964 Riverside USRRC, where he finished 11th. Pete Voedodsky qualified for the 1964 ARRC and finished third-in-class. The Mk.4 was as competitive as any front-engined car of its time.

The Townsend Mk.4 (No. 62) takes on a Maserati, a Lotus, and a Genie. *Owen Gibson collection*

Townsend Mk.5

In 1965, Townsend joined the midengined revolution with a Genielike special built from cannibalized parts from the Mk.4, a modified Genie body, and BMC transaxle (sourced from Huffaker). It had a steel tube space frame and conventional coil-over suspension. The engine was originally the Pontiac from the Mk.4 but was replaced with a 427 L-88 Chevy (iron block with aluminum heads). The Chevy engine pushed the BMC transaxle past its breaking point, so a ZF transaxle was substituted. Although the Mk.5 was no match for a McLaren (after all, what was?), it finished an excellent fourth-in-class at the 1966 ARRC, driven by Voedodsky. Townsend continued to campaign the car through the late 1960s.

The Townsend Mk.5, shown leading a Ford GT40, was the only mid-engined Townsend design. *Owen Gibson collection*

Although Townsend built no more road racing cars, he kept busy campaigning some of the fastest Pro-Stock dragsters in the country and even owned a Chevelle stock car that ran in the *Motor Trend* 500 at Riverside in 1969. He is still building hot cars and street rods in his shop in Tucson.

TOWNSEND SPECIALS

TOWNSEND MK.1

Constructors	Frank Townsend, Robert Townsend, Jack Voedodsky, and Pete Voedodsky
Location built	Tucson, Arizona
Year built	1957
Engine	Oldsmobile V-8
Gearbox	four-speed
Chassis	space frame
Front suspension	independent, coil springs
Rear suspension	live axle
Brakes	drum
Body material	fiberglass

TOWNSEND MK.2

Constructors	Frank Townsend, Robert Townsend, Jack Voedodsky, Pete Voedodsky, Butch McDaniel, and Larry Randell
Location built	Tucson, Arizona
Year built	1958
Engine	Pontiac V-8
Gearbox	four-speed
Chassis	space frame
Front suspension	independent, coil springs
Rear suspension	live axle
Brakes	drum
Body material	fiberglass
Wheelbase	102 inches

TOWNSEND MK.3 AND 4

Constructor	Frank Townsend
Location built	Tucson, Arizona
Body by	Devin Enterprises (Mk.3 only)
Year built	1962
Engine	Pontiac V-8
Gearbox	four-speed
Chassis	space frame
Front suspension	independent, coil springs
Rear suspension	live axle
Brakes	drum/disc
Body material	fiberglass
Wheelbase	92 inches
Weight, approx.	1,800 pounds

TOWNSEND MK.5

Constructor	Frank Townsend
Location built	Tucson, Arizona
Year built	1965
Engine	Pontiac/Chevy V-8
Gearbox	four-speed BMC and five-speed ZF
Chassis	space frame
Front suspension	independent, coil springs
Rear suspension	independent, coil springs
Brakes	disc
Body material	fiberglass

We Talk With Frank Townsend.

AUTHOR: Why did you decide to build your own car instead of just buying one?

TOWNSEND: The cars we were looking at were in the $10,000 range and I didn't have that kind of money. Financial was the number one reason, and the challenge of doing it myself was the number two reason. I've always been that way; I've been in auto racing since I was 12 years old, starting in micromidget racing.

AUTHOR: What was it about Pontiacs that you liked?

TOWNSEND: Pontiac was picked because it was a lightweight engine, about 40 pounds more than a Chevy small-block. When we started racing in 1968, the biggest Chevy you could get was a 283 and the Pontiac was a 371. So it was an easy way of getting around 90 extra inches, and the Pontiac was reliable and made good power. The early ones even had forged rods.

AUTHOR: I've heard you had some aluminum-block Pontiacs.

TOWNSEND: I had two of them. They were sold to me; Pontiac couldn't give them to me. We were running NASCAR cylinder heads, which were all hollowed out and had no heat risers. The engine, ready to run, was about 400 pounds. It was a 389-inch engine made from a 371 by putting in a 389 crank. As I recall, we had block Number 3 and block Number 10; Pontiac only built ten of them.

AUTHOR: About how much power do you think you got?

TOWNSEND: We figured we were getting about 450 horsepower out of them. That was using a Grand National 421 head with NASCAR connecting rods and Forged True pistons. It was basically all NASCAR stuff.

AUTHOR: What engine did you use in the last midengined car?

TOWNSEND: I built the chassis to take a 427 Chevy, but we still had the Pontiac so we used it, because it was light and proven. But when we got serious about racing, it was underpowered so we switched to a 427 engine, basically an L-88. Pete [Voedodsky] was spending the money on the car, and he decided to go to law school so we passed on the aluminum block. That would have been the next step.

AUTHOR: Did you like drag racing or road racing best?

TOWNSEND: I think road racing was more of a challenge. The thing I like about road racing is that you can make a small error and make up for it later. In drag racing, if you snooze, you lose. I definitely preferred the road racing; it involved horsepower, it involved chassis setup, it involved a lot of things.

The other day, I saw a special on Max Balchowsky. We used to run against him a lot. The way he laid out a frame on the floor and drew chalk marks is the same way I built the last car. I laid quart paint cans on the floor, set the tubing on top and that was the ride height. Then I drew the lines on the floor. For the earlier cars I drew up blueprints, though we didn't always follow them. That was the way a lot of people did things back then. I had a couple of fellows from the university come in, and they laughed at me when they saw that stuff on the floor, but that was the way the things got built.

Troutman-Barnes Special

Dick Troutman and Tom Barnes met in 1949 while working at Frank Kurtis' famed Kurtis Kraft of Glendale, California. Troutman was an experienced metal shaper from his days at Lockheed, and

The Troutman-Barnes Special had many famous drivers. *Allen Kuhn*

Barnes was a skilled machinist. The two men's skills were further sharpened by experience building Indy cars with Kurtis. While the two men had different backgrounds and dissimilar skill sets, they shared a common passion for race cars. So it was only natural that they became friends, and eventually they decided to build a race car of their own design. That decision changed everything. The Troutman-Barnes Special launched their careers, ultimately taking them to the zenith of the field. The Reventlow Scarabs and Hall's Chaparral I later

Chuck Daigh in the Troutman-Barnes Special leads Bill Friedauer in an Austin Healey 100S at Santa Barbara in 1956. *Allen Kuhn*

246

The Troutman-Barnes Special predated the lovely Scarabs. This car had a variety of Ford engines. *Harold Pace*

the two engine side panels, which forced cool air into the engine compartment. The body was finished in icebox white, which complemented and accentuated the car's lovely lines. As an added touch, Troutman and Barnes fitted the car with a short purposeful windscreen and Indy-style Halibrand mag wheels.

The car was initially propelled by a Mercury flathead V-8. The motor was bored and stroked and had aluminum cylinder heads, a triple carburetor intake manifold, and tubular headers. In that config-uration, the car was fitted with a Ford three-speed gearbox with Zephyr gears. As it was developed, Troutman and Barnes switched to a 347-ci over-head valve V-8 from a Ford T-Bird. With Hilborn fuel injection and 9.5:1 compression, the engine produced 335 horsepower at 5,800 rpm. In this configuration, drive went through a Jaguar (C-Type) four-speed gearbox.

The finished car was an absolute jewel box in every manner and was extremely reliable and competitive. Ken Miles raced the car on numerous occasions in between his R-1 and R-2 projects. Later, Chuck Daigh took the wheel for the 1955, 1956, and 1957 seasons. In 1955, Daigh ran second at Santa Barbara in September, second at Torrey Pines in October, and third at Palm Springs in December. In March 1956, Daigh finished third at Santa Barbara. In 1957, Daigh finished second at Paramount Ranch in March, second at a Hawaiian race in April, first at Paramount Ranch in June, and first at Santa Barbara in September.

The Troutman-Barnes Special was sold to Jimmy Pfluger of Honolulu, Hawaii, in November 1957, and Troutman and Barnes went to work on Reventlow's Scarab project. Pfluger renamed the car the Fury Special. Daigh raced the car in July 1959 at the first USAC-sanctioned professional road race at Riverside. Powered by a Scarab-Chevy V-8, the car was in the lead for the first 15 laps but ultimately finished sixth.

Today, the car still exists and is actively raced in vintage events.

made them one of the greatest American race car construction teams of all time.

The Troutman-Barnes Special was built in Troutman's garage in Los Angeles, California. A space frame was constructed from 2-inch tubing with smaller tubes serving as side members and braces. An independent front suspension of the team's own design incorporated lower A-arms and transverse leaf springs. The rear suspension was live axle with transverse leaf springs and a compli-cated setup with cross springing and floating radius rods. Braking was accomplished with 11-inch Ford-Bendix drums (3-inch-wide drums in the front, 2 1/2-inch-wide drums at the rear), which were heavily drilled and ducted to dissipate heat. Steering was by an MG rack and pinion.

The aluminum body was an original design and was equally well crafted and beautiful. Nine body panels were affixed to the frame with Dzus fasteners for easy on and off. The car sometimes ran without

Andre Capella's Twareg Special sported a Chrysler engine.
Andre Capella collection

Twareg Special

Andre Capella (he later changed his name to Gessner) of Seal Beach, California, built the Twareg Special in 1958. Capella was a self-described wanderer, and it was natural that he named the car after a nomadic African tribe.

He built the car on a space frame chassis of his own design. The front suspension was Ford live axle and the rear was a de Dion unit from an Allard (the rear suspension became independent in 1961). Capella said that he got most of the other components from the junkyard, including the Chrysler Hemis. He recalls paying $50 each for engines, which was important at the time because he blew several of them up trying to wind them to 6,500 rpm.

The brakes were drums front and rear, and Capella recalls that they didn't work very well. Later, he bought a set of Jaguar disc brakes from Shelby for the rear, and the car stopped much better. The gearbox was a Ford three-speed, and the body was a fiberglass beauty.

TWAREG SPECIAL	
Constructor	Andre Capella
Location built	Seal Beach, California
Body by	Bob Sorrell
Year built	1958
Engine	Chrysler Hemi V-8 (331 ci)
Gearbox	Ford three-speed
Chassis	space frame
Front suspension	live axle
Rear suspension	de Dion
Brakes	drum
Body material	fiberglass
Weight, approx	2,200 pounds
Wheelbase	95 inches
Length	150 inches
Height	30 inches
Cost when new	$1,500

We Talk With Andre Capella.

AUTHOR: Where did the body come from?

CAPELLA: The car had a Sorrell body. Bob Sorrell gave me that body. I was a very poor guy. I had no money. So a lot of people gave me stuff, luckily, or I probably never would have been able to race at all. I painted the car gold. Later, I put a white flame job on it.

AUTHOR: Tell me about Sorrell.

CAPELLA: He had a place up in Hollywood, and he did a lot of designing and drawing. He was way ahead of his time on a lot of his drawings of cars. He had some really good ideas for bodies and cars. He was a nice guy, but you know he didn't have the bucks either; he wasn't connected. That's probably what held him back. That's why he probably gave me the body; he was looking for some exposure.

248

AUTHOR: What kind of training did you have to build your own car?

CAPELLA: I was a machinist. I was pretty innovative for being a dumb kid.

AUTHOR: Was the car successful?

CAPELLA: The car went fast, but it wasn't a finisher; you know I really didn't finish many races. Although at a Speed Week in Colorado one time, I had top straightaway time of 155—faster than the Birdcages and Ken Miles' Porsche. The car did really good in several races but it always broke. It was a lot of fun, because I drove it sideways. That's the way it went around corners—sideways. The problem was I didn't know what I was doing a lot and neither did anyone else. Balchowsky was the one who helped me the most. The car never failed to qualify for the Riverside Grand Prix.

AUTHOR: What happened to the Twareg? Does it still exist?

CAPELLA: No. I just kept cutting it up and changing it, until there was nothing left. What I did was use some of the pieces from the Twareg when I built the Front-Runner Special.

Uihlein MG Special

The Uihlein MG was a very well thought-out design that just never ran the way it should have. While he was in school, David Uihlein worked summers at the race shop of Carl and Tudy Marchese. Although he had apprenticed in his family business (Schlitz Brewing), he wanted to build an American racing car to take on the OSCAs and Porsches in the 1,500-cc class. Starting with a pile of MG parts, he built a sophisticated twin cam conversion for the MG TD engine. The block and bottom end were from an MG TD 1,250-cc XPAG engine. In an article in *Speed Age*, Uihlein said he picked the MG block because he planned to sell copies of his race motor and the MG block was plenty strong and cheaper than the Offy midget engine.

The Uihlein MG Special had a long nose and a one-off MG engine. *Pete Lyons*

Uihlein fabricated a twin cam cylinder head with hemispherical combustion chambers and a gear drivetrain mounted on ball bearings. The cross-flow head was cast from nickel-alloy steel, and the stock cam was left in the block to drive the oil pump and distributor. Twin SU carburetors were fitted on the left side of the engine. Big 1 7/16-inch-diameter valves were installed with valve springs of 250-pound tension. Power was estimated at 90 horsepower.

UIHLEIN MG SPECIAL

Constructor	**David L. Uihlein**
Location built	**Milwaukee, Wisconsin**
Year built	**1953**
Engine	**MG TD twin cam conversion**
Gearbox	**four-speed**
Chassis	**ladder frame**
Front suspension	**independent**
Rear suspension	**live axle**
Brakes	**drum**
Body material	**aluminum**

The engine was installed in a cut-down MG TD special with a cigar-shaped aluminum body built by Joe Silnas, an Indy car builder. The new body cut 600 pounds off the weight of the stock TD. The bright purple car was driven by Karl Brocken, but proved to be no faster than other MG specials. It is still owned by its builder, David Uihlein, now a noted car collector.

Van Dyke Special

See Barlow Simcas entry.

Vogel/Balchowsky Special

This special began life in the 1940s when dry lakester Jimmy Summers of Los Angeles, California, built a channeled '32 Ford roadster. In the early 1950s, the car came to be owned by Fred Vogel, with Max Balchowsky serving as the car's driver and mechanic. These were the earliest days of

Constructor	Max Balchowsky (built from Jimmy Summers' 1932 Ford roadster)
Location built	California
Years built	1940s and 1952
Engine	various
Gearbox	various
Chassis	1932 Ford ladder
Front suspension	live axle
Rear suspension	live axle
Brakes	drum
Weight, approx.	2,700 pounds

racing for Balchowsky, and the fabulous Old Yallers were hardly a twinkle in his eye.

The special's first outing was at Torrey Pines in December 1952. The car was powered by a LaSalle motor and was entered in the first race, which was for novice drivers. As the green flag dropped, Balchowsky powered the car into the lead. Unfortunately, the car broke a few laps later.

Not dissuaded by this first failure, Balchowsky went to work improving the car, one piece at a time. The Ford hydraulic brakes were discarded and larger Lincoln brakes (1949 to 1951 units) were installed. The old steering mechanism was exchanged for a better system from a Dodge pickup truck. The original Ford leaf springs were removed, and lighter units with more travel were installed. That simple spring swap made all the difference in the handling characteristics of the Vogel/Balchowsky Special.

Next, Balchowsky turned his attention to the driveline. He tried various gearboxes, including a Ford three-speed with Zephyr gears and a LaSalle three-speed. At one point, the car even ran with a Hydra-matic transmission out of a Sherman tank.

As he had done with the gearbox, Balchowsky experimented with the special's powerplant. The LaSalle motor, originally built by Yam Oka of Glendale, California, was eventually set aside and the car ran with a series of overhead valve V-8

engines. These included units from Buick, Chrysler, Oldsmobile, Cadillac, and DeSoto. Balchowsky liked the Buick the best, and the car raced most often in that configuration.

The Vogel/Balchowsky Special was never much of a winner at the racetrack, but it did serve as an important stepping stone in Balchowsky's illustrious career. In fact, based on the ultimate choice of the Buick engine, that car, plus a gallon of yellow paint, could have been considered Old Yaller 0.5.

Volvo Special

See Priest Volvo entry.

Von Neumann MG Special

Back in the early 1950s, John von Neumann owned and ran Competition Motors on Ventura Boulevard in North Hollywood, California. Among other things, his shop specialized in MGs. It was therefore only natural for von Neumann to select the MG TD

as a starting point for his plan to build a winning race car.

The chassis for von Neumann's special was MG with a number of modifications. Von Neumann cut the front section of the frame so that it terminated at the radiator. The car was lowered by cutting a portion of a coil from each front spring, and the rear suspension was modified by removing leaves from the semielliptic springs and adding trailing traction bars. The car was fitted with larger drum brakes with fins for cooling.

Emil Diedt performed the body modifications. Diedt was a skilled aluminum worker, and he essentially rebuilt and reworked most of the body. New alloy fenders were fabricated, as were the hood, rear fenders, firewall, floorboards, and fuel tank. New alloy doors were constructed, and the hinge mechanism was reversed and relocated at the front of the door. The body was lowered 3 inches relative to the frame, and the car was finished off with 16-inch Borrani wire knock-offs.

The MG motor was built up to competition specifications. The compression was set at 9.5:1, and the valves were enlarged. Induction was via

Johnny von Neumann built one of the fastest MG Specials on the West Coast before he switched to Ferraris and Porsches.
Harold Pace

250

John von Neumann was a pivotal character in American racing, and his MG was one of the fastest on the West Coast. *Harold Pace*

Palm Springs, behind the much more powerful foreign entrants (Ferrari, Allard, and Jaguar). The car won its class at the Sandberg Hillclimb a few weeks later. Roger Barlow's Barlow Simca beat the special in class at the second races at Pebble Beach. By the start of the 1952 season, the car had scored seven wins and four second-place finishes.

The car is currently owned and vintage raced by Don Martine.

Votorini

Bob Allinger of Palo Alto, California, built the Votorini. The nifty racer was initially constructed as

The von Neumann MG looked good from any angle. *Harold Pace*

a 1 1/2-inch SU carb system, and exhaust was by individual headers and straight pipes. Von Neumann used twin electric fuel pumps and a magneto from Lucas. Power output was 86 horsepower for the 1,500-cc motor and 75 horsepower in 1320-cc trim. To improve performance, Von Neumann used an MG TC gearbox because of its more desirable (as compared to an MG TD) gear ratios.

Von Neumann's plan worked, and the car was an out and out winner. Its first outing was at Pebble Beach in November 1950. Von Neumann won the Cypress Point Light Car Race for cars of 750-cc to 1,500-cc displacement (classes G and F). In February 1951, von Neumann won another class race at Carrell Speedway. In April 1951, the car finished a respectable sixth in the feature race at

The Votorini first ran as a modified, and then was converted to a Formula Junior. *Robert Rolofson Jr.; Robert H. Rolofson III collection*

a sports car special with fenders, lights, and a spare tire. The car later ran as a Formula Junior when that equipment was removed.

The body was attractive and purposeful, with the drive on the right. The large grille fed the radiator, which was cooled by an electric fan. The fuel tank rode low in the rear section just behind the axle and was accessible through a large trunk lid.

The front suspension was live axle with coil springs and shock absorbers; the rear suspension was also live axle. Drum brakes were used at all four corners.

Allinger powered the car with a 1,100-cc Fiat four-cylinder with twin SU carburetors and a Scintilla Vertex magneto.

VOTORINI

Constructor	**Bob Allinger**
Location built	**Palo Alto, California**
Year built	**early 1950s**
Engine	**1,100-cc Fiat four-cylinder**
Chassis	**ladder**
Front suspension	**live axle**
Rear suspension	**live axle**
Brakes	**drum**

Ward/McKee Cooper-Buick

The Ward/McKee Cooper-Buick, built in 1961, may well be the first example of a special to arise from stuffing an American V-8 thumper into a rear-engined European sports racer. Following his success at the Indy 500, including a win in 1959, Roger Ward purchased a '59 Cooper Monaco from Jack Brabham. He then hired Bob McKee to install a 254-ci Buick V-8 to turn the thing into a race car with an astounding weight-to-horsepower quotient of 4.4-to-1. Additional modifications were performed on the chassis and suspension. Ward raced the car at Riverside, Laguna Seca, and Mosport in 1961 and failed to finish. He was also a nonstarter at Nassau. In 1962, McKee made significant changes to the rear suspension, which became a twin wishbone, and the car received a transaxle designed by Peter Weisman. The car had a second engine swap in late 1962, when it received a Ford V-8. Ed Hamill bought the car and raced it for a few years.

WARD/MCKEE COOPER-BUICK

Constructor	**Bob McKee**
Year built	**1961**
Engine	**Buick V-8 (254 ci)**
Gearbox	**Cooper Knight five-speed**
Chassis	**1959 Cooper Monaco**
Weight, approx.	**1,100 pounds**

Webster Specials

Racing cars always have a personality. Some are brutal and crude, others simple and workmanlike. A very few can be considered works of art, due to meticulous standards of workmanship. Of those, only a handful are both exquisite and fast. The Scarabs come to mind, some Indy roadsters, and

the Websters. Never heard of them? Well, you should have. They were drop-dead gorgeous and, for a brief time in the mid-1960s, one was the fastest under-2-liter racing car in America.

The Websters were the brainchild of Marvin Webster, who was heavily involved in racing midgets and quarter-midgets in the 1950s. His son was the quarter-midget national champion in 1958. Webster had made enough money in marine electronics to indulge his racing effort, but when his son outgrew midgets, Webster was out of a hobby. He went to a sports car race at Laguna Seca and got hooked. Soon, Webster had a pair of Formula Juniors and a Lotus 23 and was making his own cranks, rods, and pistons to go in them.

Webster 2-Liter

But the car that everyone remembers best is the one-off Webster 2-liter built in 1963–1964. The chassis was about the same size as a Lotus 23 (causing it to sometimes be incorrectly identified as a modified 23) with scuttle-hoop bulkheads. It was made from 1 1/4-inch mild steel tubing, and there was extra bracing along the cockpit sides. The frame rails carried water and oil to the midmounted Climax engine. The suspension was conventional race car practice, with unequal-length A-arms and coil-over Armstrong shocks in front and reversed wishbones in back with radius rods. Webster cast his own drilled brake rotors, gripped by Girling calipers. American Racing Equipment 13-inch wheels carried Goodyear racing tires.

Aerodynamicist Bob Herda designed the purposeful body, which Jack Hagemann paneled in aluminum. The driver sat on the right, and a 27-gallon aluminum fuel tank ran along the left side of the cockpit area.

Starting with a 1,500-cc Coventry-Climax FPF, Webster substituted a head from a 2.5 FPF that had larger valves. It was fitted with special Webster-made ductile iron sleeves that combined the 2.5 Climax bore size with the 1,500 crank stroke to net

WEBSTER SPECIALS

WEBSTER 2-LITER

Constructor	**Marvin Webster**
Location built	**California**
Body by	**Bob Herda and Jack Hagemann**
Years built	**1963–1964**
Engine	**Coventry-Climax FPF**
Gearbox	**Porsche five-speed**
Chassis	**space frame**
Front suspension	**independent, coil springs**
Rear suspension	**independent, coil springs**
Brakes	**disc**
Body material	**aluminum**
Wheelbase	**91 inches**

WEBSTER V-8

Constructor	**Marvin Webster**
Location built	**California**
Body by	**Bob Herda and Jack Hagemann**
Year built	**1964**
Engine	**Oldsmobile V-8, 255 ci**
Gearbox	**ZF five-speed**
Chassis	**space frame**
Front suspension	**independent, coil springs**
Rear suspension	**independent, coil springs**
Brakes	**disc**
Body material	**aluminum**
Weight, approx.	**1,250 pounds**

1,996 cc, which neatly fit in the 2-liter racing class. Webster designed his own 4130 tubular rods and pistons, made by Forged True. The intake ports were hogged out to 1.625 inches and 58-millimeter side-draft Webers with 45-millimeter chokes were fitted. Exhaust ports were reduced in size, and Winfield cams gave 200 horsepower at 9,000 rpm, a real screamer for its day. The power was transmitted through a Porsche RSK five-speed transaxle.

Sports Car Graphic featured the car in its November 1964 issue and even put it on the cover, with the body off, to show the incredible standard of finish. The development driver was Tony Settember, who had raced Formula 1 in Europe and was very impressed with the car.

However, the first driver to taste blood in the Webster was Jerry Titus, who drove it to a win at the 1964 SCCA ARRC race. Although it ran in the D-Modified class, Titus easily outdistanced the bigger C-Modifieds, except for a Cooper-Chevy that barely nipped him at the line. And it was the first time Titus had driven the car!

The Webster then went on the 1965 USRRC trail, but luck was not with it. Titus drove it without success. The Webster 2-liter was retired and is currently undergoing restoration.

Webster V-8

Webster built a new car for the 1964 season, this time with an aluminum Oldsmobile V-8 engine.

Jerry Eisert built the space frame chassis, and Jack Hagemann fashioned the handsome aluminum body. A five-speed ZF gearbox was used, and the Olds breathed through four Weber 48-millimeter carburetors. It appeared halfway through the 1964 season, driven by Ed Leslie and Tony Settember with few results.

The next year, it ran in the Can-Am series, and Titus managed an incredible sixth overall in the Las Vegas round. Leslie had a DNF at Riverside and that was it. Reportedly a third Webster was built. The V-8 has been restored and competes in vintage racing, driven by Terry Miller. Webster later found fame with its line of excellent Webster gearboxes.

Wolverine

The Wolverine was a one-off sports-racer driven by Jerry Hansen. Hansen won more SCCA National Championships than anyone, but not in this car. It was designed by Lee Dykstra and had a Chevy V-8 for power. It looked great, with a pincer-shaped nose and rounded bodywork. Hansen ran it in Can-Am and USRRC races in 1966. At the Mid-Ohio USRRC, he failed to finish, and at the St. Jovite Can-Am, he finished 20th. The Wolverine also ran in SCCA races.

WOLVERINE

Year built	**1966**
Engine	**Chevy V-8**
Front suspension	**independent**
Rear suspension	**independent**
Brakes	**disc**

The Webster V-8 was one of the most beautiful specials of all time. *Terry and Joan Miller collection*

Wright Specials

Architect Vale Wright was a hard-core car guy who sold very nice kit car bodies and built two specials

Vale Wright built Lil Stinker from a midget circle track car. *Bob Canaan; Ron Kellogg collection*

Vale Wright sold these Cisitalia-replica bodies to fit on MG chassis. *Dean Batchelor*

WRIGHT SPECIALS

LIL STINKER

Constructor	**Vale Wright**
Location built	**Berkeley, California**
Year built	**1954**
Engine	**Ford V-8 60**
Gearbox	**four-speed**
Chassis	**ladder**
Front suspension	**live axle**
Rear suspension	**live axle**
Brakes	**drum**
Body material	**fiberglass**
Weight, approx.	**1,450 pounds**

WRIGHT RENAULT SPECIAL

Constructor	**Vale Wright**
Location built	**Berkeley, California**
Year built	**1956**
Engine	**Renault Dauphine**
Gearbox	**four-speed**
Chassis	**ladder**
Front suspension	**independent**
Rear suspension	**swing axle**
Brakes	**drum**
Body material	**fiberglass**
Wheelbase	**78 inches**
Weight, approx.	**862 pounds**

that were raced on the West Coast in the early 1950s. In 1951, he developed a lovely fiberglass body kit that fit on an MG T-Series chassis. The body resembled the Cisitalia Nuvolari Spyder with an oval grille and tiny tail fins.

When Wright decided to build a racing car in 1954, he wanted to use his kit body, but the tail section was too heavy, so he settled on two nose sections fitted back to back. His first special was named Lil Stinker and was based on an old circle-track midget powered by a Ford V-8 60 engine. Wright lengthened and widened the frame to fit the two-seat body. The midget axles, differential, steering, brakes, and wheels were used pretty much as they were.

The old 134-ci flathead midget engine soon expired at Pebble Beach. It was then rebuilt with a Winfield cam, twin Stromberg 81 carburetors, and Eddie Meyer heads to produce 100 horsepower. A Clements adapter allowed use of an MG TC transmission.

The second Wright special, which came out in 1956, was a midengined H-Modified based on Renault Dauphine running gear. Wright bought a wrecked Renault for $125 and built a simple ladder frame from 2 1/4-inch tubing. The Dauphine suspension was used in mildly modified form. Like the first special, it used the twin-front-end body concept, but without the headlights, and a tall headrest covered the roll bar. Total cost was around $800.

X-Ray Special

The X-Ray Special was a racer that never actually raced. It was a prototype race car built in 1955, constructed on a one-off steel tube frame. Front suspension was by trailing arms with transverse leaf springs. A de Dion unit was at the rear. The body was a real showstopper, a curvaceous, sexy left-hand-drive roadster with a short windscreen, sidepipes, and wire wheels. Although it never made it to the track, it was ready. Its competition-prepared Chrysler Hemi V-8 pumped out a respectable 275 ponies.

Yeovil

George Clowes and his wife, Allison, built this one-off Formula Junior in 1960. She welded up the space frame (her first welding job); the rear-engined racer used a Goliath Tiger engine and a Volkswagen gearbox. The Goliath engine was modified to produce over 65 horsepower, with dual Holley carburetors on fabricated manifolds. Volkswagen rear suspension was used as well.

The front suspension, brakes, and steering were based on Fiat Topolino parts, and an aluminum body was made.

YEOVIL

Constructors	George and Allison Clowes
Location built	Chicago, Illinois
Year built	1960
Engine	Goliath Tiger
Gearbox	Volkswagen four-speed
Chassis	space frame
Front suspension	independent
Rear suspension	swing axle
Brakes	Fiat drums
Body material	aluminum
Weight, approx.	880 pounds
Cost when new	$1,850

Zerex Special

Roger Penske was used to fixing up rough sports cars. Before he was old enough to drive, he bought a nasty MG TD and got it running. He sold that and

bought an MG TC, then passed it on and bought a 1954 Ford business coupe, squeezing in a big Olds engine. After getting a job at Alcoa Aluminum, Penske started buying and fixing up older cars and selling them for a profit. His experience in making money and repairing damaged cars paid off when he decided to build one of the pivotal specials in American racing history.

Penske started road racing in a Corvette, then switched to the Porsche RS Spyder he bought from Bob Holbert. After racing a series of Porsches and a Maserati Birdcage, he bought a Cooper Monaco. But after problems with Porsche and Cooper, Penske became discouraged about buying European racing cars. He felt like the customers always got the second-best equipment, while the factory drivers had the best of everything. Of course, he was right.

His experience racing Coopers led him to Briggs Cunningham's shop in 1961 to look over a Cooper-Maserati. In the back of the shop was a Cooper

255

Roger Penske posed with the Zerex Special (and a starlet). *Allen Kuhn*

The Zerex Special ran at Riverside in 1963. *Allen Kuhn*

Formula 1 car that Walt Hansgen had wrecked at Watkins Glen. Penske thought it might be useful for parts, so he swapped Cunningham some Maserati spares for it.

When Penske got the chassis home to Wayne, Pennsylvania, he had mechanic Roy Gane and friend Jim Soley completely rebuild the chassis. They had to throw away and replace over a fourth of the tubes before it was straight again. All the wishbones had been torn away from the chassis, and the wheels were all bent. But when it was completed, Penske was looking over the pristine chassis and got the idea to build it into a sports car.

Penske wanted to keep the chassis as it was and simply install a full-width body to cover the tires. Center-seat cars had been built before, including Pete Lovely's Pooper. Since the rules required two seats, a vestigial one would be installed to one side, covered by the body (the rules didn't say a passenger had to be able to actually get in the car). Penske ran his idea past USAC officials (he planned to run in their pro series) and the organizers of the Times Grand Prix pro race. They all gave him the green light.

Veteran car builder Bob Webb hammered the aluminum body with help from Roy Gane and Larry Tidmarsh. When new, the F1 car ran a 1.5-liter Coventry-Climax FPF four-cylinder engine. But for his special, Penske bought a 2.7-liter Climax FPF that had been Jack Brabham's backup engine at

Indianapolis in 1959. At that time, Climax had only built a few 2.7s and wasn't anxious to build more, so it was a valuable find. Gane rebuilt the 250-horsepower engine in his Updraught Engineering shop, and it ran faultlessly. The combination of the Formula 1 chassis and the rare and powerful 2.7 Climax gave Penske an edge over the factory-built cars from Europe.

The Cooper running gear was left as-is, with Girling discs (10 1/4-inch-diameter front and 9 3/4-inch rear) and cast magnesium rear uprights. Triumph Herald uprights were used in front along with Morris Minor rack-and-pinion steering. The new special was named the Zerex Special, as Penske had convinced DuPont (maker of Zerex antifreeze) to sponsor his racing efforts. It was also sometimes called the Zerex-Durlite Special.

First time out for the new car was at Riverside in October 1962, and as soon as the Zerex got off the trailer, the line started forming to file protests. Some said it wasn't a two-seater, but Penske removed a small metal panel and wedged himself down into the tiny passenger seat. One by one he showed that he had met the letter, if not the intent, of the regulations. The race was ferocious, with Jim Hall in a front-engined Chaparral and Dan Gurney in a

256

The Zerex Special put Roger Penske on the map. *Allen Kuhn*

Lotus 19 fighting Penske all the way, But in the end, the Zerex Special was the winner.

The next weekend, Penske was at Laguna Seca for the Pacific Grand Prix, where he squared off with Gurney and Lloyd Ruby, both in Lotus 19s. The race ran in two heats, with the winner determined by an aggregate of the two. In the first heat, the two Loti left Penske behind, with Ruby falling back to let Penske take second. In the second heat, Ruby came back to win, with Penske again in second. It was enough to give Penske the overall victory. The Zerex Special was then two for two.

Right after Laguna Seca, the SCCA bowed to a thunderous round of protests and outlawed the Zerex. Gane went back to work and moved the seat just off center to make it legal again. Penske won the Puerto Rican Grand Prix in November and was crowned the 1962 USAC Sports Car Champion.

The next season, Penske was forced to make major revisions to the car. The SCCA now insisted on two full seats, so the chassis was remade with a wider center section. Penske also sold the car (along with his services) to John Mecom. Penske won at both Marlboro and Cumberland at the start of the season. After that, the magic was over. Penske won at Brands Hatch, England, but otherwise was out of the hunt. Mecom decided to fit an aluminum Olds V-8 like he ran in some of his other cars, but instead sold the package to Bruce McLaren.

McLaren took the car to England and picked up wins at Aintree and Silverstone in 1964. McLaren used the Zerex as the development car for his planned McLaren sports-racers and installed the Olds he had bought with the car from Mecom. In that form, McLaren took the car to Mosport in Canada, where he picked up a win. Then it was back to England for another win at Brands Hatch.

After its front-line career was over, the old Zerex returned to the United States and was sold to Dave Morgan, who ran it in the Southwest division of the SCCA in the mid-1960s. It has supposedly survived but has not been seen in some time.

FOUR

Engine Swap Specials

Overview

In the 1950s and 1960s, hundreds of racing cars were subjected to engine swaps. While not technically specials, they were definitely Americanized. Few worked satisfactorily, as these swaps typically took place after the chassis had become obsolete (and thus cheaper). Here are some of the better-known cross-breeds.

Cooper

Cooper Monaco-Chevy

After Shelby American ordered special Monacos set up for Ford V-8s, Cooper offered similar chassis for sale. Some were fitted with Chevy V-8s.

Cunningham Cooper-Buick

Briggs Cunningham bought a used Cooper Monaco Mk.III and had Reventlow Automotive install a 3.8-liter aluminum Buick V-8. It won at Bridgehampton in 1963.

Sharp Cooper Maserati

Hap Sharp (in his pre-Chaparral days) bought a new Cooper Monaco, but reasoned he would not be sold as hot a Coventry-Climax engine as the factory cars were getting, so he installed a one-off 2,298-cc Maserati engine. Later, equipped with a 2.9-liter engine, it was very competitive in the early 1960s.

Telar Special

Roger Penske and John Mecom built a Chevy-powered Cooper Monaco. Penske had connections at Chevy and got an all-aluminum Chevy engine. The car was quick but no world-beater.

Ward Cooper Buick

Bob McKee converted this Cooper Monaco to aluminum V-8 power for Indy starter Roger Ward. It proved fast but prone to overheating.

Ferrari

The Bastard

In the late 1950s, Jim Hall and Carroll Shelby had a car dealership in Dallas, and they occasionally raced a primer-gray Ferrari Monza with a Chevy engine. It was called the Bastard and as a point of honor, was never washed.

Jones Ferrari-Chevy

R. David Jones, later president of the SCCA, raced a Chevy-powered Ferrari Testa Rossa in the Texas area.

Reed Ferrari

A Ferrari 250 Testa Rossa TR59 was reengined several times by owner George Reed in the early 1960s. First, a bigger Ferrari 290 MM engine was installed, followed by a 4.5-liter 375 MM engine. Finally, a 427 Ford stock car engine was squeezed in. Reed raced the car at Nassau and tracks in the Northeast and Canada.

Tilp Ferrari-Offy

George Tilp installed an Offenhauser Champ car engine in a Ferrari Mondial. Walt Hansgen drove it briefly.

Von Neumann 625TRC/Chevy

John von Neumann owned a special Ferrari 625 TRC that he reengined several times with various larger Ferrari engines. After he sold the car in the late 1950s, it was reengined with a Chevy V-8 and raced on the West Coast.

Jaguar

Dunbar-Jaguar

Jerry Dunbar had a Chevy-powered D-Jag he raced in the early 1960s.

A number of Cooper Monacos were fitted with Chevy V-8s. *Allen Kuhn*

258

Ensley Jaguar-Chevy

Jack Ensley bought an engineless D-Type Jaguar that Chevrolet had considered fitting with a Chevy V-8. Ensley's mechanic, Joe Silnas, did the job.

Johnson XK-SS

Delmo Johnson bought Bob Stonedale's XK-SS (a *Road & Track* road test car) and installed a Chevy V-8. It was raced in the Texas area in the 1950s and 1960s.

Krause Jaguar-Chevy

Billy Krause was a hard-charger who slipped a full-race Chevy engine into a D-Type Jaguar. The car was very quick and ran near the front in California road racing and at the Pikes Peak Hillclimb.

The Escherich Lotus wore some odd hood projections to cover the flat-four Porsche engine. *Allen Kuhn*

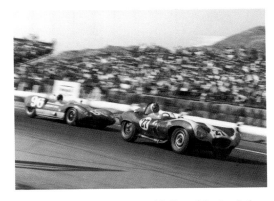

Bill Krause slides his D-Jaguar with Chevy bite ahead of a Lotus 19. *Allen Kuhn*

Teague Jaguar

Marshall Teague ran a Chevy-powered D-Jaguar in the late 1950s.

Lotus

Arciero Lotus-Chevy

The Lotus 19 in which Dan Gurney won the 1962 Daytona Continental was later repowered with a Chevy V-8 and raced by Bobby Unser in 1964.

Escherich Lotus-Porsche

Dr. William Escherich had one of the oddest engine swaps of all—a Porsche four-cam engine stuffed in the front of a Lotus Mk.IX. The engine was removed from the Porsche 550 actor James Dean was driving at the time of his death.

Grant Lotus 19 Olds/Chevy

Jerry Grant bought a partially completed Lotus 19 that was intended for an Oldsmobile aluminum V-8. Tom Carstens had started the job, but Grant completed the car and campaigned it in 1963 before having Trevor Harris reengineer the entire car to take a 400-horsepower Traco Chevy. It proved to be as fast as a Chaparral 2, but not as reliable.

Jerry Grant started with an aluminum Olds in this Lotus 19, and then switched to a big Chevy. *Allen Kuhn*

Gurney Lotus 19B

This was not an engine swap, but a one-off car built in England specifically for Dan Gurney, complete with a Ford V-8. Contrary to published articles, this was not the same Lotus 19 he won the 1962 Daytona race with (see Arciero Lotus-Chevy entry above).

Harrison Special

The J. Frank Harrison team ran a Lotus 19 in 1963 for driver Lloyd Ruby. The Climax engine was replaced with a Shelby-worked Ford 289, and an all-new body was installed. Jerry Eisert built the car. Ruby won the 1963 Kent USRRC race in that car.

The J. Frank Harrison team radically transformed this Lotus 19 with a Ford V-8 and special bodywork. Driver Lloyd won the 1963 Kent USRRC race in this car. *Allen Kuhn*

LeMay Lotus-Offenhauser

Alan LeMay raced a Lotus Mk.VI powered by an Offenhauser midget engine in the mid-1950s.

Mecom Lotus 19

Originally Climax-powered, this Lotus was reengined at Reventlow Automotive with an Oldsmobile V-8 and driven by Augie Pabst and John Cannon.

Nethercutt Lotus 15-Ferrari

Jack Nethercutt installed a four-cylinder Ferrari engine into a Lotus 15 and ran it in the early 1960s.

This little Lotus 15, owned by Jack Nethercutt, packed Ferrari punch. *Allen Kuhn*

Rosebud Lotus 19-Ferrari

After Innes Ireland won the Nassau Trophy Race in 1962, the Rosebud team removed the Climax engine from its Lotus 19 and installed a warmed-over Ferrari Testa Rossa engine. The car ran at the Northwest Grand Prix, where it was badly damaged in an accident. It was rebuilt on a new chassis and ran once more at Laguna Seca in 1964, by which time it was outdated. It was donated to the Victoria, Texas, high school auto shop class.

Maserati

Connell Maserati-Ferrari

Texan Alan Connell installed a Ferrari Testa Rossa V-12 in a long-tail Maserati Birdcage and raced it in the early 1960s.

Cunningham Maserati-Ford

Briggs Cunningham had a Maserati T-151 coupe that he stuffed with a Ford 427-ci stock car engine. The car was wrecked and burned to the ground in its first race.

Dixon Maserati-Chevy

Bill Dixon pepped up a Maserati 300S with a 351-ci Chevy engine. It was fitted with four side-draft Webers on a manifold made out of flex tubing.

Edgar Maserati-Pontiac

John Edgar had a Maserati 450S with a Pontiac V-8 that ran in 1958 and 1959 with Indy driver Jim Rathman at the wheel.

Miscellaneous

Abarth-McCulloch

Herbert Johnson installed a McCulloch flat-four 1,500-cc target drone engine in a 1950 Abarth 205 Vignale Berlinetta. It raced once in 1954 but overheated and retired.

Alfa-Cadillac

Tom Bamford raced a prewar Alfa Romeo Grand Prix car with a Cadillac engine in the early 1950s.

Arnolt-Chevy

Ed Rahal (uncle of Indy star Bobby Rahal) briefly raced an Arnolt-Bristol powered by a Chevy V-8.

Doretti-Buick

In the mid-1950s, Max Balchowsky built a short run of Buick-powered Doretti sports cars. Although these were intended primarily as road cars, Balchowsky raced at least one of them before building Old Yaller I.

HRG-Offy

P. Iselin inserted an Offy Midget engine into an upright British HRG in the early 1950s. He finished sixth in a handicap race at the Allentown airport in 1952.

Michaels Bandini-Offy

Dave Michaels drove a cycle-fendered Bandini fitted with an Offy Midget engine to many wins in the early 1950s (see Meyer Drake Engines entry, Chapter 6).

The Michaels Bandini-Offy (No.50) was one of the quickest of the Offy midget-powered racers.
Stuart Schaller collection

Tilp Aston Martin-Offy

George Tilp installed an Offenhauser Champ car engine in an Aston Martin DB-2 coupe in the 1950s. The engine was later transferred to his Ferrari Mondial (see Tilp Ferrari-Offy entry above).

2JR

Stock car builder Bill Stroppe built a stripped MG TC special in the early 1950s, powered by a full-house Ford V-8 60 engine. Phil Hill drove the car to several wins. Other MGs were also fitted with the V-8 60 engine.

Vinegaroon Elva-Maserati

This Elva Mk.6 was fitted with a four-cylinder Maserati engine. It was built in 1964 for actor Dan Blocker's racing team.

Actor Dan Blocker owned this potent but star-crossed Elva, powered by a Maserati engine (No.15). *Allen Kuhn*

Alken

The Alken Corporation offered one of the first kit car bodies intended for use on the Volkswagen chassis. The Alken D-2 came out in 1958 and was an attractive, if expensive, route to improving the appearance of the VW Beetle. The car was designed by industrial designer Bill Pierson and was built in Venice, California. A complete kit, including the body, windshield frame, doors, and front and rear deck lids, could be had for $1,295. For an extra $100, Alken would hang the doors and deck lids. Other options included fiberglass seats and the associated hardware ($65.50), a removable hardtop ($195), plexiglass side screens ($45 per pair), and roll-up windows ($95 per pair).

Although the bodies were not intended for racing, Alken built a single "works" racing car to showcase the new body. It was raced at Riverside in 1958 and promptly disappeared. Alken was out of business by the early 1960s.

ALKEN	
Alken Corporation	
2100 Zeno Place	
Venice, California	
Years built	**starting in 1958**
Kit Products	**fiberglass roadster body**
Body styles	**one**

Almquist

This kit body builder of the 1950s and 1960s came to the business when Ed Almquist purchased the stock of fiberglass bodies from Clearfield Plastics. The body became the Almquist Sabre I, which was a lovely 124-inch-long roadster that could accommodate chassis with a wheelbase of 72 to 82 inches. It featured a unique headlight option that allowed the customer to specify grille or fender mounting. The Sabre I was followed by the Sabre II, which was similar roadster design, but was 134 inches long and could accommodate chassis wheelbases of 82 to 92 inches. Both were $295 and were Almquist's all-time best sellers. The Sabre 750 followed and was essentially a Sabre I or II shell with a reworked rear deck to allow for a rear-engined chassis. The Sabre 750 cost $295 and was offered in two sizes, one for a Volkswagen chassis and the other for a Renault chassis. All three Sabre models weighed in at approximately 75 pounds.

The Almquist Speedster was offered in three sizes at a price of $495. The Speedster I body was 156 inches long and accommodated wheelbases of 94 to 106 inches. The Speedster II and III bodies were 166 inches long and accommodated wheelbases of 106 to 116 inches. The only real difference between the Speedster II and III was that the latter had quad headlight receptacles located in the fenders. The speedster series bodies weighed approximately 110 pounds.

ALMQUIST	
Ed Almquist	
Almquist Engineering	
Milford, Pennsylvania	
Constructor	**Ed Almquist/Almquist Engineering**
Years built	**1950s and 1960s**
Kit Products	**fiberglass roadster bodies**
Body styles	**nine available (see text)**
Body material	**fiberglass**
Wheelbase range	**72 to 118 inches**

261

The Almquist Speedster was a popular kit car body in the mid-1950s. *Robert Rolofson Jr.; Robert H. Rolofson III collection*

Almquist Speedster I.

Ambro

Dewey Brohaugh and William E. Aldrich-Ames built a Triumph-powered race car in 1961 (see Ambro entry, Chapter 2) and offered copies of its lovely fiberglass body to specials builders. The body was a combination of Lister and Maserati Birdcage styling elements, and some panels were actually molded off an original T-61 Maserati. The bodies were made of 1/8-inch fiberglass and were molded in six panels. The nose and tail were separate pieces, as were the doors and the two lower roll panels. The body could be made to fit 88- to 102-inch-wheelbase chassis, with 45.5- to 52-inch track. The body weighed around 80 pounds. Ambro recommended that the body be mounted on an inner structure made from conduit tubing, and the instruction manual showed drawings of the recommended structure. The complete body retailed for $349, and the various panels could be ordered separately. There was no frame or inner framework

The Ambro bodies had elements of Lister and Maserati bodywork. *Harold Pace*

offered. Ambro bodies were fitted to a number of specials. At least one was fitted to a Bristol-powered special that raced on the East Coast; another was fitted to a Peerless chassis that is still being run in vintage racing. One was used on a DKW-powered H-Modified in Texas, while at the other extreme, an Ambro body ended up on a Buick-powered special called the Mustang. Around 40 bodies were built before the project was sold to Jerry Scrabeck of Rochester, Minnesota, in 1964. Scrabeck sold about

another dozen bodies. In the 1990s, the body was reborn by Bill Bonadio, with the help and approval of Brohaugh, for the Dio Tipo kit car.

AMBRO	
Ambro Ltd.	
1339 Third Avenue S.W.	
Rochester, Minnesota	
Constructors	**Dewey Brohaugh and William E. Aldrich-Ames**
Years built	**1961–1964**
Kit products	**fiberglass roadster body**
Body styles	**one**
Wheelbase range	**88 to 102 inches**

Atlas/Allied

Roy Kinch and Mickey Thompson founded the Atlas Fiber-Glass Company in the early 1950s; both men later found fame at Bonneville. They offered both a roadster and coupe body. The mold for the body was pulled off of a Cisitalia 202 Grand Sport, which was a lovely Pininfarina design. The body was initially offered in a size intended for MG TC and MG TD chassis. Later, two larger sizes were offered. The company name was eventually changed to the Allied Fiber-Glass Company.

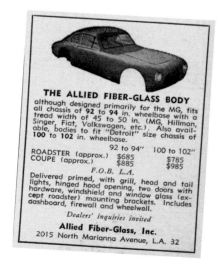

THE ALLIED FIBER-GLASS BODY although designed primarily for the MG, fits all chassis of 92 to 94 in. wheelbase with a tread width of 45 to 50 in. (MG, Hillman, Singer, Fiat, Volkswagen, etc.). Also available, bodies to fit "Detroit" size chassis of 100 to 102 in. wheelbase.

	92 to 94"	100 to 102"
ROADSTER (approx.)	$685	$785
COUPE (approx.)	$885	$985

F.O.B. L.A.

Delivered primed, with grill, head and tail lights, hinged hood opening, two doors with hardware, windshield and window glass (except roadster) mounting brackets. Includes dashboard, firewall and wheelwell.

Dealers' inquiries invited

Allied Fiber-Glass, Inc.
2015 North Marianna Avenue, L.A. 32

The Allied bodies were copies of the Italian Cisitalia coupe. *Allen Kuhn*

ATLAS/ALLIED	
Atlas Fiber-Glass Company/Allied	
Fiber-Glass Company	
California	
Constructors	**Roy Kinch and Mickey Thompson**
Years built	**starting in the early 1950s**
Kit Products	**fiberglass roadster body; fiberglass coupe body**

Bangert

Noel Bangert designed his first fiberglass body in the early 1950s, and by 1954 he was in the kit car business. His first design was a cigar-shaped roadster that would accommodate chassis with a wheelbase of 98 to 118 inches. The design so impressed Hollywood Plastics that it offered the body for sale through company advertisements for $395.

In 1955, *Road & Track* featured Bangert's second design, also a cigar-shaped roadster but now with winglike fenders and open wheel arches. This was a popular choice for racers, as the body weighed in at only 125 pounds and could accommodate a wheelbase of 90 to 104 inches.

Bangert's third body style was designed to be more streamlined to improve aerodynamics. The impetus for this was the experience he gained with

John Teverbaugh, who set a Bonneville record of 153.84 miles per hour in a Bangert-bodied (second design), 1956 Chrysler-powered roadster. Although the third design was an improvement over the second, Teverbaugh failed to set another record.

Bangert also offered a simple ladder frame constructed of 2- and 3-inch rectangular tubing. It was set up to accept prewar Ford suspension and Lincoln brakes. A frame was also offered.

Bocar

Denver-based Bocar (see Bocar entry, Chapter 2) built complete customer racing cars, but it also sold bodies and chassis that were built into race cars. The X-1 body used on the XP-4 and XP-5 Bocars was designed to fit wheelbases from 86 to 94 inches. The $585 basic body was a one-piece fiberglass shell

with molded-in headlights and taillights. For an extra $44, the hood or trunk lid could be installed with provision for Dzus fasteners. Clear plastic headlight covers were $22, and a headrest (left or right side) was only $22. Most Bocars did not have doors, but one or two could be cut out at the factory or by the owner. A cockpit liner with a firewall, tunnel, and floorboards was $275 extra. The bodies were shipped in lacquer primer. A rare option was a removable hardtop with a built-in windshield.

The chrome-moly space frame chassis set up for VW front suspension sold for $995. For an extra $295, a complete VW front end was installed, and the rear suspension with VW torsion bars and shocks was $300. The rear axle housing was usually a modified Chevy unit with Positraction, and Bocar would sell a new one for $135. The usual brakes were Buick Alfin drums, and for $268

Bocar would sell you a full set, modified and ready to bolt on. Although steel wheels were standard, Bocar also sold Borrani wires with knock-off hubs for $685. For $4,325.28 you could have everything you needed to build your own XP-5. Bocar also offered the longer XP-6/XP-7 body with 102- to 104-inch wheelbase and the 101-inch-wheelbase Stiletto, although few were sold. One Stiletto body

was fitted to an H-Modified DKW-powered special that was run in Colorado.

A number of specials were built with Bocar bodies, but perhaps the best known was the Peterson Special (see Chapter 3). Wendell Burgess also built one on a Henry J. chassis (with Chevy power) and raced it in Colorado. Bocar kits were also built on Triumph and Jaguar chassis, among others.

Most Bocar kit chassis did not have chassis numbers, but some bodies had numbers spray-painted on the inside of a fender.

263

Byers

If Bill Devin had a rival in the production kit body business, it was definitely Jim Byers. Byers only sold two styles (Devin sold more than two dozen), but his fiberglass roadster bodies were beautifully styled and finely crafted works of art. Like Devin, Byers was committed to delivering a high-quality product and only the smoothest of body skins were allowed to leave his shop.

Byers' first design was the SR-100. This was a magnificent swoopy roadster body. The SR-100 was designed for a wheelbase of 99 to 101 inches but was engineered to be easily modified for other wheelbases. The body was made to accept a stock Corvette windshield, which was a real plus for the home-builder. The large engine compartment and grille opening made stuffing a monster V-8 and radiator under the hood a breeze. With a weight of 95 pounds and a cost of $345 to $595 (depending

This Byers SR-100 body is on a Kurtis 500KK chassis with DeSoto Hemi power. It was called the Salem Special. *Harold Pace*

264

upon trim and hardware), the SR-100 was a favorite of many racers of the day.

Byers' second body was the CR-90. This body weighed 75 pounds and was intended for wheelbases ranging from 88 to 92 inches. Like the first car, the CR-90 was a beautiful open roadster suitable for racing. A faired-in headrest was designed to house a roll bar, and it gave the car a racy appearance. The price ranged from $325 to $465.

In 1960, Byers sold his molds to Victress Manufacturing, which continued to produce the bodies. Later, the molds were sold to LaDawri and still later to Kellison.

BYERS

Byers
118 Sheldon Street
El Segundo, California

Constructor .... **Jim Byers**
Years built **1957–1960**
Kit products .... **fiberglass roadster bodies**
Body styles .... **two**
Wheelbase range .... **88 to 101 inches (modifiable for other wheelbases)**

Devin

Bill Devin is perhaps best known for his gorgeous fiberglass bodies. Following his first foray into the world of fiberglass on the Devin Panhard, Devin hit on the idea of making bodies for racers, gearheads, and the shade tree set around 1956. Using an ingenious array of modular molds, Devin was able to manufacture bodies in 27 different sizes to fit virtually any road or race car (sizes A through X, and sizes V-6, W-6, and X-6). The smallest body available would accommodate an H-Mod racer with a wheelbase of 82 to 84 inches and an overall length of 145 inches. The largest body would accommodate a big-bore racer with a 102- to 106-inch wheelbase and an overall length of 169 inches. The bodies cost $295, and the average freight charge was an additional $10. (Those were the days!) Extras available for an additional charge included: a removable headrest ($25), a cockpit liner ($75), and reinforcements for the deck and hood openings ($25 for each).

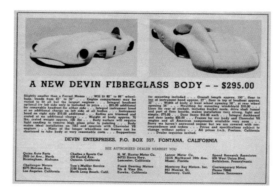

The business boomed, with Devin selling thousands of units through a network of dealers in each of the 50 states. Devin's bodies were not only beautiful, but the quality was the best available by a long shot, and the price was more than reasonable. Devin was uncompromising in the development and maintenance of the master molds, and the smooth bodies that they produced clearly evidenced that point. He was equally dogmatic about the fiberglass product employed. Each Devin body was hand laid,

Small Devin kit bodies were used on hundreds of Crosley-powered modifieds. *Harold Pace*

using a high-quality, durable, translucent fiberglass cloth rather than the inferior mat material utilized by so many builders of the day. Devin could have made a fortune had he stuck with the $295-body business. But in typical Devin fashion, he grew fidgety for a new challenge. (He was dreaming up the Devin SS.) Although Devin achieved great financial success in the body business, he made no secret of the fact that he never really liked making them.

Numerous racing specials of the day were adorned in a beautiful Devin body. Ak Miller was very successful in his numerous Devin-bodied sports cars. The Moonbeam, built by speed equipment guru Dean Moon, was a very successful Salt Flats and drag race special. Other Devin-bodied specials include the Chevy-powered Del Mar Mk.II, the three Echidnas, and the third Morgensen Special.

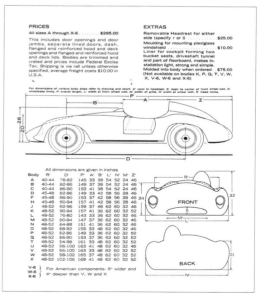

PRICES
All sizes A through X-6 .... $295.00

This includes door openings and door jambs, separate lined doors, dash, flanged and reinforced hood and deck openings and flanged and reinforced hood and deck lids. Bodies are trimmed and crated and prices include Federal Excise Tax. Shipping is via rail unless otherwise specified, average freight costs $10.00 in U.S.A.

EXTRAS
Removable Headrest for either side (specify r or l) $25.00
Moulding for mounting plexiglass windshield $10.00
Liner for cockpit forming two bucket seats, driveshaft tunnel and part of floorboard, makes installation light, strong and simple. Molded into body when ordered .... $75.00 (Not available on bodies K, P, Q, T, V, W, X, V-6, W-6 and X-6)

Body	R'	D'	P	A'	B'	L'	N'	M'	Z'
A	40-44	78-82	145	33	38	54	52	24	46
B	40-44	82-86	149	37	38	54	52	24	46
C	40-44	86-90	153	41	38	54	52	24	46
D	45-48	82-86	149	33	42	58	56	28	46
F	45-48	86-90	153	37	42	58	56	28	46
H	45-48	90-94	157	41	42	58	56	28	46
J	48-52	92-96	159	37	48	62	60	32	46
K	48-52	90-94	157	41	36	62	60	32	52
L	48-52	76-80	143	33	36	62	60	32	46
M	48-52	80-84	147	37	36	62	60	32	46
N	48-52	84-88	151	41	36	62	60	32	46
O	48-52	88-92	155	33	48	62	60	32	52
P	48-52	82-86	149	33	36	62	60	32	52
Q	48-52	86-90	153	37	36	62	60	32	52
T	48-52	94-98	161	33	48	62	60	32	52
U	48-52	96-100	163	41	48	62	60	32	52
V	48-52	96-100	163	33	48	62	60	32	52
W	48-52	98-102	165	37	48	62	60	32	52
X	48-52	1C2-106	169	41	48	62	60	32	52
V-6									
W-6	For American components: 6" wider and								
X-6	4" deeper than V, W and X								

All dimensions are given in inches

FRONT

BACK

The beautiful $295 Devin bodies were very popular on V-8 specials. *Chris Wickersham*

DEVIN

**Devin Enterprises
44500 Sierra Highway
Lancaster, California**

**Devin Enterprises
9800 Rush Street
El Monte, California**

**Devin Sports Cars
35089 San Carlos Street
Yucaipa, California**

Constructor . . . . **Bill Devin**
Kit Products . . . . **fiberglass roadster bodies**
Body styles . . . . **27 available (see text)**
Wheelbase range . . . . **78 to 106 inches**
Length range . . . . **145 to 169 inches**
Number built . . . . **one**

Fiberfab

One of the most difficult kit car stories to tell is that of Fiberfab, which began producing fiberglass bodies around 1964. Over the years, the company has changed ownership numerous times and has been "headquartered" in, at least, the following cities: Palo Alto, California; Sunnyvale, California; Santa Clara, California; Freemont, California; Cleveland, Ohio; Pittsburgh, Pennsylvania; and Minneapolis, Minnesota.

Fiberfab produced some 14 models, including the following: Fiberfab GT (the first design, which was a coupe similar to the first Ford GT40); Aztec (the Fiberfab GT with a new name); Azteca (a convertible version of the Aztec); Aztec II (an updated version of the Aztec); Centurion (essentially a replica of the Corvette Sting Ray prototype); Caribee (an unattractive gull-winged-door kit coupe); Banshee (the Caribee with a new name); Avenger (a Ford GT lookalike); Valkyrie (a more muscular version of the Avenger); GTX (later version of the Valkyrie); Jamaican (a replacement version of the Banshee); and the Aztec 7 (styled after the Alfa Romeo Carabo show car).

Of all the Fiberfab designs, it is likely that only the Avenger, Valkyrie, and GTX were used on race cars in period.

The Avenger was one of Fiberfab's successful models; with thousands of units sold, it made a big impact on the kit car market. While it was not a direct copy of the Ford GT, its influence was undeniable. Because the kit was relatively easy to assemble, many were actually completed. That was not so common of kit cars in the 1960s.

The Valkyrie was a muscular version of the Avenger, available in turnkey form for $12,500 or as a kit for $1,595. This was a well-designed, mid-engined, V-8-powered sports car coupe with a Corvair transaxle. The GTX was the last version of the Valkyrie and only a few were sold. It was intended to use a Hewland racing transaxle or a ZF unit and would accommodate a big-block Chevy V-8. Some Valkyries and GTXs were raced in the SCCA but were not competitive when pitted against the Lolas and McLarens of their class.

In addition to fiberglass bodies and car kits, Fiberfab offered a number of kit frames and chassis of various types and configurations.

The Fiberfab Avenger and Valkyrie bodies were used on a few club racers in the 1960s. *Harold Pace*

FIBERFAB

**Fiberfab
United States**

Constructors . . . . **numerous**
Years built . . . . **starting in 1964**
Kit products . . . . **fiberglass convertible bodies; fiberglass coupe bodies; various frames and chassis**
Body styles . . . . **14 (see text)**

265

Fibersport

Fibersport began as a manufacturer of complete Crosley-based racing cars in 1953, but quickly entered the kit car market selling bodies and frames. (See Fibersport entry, Chapter 2).

FIBERSPORT

**Fibersport
Bloomington, Illinois**

Constructors . . . . **John Mays, Bill Mays, and John Burmaster**
Years built . . . . **starting in 1953**
Kit products . . . . **fiberglass roadster bodies; frames and chassis**
Body styles . . . . **two (one race version, one street version)**

Glasspar

The Glasspar Company was a fiberglass boat manufacturer that got into the car body business quite by accident. Around 1950, Air Force Major Kenneth Brooks was looking for someone to build him a one-off roadster. When no one else seemed interested, Glasspar's co-owner and chief designer, Bill Tritt, answered his friend's call for help. The car was built with Willys running gear and became known as the Brooks Boxer. It received substantial media attention and business interest from the U.S. Rubber Company; its Naugatuck Division produced fiberglass resin. The publicity convinced Tritt to go into production in 1951.

The first production body was a modified version of Brooks' shell known as the G-2. It was a lovely sports car body with a door on the passenger's (right) side but without one for the driver. Glasspar also offered a ladder frame built by the Mameco Company and designed to accept Ford running gear.

In order to promote the sale of G-2 bodies, Glasspar built a race car that competed throughout California. The car was powered by a flathead Mercury engine and rode on a one-off tube frame fabricated by Shorty Post. Dick Morgensen built a Cadillac-powered Glasspar and ran seventh at Torrey Pines in December 1952. The 1951 Comet ran with an MG TD chassis, a flathead Mercury motor, and a Glasspar G-2 body.

Glasspar made one of the first fiberglass kit car bodies in the United States. *Harold Pace*

After the G-2, Tritt worked on several other car-related designs, including fully assembled cars and various other body designs.

GLASSPAR	
Glasspar Company	
Santa Ana, California	
Constructor	**Bill Tritt**
Years built	**starting in 1951**
Kit products	**fiberglass roadster bodies; ladder frame**

The Kellison convertible body was popular on many specials. This one is on an MGA chassis with Chevy V-8 power. *Harold Pace*

Kellison coupes were great looking bodies used on a few racing cars. *Harold Pace*

Kellison

Ex-fighter pilot Jim Kellison formed Kellison Engineering & Manufacturing Company in 1954. Over time, Kellison became one of the most successful and prolific of all the kit car builders. His designs were not only innovative and attractive but have stood the test of time with a constant replenishing supply of modern-day fans. The bodies could be purchased as bare uncut units (as pulled from the mold) or as complete units including the floorpan, inner wheelwells, fender and door opening reinforcements, and firewall.

Kellison built a number of open-cockpit roadster bodies used on race cars. The first one was the J-2 roadster. The body had a length of 169 inches and was designed for 102-inch wheelbases. The price was $380 bare and $500 complete. The J-3 roadster had a length of 165 inches for shorter wheelbase cars of 98 inches. Prices were $400 for a bare body and $520 complete. A shorter K-2 roadster was also offered. The body was 154 inches long and fit 86- to 88-inch wheelbases. A bare body could be had for $365; a complete body was $485. The Kellison roadsters could be purchased with or without a head fairing.

Kellison's first closed-cockpit car was the J-4 Grande Turismo Coupe. It measured 165 inches in length and was designed for wheelbases of 98 to 102 inches. The coupe, designed to run as a front-engined V-8, stood just 39 inches tall—a full inch shorter than the Ford GT40! The J-4 sold for $365 bare and $605 complete. The K-3 Grande Turismo Coupe had a double-bubble roofline and was 154 inches long with wheelbase options of 86 to 88 inches. The overall height was a startling 38 inches. List price was $390 bare and $570 complete.

In addition to fiberglass roadster and coupe bodies, Kellison offered a $5 plan set for a tube frame and at least two finished frames to mate with his bodies. He offered the first frame in 1958. It was a box-type frame designed by Chuck Manning. It carried a live axle at each end and was built up from 4-inch tubing with a 0.60-inch wall thickness. Later, he offered a frame that used early Corvette suspension at the front and rear.

For information on the complete racing cars that Kellison manufactured, see Chapter 2.

KELLISON

**Kellison Engineering & Manufacturing Company
905 Sutter Street
Folsom, California**

Constructor	**Jim Kellison**
Years built	**starting in 1954**
Kit products	**fiberglass roadster bodies; fiberglass coupe bodies; chassis; chassis plans**
Wheelbase range	**86 to 102 inches**
Length range	**154 to 169 inches**

Kurtis

Frank Kurtis built some of the most fabulous road racing cars of the 1950s and early 1960s. Many of the cars, including the Kurtis Sports Car (KSC) and Kurtis 500S, were sold as completed factory cars or as kits. Those cars are covered in Chapter 2 (see Kurtis entry). This section covers the Kurtis chassis kit.

Kurtis 500KK Chassis

Shortly after the introduction of his cycle-fendered 500S race car in 1953, Kurtis announced the introduction of a kit chassis intended to fill the needs of the backyard hot rodder and race car home-builder. The tube chassis was similar to that of the 500S but with a few differences.

The all-new 500KK had a central deep-channel frame rail construction similar to the 500S, but the KK rails were not as tall and not as stout. Kurtis diminished the frame rail height in the KK chassis in order to make body mounting easier for the hobbyist and homebuilder. With the diminished frame rail height, the frame tubes were placed closer together in the frame section, and the overall strength and stiffness of the

Bill Boldt raced this Pontiac-powered Kurtis 500KK. The body builder is unknown. *Allen Kuhn*

chassis were reduced. In order to counterbalance that effect, Kurtis installed an X-member built from the same stock as the KK channel frame rails; no lightening holes were drilled in the X-member.

The suspension for the KK chassis was the same as the 500S, both up front and in the rear. The rear axle was a 1940 Ford-type, installed to allow for the use of a Halibrand quick-change unit.

The bare frame weighed in at less than 100 pounds and tipped the scales at 770 pounds with the brakes, steering gear, shocks, radiator, and wheels installed. The standard KK frame length was 158 inches, but Kurtis would customize the wheelbase from 88 to 100 inches, as the customer desired.

Kurtis sold the frame/chassis and components in any state of finish that the customer desired. The bare frame was $399. Other components were available as follows: front and rear suspension, $391.20; steering gear (no column), $92.69; rear end housing, $89.86; running gear (including standard Ford spindles,

The Kurtis 500KK was a chassis kit for use with kit car bodies. This example has a Byers SR-100 body and is powered by a DeSoto Hemi. In the 1950s, it was called the Salem Special. *Harold Pace*

hubs, drums, brakes, and wheels), $228.19; and radiator and shocks, $89.06. For the customer who wanted to go as far as possible, Kurtis would deliver a chassis complete with Ford 11-inch hydraulic brakes, Gemmer steering gear, 50/50 tube shocks, a custom radiator, and 15- or 16-inch Ford wheels for the sum of $1,290.

The best estimate is that approximately 60 Kurtis 500KK chassis were built. Between 18 and 20 were used to construct the Kurtis 500M cars, so some-

KURTIS

Kurtis Kraft
6215 South San Pedro Street
Glendale, California

1107 East Colorado Boulevard
Glendale, California

Alger Street
Glendale, California

Constructor	**Frank Kurtis**
Years built	**1954–1955**
Kit Products	**ladder chassis**
Wheelbase range	**88 to100 inches**
Chassis length	**158 inches (average)**
Chassis width	**40 inches**
Chassis track	**58 inches**
Number built	**approximately 60 (including 18 to 20 used in the construction of the 500M)**
Price when new	**$399 to $1290 (depending on components and state of finish)**

where between 40 and 42 were probably used to build specials. A variety of fiberglass bodies were used to build a racing car on a 500KK chassis, including those from Allied/Atlas (coupes), Bangert, Byers, Glasspar, Sorrell, Victress, and Woodhill. In addition, several KK chassis were clothed in alloy bodies from California Metal Shaping, Charles Lyons, and others.

LaDawri

Les Dawes of LaDawri of Long Beach, California, produced some of the more finely constructed fiberglass bodies of the 1950s and 1960s. Dawes' bodies benefited from his attention to detail and commitment to produce a high-quality, rigid shell. He augmented body rigidity by laminating strengthening panels into the shell in vital areas of stress. Overall body fit was very good, and the doors were even relatively easy to hang. Those qualities made the LaDawri product an attractive option for kit car enthusiasts of the day. A total of 19 models of LaDawri bodies were available during the company's rise and fall. Many were original LaDawri designs, but some body molds were acquired from smaller companies. Some LaDawri bodies were beautiful, while others were visually challenged, but they were all interesting in their own right.

Sports Car Bodies

LaDawri produced a total of five sports car bodies. The first was the Conquest, and it was actually the first original LaDawri design. The body was designed to be mounted on a chassis with a wheelbase of 100 to 104 inches and was featured on the cover of *Road & Track* in July 1957. The following year, Dawes added another original body design to the LaDawri line-up—the Quest GT. The Quest GT was a modification of the Conquest body intended for chassis with a wheelbase of 92 to 98 inches. Chassis commonly used with the Quest GT body included Volkswagen, MG, and Austin-Healey. Another modification of the Conquest involved

restyling the nose and dual grille openings. The resulting body, known as the Daytona, had a single, full-width grille and the same wheelbase options as the Conquest. Two diminutive versions of the Daytona followed for smaller chassis. The Sebring was available for chassis of 92 to 98 inches, and the Del Mar covered the market for chassis of 84 to 92 inches.

All five sports car models were designed to accept a production windshield and had an attractive molded-in dash. A roll bar was built into the frame of the windshield, and well-designed bucket seats were available.

Race Car Bodies

In 1961, Dawes purchased a stable of body molds from Victress and renamed each of the bodies. Two of the bodies were constructed as thin body shells without inner panels or bulkheads, to be used on competition race roadsters. The delightful Victress S-1A body became the LaDawri Vixen. The Vixen body was 168 inches long, 69 inches wide, and was appropriate for chassis with a 98- to 102-inch wheelbase. The Victress S-5 was renamed the LaDawri Cheetah and measured 156 inches in length, 60 inches in width, and was intended for chassis with a wheelbase of 92 to 96 inches.

In 1963, Dawes made a deal to lease body molds from Ralph Starkweather to produce the LaDawri Firestar Mk.II. It was the same mold that Starkweather had used to form the shell for his race car, the Starkweather Crosley (see Starkweather Crosley entry, Chapter 3). The body was delivered as a one-piece shell and was a real head-turner, with a cowl height of only 23 inches. The shell was light-weight (just 40 pounds) and was appropriate for chassis with a wheelbase of 76 to 86 inches. The length was 124 inches and the width was 56 inches. The Firestar was LaDawri's answer to the H-Mod racer looking for a lightweight, low-cost body shell. Suggested chassis included Crosley, Fiat, Metropolitan, and Sprite. The body was $195 with a built-in headrest on the right or $220 with the head-rest supplied as a separate piece.

By 1965, the kit car market was receding, and Dawes' business was in trouble. Aerospace engineer Clark Adams designed a new and stylish racing coupe with the intent of creating a one-body-fits-all product. The body was dubbed the LaDawri Formula Libre and could be adapted for use with a front-, mid-, and rear-engine chassis. Entry into the beautiful Formula Libre was via a tilt-forward canopy, and specially constructed reclining seats allowed the driver to fit under the low roofline. As an alternative to the tilt canopy, gullwing doors could be ordered. In fact, Dawes would customize the Formula Libre to the exact specifications of the customer in order to make the body fit the intended chassis. A few of the

Formula Libre bodies were used on the well-known Fiat-powered PBS racing cars.

Other Bodies

Three additional molds were purchased from Victress and used to construct a LaDawri body. The Victress C-2 coupe became the LaDawri Sicilian (wheelbase 90 to 98 inches, length 157 inches, width 63 inches), and the Victress C-3 coupe became the LaDawri Castilian (wheelbase 98 to 108 inches, length 165 inches, width 70 inches). The Victress S-4 con-vertible became the LaDawri Cavalier (wheelbase 108 to 120 inches, length 187 inches, width 71 inches); a shortened version of the Cavalier became the LaDawri Conquistador (wheelbase 92 to 110 inches).

Manning

Chuck Manning built a highly successful special in the early 1950s (see Manning Mercury Special entry, Chapter 3), and wrote a series of articles for *Road & Track* on building a racing car. There was quite a bit of interest, so he wrote up and sold sets of plans for building copies of his special.

The Manning plan set led to many specials like this one. *Harold Pace*

Manning Plan Set

Manning's plans showed all the dimensions used to build a tube-frame special with a flathead Mercury engine. A number of cars were built more or less from these plans, including the Monsterati and the Schaghticoke Special (see Monsterati and Schaghticoke Special entries, Chapter 4).

Manning later designed frames for the Kellison Kit Car Company.

Sorrell Engineering

Bob Sorrell had a shop on Felton Avenue in Inglewood, California. He was a skilled fabricator, well known for his work with tin, aluminum, and fiber-glass. Many of the great race cars of the day passed through Sorrell's shop to have him do such things as form the bulkheads or fabricate the firewall. Road racers, drag racers, and the speed record set equally appreciated Sorrell's work. More than one who knew him well have described him as a "genius with automotive design" or "way ahead of his time."

Sorrell began building fiberglass bodies in the early 1950s. In October 1955, the first of a multi-installment article featuring his fiberglass shells appeared in *Car Craft*. His somewhat unique construction technique involved fastening wooden templates together at 10-inch intervals. He would then fill in the gaps with chicken wire, paper, and plaster to form a buck. The buck was then used to pull a mold.

One of his more popular designs was the Sorrell SR-100. The beautiful roadster body was designed to fit chassis with wheelbases from 95 to 100 inches and could be purchased for $500. Although it bore the same name as one of Jim Byers' shells, there was no relation or similarity. The Sorrell SR-100 was a slick, aerodynamic skin and therefore popular with both road racing and dry lakes racers. Denny Larsen set a D-Modified record of 178.068 miles per hour in a Chrysler-powered Sorrell SR-100 with a custom-fabbed bubble top. Sorrell so liked the bubble top that he added an optional teardrop-shaped hardtop to his product line.

Another popular Sorrell design was the SR-190. The fiberglass coupe body had a price of $575 and was designed to bolt directly onto a stock Austin-Healey 100/4 or 100/6 chassis. Sorrell also offered the coupe top as a separate item to Healey owners for $295. For non-Healey customers, the body could be stretched to accommodate a chassis with a wheelbase up to 100 inches.

In addition to the production shells, Sorrell made a number of one-off fiberglass creations for race cars along the way. Some were beautiful, some were quirky looking, but they all shared the outrageous Sorrell flare.

Sports Car Engineering

The Microplas Mistral body was one of the loveliest and most popular fiberglass kit shells produced in England. Because of its success in Europe, American-based Sports Car Engineering began to sell the Mistral body in the United States. It is unclear whether the company simply acted as a sales agent for Microplas or actually had a set of molds from which it produced bodies domestically.

The Mistral body was available in two sizes. For $295, the customer could order a skin for wheelbases of 84 to 94 inches. For $345, a Mistral body for larger cars with wheelbases from 94 to 102 inches could be purchased.

Sports Car Engineering also offered two chassis options, one street chassis and one racing chassis. The latter was a 100-inch wheelbase light tube frame. With the suspension hung, the racing chassis could be purchased for $495.

Several American specials of the day were clothed in a fiberglass Mistral body. Perhaps the best known was the Arciero Special.

Vale

Vale Wright began to design a stylish new fiberglass body for his MG TC in December 1951. It was obviously inspired by the Cisitalia Nuvolari Spyder. Wright was a talented architect/designer/artist, and the new body turned out so well that he decided to go into business making the shell for other customers. Wright showed a prototype at the 1952 Oakland International Sports Car Show that was very well received by the press and public. Production ceased around 1958.

VALE	
Constructor	Vale Wright
Years built	1951–1958
Kit products	fiberglass roadster body
Wheelbase range	under 100 inches

Victress

The Victress Manufacturing Company was founded in the early 1950s by William "Doc" Boyce-Smith and quickly grew to be a leader in the emerging kit body industry. Boyce-Smith studied engineering at UCLA and was an experienced circle track and dry lakes racer. He also had significant expertise in all aspects of fiberglass construction, owing to his time spent working for Lockheed's plastics division.

While he had the inclination and know-how, Boyce-Smith knew that he needed help. He called on Merrill Powell, a former rodder and graduate of Los Angeles' prestigious Art Center College of Design, to serve as the company's chief of design and Bill Powell (who was of no family relation) to serve as the company's production manager.

The first Victress body was the S-1A. The gorgeous fiberglass roadster body had a sleek, aerodynamic appearance, and was actually wind tunnel tested in the early 1950s. Apparently, the engineering exercise paid off, as Guy Mabee drove a Chrysler-powered Victress S-1A-bodied special to a top speed of 203.105 miles per hour at Bonneville in 1953.

The S-1A was designed to fit a wheelbase of 99 inches, and many builders of the era used a modified 1941 Ford chassis. Builders adapted other frames, and Victress even offered a frame kit produced by the Mameco Company, which also built frames for Glasspar.

Victress offered the S-5, a smaller roadster version of the S-1A. The body was appropriate for chassis with a 94-inch wheelbase, such as the MG TC, MG TD, and MG TF. Victress also offered a kit frame to fit the S-5 body.

VICTRESS	
Victress Manufacturing Company	
11823 Sherman Way	
North Hollywood, California	
Constructors	William "Doc" Boyce-Smith, Merrill Powell, Bill Powell
Years built	early 1950s to 1961
Kit products	fiberglass roadster bodies; fiberglass coupe bodies; ladder frames
Body styles	six
Wheelbase range	94 to 118 inches

By the late 1950s, Victress had introduced two fiberglass coupes, the C-2 and C-3. The C-2 was intended for MG and Volkswagen chassis and had a 94-inch wheelbase. A C-2-bodied Chrysler special was clocked at Bonneville at 155 miles per hour in period. The C-3 looked similar to the C-2 but fit chassis with a wheelbase of 98 to 102 inches.

A DR-1 dragster body (wheelbases 100 to 118 inches) was later added to the Victress line-up, as were Jim Byers' bodies after the purchase of his molds in 1960. By 1961, Victress had too much governmental contract business to stay focused on car bodies, and the company sold its molds to LaDawri.

WOODHILL WILDFIRE	
Constructor	B. R. "Woody" Woodhill
Years built	1952–1963
Kit products	fiberglass roadster body

Woodhill Wildfire

Tony Curtis drove the Woodhill Wildfire-bodied Idaho Potato Special to a stunning victory in Universal International's 1954 motion picture *Johnny Dark*. Although few racing cars of the day were actually clothed in one of B. R. "Woody" Woodhill's roadster bodies, it was apparently sexy enough to land Piper Laurie in Curtis' arms.

SIX

American Racing Engines

Buick

Nailhead V-8

The big Buick overhead valve (OHV) engine came out in 1953. It was heavy and limited in breathing capability (due to small valves, hence the Nailhead nickname), but produced loads of torque. First introduced at 332 ci, it grew to 364 ci in 1957 and 401 ci in 1959. The Nailheads were most famous when installed in the Old Yaller racers of Max Balchowsky, who was the foremost expert on Nailhead race prep. He equipped them with log manifolds and six Stromberg carburetors. A few other specials were built around the Nailheads, but generally they were obsolete by the late 1950s.

The Buick Nailhead got its best rides in Max Balchowsky's Old Yallers. *Harold Pace*

B-O-P V-8

In 1961, General Motors introduced an all-aluminum V-8 engine to power new small sedans from Buick, Oldsmobile, and Pontiac, which led to the B-O-P engine moniker. The Buick and

The little Buick B-O-P V-8 was popular in mid-engined cars like this Genie. *Harold Pace*

Oldsmobile versions were slightly different; the Olds had better cylinder heads and the Buick was slightly more compact. Pontiac used the Olds version. The engines weighed only 266 pounds (less than a Coventry-Climax FPF) and were immediately swapped into a variety of small English sports-racers. The B-O-P V-8 was also the engine of choice for early USRRC racers like the Genies and the midengined Scarab. Famed engine builder Traco made its reputation with hot versions of the engine that produced over 320 horsepower from 215 ci. However, by the late 1960s, the Chevy V-8 had taken over, and the little V-8 slipped away.

Cadillac

Cadillac led the American auto industry in the power race by introducing its 331-ci OHV V-8 in 1949. It was muscular, if heavy, at 645 pounds. Of course, it had the considerable torque needed to pull a 4,500-pound luxury car around. Frick-Tappet Motors installed Cadillac engines in its speedy Fordillac and Studillac muscle cars. Briggs Cunningham was so impressed with the engines that he built up two

The Cadillac V-8 was popular in Allards and specials in the early 1950s. *Harold Pace*

Cadillacs to run Le Mans in 1950. Sydney Allard liked what he saw and soon Cadillac-powered Allards were mopping up on American racetracks. The Cadillacs were competitive until the mid-1950s, when the Chevy took over.

Chevrolet

Small-Block V-8

Soon after its introduction in 1955, the Chevy 265-ci V-8 became the darling of the hot rod set. It produced as much power in stock form as a full-race Ford flathead and weighed the same at about 540 pounds. Speed part manufacturers like Edelbrock, Isky, and Hillborn jumped on the bandwagon, and soon the small-block Chevy became the most popular engine ever built. And it's still in production and winning races today. The first Chevy-powered road racer was the Stovebolt, and when the larger 283-ci version came out in 1957, everybody from Brian Lister in England to Lance Reventlow in California began wedging the engines into their chassis. The small-block Chevy went on to dominate the USRRC, the early Can-Am, and the F-5000 series, and it was highly successful in the Trans-Am and in production car racing in Corvettes. Race car builders tried a number of bore and stroke combinations to come up with a variety of displacements, most commonly 301 (to fit in the under-5-liter class), 339, 350, 377, and 402 ci. All-aluminum engines were used by Roger Penske (in a Cooper Monaco) and in the early Chaparrals.

The Stovebolt Special used an untried Chevy V-8 with three carburetors. *Harold Pace*

Big-Block V-8

The Chevy 396-ci engine came out in 1965 to replace the heavy and antiquated 409. The Chevy was a development of a secretive stock car engine program called "the Mystery Motor," but some of the best design features were lost to cost-saving measures. Still, the big-block Chevy grew into a race winner in Corvettes and Can-Am cars. In 1966, it swelled to 427 ci, and in the Can-Am series, engines as big as 494 ci were common. All-aluminum ZL-1 versions were also available directly from Chevrolet. The 700-plus-horsepower Chevy big-block dominated the Can-Am until the arrival of the Porsche 917.

Chrysler

Although Chrysler has made many excellent race engines, only a handful have been used in road racing cars. The small-block Chrysler was tried in some F-5000 cars but without much success. The big Hemi was a potent power-producer, but fatally heavy at 765 pounds. The Chryslers carried Briggs Cunningham to Le Mans in the 1950s (and nearly won), while the last serious effort was in the Hussein I in the mid-1960s. The big Chryslers never tallied up much in the win column, but they were used in specials, like the Barneson-Chrysler, and in many Allards. The early Hemis, as used in the Cunninghams, displaced 331 ci, while the later versions had 426 ci. Chrysler division DeSoto also had a smaller 276-ci Hemi engine that was used in some specials.

Chrysler Hemis were heavy but powerful. Hillborn fuel injection was a common period modification. *Harold Pace*

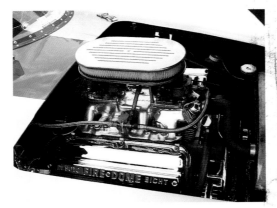

Chrysler also built the DeSoto Firedome V-8, a smaller version of the Hemi. This one lives in a Kurtis chassis. *Harold Pace*

Crosley

Crosley built slow, drab economy cars prior to World War II, but afterward the company knew it needed more sophistication than its old air-cooled twin could produce. Crosley bought the production rights to a lightweight, water-cooled, four-cylinder engine designed by Californian Lloyd Taylor (who later built the Taylor Super Sport engine). The tiny 44-ci engine was intended to drive generators on PT boats, but it proved to be a powerhouse in small-bore road racing cars. The first ones were called the COBRA engines (for their COpper BRAzed construction). The block was cast from thin-wall steel, while the head, ports, and water jackets were brazed together from thin sheet steel. The tiny engine weighed 59 pounds and could be easily carried around by one man.

The Crosley engines turned out to be potent power-producers for their size, even though the welded metal assembly proved to be a maintenance disaster. Soon, the COBRA engine gave way to the CIBA engine, which was basically the same dimensions but used a cast-iron block and integral cylinder

273

Many H-Modified racing cars used the versatile Crosley engine. *Harold Pace*

head. Racing car builders quickly discovered the engine and modified it for small-displacement classes, where it proved superior to the small Fiat engines used previously. Italian tuning firm Bandini even cut off the Crosley head and used the bottom end as the basis for its own twin cam racing engines. One of the first to hop up the Crosley was Nick Brajevich, who offered the Braje line of manifolds and internal parts. In stock form, the Crosley produced only 26 horsepower, but racing versions were getting over 60 horsepower in the early 1950s. The Crosley engine dominated H-Modified racing during most of the 1950s.

Ford
Flathead V-8

The Ford flathead V-8 was one of the most popular powerplants for special builders in the early 1950s. The legendary engine was introduced in 1932 and built until 1953. There were a number of varieties, including Mercury versions that were larger and more powerful. Originally introduced in 221-ci form, the flathead grew first to 239.4 ci, then finally to 255.4 ci. By boring and stroking, the flathead could be hogged out to as much as 296 ci, but going that big was asking for trouble.

This flathead Mercury sports triple carburetors and Edelbrock heads. *Harold Pace*

Racers ditched the stock heads and replaced them with high-performance parts (usually aluminum) from Edelbrock, Eddie Meyer, Evans, Navarro, Sharp, Offenhauser, Smith, Tattersfield, and Weiand. Intake manifolds were available to mount up to six Stromberg or Holley carburetors. Most road racers used triple Stromberg 97s. The flathead weighed a little under 550 pounds and produced about 230 horsepower in full-race tune. Although quick, they were plagued by overheating problems.

Ford also produced the V-8 60, a smaller 136-ci version of the flathead. They were only made from 1937 to 1940, but they proved popular with midget racers and special builders who could not afford Offys. A number of them were swapped into MG TCs, but they had a short competitive life. By the mid-1950s, they were obsolete in road racing.

A few racers managed to get their hands on the rare and expensive Ardun overhead valve conversions for the flathead. Designed by Zora Arkus-Duntov, they were technically superior but never developed properly in their day.

Y-Block

The Y-block engine (so named for its deep crankcase, which made the engine Y-shaped) was Ford's first OHV design, and it replaced the flathead in 1954. Although it was a decent engine, it was heavy, at 625 pounds, and seldom used in road racing cars. Among the few Y-block-powered road racers were the Battlebirds and the Troutman and Barnes Special.

Fairlane V-8

The lightweight Ford small-block engine came out in 1961 in 221-ci form but soon grew to 260 ci and then 289 ci. At only 470 pounds, it was considerably lighter than the Chevy small-block. Carroll Shelby developed the little Ford into a potent race engine that produced around 375 horsepower with four Weber carburetors. The engines were used in the Cobras, GT-350s, Ford GTs, King Cobras, and many

The Ford 289 was installed in everything from Cobras to sports-racers. *Harold Pace*

specials until the late 1960s. An aluminum-block version of the Indy Fairlane engine was tried in the early Ford GTs without success. Dan Gurney developed the famed Gurney-Weslake heads for the small Ford engine and won Ford's only Can-Am victory at Bridgehampton in 1966. The engines were also used in the Wyer team Ford GTs in 1968 and 1969.

FE Big Block

The Ford 427 was a highly successful stock car and drag racing engine, but its main success in road racing was earned in the Cobra 427. Some were tried in Can-Am and USRRC cars, but they were generally too heavy (660 pounds) to take on the Chevrolets.

Others

Various Ford engines were tried in road racing cars, including the four-cam Indy engine and a 477-ci version of the 429 Semi-Hemi engine that Holman-Moody stuffed in a Can-Am car. They were quick but temperamental and had little impact. A few early Can-Am cars (like the Honker II) tried the Ford 351-ci engine, but it was not competitive with the big-block Chevys.

McAfee Engineering

Ernie McAfee was an accomplished racing driver and the tuning wizard who built John Edgar's phenomenal supercharged MG TC (Ernie was no relation to ace Porsche pusher Jack McAfee, who sometimes worked for him). From his race shop, McAfee Engineering in North Hollywood, California, McAfee was an indispensable part of Edgar's racing team, and they began importing Siata sports cars from Italy. For a while, McAfee also partnered with Bill Devin of Devin sports car fame, but that didn't last.

The small Siata Amicas arrived at McAfee's shop less engine, where a variety of powerplants, mostly Crosleys but sometimes a Simca or an MG, were installed. In 1952, McAfee was involved in two projects that involved original engine designs for the Siata chassis.

Barker Midget

Bob Barker built a lovely little twin cam four-cylinder engine for use in circle-track midget racers. It was a promising design intended to do battle with the Offy midget engine. However, Barker was killed in a crash, and McAfee picked up the rights to build the engine for sports car racing. It was destroked to bring displacement down to 1,500 cc and adapted to a single carburetor to make it easier to service. It was a beautiful little mill and filled the engine bay of the diminutive Siata. Its first appearance was at Torrey Pines in 1952, where Jack McAfee drove it hard and pushed the leaders until he ran out of brakes. After that, no more was heard of the engine.

Twin Triumph

Another McAfee Siata swap involved attaching two Triumph two-banger motorcycle engines together with a transfer case. An extra output shaft drove an S.C.O.T. supercharger for even more power. The blower breathed through a single Solex carburetor.

The two 500-cc engines would have put it in the 1,000-cc class, but the blower bumped it up into the 1,500-cc class, where it would have been mincemeat for the first Porsche 550 or OSCA that showed up. The whole thing drove through an MG TC gearbox and a Studebaker clutch. It ran at Torrey Pines, but differential problems kept it out of the race.

McAfee was a popular figure in the 1950s racing scene. When he was killed driving a Ferrari at Pebble Beach in 1956, it was the last year for racing at the venue where the famous concours is held today.

Meyer & Drake

For years the only successful purpose-built racing engine available for sale in America was the venerable Offenhauser, owned and built by the Meyer & Drake Engineering Company after 1946. It ruled the speedways and bull rings, but on a road circuit it was hard to make it cut the mustard.

Champ Car Engines

Several big Offys were tried in the 1950s, most notably by Briggs Cunningham in his C-6R. Cunningham needed a 3-liter engine to run at Le Mans in 1955, so a 220-ci Offy was destroked to 180 ci and fed by two Weber 50DCOE3 side-draft carburetors. The engine vibrated so badly it caused the gas in the bowls to foam up, so the carbs were solid-mounted on the chassis and connected to the engine with flexible hoses. Team engineer Phil Walters switched the Bendix magneto to a Lucas distributor. A peak power output of 270 horsepower was reached in testing. Meyer & Drake provided a bell housing to accept a billet flywheel with a Cadillac ring gear and starter. But to run at Le Mans, the engine had to be modified to run on the low-octane French gasoline, so lower compression pistons were substituted and the cam and ignition timing were backed down. The modifications cost lots of power and caused overheating. At Le Mans, the Offy burned a piston and retired. It was repaired and run at Elkhart Lake, where it repeated the performance. Out it came and in went a Jaguar mill.

Lance Reventlow built his Chevy-powered Scarab sports-racers with the intention of running them in European events, but in 1958, the FIA dropped the displacement limit to 3-liters. He had engine wizards Travers and Coons build up a 180-ci Offy to see how it would work. It didn't. Installed in Scarab Chassis Number 003, it ran only once, at Santa Barbara, where it was so slow a Corvette passed it on the straight. Then it vibrated so badly the shift linkage fell apart. The Offy was removed and installed in the first Scarab Formula 1 car for testing while a new engine (also a turkey) was being readied.

The Meyer Drake was a classic racing engine at Indy but never worked out on road courses. *Harold Pace*

An Offy engine powered the Beavis Offy Special.
Bob Tronolone

275

One of the few privateer users of the big Offy was George Tilp, who installed a 180-ci Offy in an Aston Martin DB-2 (which failed to start at Sebring in 1954), then transferred it to a Ferrari Mondial chassis. It was adapted to a four-speed transmission, fitted with a Vertex magneto, and fed by Weber carburetors. Later, it was changed over to Bosch fuel injection. Walt Hansgen drove the Ferrari-Offy in SCCA races before it expired in grand fashion at Cumberland Airport in Maryland.

In a low-budget approach much more successful than either Cunningham or Reventlow's efforts, Ted Cannon and Jim Seely pieced together a 270-ci Offy from junk parts (see Cannon Specials). The engine was laid over and ran dual Stromberg carbs with a Ford V-8 distributor. It was quick on occasion but failed to make much of an impact.

The big 220-, 250-, and 270-ci monsters proved to be virtually impossible to keep alive on gasoline instead of their normal diet of alcohol, and they vibrated so badly they shook everything apart. When detuned to the point of reliability, the engines didn't provide enough power. However, the Offenhauser midget engine (designed for the popular class of small oval track cars) proved to be a winner in small-displacement classes for a short time in the mid-1950s.

1500 Sport Engines

The midget Offy was similar in design and appearance to its big brother but had only two valves, versus four for the bigger engines. They were highly successful and became required equipment for any winning midget team. The 1,500-cc Offys were also known as 91 models for their cubic inches. Although some road racers converted midget engines on their own, Meyer & Drake offered a special version of the midget engine called the 1500 Sports. Special manifolds were designed to take two SU or twin two-barrel side-draft Weber carburetors, and a gear-driven Lucas distributor replaced the usual magneto. Up front, a pair of timing chains

replaced the gear tower used on roundy-round engines. At the rear, the engine was modified to accept a clutch, flywheel, and MG TC gearbox (midget engines used a direct-drive "in-and-out" box). The rear of the intake cam had a special adapter made to accept a tachometer take-off and a fuel pump drive. A belt-driven generator was adapted, as was a starter. (Midgets were push started and needed no starter.)

George Beavis built a special (see Beavis Offenhauser entry, Chapter 3) powered by the first 1500 Sports engine delivered in 1953. He had a 106-ci version as well, which he mounted on its side in his F2 car. Working closely with Meyer & Drake, Beavis built the fastest of the Offy road racers and won his class at Torrey Pines, Palm Springs, Santa Barbara, and Willow Springs. In 1954, Beavis even built a one-off 1,750-cc Offy to run in a 2-liter race at Palm Springs, where he beat a Ferrari 500 Mondial by over a lap.

Oklahoma oilman and Indy car owner Jack Hinkle raced a Kurtis 500X with a special twin-plug Offy, although the chassis was a bit heavy for the engine power. Owner William Escherich repowered the ex-Barlow Simca with an Offy. Allen Le May installed one in a Lotus, and another was shoehorned into a Lester. Movie idol James Dean ordered a Lotus Mk.10, which he intended to power with an Offy, but it was not completed before his death.

Engineers at Borg-Warner also dropped a supercharged Offy into a Cisitalia in 1950 to promote the Pesco line of fuel pumps and superchargers. The 88.9-ci blown Offy put out a remarkable 160 horsepower, but its racing record is unknown.

The best trophy-collector of them all was Dave Michaels, who shoehorned an Offy midget mill into an Italian Bandini sports-racer in 1954. Jim Mathews owned the car, and Fred Sinon owned the engine. Starting with a 1,625-cc midget engine (not the Sports package), Michaels Engineering in New Jersey built a bomb that held the 2-liter lap record at Thompson for a year and a half. The engine was

originally installed in Sinon's MG TD and was remarkably stock. Side-draft Riley carbs were mounted on a manifold designed for alcohol fuel, although the Bandini ran on gasoline. Two sets of cams were used, depending on where the power needed to come in for a given track. The engine was adapted to a four-speed Siata transmission. Power was estimated at 115 horsepower, and the Offy-Bandini was a winner.

Scarab Formula 1

Offenhauser engineer Leo Goosen designed an all-new four-cylinder engine for the Scarab Formula One. It was a laydown design, with twin plugs per cylinder and a desmodromic valve train that used secondary cams instead of springs to close the valves. Goosen was against the desmo setup on development grounds, but Reventlow insisted. The engine never produced competitive power and was unreliable to boot.

Smith Jiggler

Texan T. Noah "Tiny" Smith engineered a semioverhead valve conversion for the Ford flathead V-8 60 engine. The small 136-ci Ford (manufactured from 1937 to 1940) was popular as an alternative to the expensive Offenhauser in midget circle track racing. The Smith conversion used rocker arms above the head to operate exhaust valves housed in ports in the new heads. The intake valves remained in their standard location in the block. The overhead rockers "jiggled" around, leading to the name Smith Jiggler for the little engine.

In 1954, Smith advertised that he had adapted the Jiggler V-8 60 for use in small modified sports cars. The standard sports car engine had 2.6-inch

bore and 3.2-inch stroke, to produce 134 ci. The compression ratio was 9:1. A hotter race version had 2.4375-inch bore and 3.2-inch stroke for 119.3 ci (to fit in a smaller displacement class). The complete engine weighed 325 pounds and was said to fit in MG sports cars. They were sold in kit or assembled form. If you already had a V-8 60, the Jiggler conversion kit was $450. A complete standard engine cost $750, and a full-race unit was $1,050.

The Smith engines were known to have cooling problems relating to the lack of water passages in the heads. Smith was located in San Antonio, Texas.

of the engine to 180 pounds, less than half that of a Triumph TR-3 and an impressive achievement even today. The initial concept was a SOHC design with a compression chamber and port assembled from five steel stampings and two steel valve seats. Once assembled, the unit was furnace-brazed together.

The outer walls of the block and head assembly were 0.074 steel, and the cylinders were chrome-moly tube. The fabricated assembly allowed excellent cooling, eliminating hot spots that can occur in cast engines. Ford six-cylinder connecting rods were used, along with Jahns 12:1 pistons. A barrel-type crankcase (similar to Offy practice) was cast in aluminum with iron bearing webs mounted into the crankcase with through-bolts. The crankshaft was cast with a hollow core to save weight and allow better grain structure during the casting operation. The first test engines produced 145 horsepower, which was impressive for a 2-liter engine. Price was expected to be $800 each in 1958. However, durability problems prevented that version from being marketed.

A twin cam version followed in 1959, with hemispherical combustion chambers, and Ted Tyce stepped in as a sponsor. Compression was now up to 14:1, and Edsel valves (1 13/16-inch intake and

exhaust) were used for ease of replacement in the field. The two cams were driven by chain and could be quickly changed for testing. The engine was designed to run up to 10,000 rpm, and desmodromic valve operation was considered. A Lucas distributor was standard, with a magneto optional. Various carburetors were tried, as was Hillborn fuel injection.

Three engine sizes could be accommodated, all with the same 3.50-inch bore. The smallest 91-ci version was designed to use a variety of transmissions, while the 120- and 135-ci versions were intended for the Chevrolet four-speed. The 91-ci version produced 115 horsepower, the 120-ci version 150 horsepower, and the big engine 175 horsepower (an impressive figure even by late 1960s standards). Price in 1960 was up to $1,450, but it appears that few twin cams, if any, were ever raced.

The Super Sport Special (see Super Sport Special entry, Chapter 3) was a revamped MG special converted in 1958 to take the experimental SOHC Taylor engine fitted with Hillborn fuel injection. With an estimated 160 horsepower, it was clocked at 162 miles per hour, but the engine could not be made reliable and soon disappeared without a trace. A shame—it had great potential.

Taylor Super Sport

There are lots of American specials, but only a handful of American road racing engines. The most ambitious attempt at a purebred small-bore racing engine was the Taylor Super Sport, also known as the Tyce-Taylor, which first appeared in the late 1950s. Lloyd Taylor made his mark on engine design when he penned the original Crosley COBRA fabricated-block economy car engine. The tiny Crosley proved to be a potent racing engine, and in 1957, Taylor basically scaled up the concept for a 2-liter racing engine.

By using an aluminum crankcase and a fabricated block and head assembly, Taylor held the total weight

The Taylor Super Sport engine had a family resemblance to the smaller Crosley.
Robert Rolofson Jr.; Robert H. Rolofson III collection

SEVEN

Racing Classes

One of the most confusing things about researching vintage racing cars is the bewildering number of classes that have been used over the years. Regulations were always in a state of flux and local race organizers were prone to invent new classes to suit local interest, like Powder Puff (women only) races and events featuring solely MGs or Jaguars.

American sports car racing started out with a number of clubs hosting races, but the dominant club ended up being the Sports Car Club of America (SCCA). The group put on professional events, as did the United States Auto Club (USAC). There was also the high-profile California Sports Car Club (CSCC), with its own classes and production car preparation regulations. Here is a timeline of the major classes and changes over the years.

278

1950–1954

In the early 1950s, the SCCA broke racing cars into four basic types, based almost completely on FIA classes and regulations. However, the SCCA did require the use of pump gas in all engines. Formula 3 was not originally an SCCA class, but the cars were raced in America from the early 1950s on.

Production Cars

Production cars were street sports cars basically in stock form. To be eligible, at least 500 examples of the car had to have been sold. In the early 1950s, the only permissible modifications were changes to the jets and spark plugs. The wheels had to be stock, and the tires had to be the same size as originally fitted. Hub caps and fender spats could be removed, but the air cleaners, bumpers, and trim could not. Special high-performance option packages, like the MG TD Mk.II, offered by the factory but not fitted to at least 500 examples were not allowed. The production car classes were divided by engine displacement as follows:

Production Car Class A:	Over 5,500 cc
Production Car Class B:	5,000 cc to 5,500 cc
Production Car Class C:	3,000 cc to 5,000 cc
Production Car Class D:	2,000 cc to 3,000 cc
Production Car Class E:	1,500 cc to 2,000 cc
Production Car Class F:	1,100 cc to 1,500 cc
Production Car Class G:	750 cc to 1,100 cc
Production Car Class H:	500 cc to 750 cc
Production Car Class I:	350 cc to 500 cc
Production Car Class J:	Under 350 cc

Sports Cars

The sports cars were pure racing cars that had to meet the FIA regulations used in Europe, including at least one working door, two seats, and many other requirements. Supercharged cars were moved up one class. The sports car classes were divided by engine displacement as follows:

Sports Car Class A:	Over 5,500 cc
Sports Car Class B:	5,000 cc to 5,500 cc
Sports Car Class C:	3,000 cc to 5,000 cc
Sports Car Class D:	2,000 cc to 3,000 cc
Sports Car Class E:	1,500 cc to 2,000 cc
Sports Car Class F:	1,100 cc to 1,500 cc
Sports Car Class G:	750 cc to 1,100 cc
Sports Car Class H:	500 cc to 750 cc
Sports Car Class I:	350 cc to 500 cc
Sports Car Class J:	Under 350 cc

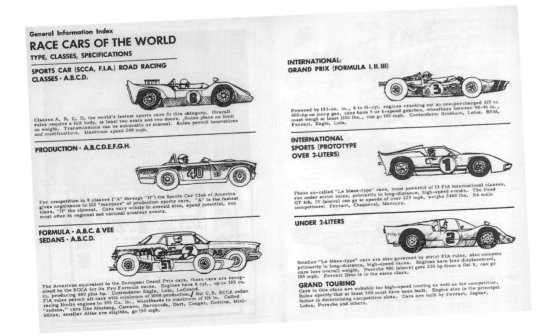

General Information Index
RACE CARS OF THE WORLD
TYPE, CLASSES, SPECIFICATIONS

SPORTS CAR (SCCA, F.I.A.) ROAD RACING CLASSES · A.B.C.D

Classes A, B, C, D, the world's fastest sports cars fit this category. Overall rules require a full body, at least two seats and two doors. Rules place no limit on weight. Transmissions can be automatic or manual. Rules permit innovations and modifications. Maximum speed 200 mph.

PRODUCTION · A.B.C.D.E.F.G.H.

For competition in 8 classes ("A" through "H") the Sports Car Club of America gives cognizance to 122 "marques" of production sports cars. "A" is the fastest class, "H" the slowest. Cars vary widely in overall size, speed potential, run most often in regional and national amateur events.

FORMULA · A.B.C. & VEE
SEDANS · A.B.C.D.

The American equivalent to the European Grand Prix cars, these cars are recognized by the SCCA for its Pro Formula races. Engines have 8 cyl., up to 305 cu. in., producing 400 plus hp. Contenders: Eagle, Lola, LeGrand. FIA rules permit all cars with minimum of 1000 production. But U.S. SCCA sedan racing limits engines to 305 Cu. In., wheelbases to maximum of 116 in. Called "sedans," cars like Mustang, Camaro, Barracuda, Dart, Cougar, Cortina, Mini-Minor, smaller Alfas are eligible, go 150 mph.

INTERNATIONAL:
GRAND PRIX (FORMULA I. II. III)

Powered by 183-cu. in., 8 to 16-cyl. engines cranking out an unsupercharged 325 to 400-hp on pump gas, cars have 5 or 6-speed gearbox, wheelbase between 90-96 in., must weigh at least 1100 lbs., can go 190 mph. Contenders: Brabham, Lotus, BRM, Ferrari, Eagle, Lola.

INTERNATIONAL
SPORTS (PROTOTYPE
OVER 2-LITERS)

These so-called "Le Mans-type" cars, most powerful of 13 FIA international classes, run under strict rules, primarily in long-distance, high-speed events. The Ford GT Mk. IV (above) can go at speeds of over 225 mph, weighs 2400 lbs. Its main competitors: Ferrari, Chaparral, Mercury.

UNDER 2-LITERS

Smaller "Le Mans-type" cars are also governed by strict FIA rules, also compete primarily in long-distance. Engines have less displacement, cars less overall weight. Porsche 906 (above) gets 200 hp from a flat 8, can go 165 mph. Ferrari Dino is in the same class.

GRAND TOURING

Cars in this class are suitable for high-speed touring as well as for competition. Rules specify that at least 500 must have been built. Engine size is the principal factor in determining competitive slots. Cars are built by Ferrari, Jaguar, Lotus, Porsche and others.

As an example, a standard 1,500-cc Porsche 356 would have run in Production Class F, while a piping hot 550 Spyder with the same size engine would have been in Sports Car Class F.

Unrestricted

The unrestricted class included cars that did not fit into any of the other classes but were safe to be raced.

Formula 3

Amateur formula car racing in America started with Formula 3, a class that started in England right after World War II for single-seat, open-wheel cars. The cars were restricted to 500-cc engines (mostly air-cooled motorcycle units) with unrestricted valve gears or 750-cc engines with L-heads or water-cooled OHV engines. The minimum weight was 440 pounds, and the rest was pretty much up to the builder.

1959

By 1959, the SCCA had revised its classes. Production car class regulations were liberalized every year, allowing more modifications to be performed.

Production Cars

The number of cars necessary for approval to race in the production car class was dropped to 150 cars, and the list of allowable modifications swelled to include removing the bumpers and windshield, port matching the heads, and balancing the engine. However, all internal engine and running gear parts had to be standard or optional from the factory. The production car classes were then divided by engine displacement as follows:

Production Car Class A:	Over 5,000 cc
Production Car Class B:	Over 3,500 cc to 5,000 cc
Production Car Class C:	Over 2,700 cc to 3,500 cc
Production Car Class D:	Over 2,000 cc to 2,700 cc
Production Car Class E:	Over 1,600 cc to 2,000 cc
Production Car Class F:	Over 1,300 cc to 1,600 cc
Production Car Class G:	Over 1,000 cc to 1,300 cc
Production Car Class H:	Over 750 cc to 1,000 cc
Production Car Class I:	Over 500 cc to 750 cc
Production Car Class J:	Over 350 cc to 500 cc
Production Car Class K:	Below 350 cc

Modified

The sports car class cars were called modifieds, as many of them were modified from production cars. There was a set of dimensions for the cockpit area, and two seats had to be provided. A complete electrical system was required, including lights, a horn, and a generator. The modified classes were divided by engine displacement as follows:

Modified Class A:	Over 8,000 cc
Modified Class B:	Over 5,000 cc to 8,000 cc
Modified Class C:	Over 3,000 cc to 5,000 cc
Modified Class D:	Over 2,000 cc to 3,000 cc
Modified Class E:	Over 1,500 cc to 2,000 cc
Modified Class F:	Over 1,100 cc to 1,500 cc
Modified Class G:	Over 750 cc to 1,100 cc
Modified Class H:	Over 500 cc to 750 cc
Modified Class I:	Over 350 cc to 500 cc
Modified Class J:	350 cc or less

Restricted

The unrestricted class became known as the restricted class. (Go figure.) It was not an official SCCA class, but if enough cars showed up, the race organizers could provide the class.

Formula Junior

A new class of FIA-approved single-seaters joined Formula 3, and the SCCA began putting on

races for them. Formula Juniors were required to have a 1,100-cc maximum displacement with overhead valves and an engine, gearbox, and brakes from a high-volume production car. The first wave of cars was front-engined, but soon more expensive mid-engined models began to dominate the class. Escalating costs and rapid development caused the class to begin to fail as early as 1962. Some SCCA regions started separate classes for front-engined Juniors, but by 1964, the class had run its course and was absorbed into Formula C.

American Formula Junior

The SCCA didn't have much interest in formula car racing, so the Formula Racing Association (FRA, formerly known as the 500-cc Club of America) sprang up to put on single-seater events. The FRA normally ran Formula 3 and Formula Libre classes, but when the FIA Formula Junior regulations came out, the FRA thought it could do better. The rules were based on the FIA regs, but also allowed several alternate engines more suited to American conditions, like the Crosley 750 and the MG T-series. Each engine type was tied to a different minimum car weight. The FRA also allowed motorcycle gearboxes, and brakes were free. The California Sports Car Club accepted the FRA regulations, which they called Formula B, but the SCCA did not. Few cars were built.

1960

Production Cars

In 1960, the SCCA made a major change to its previous production class rules. The SCCA abandoned the FIA displacement-based class divisions and instead classified cars by relative performance. The change was principally brought on by the

Porsche 356 Carrera. The car was very expensive and capable of making mincemeat out of OHV Porsches and MGAs, which together made up a large part of SCCA small-bore race groups. From that point on, there were eight classes (A through H-Production) for production cars. An I-Production Class (principally for Berkeleys) was briefly recognized. The makeup changed every year as new models were introduced and existing models moved up or down the class order, depending on how they were doing. Class-dominating cars moved up; hopelessly slow cars could move down or were given more allowable options.

Formula Libre

The restricted class was replaced by Formula Libre, which theoretically allowed open-wheeled cars of all types. However, Formula Libre races were frequently thrown open to anything on wheels.

1962

Formula 4

The FRA added a class of its own when it updated Formula 3 into Formula 4. The regs called for a 500-cc unrestricted engine or a 750-cc engine with no more than one overhead cam. When the SCCA announced its formula car rules in 1965, the FRA was disbanded and Formula 4, which was never particularly popular, was absorbed into Formula C.

Intercontinental Formula

Intercontinental Formula began in England in 1960 as an ill-fated concept to rival Formula 1. The class allowed 3-liter pure racing engines developed out of 2.5-liter Formula 1 engines. There was no interest in the class in America until the organizers worked a deal with USAC to allow highly modified stock-block V-8s as well. However, the FIA quashed

the deal and no Intercontinental races ran in the United States. Scarab built the only car intended for the formula.

Formula 366

Formula 366 was a proposed formula for single-seaters powered by 6-liter V-8 engines. The class never got off the ground but generated a lot of talk in car magazines.

1963

USRRC

The USRRC was the first SCCA pro series for big V-8 sports-racers ran by FIA Group 9 (later Group 7) regulations. There were no restrictions on engine size or design, weight, or tire size. Two seats and a full-width body were required, and there were minimum cockpit dimensions. The USRRC also had an under-2-liter sports-racer class and separate events for GT cars like Cobras and Porsche 904s.

1964

Formula Vee

This brilliant class was introduced in 1964 for formula cars built from 1,200-cc Volkswagen parts. The specifications were very rigid, and the VW engine, gearbox, suspension, and brakes were kept close to stock. Formula Vee ultimately proved to be the SCCA's most successful class.

Formula S

The popularity of Formula Vee prompted a proposed class for Saab-based single-seaters using 850-cc GT engines with some Saab suspension and

brake parts. The class was never recognized by the SCCA, and cars built to Formula S rules ran in Formula C.

1965

Modified

In 1965, the SCCA condensed its modified (M) classes as follows:

C/M: Over 3,000 cc
D/M: Over 2,000 cc to 3,000 cc
E/M: Over 1,600 cc to 2,000 cc
F/M: Over 1,150 cc to 1,600 cc
G/M: Over 850 cc to 1,150 cc
H/M: 850 cc or less

Formula SCCA

Due to the growing popularity of formula car racing, the SCCA finally adopted a series of classes for them. The classes were as follows:

Formula A: Over 1,600 cc to 3,000 cc
Formula B: Over 1,100 cc to 1,600 cc
Formula C: 1,100 cc or less

1966

Sedans

New SCCA classes were implemented to accommodate increasing numbers of sedans, resulting in the formation of the Trans-Am series.

A-Sedan: Over 2,000 cc to 5,000 cc
B-Sedan: Over 1,300 cc to 2,000 cc
C-Sedan: Over 1,000 cc to 1,300 cc
D-Sedan: 1,000 cc or less

Can-Am Series

The legendary professional series ran by FIA Group 7 regulations, a development of Group 9. Almost anything was permitted.

1967

Sports-Racing

The SCCA modified category was renamed the sports-racing category to reflect the fact that most of the cars were purpose-built racing cars, not modified production cars. The classes were the same.

1968

Formula A/Formula 5000

Formula A allowed 5-liter, production-based pushrod engines, leading to the Formula 5000 Championship pro series.

VSR

A number of Formula Vee manufacturers attempted to start a new SCCA class for Volkswagen-based sports-racers. VSR would have been based on VW Type 3 (Squareback and Notchback body styles) 1,600-cc running gear and suspension. Although several cars were built, the SCCA never approved the class.

1969

Formula Ford

This single-seater class had as strong an impact as Formula Vee, but did not hold its popularity as

long. It was enormously successful as a training ground for future stars and as a way to go fast on a budget.

Sports-Racing

The SCCA reduced the number of sports-racing (SR) classes to four as follows:

A/SR: Over 2,000 cc
B/SR: Over 1,300 cc to 2,000 cc
C/SR: Over 850 cc to 1,300 cc
D/SR: 850 cc and under

1970

Formula Super Vee

A step up from Formula Vee, cars in Formula Super Vee (FSV) used full-race 1,600-cc Volkswagen Type 4 engines in sophisticated Formula Ford-style chassis. FSV spawned a popular pro series backed by VW of America.

NATIONAL SANCTION NO. 72-N-36S

National Championship and Formula *Ford* CHAMPIONSHIP

SANCTION NO. 72-RS-81S

St. Louis Region ● Sports Car Club of America

It's road racing at its finest at Mid-America Raceways. With auto and pedestrian cross-over bridges to the infield and the paddock, you can see the turns of your choice . . . cross over the bridge and see all the circuit.

LAP RECORDS

CLASS	DRIVER	CAR	TIME	REGION	AVERAGE SPEED (MPH)	DATE
AP	Charlie Kemp	Corvette	1:58.6	Miss	86.813	5/72
BP	Allan Barker	Corvette	1:59.4	Kent.	86.231	5/72
CP	John McComb	Triumph TR6	2:02.8	Wichita	83.844	5/72
DP	John McComb	Datsun 2000	2:06.0	Wichita	81.714	5/70
EP	Ray Kraftson	MGB	2:11.4	St. Louis	78.356	5/71
FP	Aubrey O'Connor	Tr Spitfire	2:12.0	Chicago	78.000	5/72
GP	Gordon Smiley	Tr Spitfire	2:13.0	Kansas City	77.414	7/70
HP	Andy Fulton	AH Sprite	2:21.0	Detroit	73.021	7/70
*ASR	Fred Parkhill	McLaren 8E	1:48.2	NE Okla	95.157	5/72
BSR	Pete Harrison	Lola T212	1:56.4	Atlanta	89.454	6/71
CSR	Bob Klempel	Lotus Alfa	2:07.0	St. Louis	81.071	7/70
DSR	Dick Durant	Dubury Saab	2:08.0	St. Louis	80.437	7/70
AS	Allan Barker	Camaro	2:04.6	Kent	82.632	5/71
BS	Horst Kwech	Alfa Romeo	2:12.0	Chicago	78.000	9/68
CS	Britt Brown	Austin Cooper	2:15.0	St. Louis	76.267	7/70
	Dan Hugh	Austin Cooper	2:15.0	So. Ind.	76.267	7/70
	Roger Mitchell	Austin Cooper	2:15.0	St. Louis	76.267	7/70
SSS	Jimmy O'Dell	Opel 57	2:38.4	Kansas City	65.000	5/72
FA	Charles Dietrich	Lola T142	1:52.0		91.929	9/69
FB	Gordon Smiley	Merlyn Mk 21	1:52.6	Kansas City	91.439	5/72
FC	Charles Grauel	Brabham BT15	2:03.6	Wichita	83.301	6/71
FV	J. Edwin Leamen	Zink	2:12.0	SIR	78.000	7/70
FF	Gordon Smiley	Merlyn	2:00.0	Kansas City	85.800	5/71
FSV	Joe Wedig	Hawke	2:02.3	SIR	84.186	5/71

*Indicates Track Record

Cars by Year(s) of Construction

1939
Ardent Alligator
Bu-Merc

1947
Payne Special

1948
Butterball Special

1949
Baldwin Mercury Special
Brundage Duesenberg-Ford
Fitch Type B
Ingalls Special
Kurtis Sports Car (KSC)

late 1940s
Darwin Special
Flying Banana

1950
Altemus Auto-Banker
Cannon Mk.I
Edgar MG TC
Edwards Special
Kurtis Sports Car (KSC)
Le Monstre
Seifried Special
Von Neumann MG Special

1951
Barlow Simca Number 1
Comet
Coppel MG TC
Croslahti
Croslahti B
Cunningham C-1
Cunningham C-2R
David MG TD
Devin-Crosley Super Sport
Fitch-Whitmore Jaguar
Le Biplace Torpedo
Manning Mercury Special
Morgensen Special (1)
Parkinson Jaguar
Schrafft-Fitch Crosley
Troutman-Barnes Special

1952
Aardvark

Ak Miller's Caballo de Hierro
Barlow Simca Number 2
Bathtub
Beast
Beavis Offenhauser-First
 Version
Brundage VW Special
Cannon Mk.II
Cunningham C-4R
Cunningham C-4RK
Edwards Special (2)
Excalibur J
Eyerly Crosley
Fibersport-Crosley
Gillespie MG TD
Hansgen Jaguar
John Bull Special
Louis Van Dyke International
 Motors Simca Special
Multiplex 186
PBX Crosley Special
Tatum-GMC
Vogel/Balchowsky Special

1953
Beavis Offenhauser-Second
 Version
Cannon Mk.IV
Cunningham C-5R
Davis Special
Edwards / Blume Special
Eliminator
Fageol Twin-Porsche
Fibersport-Crosley
Georgette
Hughes-Kircher Special
Kurtis 500S
Mabee Drilling Special
Miles R-1
Morgensen Special (2)
Multiplex 186
Pickford Jaguar
Swiss Cheese Special
Tatum-GMC
Uihlein MG Special

early 1950s
Austin Chevy Special
D and D Special
Georgette-the-Racer
Leson Simca
Meyer Special

Morgan Special
Satcher Special
Seifried Crosley
Singer Special
Sorrell-Manning Special

1954
Arnolt Bristol Bolide
Cheetah (John Plaisted)
Devin Panhard
El Toro (1)
Fibersport-Crosley
James Special
Kurtis 500S
Lil Stinker
Lipe Pooper
Lovely VW-Porsche Special
Mar-Chris Special
Marston Healey
Miles R-2 (The Flying Shingle)
Multiplex 186
Nichols Panhard
Sadler Mk.1
Siam Special

1955
Arnolt Bristol Bolide
Baldwin Mark II
Barneson-Hagemann Chrysler
Cunningham C-6R
Dane Formula 3
Fairchild Panhard
Fibersport-Crosley
Hagemann GMC
Hansen Special
Jomar Mk.I (Dellow-Jomar)
Kurtis 500M
Kurtis 500S
Kurtis 500X
Lovely Pooper
Lowe's Frazer-Nash
Miller Specials
Orgeron Talbot-Lago
Sadler Mk.2
Schaghticoke Special

1956
Ak Miller's Caballo II
Arnolt Bristol Bolide
Baird-Jag Special
Bud Hand Special
Cleary Special

Corvette SR-1
Corvette SR-2
Corvette SS
Durlite Special
Fibersport-Crosley
FoMoCo Special
Jomar Mk.II
Lucas-Whitehead Climax
Miles R-3 (The Pooper)
Miller Specials
Monsterati
Porter SLS
Reynolds Wrap Special
Silver Bomb
Stovebolt Special
Super Sport Special
Wright Renault Special

mid-1950s
Flying Triangle
Gounis Fiat-Crosley
Jaybird Mark X
Jones-De Camp Crosley
Miller-Sparks Crosley
Morlang Porsche
Priest Volvo
Seifried Crosley
Simon LaDawri-Packard

1957
Andree Special
Arnolt Bristol Bolide
Battlebirds
Beavis Offenhauser-Third
 Version
Cozzi Jaguar
Devin Ryan Special
Eave Chevy Special
Elwood Porsche Special
Exner Simca Special
Fibersport-Crosley
Jabro Mk.1
Jabro Mk.2
Jomar Mk.II
Jomar Mk.III
Jomar Notchback Coupe
 (Mk.I road car)
Jomar Roadster
Knoop Chevy
Little Digger
Manta Ray
Miller Specials

Old Yaller I
Pink Elephant I
Plass Mistral
Rattenbury Crosley
Tanner T-1
Townsend Mk.1

1958
Ak Miller's Devin-Chevy
Arnolt Bristol Bolide
Bocar XP-4
Bocar XP-5
Devin D
Devin SS (Irish chassis cars)
Double-Ender
Echidnas
El Toro (2)
Fibersport-Crosley
Hall-Scott Special
Holynski 1
Jabro Mk.1
Jabro Mk.2
Jomar Fastback Coupe
 (MkII road car)
Jomar Mk.II
Jomar Mk.III
Jomar Notchback Coupe
 (Mk.I road car)
La Boa Mk.1
Long Renault Special
Mangham-Davis Special
Masterson Batmobile
Miller Specials
MPX Crosley
Papier Mache Special
Peterson Special
Pink Elephant II
Rutan Porsche Special
Sanitary Special
Scarab Mk.I
Scarab Mk.II
Starkweather Crosley
Tholen Crosley
Townsend Mk.2
Twareg Special

1959
Ak Miller's Devin-Olds
Arnolt Bristol Bolide
BMC Mk.1 Formula Jr.
Bocar XP-4
Bocar XP-5

Bourgeault Formula Junior
Burnett Mk.1
Chukkar Mark II
Corvette Sting Ray Racer
Devin C
Devin D
Devin SS (California chassis cars)
DKW Formula Junior
Durlite Too
Echidnas
El Toro (3)
Ferret
Fibersport-Crosley
Formula III Echo
Hixon Special
Hummingbird
Jabro Mk.1
Jabro Mk.2
Jocko Formula Junior
Jomar Fastback Coupe (Mk.II road car)
Jomar Mk.III
Jomar SSR1 Formula 2 Racer (Jomar Single-Seater)
Jones Racing Team Special
Kellison J-4 Competition Coupe
Lo-Test Special
Mickey Mouse Special
Mighty Mouse Special
Miller Specials
Old Yaller II
Peyote Mk.II
Peyote Special
Philson-Falcon
Pink Elephant III
Sadler Formula Junior
Sadler Formula 3
Sadler Mk.3
Sadler Mk.4
Sadler-Meyer Special
Scarab Formula 1
SHE Special
Shingle Corvette
Tanner T-2
Votorini
Zeter Mk.1 Formula Junior

late 1950s

Fubar
Keck Spyder

Morgensen Special (3)
Pink Elephant IV
Pink Elephant V
Shiva

1960

Albi Devin Special
Apache
Arnolt Bristol Bolide
Begra Mk.1
BMC Mk.1 Formula Jr.
BMC Mk.2 Formula Jr.
Bocar XP-5
Bocar XP-6
Bocar XP-7
Bocar XP-7R
Civit Jr.
Dane Formula Juniors (Front engine)
Devin C
Devin D
Devin-Roosevelt
Dolphin Formula Junior
Dolphin Formula 2
Fibersport-Crosley
Forsgrini Specials
HSM Formula Junior
Jabro Mk.1
Jabro Mk.2
Jabro Mk.3
Miller Specials
Old Yaller III
Old Yaller IV
Phoenix Saab
PMY-2
Powell Formula Junior
Sadler Formula Libre (Mid-engine)
Scarab Formula 1
Sorrell-Larkin Special
Tanner T-3
Tanner T-4
Teakettle (MG TD) Special
Thundermug
Yeovil
Zeter Mk.2 Formula Junior

1961

Ambro
Apache
Arnolt Bristol Bolide
Begra Mk.2

BMC Mk.2 Formula Jr.
Bocar Stiletto
Bocar XP-5
Bocar XP-7
Bocar XP-7R
Campbell Special
Chaparral I
Dailu Mk.I
Dane Formula Juniors (Mid-engine)
Devin C
Devin D
Dolphin International
Dolphin Sports-Racers
Fibersport-Crosley
Forsgrini Specials
Grady 1
Grady 2
Jabro Mk.1
Jabro Mk.2
Jabro Mk.3
Jack Baker's Black Jack Special
Old Yaller IV
Old Yaller V
Old Yaller VI
PMY-3
Sadler Mk.5
Santee SS
Scarab Intercontinental
Ward/McKee Cooper-Buick

1962

Apache
Arnolt Bristol Bolide
Beach Mk.5
Beach Mk.5B
Beach Mk.5C
Begra Mk.3
BMC Mk.2 Formula Jr.
Bobsy SR1
Cobra Mk.1 (race cars)
Dailu Mk.II
Devin C
Devin D
Dolphin Sports-Racers
Fibersport-Crosley
Forsgrini Specials
Grady 1
Hawaiian Special
Holynski Scimitar
Jabro Mk.1

Jabro Mk.2
Jabro Mk.3
Kurtis Aguila
La Boa Mk.2
La Boa Mk.3
LeGrand Cheetah Mk.1
Old Yaller VII
Old Yaller VIII
Scarab Mid-Engined Sports-Racer
Tanner T-5
Tanner T-6
Townsend Mk.3
Townsend Mk.4
Zerex Special
Zink Petit

1963

Arnolt Bristol Bolide
Beach Mk.4
Beach Mk.4B
Beach Mk.4C
Beach Mk.5
Beach Mk.5B
Beach Mk.5C
BMC MK.6 Formula Jr.
Bobsy SR2
Chaparral 2A
Chaparral 2C
Cheetah (Bill Thomas)
Cobra Mk.1 (race cars)
Cobra Mk.2 (race cars)
Corvette Grand Sport
Dailu Mk.III
Dailu Mk.IV
Delfosse Mini-Junior
Devin C
Devin D
Dolphin Sports-Racers
Excalibur Hawk
Excalibur Mk.VI
Ford GT Mk.I
Formcar Formula Vees
Forsgrini Specials
Genie Mk.4
Genie Mk.5
Genie Mk.8
Genie Mk.10
Grady 2
Hussein I
Jabro Mk.1
Jabro Mk.2

Jabro Mk.3
King Cobra
La Boa Mk.2
La Boa Mk.3
LeGrand Cheetah Mk.1
Old Yaller IX
Odenborg Mercury H-Modified
Porphin
Sardini
Scorpion
Tomcat
Webster 2-Liter
Zink Petit

1964

Ausca Sports-Racer
Autodynamics D-1Mk.1
Formula Vee
Beach Mk.4
Beach Mk.4B
Beach Mk.4C
Beach Mk.5
Beach Mk.5B
Beach Mk.5C
Bobsy SR2
Burnett Mk.2
Cheetah (Bill Thomas)
Cobra 427 Competition
Cobra 427 S/C
Cobra Daytona Coupe
Cobra Mk.2 (race cars)
Crusader Formula Vees
Devin C
Devin D
Dolphin Sports-Racers
Durant Devin-Pontiac
Ford GT Mk.I
Formcar Formula Vees
Forsgrini Specials
Front-Runner Special
Genie Mk.4
Genie Mk.5
Genie Mk.8
Genie Mk.10
Hamil SR-2
Hamil SR-3
King Cobra
La Boa Mk.2
La Boa Mk.3
LeGrand Cheetah Mk.1
LeGrand Cheetah Mk.2
McKee Mk.I

McKee Mk.II
McKee Mk.III
Sardini
Sceptre
SPAD
Vanguard Formula Vee
Webster V-8
Zink Z-4

1965

Autodynamics D-1A Mk.2
Formula Vee
Beach Mk.4
Beach Mk.4B
Beach Mk.4B/SRV
Beach Mk.4C
Beach Mk.5
Beach Mk.5B
Beach Mk.5C
Beach Mk.8
Bobsy SR3
Bourgeault Formula B/C
Bourgeault Sports-Racers
Brand X (Davis)
Capella
Cheetah (Bill Thomas)
Cobra 427 Competition
Cobra 427 S/C
Cobra Daytona Coupe
Crusader Formula Vees
CRV/Piranha
Dailu Mk.V
Devin C
Devin D
Durant Devin-Chevy
Ford GT Mk.I
Ford GT Mk.II
Formcar Formula Vees
Forsgrini Specials
Genie Mk.4
Genie Mk.5
Genie Mk.8
Genie Mk.10
Genie Mk.11
Hamill SR-3
La Boa Mk.2
La Boa Mk.3
LeGrand Cheetah Mk.1
LeGrand Cheetah Mk.2
LeGrand Mk.3
LeGrand Mk.3B
Lynx A

McKee Mk.IV
McKee Mk.V
Mirage
PAM Project Group 7
PBS Mk.1
PBS Mk.2
Quantum Formula S
Sardini
Shark Formula Vee
Shelby GT-350R
Townsend Mk.5
Zeitler Formula Vee
Zink Z-5

1966

Autodynamics D-3 Formula B
Beach Mk.4
Beach Mk.4B
Beach Mk.4B/SRV
Beach Mk.4C
Beach Mk.5
Beach Mk.5B
Beach Mk.5C
Beach Mk.8
Bourgeault Formula B/C
Bourgeault Sports-Racers
Chaparral 2D
Chaparral 2E
Crusader Formula Vees
CRV/Piranha
Eagle-Climax Formula 1
Eagle-Weslake Formula 1
Ford GT Mk.I
Ford GT Mk.II
Forsgrini Specials
Hamill SR-3
Holman-Moody Honker II
La Boa Mk.2
LeGrand Mk.3
LeGrand Mk.3B
LeGrand Mk.4
LeGrand Mk.5 F3
Lynx Mk.II/B
McKee Mk.VI
Shark Formula Vee
Templeton Ringwraith
Wolverine
Yenko Stinger
Zeitler Formula Vee
Zink Z-5

mid-1960s

Ausca Formula Vee
Evans Saab Special
Kangaroo-Fiat
PAM Special
Platypus-Porsche
Tanner T-7

1967

Ausca Formula B
Autodynamics D-7
Beach Mk.4
Beach Mk.4B
Beach Mk.4B/SRV
Beach Mk.4C
Beach Mk.5
Beach Mk.5B
Beach Mk.5C
Beach Mk.8
Bobsy Vega Formula Vee
Bourgeault Formula B/C
Bourgeault Sports-Racers
Brand X (Christ)
Caldwell D-7
Chaparral 2F
Crusader Formula Vees
CRV/Piranha
Eagle-Weslake Formula 1
Ford G7A
Ford GT Mk.I
Ford GT MK.IV
Forsgrini Specials
Howmet Falcon
King Cobra Group 7
La Boa Mk.2
La Boa Mk.3
LeGrand Mk.6
Lynx Mk.II/B
McKee Mk.VII
RCA FV
Shark Formula Vee
Templeton Shadowfax
Yenko Stinger
Zeitler Formula Vee
Zink Z-5

1968

Ak Miller's Devin-Ford
Autodynamics D-4A Mk.4
Formula Vee
Beach Mk.4
Beach Mk.4B
Beach Mk.4B/SRV

Beach Mk.4C
Beach Mk.5
Beach Mk.5B
Beach Mk.5C
Beach Type 11 FB
Beach Type 11 FC
Beach Type 11 Formula Ford
Bourgeault Formula B/C
Bourgeault Sports-Racers
Burnett Mk.3
Chaparral 2G
Crusader Formula Vees
Crusader VSR
CRV/Piranha
Eagle Formula A (Eagle
Formula 5000)
Eagle-Weslake Formula 1
Eisert F-A
Forsgrini Mk.10 F5000
Forsgrini Mk.10 FC
Forsgrini Mk.11 F5000
Forsgrini Mk.12 FF
Forsgrini Mk.14 F5000
Howmet Turbine
Irons FC
Kellison Formula Vee
La Boa Mk.2
La Boa Mk.3
LeGrand Mk.7
LeGrand Mk.10
Lynx C
Lynx Mk.II/B
McKee Mk.8 F5000
NTM Mk.1
NTM Mk.2
R.A.C.E. Formula Ford
Rattler
Shark Formula Vee
Sidewinder
Spectre HR-1 FA
Vulcan Formula A
Yenko Stinger
Zeitler Formula Vee
Zink Z-5
Zink Z-8

1969

Armco Cro-Sal Can-Am
Autodynamics D-4B Mk.5
Formula Vee
Beach Mk.4B/SRV
Caldwell D-9 Formula Ford

Chaparral 2H
Crusader Formula Vees
Eagle Formula A (Eagle
Formula 5000)
Eisert F-A
Forsgrini Mk.10 F5000
Forsgrini Mk.11 F5000
Forsgrini Mk.12 FF
Forsgrini Mk.14 F5000
Keil Porsche
LeGrand Mk.11
Lynx Mk.II/B
McKee Mk.11 F5000
NTM Mk.1
NTM Mk.2
Ti22 Mk.1
Vulcan Formula A
Yenko Stinger
Zeitler Formula Super Vee
Zeitler Formula Vee
Zink Z-5
Zink Z-9

1970

Anvil
Autodynamics D-4B Mk.5
Formula Vee
Beach SV16 Formula Super
Vee
Bobsy SR4
Burnett Mk.4
Caldwell D-9B Formula Ford
Caldwell D-10 FSV
Chaparral 2J
Crusader Formula Vee Wedge
Eisert F-A
Forsgrini Mk.10 F5000
Forsgrini Mk.11 F5000
Forsgrini Mk.14 F5000
Lynx D
Lynx Mk.II/B
McKee Mk.12 F5000
Quasar SR
Ti22 Mk.2
Vulcan Formula A
Zeitler Formula Super Vee
Zeitler Formula Vee
Zink Z-5

Cars by Constructor

Hans Adams
Platypus-Porsche

John Albi
Albi Devin Special

William Aldrich-Ames
Ambro

Bob Allinger
Votorini

Bill Ames
Peyote Mk.II
Peyote Special

Jack Anderson
Swiss Cheese Special

Frank Arciero
Arciero Special

S. H. "Wacky" Arnolt
Arnolt Bristol Bolide

Bob Arnt
Singer Special

Addison Austin
Austin Chevy Special

Jack Baird
Baird-Jag Special

Jack Baker
El Toro (1)
El Toro (2)
El Toro (3)
Goldenrod Jack Baker's Black Jack Special

Max Balchowsky
Old Yaller I
Old Yaller II
Old Yaller III
Old Yaller IV
Old Yaller V
Old Yaller VI
Old Yaller VII

Old Yaller VIII
Old Yaller IX
Vogel/Balchowsky Special

Willis Baldwin
Baldwin Mark II
Baldwin Mercury Special
Payne Special

Dean Banks
Aardvark

Roger Barlow
Barlow Simca Number 1
Barlow Simca Number 2
Louis Van Dyke International
Motors Simca Special

Tom Barnes
Scorpion
Troutman-Barnes Special

Ed Bassage
Morgan Special

Dean Batchelor
Silver Bomb

Harold Baumann
HSM Formula Junior

Al Baurle
La Boa Mk.1
La Boa Mk.2
La Boa Mk.3
La Boa R.A.C.E. Formula Ford

Gene Beach
Beach Mk.4
Beach Mk.4B
Beach Mk.4B/SRV
Beach Mk.4C
Beach Mk.5
Beach Mk.5B
Beach Mk.5C
Beach Mk.8
Beach SV16 Formula Super Vee
Beach Type 11 FB
Beach Type 11 FC
Beach Type 11 Formula Ford
Begra Mk.1

Begra Mk.2
Begra Mk.3

George Beavis
Beavis Offenhauser-First Version
Beavis Offenhauser-Second Version
Beavis Offenhauser-Third Version

Scott Beckett
Lo-Test Special

Bob Bentzinger
PBX Crosley Special

Manuel Betes
Flying Triangle

Don Bolen
SPAD

Nade Bourgeault
Bourgeault Formula B/C
Bourgeault Formula Junior
Bourgeault Sports-Racers
Keck Spyder

Bill Bradley
Civit Jr.

Mark Bratton
Rattler

Merle Brennan
Masterson Batmobile

James Broadwell
Jabro Mk.1
Jabro Mk.2
Jabro Mk.3

Dewey Brohaugh
Ambro

Ira J. Brundage
Brundage Duesenberg-Ford

Herbert Brundage
Formcar Formula Vees

Brundage Motors
Brundage VW Special

Peter Bryant
Bryant Ti22 Mk.1
Bryant Ti22 Mk.2

Kelly Buchanan
Singer Special

Bob Buck
Keil Porsche

Charles A. Bull
John Bull Special

Stan Burnett
Burnett Mk.1
Burnett Mk.2
Burnett Mk.3

Archie J. Butterworth
Butterball Special

Ray Caldwell
Autodynamics D-1A Mk.2 Formula Vee
Autodynamics D-1B Mk.3 Formula Vee
Autodynamics D-1Mk.1 Formula Vee
Autodynamics D-3 Formula B
Autodynamics D-4 Mk.4 Formula Vee
Autodynamics D-4B Mk.5 Formula Vee
Caldwell D-7
Caldwell D-9 Formula Ford
Caldwell D-9B Formula Ford
Caldwell D-10 FSV
Caldwell D-13 Formula Vee

John Camden
Civit Jr.

Ted Cannon
Cannon Mk.I
Cannon Mk.II
Cannon Mk.IV

Andre Capella (Gessner)
Capella
Front-Runner Special
Twareg Special

Bob Carnes
Bocar Stiletto
Bocar XP-4
Bocar XP-5
Bocar XP-6
Bocar XP-7
Bocar XP-7R

Tom Carstens
Stovebolt Special

Luigi Cassiani
Dailu Mk.I
Dailu Mk.II
Dailu Mk.III
Dailu Mk.IV
Dailu Mk.V

James Cassidy
John Bull Special

Jim Chaffe
Pink Elephant I
Pink Elephant II
Pink Elephant III
Pink Elephant IV
Pink Elephant V

Wally Chapman
Schaghticoke Special

Joe Christ
Brand X (Christ)

Micheal Cleary
Cleary Special

Paul Clovis
Comet

Allison Clowes
Yeovil

George Clowes
Yeovil

Miles Collier
Ardent Alligator

Sam Collier
Ardent Alligator

Harry Constant
Civit Jr.

Frank Coons
Battlebirds

Alfred Coppel
Coppel MG TC

C.W. "Chuck" Cornett
Chukkar Mark II

Ron Courtney
Sceptre

Charlie Cox
Goldenrod

Dan Cozzi
Cozzi Jaguar

John Crosswaite
Dolphin Formula Junior
Dolphin Formula 2
Dolphin International
Dolphin Sports-Racers
Porphin

Briggs Swift Cunningham
Bu-Merc
Cunningham C-1
Cunningham C-2R
Cunningham C-4R
Cunningham C-4RK
Cunningham C-5R
Cunningham C-6R
Le Monstre

Stuart Dane
Dane Formula 3
Dane Formula Juniors
(Front engine)

Dane Formula Juniors
(Mid-engine)

David Dangerfield
Simon LaDawri-Packard

Bill David
David MG TD

Bob Davis
Davis Special

Dan Davis
Brand X (Davis)

Frank Davis
Mangham-Davis Special

Peter Dawson
Ferret

Lyn De Camp
Jones-De Camp Crosley

Curt Delfosse
Delfosse Mini-Junior

Bill Devin
Devin C
Devin D
Devin-Panhard
Devin SS
Devin-Crosley Super Sport
Devin-Roosevelt

Emil Diedt
Edwards Special
Edgar MG TC

James Dobson
Altemus Auto-Banker

Emmet Draddy
Sidewinder

Dave Dunbar
Fubar

Zora Arkus-Duntov
Corvette Grand Sport
Corvette SR-1
Corvette SR-2

Corvette SS
Corvette Sting Ray Racer

Dick Durant
Durant Devin-Chevy
Durant Devin-Pontiac

Larry Eave
Eave Chevy Special

John Edgar
Edgar MG TC

Forrest Edwards
Edwards / Blume Special

Stirling Edwards
Edwards Special (2)

Bob Eelsing
Shingle Corvettie

Ike Eichelbarger
Keil Porsche

Jerry Eisert
Eisert F-A
Webster V-8

Jack Ensley
SHE Special

Tom Evans
Evans Saab Special

Harry Eyerly
Eyerly Crosley

Wayne Ewing
Campbell Special

Virgil Exner, Jr.
Exner Simca Special

Lou Fageol
Fageol Twin-Porsche

Jerry Fairchild
Fairchild Panhard

Richard Finch
Finch F3

John Fitch
Fitch Type B
Fitch-Whitmore Jaguar
Schrafft-Fitch Crosley

Ford Motor Company
Ford G7A
Ford GT Mk.I
Ford GT Mk.II
Ford GT MK.IV

Dale Forsgren
Forsgrini Specials

Lyle Forsgren
Forsgrini Specials
Forsgrini Mk.10 FC
Forsgrini Mk.12 FF
Forsgrini Mk.10 F5000
Forsgrini Mk.11 F5000
Forsgrini Mk.14 F5000

Jim Frostrom
Silver Bomb

Johnny Gable
Anvil

Charles Gardner
Jones-De Camp Crosley

Joe Goss
Super Sport Special

Charles Gounis
Gounis Fiat-Crosley

Ron Grable
Spectre HR-1 FA

Henry Grady
Begra Mk.1
Begra Mk.2
Grady 1
Grady 2

Jim Granger
Hawaiian Special

David Greenblatt
Dailu Mk.I
Dailu Mk.II
Dailu Mk.III
Dailu Mk.IV
Dailu Mk.V

Ed Grierson
Echidnas
El Toro (1)

Bob Guest
Monsterati

Dan Gurney
Eagle Formula A
(Eagle Formula 5000)
Eagle-Climax Formula 1
Eagle-Weslake Formula 1

Jack Hagemann
Barneson-Hagemann Chrysler
David MG TD
Gillespie MG TD
Hagemann GMC
Leson Simca

Jim Hall
Chaparral I
Chaparral 2A
Chaparral 2C
Chaparral 2D
Chaparral 2E
Chaparral 2F
Chaparral 2G
Chaparral 2H
Chaparral 2J

Chalmers "Chal" Hall
Hall-Scott Special
Little Digger

Ed Hamill
Hamill SR-2
Hamill SR-3

Scott Hamilton
Odenborg Mercury H-Modified
Sceptre

Bud Hand
Bud Hand Special

Ray Hansen
Hansen Special

Walt Hansgen
Hansgen Jaguar

Jim Harcum
Mickey Mouse Special
Mighty Mouse Special

George Harm
Chukkar Mark II

Bill Harper
Coppel MG TC

Doug Harrison
Ak Miller's Caballo de Hierro
Ak Miller's Caballo II

Haverford Sport Motor
HSM Formula Jr.

Ray Heppenstall
Howmet Falcon
Howmet Turbine
HSM Formula Junior

Kenneth Hill
Flying Banana

Roger Hill
Tomcat

Ray Hixon
Hixon Special

Karl Hloch
Mickey Mouse Special
Mighty Mouse Special

Emil Hoffman
Hansgen Jaguar

Bob Hollbrook
Beast

Holman-Moody
Holman-Moody Honker II

Dick Holynski
Holynski 1
Holynski Scimitar
H. Hudler SHE Special

H. Hudler
SHE Special

Joe Huffaker
BMC Mk.1 Formula Jr.
BMC Mk.2 Formula Jr.
BMC MK.6 Formula Jr.
Genie Mk.4
Genie Mk.5
Genie Mk.8
Genie Mk.10
Genie Mk.11
Knoop Chevy
Marston Healey

Boyd Hugh
Morgensen Special (2)

Charles Hughes
Hughes-Kircher Special

Robert "Bud" Hull
Dolphin Formula Junior
Dolphin Formula 2
Dolphin International
Dolphin Sports-Racers
Porphin

Ed Ingalls
Ingalls Special

Ray Ingalls
Sanitary Special

Charlie Irons
Irons FC

Don James
James Special

Bill Jankowski
Monsterati

Harry Jones
Jones Racing Team Special
Jones-De Camp Crosley

Joe Jordan
Jaybird Mark X

Ronnie Kaplan
Apache

Jim Kellison
Kellison Formula Vee
Kellison J-4 Competition Coupe

Chris Kennedy
Ferret

Harry Alden King
Hummingbird

Kurt Kircher
Hughes-Kircher Special

Herman Kluge
John Bull Special

Frank Kurtis
Kurtis 500M
Kurtis 500S
Kurtis 500X
Kurtis Aguila
Kurtis Sports Car (KSC)

Horst Kwech
Ausca Formula B
Ausca Formula Vee
Ausca Sports-Racer

Pete Laffe
Mickey Mouse Special
Mighty Mouse Special

Abbott Lahti
Croslahti
Croslahti B

Chet Lancaster
Georgette-the-Racer

Jim Larkin
Chukkar Mark II

Reynolds Wrap Special
Sorrell-Larkin Special

Bill Larson
Echidnas

Aldin "Red" LeGrand
LeGrand Cheetah Mk.1
LeGrand Cheetah Mk.2
LeGrand Mk.3
LeGrand Mk.3B
LeGrand Mk.4
LeGrand Mk.5 F3
LeGrand Mk.6
LeGrand Mk.7
LeGrand Mk.10
LeGrand Mk.11

Lujie Lesovsky
Edwards Special

Don Lewis
James Special

Ingvar Lindqvist
Double-Ender

Gordon Lipe
Lipe Pooper

Duffy Livingston
Eliminator

Al Long
Long Renault Special

Pete Lovely
Lovely Pooper

Jim Lowe
Lowe's Frazer-Nash

Harry Lucas
Lucas-Whitehead Climax

Guy Mabee
Mabee Drilling Special

Joe Mabee
Mabee Drilling Special

"Jocko" Maggiacomo
Jocko Formula Junior

Stormy Mangham
Mangham-Davis Special

Henry Manney III
Georgette-the-Racer

Charles "Chuck" Manning
Manning Mercury Special
Sorrell-Manning Special

Walter Manske
MPX Crosley

Phillip Martin
PMY-2
PMY-3

Walt Martin
Papier Mache Special
PMY-2
PMY-3

John "Bat" Masterson
Masterson Batmobile

Bill Mays
Fibersport-Crosley

John C. Mays
Fibersport-Crosley

Ernie McAfee
Edgar MG TC

John McCann
Santee SS
Teakettle (MG TD) Special

Butch McDaniel
Townsend Mk.2

Bob McKee
Armco Cro-Sal Can-Am
McKee Mk.I

Cars by Racing Class

PRODUCTION

A Production
Cobra Mk.1 (race cars)
Cobra Mk.2 (race cars)
Cobra 427 Competition
Cobra 427 S/C

B Production
Shelby GT-350R

C Production
Arnolt Bristol Bolide

D Production
Yenko Stinger

E Production
Arnolt Bristol Bolide

SPORTS

Sports B
Bu-Merc
Cheetah (John Plaisted)
El Toro (1)
El Toro (2)
Kurtis 500S
Mabee Drilling Special
Meyer Special
Morgensen Special (1)
Edwards Special (2)
Sorrell-Manning Special
Vogel/Balchowsky Special

Sports C
Altemus Auto-Banker
Ardent Alligator
Austin Chevy Special
Baldwin Mercury Special
Brundage Duesenberg-Ford
Butterball Special
Cannon Mk.I
Cannon Mk.IV
Comet
Darwin Special
Davis Special
Fageol Twin-Porsche
Fitch-Whitmore Jaguar
Flying Banana
Hansgen Jaguar
Hughes-Kircher Special
Ingalls Special

James Special
Kurtis 500S
Kurtis Sports Car (KSC)
Manning Mercury Special
Morgensen Special (2)
Parkinson Jaguar
Payne Special
Pickford Jaguar
Satcher Special
Seifried Special
Tatum-GMC
Troutman-Barnes Special
Vogel/Balchowsky Special

Sports D
Cannon Mk.II
Excalibur J
Fitch Type B
Hughes-Kircher Special

Sports E
Beavis Offenhauser-First Version
Edgar MG TC
Lil Stinker

Sports F
Barlow Simca Number 1
Barlow Simca Number 2
Beavis Offenhauser-Second
  Version
Brundage VW Special
Coppel MG TC
D and D Special
David MG TD
Edwards / Blume Special
Edwards Special
Gillespie MG TD
John Bull Special
Leson Simca
Lipe Pooper
Louis Van Dyke International
  Motors Simca Special
Lovely VW-Porsche Special
Mar-Chris Special
Miles R-1
Miles R-2 (The Flying Shingle)
Multiplex 186
Sadler Mk.1
Singer Special
Swiss Cheese Special
Uihlein MG Special
von Neumann MG Special

Sports G
Bathtub
Devin-Panhard (with blower)

Sports H
Aardvark
Beast
Croslahti
Croslahti B
Devin-Panhard
Devin-Crosley Super Sport
Eyerly Crosley
Fibersport-Crosley
Georgette
Georgette-the-Racer
Le Biplace Torpedo
Nichols Panhard
PBX Crosley Special
Schrafft-Fitch Crosley
Seifried Crosley
Siam Special

MODIFIED

B-Modified
Ak Miller's Caballo II
Ak Miller's Devin-Olds
Apache (Bud Gates)
Barneson-Hagemann Chrysler
Battlebirds
Bocar Stiletto
Bocar XP-4
Bocar XP-5
Bocar XP-6
Bocar XP-7
Bocar XP-7R
Bourgeault Sports-Racers
Burnett Mk.2
Burnett Mk.3
Chaparral 2A
Chaparral 2C
Cheetah (Bill Thomas)
Chukkar Mark II
Dailu Specials
Devin SS
Durant Devin-Pontiac
Echidnas
El Toro (3)
Excalibur Mk.VI
FoMoCo Special
Front-Runner Special
Genie Mk.8
Genie Mk.10

Hamill SR-2
Hamill SR-3
Hummingbird
Hussein I
King Cobra
Kurtis 500M
Kurtis 500S
Kurtis 500X
Lo-Test Special
Mangham-Davis Special
Masterson Batmobile
McKee Mk.I
McKee Mk.II
McKee Mk.III
McKee Mk.IV
McKee Mk.V
Mirage
Monsterati
Old Yaller II
Old Yaller III
Old Yaller IV
Old Yaller V
Old Yaller VI
Old Yaller VII
Old Yaller VIII
Old Yaller IX
PAM Project Group 7
Sadler-Meyer Special
Scarab Mk.I
Scarab Mk.II
Scorpion
Simon LaDawri-Packard
Townsend Mk.3
Townsend Mk.4
Townsend Mk.5
Twareg Special

C-Modified
Ak Miller's Devin-Chevy
Albi Devin Special
Baird-Jag Special
Baldwin Mark II
Battlebirds
Bocar XP-4
Bocar XP-5
Bocar XP-7
Burnett Mk.1
Campbell Special
Capella
Chaparral I
Chaparral 2D
Chaparral 2E

Corvette Grand Sport
Corvette SR-2
Corvette Sting Ray Racer
Cozzi Jaguar
Dailu Specials
Devin Ryan Special
Devin SS
Durant Devin-Chevy
Eave Chevy Special
Echidnas
Eliminator
Excalibur Hawk
Hagemann GMC
Hamill SR-2
Hamill SR-3
Hansen Special
Hawaiian Special
Hixon Special
Holman-Moody Honker II
Holynski 1
Jack Baker's Black Jack
  Special
James Special
Kellison J-4 Competition
  Coupe
Knoop Chevy
Kurtis 500S
Kurtis 500X
Kurtis Aguila
Mangham-Davis Special
McKee Mk.VI
Morgensen Special (3)
Old Yaller I
Peterson Special
Philson-Falcon
Pink Elephant II
Pink Elephant III
Pink Elephant IV
Pink Elephant V
Porter SLS
Reynolds Wrap Special
Sadler Mk.2
Sadler Mk.3
Sadler Mk.4
Sadler Mk.5
Santee SS
Scarab Mk.I
Scarab Mk.II
Scarab Mid-Engined
  Sports-Racer
Schaghticoke Special
SHE Special

Silver Bomb
Sorrell-Larkin Special
Stovebolt Special
Teakettle (MG TD) Special
Tomcat
Townsend Mk.1
Townsend Mk.2
Ward/McKee Cooper-Buick
Webster V-8
Wolverine

D-Modified
CRV/Piranha
Devin C
Genie Mk.5
Marston Healey
Pink Elephant IV
Pink Elephant V
Webster 2-Liter
Zerex Special

E-Modified
Ambro
Ausca Sports-Racer
Beach Mk.4
Beach Mk.4B
Beach Mk.4C
Bobsy SR3
Brand X (Davis)
Devin D
Durlite Too
Genie Mk.4
Keck Spyder
La Boa Mk.3
LeGrand Mk.4
Lowe's Frazer-Nash
Mickey Mouse Special
Mighty Mouse Special
Morlang Porsche
PAM Special
Peyote Mk.II
Peyote Special
Platypus-Porsche
Porphin
Priest Volvo
Sadler Mk.2
Shingle Corvettie
Super Sport Special

F-Modified
Beach Mk.4
Beach Mk.4B

Beach Mk.4C
Beavis Offenhauser-Third
  Version
Bobsy SR2
Bobsy SR3
Bourgeault Sports-Racers
Bud Hand Special
Crusader VSR
Devin D
Durlite Special
Elwood Porsche Special
Exner Simca Special
Ferret
Jomar Mk.I (Dellow-Jomar)
Jomar Mk.II (with blower)
Jomar Mk.III (with blower)
La Boa Mk.3
LeGrand Mk.4
Lovely Pooper
Miles R-3 (The Pooper)
Pink Elephant I
Plass Mistral
Sceptre

G-Modified
Beach Mk.4
Beach Mk.4B
Beach Mk.4C
Bobsy SR2
Bobsy SR3
Bourgeault Sports-Racers
Dolphin Sports-Racers
Forsgrini Specials
Grady 1
Jomar Fastback Coupe
  (Mk.II road car)
Jomar Mk.II
Jomar Mk.III
Jomar Notchback Coupe
  (Mk.I road car)
Jomar Roadster
La Boa Mk.3
LeGrand Mk.4
Lucas-Whitehead Climax
Shiva

H-Modified
Beach Mk.4
Beach Mk.4B
Beach Mk.4C
Begra Mk.1
Begra Mk.2

Begra Mk.3
Bobsy SR1
Bobsy SR3
Cleary Special
Devin-Roosevelt
Dolphin Sports-Racers
Double-Ender
Evans Saab Special
Fairchild Panhard
Fibersport-Crosley
Flying Triangle
Forsgrini Specials
Genie Mk.11
Gounis Fiat-Crosley
Grady 2
Hall-Scott Special
Jabro Mk.1
Jabro Mk.2
Jabro Mk.3
Jaybird Mark X
Jones Racing Team
  Special
Jones-De Camp
  Crosley
Kangaroo-Fiat
La Boa Mk.1
La Boa Mk.2
La Boa Mk.3
LeGrand Cheetah
  Mk.2
LeGrand Mk.4
Little Digger
Long Renault Special
Manta Ray
Miller Specials
Miller-Sparks Crosley
Morgan Special
MPX Crosley
Odenborg Mercury
  H-Modified
Papier Mache Special
PBS Mk.1
PBS Mk.2
Phoenix Saab
PMY-2
PMY-3
Rattenbury Crosley
Sanitary Special
SPAD
Starkweather Crosley
Tanner T-1
Tanner T-2

Tanner T-3
Tanner T-4
Tanner T-5
Tanner T-6
Tanner T-7
Tholen Crosley
Thundermug
Wright Renault Special
Zink Petit

SPORTS RACER

A Sports Racer
Armco Cro-Sal Can-Am
Burnett Mk.4
Caldwell D-7
Chaparral 2H
Chaparral 2J
Ti22 Mk.1
Ti22 Mk.2

B Sports Racer
Keil Porsche
Quasar SR

C Sports Racer
Ak Miller's Devin-Ford
Burnett Mk.3
Chaparral 2F
Chaparral 2G
Ford G7A
King Cobra Group 7
McKee Mk.VII
Quasar SR
Sidewinder

D Sports Racer
Quasar SR

F Sports Racer
Zink Z-8

H Sports Racer
Brand X (Christ)
NTM Mk.1
NTM Mk.2
Rattler

FORMULA

Formula A
Eagle Formula A (Eagle
  Formula 5000)

Eisert F-A
Forsgrini Mk.10 F5000
Forsgrini Mk.14 F5000
LeGrand Mk.7
LeGrand Mk.11
McKee Mk.8 F5000
McKee Mk.11 F5000
McKee Mk.12 F5000
Spectre HR-1 FA
Vulcan Formula A

Formula B
Ausca Formula B
Autodynamics D-3 Formula
  B
Beach Type 11 FB
Bourgeault Formula B/C
LeGrand Mk.3B
LeGrand Mk.6

Formula C
Beach Type 11 FC
Bourgeault Formula B/C
Forsgrini Mk.10 FC
Irons FC
LeGrand Mk.3
LeGrand Mk.6
Quantum Formula S

Formula 1
Eagle-Climax Formula 1
Eagle-Weslake Formula 1
Scarab Formula 1

Formula 2
Dolphin Formula 2
Andree Special

Formula 3
Dane Formula 3
Formula 3 Echo
LeGrand Mk.5 F3
Sadler Formula 3

Formula 4
Delfosse Mini-Junior
LeGrand Cheetah Mk.1

Formula Ford
Beach Type 11 Formula Ford
Caldwell D-9 Formula Ford
Caldwell D-9B Formula Ford

Forsgrini Mk.12 FF
LeGrand Mk.10
Lynx C
R.A.C.E. Formula Ford

Formula Junior
Apache (Formula Junior)
BMC Mk.1 Formula Jr.
BMC Mk.2 Formula Jr.
BMC Mk.6 Formula Jr.
Bourgeault Formula Junior
Civit Jr.
Dane Formula Juniors (Front engine)
Dane Formula Juniors (Mid-engine)
DKW Formula Junior
Dolphin Formula Junior
Dolphin International
HSM Formula Junior
Jocko Formula Junior
Powell Formula Junior

Sadler Formula Junior
Votorini
Yeovil
Zeter Mk.1 Formula Junior
Zeter Mk.2 Formula Junior

Formula Libre
Holynski Scimitar
Jomar SSR1 Formula 2 Racer
Kurtis Aguila
Orgeron Talbot-Lago
Sadler Formula Libre (Mid-engine)
Scarab Intercontinental

Formula Super Vee
Beach SV16 Formula Super Vee
Caldwell D-10 FSV
Lynx D
Zeitler Formula Super Vee
Zink Z-9

Formula Vee
Anvil
Ausca Formula Vee
Autodynamics D-1Mk.1 Formula Vee
Autodynamics D-4 Mk.4
Formula Vee
Autodynamics D-4A Mk.4 Formula Vee
Autodynamics D-4B Mk.5 Formula Vee
Beach Mk.5
Beach Mk.5B
Beach Mk.5C
Bobsy Vega Formula Vee
Crusader Formula Vees
Crusader Formula Vee Wedge
Formcar Formula Vees
Kellison Formula Vee
Lynx A
Lynx Mk.II/B
RCA FV

Sardini
Shark Formula Vee
Templeton Ringwraith
Templeton Shadowfax
Vanguard Formula Vee
Zeitler Formula Vee
Zink Z-4
Zink Z-5

FIA & MISC.

FIA GT
Cobra Mk.1 (race cars)
Cobra Mk.2 (race cars)
Cobra Daytona Coupe
Corvette Grand Sport
Corvette SR-1
Ford GT Mk.I

FIA Prototype
Beach Mk.8
Corvette SS

Cunningham C-1
Cunningham C-2R
Cunningham C-4R
Cunningham C-4RK
Cunningham C-5R
Cunningham C-6R
Ford GT Mk.I
Ford GT Mk.II
Ford GT MK.IV
Howmet Falcon
Howmet Turbine
Le Monstre

FIA Sports
Ak Miller's Caballo de Hierro
USAC under 2-liter
Rutan Porsche Special

Bibliography

Ak Miller's Caballo de Hierro
Hot Rod, February 1954
Hot Rod, January 1955

Altemus Auto-Banker
Motor Trend, July 1951

Apache
Road & Track, April 1960
Sports Car Illustrated, March 1960

Arnolt
Automobile Quarterly, Vol.15 No. 4
Road & Track, February 1956
Sports Car Illustrated, July 1956

Autodynamics
Sports Car Graphic, September 1967
Sports Car, December 1972

AVS Shadow
Road & Track, August 1969
Road & Track, May 1971

Baird-Jag Special
Sports Car Illustrated, February 1957

Baldwin Mercury Special
Road & Track, May 1950

Barlow Simca
Road & Track, July 1951
Road & Track, October 1951

Battlebirds
T-Bird, 40 Years of Thunder
   by John Gunnell, Krause
   Publications, 1995
Sports Car Illustrated, July 1957

Beast
Car and Driver, February 1961

Beavis Offenhauser
Car Craft, March 1954

BMC-Mk.2
Sports Car Graphic, October 1961

BMC-Mk.6
Sports Car Graphic, June 1963

BMC-Formula Junior engines
Sports Car Graphic, June 1962

Bobsy SR2
Road & Track, March 1964
Sports Car Graphic, July 1964

Bobsy SR3
Sports Car Graphic, June 1966

Bobsy Vega Formula Vee
Road & Track, April 1968

Bocar-General
Automobile Quarterly,
   Vol. 31, No. 2, 1993

Bocar XP-5
Motor Trend, June 1959
Sports Car Graphic, June 1959

Bocar XP-6
Sports Car Illustrated, January 1960

Bocar XP-7
Popular Science, January 1961

Bocar Stiletto
Motor Life, July 1961

Bourgeault
Motor Sport International,
   November 1965

Brundage Duesenberg-Ford
Road & Track, February 1950
   (cover, feature)

Brundage VW Special
Excellence, February 2004

Burnett Special
Can-Am by Pete Lyons,
   MBI Publishing Company, 2002

Campbell Special
Sports Car Graphic, December 1961

Cannon-Offenhauser Mk.IV
Road & Track, February 1955

Chaparral
Chaparral by Richard Falconer,
   MBI Publishing Company, 1992
Chevrolet—Racing by
   Paul Van Valkenburgh, SAE
   International, 2000
Sports Car Graphic, August 1961

Car and Driver, July 1964
Road & Track, December 1966

Cheetah (Bill Thomas)
Sports Car Graphic, November 1963
Hot Rod, March 1964
Automobile Quarterly,
   Vol. 19, No. 3, 1981
Sports Car Graphic, July 1964

Cheetah (Plaisted)
Hot Rod, September 1958

Chevrolet
*Corvette, America's Star-Spangled
   Sports Car* by Karl Ludvigsen,
   Automobile Quarterly, 1978
Chevrolet—Racing by
   Paul Van Valkenburgh, SAE
   International, 2000
Adventure on Wheels by John Fitch,
   G. P. Putnum's Sons, 1959
Zora Arkus-Duntov by Jerry Burton,
   Bentley Publishers, 2002

Cleary Special
Vintage Motorsport, March/April 2004

Comet Special
Vintage Motorsport, July/August 1993

Cunningham
Cunningham by Dean Batchelor
   and Albert R. Bochroch,
   MBI Publishing Company, 1993
Sports Cars and Hot Rods,
   December 1953
Road & Track, October 1950
Road & Track, June 1951
Mechanix Illustrated, July 1951
Road & Track, January 1952

Dane
Road & Track July, 1961
Sports Car Graphic, April 1963
West Coast Sports Car Journal, January
   1957

Delfose
Sports Car Graphic, November 1963

Devin C
Sports Car Graphic, January 1962

Devin D
Sports Car Graphic, May 1961
Thoroughbred and Classic Cars,
   November 1999

Devin-General
Car and Driver, July 1961
Vintage Motorsport, March/April 1991
Automobile Quarterly,
   Vol. 23, No. 3, 1985
Kit Car, May 1989
Petersen's Sports Car Classics,
   No. 2, 1982
Kit Car Illustrated, October 1987
Kit Car, July 1986

Devin Panhard
Sports Car Illustrated, May 1957

Devin-Roosevelt
Sportscar Specials,
   Trend Book No. 196

Devin SS
Sports Car Illustrated, July 1959
Road & Track, July 1959
Classic and Sports Car, March 1991
Road & Track, August 1991

Dolphin Formula Junior
Sports Car Illustrated,
   December 1960

Dolphin
Vintage Motorsport, Vol. 5, 1993

Eagle
Road & Track, April 1966
Sports Car Graphic, April 1966
Road & Track, May 1966
Road & Track, June 1966
Sports Car Graphic, April 1967
Gurney's Eagles by Karl Ludvigsen, MBI
   Publishing Company, 1992
American Grand Prix Racing by
   Tim Considine, MBI Publishing
   Company, 1997

Eave Chevy Special
Sports Car Illustrated, November 1957

Edgar MG TC
Road & Track, January 1952

Edwards/Blume Special
Road & Track, September 1954

Excalibur
Auto Sport Review, May 1952
Road & Track, January 1953
Car Life, March 1954
Road & Track, May 1963

Exner Simca Special
Road & Track, April 1959
Classic & Sports Car, May 2004

Eyerly Crosley
Road & Track, January 1957
Car and Driver, February 1957

Fibersport
Auto Sport Review, December 1953
Road & Track, July 1958

Ford G7A
Sports Car Graphic, October 1967

Ford GT
*Ford GT40 Production and Racing
   History* by Trevor Legate,
   Veloce Publishing, 2001
Car and Driver, June 1965
Road & Track, May 1965
Road & Track, May 1966
Road & Track, October 1966
Road & Track, March 1967
Road & Track, January 1968

Formcar
Today's Motor Sports, June 1961
Foreign Car Guide, November 1963
Foreign Car Guide, December 1963
Car and Driver, May 1963
Auto Topics, June 1965
Grassroots Motorsports,
   September 1999

Front-Runner Special
Hot Rod Parts Illustrated,
   November 1964

Genie-Corvair
Sports Car Graphic, January 1963
Genie-Mk.4
Sports Car Graphic, November 1962

Genie-Mk.8
Sports Car Graphic, August 1963

Georgette
Auto, February 1953

Hamill
Can-Am Photo History by Pete Lyons,
MBI Publishing Company, 2002

Hansen Special
Hot Rod, January 1956

Hawaiian Special
Sports Car Graphic, March 1963

Hixon Special
On The Grid, September 1961

Holynski Scimitar
Hot Rod, December 1964

Hughes-Kircher Special
Road & Track, January 1955
Road & Track, December 1955

Hummingbird
Machine Design, 1968

Jabro
Sports Car, March-April 1957
Car and Driver, January 1962

John Bull Special
Car Life, September 1954

Jomar
Automobile Quarterly,
Vol. 35, No.2, 1996

Jones-De Camp Crosley
Road & Track, August 1958

Kellison
Motor Trend, December 1959
Sports Car, December 1968

Knoop Huffaker
Hot Rod, October 1958

Kurtis-General
*Kurtis-Kraft: Masterworks of Speed and
Style* by Gordon Eliot White, MBI
Publishing Company, 2001

Kurtis 500 KK Chassis
Road & Track, October 1953

Kurtis 500M
Road & Track, May 1954
Autoweek, July 1988

Kurtis 500S
Road & Track, April 1953
Road & Track, October 1953

Kurtis Sports Car (KSC)
Motor Trend, October 1949

Kurtis 500X
Automobile Quarterly,
Vol. 31, No. 2, 1993

LaDawri Conquest
Road & Track, July 1957

Le Biplace Torpedo
Road & Track, February 1958

LeGrand
Sports Car Graphic, November 1963
Sports Car Graphic, June 1965
Road & Track, July 1966
Road & Track, November 1967
Road & Track, July 1968
Victory Lane, April 1989

Lynx Cars
Road & Track, July 1976

Mabee Drilling Special
Victory Lane, July 1995

Mangham-Davis Special
Motor Trend, November 1958

Manning Special
Road & Track, November 1951

McAfee Engineering
Auto Speed and Sport, October 1952

McKee
Road & Track, February 1967

McKee Armco Cro-Sal Can-Am
Sports Car Graphic, July 1969
Car Craft, September 1954

McKee Chevette
Sports Car Graphic, August 1964

Meyer-Drake Engines
Offenhauser by Gordon White,
MBI Publishing Company, 1996
Sports Car Illustrated, October 1956
Sports Car Illustrated, June 1957

Meyer Special
Sports Car Illustrated, April 1956

Miles Specials
Sportscar Specials by Bob Rolofson,
Petersen Publishing, 1958
Road & Track, December 1953
Road & Track, April 1955
Road & Track, May 1955

Miller
Victory Lane, May 1988

Mirage
Sports Car Graphic, February 1965

Morgan Special
Hot Rod, May 1958

Nichols Panhard
Victory Lane, August 1988

Odenborg Specials
Sports Car Graphic, January 1964
Sports Car Graphic, January 1965

Old Yaller-General
Sports Car Illustrated, August 1960
Automobile Quarterly, Vol. 39, No. 1,
May 1999

Old Yaller I
Sports Car Illustrated, May 1957

Old Yaller IV
Sports Car Graphic, July 1961

PAM Project Group 7
Sports Car Graphic, October 1966

Papier Mache Special
Sports Car Illustrated, January 1960

PBS
Road & Track, January 1967

PBX Crosley Special
Car and Driver, July 1956

Porphin
Sports Car Graphic, August 1963
Excellence, May 2002

Porter SLS
Road & Track, September 1956
Sports Car International,
November 1956
Sports Car International, June 1957
Sports Car International,
November 1957

Powell Formula Junior
Sports Car Graphic, May 1961

Pupilidy VW
Sports Cars International, April 1956

Quantum
Sports Car Graphic, July 1965
Autoweek, December 2, 1991

Rattenbury Crosley
Road & Track, April 1957

Scarab
*Scarab, Race Log of the All-American
Specials 1957–1965* by Preston
Lerner, MBI Publishing Company,
1991
Road & Track, February 1958
Road & Track, June 1958
Sports Car Illustrated, June 1958
Sportscar Quarterly, Fall 1958
Road & Track, February 1959
Road & Track, April 1959
Sports Car Graphic, December 1959
Road & Track, July 1960
Sports Car Graphic, December 1962
Sports Car Graphic, March 1964

Seifried Special
Mechanix Illustrated,
Sept 1952 (Cover)

Shelby American
Carroll Shelby's Racing Cobra by Dave
Friedman and John Christy, Osprey
Publishing
The Carroll Shelby Story by Carroll
Shelby, Simon & Schuster, 1967
*Cobra: GT-350: GT-500 A Production
History and Owner Registry*
by Shelby American Automobile
Club, SAAC, 1982
Ford Cobra Guide by Bill Carroll, Sports
Car Press, 1964
Road & Track, May 1965
Road & Track, June 1995
Victory Lane, December 1997

SHE Special
Hot Rod, March 1960

SPAD
Sports Car Graphic, July 1964

Starkweather Crosley
Sports Car Graphic, March 1960

Stovebolt Special
Car Life, July 1955
Sports Car Illustrated,
September 1956
Classic and Sportscar, May 1987
Alf Francis, Racing Mechanic
by Alf Francis, Haynes, 1991

Super Sport Special
Sportscar Specials 1960 by Bob
Rolofson, Petersen Publishing,
1960

Tanner
Sports Car Illustrated, March 1957

Tatum-GMC
Hot Rod, October 1953
Motorlife, September 1954

Taylor Super Sport Engine
Road & Track, May 1958
Sports Car Graphic, April 1960

Townsend
Sports Car Graphic, December 1962

Uihlein MG Special
Speed Age, September 1953

Von Neumann MG Special
Road & Track, August 1951
Road & Track, January 1952 (display
advertisement on page 48)

Webster Special
Sports Car Graphic, November 1964

Wright Specials
Car Craft, October 1954
Sports Cars Illustrated, October 1956

Yenko
Sports Car, June 1966
Sports Car Graphic, May 1966
Car and Driver, June 1966

Zeitler
Vintage Racecar Journal, June 2001

Zerex Special
Pro Sports Car Racing by Dave
Friedman, MBI Publishing
Company, 1999
Car and Driver, January 1963

Zink
Sports Car, August 1968

Index

301

∘ Hixon Special ∘ Holman-Moody Honker II ∘ Holynski 1 ∘ Holynski Scimitar ∘ Howmet Falcon ∘ Howmet Turbine ∘ HSM Formula Junior ∘ Hughes-Kircher Special ∘ Hummingbird ∘ Hussein I ∘ Ingalls Special ∘ Irons FC ∘ Jabro Mk.1 ∘ Jabro Mk.2 ∘ Jabro Mk.3 ∘ Jack Baker's Black Jack Special ∘ James Special ∘ Jaybird Mark X ∘ Jocko Formula Junior ∘ John Bull Special ∘ Jomar Mk.I ∘ Jomar Mk.II ∘ Jomar Mk.III ∘ Jomar Fastback Coupe ∘ Jomar Notchback Coupe ∘ Jomar Roadster ∘ Jomar SSR1 Formula 2 Racer ∘ Jones Racing Team Special ∘ Jones-De Camp Crosley ∘ Kangaroo-Fiat ∘ Keck Spyder ∘ Keil Porsche ∘ Kellison Formula Vee ∘ Kellison J-4 Competition Coupe ∘ King Cobra ∘ King Cobra Group 7 ∘ Kurtis 500KK ∘ Kurtis 500M ∘ Kurtis 500S ∘ Kurtis 500X ∘ Kurtis Aguila ∘ Kurtis Sports Car ∘ La Boa Mk.1 ∘ La Boa Mk.2 ∘ La Boa Mk.3 ∘ Le Biplace Torpedo ∘ Le Monstre ∘ LeGrand Cheetah Mk.1 ∘ LeGrand Cheetah Mk.2 ∘ LeGrand Mk.3 ∘ LeGrand Mk.3B ∘ LeGrand Mk.4 ∘ LeGrand Mk.5 F3 ∘ LeGrand Mk.6 ∘ LeGrand Mk.7 ∘ LeGrand Mk.10 ∘ LeGrand Mk.11 ∘ Leson Simca ∘ Lil Stinker ∘ Lipe Pooper ∘ Little Digger ∘ Long Renault Special ∘ Lo-Test Special ∘ Louis Van Dyke International Motors Simca Special ∘ Lovely Pooper ∘ Lovely VW-Porsche Special ∘ Lowe's Frazer-Nash ∘ Lucas-Whitehead Climax ∘ Lynx A ∘ Lynx C ∘ Lynx D ∘ Lynx Mk.II/B ∘ Mabee Drilling Special ∘ Mangham-Davis Special ∘ Manning Mercury Special ∘ Manta Ray ∘ Mar-Chris Special ∘ Masterson Batmobile ∘ McKee Mk.I ∘ McKee Mk.II ∘ McKee Mk.III ∘ McKee Mk.IV ∘ McKee Mk.V ∘ McKee Mk.VI ∘ McKee Mk.VII ∘ McKee Mk.8 F-5000 ∘ McKee Mk.11 F-5000 ∘ McKee Mk.12 F-5000 ∘ Meyer Special ∘ Mickey Mouse Special ∘ Mighty Mouse Special ∘ Miles R-1 ∘ Miles R-2 ∘ Miles R-3 ∘ Miller Specials ∘ Miller-Sparks Crosley ∘ Mirage ∘ Monsterati ∘ Morgan Special ∘ Morgensen Special (1) ∘ Morgensen Special (2) ∘ Morgensen Special (3) Morlang Porsche ∘ MPX Crosley ∘ Multiplex 186 ∘ Nichols Panhard ∘ NTM Mk.1 ∘ NTM Mk.2 ∘ Odenborg Mercury H-Modified ∘ Old Yaller I ∘ Old Yaller II ∘ Old Yaller III ∘ Old Yaller IV ∘ Old Yaller V ∘ Old Yaller VI ∘ Old Yaller VII ∘ Old Yaller VIII ∘ Old Yaller IX ∘ Orgeron Talbot-Lago ∘